Why Word? Why Beginning WordBasic P

Word is not only a complete word processor that can be us‹
contains a complete underlying programming language, Wor‹
just a macro language used to automate keystrokes; it's the ᴠ ......ᴄᴇ ᴏғ Word itself,
packaged in a form easily accessible to the intrepid user.

After giving you a thorough introduction to the WordBasic language syntax and construction, we'll show you how to create your own time saving, performance improving utilities in WordBasic. Clearly explained examples show just what you can achieve, from simple text insertion to complete survey reporting, all in WordBasic. Let *Beginning WordBasic Programming* be your first step along the path to achieving complete office automation.

What is Wrox Press?

Wrox Press is a computer book publisher which promotes clear, jargon-free programming and database titles that fulfill your real demands. We publish for everyone, from the novice through to the experienced programmer. To ensure our books meet your needs, we carry out continuous research on all our titles. Through our dialog with you, we can craft the book you really need.

We welcome suggestions and take all of them to heart - your input is paramount in creating the next great Wrox title. Use the reply card inside this book or contact us at:

feedback@wrox.com

Compuserve 100063, 2152

http://www.wrox.com/

Wrox Press Ltd.
2710 W. Touhy
Chicago
IL 60645
USA

Tel: +1 (312) 465 3559

Fax: +1 (312) 465 4063

Visit The Wrox Press
DEVELOPERS' REFERENCE
On The Web

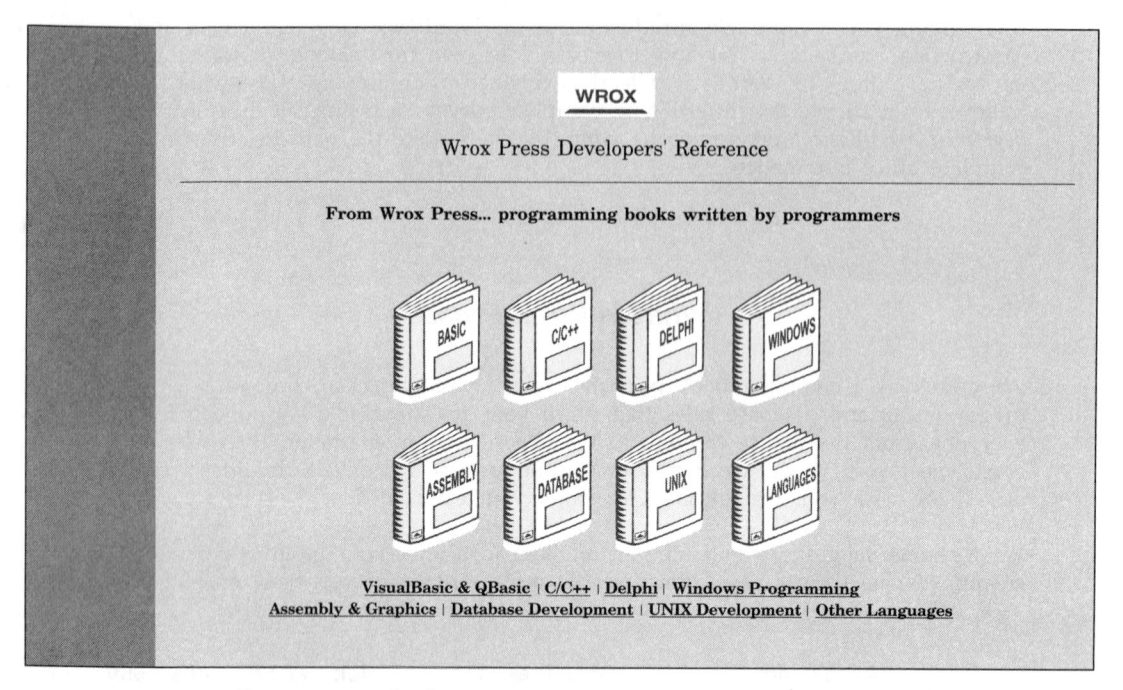

WROX

Wrox Press Developers' Reference

From Wrox Press... programming books written by programmers

VisualBasic & QBasic | C/C++ | Delphi | Windows Programming
Assembly & Graphics | Database Development | UNIX Development | Other Languages

http://www.wrox.com/

Our web site is now organized by subject area for easy reference. Whether you're into QBasic or Assembly or anything in between, check us out:

- See our latest titles
- Read book reviews on-line
- Download free source code
- Connect to other hot sites
- Search for a store near you
- Get an update of our publication schedule
- Visit 'Wrox in Progress' – gives us advanced feedback on the next best-seller

Beginning WordBasic Programming

Alex Homer

Wrox Press Ltd.®

Beginning WordBasic Programming

© 1996 Wrox Press

All rights reserved. No part of this book may be reproduced, stored in a retrieval system or transmitted in any form or by any means - electronic, electro static, mechanical, photocopying, recording or otherwise, without the prior written permission of the publisher, except in the case of brief quotations embodied in critical articles or reviews.

The author and publisher have made every effort in the preparation of this book and disk to ensure the accuracy of the information. However, the information contained in this book and disk is sold without warranty, either express or implied. Neither the author, Wrox Press nor its dealers or distributors will be held liable for any damages caused or alleged to be caused either directly or indirectly by this book or disk.

WROX

Published by Wrox Press Ltd. Site 16, 20 James Road, Birmingham, B11 2BA, UK
Printed in Canada
1 2 3 4 5 TRI 99 98 97 96

Library of Congress Catalog no. 96-60776
ISBN 1-874416-86-9

Trademark Acknowledgements

Wrox has endeavored to provide trademark information about all the companies and products mentioned in this book by the appropriate use of capitals. However, Wrox cannot guarantee the accuracy of this information.

Windows 95 and Windows NT are trademarks of Microsoft Corporation. Delphi is a trademark of Borland International Inc.

Credits

Author
Alex Homer

Development Editor
Graham McLaughlin

Technical Editor
Darren Gill

English Editor
Melanie Orgee

Technical Reviewers
Norman Powroz
Andy Kramek
Douglas Shand

Production Manager
Greg Powell

Design/Layout
Neil Gallagher
Andrew Guillaume

Proof Readers
Melanie Orgee
Pam Brand
Joanne Sawyer

Index
Simon Gilks

Cover Design
Third Wave

For more information on Third Wave, contact Ross Alderson on 44-121 236 6616
Cover photograph supplied by The Image Bank

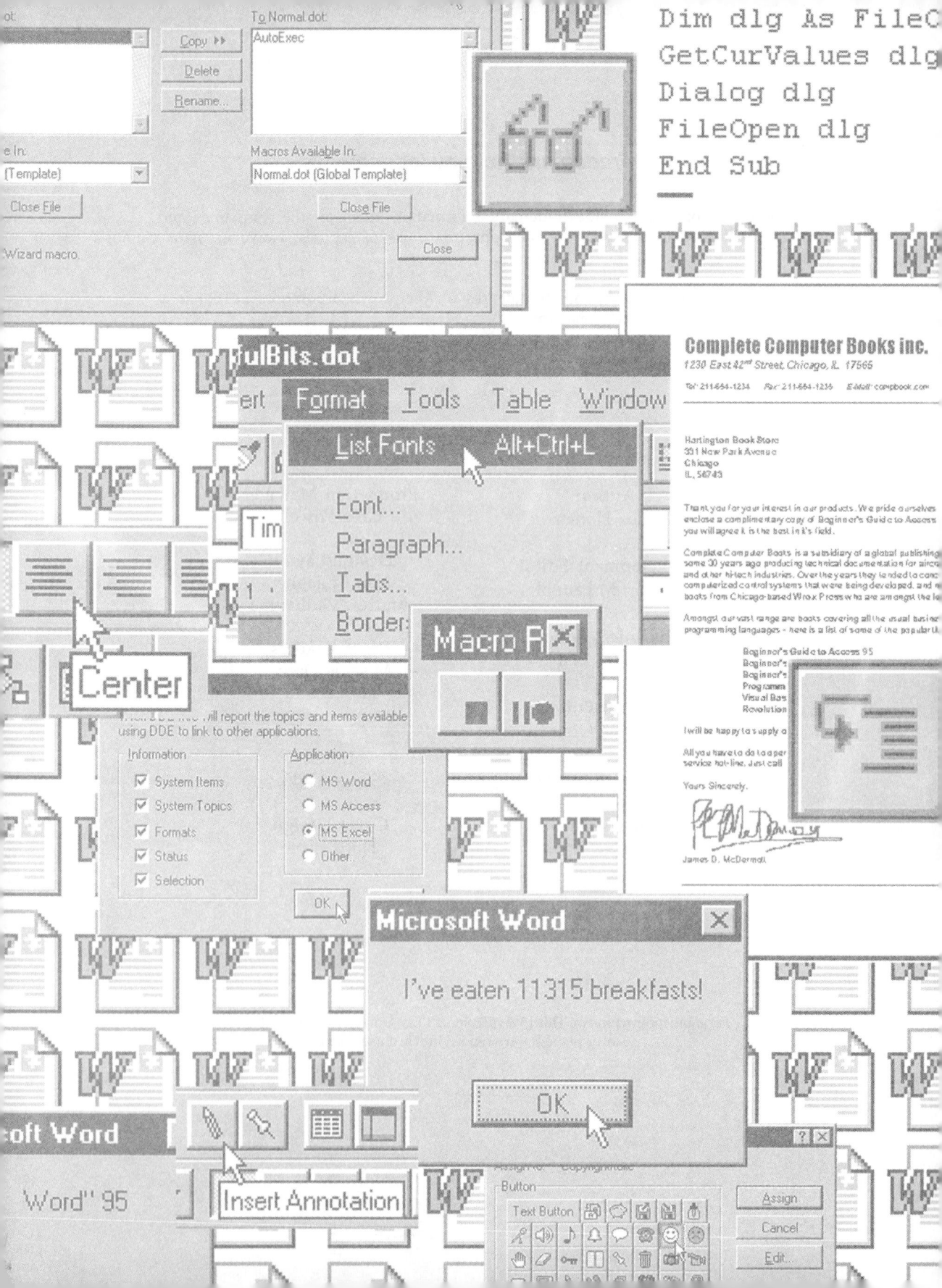

```
Dim dlg As FileO
GetCurValues dlg
Dialog dlg
FileOpen dlg
End Sub
```

Beginning WordBasic Programming

Summary of Contents

	Introduction	1
Part 1	**All About WordBasic**	**5**
Chapter 1	Introducing WordBasic	7
Chapter 2	WordBasic Fundamentals	37
Chapter 3	Communicating With Your Users	87
Chapter 4	Working with Documents	135
Part 2	**Word in the Workplace**	**185**
Chapter 5	Wizards and Add-in Utilities	187
Chapter 6	Word in a Publishing Environment	229
Chapter 7	Creating Web Pages for the Internet	273
Chapter 8	Creating Windows 95 Help	321
Chapter 9	Compiling Windows Help Files	363
Part 3	**Word and the Outside World**	**411**
Chapter 10	The Problems of Sharing Documents	413
Chapter 11	Using Fields and Forms in Word	449
Chapter 12	Sharing and Analyzing Data	487
Chapter 13	Using Objects in Your Documents	525
Chapter 14	E-mail, Address Books and Mail Merge	565
	Index	603

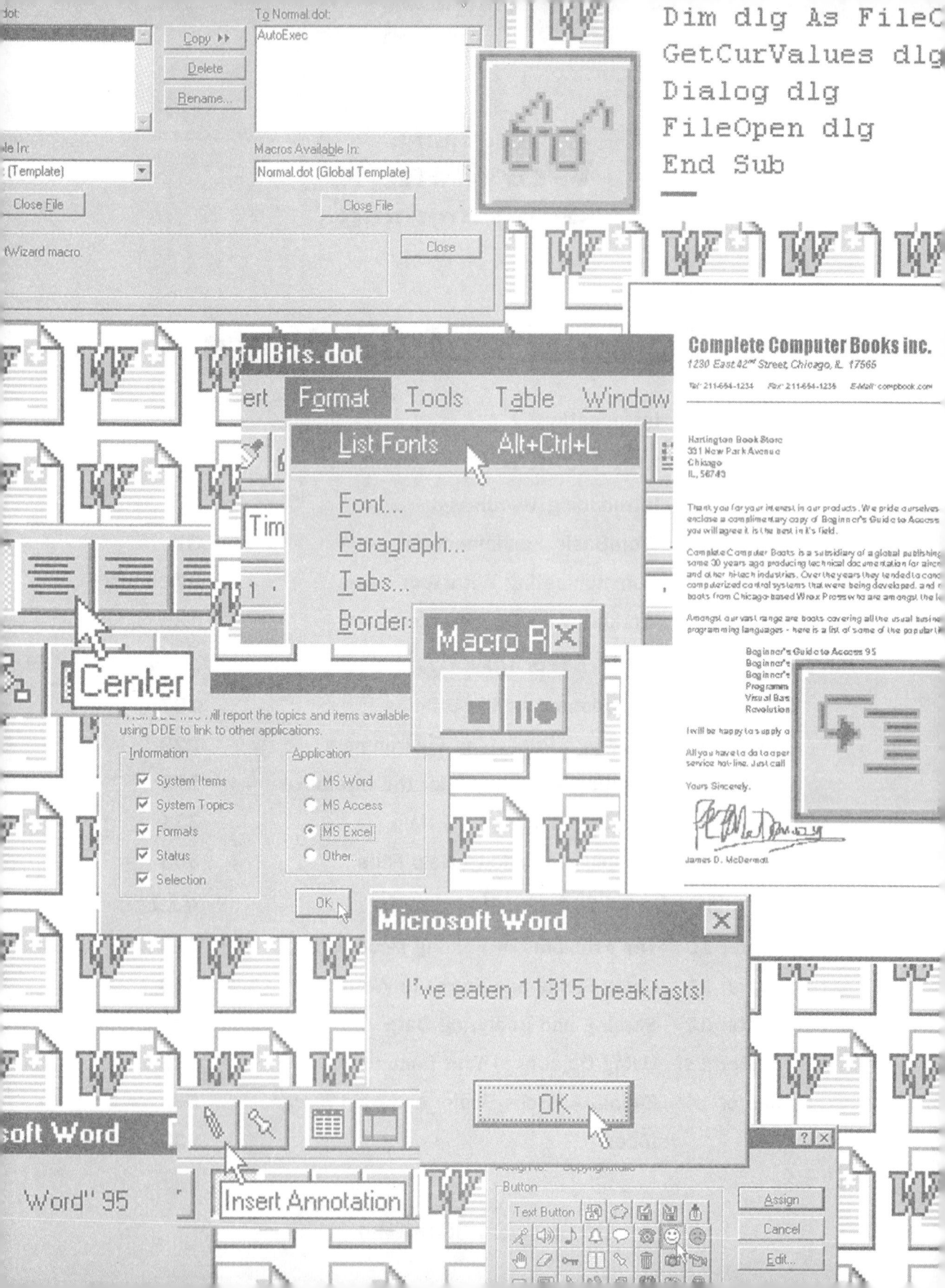

```
Dim dlg As FileO
GetCurValues dlg
Dialog dlg
FileOpen dlg
End Sub
```

I've eaten 11315 breakfasts!

Beginning WordBasic Programming

Table of Contents

Introduction — 1
- What's this Book About? — 1
- What You Need to Use this Book — 2
- How this Book is Organized — 2
- Conventions Used — 3
- Tell Us What You Think — 4

Part 1 — All About WordBasic — 5

Chapter 1 — Introducing WordBasic — 7

- What Is a Word Application? — 7
- An Overview of WordBasic and Macros — 11
  - Three Ways of Using WordBasic — 11
  - Where and How Macros are Stored — 13
- Writing Your First Macro — 19
  - Recording Macros Automatically — 26
  - What Gets Stored in a Document? — 31
  - Stopping a Macro while It's Running — 34
- Summary — 34

Chapter 2 — WordBasic Fundamentals — 37

- Introduction — 37
- WordBasic Language Fundamentals — 38
  - Variables — 38
  - WordBasic's Data Types — 39
  - Operators and Expressions — 43
  - WordBasic's Built-in Statements — 47
  - WordBasic's Built-in Functions — 50
  - User-defined Procedures — 54

		Controlling Execution of Your Code	61
		WordBasic Control Structures	62
		Coping with Errors	68
		Setting Break Points	71
		Useful Techniques with Control Structures	73
		Summary	85
Chapter 3	**Communicating With Your Users**		**87**
		Introduction	87
		WordBasic's Input and Output Statements	87
		Using the Status Bar	88
		Using Standard Message and Input Windows	90
		Using Word's Built-in Dialogs	98
		What Is a Dialog Record?	99
		Displaying a Built-in Dialog	102
		Creating Your Own Custom Dialogs	107
		What Is a Custom Dialog?	107
		How a Custom Dialog is Used	113
		Putting It All Together	119
		Introducing Dynamic Dialogs	122
		The Dialog Definition Statement	122
		The Dialog Function	123
		WordBasic Dialog Procedures	126
		Summary	133
Chapter 4	**Working with Documents**		**135**
		Introduction	135
		Editing, Finding and Selecting in a Document	135
		Moving and Selecting	136
		Inserting and Deleting	142
		Formatting Text	143
		Working with Tables	147
		Searching and Replacing	149
		Using Bookmarks	153
		Going to a Point in a Document	158
		Saving Information Globally and in Documents	162
		Storing Information in a Template	164
		Storing Information in a Document	166
		Storing Information in .ini Files and the Registry	167
		Using Document Properties	168
		Making Macros Available to Your Users	169
		Setting a Key Combination for a Macro	169
		Adding Macros to Your Toolbars	171
		Adding Macros to Your Menus	173
		Replacing Word Commands	176
		Macros that Run Automatically	179
		Summary	182

Part 2 Word in the Workplace 185

Chapter 5 Wizards and Add-in Utilities 187

Introduction 187
Creating WordBasic Wizards 188
   What is a Wizard? 188
Word Add-in Utilities 211
   What are Add-ins? 211
   Introducing Wrox Zip 211
   Using Zip Manager 216
Extending the Power of WordBasic 218
   What are DLLs? 219
Summary 227

Chapter 6 Word in a Publishing Environment 229

Introduction 229
Managing Large Documents 230
   Using Master Documents and Subdocuments 230
   Other Ways to Build a Master Document 238
Protecting Your Documents 241
   Applying a Password to a Document 241
   Preventing Changes to the Original Text 243
Controlling Changes to Your Documents 244
   Using Revisions in a Document 244
   Using Annotations in a Document 245
   Adding Edit History to a Document 245
Creating Indexes and Tables of Contents 249
   Creating a Table of Contents 249
   Indexing Your Documents 250
Managing Pictures in a Document 258
   Using WroxPic to Manage Pictures in a Document 258
Better Printing with WordBasic 264
   Taking Over Word's Printing Commands 264
   Creating Your Own Print Dialog 265
   Installing the WroxPBS Duplex Print Utility 265
Summary 270

Chapter 7 Creating Web Pages for the Internet 273

Introduction 273
Why do I Need to Know about the Internet? 274
   How does the World Wide Web Work? 274
Creating Web Pages as HTML Text Files 279
   The Structure of a Web Page 280
   Making Web Page Creation Easier 290
   Viewing Your Web Pages 297
   Paragraphs, Line Breaks, Centered Text and Ruled Lines 299

	Using Graphic Images in Your Web Pages	301
	Inserting Hypertext Links into Your Web Pages	303
	Adding Extra Features to Your Web Pages	307
	Using Tables in Your Web Pages	307
	Using Forms and Controls in Your Web Pages	310
	Including Clickable Image Maps in Your Pages	312
	Other Miscellaneous HTML Tags	315
	Summary	318
Chapter 8	**Creating Windows 95 Help**	**321**
	Introduction	321
	Introducing Windows 95 Help	322
	Different Kinds of Help	322
	An Overview of a Help Project	331
	The Tools You Need	332
	Creating Topic Files	334
	The Structure of a Topic File	334
	Planning a Help File	336
	Writing the Topics	340
	Other Topic Footnotes	351
	Printing Footnote Reports	357
	Reference of Help File Footnote Types	359
	Summary	361
Chapter 9	**Compiling Windows Help Files**	**363**
	Introduction	363
	Creating a Project File	364
	The Sections of a Project File	364
	Compiling a Help File	372
	Using Help Author Mode	373
	Viewing WinHelp Messages	374
	Compiling and Viewing Your Help File	375
	Adding Extra Features to a Help File	379
	Graphics that Respond to the User	379
	Using Sound and Video Clips	382
	Changing the Way Hot Spots Look and Work	385
	More about Help File Macros	394
	Where are Macros Used?	395
	Setting the Color of Pop-ups	396
	Setting and Using Help File Markers	397
	Running Other Programs	398
	Creating a Contents List	399
	Linking Help to Your Application	405
	Context-sensitive Help	405
	Opening a Help File from Your Application	406

	Coping with Errors in a Help File	407
	Errors, Warnings and Notes	408
	Help Files that Misbehave	408
	Testing the Contents File	409
	Summary	409

Part 3   Word and the Outside World   411

Chapter 10   The Problems of Sharing Documents   413

Introduction	413
Managing Document Templates on a Network	414
Workgroup Templates	414
Protecting Templates from Changes	414
Adding Pages to the Template Dialog	415
Sharing Documents Over a Network	415
Simultaneous Editing of Documents	416
Comparing Different Versions of a Document	417
Automating Simultaneous Editing of a Document	417
Protecting Yourself from Viruses	426
How Document Viruses Work	427
Fighting the Virus Threat	428
Summary	446

Chapter 11   Using Fields and Forms in Word   449

Introduction	449
What are Word Fields?	450
Viewing the Field or the Result	450
Types of Word Field	451
Using Simple Field Types to Display Information	451
Using Button Fields to Carry Out an Action	461
What are Electronic Forms?	464
What are Form Fields?	465
The Wrox Reader Survey Form	469
Summary	485

Chapter 12   Sharing and Analyzing Data   487

Introduction	487
Using the Wrox Survey Results	488
Turning Data into Information	488
Analyzing Data in Word	490
Disk Files and WordBasic	490
Using the Survey Results in Excel and Access	501
Importing the Data into Excel	502
Analyzing the Data in Excel	503

	Importing the Data into Access	505
	Using the Data We've Collected in Access	507
	Getting the Information Back into Word	508
	An Overview of DDE and OLE	508
	Using DDE with WordBasic	510
	Hints and Tips for DDE with Word	518
	Summary	523
Chapter 13	**Using Objects in Your Documents**	**525**
	Introduction	525
	The Future of Object Technology	526
	What is an Object?	526
	What is Object Linking and Embedding?	526
	Using Word's Menus to Work with Objects	529
	Inserting Objects into Your Documents	530
	Working with Objects in Your Document	534
	Inserting Our Survey Data into a Document	536
	How Word Stores Objects	541
	The {EMBED} Field	542
	The {LINK} Field	542
	Other Types of Fields	543
	Manipulating Objects with WordBasic	544
	WordBasic Statements for Manipulating Objects	545
	Keeping Your Document Logo up to Date	548
	Maintaining an Audit Log of Data Use	551
	Sharing Your Compound Documents	556
	Using Word as an OLE Server	559
	A Brief Look at OLE Automation	559
	OLE Automation and Visual Basic	560
	Summary	563
Chapter 14	**E-mail, Address Books and Mail Merge**	**565**
	Introduction	565
	Using an Address Book	566
	The Microsoft Exchange Personal Address Book	566
	Using WordBasic with Your Default Address Book	568
	Using Addresses in Your Documents	578
	Sending Documents with Exchange	582
	Sending E-mail Direct from Word	582
	Routing a Document from Word	583
	Sending Faxes from Word	585
	Using Mail Merge with Word	587
	What is Mail Merge?	587
	Using Mail Merge with Our Survey Data	588
	Using Mail Merge from WordBasic	598
	Summary	600
	Index	**603**

Table Of Contents

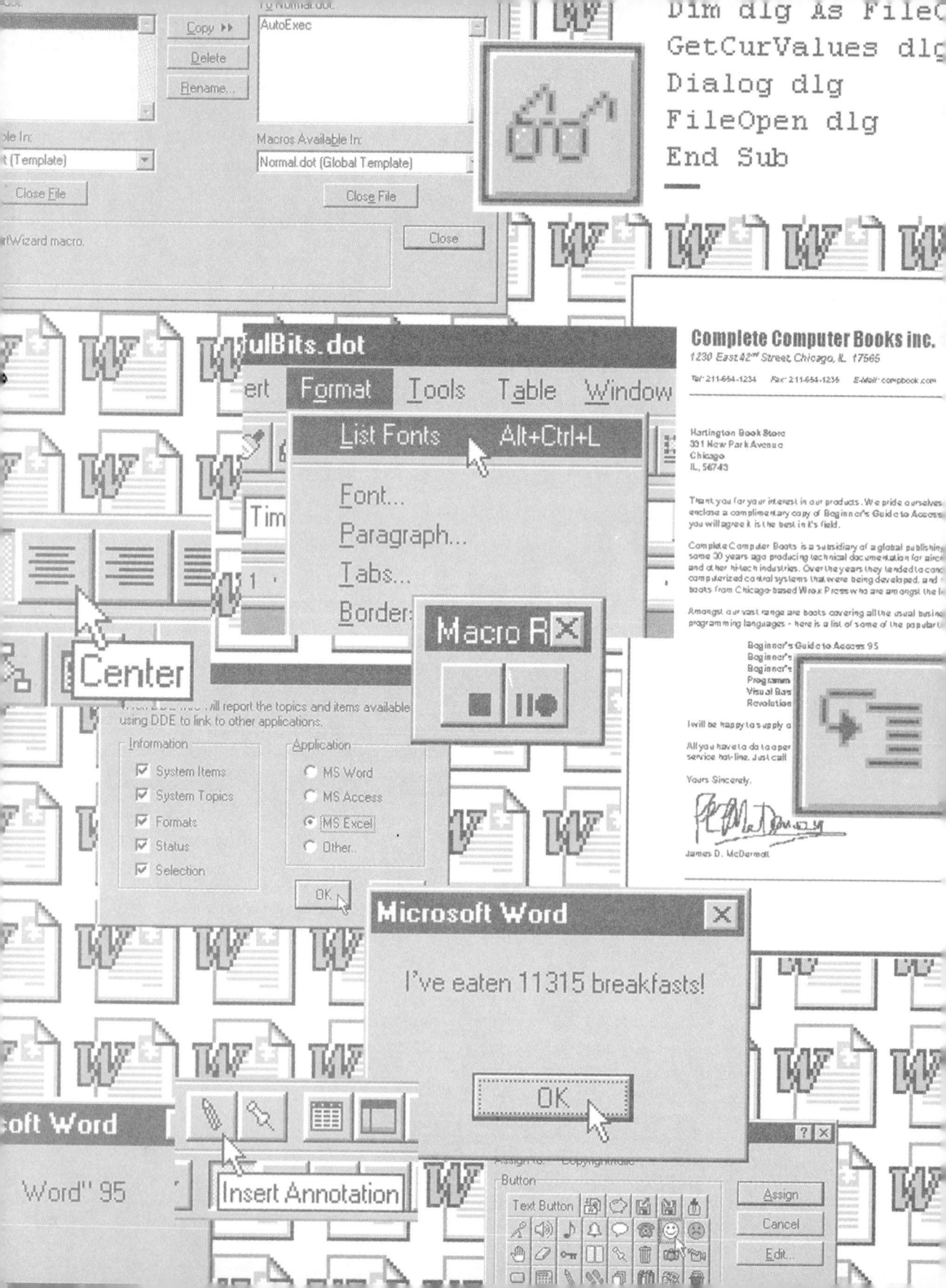

```
Dim dlg As FileO
GetCurValues dlg
Dialog dlg
FileOpen dlg
End Sub
```

Beginning WordBasic Programming

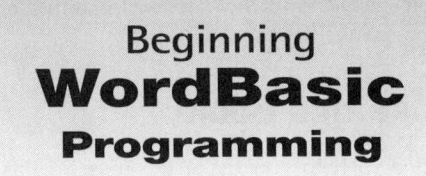

Introduction

Microsoft Word 95 is a *big* application, not only because of the vast tracts of your hard disk it consumes, but also because of the huge variety of options and features it contains. If you just use it to produce the occasional document, business letter or direct mailing, you probably take advantage of only a third of these features. Even Word's 'Intellisense' automation that helps you get the job done quicker can be used in a much more powerful context. For example, you'll have seen how Word changes *teh* to *the* as you type. This is the AutoCorrect feature at work behind the scenes, but did you know that you can create your own AutoCorrect entries, so that you just have to type *TYI* and Word will change it to *Thank you for your inquiry* automatically. Just think how much time that could save you!

When you're using an application all the time, as we do when we produce books like this, you just don't have the time to learn how it can actually *save* you time. You're too busy getting the job in hand finished. In this book we'll show you, in easy to follow bite-sized chunks, many of the ways that you can become more productive and efficient in your everyday tasks.

So we won't be telling you how to accomplish the basic word-processing tasks, like creating a document, printing and saving it, and how you format text. We'll assume that you already know how to use Word as an advanced typewriter. In fact, if that's all you need to do, you probably won't find a lot that is directly applicable here, but read on. Once you know a bit more about how Word works, you'll be surprised just how much easier you can make even the simplest tasks.

What's this Book About?

Basically, word-processing involves two stages: you insert text, pictures and other objects into a document, then manipulate and format them to get the end result that you need. However, Microsoft Word can accomplish a lot more than this and lets you automate many of the repetitive tasks that take up your time. While we can't guess exactly what uses you make of Word, we can show you many different advanced features at work.

For example, we'll show you how to use data from another application, such as a chart from Microsoft Excel, in your documents, or create personalised direct mailings using your address database from Microsoft Access.

You won't need to be a programming expert or software developer to use this book. Each chapter includes step-by-step guides, as well as a discussion of more advanced methods for you to experiment with. What you *will* learn is how to write simple chunks of code using Word's built-in programming language, WordBasic.

What You Need to Use this Book

The essential ingredient needed to help you make the most of this book is a copy of Microsoft Word for Office 95. Some of the chapters in the book tackle specific areas of development and do require some additional applications. For example, in Chapter 7 we discuss how to create HTML documents for the World Wide Web. There are many such browsers available on the market, but we have chosen to use Microsoft Internet Explorer, which is freely available for download from the Microsoft web site at:

> http://www.microsoft.com/

We also show you how to create WinHelp Help files for the applications that you develop. To fully appreciate these chapters, you'll need a copy of the Windows Help Compiler Version 4 and Help Workshop. You can get these from almost any professional Windows Application development tools or with the WinHelp Developers Kit.

For the final part of the book, we make use of some of the other Office95 applications to help us manipulate pieces of information. For these chapters we use Access, Excel and, finally, Exchange to demonstrate just what can be done in the world of Word.

How this Book is Organized

We've divided the book into chapters, each dealing with an individual topic. For instance, there's a chapter devoted to using Word in a publishing environment, such as producing a book or other technical document. It shows you how to get more from features such as annotations, indexing and tables of contents. It also demonstrates how you can produce WordBasic routines to automate the repetitive tasks that publishing often involves. The techniques covered in the chapter are often applicable to other situations, but doing things this way hopefully makes it easier for you to find related topics.

Other chapters are arranged in a similar way, covering features that you may never have used before and then looking at ways you can automate these and other related tasks. We'll also show you how you can modify the Word interface itself by changing the menus and toolbars to suit your own particular needs.

The one exception to this approach is our coverage of WordBasic itself. If you haven't come across WordBasic before, you'll need some introduction so we've provided this in the first few chapters, where we show you how to create WordBasic routines and then the various ways you can use them.

So, the book is divided into three parts:

Part 1: All About WordBasic is this introduction to WordBasic. It starts with a quick run through creating your first WordBasic program and discusses how documents, templates and macros fit together. We then go into the various language elements of WordBasic and look at how to communicate with your users through the use of message windows and dialog boxes. We finish off with a look at you how you can build more complicated routines and include them within the Word interface.

Part 2: Word in the Workplace then picks up on these techniques and shows how they can be related to your everyday tasks. In each chapter, you'll also find examples and explanations of Word's more advanced built-in features. We'll cover techniques which vastly extend the power of Word, and show how you can use Word to help create Windows 95 Help files and World Wide Web pages. We'll also look at you how you can make Word more effective when more than one person is working with a document. In a workgroup or multi-user environment, you need to keep track of the changes made by individual users and manage the revisions of a document.

Part 3: Word and the Outside World is about how you link your work in Word to the outside world. We look both at how you can use Word with other applications on your own machine or network and then generally in a wider context. This could be simple e-mail, or the exciting world of the Internet.

Once you've mastered the simple WordBasic techniques, you can continue through each chapter, learning more about the power of Microsoft Word, or just dive straight into any part of the book to explore individual techniques.

Conventions Used

We use a number of different styles of text and layout in the book to help differentiate between the different kinds of information. Here are examples of the styles we use and an explanation of what they mean:

> **FYI** Extra details, for your information, come in boxes like this.

- **Important words** are in a bold type font.
- Words that appear on the screen, such as menu options, are a similar font to the one used on screen, for example, the File menu.
- Keys that you press on the keyboard, like *Ctrl* and *Enter*, are in italics.
- All filenames are in this style: `Wineshop.mdb`.
- Function names look like this: `sizeof`
- Code which is new, important or discussed will be shown in the following format:

```
Sub MAIN
    Insert "1996 - Wrox Press"
    Italic
End Sub
```

- Code which has previously been discussed, or is unimportant to the current discussion will be shown as:

```
Sub MAIN
    Insert "1996 - Wrox Press"
    Italic
End Sub
```

Tell Us What You Think

We have tried to make this book as accurate and enjoyable for you as possible, but what really matters is what the book actually does for you. Please let us know your views, whether positive or negative, either by returning the reply card in the back of the book or by contacting us at Wrox Press by any of the following methods:

feedback@wrox.com
http://www.wrox.com/
Compuserve: 100063,2152

We have made every effort to make sure there are no errors in the text or the code. However, to err is human and as such we recognize the need to keep you, the reader, informed of these mistakes as they are spotted and amended. Please visit our web site for the latest errata sheet, or call us on **1 800 USE WROX** and we'll gladly send it to you by post.

If you spot a mistake for which there is no reference on the errata sheet, please get in touch and let us know. We'll endeavor to solve the problem and get back to you with the solution as soon as humanly possible. This not only helps you, but others who may come across the same problem.

If you like the utilities provided with this book and you want to see more Bitsoft Utility software then point your browser at **http://dspace.dial.pipex.com/bitsoft/**, where you'll find all the latest information on Bitsoft Utility and data archive software.

Finally, thank you for buying this book, or if you're just browsing in the store, please buy and enjoy!

Part 1

All About WordBasic

If you haven't yet explored Word's built-in programming environment, you're in for a treat. WordBasic is a relatively simple language which very closely mirrors the functions you use every day in Word. Unlike most modern computer languages, it contains no classes, units, compiler, or any other of the complex-sounding terms that are today's buzz-words. And there are no plus signs after the name to frighten away the faint-hearted.

WordBasic is still a very powerful tool, bearing the origins of Microsoft's Visual Basic and VBA (Visual Basic for Applications). If you can use VB or VBA, you'll have no problem picking up WordBasic, but even if you've never programmed anything more complicated than your video recorder, you can still become proficient enough to impress your colleagues in no time at all.

In Part 1 we'll start with an overview of the way WordBasic interfaces with Word and use realistic and useful examples to build up your knowledge of the language. Even if you're already a WordBasic expert, spare the time to skip through this section and have a play with the sample Book Order application.

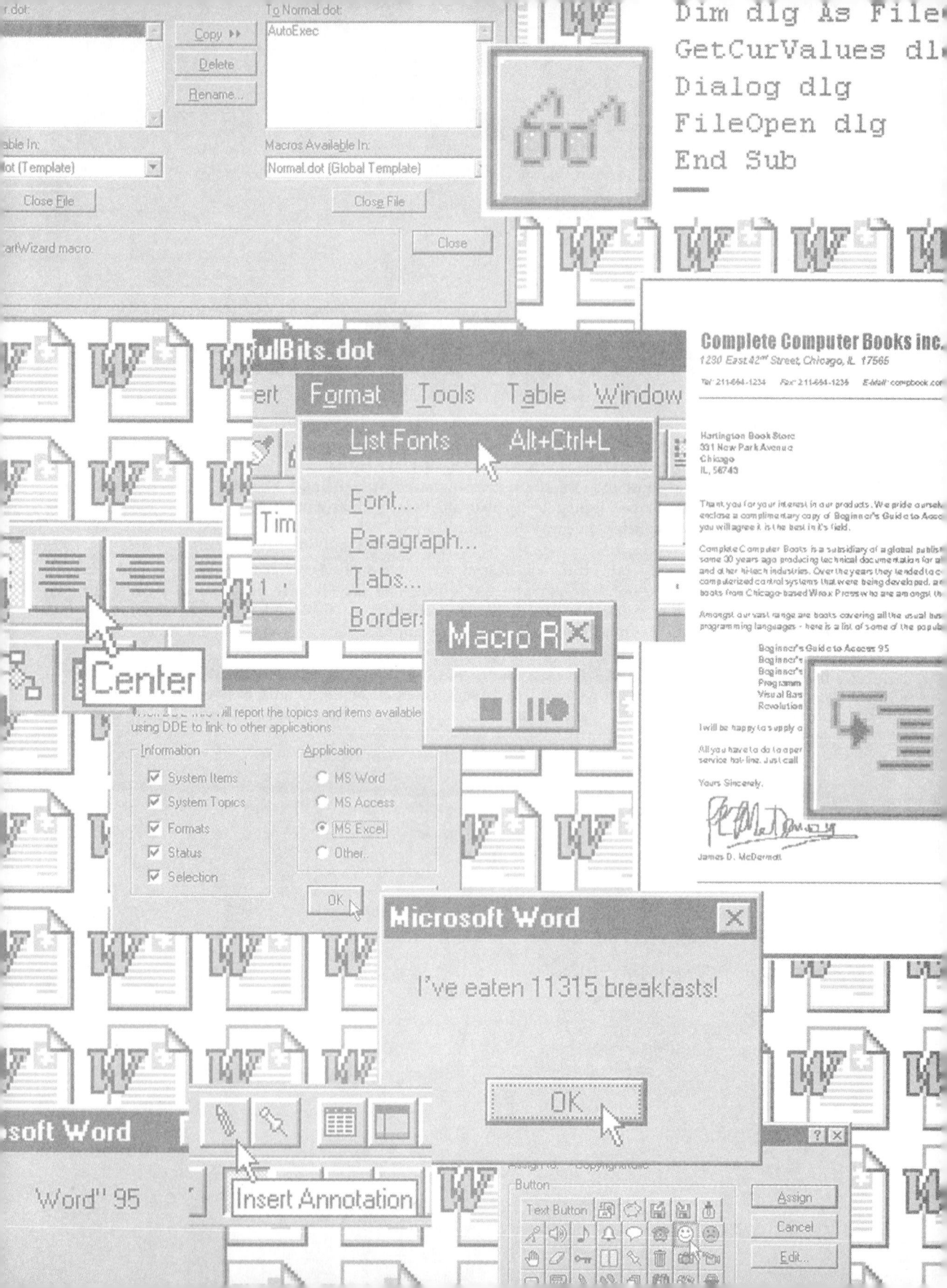

Introducing WordBasic

This book is about developing solutions for your business needs and using Microsoft Word in the real world. In these first few chapters, we'll look at how you can use Word as an *application* rather than just as a word processor, which lets you take advantage of Word's programming facilities to exert control and automate both complex and simple, but repetitive, tasks.

You may be thinking now that Word itself is an application. And what do we mean by *developing solutions*? To answer these questions, we'll first look at one of the samples included on the disk that accompanies this book. Then we'll examine in more depth what Word's programming language, WordBasic, actually is and how it interfaces with Word itself. Finally, we'll show you some simple ways to use WordBasic. So, in this chapter we'll see:

- How Word can make your work more efficient
- What WordBasic actually is
- Where, and how, macros are stored
- Some simple uses for WordBasic and macros

What Is a Word Application?

When you start Word from Windows 95 Start menu, it doesn't actually do very much. Once the fancy start-up screen has gone, all you have is a few menus and toolbars and a lot of blank white page. You can sit back and watch it for an hour or so, but other than a blinking cursor there's not a lot happening. So, instead, try this out...

Try It Out - An Inquiry Handling System

This example uses one of the sample files supplied with this book which you'll need to install on your computer. By default, they are placed in the folder `C:\BegWord` on your hard disk. The application produces a standard letter in response to an order for, or inquiry about, the range of books sold by the fictitious company Complete Computer Books Inc.

1 Open My Computer or Explorer and move to the folder where you installed the sample files. This will be **C:\BegWord** unless you changed the folder when you installed them. Double-click on the file **Book Order.dot**. Word starts up and a welcome screen is displayed.

> **FYI** You can disable the automatic starting of a Word application (you'll see more of this later in the book). If you don't see the welcome screen, select **Macro...** from Word's **Tools** menu and in the list of macros select **AutoNew** and click the **Run** button.

2 The first screen allows you to select whether this is an order and for how many copies, or an inquiry, and whether we want to send a sample. You can also specify whether it will be sent to the customer by post/fax or e-mail. For now, select Inquiry and Enclose a Complimentary copy. Make sure that Post/Fax is selected in the second frame.

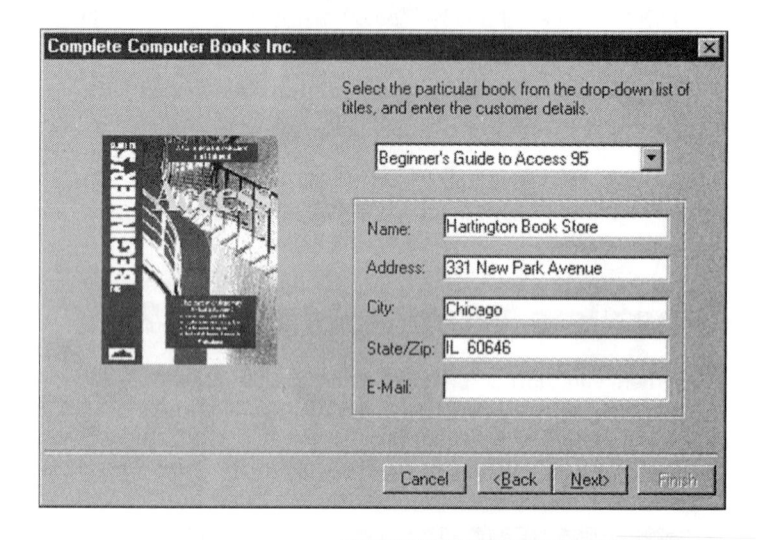

3 Click Next. Here we enter the customer's name, address and their e-mail address if we're sending it this way. In the drop-down list above, we can select the particular book that we're sending, which displays a picture of the cover.

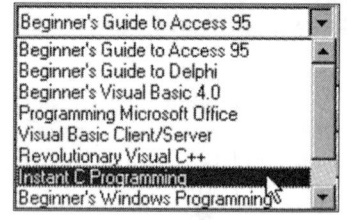

4 Click Next again. Now we can select which sections we want in the letter. The How to open a trading account option is only selected by default if we're dealing with an inquiry. If we're dealing with an order, this is turned off, but we can select it if we need to. Select the ones you want to include. Notice how the preview changes when you click on the Include the Cover picture option.

5 Click Next and we come to the final screen. Here we can change the suggested file name and decide if we want to edit the letter manually before we send it. Leave this set to No, it's ready to send now.

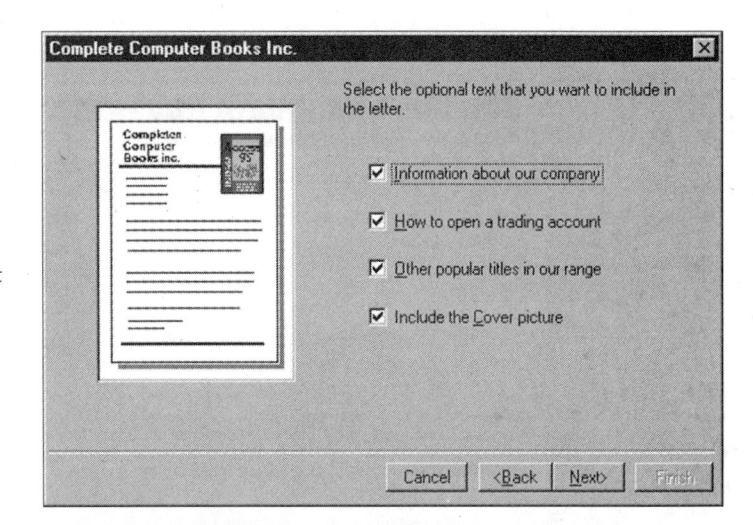

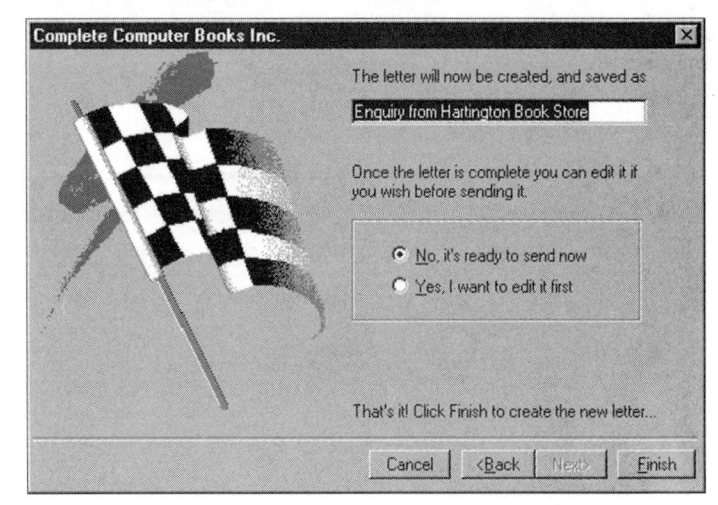

6 Click Finish and the letter is created, then the Print dialog opens. Select the printer you want to send it to, or your fax software driver if you want to fax it. Then click OK. Word prints the letter and closes down, returning you to the Windows desktop.

The final letter is attractive, personalized and, of course, pre-addressed for you ready to pop in an envelope and post. Think how much time that could save you every day if you have to handle a lot of orders and inquiries

> **Complete Computer Books inc.**
> 1230 East 42nd Street, Chicago, IL 17565
> Tel:211-654-1234   Fax:211-654-1235   E-Mail:compbook.com
>
> Harligton Book Store
> 331 New Park Avenue
> Chicago
> IL, 58743
>
> Thank you for your interest in our products. We pride ourselves not only on the quality and enclose a complimentary copy of Beginner's Guide to Access 95 for you to look at. I'm sure you will agree it is the best in it's field.
>
> Complete Computer Books is a subsidiary of a global publishing company which started out some 30 years ago producing technical documentation for aircraft manufacturers, car makers and other hi-tech industries. Over the years they tended to concentrate more and more on the computerzed control systems that were being developed and now are the world's foremost of books from Chicago-based Wrox Press who are amongst the leaders in this field.
>
> Amongst our vast range are books covering all the usual business applications and the major programming languages - here is a list of some of the popular titles:
>
> > Beginner's Guide to Access 95
> > Beginner's Guide to Delphi
> > Beginner's Visual Basic 4.0
> > Programming Microsoft Office
> > Visual Basic Client/Server
> > Revolutionary Visual C++
>
> I will be happy to supply our full catalogue on request.
>
> All you have to do to open a trading account with us is call John or Margaret on our customer service hot-line. Just call 800-123-4587 now.
>
> Yours sincerely
>
> *[signature]*
>
> James D. McDermott

We'll be taking this sample application to pieces in the next few chapters to see how it works. In the meantime, play around with it if you like. You can try sending the letter by e-mail, though you must have Microsoft Exchange installed to do so. If you haven't, the **E-Mail** option on the first screen will not be available.

The application will add entries to your address book for each letter you send by e-mail. However, it uses a very simple mail-handling method and you may well get error messages as you send it if your default address book setting is not **Personal Address Book**. In later chapters, we'll look in more detail at how you can interface with Microsoft Exchange and use Word with various online services directly.

An Overview of WordBasic and Macros

The application you've just seen uses the built-in programming language WordBasic—nothing else. WordBasic can quite easily cope with quite complex tasks like this with a remarkably small amount of code.

However, although WordBasic resembles the more usual Basics, it works in a fundamentally different way. Microsoft Word itself is actually built around WordBasic; you can use it to directly execute a function in Word, or you can take advantage of individual functions and dialog boxes that are already part of Word. When Word is running in the normal way, the actions you take selecting from the menus or clicking buttons execute these internal functions in exactly the same way as when you use them within WordBasic code.

Each of these segments of code, whether part of Word or ones you've written yourself, are called **macros**. The ones that are part of Word itself (that you execute from a menu or toolbar button) are often referred to as *built-in commands* or *functions*.

Three Ways of Using WordBasic

Let's take a quick overview of the three different ways you can interact with Word using WordBasic macros. You'll probably find it useful to come back to these diagrams as you progress through the book. *Don't worry about what the instructions in the macro actually mean*, just get a feel for the differences between the methods for now. We'll be covering each type in detail as we work through the next few chapters.

Method One: Executing a Built-in Word Function Directly

When you call a built-in macro or command in Word, it executes (in most cases) exactly as if you had selected it from a menu or toolbar button, or pressed a key, or a combination of keys on the keyboard.

This is the simplest way to use WordBasic and is handy for things like formatting text and other simple tasks. In the case opposite, the **CharLeft** instruction in the macro moves the insertion point (flashing text cursor) to the left by one place.

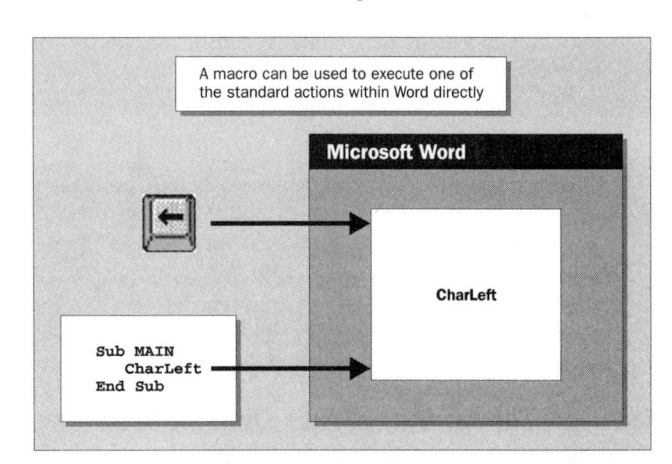

A macro can be used to execute one of the standard actions within Word directly

Microsoft Word

CharLeft

```
Sub MAIN
    CharLeft
End Sub
```

Method Two: Using Word's Built-in Dialog Boxes

The second method involves **dialogs**, the windows that offer you a choice of settings or actions when you're using Word. The example here uses the FilePrint dialog which is the one that you see when you select Print from the File menu.

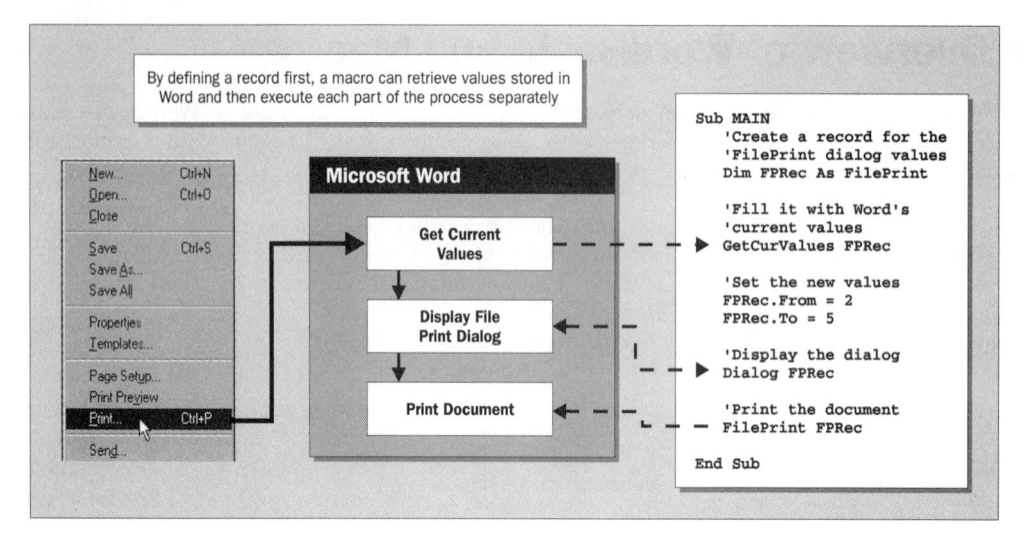

```
                    By defining a record first, a macro can retrieve values stored in
                    Word and then execute each part of the process separately
                                                                                    Sub MAIN
                                                                                        'Create a record for the
                                                                                        'FilePrint dialog values
   New...         Ctrl+N        Microsoft Word                                          Dim FPRec As FilePrint
   Open...        Ctrl+O
   Close                                                                                'Fill it with Word's
                                      Get Current                                       'current values
   Save           Ctrl+S              Values                                        ▶   GetCurValues FPRec
   Save As...
   Save All                                                                             'Set the new values
                                                                                        FPRec.From = 2
   Properties                       Display File                                        FPRec.To = 5
   Templates...                     Print Dialog
                                                                                        'Display the dialog
   Page Setup...                                                                    ▶   Dialog FPRec
   Print Preview
   Print...       Ctrl+P            Print Document                                      'Print the document
                                                                                        FilePrint FPRec
   Send...
                                                                                    End Sub
```

This method looks a lot more complicated than it really is. When you select File | Print in Word, a chain of events is set in motion. First, the settings for your printer and the current document are retrieved and then the Print dialog opens with these values displayed. For example, it shows which printer is currently selected, the range of pages to print, etc. You can change the values in the dialog from the ones that Word has retrieved and when you click OK, Word runs the built-in command that prints the document, using the values from the dialog. Follow the thick lines in the diagram to see this.

We can carry out this chain of events in code, using WordBasic. The example shows the macro first creating a record (simply a set of locations in memory which correspond to the settings and options available in the dialog) to store the values for the Print dialog. Here, it's called **FPRec**. The macro then gets the current values to fill the dialog box from Word and places them in this record.

Now it can change the values as required. Here, it sets the range of pages to print from 2–5. The next step is to display the Print dialog on screen where the user can change the values themselves as usual. When they click OK this time, however, Word passes control back to our macro with the record **FPRec** holding the latest values from the dialog. To actually start the printing process with these values, we have to use another instruction. You can see from the dotted lines in the diagram how each part of the macro is linked to functions within Word itself. So, you can use the powerful built-in functions of Word, including most of the screen dialogs, but control each step of the process yourself.

Method Three: Using Your Own Custom Dialog Boxes

In the previous example, we used the functionality within Word to do all the work; we just told it which built-in function to execute and what values to use. However, we can also create far more complex macros which don't depend on the standard dialogs that are part of Word.

> A macro can simply retrieve and set individual values within Word directly and use them in custom dialogs to interact with the user

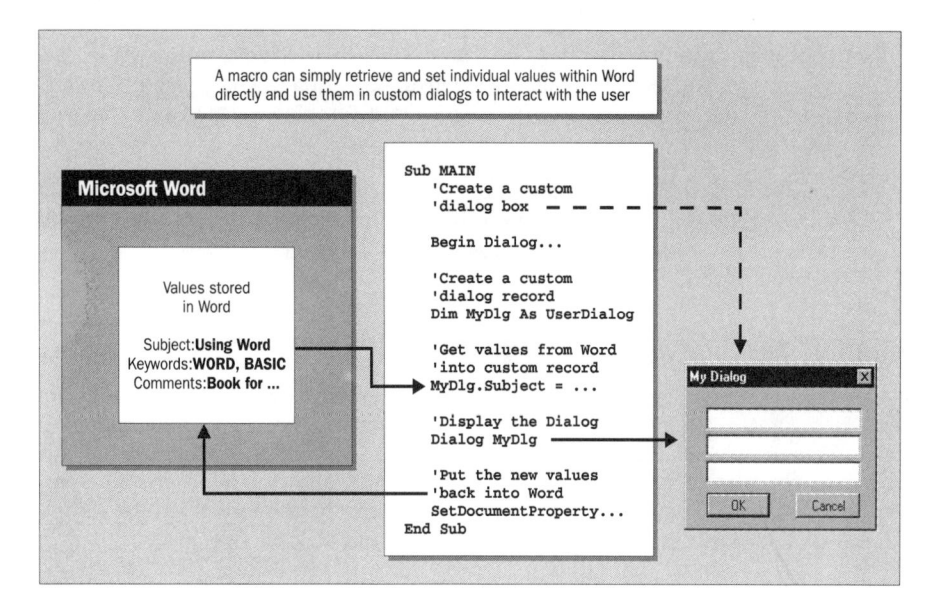

```
Sub MAIN
    'Create a custom
    'dialog box

    Begin Dialog...

    'Create a custom
    'dialog record
    Dim MyDlg As UserDialog

    'Get values from Word
    'into custom record
    MyDlg.Subject = ...

    'Display the Dialog
    Dialog MyDlg

    'Put the new values
    'back into Word
    SetDocumentProperty...
End Sub
```

Microsoft Word — Values stored in Word
Subject: **Using Word**
Keywords: **WORD, BASIC**
Comments: **Book for ...**

The third method, shown above, allows us to create our own custom dialog and define a record to store its values. Then we can access the individual values, option settings and text within Word directly and place them in our record in any way we want. Finally, we display our dialog, interact with the user and, when they click OK, we place the changed values back in Word again.

This is fundamentally different from the previous method: it doesn't use the built-in dialogs or standard records for storing their values. Despite the overhead of a more complex macro, it does have many other advantages. Again, we'll see more of this later on. In particular, though, you're free to design a totally different interface to Word, which manipulates the document and its environment without being tied to the standard built-in functions.

Where and How Macros are Stored

By now, you should be bursting with ideas of how WordBasic can solve some of your problems, but be patient—we'll come to the 'nuts and bolts' bit soon. The first thing that we *must* consider—and that it's very important you grasp before we go any further— is where the magic to produce our application actually comes from when we run it.

It's fairly obvious that the inquiry handling system we looked at earlier is something to do with the template **Book Order.dot**. You began by double-clicking on it to start Word and run the inquiry application. This template contains all the elements that produce the dialog boxes, pictures, the text and graphics for the letter and, of course, the code that ties it all together.

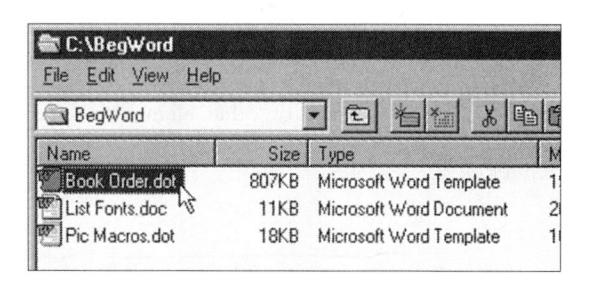

Name	Size	Type
Book Order.dot	807KB	Microsoft Word Template
List Fonts.doc	11KB	Microsoft Word Document
Pic Macros.dot	18KB	Microsoft Word Template

C:\BegWord

> **FYI** Word templates use the file extension .dot rather than .doc (a normal Word document). You can set up Windows 95 so that the extension part of a file name isn't visible. However, you'll see the file's type listed as **Microsoft Word Template** in **My Computer** or **Explorer** file list windows.
>
> If you want to turn on the display of the file extensions, open **My Computer** or **Explorer** and select **Options...** from the **View** menu. In the **Options** dialog, select the **View** tab, and turn off the **Hide MSDOS file extensions...** option.

Understanding Templates and Context

One of the ways that you customize Word when you use it to produce letters or other documents is to create a template which already contains, for example, your name and address. Each time you base a new document on this template, your name and address is automatically inserted. When you select New from the File menu, Word allows you to choose from different templates. However, you may not appreciate that you can have more than one template loaded at any one time—in fact, most of the time you probably have at least two loaded.

The templates (and other add-ins) that are loaded at any one time define the context in Word and since you can have more than one template loaded, you have a choice of where you store your macros and the other elements required for your applications. There are four parts of the context that are important:

- The active template
- The global context
- The Normal template
- The built-in commands

You can think of these as forming a hierarchy. At the bottom are the built-in commands and functions that are part of Word, and at the top are the macros, text and other objects in the active template (the one you based the current document on). Notice that the normal template, called **Normal.dot**, is always loaded when you open a document, even if that document is based on a different template. So, any macros in **Normal.dot** are always available. If you delete **Normal.dot**, Word will obligingly create a new one for you automatically (of course, you'll lose anything you stored in it originally).

So what is the global context? Well, here the uncertainty often arises. It's a shame that Microsoft didn't use the name **Global.dot** for the normal template, because effectively they are the same thing, with one major difference. If you base a document on **MyLetter.dot**, you'll find you have both **MyLetter.dot** and **Normal.dot** loaded automatically. However, if you have another template called **UsefulBits.dot**, you can load this *as well*. It appears as part of the global context, so any macros or other elements it contains are available. However, the format and content of the active document, which is based on the active template **MyLetter.dot**, don't change.

```
        MyLetter.dot          ◄──  The Active Template

       UsefulBits.dot         ◄──  Global Add-ins and Templates

       Normal.dot             ◄──  The Normal Template

    Word's Built-In Commands and Functions
```

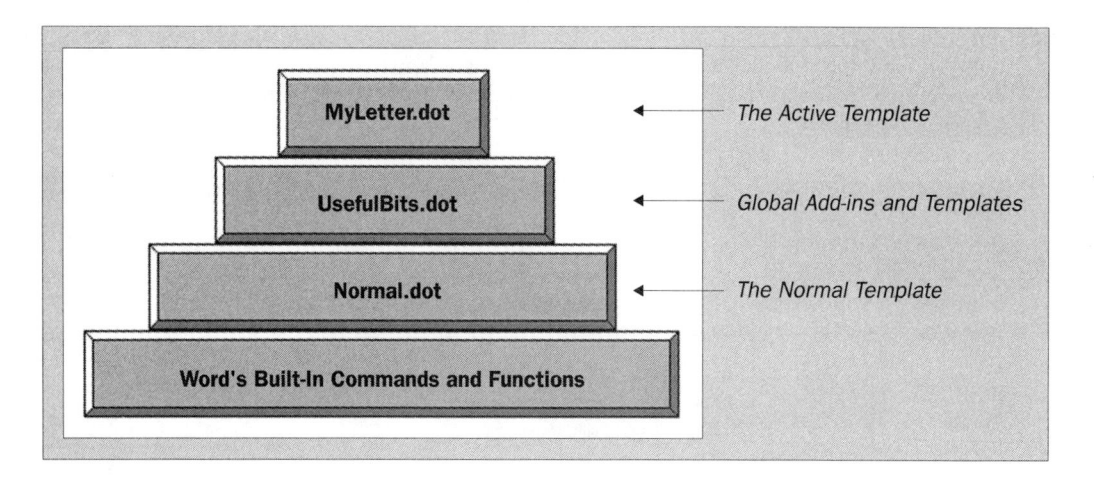

The Template Organizer

OK, let's take a look at these different contexts. Word includes a clever tool, called the Organizer, which we'll use to see the different elements included in the sample Book Order application. Because we've been using the word *elements* in the previous sections, rather than just saying *macros*, you won't be surprised to find there are other things in this template as well. We'll see what else is stored there.

Try It Out - Using the Template Organizer

Again, we'll be using one of the sample files supplied with this book. These will have been placed in the **C:\BegWord** folder on your hard disk, unless you changed the defaults during installation.

1 Start Microsoft Word from the Start menu. Open the sample file **Book Order.dot** while holding down the *Shift* key. This stops the application running automatically when you open the file.

2 Select Templates from the File menu and in the Templates and Add-Ins dialog click the Organizer... button. The Organizer dialog appears. This shows the Styles, AutoText entries, Toolbars and Macros that are stored in a document template. Make sure the Macros tab is selected.

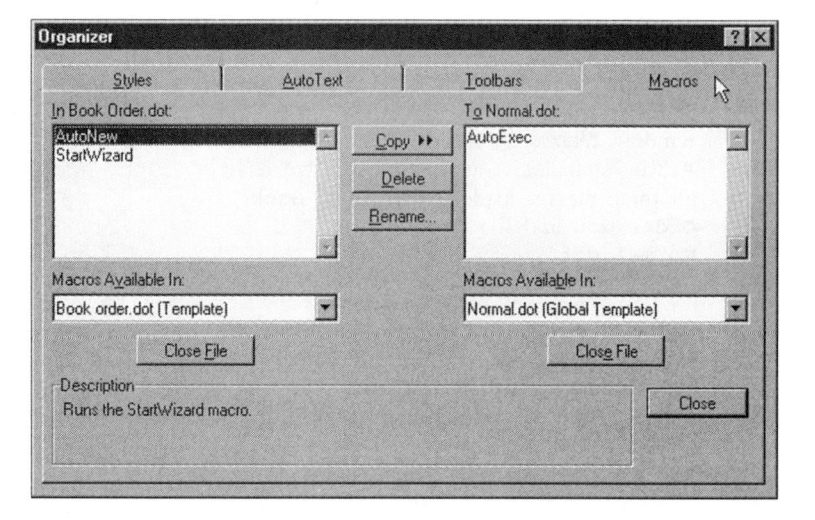

15

3   You can view the contents of two different templates at a time—in this case, our **Book Order** template and the default **Normal** template. Here you can see that our **Book Order** template contains two macros, `AutoNew` and `StartWizard`. The **Normal** template only contains one, called `AutoExec`.

4   Click the **AutoText** tab. Now you can see a list of **AutoText** entries in the **Book Order** template. If you select one, you'll see the parts of the text that make up our letter appear in the lower frame. However, some of the **AutoText** entries produce **EMBED PBrush** instead. These are the graphics (book covers, etc.) used by the application.

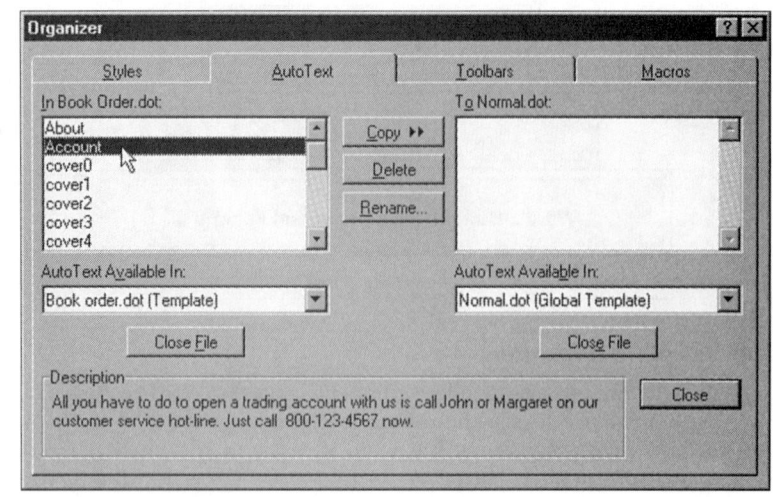

5   There are no toolbars in our application, and no special styles other than those set by default. If you want to explore, though, go right ahead.

6   Click the **Close** button to close the **Organizer** dialog. Then, from Word's **Tools** menu, select **Macro....** The **Macro** dialog opens. Notice that this also contains an **Organizer...** button. You can open **Organizer** either this way or with the **File | Templates...** command we used earlier.

7   The **Macro** dialog shows only the macros that are *actually loaded*, whereas the **Organizer** window showed what was stored in the template. At the bottom of the window, **Macros Available In:** is set to **All Active Templates**. You can see that we have all three macros loaded—two from `Book Order.dot` and the one from `Normal.dot`.

8   In the drop-down list at the bottom of the **Macros** dialog, you can select the context for which you want to see the loaded macros. For example, selecting **Book Order.dot (Template)** will only show the two macros stored there.

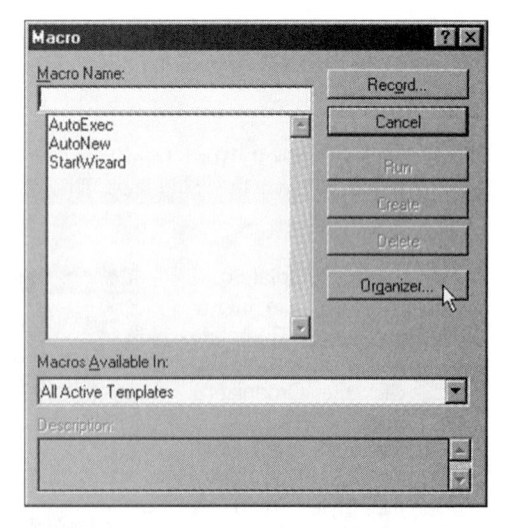

What We've Seen

So, the Organizer and Macro dialogs are useful tools for examining macros (and all the other items that are stored in a template).

Organizer displays the actual contents of any template, whether or not it's loaded or active at the time. By default, it shows the currently active template(s), in our case Book Order, and the Normal template. However, you can use the Close File button to close the templates that are currently displayed, then open another one to see what it contains.

That's not all that Organizer can do: you can use the Copy, Delete and Rename... buttons to manage the individual items in the template, or to copy them between any two templates. You'll see more of this later.

The Macro dialog, on the other hand, is useful to indicate which macros are current in each context. You can elect to include all active templates, the template on which the document is based, any globally loaded templates or add-ins, the Normal template and all Word's built-in commands.

You should also have picked from this exercise that the Normal template is *always* loaded, even if you specify a different one as the basis for a document, like we did in this example.

Using the Correct Template to Store Macros

Well, now you know that macros are stored in a template, but we've discovered that there can be several templates loaded at one time. So which one do you use? The answer to this depends on what you want your macro to do and when you want to use it.

If you want your macro to be universally available each time you start Word, the answer is simple: drop it into your Normal template which is loaded by default, as we saw in the previous section. However, this has an obvious downside: if you put *all* your macros there, the template will soon become very large and very overcrowded. For instance, because of the graphics it contains, our Book Order template is over 800KB on its own. If you loaded this each time you used Word, you would be wasting memory and increasing the time taken to load it and save any changes you may make to the template.

> **FYI** By default, Word automatically saves changes to a template when you close a document based on it. So, even simply changing the details of a style would mean resaving the whole template.

Alternatively, if the macro you want is stored in a different template to the one your document is based on, you have to consciously load that template before you can use the macro. That means remembering what the template is called. If there are a lot of other macros in that template, you end up loading them all just to get at the one you want. Again, you're wasting valuable memory and, as we all know, Windows 95 and Word between them take up enough to start with.

All of this means that, to judge where best to place it, you need to have a pretty clear idea of how the macro will be used. Of course, if it's only simple and contains no space-hogging graphic images, you can tuck it into a corner of **Normal.dot** with no problems. Otherwise, here are a few suggestions:

Macros which:	Are best stored in:
Are very large and complex, or contain a lot of graphics and text	Individual templates—one for each function or group of functions.
You use very rarely, and then only for specialized purposes	A template for all the ones with related purposes.
Are medium to large, and used regularly	One or more 'utility' templates—grouped by task and containing several macros in each.
Are small and used regularly with a particular document type	That document type's template.
Are small and used regularly with all types of document	`Normal.dot`

Remember, you can always move macros around, from one template to another, using the Organizer dialog. You can also create 'utility' templates containing sets of macros that are just plain useful, then load this template together with the one your document is based on—just like the hypothetical UsefulBits template we came across when we looked at how contexts work earlier.

> **FYI** Many of the macros we'll be using in this book are supplied with the samples on the accompanying disk—in the file `UsefulBits.dot`. The default folder for these is `C:\BegWord`, unless you changed it while installing them. We'll be creating a new template called `UsefulBits.dot` in your default **Templates** folder, and you can copy macros to it from our sample template if you wish.

Loading a Template Globally

So let's assume you've got a template, such as UsefulBits, which contains macros that you want to use while you've got a different template loaded. For example, you could be writing a letter based on your Bank Letter template. Any macros in your Normal template are already available, because `Normal.dot` is always loaded. So how do you load `UsefulBits.dot` as well? Easy—select Templates... form the File menu to open the Templates and Add-ins dialog.

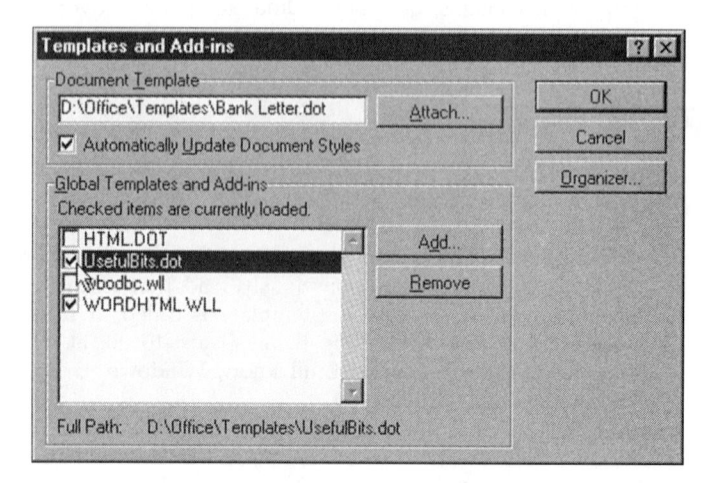

The lower section of this dialog shows the templates and add-ins that are currently loaded. You can pick the ones you want to use by placing a tick in the box next to them, or deselect them by clicking again to remove the tick. If the template you want isn't shown, you will need to add it to the list. Click the A_dd... button and the Add Template dialog allows you move to the folder where it's stored and select it. To remove one from the list altogether, select it and click the Remove button. Notice that the bottom of the dialog shows the full path to the template or add-in.

You can also use this dialog to change the template that is linked to the currently active document. In the figure on the previous page, you can see it's set to Bank Letter.dot—the one the document was based on when we created it. Click the A_ttach... button and you can specify a different one and optionally update all the styles in the document to the ones in the new template. If you don't select this option, existing text isn't reformatted to match the new styles.

> **FYI** The term *add-in* is used to identify a special kind of file that contains code routines. These are written in another language, such as C++, which is much faster and more compact than WordBasic and allows you to accomplish tasks which are otherwise not possible. They can be identified by the file extension of `.wll` (*Word Link Library*).

Using Word's Startup Folder

If you want a template to be loaded globally each time you start Word, you simply place it in the **Startup** folder. This is created by the **Setup** program, within the folder where you installed Word. Any add-ins you place there are also loaded automatically each time you fire up Word.

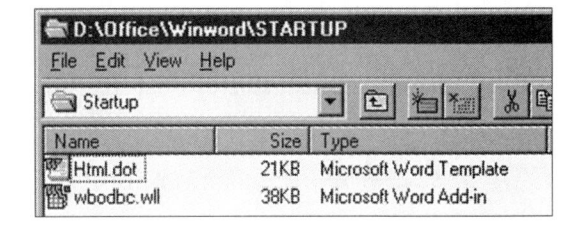

The Priority of Templates

One other aspect of using global templates is knowing which macro will be executed if you have two (or more) with the same name. Word searches through all its loaded templates in a fixed order and runs the first macro with the correct name that it finds. The order of searching is:

1 The active template (the one the currently active document is based on)

2 The Normal template (`Normal.dot`)

3 All the global templates that are currently loaded

Writing Your First Macro

Now that we know what macros are and where we store them, it's time to create a few. Let's start with the simplest type: those which just execute Word's standard functions. We'll come to the more complex types that use dialog boxes in the next chapter. However, here we'll aim for something that is at least moderately useful. Suppose we produce a lot of technical or other documentation and need to include a copyright notice in the documents—something along the lines of ©1996 – Alex Homer, Wrox Press.

Try It Out - Automating the Copyright Text

One of the most basic and useful macro instructions is the **Insert** statement. This simply places text or other objects in the document at the current insertion point (the text cursor position). Before we can create this macro, we have to decide where we're going to store it. So that we don't interfere with our Normal template, we'll create a new one to hold all the useful routines we'll be building in these next chapters.

1 Create a new document template by selecting New... from the File menu and selecting Template in the Create New section (bottom right) of the dialog.

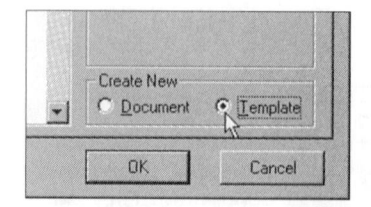

2 Click OK to create the new template. You'll see the title is Template1 which indicates we're editing a template, not a document.

3 Select Macro... from the Tools menu to open the Macro dialog and make sure you select Template1 in the Macros Available In: drop-down list. This ensures we store the macro in our new template, not in **Normal.dot** which is the default.

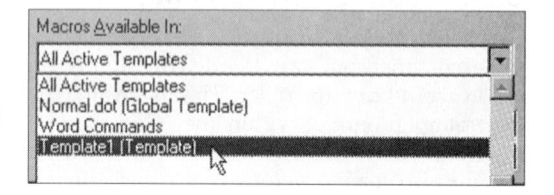

4 In the Macro Name: box type CopyrightText as the name for the new macro. Enter a Description which will be displayed in the status bar, and the Macro and Organizer dialogs, to help identify it later. Then click the Create button—we're creating the new macro from scratch.

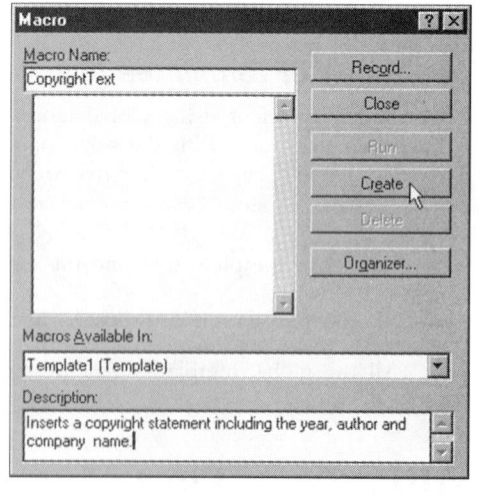

5 Word opens the macro editing window which is basically a normal document window but with an extra toolbar. This contains buttons for many of the commands you use to work with macros. You'll also find that some of the normal menus have changed. A lot of commands are disabled because they're not applicable to macro editing and many of the standard toolbar buttons will not work.

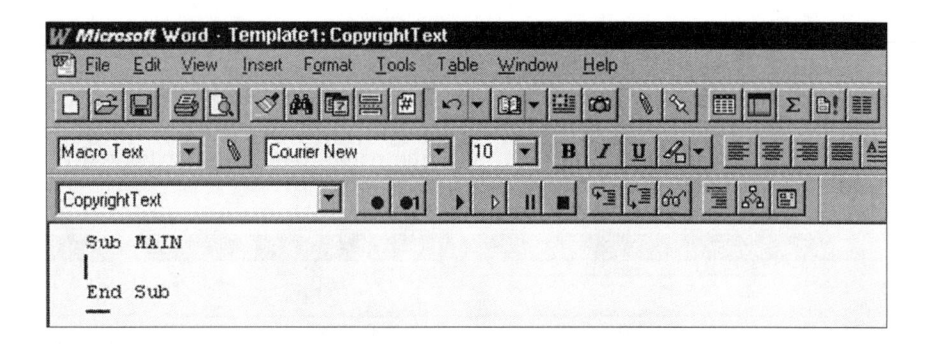

FYI Remember that it's possible to hide toolbars. If you don't see the macro editing toolbar, you can display it by right-clicking any other toolbar and selecting the **Macro** toolbar. Alternatively, select **Toolbars** from the **View** menu, and make sure the entry for the **Macro** toolbar is ticked.

6 The important part, of course, is the macro editing area. Word has automatically placed the outline of our macro there, and the text cursor is ready to enter the code that makes it work. Type,

```
Insert "©1996 - Alex Homer, Wrox Press"
```

in between the **Sub MAIN** and **End Sub** lines. (You can substitute your own name and details!) To get the © symbol press *Ctrl-Alt-C*.

```
Sub MAIN
Insert "©1996 - Alex Homer, Wrox Press"
End Sub
```

7 Now we can test it out. Leave the CopyrightText macro window open and switch back to the normal Template1 window using the Window menu. This way the Macro toolbar is still shown and we can use it to run our new macro. Click the Start button on the Macro toolbar and Word inserts the copyright text into the currently active document, in this case, our template.

> ©1996 - Alex Homer, Wrox Press

FYI If you try to run the macro while the **Macro** window is active you'll get an error message. Most macro commands only work when a document window (including, of course, the template's own document) is the currently active window.

8 The final task is to save the new template. If you've got the macro editing window open, you'll find the File menu now contains a Save Template command. If the current window is the template's document window, the normal Save As command is shown. Select either of these and the Save As dialog opens. You'll see that Word suggests the default `Templates` folder, as you're saving a new template. Enter the name UsefulBits.dot for the file name and hit the Save button.

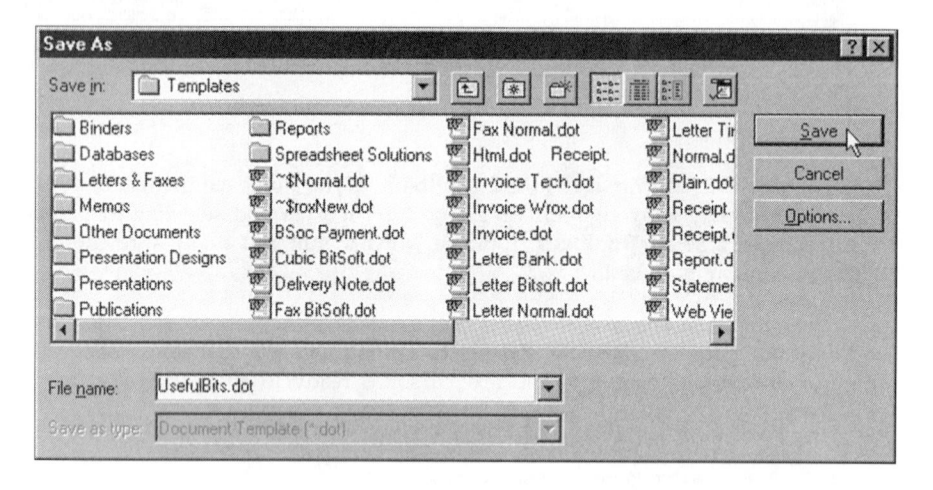

Well, that was easy enough. If you look back at the CopyrightText macro window, you'll see there's a drop-down list box which contains the name of our macro, CopyrightText. Under that is the code of our macro. The line **Sub MAIN** defines where the macro starts, and **End Sub** where it finishes (we said it was simple). In between are all the lines of code that Word executes when we run the macro, in our case just the **Insert** statement. However, there can be as many lines as you need. Remember, also, that when you create a macro, you should specify where you want it stored using the list in the Macro dialog. If you don't specify an alternative, it will be placed in your Normal template.

We could have achieved the same results as our new macro using Word's built-in AutoCorrect feature. If you haven't seen this before, open the Tools menu and select AutoCorrect.... You enter some text in the Replace: box to identify your entry and then type the actual text you want in the final document in the With: box. Word includes a selection already set up for you, including 'smiley' faces, arrows, and common misspellings.

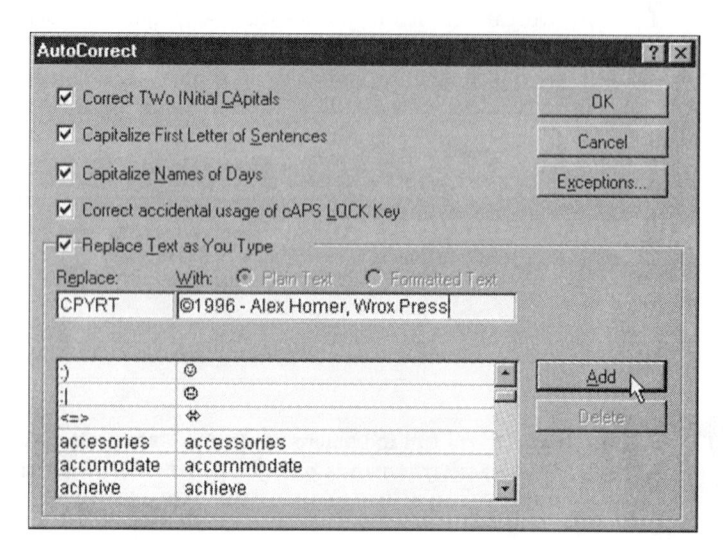

So we could enter something like CPYRT in the R̲eplace: box, and the full copyright expression in the W̲ith: box, so that Word will perform the replacement automatically every time we typed CPYRT.

Try It Out - Improving Our Copyright Macro

So let's be a bit cleverer. We'll change our macro so that it inserts the *current* year rather than the fixed text 1996. And while we're about it, let's also see if Word knows our name without being told. If it does, the macro will work on another machine without being changed.

1 The first step is to open the macro we created earlier for editing. If you have closed the UsefulBits template, open it again by selecting it from the F̲ile menu's recently used files list, or use the F̲ile | O̲pen... command and set the Files of Type: to Document Templates (*.dot).

2 Select M̲acro... from the T̲ools menu and in the Macros dialog select the CopyrightText macro we created earlier. Then click the E̲dit button.

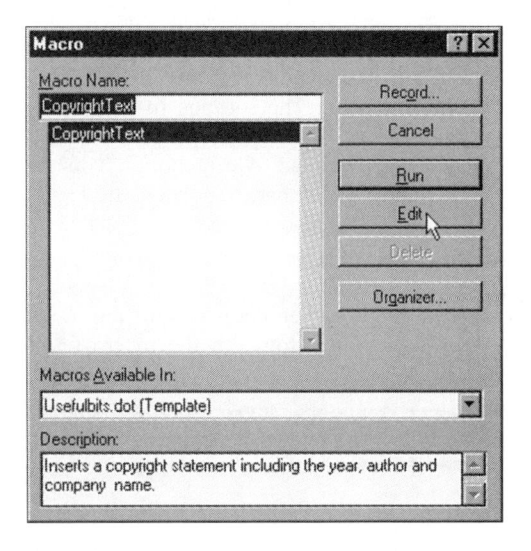

3 The macro editing window opens with the original `CopyrightText` macro shown. We'll change it to make it independent of the machine it's running on. The first step is to get Word to use the current year. We do this with the statement:

```
Insert "©" + Str$(Year(Now())) + " - "
```

FYI — This uses three of WordBasic's built-in functions. `Now()` returns the current date and time set in the computer's operating system. `Year()` takes a date and returns the year as a number. `Str$()` takes a number and converts it into a string with either a space or a minus sign added to the left. You'll see all these terms discussed in more detail in the next chapter. If you aren't familiar with them, just accept them for now and we'll fill you in later on.

By placing a plus sign between the different elements, we tell Word to compound them into a single piece of text and insert it in the document.

```
REM CopyrightText Macro
Sub MAIN
    Insert "©" + Str$(Year(Now())) + " - "
End Sub
```

4 Switch to the template's document window and click the Start button on the Macro toolbar. The first part of the copyright text is inserted, using the current year.

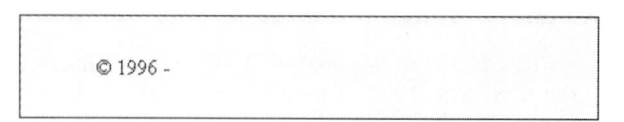

© 1996 -

5 Back in the macro window, we now need to add the author and company name. These are actually stored in all the documents and templates you create. To see them, select Properties from the File menu and open the Summary page. The settings in a new document are those you specified when you installed Word, though you can change them here. You may find that Word has also suggested a Title for the document.

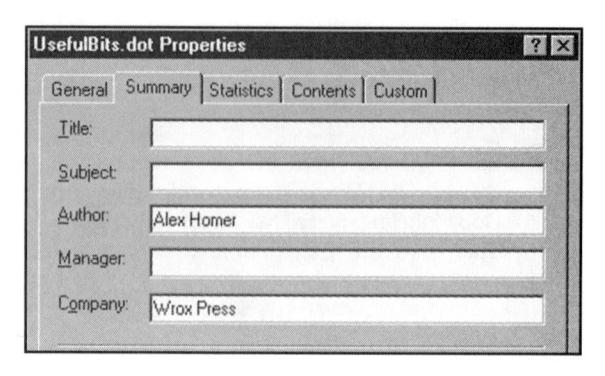

UsefulBits.dot Properties
General | Summary | Statistics | Contents | Custom
Title:
Subject:
Author: Alex Homer
Manager:
Company: Wrox Press

6 We get at these properties using the **GetDocumentProperty$** function that is part of WordBasic's repertoire. In the macro window, add the lines

```
Insert GetDocumentProperty$("Author") + ", "
Insert GetDocumentProperty$("Company")
InsertPara
```

to your macro. These return the values of the **Author** and **Company** from the list of properties that are stored within the document. Again, we've used the plus sign to compound the parts of the text, and we've added a third line which simply inserts a carriage return, just as you press *Return* when typing.

```
Sub MAIN
    Insert "©" + Str$(Year(Now())) + " - "
    Insert GetDocumentProperty$("Author") + ", "
    Insert GetDocumentProperty$("Company")
    InsertPara
End Sub
```

7 Now switch back to the template's document window and place the text cursor on a new line. Click the Start button on the Macro toolbar. The macro now inserts the complete copyright statement and moves the cursor to the next line.

© 1996 - Alex Homer, Wrox Press

8 Close and save the template. If you currently have the macro window open, you'll be prompted to save the changes to the macro, as well as those to the actual template text. Select Yes.

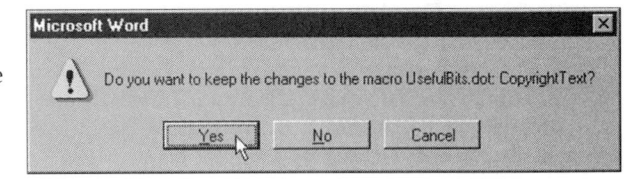

How It Works

All we've done is change the way that the text is generated. In the earlier example, we used the fixed text ©1996 - Alex Homer, Wrox Press and inserted it into the document using the `Insert` statement. This time, we've got Word to supply the year, author and company name instead. The built-in functions that are part of WordBasic can supply the current date and format it so that it appears only as the year. The properties that are stored in all documents can be retrieved using other WordBasic functions. We'll be explaining in more depth, over the next few chapters, exactly how each of these functions are used.

So we've now got a macro that does something useful, something that would be quite complicated to achieve any other way. Yet this is still only using WordBasic at the simplest level. We've got a lot more territory to explore yet, as you'll see.

You've also seen here how you create a new macro and edit an existing one. The heart of the process is the Macro dialog (select Macro... from the Tools menu), and it's here you can Run, Create and Delete macros. You can also open the Organizer dialog we met earlier, which will Rename them and move them from one template to another.

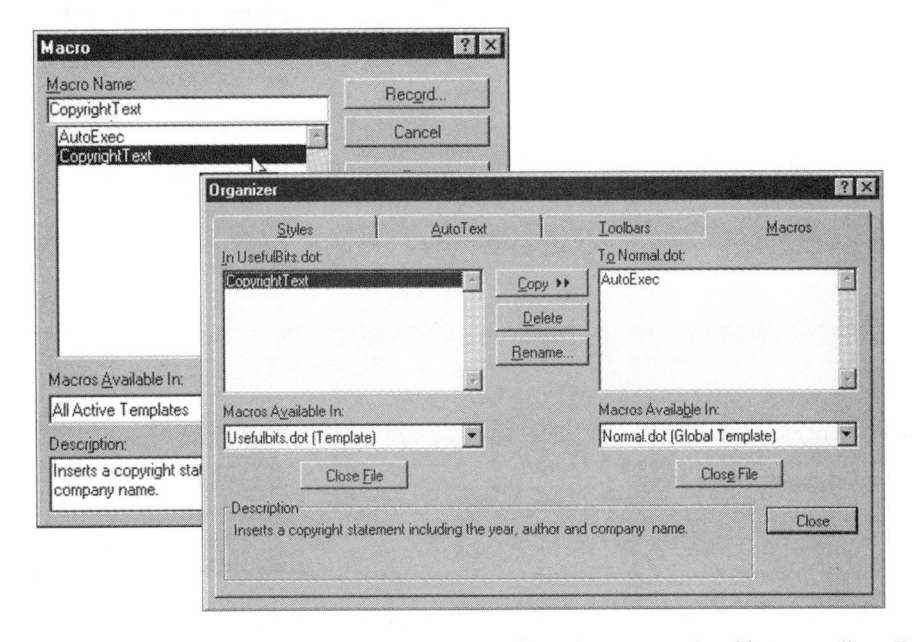

In these examples, we've run our macros using the Start button on the Macro toolbar. Remember that, although you can see the macro sheet and the associated toolbar while you're writing a macro, you don't see it when you're editing a document based on that template. Even though your users can run a macro by opening the Macro dialog, selecting the one they want and clicking the Run button, it looks much better and is more efficient if you offer them a more intuitive way to start the macro.

You can arrange to start a macro in response to a toolbar button, menu command, or special key combination while you're working on a document. We'll see how this is done as we create more macros throughout this part of the book.

Recording Macros Automatically

You'll no doubt have noticed that the Macro dialog also contains a button to record a macro. Like most other macro languages, you can create a WordBasic routine by carrying out the commands which you want to automate using the keyboard and have Word record them for you. However, unlike other simple macro languages, Word doesn't record the actual keystrokes—it converts them into WordBasic statements.

This can be very useful. If you don't know which statement you need, you can record the action that carries it out using the mouse and keyboard, then view the completed macro afterwards. To make life even easier, Word has a function which records just one command, then automatically switches recording off.

Recording the Next Command

For example, if you want to add an instruction to center the current paragraph you just:

1 Position the cursor in your macro where you want the statement to be.

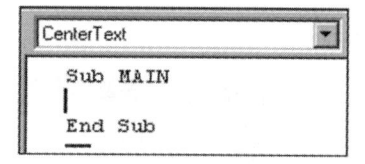

2 Switch to the document window and click the Record Next Command button.

3 Click the Center button on the toolbar (or press *Ctrl-E*).

When you go back to the macro editing window again, you find the statement **CenterPara** has been inserted for you. This will carry out the action you want when you run the macro.

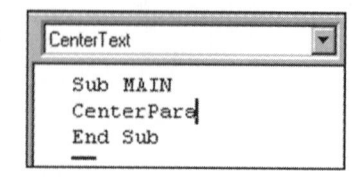

Before we leave this chapter, we'll have a go at recording a more complex macro, then see what the result is. We'll also come across one of the problems with this method and see how to resolve it.

Try It Out - Recording a Macro

We'll try recording a macro similar to the `CopyrightText` we created earlier. As well as inserting the text, we'll also format it as italic.

1 If you've closed the UsefulBits template, open it again by selecting it from the File menu's recently used files list, or use the File | Open... command and set the Files of type: to Document Templates (*.dot).

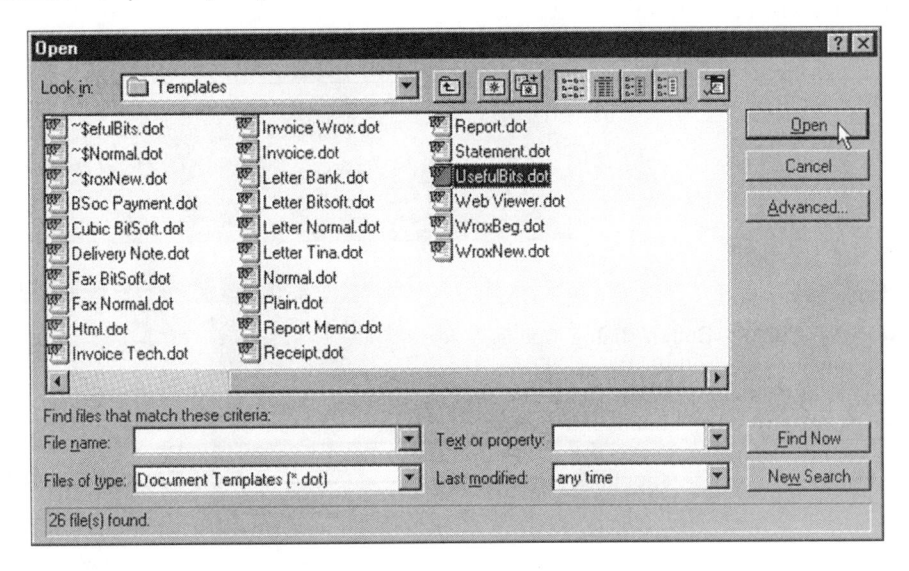

2 Select Macro... from the Tools menu, and in the Macros dialog change the Macros Available In: to UsefulBits.dot (Template) so that the new macro is created in this template, rather than Normal.dot.

3 Enter the name CopyrightItalic for the new macro, type in a Description and this time click the Record button.

4 Now the Record Macro... dialog opens. Here we choose where and how we install our new macro in the Word interface, so that our users can run it. For the time being, we'll use the Toolbars option. Click the Toolbars button.

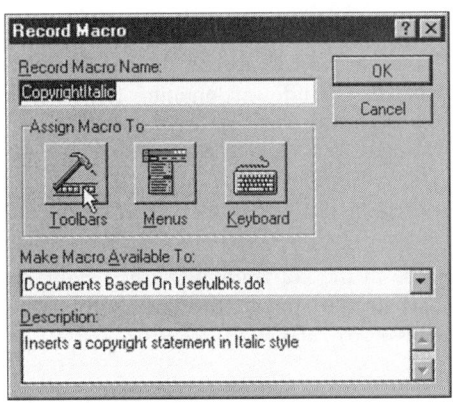

5 This opens the Customize window. Select the CopyrightItalic macro that we're about to create and, holding the left mouse button, drag it onto one of the existing toolbars. As you drag, the cursor shows a gray square and when you let go, a blank button is placed on that toolbar.

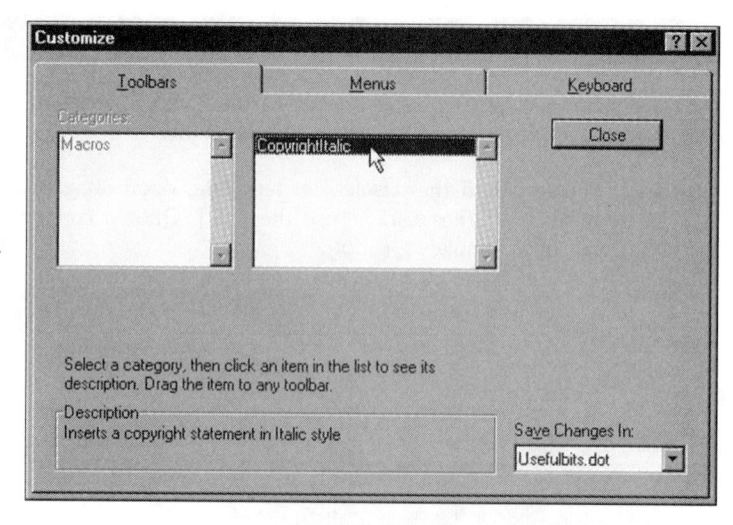

6 Next the Custom Button dialog opens. Select a picture for the button. We've chosen the 'smiley' face, mainly because none of the others are any more suitable! If you're feeling artistic, you can use the Edit... button to change one of the supplied pictures.

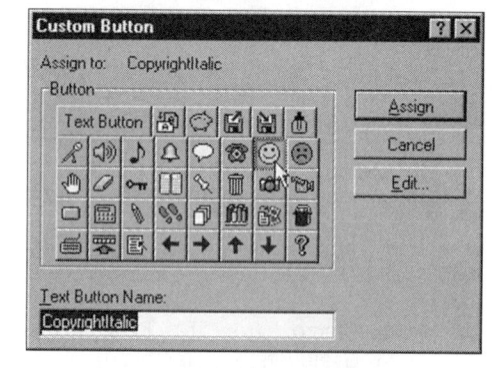

7 Click Assign and the picture appears on the new button.

8 Now we start to record the macro. Word automatically opens the Macro Recorder window containing two buttons. One is the Stop button and the other allows us to pause the recording part way through. The cursor also changes to look like a cassette tape, showing that we're already recording. Every action we take now will be translated into WordBasic statements and stored in the new macro.

9 Type in the copyright text, then hold down the *Shift* key and use the left arrow key to move back to the start of the line, highlighting (or selecting) all the text. To type the © symbol, press *Ctrl-Alt-C*.

© 1996 - Alex Homer, Wrox Press

> **FYI** Notice that you can't use the mouse to select or manipulate text while you're recording. Word just ignores it. You can, however, use it to select items from menus, click toolbar buttons and scroll the window.

10 Select Font from the Format menu. In the Font dialog, set the Font Style to Italic, then click OK.

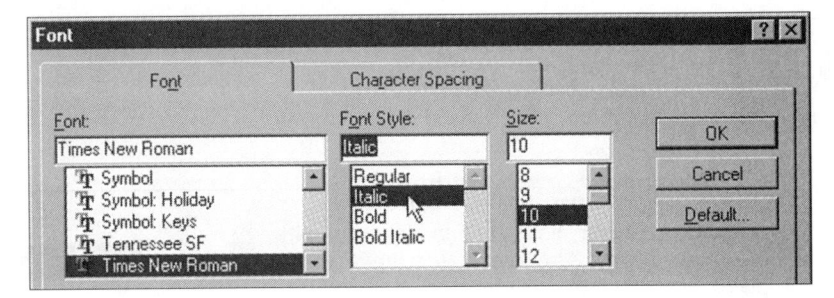

11 We've finished recording, so click the Stop button in the Macro Recorder window.

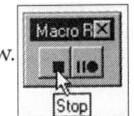

12 Now we can examine the macro. Select Macros from the Tools menu and in the Macros dialog select our new CopyrightItalic macro. Click Edit to open it.

```
Sub MAIN
Insert "© 1996 - Alex Homer, Wrox Press"
CharLeft 31, 1
FormatFont .Points = "10", .Underline = 0, .Color = 0, .Strikethrough
= 0, .Superscript = 0, .Subscript = 0, .Hidden = 0, .SmallCaps = 0,
.AllCaps = 0, .Spacing = "0 pt", .Position = "0 pt", .Kerning = 0,
.KerningMin = "", .Tab = "0", .Font = "Times New Roman", .Bold = 0,
.Italic = 1, .Outline = 0, .Shadow = 0
End Sub
```

How It Works

The first part of the macro looks familiar. You can see the same **Insert** statement that we saw in the first macro, just as we typed it in. The next line uses the **CharLeft** statement to move the cursor left 31 places (to the start of the line). It also has an extra argument—the number 1 after the comma—which tells Word to select the text as it moves the cursor.

However, the next five lines, which all form one statement, look formidable. These are the various options in the Font dialog that we could have selected. You'll see that the **Italic** argument (on the last line) is set to **1**. This means that we 'turned on' italic format for the text.

To see the macro at work, switch back to the template's document window and place the cursor on a new line. Place the mouse-pointer over the new toolbar button and you'll see the name of our macro appear—Word has automatically added a ToolTip for us. The description we placed in the Macros dialog when we created the macro is shown in the status bar at the bottom of the screen.

When you hold the mouse-pointer over the button for a few seconds, a ToolTip appears describing its function.

FYI You'll notice that the ToolTip has a space between the words **Copyright** and **Italic**. You can't include a space in the name of a macro, but Word automatically adds a space before any capital letters in the name when it creates the ToolTip.

Click our new toolbar button to run the macro and you'll see the text you typed originally. It's also formatted in italic, as with the original text. Also notice that the Font dialog *does not* open. Simply using a statement that sets the font dialog options like this doesn't actually open the dialog so that the user can choose the options they want—it just gets on and does it. We'll look at how to show the dialog in the next chapter.

When It Doesn't Work

However, there's a slight problem here. Our original document used the Normal style which was Times New Roman font. When we run the macro, we get Times New Roman Italic. But try this. On a new line, change the font to something else—here we've used Arial Black—and make sure you select Normal for the Font Style. Then type some text, press *Return* and click the new Copyright Italic toolbar button. Word adds the copyright notice, but it's still in Times New Roman Italic instead of Arial Black Italic.

This might be what you want. However, we expected to get the same font, but in italic format. The reason we didn't is simple. That five line statement at the end of our macro specifies *all* the arguments for the Font dialog:

```
FormatFont .Points = "10", .Underline = 0, .Color = 0, .Strikethrough = 0, .Super-
script = 0, .Subscript = 0, .Hidden = 0, .SmallCaps = 0, .AllCaps = 0, .Spacing =
"0 pt", .Position = "0 pt", .Kerning = 0, .KerningMin = "", .Tab = "0", .Font =
"Times New Roman", .Bold = 0, .Italic = 1, .Outline = 0, .Shadow = 0
```

You can see that the **Font** argument (line 4) is setting the font to Times New Roman. If we want to leave an argument set to its current value, we just omit it from the statement. So, to just change the style to italic, but not change the font, we omit all the arguments except this one.

```
FormatFont .Italic = 1
```

In fact, we can do it even more simply. The statement **Italic** is equivalent to just hitting the normal Italic button on the toolbar. If we had done this as we recorded the macro, we would have found this as our new macro instead:

```
Sub MAIN
    Insert "© 1996 - Alex Homer, Wrox Press"
```

```
    CharLeft 31,1
    Italic
End Sub
```

If you edit the `CopyrightItalic` macro to read like this, you get the result you would expect:

> **This is the font I want**
> © *1996 - Alex Homer, Wrox Press*

What Gets Stored in a Document?

When you create a new document based on a template, the styles you've defined for that document (or that have been inherited from its template) are stored within the document. What doesn't get stored there are any macros, toolbars or auto text entries that are in the template.

Loading the document again only gives you access to macros and other items that are available in the templates that are currently active, and not necessarily the ones that were in the original template. In other words, if you create a new document using the Book Order template and give it to another user who doesn't have the template, they will be able to load the document but they won't get a copy of the macros, toolbars or autotext entries with it.

To explain this more precisely, remember that you can have more than one template loaded, or active. When your user loads the document based on the Book Order template, they will most likely only have their Normal template loaded, so they'll only see any macros, toolbars or autotext entries stored in it, and not those in the original Book Order template.

Where are Templates Stored?

As you saw earlier, Word expects to find a template called Normal in its `Template` folder on your disk—the default is `MSOffice\Templates`, but depends on the options you selected when you installed Word 95 or Office 95. You can tell what the default folder is and change it by opening the Options dialog. Select Options from the Tools menu and look at the File Locations page:

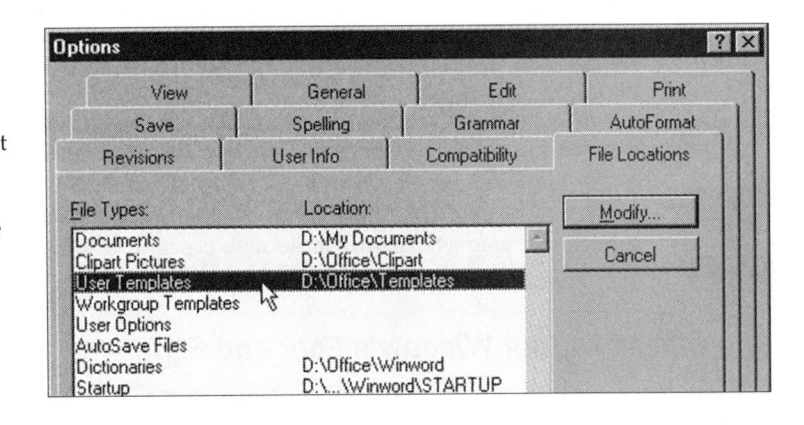

You don't have to store your templates in the default folder, but if you don't, they won't be available in Word's File | New... dialog. To create a document based on them you have to open the template directly using My Computer or Explorer, like we did with our Book Order template at the beginning of the chapter. Of course, you can also create a shortcut to frequently used templates on your desktop. Double-clicking this will then start Word and create a blank document using that template.

Distributing Your Application

OK, so we haven't even created an application yet... but while we're talking about the items that actually get stored in a document, it makes sense to consider how this affects the way you get the application to your users.

As you've seen, the document itself only contains the styles that were defined for it, not the other items that go to make up an application. So, to get the actual code that does the work, your user has to have a copy of the template. There are two things that you must bear in mind:

- If your application is stored in **Normal.dot**, they will have to replace their own copy of **Normal.dot** with your new version. This means they will lose any existing macros, styles, AutoText entries and toolbars they have defined for their own use—and you won't be on their next list of party guests. If you must use **Normal.dot**, you need to arrange for their existing macros, etc. to be copied into your new version, or your applications code copied into their existing Normal template.

- Once you supply your users with the application template, they have free access to all the contents—unlike a normal executable program which is contained in a single file that can't be viewed. If you need to keep the implementation secret for any reason, this can be a problem. The answer is to encrypt your macros before you distribute the application.

Encrypting Macros

You can make a copy of your macros in such a way that the code is encrypted (or protected). Encryption ensures that the macros can't be opened for viewing and editing in the Macro dialog. However, this process is one-way only. Once you've encrypted them, neither you nor your users can unencrypt them. So you *must* keep a copy of the original in case you ever need to edit it again. An ideal way is to store them normally on your own machine and only encrypt the ones you distribute.

There's one situation that's worth considering, though. No doubt you've heard about document viruses that can damage the data on your machine just from loading the document. This is a worrying aspect, as we're all used to the risk of viruses in executable (program) files and should already be taking appropriate precautions. But with a document, it's a lot more difficult to be sure of what's actually in it. Most users are likely to be highly suspicious of documents which contain encrypted macros that they can't check out themselves.

> **FYI** Later on, in Part 2, we'll look at how you go about encrypting your macros and how you can protect yourself against these new types of document viruses.

The Macro Editing Window's Font and Style

One other quick diversion here may just make your life easier if you don't like the standard font and style used for text in the macro editing window. This is always formatted in the built-in style Macro Text. You can't change the Macro Text style while a macro editing window is open, but you can when a document window is open.

Try It Out - Changing the Style of the Macro Editing Window

1 Switch to the template's document window and enter some text. Select your text and, in the **Style** box on the toolbar, select **Macro Text** as the new style. If it doesn't exist, just type it in, making sure you include the correct capitalization and the space. Press *Return*.

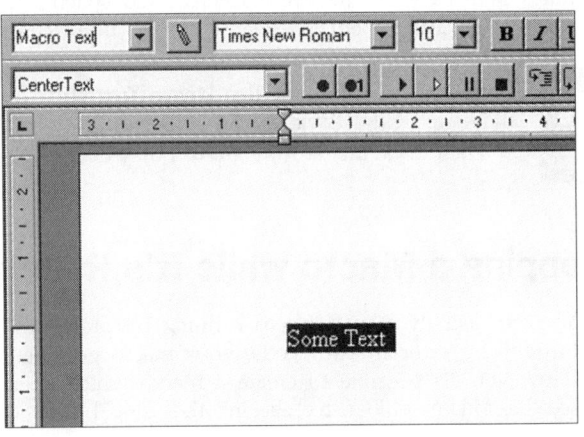

2 The text is formatted in Courier 10pt, the usual style for macro text. While it's still selected, change the font and size and add bold/italic or other formatting as required. You can see we've gone for the classical style. Then re-open the **Style** list and click **Macro Text** again.

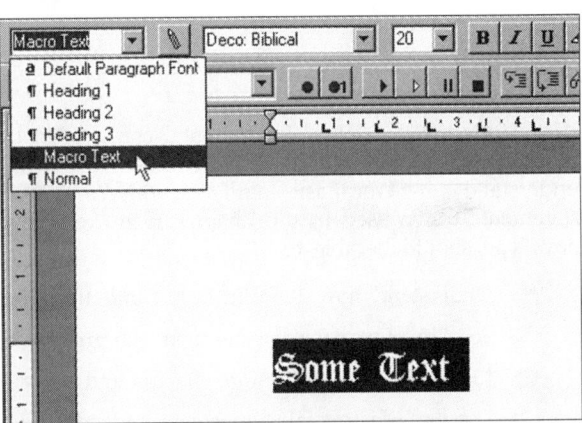

3 The **Reapply Style** dialog opens. Select the first option, **R**edefine the style using the selection as an example, and click OK.

4 Switch back to the macro editing window and you'll see your text displayed in the new style.

As you can see, if you don't choose your font and size carefully, it's easy to make your macros quite illegible. So, if you decide to change the **Macro Text** style, be sure to choose something that's both easy on the eye and has fixed spacing (i.e. a non-proportional font), otherwise you'll find that reading them afterwards can be quite confusing.

> **FYI** You can also modify the **Macro Text** style directly by selecting **Style** from the **Format** menu. In the **Style** dialog, change the **List:** setting to **All Styles** and select **Macro Text**. Then click the **Modify** button and change the existing style as required.

Stopping a Macro while It's Running

You can usually stop a macro running by pressing the *Escape* key. If for some reason, probably through an error in your code, your macro gets tied in knots and locks up Word, try this. (However, it's possible to create a macro which doesn't stop when you press *Escape*.) If you can see the **Macro** toolbar, try clicking the **Stop** button there instead.

Summary

We've introduced a lot of fundamental concepts in this chapter, but not much actual code. This is intentional. Before we go on to look at WordBasic code in more detail, it's important that you understand how WordBasic interfaces with Word itself. We'll also be following up some of the statements we've used in this chapter to make sure you understand what's going on. But, by now, you should be able to:

- Understand how WordBasic fits into the Word environment
- See how templates are used and appreciate the idea of contexts
- Judge where best to store macros and associated items
- Use the Macro dialog to create and edit macros
- Use the Organizer dialog to view the contents of a template
- Record a complete macro, or just a single statement

WordBasic is a fundamental part of the way Word operates, so you can seamlessly integrate macros with Word's own functionality to extend the power of Word itself. In the next few chapters, we'll be assuming you've absorbed these concepts and we'll start to use WordBasic in anger. In particular, we'll take a closer look at the workings of the **Book Order** application you saw at the beginning of the chapter.

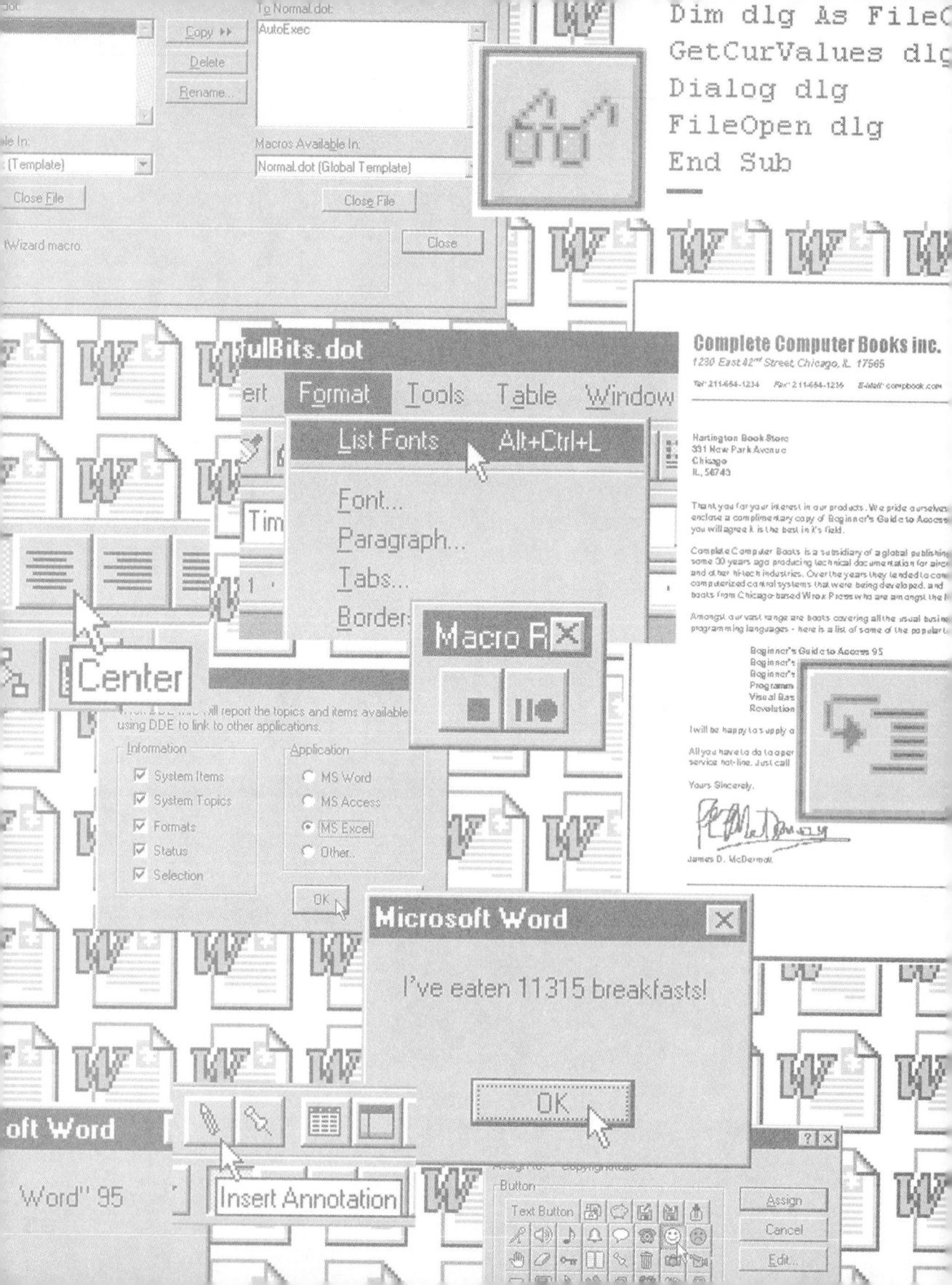

```
Dim dlg As FileO
GetCurValues dlg
Dialog dlg
FileOpen dlg
End Sub
```

WordBasic Fundamentals

Introduction

The aim of this chapter is to introduce you to the fundamentals of WordBasic. If you have used other versions of Basic, you'll find much of this is familiar. If not, all you need to know is here. WordBasic is a great deal simpler than Microsoft's other application languages, so we'll be working at a fairly brisk pace.

We need to catch up on the various statements you met in the example macros in Chapter 1 and explain a little more about how they work. We'll also examine how you control the execution of your code by repeating a block of statements, or selectively executing them. Many of the examples are taken from the sample Book Order application and we'll be creating some useful routines for you to use in your own code.

So, in this chapter we'll cover:

- Variables, data types, operators, statements and functions
- Creating your own procedures and using them in your code
- Different ways of controlling execution and responding to errors
- How you put these techniques to work in your own macros

By the end of this chapter, you'll be ready to start creating powerful macros which can make your work easier and more productive.

WordBasic Language Fundamentals

The first things we need to look at in this chapter are the different elements of WordBasic that you use to construct a macro. These include:

- What variables are and how they're used
- The different data types available in WordBasic
- How you create expressions using simple operators
- The built-in functions and subroutines that are part of Word
- How you create and use your own procedures

We'll start with a look at how you can create and use variables.

Variables

You will often want to write a macro to store values, either temporarily in memory while the macro is running, as part of a particular document so that they're available when the document is open, or even permanently so that they can be used in any document.

To make values permanently available, you would normally store them outside Word, either in a file on disk or in the Windows **registry** files. We'll be looking at this is in a later chapter. To store values within a document, you use **document variables**. These store the values within a document that is currently active and allow you to set and retrieve values from that document. Again, we'll be coming back to these later. In this section, we'll be examining how you can temporarily store values in variables, so that you can use them within a macro. When the macro ends, the values are lost; they are held in memory only while the macro is actually executing.

To identify the values in memory, when we create them, we give each one a unique name. This can be up to 80 characters long, starting with a letter. The rest of the name can be a mixture of letters, numbers and the underscore character only—no spaces are allowed. Some legal variable names are:

```
x
MyNumber
Days_in_a_Year
```

You should try to make a variable's name as meaningful as possible. **x** isn't exactly informative. When you come back to adapt your macro in a month's time, you won't find it gives you any clues about what values are stored in the variables! Once you've appropriately named the variable, then you can assign values to it:

```
MyNumber = 42
Days_in_a_Year = 365
```

You retrieve the values stored in a variable in a similar way. You can also assign one variable's value to another variable, or use it as part of a statement:

```
MyNumber = Days_in_a_Year
Print MyNumber
```

Here we've assigned the value of **Days_in_a_Year** to **MyNumber** and then used Word's **Print** statement to print its value. You change the value stored in a variable simply by assigning another value to it.

WordBasic's Data Types

You may have heard programming experts use the term *strongly typed*. Languages such as C, C++ and Pascal support many different types of variable and are very strict in the way that they are used. Visual Basic and its offshoots are less so; they allow you to interchange values between certain data types quite freely. WordBasic, though, is something of an odd-ball in this area. It only supports two elementary data types, but it's quite strict in the way it carries out type checking when you try to assign values between them. Let's see what this means in more detail.

Elementary Data Types

Elementary data types are the 'root' of any language. You've seen how you can store values in memory and retrieve them again by giving them a name. They become variables. However, you can't assign just any value to a variable. If you want to store the value 42, Word does so by setting the values in memory to the number 42. But when you come to store the title of a book—*Instant WordBasic*, for example—Word has to use a different technique. Text values, such as our book title, are called **strings**. They are, in effect, a string of characters. So Word has to be able to handle both ordinary number and string-type variables.

Number Data Types

A number-type variable in WordBasic can hold positive or negative values that are whole numbers (integers) or numbers which have a fractional part (real numbers). There's also a set of functions which allow you to set the number of decimal places you want to be contained and convert real values to integer values. A number-type variable can be assigned values such as:

```
MyNumber = 42
AnotherNumber = -256.671
SmallNumber = 0.0001
```

Word stores number-type variables with up to 14 digits precision and the largest value you can assign to it is $1.7976931348623 \times 10^{308}$, which is likely to be plenty big enough for anything we need!

One special aspect of using number-types is the way WordBasic handles the two special values **True** and **False**. You'll see how we use these when we come to look at control structures in a later section of this chapter. Like most other languages, WordBasic defines **True** = **-1** and **False** = **0**. These values can be stored in a number-type variable, although WordBasic actually treats *any* non-zero number as being **True**, and only zero as being **False**.

FYI This is important because many of Word's built-in functions are less than intuitive when it comes to the values they return. As you'll see later on, you need to be careful how you test the 'truth' of a function's result.

You may see the keyword **Let** used to assign values to variables:

```
Let MyNumber = 42
```

This is entirely optional and only included for compatibility with earlier versions of WordBasic. We won't be using it in our code.

String Data Types

To store strings, WordBasic uses a different data type. So that Word can differentiate between number and string-type variables, it insists that you add a suffix **$** to the end of a variable name if it's going to be used to store string values. (A single character is also classed as a string.) A WordBasic string can hold up to 65,280 characters.

We assign a string to a string-type variable in the same way as we do with a number-type:

```
MyName$ = "Alex Homer"
MyFirstInitial$ = "A"
```

Notice that strings can contain spaces and that we place quotes around them to indicate to WordBasic that they are strings. If we didn't, it would treat the string as a variable name. If you want to include a quotation mark (") within a string, you use the equivalent character code:

```
"Today's word is " + Chr$(34) + "WordBasic" + Chr$(34)
```

This will produce the string **Today's word is "WordBasic"**. The plus sign is just the way you indicate to Word that you want it to join the various strings together to make a single string.

FYI There is also a short-cut method. If you type two quotation marks together in a string, Word will automatically change it to the correct format when you save or run the macro.

Compound Data Types

The two data types, number and string, are called **elementary** data types because we can use them to build other data types, usually referred to as **compound** data types. Many languages offer you a choice of ways to do this, but again WordBasic is a little more limited. You can create arrays and... er... well, that's it actually. So let's look at arrays.

Arrays

An array is a structure containing several variables *of the same type.* You can think of an ordinary array as a row of boxes:

Each box can contain one value and you set and retrieve these values by referring to their index (or subscript). The first box is always indexed **0**, and we generally call each value an element of the array. The number of elements is limited only by the amount of memory available.

You can also create an array with more than one dimension. In this case, it becomes more like a set of pigeon holes:

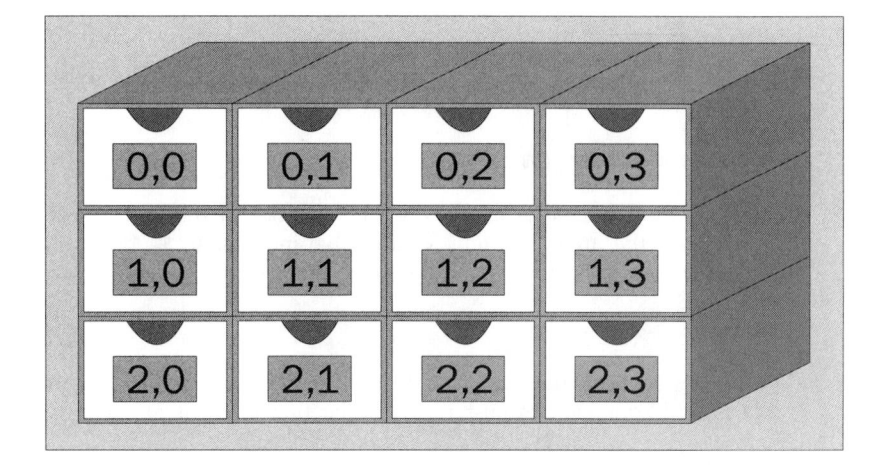

Now we need to use two indexes to define each element, one for the row and one for the column. You can go further; there's no limit (other than memory space) to the number of dimensions that you can create, but, if you need more than two, you should perhaps be looking at how you can simplify your code. While you may need three dimensions for spatial calculations, you'll need to be a sci-fi fan to visualize values stored in the fourth dimension.

WordBasic includes a function that you can use to sort the elements in an array, which makes them attractive for all kind of storage scenarios. We'll be looking at sorting arrays in more detail in Part 2.

> **FYI** There is, in fact, another data type available in Word: the dialog record. This is a way of storing the information that Word uses to fill the controls in a dialog. We'll be looking in detail at dialog records in Chapter 3.

Declaring Variables in Your Code

In many languages, you have to tell the program what variables you'll be using at the start. This is called **declaring** variables. With a couple of exceptions, WordBasic is more forgiving. It allows you just to use a new variable name anywhere in your code and it obligingly creates the variables as it meets them. If the name ends in a **$** then it creates a string-type variable, otherwise it creates a number-type variable.

You can, however, declare your variables 'up front' if you want to. This is a good idea in a complex macro because it means you can add comments which identify them, or explain what values they will hold. To declare a variable, you use the **Dim** statement, usually as the first line(s) of the macro:

```
Sub MAIN
    Dim MyNumber      'declare a number-type variable called MyNumber
```

```
        Dim MyString$    'declare a string-type variable called MyString$
        ...
        ...
End Sub
```

Declaring Array Variables

While the declaration of elementary variables is optional, arrays must *always* be declared before you use them. So, to declare an array to hold four numbers, we could use:

```
Dim MyFourNumbers(3)
```

Because the first element is indexed **0**, the number in the brackets is one less than the number of elements in the array; the four values have indexes **0**, **1**, **2** and **3**. To declare an array to hold the names of the months of the year, we need to use string variables:

```
Dim MonthNames$(11)
```

However, this makes **January** month number **0**, rather than the more usual month number **1**. We can avoid confusion by just ignoring the first element of the array:

```
Dim MonthNames$(12)
MonthName$(0) = ""
MonthName$(1) = "January"
MonthName$(2) = "February"
...
```

We've set element **0** to an empty string, and element **1** to **January**. Now the months have a more intuitive index number. Notice how we refer to the individual elements of the array in code, using the array variable name followed by the element we want in brackets.

Once you've declared an array, you can resize it using the **ReDim** statement. This allows you to change the size of an array that has already been declared. For example:

```
Dim MyValues(49)       'make room for 50 values
...
...    work with the values in the array
...
ReDim MyValue(99)      'make room for 100 values
...
```

One point to note is that when you resize an array, all the values in it are lost; WordBasic re-initializes it. However, you can use this method to save memory. If an array is no longer required, you just **ReDim** it to a single element and WordBasic releases the rest of the memory to your application. You can also minimize memory requirements by reusing the original array, rather than declaring another one.

Declaring Multidimensional Arrays

To declare an array with more than one dimension, you just add extra indexes to the brackets in the **Dim** statement, separated by commas. So the statement,

```
Dim ChessBoard$(7,7)
```

will create an array to hold the squares of a chess board. You can then store the name of each piece in the appropriate square to represent a game of chess in progress:

```
ChessBoard$(1,1) = "Black Pawn"
ChessBoard$(5,3) = "White King"
```

Declaring Shared Variables

So far, we've looked at how to declare variables of different types. Each of these is declared within a procedure, i.e. between the **Sub MAIN** and **End Sub** lines (generally, immediately after **Sub MAIN**). Remember that you don't have to consciously declare ordinary number or string-type variables, WordBasic 'declares' them automatically when they are first used.

Because all these variables are declared within a procedure, their values are lost when that procedure ends i.e. at the **End Sub** line. However, we can place more than one procedure in a macro (you'll see more of this later). If we want to use the value stored in a variable in *all* these procedures, we need to declare it as shared. In other programming languages, this is equivalent to the variable being global.

> **FYI** Remember that a macro can contain more than one procedure. Up to now, the ones we've seen only contain the procedure that starts with **Sub MAIN** and finishes at **End Sub**. In a later section, you'll see macros that have other procedures, as well as a **Sub MAIN**.

To declare a shared variable, we place the declaration outside the **Sub MAIN** and **End Sub** lines and precede it with the keyword **Shared**:

```
Dim Shared MyValue

Sub MAIN
    'this is the main subroutine of the macro
    MyValue = 10
End Sub

Sub DoSomethingElse
    'this is another subroutine in the same macro
    MyValue = MyValue + 1
End Sub
```

The variable **MyValue** can be accessed in both the subroutines because we've declared it outside both of them as shared. You'll hear the word *scope* used to indicate in which parts of a program a particular variable can be accessed. Here, our variable **MyValue** is in scope for the whole macro, in other words, it's globally accessible.

Operators and Expressions

Once we've declared our variables and assigned values to them, we need to be able to manipulate these values. For example, we may need to add numbers together, or join strings, and, of course, we need to be able to test the values to see if they meet certain conditions. All these are the province of WordBasic operators. When we combine values and operators in a statement, we're creating an expression.

Numeric Operators

Numeric operators are those familiar symbols that you learned about in your first day at school. They are used to manipulate numbers mathematically.

Operator	What it does	Example
+	Adds two numbers together.	5 + 2 = 7
-	Subtracts one number from another.	10 - 6 = 4
*	Multiplies two numbers together.	3 * 2 = 6
/	Divides one number by another, giving a result including any fractional part.	7 / 2 = 3.5
MOD	Modular division. Divides one number by another and returns only the remainder.	15 MOD 4 = 3

String Operator

There's only one string operator in WordBasic: the **string concatenation** operator. Notice that it uses the same symbol as the numeric addition operator.

Operator	What it does	Example
+	The string concatenation operator. Joins two strings together. Remember to include a space in one string if you don't want the words to run together.	"Word" + "Basic" = "WordBasic"

Comparison Operators

These operate on either number or string variables. When number variables are compared, the normal rules of mathematics apply, but when strings are compared, the order is that of the standard ANSI character set. This is generally spaces first, followed by punctuation marks (full stops, commas, etc.), followed by the characters 1 – 9 and then the letters A – Z. The comparison is case-insensitive, so *a* isn't the same as *A*.

If the first letter of both strings is the same, WordBasic compares the next letter, and so on to the end of the string. If all the letters are the same and one string is longer than the other, the shorter one is 'less' than the longer one.

Operator	What it does	Example
=	Tests whether two values are equal.	7 = 7 - **True** 3 = 7 - **False**
<>	Tests whether two values are *not* equal.	3 <> 7 - **True** 7 <> 7 - **False**

Table Continued on Following Page

Operator	What it does	Example	
<	Tests whether the first value is less than the second one.	3 < 7 - 7 < 7 -	True False
<=	Tests whether the first value is less than or equal to the second one.	3 <= 7 - 9 <= 7 -	True False
>	Tests whether the first value is greater than the second one.	7 > 3 - 7 > 7 -	True False
>=	Tests whether the first value is greater than or equal to the second one.	7 >= 7 - 3 >= 7 -	True False

Logical Operators

These operators are used to combine the results of two other operations. When you perform a comparison using, for example, the > operator, WordBasic returns the result **True** or **False**. These logical operators can be used to combine the results of two (or more) other operations. In the Example column we've used **True** and **False** to represent the result of these operations. We'll show you in more detail how they're applied in WordBasic later in this chapter.

Operator	What it does	Example
OR	Evaluates to **True** if *either* or *both* of the values is **True**. If both are **False**, the result is **False**.	True OR True = True True OR False = True False OR True = True False OR False = False
AND	Evaluates to **True** only if *both* values are **True**. If *either* is **False**, the result is **False**.	True AND True = True True AND False = False False AND True = False False AND False = False
NOT	Reverses the 'truth' of a value.	NOT False = True NOT True = False

FYI Remember that WordBasic accepts only zero as **False**, but *any* non-zero value as **True**. The NOT operator, however, doesn't convert all non-zero values to **False**. NOT(0) evaluates to **True** (-1) and NOT(-1) evaluates to **False** (0). But NOT(1) does *not* evaluate to **False**.

What Are Expressions?

Now that we know what operators are available, we can use them to create expressions. An **expression** is simply a series of values and operators that can be evaluated to produce a result:

```
(7 * 3) + 6            'evaluates to 27
```

```
(6 > 3) OR (4 = 9)      'evaluates to True
"Word " + "95"          'evaluates to "Word 95"
```

We generally assign the result of an expression to another variable, or use it as a test for a control structure. Control structures are covered in a later section, but, for now, here are some examples of how we can assign the result to a variable. Notice that the variable can itself be used in an expression:

```
Sub MAIN
    MyAge = 21                           'set variable MyAge to 21
    Days_in_a_Year = 365                 'set the number of days in a year
    MyAge = MyAge + 10                   'sometimes I tell lies
    Breakfasts = MyAge * Days_in_a_Year
    Message$ = "I've eaten" + Str$(Breakfasts) + " breakfasts!"
    MsgBox Message$
End Sub
```

If you type this into a macro and run it, you'll see the text in the **Message$** variable displayed in a standard *Windows* message box:

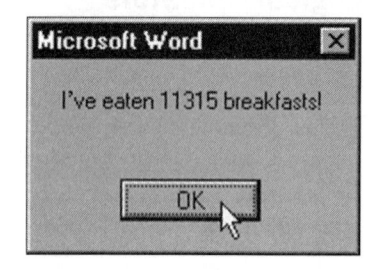

> **FYI** This example uses two statements that we haven't really discussed so far: `Str$()` and `MsgBox`. `Str$()` converts a value stored in the number-type variable into a string (preceded by a space or minus sign), and `MsgBox` displays a string in a standard Windows message box. You can find this example in the `UsefulBits` template in your samples folder.

How Expressions Are Evaluated

When WordBasic evaluates an expression, it does so in a particular order. Generally, this is the order you would expect, but you have to be careful when you use the numeric operators. There's a fixed order of precedence. Operators that have the same precedence are evaluated from left to right in the expression:

1 Multiplication and division operations

2 Addition and subtraction operations

3 String concatenation

4 Comparison operators

5 Logical operators

You can change the order of precedence by using parentheses (brackets) in the expression.

Operations within the brackets are evaluated first, in the normal order of precedence. If you nest one set of brackets within another, the innermost operation is evaluated first.

For example, if you evaluate the expression

```
7 + 3 * 2
```

you find that WordBasic evaluates the operation **3 * 2** first, because multiplication has a higher order of precedence than addition. It then adds **7**, giving the result **13**. What you may have expected when you wrote the expression is the result **20**—in other words for the addition to be performed first. To get this answer you use brackets:

```
(7 + 3) * 2
```

You may also find problems occurring when you use logical and comparison operators together. To make sure you get the result you want, you can always enclose each operation in brackets. WordBasic will then evaluate the innermost one first, then work outwards, and finally left to right.

```
(6 < (4 + 1)) AND ("Fred" > "Bill")
```

The order of evaluation here is

```
4 + 1 = 5
6 < 5 = False
"Fred" > "Bill" = True        'because "F" comes after "B"
False AND True = False
```

so the entire expression evaluates to **False**.

WordBasic's Built-in Statements

In Chapter 1, we used several of WordBasic's own built-in statements, such as **Insert** and **Italic**. These are routines within Word that carry out an action—we saw them inserting text into our documents and switching the font to italic. There are literally hundreds of these routines available to you, from moving the cursor right or left to creating a complete table of contents for your document.

In many cases, there are several different ways to achieve the same result. For example, you saw how we could change text to italic using the **FormatFont** statement:

```
FormatFont .Italic = 1
```

We did the same thing using the single statement **Italic**. This is equivalent to clicking the Italic button on the Formatting toolbar. However, it actually *toggles* the state of the font, switching it from normal to italic and back again. If the font is already italic, it's changed back to normal when you execute the statement. You can add an argument to the **Italic** statement to specify the result you want:

```
Italic 1    ' changes the font to italic
Italic 0    ' changes the font to non-italic
```

So, while **Italic** on its own toggles italics on and off, **Italic 1** always sets it to italic, the same as **FormatFont .Italic = 1**. As we saw, though, the **FormatFont** statement can do a lot more. You can add many different arguments to set the other attributes of the text. Our **CopyrightItalic** example in Chapter 1 originally used the full version of this statement:

```
Sub MAIN
Insert "© 1996 - Alex Homer, Wrox Press"
CharLeft 31, 1
FormatFont .Points = "10", .Underline = 0, .Color = 0, .Strikethrough
= 0, .Superscript = 0, .Subscript = 0, .Hidden = 0, .SmallCaps = 0,
.AllCaps = 0, .Spacing = "0 pt", .Position = "0 pt", .Kerning = 0,
.KerningMin = "", .Tab = "0", .Font = "Times New Roman", .Bold = 0,
.Italic = 1, .Outline = 0, .Shadow = 0
End Sub
```

> **FYI** Arguments are the 'extra items' of information that you supply to a statement (or function) which tell it more precisely what you want it to do. We'll be looking at how arguments are used more fully as we progress through this chapter.

Finding the Statement You Need

So how do you go about finding the statement you need if there are so many to choose from? There are several methods and, apart from the first one, they are all free!

- Buy a copy of Microsoft's *Word Developer's Kit*. It devotes over 600 pages to a detailed description of each statement and function supported in WordBasic.

- Use the Help files supplied with Word. These contain the full text of the reference section of the *Word Developer's Kit* book, which is probably why they eat up nearly 2MB of disk space. Note that you have to specify this as you install Word. If you can't find **WrdBasic.hlp** in your **Word** folder, run the **Setup** program again to install it.

- Use the Record Next Command button on the Macro toolbar to insert the statement into your macro, as we did in Chapter 1. Then place the text cursor over it and press *F1* to open the Help file and find out more about the way it works and the arguments required.

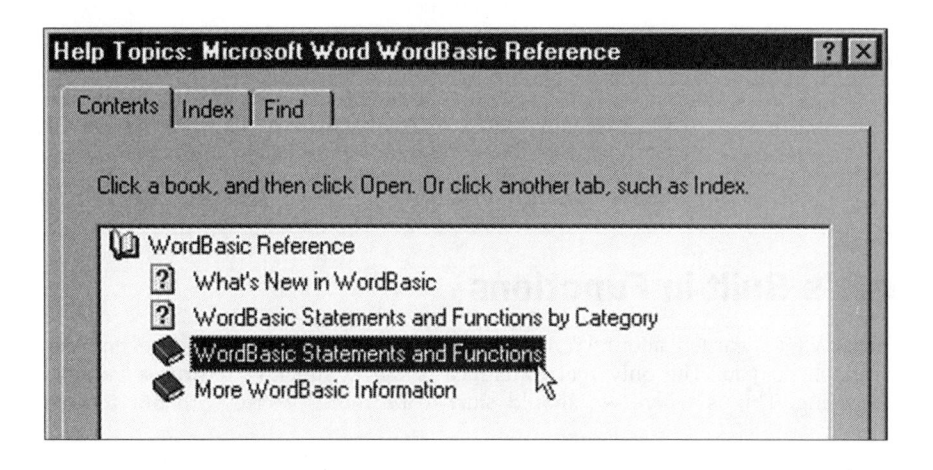

Some Common WordBasic Built-in Statements

Here's a list of some of the common statements that you are likely to come across early on. We've shown what each one does and the arguments you can specify.

Statement	What It Does	Example
CharLeft *move, select* **CharRight** *move, select* **WordLeft** *move, select* **WordRight** *move, select* **LineUp** *move, select* **LineDown** *move, select* **ParaUp** *move, select* **ParaDown** *move, select* **PageUp** *move, select* **PageDown** *move, select*	Moves the insertion point up, down, left or right. *move* is the number of characters, words, lines, paragraphs, or pages to move. If *select* = 1, the text moved over is selected.	**CharLeft** moves the insertion point one character to the left. **CharLeft 3** moves 3 characters to the left. **CharLeft 3, 1** moves three characters left and selects the text.
Insert *text$*	Inserts *text$* at the current insertion point.	**Insert "WordBasic"**
StartOfDocument **EndOfDocument**	Moves to the start or end of the current document.	**StartOfDocument** **EndOfDocument**
Bold *on* **Italic** *on* **Underline** *on* **Subscript** *on* **Superscript** *on*	Sets or toggles the current character format. *on* is optional. If *on* =1 the format is applied.	**Bold** toggles format. **Bold 0** turns bold off. **Bold 1** turns bold on.
Font *name$, size*	Changes the current font to *name$*. If *size* is used it sets the font size.	**Font "Arial"** sets the current font to Arial. **Font "Arial", 12** sets the font to Arial 12 pt.
FontSize *size*	Sets the font size to *size*.	**FontSize 12** sets the font to 12 pt.

Table Continued on Following Page

Statement	What It Does	Example
`Dim`	Declares any type of variable, and must be used for arrays.	`Dim MyValue$`
`ReDim`	Resizes an array variable	`ReDim MyVals(50)`

WordBasic's Built-in Functions

Much of what we've learned about WordBasic's statements is also true of the built-in functions that are available to you. The only real difference is that a function returns a value when it's finished executing. This is where we should start to be more precise with our terminology.

Defining Our Terminology

So that you don't get confused when we get to talking about the structure of our code later on, here are the definitions that we'll be using for the rest of the book:

- Statement: a single line of code in any macro
- Subroutine: WordBasic macros that *do not* return a value
- Function: WordBasic macros that *do* return a value
- Procedure: a general term to refer to both subroutines and functions
- Macro: a set of statements that appear in the macro window. This can contain several procedures, and there can be several macros in a single template

FYI Notice that a line of code can in fact take up more than one line on screen. WordBasic recognizes the end of a code line by the carriage return. If you want to control how a line is broken up on screen, you type a backslash immediately followed by *Return* to separate each screen line of a single statement. For example, WordBasic recognizes the following as a single line of code:

```
FormatFont .Points = "10", .Underline = 2, .Color = 3, \
.Strikethrough = 1, .Superscript = 0, .Subscript = 1, \
.Hidden = 0, .SmallCaps = 1, .AllCaps = 0, .Spacing = "0 pt", \
.Position = "0 pt", .Kerning = 1, .KerningMin = "72", \
.Tab = "0", .Font = "Arial", .Bold = 1, .Italic = 1, \
.Outline = 0, .Shadow = 0
```

How Functions are Used

When you use a Word statement in your code, you effectively give Word an instruction and let it get on with it, carrying out the action you require. However, you often need to perform an action *and* get back a result of that action. In other cases, you may just want to know something about your document, or the Word environment, but not change anything. Word provides you with a useful tool to do this: **functions**.

Many Word statements actually have two varieties, or forms. The regular form, which we have already seen and used, is called the **statement** form. The **function** form looks a lot like the statement form, but the action carried out is a little different. For example, we used the single statement

```
Italic
```

to toggle the font between normal and italic style. But if we want to know what the *current* style is, without changing it, we must use a function: `Italic()`. Notice that it's followed by a pair of empty parentheses. This is how we tell Word that we want the *function* form, not the statement. If the function required us to supply arguments, we would place them inside the brackets, separated by commas. Even if there are no arguments, we still have to include the brackets to prevent Word thinking we want the statement form of the instruction.

However, a function returns a value, so we can't use it alone on a line like we did with the statement version. Instead, we normally assign the result to a variable. The function

```
ThisIsItalic = Italic()
```

sets the variable `ThisIsItalic` to one of three values. If *none* of the currently selected text is italic it sets it to `0`, if *part* of it's italic it sets it to `-1` and, if *all* of it is italic, it sets the variable to `1`.

Of course, here we know that the function returns a value which can safely be assigned to a number-type variable (`ThisIsItalic` is a number-type variable, because it lacks the `$` suffix). When we use a function that returns a string we must assign it to a string-type variable. In WordBasic, functions that return a string value have the `$` suffix to their name in the same way as variables. For example, `Left$()` is a function which returns characters from the left-hand end of a string. But which string does it use? In this case, we have to supply arguments to tell WordBasic exactly what we want the function to do.

Using Arguments with Functions and Subroutines

The `Left$()` function will return characters from the left-hand end of a string, but we need to tell it which string to use and how many characters we want. The full syntax of the function shows that we must supply two arguments:

```
NewString$ = Left$ (OriginalString$, NumChars)
```

Notice that the second argument, the number of characters we require, is a number-type. So the function

```
NewString$ = Left$ ("WordBasic", 4)
```

will assign the value `Word` to the variable `NewString$`.

We'll be coming back to look at arguments in more detail later on, but you'll find that Word's Help file contains all the information you need about what each argument actually means, what data types it requires and what the return value indicates. As an example, place the text cursor on the word `Left$` in the macro editing window and press *F1*. Having this quantity of reference material so readily available will make developing your own macros much easier.

Beginning WordBasic Programming

WordBasic Reference

Left$()
Example

Left$(** *Source$, Count* **)

Returns the leftmost *Count* characters of *Source$*.

See also

Strings and Numbers State...
InStr()
Len()
LTrim$()
Mid$()
Right$()
RTrim$()

WordBasic Example

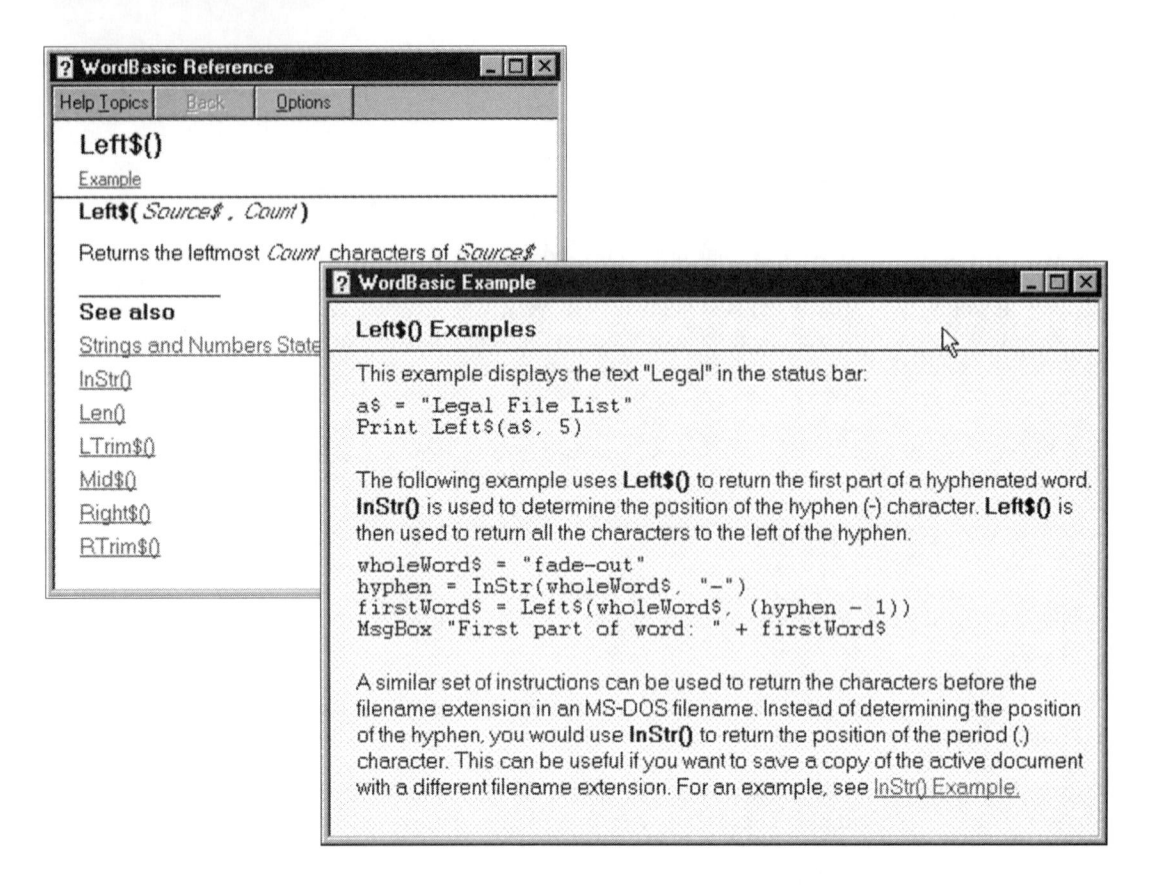

Left$() Examples

This example displays the text "Legal" in the status bar:

```
a$ = "Legal File List"
Print Left$(a$, 5)
```

The following example uses **Left$()** to return the first part of a hyphenated word. **InStr()** is used to determine the position of the hyphen (-) character. **Left$()** is then used to return all the characters to the left of the hyphen.

```
wholeWord$ = "fade-out"
hyphen = InStr(wholeWord$, "-")
firstWord$ = Left$(wholeWord$, (hyphen - 1))
MsgBox "First part of word: " + firstWord$
```

A similar set of instructions can be used to return the characters before the filename extension in an MS-DOS filename. Instead of determining the position of the hyphen, you would use **InStr()** to return the position of the period (.) character. This can be useful if you want to save a copy of the active document with a different filename extension. For an example, see InStr() Example.

Some Common WordBasic Built-in Functions

Here's a list of some of the common functions that you're likely to come across early on. We've shown what each one does, the arguments you can specify, and the value it returns:

Function	What It Does	Example
**Left$**(*string$, num*) **Right$**(*string$, num*)	Returns *num* characters from the left or right- hand end of *string$*.	`Right$("WordBasic", 5)` `= "Basic"`
**Mid$**(*string$, start, num*)	Returns *num* characters from *string$* starting at *start*.	`Mid$("WordBasic", 5,3)` `= "Bas"`
**Ltrim$**(*string$*) **Rtrim$**(*string$*)	Removes all spaces from the left or right-hand end of *string$*.	`LTrim$("  Me") = "Me"` `RTrim$("Me  ") = "Me"`
**UCase$**(*string$*) **LCase$**(*string$*)	Converts *string$* to all upper or lower case.	`UCase$("The") = "THE"` `LCase$("The") = "the"`
Len(*string$*)	Returns the number of characters in *string$*.	`Len("The") = 3`
Val(*string$*)	Returns the value of a number in *string$*.	`Val("24.12") = 24.12`

Table Continued on Following Page

Function	What It Does	Example
Str$(*num*)	Returns a string representing *num*.	**Str$(24.12) = " 24.14"**
CharLeft(*move, select*) **CharRight**(*move, select*) **WordLeft**(*move, select*) **WordRight**(*move, select*) **SentLeft**(*move, select*) **SentRight**(*move, select*) **LineUp**(*move, select*) **LineDown**(*move, select*) **ParaUp**(*move, select*) **ParaDown**(*move, select*) **PageUp**(*move, select*) **PageDown**(*move, select*)	Moves the insertion point and returns a value: **0** if the action can't be carried out at all, **-1** if it can be partly or wholly carried out. *move* is the number of characters, words, sentences, lines, paragraphs or pages to move. If *select* = **1**, the text moved over is selected.	**CharLeft(3)** moves 3 characters to the left. Returns **-1** if it can move any - *not necessarily all 3* - characters. Returns **0** if it can't move at all. **CharLeft(3, 1)** does the same, but also selects the text. **0** is equivalent to **False** **-1** is equivalent to **True**
Bold() **Italic()** **Underline()** **Subscript()** **Superscript()**	Returns a value indicating the format of the selected text: **0** if *none* of the selection is this format, **-1** if *part* is this format, **1** if *all* is this format.	**Bold()** returns **0** if none of the selection is bold, **-1** if part is bold and **1** if all is bold formatted. Notice that **-1** and **1** are equivalent to **True**, in this case indicating all or part of the selection.
Font$(*num*)	Returns the name of a font. *num* is the position in the current font list. If it's omitted, the current font is returned.	**Font$() = "Arial"** **Font$(13) = "Courier"**
FontSize()	Returns the current font size.	**FontSize() = 12**
Date$(*num*)	Returns a string representing the date in *num*. If *num* is omitted, it returns today's date.	**Date$() = Jan 26, 1996** The format is set by your current date format settings in Windows.
Time$(*num*)	Returns a string representing the time in *num*. If *num* is omitted, it returns the current time.	**Time$() = 8:37 PM** The format is set by your current time format settings in Windows.
Now()	Returns the current date and time as a number. The fractional part is the time.	**Now() = 35097.403156**
Today()	Returns the current date only as a number.	**Today() = 35097**
Day(*num*) **Month**(*num*) **Year**(*num*) **Hour**(*num*) **Minute**(*num*) **Second**(*num*)	Returns individual parts of the date or time stored in *num*. In the example, **35097** is **Feb 2, 1996**.	**Day(35097) = 2** **Month(35097) = 2** **Year(35097) = 1996**

Dates and Nesting Functions

When you work with dates in WordBasic, you'll come across date serial numbers. Windows stores dates as a number equivalent to a number of whole days followed by the time as a fractional part of a day. So mid-morning on 2nd February 1996 is expressed as **35097.453156**.

In Chapter 1 we used the statement

```
Insert "©" + Str$(Year(Now())) + " - "
```

to insert the current year into our document. This demonstrates how you can nest functions so that each uses the results of the previous one (remember WordBasic evaluates the expression in the innermost brackets first, then works outwards). This expression is evaluated as:

```
Now() = 35097.453156
Year(35097.453156) = 1996
Str$(1996) = " 1996"
```

Notice that when you use the **Str$()** function to convert a number into a string, it adds a space before positive numbers, but not before negative numbers.

```
Str$(1996) returns " 1996"
Str$(-412) returns "-412"
```

User-defined Procedures

It's time now for a little more terminology. All the procedures we've looked at in the two previous sections, built-in statements and functions, are actually part of Word itself. We use them by referring to them by name. We can also create our own subroutines or functions, and we refer to these as *user-defined procedures*. The macros we created in Chapter 1 are user-defined subroutines; they start with **Sub MAIN** and end with **End Sub**.

```
Sub MAIN
    REM CopyrightText
    Insert "©" + Str$(Year(Now())) + " - "
    Insert GetDocumentProperty$("Author") + ", "
    Insert GetDocumentProperty$("Company")
    InsertPara
End Sub
```

As we've hinted earlier, you can include more than one procedure in a macro. The macro has its own name, such as **CopyrightText**, and when you run this macro it's the **MAIN** subroutine that gets executed. When you add other procedures to a macro (by writing them in the same macro window), you give them their own names which must be unique for that macro.

Creating Your Own Subroutines

To create a subroutine called **ShowTheTime**, we just enter the procedure header, then the code that carries out the task, followed by the **End Sub** statement:

```
Sub ShowTheTime
    Message$ = "The time is " + Time$()
    MsgBox Message$
End Sub
```

To run this procedure, we must call the new subroutine from our code. It behaves just like a built-in statement: once it's finished executing, (when you click OK to clear the message box), control passes back to the **MAIN** procedure.

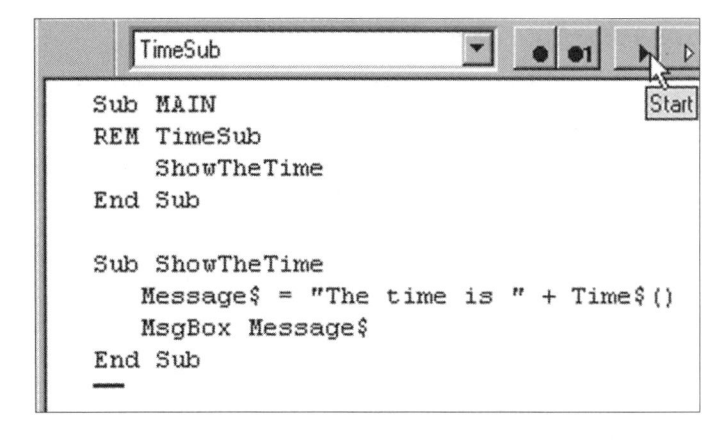

```
Sub MAIN
REM TimeSub
    ShowTheTime
End Sub

Sub ShowTheTime
    Message$ = "The time is " + Time$()
    MsgBox Message$
End Sub
```

So, when we execute the **MAIN** procedure by clicking the Start button on the Macro toolbar, it calls (executes) the statement **ShowTheTime**. This runs our user-defined procedure which displays the time:

> **FYI** You may find the keyword `Call` used to call a subroutine in some code. This is included in WordBasic for compatibility with older versions. We won't be using it in this book.

The **Time$()** function returns the current time as a string, but we can also include an argument which is a date serial number representing today's date and time. So we could adapt our procedure to display *any* time, rather than just the current one. To do this we need a way to get this number into our procedure. The answer is to add an argument to our subroutine:

```
Sub ShowTheTime (ThisTime)
    Message$ = "The time is " + Time$(ThisTime)
    MsgBox Message$
End Sub
```

Now when we call the procedure from our code, we need to supply this argument:

```
Sub MAIN
    REM TimeSub
    ShowTheTime(35097.453156)
End Sub
```

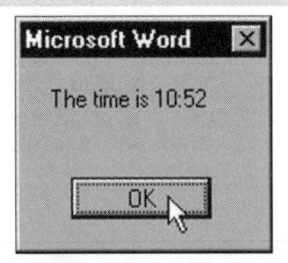

Creating Your Own Functions

In the previous section, we created the **ShowTheTime** procedure as a subroutine. It simply displays the string, The time is 12:28 (for example), in a Windows message box. However, we often need to retrieve or calculate a value for use in our code, but not necessarily display it while the procedure is running. We may want to create the time string and store it for use later in our macro, or insert it in a document.

We can do this with a user-defined function. The principle is, of course, the same as we saw with subroutines in the previous section, but now we can return a value when the function ends. We do this by assigning the value to the name of the function:

```
Function GetTheTime$
    Message$ = "The time is " + Time$()
    GetTheTime$ = Message$
End Function
```

Now the function name has to behave like a variable, because we'll be assigning a value to it. So we have to tell WordBasic what *type* of value we're going to use. Because we're creating a string within the function, we add the **$** suffix to the function's name to indicate that we'll be returning a string value. (If we were returning a number-type value, we would omit the **$** suffix.)

When we come to use our new function, we can't just call it like we did before. We have to handle the returned value by assigning it to a string variable in the calling procedure:

```
Sub MAIN
    TheTime$ = GetTheTime$
    MsgBox TheTime$
End Sub
```

When you run this example, you get the same result as with the function, but, here, the message box is being displayed by the **MAIN** subroutine, not our new function.

> **FYI** You'll see here that when you're using user-defined functions, as opposed to built-in ones, there's one major difference in syntax. If there are *no* arguments, you omit the brackets after the function name in the calling procedure. With a built-in function, you *always* have to include them.

Again, we can add an argument to the function to specify the time we want:

```
Sub MAIN
    REM TimeFunction
    TheTime$ = GetTheTime$(35097.453156)
    Print TheTime$
End Sub

Function GetTheTime$(ThisTime)
    Message$ = "The time is " + Time$(ThisTime)
    GetTheTime$ = Message$
End Function
```

In this case, we've changed the final statement in the **MAIN** procedure just to show how useful it is to create functions that return a value rather than subroutines that carry out an action. Instead of displaying the time in a message box, we're printing it in the status bar at the bottom of the Word window, using the **Print** statement. (If you can't see the status bar, turn it on in the Options dialog—select Tools | Options... and open the View tab.)

Arguments

One of the main aspects of user-defined procedures is the way you pass values between the **MAIN** procedure and the others in the macro. If you want to find out the time, you can use our **GetTheTime()** function which returns a string containing it. All you need to supply is the time you want it to use:

```
TheTime$ = GetTheTime$(35097.453156)
```

But imagine you have a more complex function which needs to process the values that are passed to it. It's quite possible that the value of the argument could be changed within the function. As a trivial example, we could have:

```
Function GetTheTime$(ThisTime)
    GetTheTime$ = "The time is " + Time$(ThisTime)
    ThisTime = ThisTime + 0.29
    TimeInUK$ = "In the UK it's " + Time$(ThisTime)
End Function
```

The function still returns the correct time, because we're assigning it directly to the function name in the first line, but now it modifies the argument **ThisTime** after it has calculated the time. If the calling procedure uses **ThisTime** again later, it will have a different value. To see this, we'll change the calling procedure as well. We'll use the **Now()** function to find the current date number, then call the function twice and display each result in a message box:

```
Sub MAIN
    TheTimeNow = Now()
    MsgBox GetTheTime$(TheTimeNow)
    MsgBox GetTheTime$(TheTimeNow)
End Sub
```

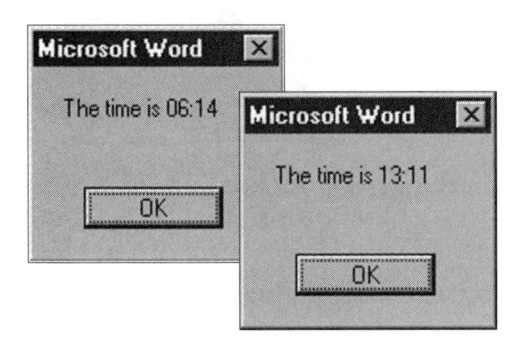

We get two different times, because the first time the function is run, it changes the value of the variable **TheTimeNow** which is passed to it as an argument. If you want to try them out, you'll find these macros in the UsefulBits template in your samples folder.

Passing Arguments by Reference

This method of using arguments is called passing values by reference, and is the default method. It has the advantage of being fast, because all WordBasic does when it calls the other procedure is to tell it where in memory the original values are stored. The procedure can then go to that location and fetch the values; and of course it can change them as well.

Passing Arguments by Value

The other method WordBasic supports is to pass arguments to a procedure by value. As the name suggests, WordBasic doesn't tell the procedure where the values are stored, but instead makes a fresh copy of the variable and passes that instead. This means that the procedure has no way of changing the original value, because it doesn't know where in memory it's stored.

To pass arguments by value, we have to enclose them individually in parentheses when we call the function from the other procedure. If there's more than one argument, you don't have to do this with all of them; you need only include those you want to pass.

To get the correct result, we need to change the code in the **MAIN** procedure:

```
Sub MAIN
    TheTimeNow = Now()
    MsgBox GetTheTime$((TheTimeNow))
    MsgBox GetTheTime$((TheTimeNow))
End Sub
```

Because you can only return one value as the result of a function, when you design functions that need to provide more than one value, you need to be able to change the values in the arguments. You must then make sure that your calling procedure is protected from changes to other arguments used in the function call.

Let's see how we can improve our **GetTheTime** code to display both the US and UK times correctly, without changing the value in the **MAIN** procedure:

```
Sub MAIN
    TheTimeNow = Now()
    USTime$ = GetTheTime$(UKTime$,(TheTimeNow))
    MsgBox USTime$ : MsgBox UKTime$
End Sub

Function GetTheTime$ (TimeInUK$, ThisTime)
    GetTheTime$ = "The time is " + Time$(ThisTime)
    ThisTime = ThisTime + 0.29
    TimeInUK$ = "In the UK it's " + Time$(ThisTime)
End Function
```

You'll see here we've used two string variables, **USTime$** and **UKTime$**, to hold the two different times. When we call the function, we pass **UKTime$** by reference and the current time number **TheTimeNow** by value.

The function changes both of these variables. When control passes back to the **MAIN** procedure, it receives the value of **USTime$** directly from the function and it picks up the new value of the **UKTime$** variable from the arguments. But because the time number variable, **TheTimeNow**, that was changed in the function was only a 'local copy', the **MAIN** routine continues to use the original (unchanged) value.

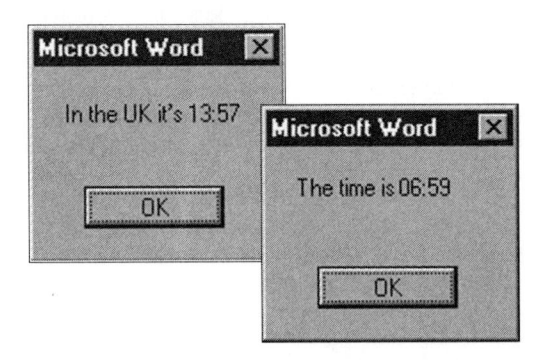

One other point to notice is that, in WordBasic, we can place more than one statement on a line by separating them with a colon (:). However, this can make your code more difficult to read, so you should only use it sparingly.

> **FYI** In the previous example, we changed the order of the arguments. This is due to a quirk in WordBasic which arises when you have mixed argument types and pass some by value. In our case, the routine only works correctly if we pass the value argument last. A better workaround for this behaviour is to declare your variables before you use them.

Named Arguments

When we used the **FormatFont** statement in Chapter 1, we specified arguments for it, using:

```
FormatFont .Italic = 1
```

This is an example of one of the WordBasic statements that supports named arguments. If you recall, there were twenty possible arguments that we could use (we saw these when we recorded the **FormatFont** action). If we used arguments in the normal way, we would have to supply all these arguments each time we called the function, even if we only wanted to specify the value for one of them.

WordBasic gets round the problem by allowing you to supply the value only for the one you want to change, using the syntax you see above. If you want to specify more than one argument, you just add them to the statement, separated with commas.

Optional Arguments

Some of WordBasic's built-in statements and functions use optional arguments. Again, we've seen this already with the **Italic** statement. We can use **Italic** to toggle the font style, **Italic 1** to set it to italic, or **Italic 0** to turn off italics altogether.

The built-in **Mid$()** function also has an optional argument:

```
Mid$("WordBasic", 5, 3)  'returns "Bas"
Mid$("WordBasic", 5)     'returns all the remaining string - i.e. "Basic"
```

Unfortunately, we can't create optional arguments in our own user-defined subroutines and functions.

Using Comments in Your Code

As your macros become more complex, it's harder to remember how they work when you come back to them a few months after you first created them. For future reference, you can place comments in your code to identify variables, describe how parts work, or just make notes. And if you expect other users to maintain your code, you need to give them a fighting chance of understanding what's going on.

To add a comment, you can use the keyword **REM**, or an apostrophe:

```
Sub MAIN
   REM this is a comment
   'and so is this
   MyValues = 42         'comment - this sets MyValues to 42
End Sub
```

It's often handy to tag a comment on the end of a line with an apostrophe, but what you see above is a perfect example of how you shouldn't comment such a line. It's obvious what **MyValues = 42** does and it certainly doesn't need the comment that we've added. However,

```
MyValues = 42      'total number of values required for control system
```

is worthwhile, because it tells you what **MyValues** actually is.

You often find **REM**s are useful for commenting out blocks of code while you're writing or testing a macro. If a set of statements is causing an error, you just add the keyword **REM** in front of it, then remove it once you clear the problem. You can add and remove **REM**s automatically using the Add/Remove REM button on the Macro toolbar.

Select the statements that you want to comment out and click the Add/Remove REM button to insert **REM** in front of each one. Click again to remove the **REM** keywords from each selected line.

```
         If PicInsertText$ = "" Then Goto LoadPic_Exit
         OldFolder$ = GetDocumentVar$("LastPictureFolder")
         If OldFolder$ = "" Then OldFolder$ = DefaultDir$(1)
REM         PicFolder$ = GetPicFolder$(OldFolder$)
REM         If PicFolder$ = "CANCEL" Then Goto LoadPic_Exit
REM         SetDocumentVar("LastPictureFolder", PicFolder$)
         ScreenUpdating 0
         EditBookmark "TempOldPosn", .Add
         Count = 0
         StartOfDocument
```

Running Procedures Stored in Other Macros

So far, all the procedures we've used have been stored in the same macro as the code that calls them, i.e. on the same macro sheet. You can, though, call procedures (either functions or subroutines) that are stored in other macros. For example, if the active document is based on **Normal.dot** and you have the **UsefulBits.dot** template loaded as a global add-in, you can use the functions stored in the UsefulBits template:

```
Sub MAIN
    TimeNow$ = TimeFunction.GetTheTime$(Now())
    MsgBox TimeNow$
End Sub
```

This creates a string variable, **TimeNow$**, and calls the **GetTheTime$()** function which is part of the **TimeFunction** macro stored in the UsefulBits template. We supply the argument for **GetTheTime$()** using the built-in WordBasic function **Now()**, which returns the current time as a serial number, then displays the time in a message box.

This is exactly the same technique that we would use if the function was stored in the same macro as our **MAIN** routine, except that now we need to tell WordBasic the name of the macro that contains the function. We do this by preceding the function name with the name of the macro and a period:

```
TimeFunction.GetTheTime$()
```

You must make sure that the template containing the macros and functions you want to use is loaded first, otherwise you'll get an 'Unknown Command, Subroutine, or Function' error message.

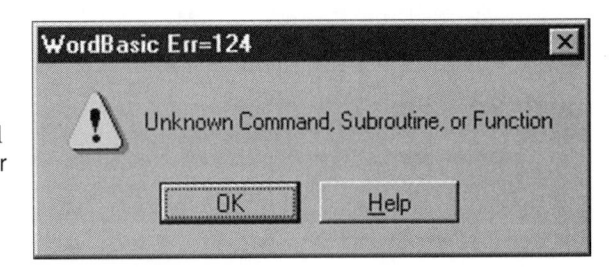

> **FYI** You can check whether a particular template is loaded as an add-in, or load and unload templates as add-ins, using the WordBasic procedures **CountAddIns()**, **AddInState**, **AddAddIn** and **ClearAddIns**. See the Help file for more details by searching on the name of each function.

Controlling Execution of Your Code

There's one major fundamental topic of the WordBasic language that we still need to look at. Like most other types of computer language, a WordBasic macro starts by executing the first line in the main procedure and works through them until it reaches the end. To write effective code, you have to be able to take decisions about which statements you want to execute, and repeat sections of code more than once. We achieve both of these by using control structures.

Again, WordBasic is much simpler than many other languages. There are only five basic methods of controlling the order of execution of your code—in other languages there are many more variations. But that doesn't mean we lose flexibility; it just means that we sometimes have to be more careful about how we design our routines.

WordBasic Control Structures

We can divide the five methods as follows:

Decision Making	Repeating Loops	Direct Jumps
If-Then-Else	For-Next	GoTo
Select-Case	While-Wend	

The modern term used to describe a control structure is a **construct**. Toss it around at your next party if you like. We'll look at each of the five types of construct in turn.

If-Then-Else

This construct allows you to execute different instructions, depending on the result of a single expression. WordBasic evaluates the expression, called the **condition**, and if it's **True,** executes the statement immediately after the **Then** keyword. If it's **False**, the statement after the **Else** keyword is executed.

```
If it's raining Then watch a chat show Else do the laundry
```

You don't have to use the **Else** part. If there's nothing to do when the expression is **False** you just omit it:

```
If it's raining Then watch a chat show
```

You can include the **Not** operator to reverse the result of the condition, so that the first part is executed when the condition is **False**:

```
If Not it's raining Then do the laundry
```

If you want to execute more than one statement for each result of the evaluation, you use the multiline version of the construct,

```
If it's raining Then
    go to the gym
    watch a chat show
End If
```

or include the **Else** part:

```
If it's raining Then
    go to the gym
    watch a chat show
Else
    do the laundry
    do the ironing
End If
```

Because WordBasic treats all non-zero numbers as **True**, you can use an expression which evaluates to an ordinary number for the condition. For example, the **Len()** function returns the number of characters in a string, so,

```
If Len(MyName$) Then MsgBox MyName$
```

gives the same result as the more wordy:

```
If Len(MyName$) > 0 Then MsgBox MyName$
```

Be wary of using these short-cuts, though. You can be fooled by functions that return non-intuitive results, such as the **Bold()** function. The statement

```
If Bold() Then MsgBox "All the selected text is bold"
```

will give the wrong result if *part* of it is bold. Remember that the **Bold()** function returns **1** if *all* the selected text is bold format, and **-1** if *part* of it is bold. Both these values will evaluate to **True** for the condition.

The **If-Then-Else** construct is ideally suited to situations where you want to execute just one set of statements, or choose between two sets depending on a single condition. If you have more than one condition which determines the outcome, you can use an extended version of **If-Then-Else** by including the **ElseIf** keyword. For example, to execute one of three statements, depending on the result two different conditions, you could use:

```
If it's raining Then
    go to the gym
ElseIf there's no clean shirts Then
    do the laundry
Else
    watch a chat show
End If
```

You can include more than one **ElseIf** section if you wish. However, there's a better way to choose between several options: a **Select-Case** construct.

Select-Case

The **Select-Case** construct is another way of choosing which statements to execute, depending on the result of evaluating a conditional expression. In this case, there's only one condition, but it can have several different results.

For example, you could have a situation where the decision is where to go each day of the week. Once you know what day it is, you can make the decision. There's only one test: 'What day is it?' Once you have the answer, you carry out the action that is appropriate for that day:

```
Select Case today
    Case Monday
        do the laundry
    Case Tuesday
        go to the gym
    Case Wednesday
        go shopping
    Case ...
        ...
    Case Else
        watch a chat show
End Select
```

You use numbers or strings in each **Case** part, depending on what data type the expression in the **Select** part evaluates to. You can include as many **Case** parts as you need. The **Case Else** part is optional, but is often included to catch the situations where a value you don't expect is generated by the **Select** expression:

```
Select Case Len(TenLetterString$)    'select on length of string
    Case 0
        MsgBox "What happened to the word?"
    Case 1, 2
        MsgBox "Is that all you could manage?"
    Case Is < 4
        MsgBox "A bit short..."
    Case 4 To 10
        MsgBox "Nice word..."
    Case Else
        MsgBox "ERROR: Only ten letters allowed!"
End Select
```

This macro above shows you some of the ways you can use the **Case** part. Starting from the top in our example, you can test for *individual* values, a *list* of values, a *condition* (using the **Is** keyword), a *range* (using the **To** keyword) and, of course, the catch-all **Else** part. The first **Case** part that matches the value is executed, and then execution jumps directly to the statement immediately after the **End Select** line.

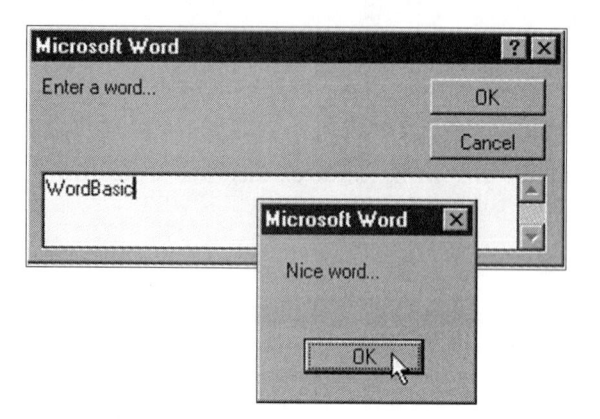

If your conditions 'overlap', like the second and third do in our example above, only the first of these is executed. For example, a value of **2** matches both of these conditions, but only the Is that all you could manage? message from the first of these is displayed.

If you want to try it out, you'll find this construct used in the macro **WordLength**. It's in the UsefulBits template in your samples folder.

For-Next

Having seen how we make decisions about which statements to execute, we now need to look at how we repeat statements more than once. The simplest loop construct to use is the **For-Next** loop.

You would normally use a **For-Next** loop when you know how many times you want to repeat the statements. Here it is in its simplest form:

```
For counter = start To end
    ...
    statements
    ...
Next counter
```

We use a counter variable, which must be a number-type, and specify the start and end values. So, to loop through the statements ten times, we could use:

```
For Count = 1 To 10
    ...
    statements
    ...
Next Count
```

Here, **Count** is our counter variable. When we enter the loop the first time, **Count** is set to **1**. Each time round, its value is incremented (**1** is added) until it's greater than the *end* value **10**. At this point, we skip over the loop and continue execution from the statement immediately after the **Next Count** line.

In a **For-Next** loop, the counter variable is available inside the loop, so the statements that are being executed repeatedly can use this value if required. If we placed the line

```
MsgBox "This is loop number" + Str$(Count)
```

inside the loop, Word would display a message showing the value of **Count** in each loop.

We aren't forced to start at **1** in a **For-Next** loop, or increment the counter variable by **1** each time round. For example,

```
For Count = 27 To -15 Step -3
```

would define a loop to run **14** times, and the value of **Count** will start at **27** and decrease by **3** every time round, till it's equal to **-15**.

One of the major uses for the **For-Next** construct is in manipulating arrays. If you remember, these are a series of values stored in a structure where you refer to each one by its index. Arrays in WordBasic always have zero as the start index. So, the code,

```
For Count = 0 To 14
    MsgBox MyValues$(Count)
Next
```

will display in turn each value in a **15** element string array called **MyValues$**. If you want to display them in reverse order:

```
For Count = 14 To 0 Step -1
    MsgBox MyValues$(Count)
Next
```

Notice that we've omitted the counter variable's name from after the **Next** in the last line of these examples. This is quite legal, though in complex code including it makes the code easier to read. This is especially true if you have nested loops.

Why would you want to nest loops? Well, remember that arrays can have more than one dimension. If we have a three-dimensional array declared as **FreePoints(359,359,359)**, perhaps used to plot points in free space, we can loop through all the points to set their initial value to zero by using the code:

```
        For X_Coord = 0 To 359
            For Y_Coord = 0 To 359
                For Z_Coord = 0 To 359
                    FreePoints(X_Coord, Y_Coord, Z_Coord) = 0
                Next Z_Coord
            Next Y_Coord
        Next X_Coord
```

While-Wend

The other loop construct is the **While-Wend** loop. Compared with other languages which often include **Do-Loop**, **Repeat-While** and **Repeat-Until**, WordBasic is rather deprived of loop constructs. However, we can manage quite well with only **While-Wend**—it just means we have to design our code with a little more care. You could argue that having too many options only encourages laziness in design!

Unlike the **For-Next** loop, we tend to use **While-Wend** when we don't know beforehand how many times we need to perform the loop.

```
While condition
    ...
    statements
    ...
Wend
```

The important point is that the condition must at some point become **False**, otherwise the loop will continue executing forever (or until you press *Escape* to stop it). So, either something inside the loop has to change a value in part of the condition, or another factor outside the loop, such as a user pressing a key, must make the condition become **False** at some point.

There are many occasions when you don't know how many times a loop will be executed. If you're prompting a user to enter a password, for example, you may decide to give them three chances to get it right. Using a **For-Next** loop is OK, but it will always execute three times—they'll be asked to enter the password again even if they get it right:

```
For Chance = 1 To 3
    get the password
    check if it's correct
Next
```

You need to exit from the loop as soon as they do get it right (hopefully, this will be the first time), and by including a variable **Chances** to check how many attempts they've had, you can still stop the loop after three tries:

```
Chances = 1
While (password is wrong) And (Chances < 4)
    get the password
    Chances = Chances + 1
Wend
If password is wrong Then failed
```

The loop will end when either of two expressions in the **While** condition becomes **False**. The user either entered the correct password, or they ran out of chances. So, all you need to do once the loop ends is to check the password again to see if you're going to let them in.

Goto

The `Goto` statement allows you to jump directly to another point in your code. Used sparingly, it can provide you with a useful way to control its execution. Just don't tell anyone you use it! `Goto` is definitely frowned upon because it's the easiest way to write 'spaghetti' code that soon becomes unreadable.

If you sit down and design your macros first, you can nearly always construct code that uses control structures other than `Goto`, which makes the code far more intelligible.

The one exception to this is error handling. We have to use labels and `Goto`s in WordBasic to control execution when we want to prevent errors from interrupting our code. You'll see more about error handling in the next few sections.

Using Labels and Line Numbers

In early versions of Basic, when windows were things you leaned out of, you identified each line of code with a line number. These days, line numbers are definitely out of fashion, but you can still use them in WordBasic if you want to. A better option, though, when you need to refer to a particular line of code in a macro is to use a label. A **label** is simply a text string followed by a colon, placed before the line you want to refer to:

```
...
Insert AuthorName$
Goto MyLabel
...
FormatFont .Italic = 1

MyLabel:
    InsertPara    'this line is referred to by MyLabel
...
```

You must place the label against the left-hand margin, otherwise Word can't locate it and you'll get an error message when you try and run the macro. Labels must be unique in a macro and can't include spaces.

Nesting Control Structures in Your Code

Now that you've seen how to create and use control structures, we'll take a quick look at how to combine them to create a program. The following example shows how you could code the decision of what to do today:

```
Select Case today
    Case monday
        If there are no clean shirts Then
            do the laundry
            While there are shirts to iron
                iron the front and back
                iron the collar
                For sleeve = 1 To 2
                    iron a sleeve
                Next
            Wend
        Else
            watch a chat show
```

```
            End If
        Case tuesday
            got to the gym
        Case wednesday
            ...
            ...
End Select
```

We use a **Select-Case** construct to decide what day it is. If it's Monday, we use an **If-Then-Else** construct to check whether we need to do the laundry, or whether we can watch a chat show. If we're out of clean shirts again, we do the laundry, then check if there are any shirts to be ironed. The **While-Wend** loop will only be entered if there are, and for each one we iron the front, back and collar, then use a **For-Next** loop to iron both sleeves.

Notice that we don't know how many shirts need ironing, so we use a **While-Wend** loop, but we know each shirt has two sleeves, so we use a **For-Next** loop.

Coping with Errors

If you've been typing in some of the examples from this chapter, you may already have encountered WordBasic error messages. When Word comes to save or execute your code, it checks to see that what you've entered is 'legal', that it agrees with the syntax of the language.

You'll notice that, as it does so, it changes the statements by capitalizing them in line with the standard syntax, adding and removing spaces between parts of each statement. If you enter

```
formatfont .italic=1
```

in a subroutine, then click the Start button on the macro toolbar, Word changes your code to read:

```
FormatFont .Italic = 1
```

However, if you've typed **formtafont** instead of **formatfont**, you get an error message when the code runs.

Click the OK button, switch to the macro window and Word has highlighted the code where the error occurred.

```
Sub MAIN
formtafont.Italic = 1
End Sub
```

You should be able to see quite easily what's wrong. Syntax errors arise generally because you have mistyped a statement, or used commas or brackets in the wrong place. Click the Help button to get advice on things to look for.

Errors like this are generally easy to find, but the other kind of errors—semantic or run-time errors—can be a lot more difficult. Here's an obvious one to start with:

```
FormatFont .Italic = 3
```

When you run this, you get an error number 159, plus a helpful message. If you hit the Help button, you get even more detailed advice. Here, the reason for the error is that the **Italic** argument to the **FormatFont** statement can only be **0** or **1**.

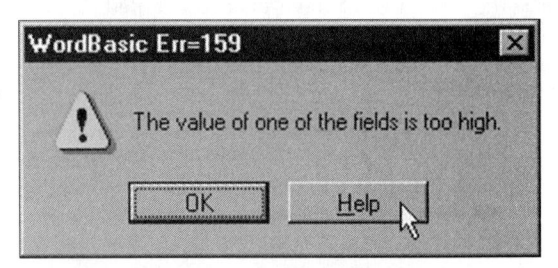

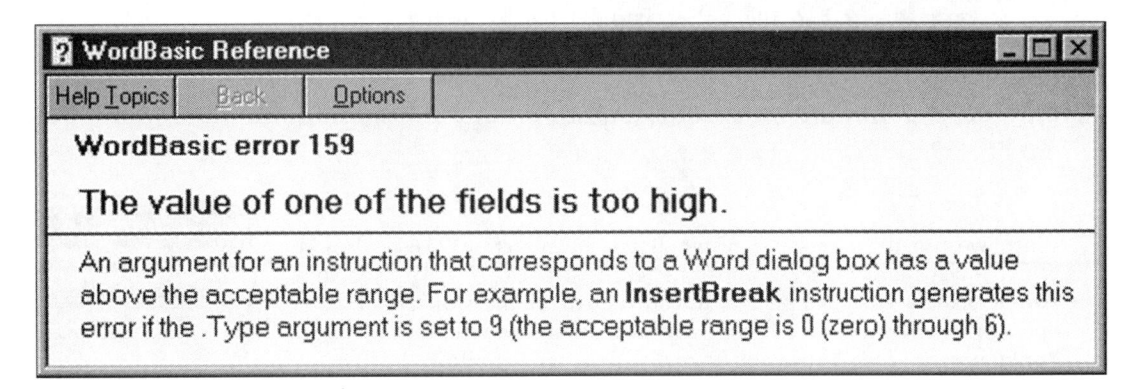

WordBasic Err=159

The value of one of the fields is too high.

[OK] [Help]

WordBasic Reference

Help Topics | Back | Options

WordBasic error 159

The value of one of the fields is too high.

An argument for an instruction that corresponds to a Word dialog box has a value above the acceptable range. For example, an **InsertBreak** instruction generates this error if the .Type argument is set to 9 (the acceptable range is 0 (zero) through 6).

Unfortunately, many errors aren't so easy to find. For example, this snippet of code gives the wrong answer:

```
Sub MAIN
    RentPayment = 125.6
    Interest = 36.24
    CashReceived$ = "Today's Cash is " + Str$(RentPayment + Interest)
    MsgBox CashRecieved$
End Sub
```

You can see that we've used a variable called **CashReceived$** to store the total as a string, and then we display it in a message box. But when we run the macro, all we get is a blank message box:

Microsoft Word

[OK]

The reason is simple. We've made a spelling mistake in the variable name in the `MsgBox` statement!

> **FYI** If, like some langauges, WordBasic forced you to predefine your variables, this error would have been prevented. When you tried to run your code, you would have been warned of your error because the variable name would have been flagged up as not having been pre-declared.

Finally, the other major source of errors is code that seems to work, but just gives the wrong answer, and then not always every time. There can be a multitude of reasons for this. You could have made a fundamental mistake when you designed the code, or you could be assuming something that's not exactly correct. Here's a sample:

```
Sub MAIN
    TaxRate = 7.5 / 100     'equivalent to 7.5 percent
    RentPayment = 125.6
    Interest = 36.24
    TaxDue = RentPayment + Interest * TaxRate
    MsgBox "Tax due is $" + Str$(TaxDue)
End Sub
```

When we run this, we get a result. But is it correct? $125.60 + $36.24 is not much more than the apparent result of $128.318 we're due to pay in tax! So what happened? If you remember the stuff about operator precedence, you'll see why: we should add the `RentPayment` and `Interest` together first, then multiply by the `TaxRate`. We need to add brackets to change the order of precedence:

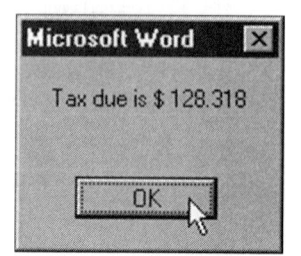

```
    TaxDue = (RentPayment + Interest) * TaxRate
```

Now we get a more likely answer.

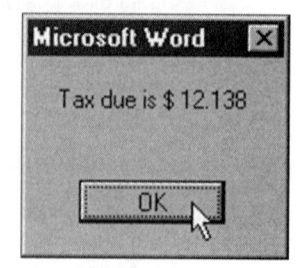

Finding Errors in Your Code

WordBasic is quite rudimentary in the support for finding errors in, or debugging, your code. If you can't see where the error is arising by examining the code, you can try stepping through it as it executes. The technique is to execute just one line or block of statements at a time and view the values of the variables. That way, you can find the statement that's causing the error.

Single-stepping through Code

To single-step through your code, you use two of the buttons on the Macro toolbar. You can execute every statement, or skip over any procedures that your code calls.

To step every statement, click the Step button. This executes one statement each time you click it, then stops. When you come to a procedure call, clicking the button takes you into the procedure, and subsequent clicks single-step you through it, then take you back into the main procedure again.

If you know that the error isn't in a particular procedure that's called from your code, you can step over it. Clicking the Step Subs button does the same as the Step button until you come to a procedure call. Instead of stepping into the procedure at that point, it runs the procedure at normal speed, then resumes single-stepping when control passes back to the main procedure again.

Setting Break Points

If you want to run part of the code at full speed—say, you know the error doesn't occur until near the end of the macro—you can set a break point. When execution reaches this point, it stops. To set a break point, you place a **Stop** statement in your code where you want to stop the code executing:

```
Stop        'stops your code and displays a message box
Stop -1     'stops your code and doesn't display a message box
```

You can then view the values of the variables, continue single-stepping through the code, or restart execution normally with the Continue button.

Viewing the Values of Variables

When execution of your macro is halted, either by a **Stop** statement or while single-stepping through the code, you can display the value of the variables that are currently in context. Remember that, unless you declare it as a **Shared** variable for that macro, a variable is only in context within the procedure in which it's declared. To open the Macro Variables dialog, click the Show Variables button on the Macro toolbar.

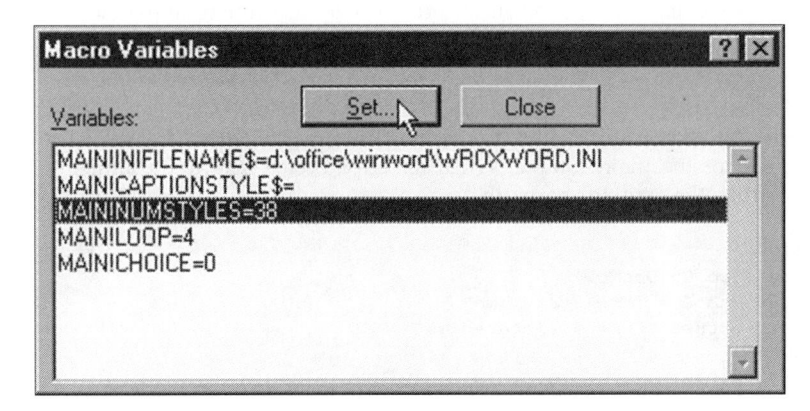

```
Macro Variables                                    ? X

Variables:           Set...         Close

MAIN!INIFILENAME$=d:\office\winword\WROXWORD.INI
MAIN!CAPTIONSTYLE$=
MAIN!NUMSTYLES=38
MAIN!LOOP=4
MAIN!CHOICE=0
```

Word shows you the current value of all the variables that are in context at that point. You can see that it uses the name of the procedure to identify where the variables are declared. In our case, they all come from the **MAIN** procedure. You can change the value currently stored in any variable by clicking the Set... button and entering a new value.

If your code is misbehaving, you may find that it reaches a certain point with an unexpected value in one of the variables. If you set a breakpoint here, you can use the Macro Variables dialog to change the value back to one that you expect, then click Continue to carry on executing the rest of the macro.

> **FYI** Word also has a facility to trace through your code. This is supposed to run the code slowly so that you can see what's happening in your macro, but you'll probably find that everything happens so quickly that it's not much help.

Run-time Error Handling Methods

When an error occurs in the code we've been using so far, Word stops execution and displays a message box describing the error. There are, though, some errors that you can't always prevent. For example, if your macro is loading a picture into a document and the picture file has been deleted for any reason, your code will fail.

You can trap this error by setting up an error handler at the beginning of your procedure, or before the section where the error is likely to occur. Once you've set up an error handler, instead of displaying the error message or stopping the code, Word will transfer execution to the statement specified by your error handler.

There are three forms of error handler statement:

On Error Goto *label*	When an error occurs, execution continues from the statement immediately after *label*.
On Error Resume Next	When an error occurs, execution continues from the statement immediately after the one where the error occurred.
On Error Goto 0	When an error occurs, execution stops and an error message box is displayed. Equivalent to 'turning off' error handling.

On Error Goto

The first form, **On Error Goto** *label*, is the most useful. You place a label in your code, usually towards the end of the main routine. When an error occurs, execution jumps to this label and you can exit from the routine gracefully:

```
Sub MAIN
On Error Goto GetOutNow
    PictureName$ = "MyPicture.bmp"
    InsertPicture .Name = PictureName$
GetOutNow:
End Sub
```

The only problem now is that if the picture is missing, nothing seems to happen; the procedure just stops. If we add an unconditional **GoTo** statement, we can arrange for execution to go one way if there's an error, or another if all is well.

```
Sub MAIN
On Error Goto GotAnError
    PictureName$ = "MyPicture.bmp"
    InsertPicture .Name = PictureName$
    Goto AllOK
GotAnError:
    MsgBox "Cannot find picture " + PictureName$
AllOK:
End Sub
```

The error trap we've set up is only active in the procedure where it occurs, so you need to create one for each procedure where there's a possibility of run-time errors arising. You can execute another **On Error** statement within a procedure whenever you like. It 'redirects' the error trap to the new label that you specify. You can also 'turn off' error handling, which effectively gives control back to Word's default error handler, by executing the statement:

```
On Error Goto 0
```

On Error Resume Next

The final form of the **On Error** statement in used when an error will not affect the macro's capability to continue. In other words, if you can allow execution to continue in the macro, even though an error has occurred, without affecting the result, you use the statement:

```
On Error Resume Next
```

When an error occurs, Word just moves to the next statement in the macro and continues execution from there. You could use this form of error handler if, for example, you are loading a picture just for decoration, so it doesn't matter if it can't be found.

Useful Techniques with Control Structures

There's been a lot of reading and not much opportunity for practice in this chapter so far. Most of what we've covered is the theory behind WordBasic, so you may already be familiar with many of the concepts we've looked at. To finish off, we'll show you the various techniques in action and build three useful macros for your own UsefulBits template. The first two of these examples are in **UsefulBits.dot** which is installed with the sample files on the disk that accompanies this book.

For all of the examples that follow you'll need to open your own UsefulBits template. If you created one in your **\Templates** folder by following the examples in Chapter 1, open it now by selecting File | Open..., changing the Files of Type: to Document Templates (*.dot), and selecting **UsefulBits.dot**.

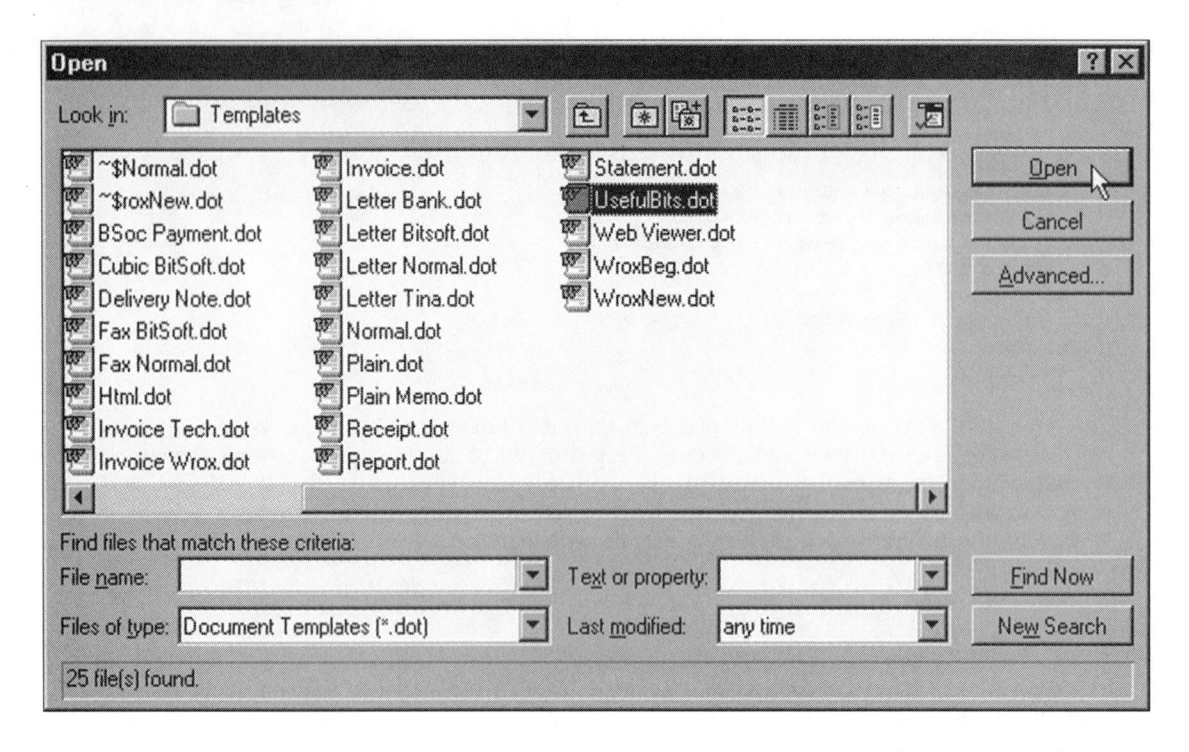

If you haven't created the UsefulBits template yet, do so now by selecting File | New..., setting the Create New option to Template, and clicking OK.

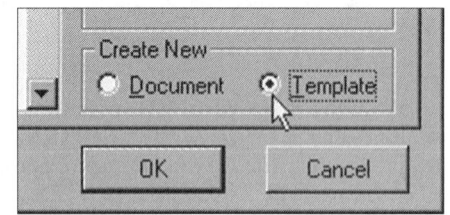

Once you've created the new template, select File | Save As... and save it as **UsefulBits.dot** in your **\Templates** folder (this will probably be **\MSOffice\Templates** or **\Winword\Template**). To find out which is your current **\Templates** folder, select Tools | Options... and open the File Locations tab.

Turning Arrays into Tables

As we saw, one of the uses of `For-Next` loops is to manipulate arrays. This example shows how you can place a set of values from an array into a table in a document. It also shows you some other functions we haven't met so far.

Try It Out - Creating a Table of Random Numbers

In this example, we'll create our new macro by copying it from the sample UsefulBits template, which will have been installed with the other sample files from the disk that accompanies this book.

1 With your own UsefulBits template open, select Macro from the Tools menu and make sure that **UsefulBits.dot** is selected for the Macros Available In: option. Select the Organizer... button.

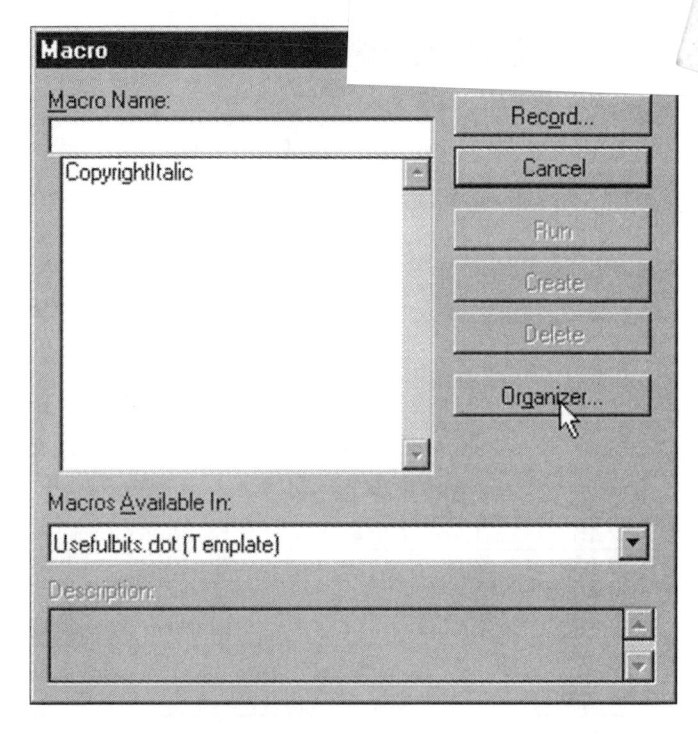

2 Open the sample UsefulBits template from the `C:\BegWord` folder, or from wherever you installed the sample files. Select the RandomTable, then click the Copy button to copy the macro into your own UsefulBits template and click Close.

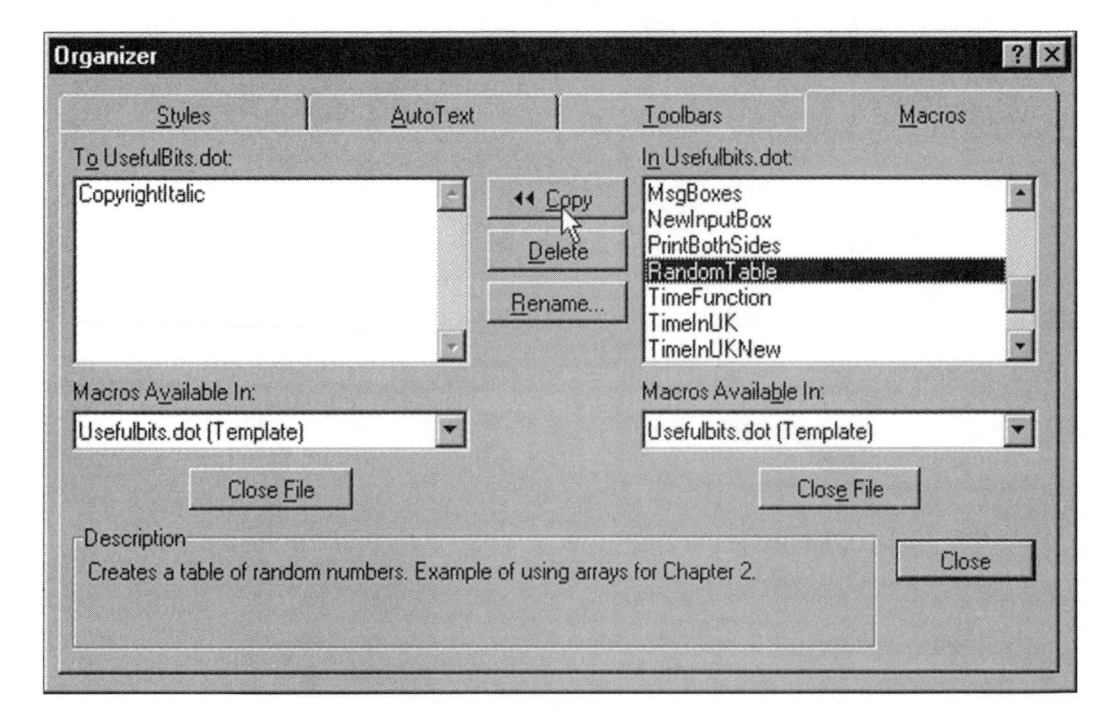

3 Again select the Tools|Macros... menu option and run the newly copied **RandomTable** macro. Then click the Start button on the Macro toolbar to run the new macro. It first creates a new document and a random-sized array of random numbers. Then it tells you how many rows and columns there will be in the new table.

> **Microsoft Word**
>
> The macro will create a table 8 columns by 9 rows, and insert the random values into it.
>
> OK

4 Click OK and the table is placed in the document.

Display of Random Numbers in a Table							
55.78	35.83	80.52	37.12	88.19	49.86	60.13	29.1
47.39	31.94	53.14	46.09	39.32	35.7	13.68	38.63
89.48	77.01	45.3	0.25	95.59	92.08	5.91	79.41
12.15	71.85	47.46	59.84	32.8	61.23	85.05	13.56
28.14	61.5	56.54	65.42	87.75	3.3	67.17	94.9
32.68	14.22	54.07	92.05	5.5	86.65	88.16	57.75
33.98	9.73	90.21	16.41	40.19	29.76	87.03	12.49
78.11	47.13	0.67	91.66	37.54	36.49	3.36	78.07
42.74	27.5	77.02	10.06	82.36	78.44	57.4	74.58

How It Works

The first thing we have to do is to make sure we have a current document window in which to insert the table. If the user has the **RandomTable** macro window open, the macro will fail because you can't (and wouldn't want to) create a table in this window. If the current window is a macro editing window, the WordBasic function **IsMacro()** will return **True**. If it does, we need to create a new document, using the statement **FileNew**. This is equivalent to selecting New from the File menu and selecting the Normal template.

```
Sub MAIN
    'check that we're not already in a table
    If SelInfo(13) >= 0 Then
        MsgBox "You must place the insertion point OUTSIDE a table"
        Goto GetOutNow
    Else
        'if macro window is current create a new document
        If IsMacro() Then FileNew
    EndIf
```

Things aren't quite that simple, though, as you can see from the code. We can't create a table within a table, so we also need to check to see if the cursor is already in an existing table. The WordBasic function **SelInfo()** can be used to return a range of information about the current selection. (If nothing is actually *selected*, the 'current selection' is just the place where the insertion point is.) **SelInfo(13)** returns the number of the row that contains the selection if it's in a table. If it isn't in a table, it returns **-1**. So we're able to warn the user if we're in an existing table and jump to the **GetOutNow** label which is just before the end of the procedure.

Now we print a message in the status bar to tell them what's happening and create two random numbers, one for the number of rows and one for the number of columns.

```
        Print "Creating array of random numbers ..."
        TotalRows = Int(Rnd() * 20) + 5
        TotalCols = Int(Rnd() * 8) + 2
```

The WordBasic function **Rnd()** returns a random number greater than or equal to zero and less than 1. Multiplying it by 20 gives us a number between 0 and 19.99999, and applying the **Int()** function to this gives us a number between 0 and 19. To ensure we always get at least 5 rows, we then add 5 to the result. This gives us a number between 5 and 24 for **TotalRows**. Similarly, multiplying by 8 and adding 2 gives us a number between 2 and 9 for **TotalCols**. This is the standard way of generating random numbers.

> **FYI** There's some discussion about whether computers can ever create truly random numbers. Currently, in most cases, the **Rnd()** function uses a 'seed', based on the internal clock, and applies complex mathematical operations to it. These are usually called *pseudo-random numbers*. In theory, the result is predictable, but the jury's still out on this one.

Now that we have the size of our array, we can declare it. Then we use two nested **For-Next** loops to fill it with random numbers. We want non-integer numbers with two decimal places. To get these, we create random numbers between 1 and 9999, then divide them by 100.

```
        Dim Randoms(TotalRows, TotalCols)    'declare a new random-sized array
        For Row = 1 To TotalRows             'and fill it with random values
            For Col = 1 To TotalCols
                Randoms(Row, Col) = Int((Rnd() * 10000) + 1) / 100
            Next Col
        Next Row
```

This is a common way of controlling the number of decimal places in a number. For example, when we are working with currency values we need two decimal places. We just multiply by 100, take the integer (whole) part of the result, then divide by 100. Note, however, that this doesn't round the result to the nearest cent; WordBasic was never designed for complex mathematical work and doesn't include a rounding function.

Now we build up a string with a message about the new table. To break the string into separate lines of the length *we* want them, we include a **Chr$(10)**:

```
        Msg$ = "The macro will create a table" + Chr$(10)
        Msg$ = Msg$ + Str$(TotalCols) + " columns by"
        Msg$ = Msg$ +  Str$(TotalRows) + " rows, and " + Chr$(10)
        Msg$ = Msg$ + " insert the random values into it."
        MsgBox Msg$
```

Next, we insert and format the new table. We're going to include a title row, so we add an extra row for this. Notice that we have to select the whole table before we can format it:

```
        'insert a table of the right size, and format it
        'we include an extra row for the heading.
        TableInsertTable .NumColumns = TotalCols, .NumRows = TotalRows + 1
        TableSelectTable
        BorderLineStyle 8              'double border
```

```
        BorderOutside
        BorderLineStyle 1          'single border
        BorderInside
        CenterPara
```

To create and format the heading row, we move to the first cell with **NextCell**, then select the current row. **TableMergeCells** makes the currently selected cells into one long one, and **ShadingPattern 4** sets the background of the selected row to 20% gray.

```
        NextCell                   'move to first cell
        TableSelectRow
        TableMergeCells
        ShadingPattern 4           '20% gray
        BorderLineStyle 2          'medium line
        BorderBottom
        Bold 1
        Insert "Display of Random Numbers in a Table"
        Bold 0
```

Now we can insert the values. We use the same two nested **For-Next** constructs to loop through the array, pulling out the values, converting them to strings and dropping them in the cells of the table. We use **NextCell** to move to the next cell each time, just like when we press the *Tab* key:

```
        For Row = 1 To TotalRows
           For Col = 1 To TotalCols
              NextCell
              Insert Str$(Randoms(Row, Col))    'insert the values
           Next Col
        Next Row
```

Finally, move back to the start of the document and the macro ends. Here's the **GetOutNow** label that we could jump to from earlier in the macro.

```
        StartOfDocument
   GetOutNow:
   End Sub
```

You'll see that there are sets of statements which mirror the standard Word menu commands, such as **TableInsertTable** and **TableSelectRow**, and that the formatting commands, like **BorderInside** and **ShadingPattern**, are broadly equivalent to those on the Borders toolbar. If you want more information about any of the statements we've used, just place the text cursor on the keyword and press *F1*.

Creating a List of Available Fonts

WordBasic includes functions which return information about the environment in which Word is operating, not just about the current document. When you're trying to produce attractive documents, you often spend time trying out different typefaces, or fonts. (If you talk to a publisher they'll tell you that typefaces and fonts are not the same thing. For our purposes, we just mean the shape and style of the letters.) To make life easier, you can print out a full list of all your installed fonts which makes choosing the right one easier.

Chapter 2 - WordBasic Fundamentals

Try It Out - Listing Available Fonts

We'll use the same technique we did in the previous example to create our new macro by copying the macro from the sample UsefulBits template provided with the book.

1 With your own UsefulBits template open, select Macro from the Tools menu, select the Organizer... tool as before and copy the `ListFonts` macro to your own UsefulBits template.

2 From the Tools|Macros dialog, select and run the ListFonts macro. A new document is created, but nothing else seems to be happening. But look at the status bar at the bottom of the window—it shows the number of fonts listed so far.

> Press ESC to stop - Listed 19 fonts so far ..

3 Once all your fonts have been listed, the screen redraws and you can see the result:

Font Name: **Deco: Biblical**

AaBbCcDdEeFfGg 1234567890

Font Name: **Deco: Billboard**

AaBbCcDdEeFfGg 1234567890

How It Works

Although this is a specific example using the fonts installed on your computer, it also demonstrates the general technique we can use to obtain information about the various objects that are part of Word and its environment. For example, we've included a very similar macro in the UsefulBits template which creates a document showing samples of all the styles stored in a template.

WordBasic contains a set of functions which return a count of the different objects in a template, and there are corresponding functions which return the names of each one. We'll be using `CountFonts()` and `Font$()` functions in our example, but if you open the Help file Index page and enter count or get, you'll see most of them listed.

First, we define the variables we're going to use. This isn't absolutely necessary, but it makes maintaining the code later a lot easier.

```
Sub MAIN
    Dim NumFonts      'total number of fonts
    Dim OldFont$      'current font of document
```

79

```
        Dim Loop            'loop counter variable
        Dim Letter          'character to print
```

As in the previous example, we need to make sure that, rather than a macro editing window, we have a document window open, otherwise we'll get an error.

```
        'if macro window is active create a new document
        If IsMacro() Then FileNewDefault
```

Now we can get the font names. **CountFonts()** returns the number of installed fonts available for use with the current printer. We declare a string array to hold their names, then use the **Font$()** function to get the name of each one. This function can be used with no arguments to return the name of the font for the currently selected text in a document, but, by providing an argument in the range **1** to **CountFonts()**, it returns the name of that particular font from the list of fonts that are installed.

Notice that our array **FontNames$** is zero-based (the first element is index **0**), while the list of fonts starts at 1. So we've declared the array size as one less than the number of fonts, and subtracted **1** from the **Loop** variable so that we fill the array starting from **0**.

```
        NumFonts = CountFonts()
        Dim FontName$(NumFonts - 1)         'declare the array
        For Loop = 1 To NumFonts            'and fill it with the names
            FontName$(Loop - 1) = Font$(Loop)
        Next
```

Word doesn't return the names of the fonts in alphabetical order, as it does when it displays them in its own dialogs and lists, so we use the **SortArray** statement to sort them. We can use **SortArray** to sort by column or by row and into ascending or descending order. If it's a two-dimensional array, we can also specify which column or row to base the sort on. In our case, however, we just use the default form of the statement to sort the array alphabetically.

```
        SortArray FontName$()               'sort into alphabetical order
```

Next, we turn off screen updating to prevent Word trying to redraw the screen every time it prints anything. This makes the routine work much more quickly, especially because, even on a good day, handling lots of fonts tends to slow Windows down. Then we save the name of the current font so that we can restore it later, and set the current font size to 12 points.

```
        ScreenUpdating 0
        OldFont$ = Font$()                  'save the current font
        FontSize 12
```

Now we can insert the font names and styles into the document. We use a **For-Next** construct to loop through the array of names. (Remember that we have to subtract one from the number of fonts because our array is zero-based.) For each font, we insert the name, then switch to that font using the **Font** *statement* (rather than the **Font()** function).

```
        For Loop = 0 To NumFonts - 1        'loop for each font
            Insert "Font Name: "
            Bold 1
            Insert FontName$(Loop)          'insert the name
            Bold 0
            InsertPara
            Font (FontName$(Loop))          'change to that font
```

To show how the font looks in different sizes, we print a pair of characters in each of seven sizes. We use a **For-Next** loop and, within it, set the size of the font to three times the value of the loop variable **Letter** plus **12**—giving us 12, 15, 18, 21, 24, 27, 30 points in turn. Then we use the **Chr$()** function to create the characters for insertion. **65** is the ASCII code for A, and **97** the code for a. So **Chr$(65)** returns the string **"A"**. As we add the increasing values of the loop variable **Letter** to it we get **Chr$(66)** - **"B"** and **Chr$(98)** - **"b",** etc.

```
        For Letter = 0 To 6                     'and print Aa to Gg
            FontSize 12 + (Letter * 3)
            Insert Chr$(65 + Letter) + Chr$(97 + Letter)
        Next
```

We include the numbers 0 to 9 in the document as well, in 14 pt size, then switch back to the original font in 12 pt and draw a line below the newly inserted text using the **BorderBottom** statement.

```
        FontSize 14
        Insert "  1234567890"
        Font(OldFont$, 12)                      'set to original font
        InsertPara
        LineUp
        BorderBottom 1                          'draw a line
        LineDown
        InsertPara
```

While we're still in the loop, we print a message in the status bar to inform the user of how things are going (it can be a long process if you have more than 50 fonts) and tell them how to interrupt it.

```
        Msg$ = "     Press ESC to stop  -  Listed"
        Msg$ = Msg$  + Str$(Loop + 1) + " fonts so far .. "
        Print Msg$
    Next
```

Finally, when all the fonts have been listed, we go back to the beginning of the document and stop.

```
        StartOfDocument
        Print "Done .."
    End Sub
```

Creating a Unique File Name

If you tried the Book Order application we discussed in Chapter 1, you'll have seen how it automatically saves the letters it creates onto your hard disk. This brings with it a problem: you have to make sure that you have a unique name for each file. Word proposes a name based on the first lines in the document, but this is a bit hit-and-miss. Instead, if that file already exists, our application adds a three digit number to the file name:

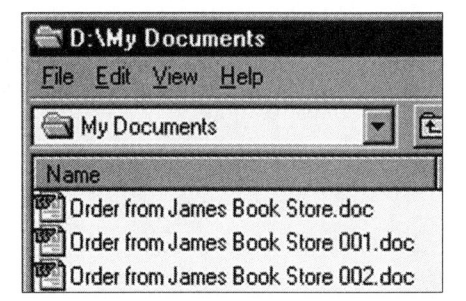

Try It Out - Creating Unique File Names

This example uses the Book Order template that's installed with the other sample files. Open it by selecting File | Open... and changing the Files of Type: to Document Templates (*.dot). Select **Book Order.dot** and hold down the *Shift* key while you click Open to stop it running automatically once it's loaded. You'll also need your own UsefulBits template open.

1 With your own UsefulBits template open, select Macro... from the Tools menu and make sure that **UsefulBits.dot** is selected for the Macros Available In: option. Enter the name UniqueFileName and fill in a brief description, then click Create.

2 Now switch to the Book Order template, select Tools | Macro..., select the StartWizard macro and click Edit.

3 Scroll down till you find the **GetFreeFileName$()** function; it's about halfway down. Select it all by dragging over it with the mouse pointer. Press *Ctrl-C* to copy it to the clipboard.

```
End Sub

Function GetFreeFileName$(FName$)
    If Files$(FName$ + ".doc") <> "" Then
        Count = 1
        FPathExtra$ = Right$("000" + LTrim$(Str$(Count)), 3)
        While Files$(FName$ + " " + FPathExtra$ + ".doc") <> ""
            Count = Count + 1
            FPathExtra$ = Right$("000" + LTrim$(Str$(Count)), 3)
        Wend
        GetFreeFileName$ = FName$ + " " + FPathExtra$
    Else
        GetFreeFileName$ = FName$
    EndIf
End Function
```

4 Switch back to your new UsefulBits template. Place the cursor *after* the **End Sub** line and press *Return* a couple of times.

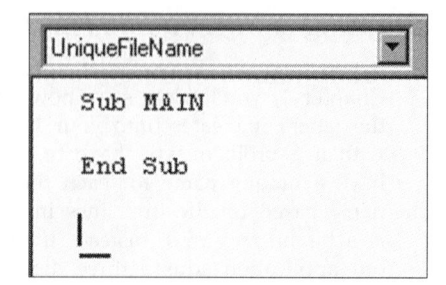

```
UniqueFileName

Sub MAIN

End Sub
```

5 Press *Ctrl-V* to place the text from the clipboard into the macro. We have to add it as a separate function because a macro must start with the usual part **Sub MAIN**. However, we'll use this to demonstrate the function at work.

6 Add the following to the **Sub MAIN** part of the macro:

```
NewFileName$ = GetFreeFileName$("Test File")
FileNewDefault
FileSaveAs .Name = NewFileName$
```

```
Sub MAIN
    NewFileName$ = GetFreeFileName$("Test File")
    FileNewDefault
    FileSaveAs .Name = NewFileName$
End Sub
```

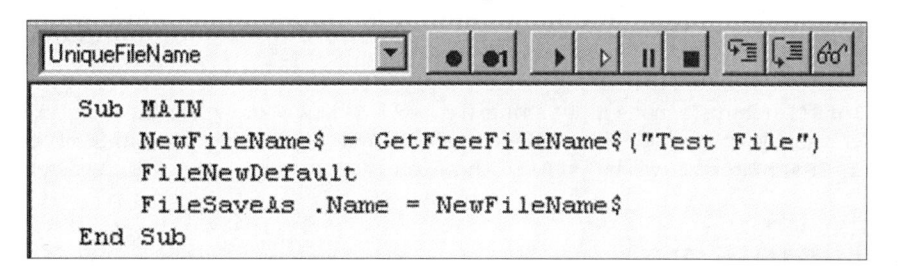

7 Click the Start button on the Macro toolbar to run the new macro. A new document is created and saved in your current folder. You can see from the title bar that it's named Test File.doc. If you run the macro several times, you will create new documents with similar incrementing file names.

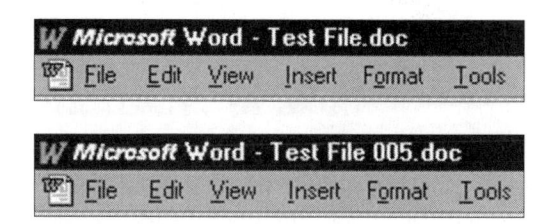

8 To save the new macro, switch back to your macro editing window and click the Save button on the standard toolbar, or select File | Save Template. Word prompts you to save the changes to the template. Click Yes. You'll also need to close all the new documents you've created.

9 To see the new file names, run My Computer or Explorer and move the folder where the documents have been stored. This will be where you loaded the last document from—it should be either the **C:\BegWord** samples folder, or your default **\Templates** folder.

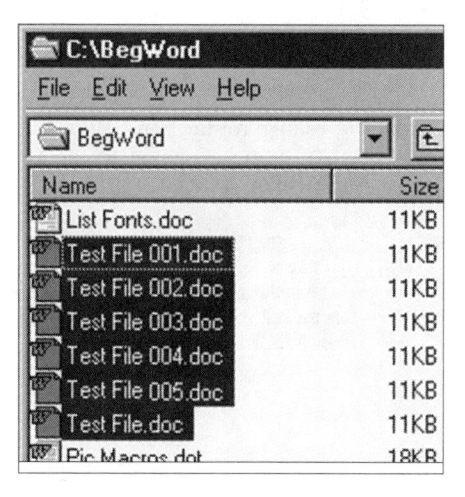

How It Works

The `GetFreeFileName$()` function is quite short and simple, but very useful. When you call the function you supply a proposed name for the file, which can include the full path if required. The first step is to add the standard **.doc** extension to the name and use the `Files$()` function to see if the file already exists.

If it does, `Files$()` returns the name of the file. This is because you can include wildcards (like the MS-DOS ***** and **?** characters) in the name. `Files$()` then returns the name of the first one that matches the pattern.

```
Function GetFreeFileName$(FName$)
    If Files$(FName$ + ".doc") <> "" Then
```

So, if `Files$()` returns a non-empty string (i.e. `<> ""`), we know the file does exist. We set the counter variable **Count** to **1**, and then create a three digit string from it. So if **Count** is equal to **1**, **FPathExtra$** will be **"001"**. The expression that does the work evaluates as:

```
Str$(1) = " 1"
LTrim$(" 1") = "1"
"000" + "1" = "0001"
Right$("0001", 3) = "001"
```

```
        Count = 1
        FPathExtra$ = Right$("000" + LTrim$(Str$(Count)), 3)
```

Now we create the full name using the new number part, such as **"Test File 001.doc"** and use the `Files$()` function again to test whether the new name is already used by an existing file. This forms the condition for the **While-Wend** loop which only executes if it does exist. Each time the loop encounters a name already in use, it adds one to **Count** and creates the next file name in sequence, then tests to see whether it exists.

```
        While Files$(FName$ + " " + FPathExtra$ + ".doc") <> ""
            Count = Count + 1
            FPathExtra$ = Right$("000" + LTrim$(Str$(Count)), 3)
        Wend
```

Once we've got a name that isn't in use, we can assign it to the function name, which returns it to the calling routine, and stop. The **Else** part of the **If-Then** construct simply assigns the originally proposed name to the function result if it didn't exist during the first test, at the top of the function.

```
        GetFreeFileName$ = FName$ + " " + FPathExtra$
    Else
        GetFreeFileName$ = FName$
    EndIf
End Function
```

Summary

In this chapter, we've devoted a lot of space to pure theory, but you need to absorb this before we go on to look at more complex code in following chapters. We're going to assume that you have a broad understanding of all the concepts we've introduced here.

We started back at the fundamental parts of the WordBasic language, examining the different elements and the way they fit together. By the end of the chapter, we had some useful routines which you can incorporate in your own code. Hopefully, these have helped to cement a real understanding of how WordBasic works.

We've covered:

- Variables, data types, operators, statements and functions
- Creating your own procedures and using them in your code
- Different ways of controlling execution and responding to errors
- How you put these techniques to work in your own macros

In the next chapter, we'll take a look at one aspect of Word that we haven't used yet: **dialogs**. These are the final link in the chain and, from there on, we can finish up the first section of the book by tidying up the loose ends and filling in on some other useful techniques. So, take a deep breath and turn the page...

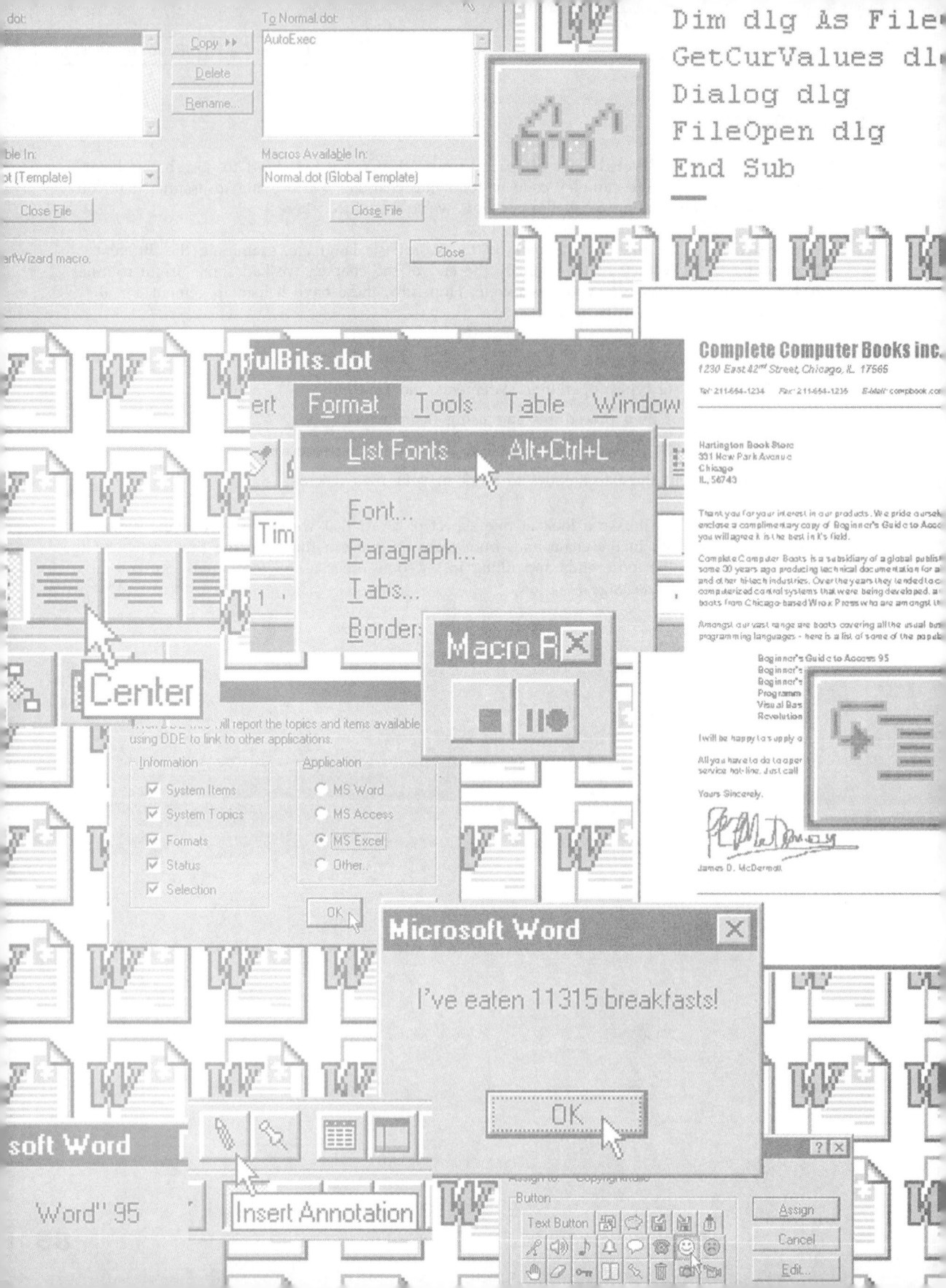

```
Dim dlg As File
GetCurValues dl
Dialog dlg
FileOpen dlg
End Sub
```

Communicating With Your Users

Introduction

Until now, we've been concentrating on the 'nuts and bolts' of WordBasic, seeing how macros work and examining the fundamental elements of the language. Now it's time to consider how we involve our users in the process. You've already seen a couple of ways of presenting information, using a Windows message box to display information, or by printing it in the status bar at the bottom of the screen.

When you use a 'real' Windows application, you spend a lot of time working with **dialog boxes**. The Book Order application we saw at the beginning of Chapter 1 uses a dialog to get the information it needs to produce a letter, and, during the process, it displays the normal Windows Print dialog so that you can choose the printer and options you require.

In this chapter, we'll look at the different ways you can communicate with your users, either getting information from them or displaying results. There are three basic methods you can use:

- Normal WordBasic input and output statements, like **MsgBox** and **Print**
- WordBasic's built-in dialogs, such as **FilePrint** and **FormatFont**
- **Custom dialogs**, which you create and manage with WordBasic code

There's a lot to cover in this chapter, so we'll be assuming that you've worked through the previous chapters, or are familiar with the concepts they cover. We'll also be giving you lots of opportunity to try out the techniques yourself.

WordBasic's Input and Output Statements

In the previous chapter, you've seen WordBasic's **MsgBox** and **Print** statements at work, and, in the **WordLength** example macro, we even sneaked an **InputBox** into the code. All these are ways of getting and displaying information in your macro.

There are four ways you can do this:

- Print information in the status bar using the **Print** statement
- Prompt for information in the status bar with the **Input** statement
- Display messages and offer options with the **MsgBox** statement
- Get text information directly using the **InputBox** statement

The first two of these use the status bar at the bottom of the screen, and the other two display normal Windows dialog boxes. We'll look at each of them in turn.

Using the Status Bar

At the bottom of the Word program window is the **status bar**. It's here that Word displays a variety of information and messages as you work, one example being the progress indicator that you see when you save a document. We've already used the status bar in our macros to display information. In the **ListFonts** macro, for example, it shows how many fonts we have listed so far.

> **FYI** If you can't see the status bar, turn it on in the **Options** dialog. Select **Tools** | **Options...** and open the **View** tab.

Printing Information in the Status Bar

We print information in the status bar using the **Print** statement. This is particularly useful because the user doesn't have to acknowledge the message, as they would with a message box, so we can display continuously updated progress information.

```
For Widget = 1 To 100
    ...
    statements to process each widget
    ...
    Print "Processing widget number"; Widget
Next
```

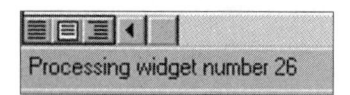

The **Print** statement is executed each time round the loop, so it can display the value of the loop variable **Widget** to show how the operation is progressing.

Notice that we don't have to convert numbers into strings to print them in the status bar, as we do with a message box. You can use **Print** to print different data types and the values of several variables at the same time. Each one is separated by a semicolon or a comma. A semicolon effectively joins the values together directly, while a comma inserts a *Tab* character between them:

The statement:	Produces:
`Print "Hooray"; 4; " Word"; "Basic"`	Hooray 4 WordBasic
`Print "Word", "Basic"`	Word Basic

Inputting Information from the Status Bar

As well as using the status bar to display information, you can also use it to **Input** values. This statement produces a prompt in the status bar, and Word will do nothing else until you enter a value and press *Return*:

```
Input "Enter a word", TheWord$
```

The text you enter is assigned to the variable **TheWord$**. If we use a number variable, such as **TheValue**, rather than a string variable, Word will automatically convert the text into a number and assign it to the number-type variable. If it can't be converted (say, if you enter non-numeric characters), it assigns zero to the variable.

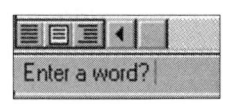

If you need to get more than one value from the user, you just add more variable names to the statement. The user enters a value for each variable, separating them with commas. The prompt is displayed until values for all of the variables have been entered:

```
Input "Enter a word and its length", TheWord$, TheLength
```

This causes a problem, however, when you want to enter values which are strings that themselves contain commas, such as addresses. In this instance, you use the **Line Input** statement to allow a string containing commas to be assigned a single string variable. Everything up to the user pressing *Return* is classed as one string value.

Having said all this, using the status bar to input information is generally not a good idea. Your macro has to stop until the values are entered, and the user probably won't think to look in the status bar, they'll just wonder why Word has 'frozen up'. The most likely response to your input prompt may be them pressing *Ctrl-Alt-Del*! Of course, you could display a message box telling them to look at the status bar, but we're supposed to be producing professional-looking applications...

FYI The Print and Input statements are also used in WordBasic to manipulate data stored in files on disk. These are generally referred to as sequential files, because they contain text or data written in a sequential manner within the file. We won't be considering these here, though you'll see more about how they can be used later in the book.

Using Standard Message and Input Windows

When you need to get information or display messages other than the progress of an operation, the generally accepted way to interface with your users is to use standard Windows message boxes. There are two types:

- **MsgBox**, which displays a text message and gives users a choice of options
- **InputBox**, which displays a text area where they can type information

Displaying Messages Using the MsgBox Statement

By now, you should be familiar with the **MsgBox** statement—we've used in earlier chapters to provide a message, or to show the result of a macro. Notice that the title of the message box is Microsoft Word, and that it just contains one option: the user has to press OK to continue.

We can do more than this, though. We can change the title to our own text and add one of the standard icons that you see in other message boxes. For example the statement,

```
MsgBox "A message box with Title and Icon", "Word Development", 64
```

creates a message box with the title Word Development and an 'information' icon. The title and icon are optional arguments to the **MsgBox** statement. You can specify a stop symbol, a question mark, an exclamation symbol, or the information sign. Each has a particular value that you use in the third argument of **MsgBox**.

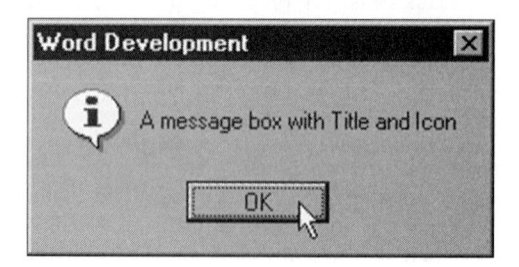

✕	Value = **16**	Used for messages which indicate a critical error has occurred, or that the user must take action to recover from an event.
?	Value = **32**	Used when the user must supply some information or acknowledge an action that's to be taken.
!	Value = **48**	Used for messages which are important, but not necessarily critical.
i	Value = **64**	Used for messages which just give the user information about a process or action that's being taken.

The message you want to display, i.e. the first argument to the statement, must be a single string. When you want to display the value of variables in a message box, you have to convert them all into one string, unlike the **Print** statement which allows you to mix data types freely and use semicolons and commas to separate them.

If you have to display anything more than a simple message, it's often easier to create the message as a string first:

```
MyVal = 4
Msg$ = "Hooray" + Str$(MyVal) + " Microsoft's" + Chr$(10) + "Word Basic !"
MsgBox Msg$, "Word Development", 32
```

This uses a number, stored in **MyVal**, which it converts into a string using the **Str$()** function, before building it into the longer message string in **Msg$**. To break the line where *we* want to, we've included **Chr$(10)**, the 'new line' character.

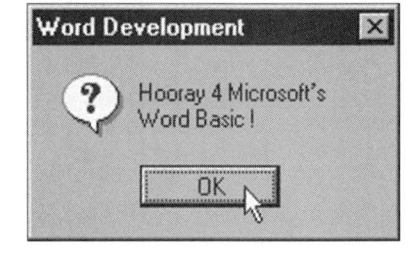

FYI
You can also use the **MsgBox** statement to output information to the status bar, like the **Print** statement we saw earlier. The most useful way is to specify -8 as the third argument. Word then displays the message using the whole width of the status bar, and it stays there until a mouse or keyboard action removes it.

Offering Choices with the MsgBox() Function

The **MsgBox** statement is used to output a message or other information, but, often, when you use a message box, you want to give users a choice of action. For example, you may display a message telling them that a particular file already exists when they try and save another with the same name. You should offer them the choice of what to do about it:

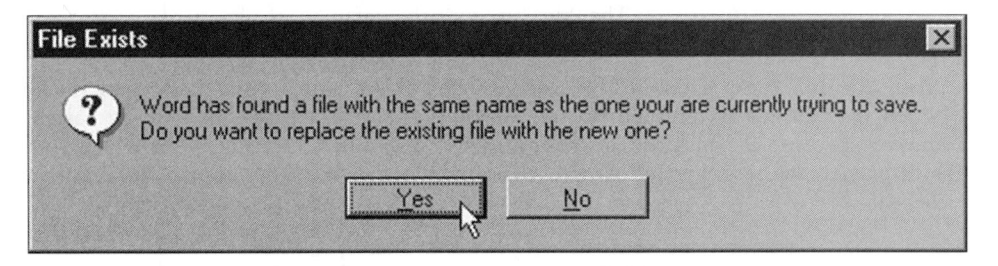

Instead of just an OK button, there are two buttons marked Yes and No. To be able to offer a choice of actions and detect which one the user selects (which button they click), we have to use the **MsgBox()** function rather than the normal **MsgBox** statement we've been using so far. The only differences are that we use different values for the third (**Type**) argument to control the number and type of buttons, and we also get a return value when the message box is closed. And of course, as it's a function, we have to enclose the arguments in brackets:

```
Msg$ = "Word has found a file with the same name as the one your are "
Msg$ = Msg$ + "currently trying to save. Do you want to replace the "
Msg$ = Msg$ + "existing file with the new one?"

Answer = MsgBox(Msg$, "File Exists", 36)
```

This creates the message box shown above. The text message is created in the variable **Msg$**, and we send this to the **MsgBox()** function, together with the title we want for the message box. But look at the third argument. **32** gives us the question mark symbol, so what does **36** do? To control the number and type of buttons, we add values to the **Type** argument, as follows:

Adding:	Displays the following buttons:
0	OK button (the default if **Type** is omitted)
1	OK and Cancel buttons
2	Abort, Retry and Ignore buttons
3	Yes, No and Cancel buttons
4	Yes and No buttons
5	Retry and Cancel buttons

So, **36** is 'Question Mark icon' (**32**) plus 'Yes and No buttons' (**4**). We can also specify which of the buttons will be the **default**, i.e. the one with the focus, and the one that will be clicked when the user presses *Return*.

Adding:	Sets the following default button:
0	The first button is the default (the default if **Type** is omitted).
256	The second button is the default.
512	The third button is the default.

When the user clicks a button, the message box closes and a value corresponding to the button they clicked is returned. In our previous example, it's assigned to the variable **Answer**. Because the buttons can have different meanings, depending on which combination is displayed, the return value simply indicates whether the first, second, or third button was clicked:

Value	Button	Meaning
-1	The first (left-most) button	OK Yes Abort
0	The second button	Cancel No Retry
1	The third button	Cancel Ignore

> **FYI** If you use -8 for the third (**Type**) argument to display the message in the status bar, the `MsgBox()` function always returns 0.

If we were using the File Exists message box example above, we could use an **If-Then** construct to save the file only if the user clicked Yes:

```
Msg$ = "Word has found a file with the same name as the one your are "
Msg$ = Msg$ + "currently trying to save. Do you want to replace the "
Msg$ = Msg$ + "existing file with the new one?"

If  MsgBox(Msg$, "File Exists", 36) = -1 Then FileSave
```

Getting Information Using the InputBox$() Function

Although we can use the `MsgBox()` function to offer choices, such as Yes/No or Abort/Retry/Ignore, we can't use it to enter information, such as text or values. To do this, we use the `InputBox$()` function.

This displays a dialog with a prompt and a text area that the user can type into. When they click OK, the text they've entered is passed back as the return value of the function, which you can then process in your macro. The statement,

```
Response$ = InputBox$("Enter a word:")
```

displays a dialog with the prompt Enter a word, and assigns the text the user types to the variable **Response$**. Notice that the variable must be a string type. To get a numeric value from the user, we have to assign the result to a string variable and then use the `Val()` function to convert the string they enter into numeric form.

```
Response$ = InputBox$("Enter a number:")
TheValue = Val(Response$)
```

If the text they enter can't be converted to a number, the `Val()` function returns zero and assigns this to **TheValue**.

Like the **MsgBox** statement, we can add a title to the input box and specify a default value:

```
Response$ = InputBox$("Enter a word:", "Word Development", "TYPE HERE")
```

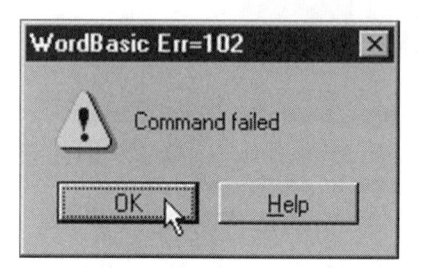

However, `InputBox$()` suffers from a few problems. For example, if the user presses the Cancel button, our macro produces an error message, so we have to trap this error by adding an error handler to the procedure.

```
Sub MAIN
    On Error Goto PressedCancel
    Response$ = InputBox$("Enter a word:", "Word Development", "TYPE HERE")
    PressedCancel:
End Sub
```

A second problem occurs when the user presses *Return* to type on the next line of the input box text area. To break the lines, Word inserts a `Chr$(11)` and `Chr$(13)` in the text rather than just the `Chr$(10)` that we used in a message box. While `Chr$(13)` (the carriage return character) does the same as our `Chr$(10)`, we get a block character for the `Chr$(11)`. Here's an example:

```
Response$ = InputBox$("Enter some text:", "Word Development", "TYPE HERE")
MsgBox Response$
```

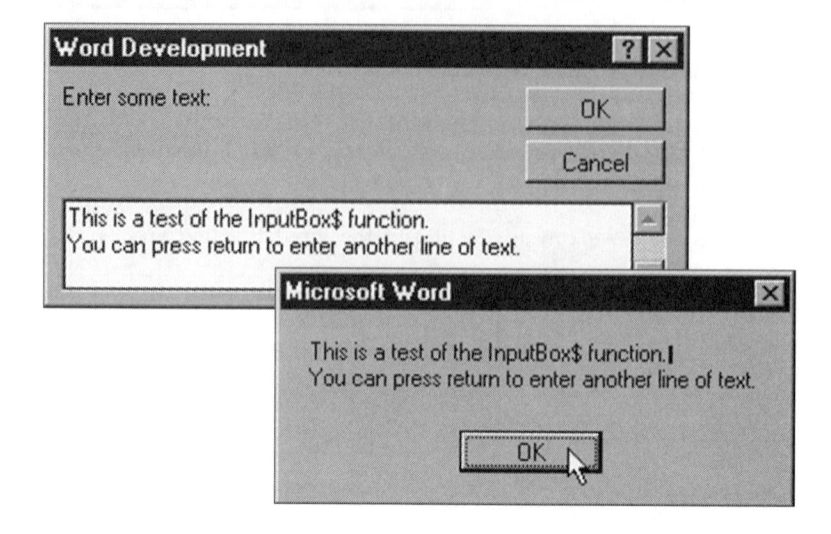

Word includes a function which will remove all nonprinting characters from a string, including our `Chr$(11)`, and replace them with a space. Adding,

```
Response$ = CleanString$(Response$)
```

replaces the all the `Chr$(11)`s with spaces.

Try It Out - Using InputBox$ and MsgBox

We'll take a look at how message boxes and input boxes can be used. This example uses a macro which is stored in the UsefulBits template supplied with the samples on the disk that accompanies this book.

1 Open the UsefulBits template from the samples folder. The default is `C:\BegWord` unless you changed this during installation.

2 Select Macro... from the Tools menu, select the MsgBoxes macro and click Edit to open it.

3 Click the Start button on the Macro toolbar and an input box opens. Enter some text, pressing *Return* between each line.

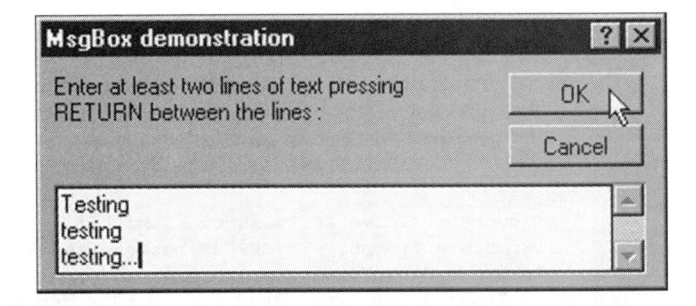

4 Click OK and the macro displays a message box asking if you want to remove the carriage returns from the text.

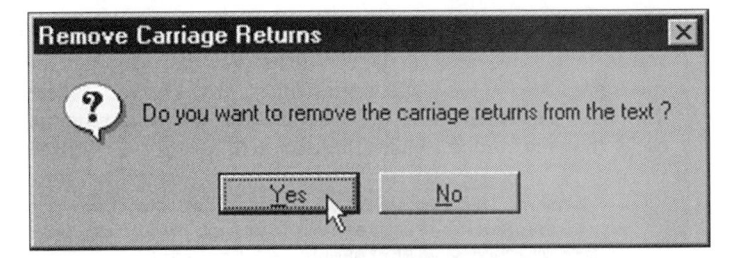

5 Click Yes, and the text is displayed without the carriage returns you entered.

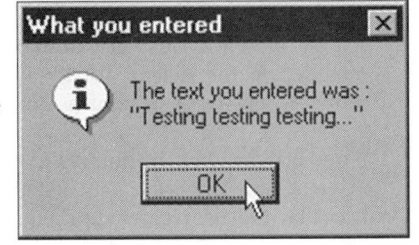

6 Now run the macro again and enter some more text. When you get to the Remove Carriage Returns prompt, this time, click No. The original text is displayed, including the `Chr$(11)`s and `Chr$(13)`s that mark where you pressed Return.

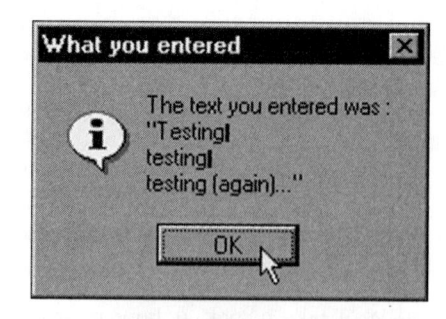

7 Run the macro for a third time and, this time, click the Cancel button in the Input Box. You get a message warning you that you pressed Cancel.

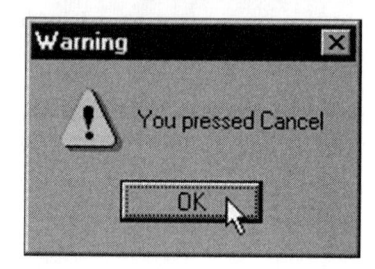

How It Works

The macro first creates a string **Prompt$** for the **InputBox$()** prompt. It then sets up an error trap so that pressing Cancel won't cause an error. Next, it displays the input box with our own title, using **Prompt$** for the prompt:

```
Sub MAIN
    Prompt$ = "Enter at least two lines of text pressing"
    Prompt$ = Prompt$ + " RETURN between the lines :"
    On Error Goto NoText
    TheText$ = InputBox$(Prompt$, "MsgBox demonstration")
```

Now we create a message string **Msg$** for our **MsgBox()** function, asking whether the user wants to remove any carriage returns. We then display the message box including our own title, specifying **36** for the Type argument so that we get Yes and No buttons and a question mark icon. The **If-Then** construct ensures that the following line will only be executed if the user clicks the Yes button, when **MsgBox** will return **-1** (**True**):

```
    Msg$ = "Do you want to remove the carriage returns from the text ?"
    If MsgBox(Msg$, "Remove Carriage Returns", 36) Then
        TheText$ = StripReturns$(TheText$)
    EndIf
```

If they did click Yes, the **StripReturns$()** function is executed. This is a user-defined function included in the macro. You'll see how it works in a while, but, for now, just accept that it removes any carriage returns from the text we send it.

Now we can display our result. We assign a new string to **Msg$**, including a **Chr$(10)** to insert a new line after the first part and using **Chr$(34)** to insert quotation marks around the text that the user entered. Then we display **Msg$** in a message box with the 'information' icon by setting the **Type** argument to **64**. Finally, we jump to the **AllOK** label and exit from the procedure:

```
    Msg$ = "The text you entered was :" + Chr$(10)
    Msg$ = Msg$ + Chr$(34) + TheText$ + Chr$(34)
    MsgBox Msg$, "What you entered", 64
    Goto AllOK
```

If the user presses Cancel in the input box, an error will occur, and execution will pass to our **NoText** label. So, here we display a message box informing them what happened. We've set the **Type** argument to **48** to display the exclamation mark icon.

```
NoText:
    MsgBox "You pressed Cancel", "Warning", 48
AllOK:
End Sub
```

Removing Carriage Returns from a String

The **MsgBoxes** macro we've just seen used a function, **StripReturns$()**, to remove carriage returns from the text. This is a user-defined function which demonstrates how you can manipulate a string using WordBasic's built-in functions:

```
Function StripReturns$(AnyText$)
   ThisText$ = CleanString$(AnyText$)
   Posn = InStr(ThisText$, Chr$(13))
   While Posn > 0
      If Posn = 1 Then
         LeftBit$ = ""
      Else
         LeftBit$ = Left$(ThisText$, Posn - 1)
      EndIf
      If Posn = Len(ThisText$) Then
         RightBit$ = ""
      Else
         RightBit$ = Mid$(ThisText$, Posn + 1)
      EndIf
      ThisText$ = LeftBit$ + RightBit$
      Posn = InStr(ThisText$, Chr$(13))
   Wend
   StripReturns$ = ThisText$
End Function
```

When you press *Return* in an input box, Word inserts a **Chr$(11)**, followed by a **Chr$(13)** at that point in the text. The first step is to remove the **Chr$(11)**s, using the **CleanString$()** function we saw earlier. It replaces each **Chr$(11)** with a space, which will then separate each line of text, so all that's left is to remove the **Chr$(13)**s.

The **InStr()** function takes two strings as arguments and returns the position of the first occurrence of the second string within the first. For example:

```
InStr("WordBasic", "Bas")     ' returns 5
```

We're using it to pinpoint the first occurrence of **Chr$(13)**. If there are none in the string, it returns zero, so we don't enter the **While-Wend** loop. We simply return the original string by assigning it to the function name in the last line of the macro.

If there are **Chr$(13)**s in the text, we enter the **While-Wend** loop. We create two strings, **LeftBit$** and **RightBit$**, which contain the parts of the string each side of the first

Chr$(13). However, to prevent errors, we need to check whether the first or last character of the string is a **Chr$(13)**. For the left part, we use:

```
If Posn = 1 Then
    LeftBit$ = ""
Else
    LeftBit$ = Left$(ThisText$, Posn - 1)
EndIf
```

This sets **LeftBit$** to an empty string if the **Chr$(13)** is the first character in the string (position **1**), or uses the **Left$()** function to split off the correct number of characters. If **Posn** was **1** and we used the **Left$()** function, we would get an error, because the second argument (number of characters) would be zero.

The other part of the string is created in **RightBit$** in much the same way, by testing whether the **Chr$(13)** is the *last* character in the string, i.e. equal to the length of the string as returned by **Len(ThisText$)**.

Now that we've got the two new parts of the string we join them together and then update the **Posn** variable with the position of the next **Chr$(13)**. If there are more to remove, the loop condition **While Posn > 0** executes the code in the loop again. Finally, we assign the result to the function name and exit from the function.

You'll find this function very useful if you work with input boxes regularly. You can copy it into your own macros from the sample UsefulBits template. Alternatively, if you load **UsefulBits.dot** as a global template (using File | Templates...) you can call it from another macro by using:

```
NoReturns$ = UsefulBits.StripReturns$(ThisText$)
```

Using Word's Built-in Dialogs

As you've seen, using the **InputBox$()** function to get information from the user isn't exactly state-of-the-art. Compared to the dialogs you work with in Word normally, it looks distinctly crude.

Remember in Chapter 1, we told you that you can use Word's standard built-in dialogs in your WordBasic macros, just as though they had been selected from the normal Word menus.

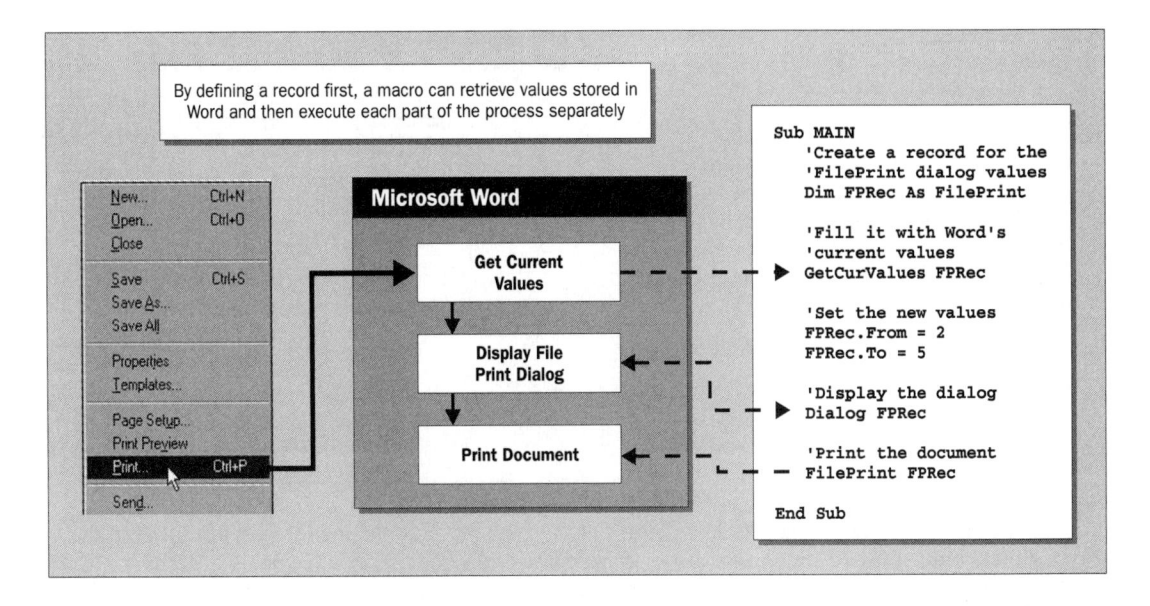

> By defining a record first, a macro can retrieve values stored in Word and then execute each part of the process separately

```
Sub MAIN
    'Create a record for the
    'FilePrint dialog values
    Dim FPRec As FilePrint

    'Fill it with Word's
    'current values
    GetCurValues FPRec

    'Set the new values
    FPRec.From = 2
    FPRec.To = 5

    'Display the dialog
    Dialog FPRec

    'Print the document
    FilePrint FPRec
End Sub
```

In this section, we'll show you how to do this and outline the different options you have. For example, you can just carry out the action of a dialog, such as **FilePrint**, without displaying the dialog at all, or you can display the dialog with your own values, rather than the ones Word suggests. You can even change the values after the user closes the dialog, before you carry out the action connected with it. You can see that you have complete control.

Before we go any further, though, we must cover some background theory. The figure shows us creating a **dialog record**. We need to find out what dialog records are.

What Is a Dialog Record?

We found in Chapter 1 that there are different types of variables. We can use elementary variables to store a single value, either a string or a number. We can also create compound variables by using an **array**. It acts like a set of variables of the same type, and each is referred to by its index within the array.

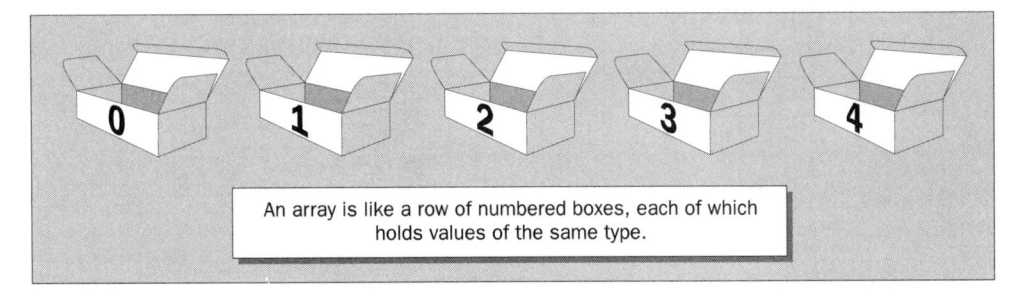

> An array is like a row of numbered boxes, each of which holds values of the same type.

In many other languages, such as Visual Basic, Pascal and C++, you can create another type of compound variable: a **record**. This is different from an array in that the elements can be of different data type, i.e. you can have some string and some number types in the same record. WordBasic doesn't support normal records, but it does provide us with **dialog records**.

If you look at a dialog, there are several options you can set. Some will be text and some will be numbers, so, to manipulate the values from the dialog, we have to have a variable that will support both types. Here's an example:

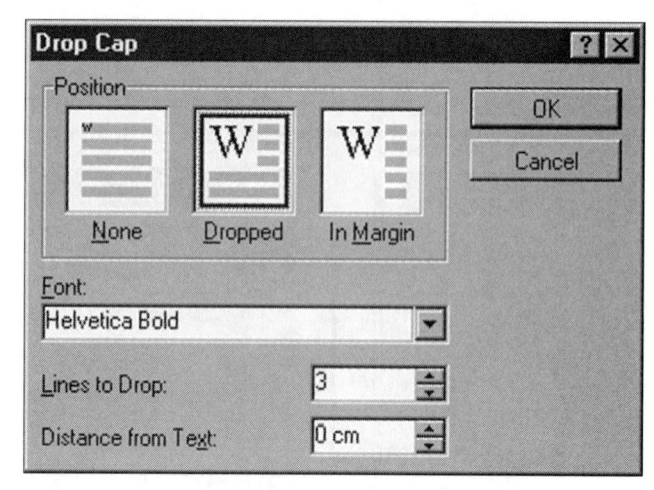

The **FormatDropCap** dialog (select Drop Cap... from the Format menu) has options for the position, font, lines to drop and distance from the text options. **Position** is a number: **0**, **1** or **2** corresponding to the options None, Dropped and In Margin. The **Font** option is text: the name of the font. The other two can be numbers or text, depending on how you enter them. In the figure, the Lines to Drop is numeric (**"3"**) and the Distance from Text is text (**"0 cm"**).

To store all of these options, we declare a dialog record of type **FormatDropCap**:

```
Dim FDCRec As FormatDropCap
```

Then, to refer to the various options within the dialog record, we use the name of that option. So, in our example, we have four variables, and we refer to each one using the syntax *RecordName.OptionName* as follows:

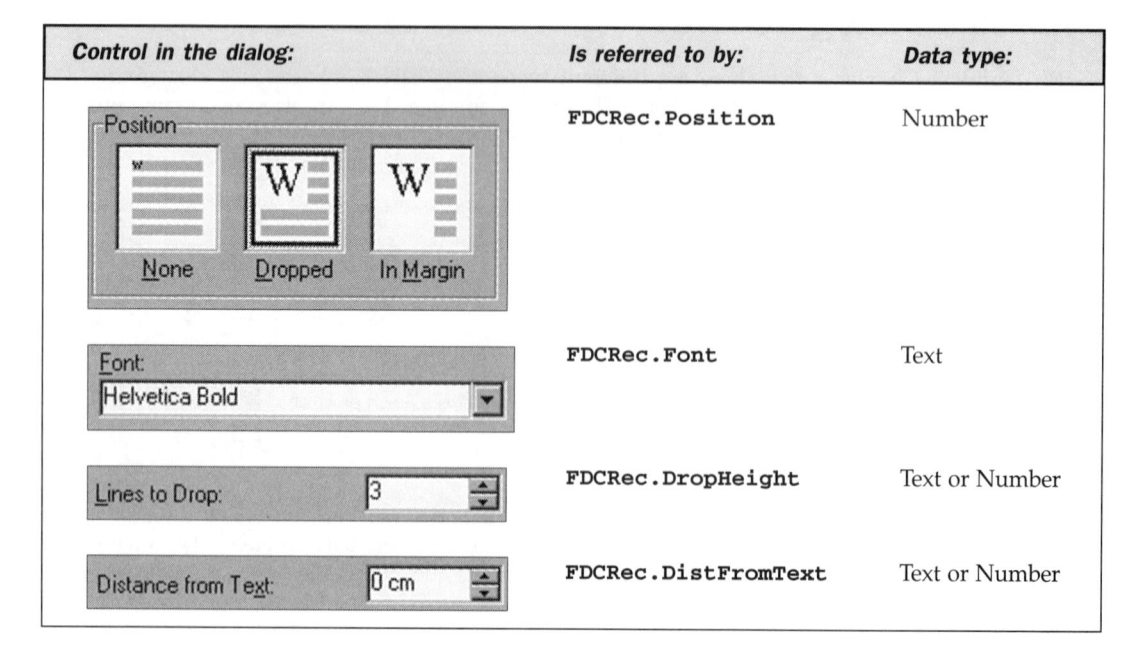

Control in the dialog:	Is referred to by:	Data type:
Position	FDCRec.Position	Number
Font	FDCRec.Font	Text
Lines to Drop	FDCRec.DropHeight	Text or Number
Distance from Text	FDCRec.DistFromText	Text or Number

Here's a fragment of code that declares our **FormatDropCap** dialog record. It then becomes a compound variable that we can use in our code. The next four lines set the values of each field of the dialog record.

```
Dim FDCRec As FormatDropCap
FDCRec.Position = 1
FDCRec.Font = "Arial"
FDCRec.DropHeight = "5"
FDCRec.DistFromText = "1.25 in"
```

Of course, we can read the current values from a dialog record:

```
CurrentFont$ = FDCRec.Font
```

Getting the Current Values into a Dialog Record

When you open the File | Print... dialog normally, it shows you the current settings for your printer, and, if you select some text and open the Format | Font... dialog from Word's menus, it shows you the current formatting of the selected text. This is why we only have to specify the arguments we want to change when we use a dialog statement, as we did in Chapter 1 to create the **CopyrightItalic** macro.

When you declare your own dialog record, the fields in it are all empty. This isn't important if you're going to set them all yourself, like the previous **FormatDropCap** example, but you can get the current values from Word into your dialog record, using the **GetCurValues** statement.

This is useful all on it's own. If you just want to retrieve a value that you know is normally shown in a dialog box, you can define the dialog record and use **GetCurValues** to fill it with the current values from Word. Then you retrieve the ones you want from your record; you don't need to display the dialog at all.

```
Dim TWCRec As ToolsWordCount
GetCurValues TWCRec
MsgBox "Document contains " + TWCRec.Words + " words."
```

This example declares a dialog record for the Tools | Word Count... dialog and gets the current values for the active document. It's then easy to display the value of the field you want in a message box:

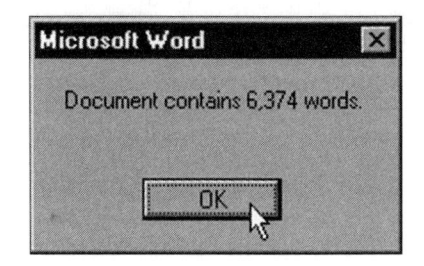

Finding the Name of a Dialog

You can declare dialog records for most of Word's built-in dialogs. The name is usually a combination of the menu commands that open that dialog—**FilePrint** and **ToolsOptionsAutoFormat** are examples. To find the one you want, try recording one macro command like we did in Chapter 1.

1 With the insertion point in your macro, switch to a document window.

2 Click the Record One Command button in the macro toolbar.

3 Open the dialog you want by selecting it from Word's menus.

4 Click OK (not Cancel) to dismiss the dialog.

```
Sub MAIN
FormatDropCap .Position = 1, .Font = "Palatino", .DropHeight = "3", .DistFromText = "0 cm"
End Sub
```

You'll see both the dialog's name and a list of all its control names (the fields) in your macro. If you want to find out more about the dialog or its fields, just place the insertion point on the dialog name in the macro window and press *F1*. Word displays help about that particular dialog.

Displaying a Built-in Dialog

Once we've created our dialog record, we can display the dialog that corresponds to it. The simplest way is to use the `Dialog` statement:

```
Dialog FDCRec
```

This will display the Drop Cap dialog with each control set to the value in our dialog record **FDCRec**. So, if we wanted to suggest particular values for the dialog we can set them in our dialog record first. Better than that, we can retrieve them after the dialog is closed. So we can control what settings the user enters...

Try It Out - Controlling the Drop Cap Dialog

Let's assume some improbable situation, but one which will help demonstrate how we can use Word's built-in dialogs. We've provided a macro that allows you to insert a dropped capital at the start of your document and nowhere else, only giving the user certain options. To save you a lot of typing, we'll use this sample **DropCaps** macro supplied in the UsefulBits template.

1 Open the UsefulBits template from the samples folder. The default is `C:\BegWord`, unless you changed this during installation.

2 Select Macro... from the Tools menu. Select the DropCaps macro and click Edit to open it.

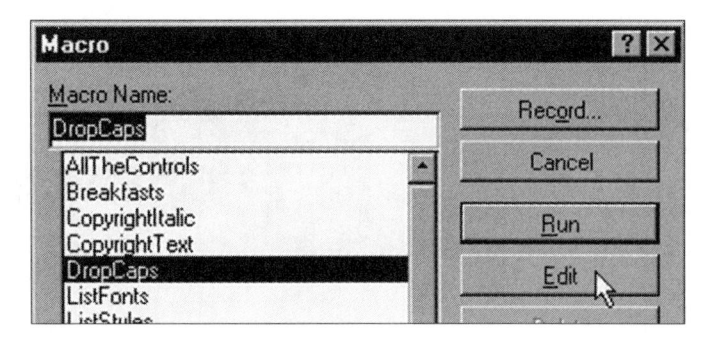

3 Switch to any other document. If you haven't got one open, you can open any that contain some existing text, or create a new one and add a few lines. Then press *Ctrl-Home* to go to the beginning of the document and click the Start button on the Macro toolbar.

4 The Drop Cap dialog opens, containing the name of the current font, but some different values for the Lines to Drop and Distance from Text options than we've seen before:

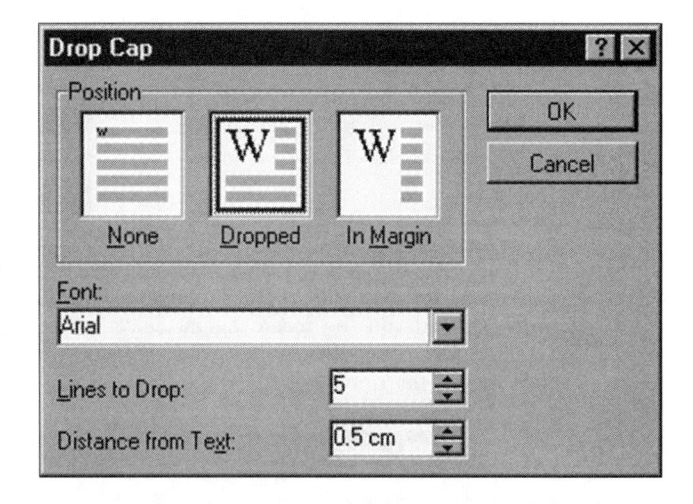

5 Change the font, and increase the Lines to Drop setting to 7.

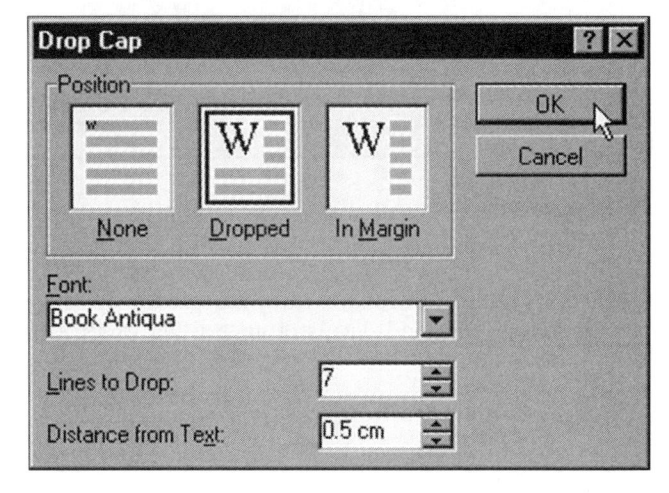

6 Click OK. You get a message telling you that the maximum height is *five* lines, then one telling you that you can't change the font.

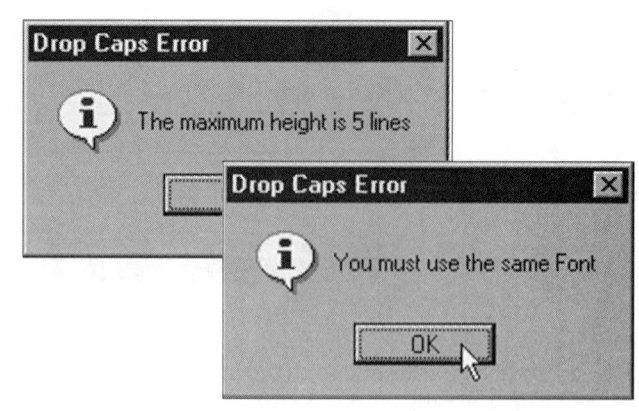

7 Finally, the dropped capital is inserted. It's in the same font as the rest of the paragraph and only five lines high:

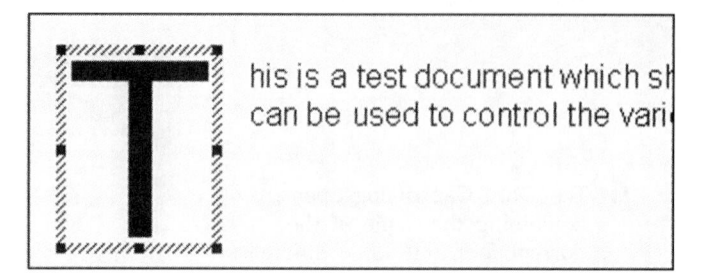

8 Now move the insertion point somewhere within the text, away from the beginning of the document, and run the macro again. Select any setting you like in the Drop Cap dialog, then click OK. This time, you're told that you can only insert a dropped capital at the beginning of the document:

How It Works

The basic workings behind this macro rest on the fact that you have to go through a fixed set of stages to use a dialog in WordBasic code. First, you declare a dialog record for that dialog; here it's **FormatDropCap**. Then you get the current values from Word to fill it. These will be the current font and details of an existing dropped capital:

```
Sub MAIN
    Dim FDCRec As FormatDropCap
    GetCurValues FDCRec          'get values from document
```

Now you can change the values in the dialog record yourself if you wish, effectively changing the 'defaults' the user would normally see. We also save the current font name, because we're going to prevent the user from choosing another:

```
        FDCRec.Position = 1           'set our default values
        FDCRec.DropHeight = "5"
        FDCRec.DistFromText = "0.5 cm"
        CurrentFont$ = FDCRec.Font    'save the current font
```

Next, you display the dialog and check how it's closed. If the user clicks OK, the value **-1** (**True**) is returned. If not, they must have pressed Cancel and so zero is returned. In this case the **If** statement evaluates to **False** and so we can skip the rest of the code if that happens.

```
        If Dialog(FDCRec) Then
```

We're limiting our users to drop heights of five lines or less and forcing them to use the same font as the rest of the paragraph. So, once the dialog has been closed (and providing the user clicked OK) we can get the values out of the dialog record and check that they still conform to our limitations. If not, we display a message:

```
        If FDCRec.DropHeight > "5" Then
            Msg$ = "The maximum height is 5 lines"
            MsgBox Msg$, "Drop Cap Error", 64
            FDCRec.DropHeight = "5"
        EndIf
        If FDCRec.Font <> CurrentFont$ Then
            Msg$ = "You must use the same Font"
            MsgBox Msg$, "Drop Cap Error", 64
            FDCRec.Font = CurrentFont$
        EndIf
```

The only other limitation is that we must be at the start of the document. In fact, we could have checked this first. Either way, we use the **AtStartOfDocument()** function which returns **True** if the cursor is right at the beginning of the document. So, if we get **True**, we carry out the dialog action to insert the dropped capital. If not, it's error message time again...

```
        If AtStartOfDocument() Then
            FormatDropCap FDCRec       'do it...
        Else
            Msg$ = "You can only insert Drop Caps at the"
            Msg$ = Msg$ + " beginning of a document."
            MsgBox Msg$, "Drop Caps Error", 48
        EndIf
    EndIf
End Sub
```

Notice the sequence of events:

1 Define a dialog record.

2 Get the current values.

3 *Retrieve or change the values if required.*

4 Display the dialog.

5 *Retrieve or change the values if required.*

6 Exit the dialog action.

We can retrieve and/or change the values in the dialog record both before and after displaying it. And we have to explicitly execute the dialog action after displaying the dialog—it isn't automatically executed.

Checking How a Dialog Is Closed

There's one fundamental problem with the method we've used above. If you click the Cancel button to dismiss the Drop Cap dialog, Word displays an error message, exactly as it did in the `InputBox$()` function earlier in the chapter. We can solve this in the same way, by placing an `On Error Goto` statement before our `Dialog` statement.

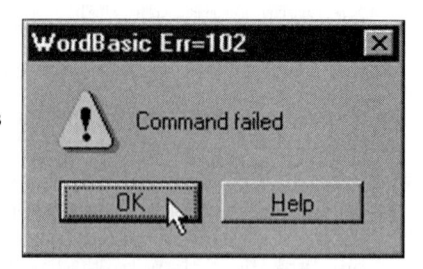

```
Sub MAIN
    On Error Goto PressedCancel    ' set the error trap
    Dim FDCRec As FormatDropCap    ' declare dialog record
    GetCurValues FDCRec            ' get the current values
    Dialog FDCRec                  ' display the dialog
    FormatDropCap FDCRec           ' execute the dialog action
PressedCancel:
End Sub
```

Now, when an error occurs, we assume that the user pressed Cancel and exit from the macro without carrying out the `FormatDropCap` action. But what happens if the insertion point is on a blank line, or is in a macro editing window? In both these cases, the macro will fail, not because the user canceled the action, but even before the dialog appears.

Instead of the statement form, we'll use the `Dialog()` function to display the dialog, which brings with it several advantages. It allows us to tell which button the user clicked to dismiss the dialog, and doesn't generate an error when they click Cancel.

```
Sub MAIN
    On Error Goto GotAnError
    Dim FDCRec As FormatDropCap
    GetCurValues FDCRec
    If Dialog(FDCRec) Then FormatDropCap FDCRec
    Goto AllOK
GotAnError:
    MsgBox "You can't insert a dropped capital here"
AllOK:
End Sub
```

In this code fragment, we set up an error trap which jumps to the `GotAnError` label if an error occurs. This displays a message telling the user what's gone wrong.

The function `Dialog (FDCRec)` then opens the Drop Cap dialog with the values set to those in our `FDCRec` variable. When the dialog is closed, it returns zero (`False`) *only* if the user has pressed Cancel. So, if the return value is non-zero (`True`), we can execute the `FormatDropCap` action, then jump directly to the end of the procedure.

In general, it's best to use the `Dialog()` function rather than the `Dialog` statement, because of the extra control it allows you to exert over your macros. The `Dialog()` function returns `-1` (`True`) if the user presses OK, or `0` (`False`) if they press Cancel.

Executing a Dialog Action without Displaying the Dialog

As you've seen, once the dialog is closed, we still need to execute the dialog box's action in our code. It doesn't occur automatically when the user clicks OK, as it would if they were using the dialog in the normal way from Word's menus. Look back to the beginning of this section where we showed you how to record the code for the Drop Cap dialog:

```
Sub MAIN
FormatDropCap .Position = 1, .Font = "Palatino", .DropHeight = "3", .DistFromText = "0 cm"
End Sub
```

Here, you can see all the arguments for the **FormatDropCap** dialog. You can see that we were actually using a dialog action, but without displaying the dialog. In this case, we used the **FormatDropCap** action, but, because we just specified the arguments we wanted to change, we didn't have to create a dialog record first. So, if we wanted to insert a decorative capital, with a gap between it and the rest of the text, we could use:

```
Sub MAIN
    Dim FFRec As FormatDropCap
    FFRec.Position = 1
    FFRec.Font = "Deco: Biblical"
    FFRec.DropHeight = 3
    FFRec.DistFromText = "0.25 cm"
    FormatDropCap FFRec
End Sub
```

This gives us the result:

> e could have carried out the same action by creating a dialog record, setting the values we want, then executing the dialog's action directly - without displaying it at all.

Creating Your Own Custom Dialogs

Having all the different Word built-in dialogs at your disposal is great, as long as you can find one that does what you need. However, there are often times when none of those that Word has to offer can do the job quite as you'd like. Then it's time to create your own.

What Is a Custom Dialog?

Custom dialogs are basically ones that you define yourself, as opposed to those that are already part of Word. You can create all kinds of dialogs to exactly meet your needs. Once you've created the new dialog, it behaves just like one of Words own, except that, when it's closed, you have to carry out any actions required yourself. For example, if you use the Drop Cap dialog to allow the user to select the format for a dropped capital in the document, you can insert the dropped capital by calling the built-in **FormatDropCap** dialog action and sending it the dialog record that you used with the Drop Cap dialog:

Beginning WordBasic Programming

```
Dim FDCRec As FormatDropCap
If Dialog(FDCRec) Then FormatDropCap FDCRec
```

However, if you're using your own custom dialog, there's no matching dialog action, so you have to carry out the task yourself using WordBasic code:

```
Dim OCDRec As UserDialog    'creates a dialog record for our new dialog
If Dialog(OCDRec) Then
    statements to carry out the action required
End If
```

Using Word's Dialog Editor

Let's have a look at how you go about creating a custom dialog. As a simple example, we'll build a better input box. The first step is to design the custom dialog, using Word's **Dialog Editor**. This tool comes as part of Word, but it isn't automatically installed. If you didn't specify it when you first installed Word 95 or Office 95, you'll have to run the set-up program again now to install it.

> **FYI** To install the **Dialog Editor** run the **Setup** program on your original program disk. If you're installing from the Office 95 disk, select **Microsoft Word**. Select **Change Option** and make sure **Dialog Editor** is selected in the list of optional components. Then click **OK** and continue with **Setup**.

Try It Out - Designing a 'Better Input Box' Dialog

We'll walk through how you create the dialog box using Dialog Editor. As you'll see in later examples, this isn't the only way to do it, but it's the quickest way to get started. Once you've created the dialog, you can modify it later on by editing your macro directly.

1 Open your own UsefulBits template from your default **\Templates** folder, select <u>M</u>acro... from the <u>T</u>ools menu and make sure that Macros Available In: is set to UsefulBits.dot. Enter NewInputBox for the macro name, and add a short description. Then click Create to open the macro editing window.

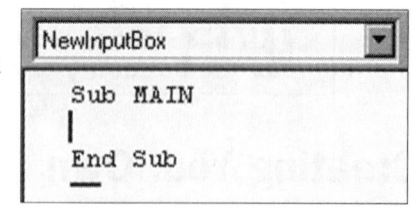

```
NewInputBox
Sub MAIN
|
End Sub
```

2 Click the Dialog Editor button on the Macro toolbar. Dialog Editor opens with a blank dialog:

108

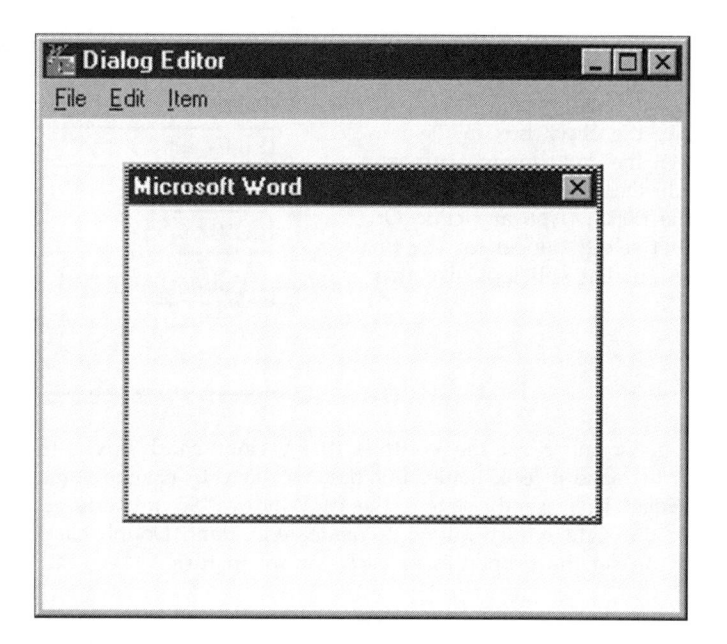

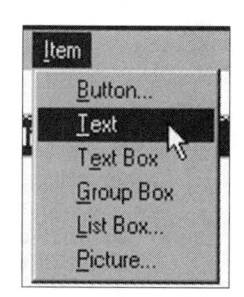

3 From the Item menu, select Text. Word places a text control in the dialog. This will act as a label where the prompt for the input box will be displayed.

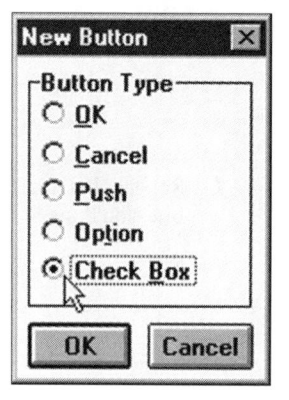

4 Add a Text Box by selecting this from the Item menu. Open the Item menu again and select Button.... Another window opens, showing the different types of button you can use. Select Check Box.

5 Click OK to place the check box in the new dialog. Then open the Item menu again and select Button.... In the New Button window, select OK for the Button Type and click OK. Do this again, but select Cancel for the final button. Your new dialog will look like this:

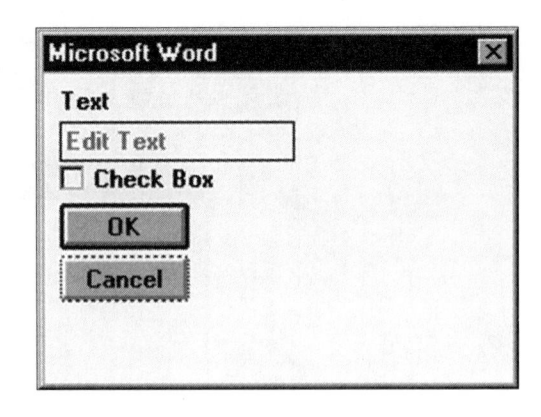

The next step is to move and resize the **controls** (the various check boxes, text boxes and buttons in a dialog) to make it look better, but first we have to change some of their properties. Dialog Editor isn't exactly state-of-the-art Windows 95 stuff—to select an item, you must double-click it; the right mouse button is made redundant. Double-clicking opens a window where you can set the properties of each control in turn.

6 Double-click on the Text control at the top of the dialog. The Text Information window opens. Change the entry for Text$ (the text that's displayed) and turn off the Auto option for the Width.

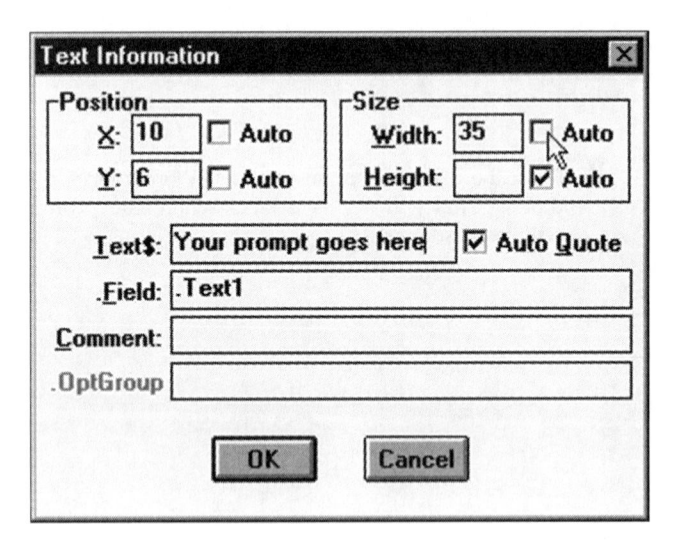

7 Repeat this for the other controls. You'll find some already have the Auto option turned off, but you'll need to change this:

Control	Property	Value
Check Box	Text$	Confirm This Input
Check Box	Width	Turn off Auto
OK Button	Height	Turn off Auto
Cancel Button	Height	Turn off Auto

8 Now you can use the mouse to resize and move the controls around. Place the pointer over the edge of a control until it turns into a double-headed arrow and drag to resize it. You'll also have to drag the dialog itself to the new size. Here's how the finished dialog should look:

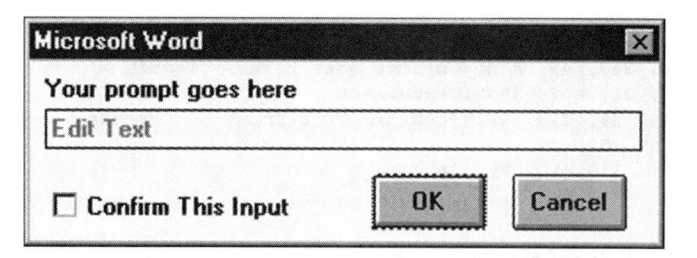

> **FYI** You can use the <u>X</u>, <u>Y</u>, <u>W</u>idth and <u>H</u>eight settings in the properties window to make sure controls are the same size and line up correctly. For example, for the two buttons, we've set **Y**, **Width** and **Height** to 52, 79 and 26.

9 Our new dialog is complete, so now we need to get it into our macro. Choose <u>S</u>elect Dialog from the <u>E</u>dit menu and press *Ctrl-C* to copy it to the clipboard. Switch back to your macro editing window and press *Ctrl-V* to paste it into the **NewInputBox** macro. It appears as a **definition**:

```
Sub MAIN
REM NewInputBox

Begin Dialog UserDialog  430, 84, "Microsoft Word"
    Text 10, 6, 363, 49, "Your Prompt goes here", .Text1
    TextBox 10, 22, 408, 18, .TextBox1
    CheckBox 16,59, 193, 16, "Confirm This Input", .CheckBox1
    OKButton 223, 52, 79, 26
    CancelButton 329, 52, 79, 26
End Dialog

End Sub
```

10 To see it in action, we have to define a dialog record for it, and display it. Add the code below to the macro, after the **End Dialog** statement:

```
Dim BIBRec As UserDialog
Response = Dialog(BIBRec)
```

11 Click the Start button on the Macro toolbar. Our new dialog is displayed.

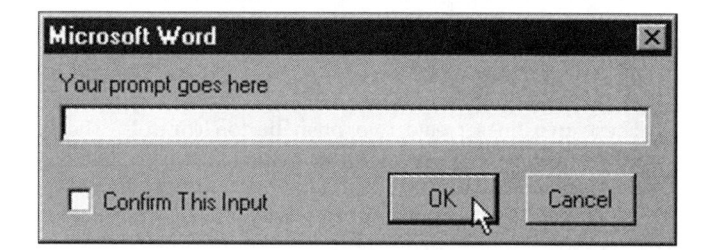

How It Works

The code that creates our custom dialog is simply a list of the controls contained between the **Begin Dialog UserDialog** and **End Dialog** statements. Dialog Editor creates a useful starting point like this, which we can go on to improve later.

```
Begin Dialog UserDialog 430, 84, "Microsoft Word"
    Text 10, 6, 363, 49, "Your prompt goes here", .Text1
    TextBox 10, 22, 408, 18, .TextBox1
    CheckBox 16, 59, 193, 16, "Confirm This Input", .CheckBox1
    OKButton 233, 52, 79, 26
    CancelButton 329, 52, 79, 26
End Dialog
```

The **Begin Dialog UserDialog** statement contains the width and height of our dialog and the title that's displayed in the window title bar. All the measurements in a dialog definition are in 'screen units'. If you want your dialog placed somewhere other than screen center, you can include the horizontal and vertical positions as well. For example,

```
Begin Dialog UserDialog 100, 50, 430, 84, "Microsoft Word"
```

would place our dialog 100 units across and 50 units down the screen. It would be 430 units wide and 84 units high, and have the title Microsoft Word.

> **FYI** A screen unit is defined as being one eighth of the system font in width, and one twelfth in height. This, however, seems to vary with different screen resolutions.

Next come the individual controls in the dialog. The way each one is declared varies slightly, depending on the type of control. In our case, we have:

```
Text 10, 6, 363, 49, "Your prompt goes here", .Text1
```

This creates a label-type text control. It's positioned at 10 units across and 6 units down in the dialog, and is sized 363 units wide by 49 units high. The text it displays is Your prompt goes here, and we refer to it by the name **Text1**. All controls use the same first four arguments for their position and size.

```
TextBox 10, 22, 408, 18, .TextBox1
```

creates a text box control where the user can enter and edit text, and is named **TextBox1**.

```
CheckBox 16, 59, 193, 16, "Confirm This Input", .CheckBox1
```

creates a check box control that the user can select or deselect by clicking. It has the caption Confirm This Input and is named **CheckBox1**.

```
OKButton 233, 52, 79, 26
CancelButton 329, 52, 79, 26
```

These two lines create two push button controls. The first has the caption OK and the second Cancel. They don't have to be named, because you can only have one of each in a dialog, and they are referred to by their type—**OKButton** and **CancelButton**.

How a Custom Dialog is Used

Having seen how relatively crude Word's **Dialog Editor** is, it will come as no surprise to learn that you don't get a full set of Windows 95 slider, tabbed dialog and gauge controls with it. You're limited to the common text, button and list controls, plus a control that will display a picture and a special 'extra' **FilePreview** control that can display a preview of a document.

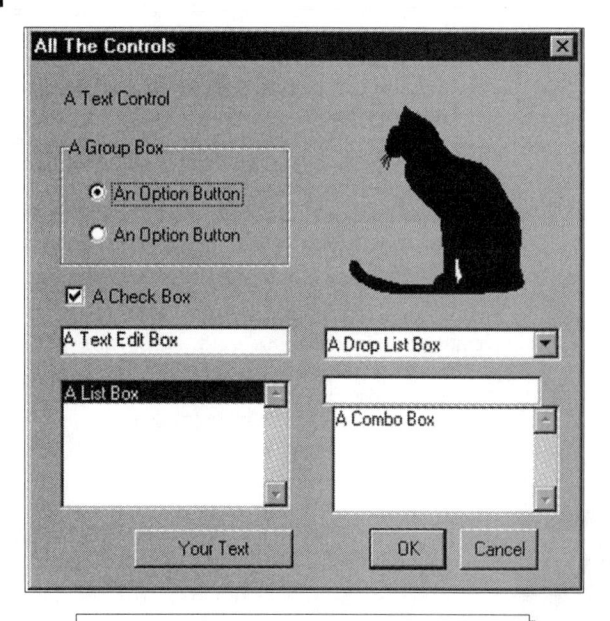

This dialog shows all the controls you can use, except for a File Preview.

Each control is listed in the **dialog definition** that creates the dialog. We've used a macro to create and display this dialog. You can examine it and try it out by opening the **UsefulBits.dot** template we've supplied from your samples folder, and running the macro **AllTheControls**.

We'll look at each part in turn later on, but the complete macro looks like this:

```
Sub MAIN
REM AllTheControls
Dim ListBox1$(0)                    ' declare arrays for the list controls
ListBox1$(0) = "A List Box"         ' .. and fill them with values
Dim ComboBox1$(0)
ComboBox1$(0) = "A Combo Box"
Dim DropListBox1$(0)
DropListBox1$(0) = "A Drop List Box"

' This is the dialog definition
Begin Dialog UserDialog 472, 304, "All The Controls"
    Text 27, 15, 150, 13, "A Text Control", .Text1
    GroupBox 24, 44, 199, 77, "A Group Box"
    OptionGroup  .OptionGroup3
```

```
        OptionButton 46, 68, 133, 16, "An Option Button", .OptionButton1
        OptionButton 46, 92, 133, 16, "An Option Button", .OptionButton2
    CheckBox 28, 128, 175, 16, "A Check Box", .CheckBox1
    TextBox 24, 153, 198, 18, .TextBox1
    ListBox 23, 184, 198, 81, ListBox1$(), .ListBox1
    DropListBox 251, 154, 207, 108, DropListBox1$(), .DropListBox1
    ComboBox 250, 182, 208, 83, ComboBox1$(), .ComboBox1
    PushButton 86, 272, 139, 24, "Your Text", .Push1
    OKButton 290, 270, 70, 26
    CancelButton 369, 270, 70, 25
    Picture 250, 24, 204, 112, "C:\Office\Clipart\cat.wmf", 0, .Picture1
End Dialog

Dim ATCRec As UserDialog            ' declare a dialog record
ATCRec.TextBox1 = "A Text Edit Box" ' set the value of the Text Box
ATCRec.CheckBox1 = 1                ' set the value of the Check Box
Result = Dialog(ATCRec)             ' display the dialog
MsgBox "Result =" + Str$(Result)    ' show the result
End Sub
```

> **FYI** If you've installed Office 95 in a different folder to the default, you may find you get **Missing Picture** instead of the picture itself. All you need to do is edit the path and name of the file in the `Picture` statement to point to an existing picture file (`.wmf` or `.bmp`) on your disk.

The Various Dialog Controls You Can Use

Control	Control Type	Description
A Text Control	`Text`	Used as a label to place fixed text, such as a prompt, in a dialog.
A Text Edit Box	`TextBox`	A normal edit box, where users can edit and update text.
☑ A Check Box	`CheckBox`	Used to select or deselect options, where any combination can be selected at one time.
A Group Box	`GroupBox`	Used to identify a set of controls, particularly option buttons where only one can be selected at a time. Can also be used just for decoration in a dialog.
⦿ An Option Button	`OptionButton`	Used to select one option from a set of mutually exclusive options. Only one can be selected at a time.

Table Continued on Following Page

Control	Control Type	Description
A List Box	`ListBox`	Displays a list of values from which one can be selected. Uses an array, the name of which is an argument in the statement that creates the control, to supply the values to fill it.
A Drop List Box	`DropListBox`	Displays a list of values, like `ListBox`, but is more compact.
A Combo Box	`ComboBox`	Displays a list of values from which the user can select, and a text edit area where they can enter new values instead of selecting an existing one.
Your Text	`PushButton`	Allows you to create buttons for any task, and label them with your own caption.
OK Cancel	`OKButton` `CancelButton`	The two standard OK and Cancel buttons which close the dialog when clicked.
Plus...	`Picture`	Displays a graphic or picture file (`.wmf` or `.bmp`), or a picture stored as an AutoText entry or in a bookmark.
And...	`FilePreview`	Displays a preview of a file, like that in the standard File, Open... dialog.

In general, each control statement in the dialog definition follows a standard form:

ControlType   X,   Y,   Width,   Height,   ValueToDisplay,   Name

where: `ControlType` is one of those shown in the table above, such as `Text`, `ListBox` or `PushButton`.

`X` and `Y` are the position within the dialog, and `Width` and `Height` are the width and height of the control itself.

`ValueToDisplay` is either a text string, indicating the value to be displayed in the control, or the name of an object that supplies the values. For a `ListBox`, `DropListBox` and `ComboBox`, `ValueToDisplay` is the name of an array variable containing the list of values to display. For a `Picture` control, it can be the filename of the picture, or its AutoText or bookmark name.

Name is the text string by which you refer to the control in a custom dialog, just like you do in a standard dialog. For example **DropHeight** is the name of the Lines to Drop control in the Drop Cap dialog we saw earlier. We use the **Name** argument to set the names we want to use for our custom dialog's controls, and these names become the names of the **fields** in the dialog record for our custom dialog.

IMPORTANT: Read the next sentence twice, because case-sensitivity is sure to catch you out one day.

> **FYI** Unlike all other variable and procedure names, the **Name** argument that you use to identify controls in a dialog definition is case-sensitive—so `txtPassword` is a different control to `txtPassWord`.

You'll get an error message if they don't match exactly, and you'll spend a long time wondering why.

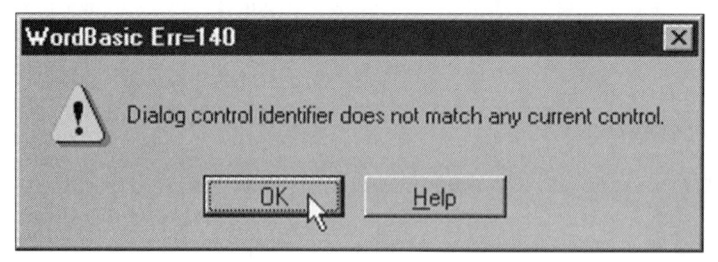

> WordBasic Err=140
>
> Dialog control identifier does not match any current control.
>
> [OK]   [Help]

Some controls, like **TextBox**, don't have a **ValueToDisplay** argument; to start with, they're empty, although you can assign values to them when the dialog is displayed. And some have extra arguments, like the **Picture** control which needs to know what the picture name argument refers to—whether it's a file, AutoText or bookmark name. You'll see the **Picture** control in use in Part 2.

The **FilePreview** control isn't available in Dialog Editor so you have to place a different control, such as **Picture**, then edit the dialog definition afterwards. You can only have one **FilePreview** control in a dialog. You'll see more later on.

The **TextBox** control normally only displays one line of text, but you can add an extra argument to make it into a multiline text box where the user can press *Return* (or *Shift-Return*) to start a new line:

```
TextBox 24, 153, 198, 18, .TextBox1, 1      'is a multi-line text box
```

Editing the Dialog Definition

Usually, you'll want to edit the dialog definition after Dialog Editor has created it. For example, we've changed the title of the dialog above to All The Controls by editing the **Begin Dialog** statement. You can also fine-tune the position and size of the controls, change the text captions, and, more importantly, make sure all the control identifiers have meaningful names. In our example, we've left them at the default (**Text1**, **Push1**, etc.) but you'll probably find it easier to work with them later if you set names that reflect their purpose.

Of course, you should add comments that will help you maintain your code in the months to come.

Setting the Tab Order and Default Button in a Dialog

When you use a dialog, pressing the *Tab* key moves the **focus** (the dotted box or text cursor which indicates the currently active control) from one control to another. If the focus jumps wildly around the dialog, it becomes difficult to use. You control the tab order by placing the statements for each control in the definition in the order you want the focus to move.

Some controls, such as a **Text** control, can't receive the focus. When the user presses *Tab*, these are skipped and the focus moves to the next one. You'll probably need to edit your definition to place the statements in the correct order as you move the controls around while you're designing the dialog.

The **default button** in a dialog is the one which is clicked when the user presses *Return*, unless another button has the focus. The default button in your dialog will be the first *button* listed in your definition, unless it is the first *control* in the definition. So, if you want the button **MyButton** to be the default, you have to place it after another control which can receive the focus, but before any other buttons.

Because a **Text** control can't receive the focus, it can't be used for this purpose. However, it's most likely that you'll already have a **TextBox**, **CheckBox**, **OptionButton** or **ListBox** of some type first in the tab order, and hence before your default button in the dialog definition.

Filling List Box and Combo Box Controls with Values

If you look back at our macro, you can see that the first thing we have to do is to declare and place values in three arrays. This is because list-type controls require an array to provide the values that fill the list. The line that defines the ordinary **list box** in the definition shows that the values for the list come from an array called **ListBox1$()**:

```
ListBox 23, 184, 198, 81, ListBox1$(), .ListBox1
```

We've only declared a single element array for each, but, of course, you would declare and fill the array to suit the items you wanted to list. In the Book Order application that you saw in Chapter 1, the array that's used for the drop-down list of book titles is declared as:

```
Dim BookList$(9)
BookList$(0) = "Beginner's Guide to Access 95"
BookList$(1) = "Beginner's Guide to Delphi"
BookList$(2) = "Beginner's Visual Basic 4.0"
BookList$(3) = "Programming Microsoft Office"
... etc.
```

Using Option Groups in a Custom Dialog

When you want to implement a set of option buttons (sometimes called *radio buttons*), you have to create an option group so that, as one is selected, all the others in the group are deselected. In the **AllTheControls** macro we've included a simple option group with two option buttons:

```
GroupBox 24, 44, 199, 77, "A Group Box"
OptionGroup  .OptionGroup3
   OptionButton 46, 68, 133, 16, "An Option Button", .OptionButton1
   OptionButton 46, 92, 133, 16, "An Option Button", .OptionButton2
```

117

First, we define a **GroupBox** control. This isn't actually necessary to make the option group work, but it provides the visual clue to the user that they can only select one option from those inside the group box.

Next, we define the group itself using the **OptionGroup** statement. Here, the group is named **OptionGroup3**. Then we can define the buttons for each option. As long as we continue to define option buttons, they're all part of the group. The end of the group is defined by a statement for a different control type, or another **OptionGroup** statement.

Filling Other Controls and Displaying Your Custom Dialog

Once you've designed your dialog, you have to display it. The first step is to create a dialog record for it, just as you would for a normal dialog. This time, you use **UserDialog** for the record type. You can only create one custom dialog at a time and, consequently, only one **UserDialog** record, but you can always define a new dialog in your macro to replace the existing definition then create a record for that one.

```
Dim ATCRec As UserDialog          ' declare a dialog record
```

The next step is to set any values you want for the controls. Here, we've placed A Text Edit Box in the **TextBox1**, and set **CheckBox1** to be ticked.

```
ATCRec.TextBox1 = "A Text Edit Box"   ' set the value of the Text Box
ATCRec.CheckBox1 = 1                  ' set the value of the Check Box
```

Now we can display the dialog using the normal **Dialog()** function. We've included a message box to display the result so that you can see what values are returned.

```
Result = Dialog(ATCRec)               ' display the dialog
MsgBox "Result =" + Str$(Result)      ' show the result
```

Checking which Button Was Pressed

If you run the **AllTheControls** macro and click the Your Text button, you may be surprised at the result. The dialog is closed and we get a result of **1**, rather than the **0** or **-1** that we've seen with Word's built-in dialogs.

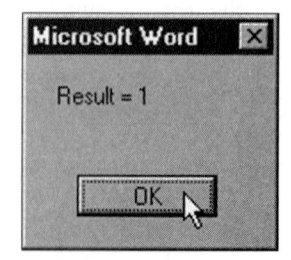

In fact, this makes sense. Pressing a button in a dialog usually means that you want to carry out some action. It may just be OK or Cancel, and the standard **OKButton** and **CancelButton** controls look after that admirably by returning **True** (**-1**) and **False** (**0**).

However, if the action you want isn't just OK or Cancel, your macro has to carry out that action. For example, if your dialog has a button marked Default, you might want to use it to set some default values in your application, rather than the ones the user sets before clicking OK. While the dialog is displayed, the macro is stopped at the **Dialog()** function. So by closing the dialog and returning a different result, Word allows you to tell which button was pressed to close the dialog. You can then carry out the actions required.

The return value is the position of the **PushButton** statement in the dialog definition, excluding the **OKButton** and **CancelButton**. In our case, we got a return value of **1**, because the Your Text button is the first normal **PushButton** in the definition. If we added more buttons, we would get values of **2**, **3**, etc.

> **FYI** You can control which button is the default in a custom dialog by adding an extra argument to the **Dialog()** function. You've seen how a dialog returns the position number of the button that was pressed to close it. If you add this number to the **Dialog()** function which displays the dialog, that button becomes the default button. For example, to display the **All The Controls** dialog with the **Your Text** button as the default we would change the code to read:
>
> ```
> Result = Dialog(ATCRec, 1)
> ```

Using the Values from a Custom Dialog

Because we declare a dialog record when we use a custom dialog, just as we do when we use a built-in dialog, we can set and retrieve the values in its **fields** in the same way. For example,

```
TheText$ = ATCRec.TextBox1              ' get the text from the TextBox
TheOption = ATCRec.OptionGroup3         ' get the OptionGroup setting
TheListIndex = ATCRec.ListBox1          ' get the index of the ListBox
TheListItem$ = ListBox1$(TheListIndex)  ' get the value from the array
```

would retrieve the values of some of the controls in our All The Controls dialog. Notice that to get the setting of the option group, we check the value of the **OptionGroup3** control, not the group box or the option buttons themselves. It returns **0** if the first option is selected, **1** if the second one is selected, etc.

The three list controls, **ListBox**, **DropListBox** and **ComboBox**, return a numeric value which is the index of the currently selected item, and not it's actual value which is, of course, a string. To get the string value, you just pull it back out of the array that you originally used to fill the list.

> **FYI** Bear in mind that you can't use the **GetCurValues** statement with a custom dialog you've created. Word doesn't know anything about the fields that you define in a custom dialog record, so it obviously can't supply any 'current values' to fill them.

Putting It All Together

To see how it all fits together we'll modify the **NewInputBox** macro we created earlier in this chapter. We'll show you how we edited the dialog definition to make it more readable and implemented some code to display the dialog and get the return values.

Beginning WordBasic Programming

Try It Out - Finishing Our 'Better Input Box' Dialog

We've supplied the code for this example in the sample UsefulBits template. The macro is named **BetterInputBox**, and is based on the one we created in the previous Try It Out.

1 Open the sample UsefulBits template, and select and open the BetterInputBox macro. Click the Start button on the Macro toolbar. You'll see the new input box appear, with a prompt, default text already entered, and the Confirm This Input checkbox ticked.

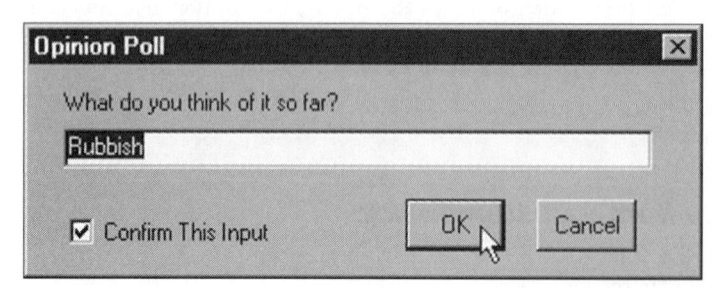

2 Change the text if you want, but leave the Confirm option set. Then click OK. The Confirm Input message appears.

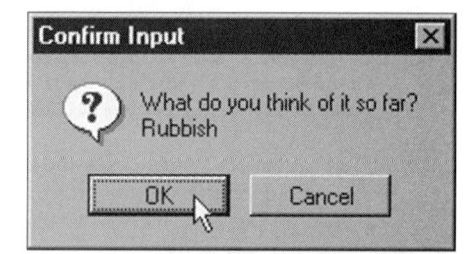

3 Click OK again, and the value you entered is displayed.

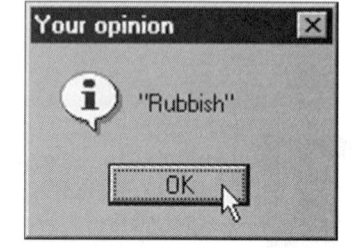

4 Run through the macro again a few times, trying different options. Try turning off the Confirm This Input option and pressing Cancel in either of the windows.

How It Works

Look first at the **function** in the **BetterInputBox** macro, called **BetterBox$()**. We've turned the original dialog definition into a function by moving it out of the **Sub MAIN - End Sub** section and adding a **Function** header. In the function header we've included arguments for the prompt, default text, dialog window title, and setting of the Confirm checkbox. Below this is an edited version of the input box dialog definition we created earlier. We've changed the names of the controls and replaced the text for the dialog window title and the Text control with the function arguments, **BBTitle$** and **BBPrompt$**.

```
Function BetterBox$(BBPrompt$, BBDefault$, BBTitle$, BBConfirm)
    Begin Dialog UserDialog 456, 94, BBTitle$
        Text 23, 10, 399, 13, BBPrompt$, .lblPrompt
        TextBox 24, 29, 404, 18, .txtTheValue
        CheckBox 27, 67, 201, 16, "Confirm This Input", .chkConfirm
        OKButton 257, 60, 70, 26
        CancelButton 347, 60, 70, 26
    End Dialog
```

So, our dialog now displays a window title and prompt corresponding to the values in the arguments to the function. But what about the default text and the Confirm checkbox? We can't set these in the dialog definition, but we can set them in the dialog record before we display the dialog:

```
Dim BIBRec As UserDialog              ' create the dialog record
BIBRec.txtTheValue = BBDefault$       ' set the default text
BIBRec.chkConfirm = BBConfirm         ' set the Confirm checkbox
```

Now we can display the dialog. If the user clicks OK, it returns **True** and we process the values in it. If the Confirm checkbox is still set, we display the Confirm This Input message box. When they click OK or Cancel to close this message box, we set the variable **Accept** to the return value, either **True (-1)** if they pressed OK, or **False (0)** if they pressed Cancel. If the Confirm checkbox was cleared by the user, we set **Accept** to **True** anyway.

```
    If Dialog(BIBRec) Then            ' show the dialog
        If BIBRec.chkConfirm Then
            Msg$ = BBPrompt$ + Chr$(10) + BIBRec.txtTheValue
            Accept = MsgBox(Msg$, "Confirm Input", 33)
        Else
            Accept = - 1              ' No Confirm so set to True
        End If
        If Accept Then BetterBox$ = BIBRec.txtTheValue
    EndIf
End Function
```

Finally, if **Accept** is **True**, we assign the value in the **TextBox** control to the name of the function, **BetterBox$()**, so that it's returned to the calling procedure.

So we can use this function in our code in a similar way to the ordinary **InputBox$()** function. In our example we set the values of the prompt, window title and default text in variables, then call the **BetterBox$()** function and assign the return value to our variable **Opinion$**. Notice we've also specified **1** for the final argument—the default setting for the Confirm checkbox.

```
Sub MAIN
    OurPrompt$ = "What do you think of it so far?"
    OurTitle$ = "Opinion Poll"
    OurDefault$ = "Rubbish"
    Opinion$ = BetterBox$(OurPrompt$, OurDefault$, OurTitle$, 1)
    If Len(Opinion$) Then
        Msg$ = Chr$(34) + Opinion$ + Chr$(34)
    Else
        Msg$ = "< None >"
    End If
    MsgBox Msg$, "Your opinion", 64
End Sub
```

We can then process the return value just as we would with the normal **InputBox$()** function. You can copy this function into your own macros and use it when you are creating applications, or load the UsefulBits template as a global template and call the function by using:

```
Response$ = BetterInputBox.BetterBox$(Prompt$, Default$, Title$, Confirm)
```

Introducing Dynamic Dialogs

In all the custom dialogs we've used so far, we've had no control over what actually happens in the dialog while it's displayed. We can only set the values in the dialog record before displaying it, and then retrieve them afterwards. However, WordBasic supports an extension to the custom dialog methods that we've already used, which lets us create and use **dynamic dialogs**.

In a dynamic dialog, we can create code that reacts to events in the dialog which occur *while the dialog is displayed*. An event can be the user clicking a button, selecting an item from a list or option group, changing the setting of a check box, typing in an edit box, or just moving the focus from one control to another. A dynamic dialog is basically designed and used in much the same way as the static custom dialogs that we've been using, but three things are different:

- The dialog definition statement in the macro
- The dialog function which allows us to respond to events in the dialog
- The WordBasic procedures that we use to work with the dialog

Basically, we need to do two things to make our static custom dialog dynamic. We have to create the dialog function, and then add its name to the dialog definition. Once we've done this Word will call our function each time an event, such as those listed above, occurs in the dialog. However, the dialog remains on screen while our new function is executing, so we can manipulate the contents of the controls in response to the user's actions.

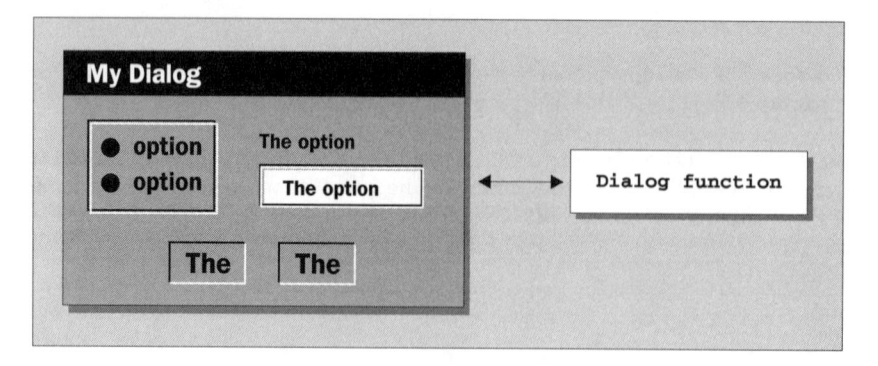

The Dialog Definition Statement

The change to the dialog definition is basic enough. We simply tell Word the name of the function that will be the dialog function for that dialog while it is displayed. To do this, we add the name to the end of the **Begin Dialog** statement, preceded by a period. So, to make the function **MyDialog()** the dialog function for our All The Controls dialog, we would use:

```
Begin Dialog UserDialog 472, 304, "All The Controls", .MyDialog
```

Now, while the All The Controls dialog is displayed, Word will call our **MyDialog()** function each time an event occurs.

Managing the Escape Key

But there's one slight problem. While a custom dialog is displayed, pressing the *Escape* key is equivalent to clicking the Cancel button in the dialog. However, a dynamic dialog behaves in a different way. Because we're running WordBasic code while the dialog is open (the code in our dialog function), pressing *Escape* will interrupt the code like it does in a normal macro. To prevent this, we have to disable the *Escape* key while our dialog is displayed:

```
DisableInput 1                  ' disable the Escape key
Result = Dialog(ATCRec)         ' display the dialog
DisableInput 0                  ' enable the Escape key again
```

The Dialog Function

The function that we use as a dialog function must conform to a fixed format, otherwise Word will raise an error. The format is similar to a normal function, but it has particular arguments that must be present. To declare the **MyDialog()** function for our All The Controls dialog, we would use:

```
Function MyDialog(ControlID$, Action, SuppValue)
    ...
    statements to respond to dialog events
    ...
    MyDialog = value
End Function
```

Although you can use different names for the arguments, you must maintain this format: one string-type and two number-type arguments. Inside the function, you handle the events by manipulating the controls in the dialog, then return a value by assigning it to the function name.

Keeping a Dynamic Dialog Displayed

If the dialog function returns the value **zero**, the dialog is closed and execution passes back to the statement in your macro after the one that originally displayed the dialog. This is normally what would happen if the user clicked OK or Cancel. But by returning any **non-zero** value, the dialog continues to be displayed. When we used the All The Controls static dialog, it closed if you pressed the Your Text button. In a dynamic dialog you can arrange for it to stay open when the user clicks a button other than OK or Cancel, by simply returning a non-zero value.

Understanding the Dialog Function Arguments

The three arguments to the dialog function identify the event that is occurring in the dialog. The first argument, **ControlID$**, is simply the name of the control that caused the event, or, in certain cases, an empty string. So, within the dialog function we can tell which control the user has clicked:

```
Function MyDialog(ControlID$, Action, SuppValue)
    RetVal = 1              'to hold dialog open by default
    Select Case ControlID$
       Case "TextBox1"
          statements to respond to TextBox1 events
       Case "Push1"
          statements to respond to Push1 events
       Case "ListBox1"
          statements to respond to ListBox1 events
       Case "OK"
          statements to respond to OK button click
          RetVal = 0        'set return value to close the dialog
       Case Else
          ' do nothing (for cases when ControlID$ is an empty string)
    End Select
    MyDialog = RetVal
End Function
```

The second argument, **Action**, is a number which identifies the type of event that has occurred. The possible values are:

Action	Action Value Meaning
1	The dialog box is being initialized before it is displayed. Here, you can set the values of controls and disable or hide them. In this case, **ControlID$** is an empty string.
2	A control *other than* a text box or the text area of a combo box has been clicked. Typing in a text box or combo box doesn't cause this action.
3	A text box or the text area of a combo box has been changed, and the user has moved to another control. The action only occurs when the focus moves, not as they enter text in the control.
4	The focus has changed in the dialog. This action is sent by the control that has just received the focus, not the one that has lost it.
5	Sent when the dialog is in the idle state. A regular succession of action 5 values are sent while the dialog is open. In this case, **ControlID$** is an empty string.
6	The dialog has been moved around on screen. This is only sent if **ScreenUpdating** is off, and again **ControlID$** is an empty string. Word will normally redraw the screen as necessary, so you only need to respond if you don't want the screen to be redrawn normally.

The third argument, **SuppValue**, supplies extra information about the event that has occurred. How the value is interpreted depends on the type of control that is generating the event. **SuppValue** has different meanings for each type of control:

Control Type	SuppValue Meaning
ListBox DropDownList ComboBox (List section)	The index of the item selected, where the first item is indexed **zero**. Corresponds to the index of the string value in the array that fills the list.
CheckBox	**1** if selected, **zero** if not.
OptionGroup	The number of the option button selected, where the first is **zero**, the second is **1**, etc.
TextBox ComboBox (Edit area)	The number of characters in the text box or the combo box's text edit area.
PushButton	A special value which identifies the button. This isn't normally used, because you can identify the button by the name returned in **ControlID$**.

If you're now completely confused, don't panic. We'll look at an example of a dialog function that uses all these arguments to decide what action to take.

The easiest way to lay out your dialog function is to use a **Select-Case** construct to examine the value of the **Action** argument first. That way, you know what type of event is occurring:

```
Function MyDialog(ControlID$, Action, SuppValue)
   RetVal = 1
   Select Case Action
      Case 1         ' initialization
         statements to set, disable, and hide controls
      Case 2         ' control clicked
         Select Case ControlID$
            Case "OptionGroup3"
               statements to respond to clicking Option Buttons
            Case "CheckBox1"
               statements to respond to clicking Check Box
            Case "OK"
               statements to respond to clicking OK button
               RetVal = 0    ' to close the dialog
            Case "Cancel"
               RetVal = 0    ' to close the dialog
         End Select
      Case 3              ' text changed and focus moved
         Select Case ControlID$
            Case "TextBox1"
               statements to respond to changes in Text Box
            Case "ComboBox1"
               statements to respond to changes in Combo Box edit area
         End Select
      Case 4              ' new control received the focus
         Select Case ControlID$
            Case "TextBox1"
               statements to respond to Text Box getting the focus
            Case "ComboBox1"
               statements to respond to Combo Box getting the focus
         End Select
```

```
            Case Else
                ' do nothing (for cases when Action is 5 or 6)
        End Select
        MyDialog = RetVal
    End Function
```

For each possible value of **Action**, we use another **Select-Case** statement to examine the value of **ControlID$**. This combination tells us what's happening to which control, and we can execute the code that's applicable.

Of course, if you don't want to respond to a particular combination of **Action** and **ControlID$**, you just ignore it by leaving it out of your function. But you must make sure you return a non-zero value for events you don't want to handle to prevent the dialog being closed when that event occurs. We've done this by setting a variable **RetVal** to **1** at the start of the function and only changing it to **0** when the OK or Cancel button is pressed.

Using the Value in the SuppValue Argument

Once your dialog function has pin-pointed which control and action combination is causing the event, you can execute statements to respond to it. To do so, you usually need to know something more about the event itself. For example, if the user has selected an item in a list box, you need to know which one they selected. The value returned in the **SuppValue** argument is the index of the item they clicked, so we can retrieve the value from the array that fills the list box:

```
    ...
    Case 2          ' control has been clicked
        Select Case ControlID$
            Case "ListBox1"
                ItemClicked$ = ListBox1$(SuppValue)
    ...
```

Here, when the user selects an item in the list box **ListBox1**, we use the value of **SuppValue** to retrieve the correct item from the array **ListBox1$()** which supplies the values to fill the list box.

Remember from our table above, that for an option group we get the index of the option button in **SuppValue**, and for a checkbox we get either **1** or **0**, depending on whether it's ticked. If the control is a text box, we get the number of characters in it. And for a combo box, we get two different results. If **Action** is **3**, we get the number of characters in the text edit area, while if it's **2**, we get the index of the item selected in the list part.

WordBasic Dialog Procedures

The only other thing that we need to know about handling dynamic dialogs is the way we set and retrieve values and change the state of the controls while the dialog is displayed. We can't use the normal method of referring to the fields in the dialog record, as we do with static custom dialogs and Word's built-in dialogs. Why not? Well, we're back to **context** again.

The Dialog Record's Context

Consider how a dialog record is declared. You have to define the dialog itself first, because this also defines the fields for the dialog record. So, the dialog record is declared *inside* the procedure that creates and displays the dialog. This is the only place that it is in context.

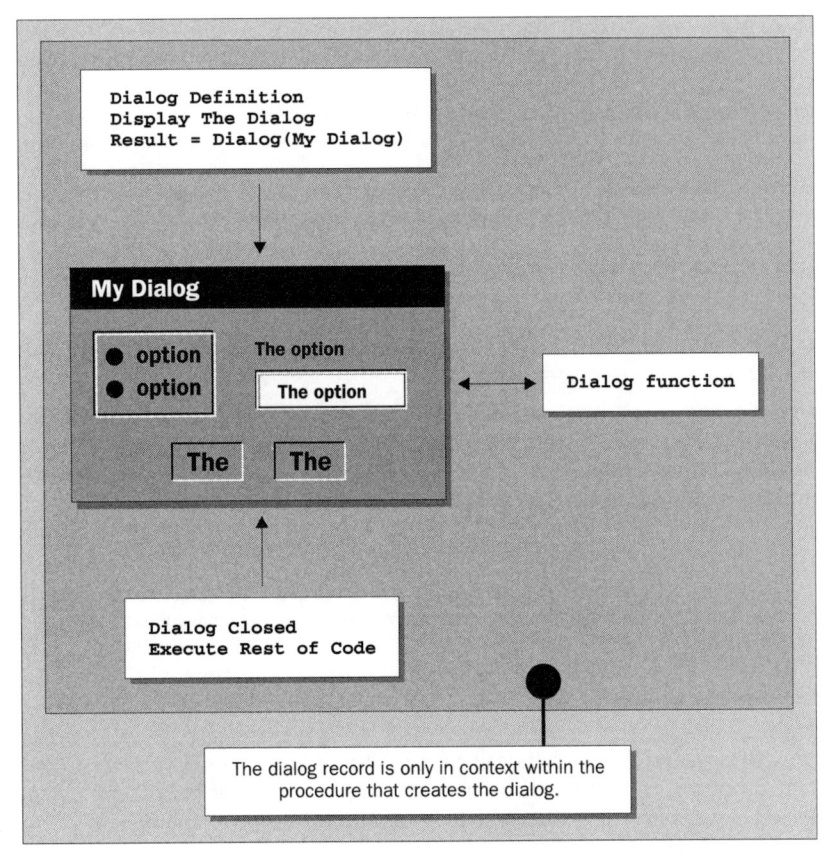

However, the dialog function is a *separate* procedure which is executed while the original procedure is stopped at the **Dialog()** statement, while the dialog is actually displayed. So the dialog record is *not* in context here. Neither can we declare it as a **Shared** variable, because we can only create it inside the procedure that creates the dialog. So how do we get at the values in the controls from within the dialog function? Easy, we use WordBasic's **dialog procedures**.

In order to work with:	You set values with:	And get values with:
Text values for a control	**DlgText**	**DlgText$()**
Numeric values for a control	**DlgValue**	**DlgValue()**
The array for a **List** control	**DlgListBoxArray**	**DlgListBoxArray()**
A **Picture** control contents	**DlgSetPicture**	n/a
A **FilePreview** control contents	**DlgFilePreview**	**DlgFilePreview()**
Showing or hiding a control	**DlgVisible**	**DlgVisible()**
Enabling or disabling a control	**DlgEnable**	**DlgEnable()**
The control that has the focus	**DlgFocus**	**DlgFocus()**
The numeric ID of a control	n/a	**DlgControlId()**

You'll see how these are used in the next couple of examples, but, basically, you just supply the identifier of the control you want to work with and any arguments required. For example:

```
DlgEnable "OK", 0                           'disables the OK button
DlgEnable "OK", 1                           'enables the OK button

DlgText "txtTheValue", "WordBasic"          'sets control's value to "WordBasic"
ThisText$ = DlgText("txtTheValue")          'retrieves the text into ThisValue$

DlgFocus "optThisOption"                    'sets the focus to this control
CurrentControlID$ = DlgFocus()              'gets ID of the control with focus
```

Notice that the control identifier is sent to the function as a string, enclosed in quotation marks. This is why the identifier is case-sensitive.

FYI

Instead of using the control identifier names, you can refer to them using their numeric identifier. When you define a dialog, each control automatically has a numeric identifier which corresponds to its position in the definition. For example:

```
Begin Dialog UserDialog 456, 94, BBTitle$
    Text 23, 10, 399, 13, BBPrompt$, .lblPrompt     'NumericID = 0
    TextBox 24, 29, 404, 18, .txtTheValue           'NumericID = 1
    OKButton 257, 60, 70, 26                        'NumericID = 2
    CancelButton 347, 60, 70, 26                    'NumericID = 3
End Dialog
```

Using the numeric identifiers can make your code run quicker. However, if you add or remove controls from the definition, those following it will be renumbered automatically, causing your macro to fail. We'll look at numeric control identifiers in more detail in Part 2.

Try It Out - Making Our 'Better Input Box' Dynamic

To see how easy it is to make our static dialog dynamic, we'll add an extra feature to the improved input box function we created earlier. If you haven't created this so far, you can use the version we've supplied. It's called BetterInputBox and is in the sample UsefulBits template.

1 Using the Organizer tool from the Tools | Macro... dialog. Open the UsefulBits template from the samples folder and your own UsefulBits template. Copy the **BetterInputBox** macro to your own UsefulBits template. Close the dialog.

2 Now we can begin editing it. Select Tools | Macro... and choose the BetterInputBox for editing. Change the dialog definition statement in the **BetterBox$()** function by adding the name of our dialog function to it:

```
Function BetterBox$(BBPrompt$, BBDefault$, BBTitle$, BBConfirm)
    Begin Dialog UserDialog 456, 94, BBTitle$, .BBFunction
        Text 23, 10, 399, 13, BBPrompt$, .lblPrompt
        TextBox 24, 29, 404, 18, .txtTheValue
```

3 Add the line **DisableInput 1** before the statement that displays the dialog, and **DisableInput 0** after it, so that pressing *Escape* won't interrupt the macro.

```
        BIBRec.chkConfirm = BBConfirm        ' set the Confirm checkbox
        DisableInput 1                       ' disable Escape key
        If Dialog(BIBRec) Then               ' show the dialog
            If BIBRec.chkConfirm Then
                Msg$ = BBPrompt$ + Chr$(10) + BIBRec.txtTheValue
                Accept = MsgBox(Msg$, "Confirm Input", 33)
            Else
                Accept = - 1                 ' no Confirm, so set to True
            End If
            If Accept Then BetterBox$ = BIBRec.txtTheValue
        EndIf
        DisableInput 0                       ' re-enable Escape key
End Function
```

4 After the **BetterBox$()** function, enter our new dialog function, called **BBFunction()**. This is the code that controls the dynamic dialog:

```
Function BBFunction(ControlID$, Action, SuppValue)
    RetVal = 1                          'to keep dialog open
    Select Case Action
        Case 2       'button or checkbox clicked
            Select Case ControlID$
                Case "OK", "Cancel"
                    RetVal = 0          'to close the dialog
                Case Else
                    'do nothing
            End Select
        Case 5       'idle
            If Len(DlgText$("txtTheValue")) Then
                DlgEnable "OK", 1       'enable OK button
            Else
                DlgEnable "OK", 0       'disable OK button
            EndIf
        Case Else
            'do nothing
    End Select
    BBFunction = RetVal
End Function
```

5 Click the Start button on the Macro toolbar. Our input box appears, looking much like before. Delete the default entry in the text box. The OK button is disabled.

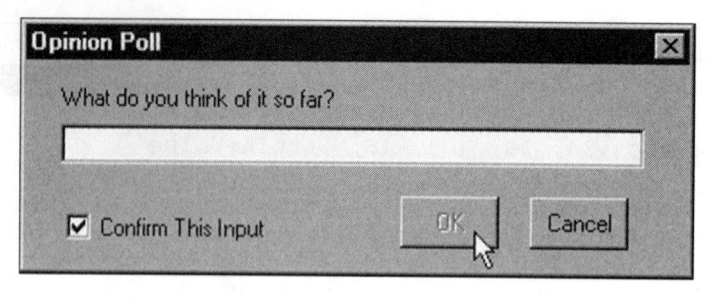

[Opinion Poll dialog screenshot: "What do you think of it so far?" with text box, "Confirm This Input" checkbox checked, OK button (disabled/being clicked), and Cancel button.]

6 As soon as you enter some text, the OK button is re-enabled. It's only available if the user has entered something in the text box, just like a real Windows dialog.

How It Works

By creating a dialog function and adding its name to the dialog definition, we have converted our input box to a dynamic dialog. Within the dialog function, all we have to do is check whether the text box has any characters in it. The best way to do this is during an **Action 5** event which occurs many times a second, during 'idle time' when Word is waiting for us to interact with the dialog.

```
Case 5    'idle
   If Len(DlgText$("txtTheValue")) Then
      DlgEnable "OK", 1        'enable OK button
   Else
      DlgEnable "OK", 0        'disable OK button
   EndIf
```

We retrieve the contents of the text box using the **DlgText$()** function and get its length using the **Len()** function. If it's non-zero (equivalent to **True**) we can enable the OK button using the **DlgEnable** statement with an argument of **1**. Otherwise, we disable it with an argument value of **zero**. But we still have to respond to **Action 2** events, because these will occur when the user clicks a button or the Confirm checkbox.

```
Case 2    'button or checkbox clicked
   Select Case ControlID$
      Case "OK", "Cancel"
         RetVal = 0            'to close the dialog
      Case Else
         'do nothing
   End Select
```

The variable **RetVal** is set to **1** at the beginning of the function, and is assigned to the function's name just before we exit from the function. The **Select-Case** construct means that we can change this value, and hence the value that the dialog function returns, depending on the events that occur. Here, we're setting it to **zero**, so that the dialog is closed when the user clicks OK or Cancel. However, if they click the Confirm checkbox, we leave it set to **1**, so that the dialog remains displayed on screen.

More Context and Shared Variables

The dialog record is now not in context within the dialog function, and it's being called repeatedly while the dialog is displayed. Each time it's called, the variables you declare within it are reinitialized and their last values are lost.

If you want to store values within your dialog function, you can use **Shared** variables declared outside all the procedures in the macro, before the **Sub MAIN** statement. To see an example of this, open the **DynamicPassword** macro which we've supplied in the sample UsefulBits template.

A Dynamic Password Dialog

You may recall in Chapter 2 that we hinted at how you could implement a Log In dialog that obtained a password from your users. If we implement this as a normal static dialog and give them three attempts to get it right, we have to display the Log In dialog three times, and we can only check the password after they click OK to close it each time.

Our new version uses a dynamic dialog that checks the password when they click the Log In button. If it's wrong, we display a message and give them two more tries. If they still get it wrong, we disable the Log In button altogether and their only option is to click Exit. (If you want to cheat, the password is WordBasic.)

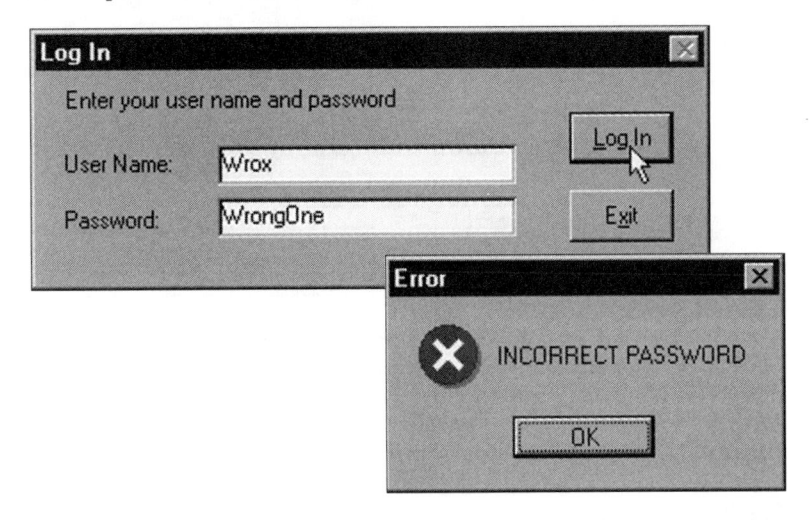

You'll see that the Log In dialog appears towards the top left of your screen because we've added the X and Y arguments to the dialog definition:

```
Begin Dialog UserDialog 100, 50, 454, 97, "Log In", .LogInFunction
```

Also, there's no OK or Cancel button; we've used two normal push-buttons and set the button text to reflect our needs more closely. And by preceding the L and x with an ampersand (&), we get these letters underlined and they act as hot keys. The user can click that button by pressing *Alt* plus the underlined letter.

```
PushButton 362, 18, 73, 26, "&Log In", .LogIn
PushButton 362, 54, 73, 26, "E&xit", .Exit
```

Notice how the Log In button, the text prompt in the dialog and the Password: text box react together. While either the User Name: or Password: boxes are empty, the Log In button is disabled, just as we saw in our 'Better Input Box' example.

```
Select Case Action
   Case 1    'initialization
      DlgEnable "LogIn", 0               'disable login button
   ...
   Case 5    'idle
      UNChars = Len(DlgText$("UserName"))    'get length of text
      PWChars = Len(DlgText$("Password"))    'in edit boxes
      If Attempts > 0 And UNChars > 0 And PWChars > 0 Then
         DlgEnable "LogIn", 1            'enable login button
      Else
         DlgEnable "LogIn", 0            'disable login button
      EndIf
   ...
```

When the user enters an incorrect password and acknowledges the message, the Password: text box is cleared and the focus moves back to it automatically. After three attempts, the prompt in the dialog changes and the Log In button is no longer available.

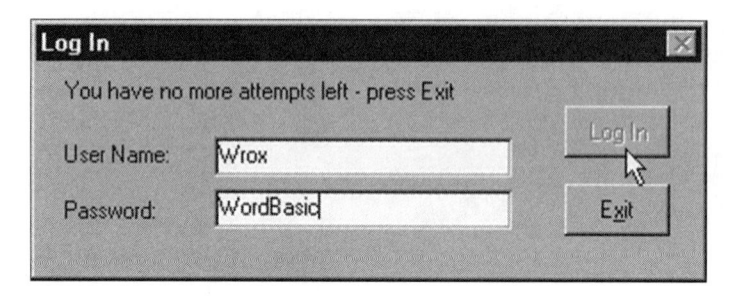

This is because we've declared the variable **Attempts** as a **Shared** variable, right at the start of the macro, so that it isn't reinitialized each time the function is called by our dialog. Before we display the dialog, we set its value to **3**, and each incorrect attempt reduces it by one. Once it reaches zero, **Action 5** events no longer enable the Log In button. Of course, **PWord$** is also declared as a **Shared** variable and set to the correct password before the dialog opens.

```
Select Case Action
   Case 2    'button clicked
      ...
      If ControlID$ = "LogIn" Then              'login button clicked
         Attempts = Attempts - 1
         If DlgText$("Password") = PWord$ Then
            RetVal = 0                          'to close dialog
         Else
            If Attempts = 0 Then
               Prompt$ = "You have no more attempts left - press Exit"
               DlgText "Prompt", Prompt$        'set dialog Text prompt
            End If
            Msg$ = "INCORRECT PASSWORD" + Chr$(10)
            MsgBox Msg$, "Error", 16
            DlgText "Password", ""              'clear password box
            DlgFocus "Password"                 'set focus to it
         End If
      End If
      ...
```

You can see here how the **DlgText** and **DlgText$()** statements are used to get and set the text values in the dialog prompt and password controls. We've also used the **DlgFocus** statement to move the focus to the password text box. In the previous section of code, we've used the **DlgEnable** statement to make the Log In button available.

Have a look at the code in the macro; select it in the Macro dialog and click Edit. We've included comments to show you how it all fits together. You'll be seeing a lot more use of dialog procedures like these in the rest of the book.

Summary

In this chapter we've looked at the different ways you can use WordBasic to communicate with those who use your macros and applications. Creating anything from the simple message box to quite sophisticated dialogs, is only limited by your ability and imagination.

But understanding how dialogs work in Word can seem quite a task. In particular, working with the static and dynamic custom dialogs that we've looked at in this chapter can seem like an uphill struggle. In reality, though, it all drops into place as you use them more and more. You'll soon find that anything less than a full-blown dynamic dialog fails to satisfy.

Dialogs are the front end of your applications, and they are what it will be judged by. No matter how clever the underlying code, if the interface appears awkward and unprofessional, your entire efforts will be judged just on this. Throughout the rest of this book, we'll continue to develop our application interfaces and help you add style and usability to the ones you create.

In this chapter you've learned about:

- WordBasic's input and output statements, like **MsgBox** and **Print**
- Word's built-in dialogs, such as **FilePrint** and **FormatFont**
- How we create custom dialogs and make them dynamic

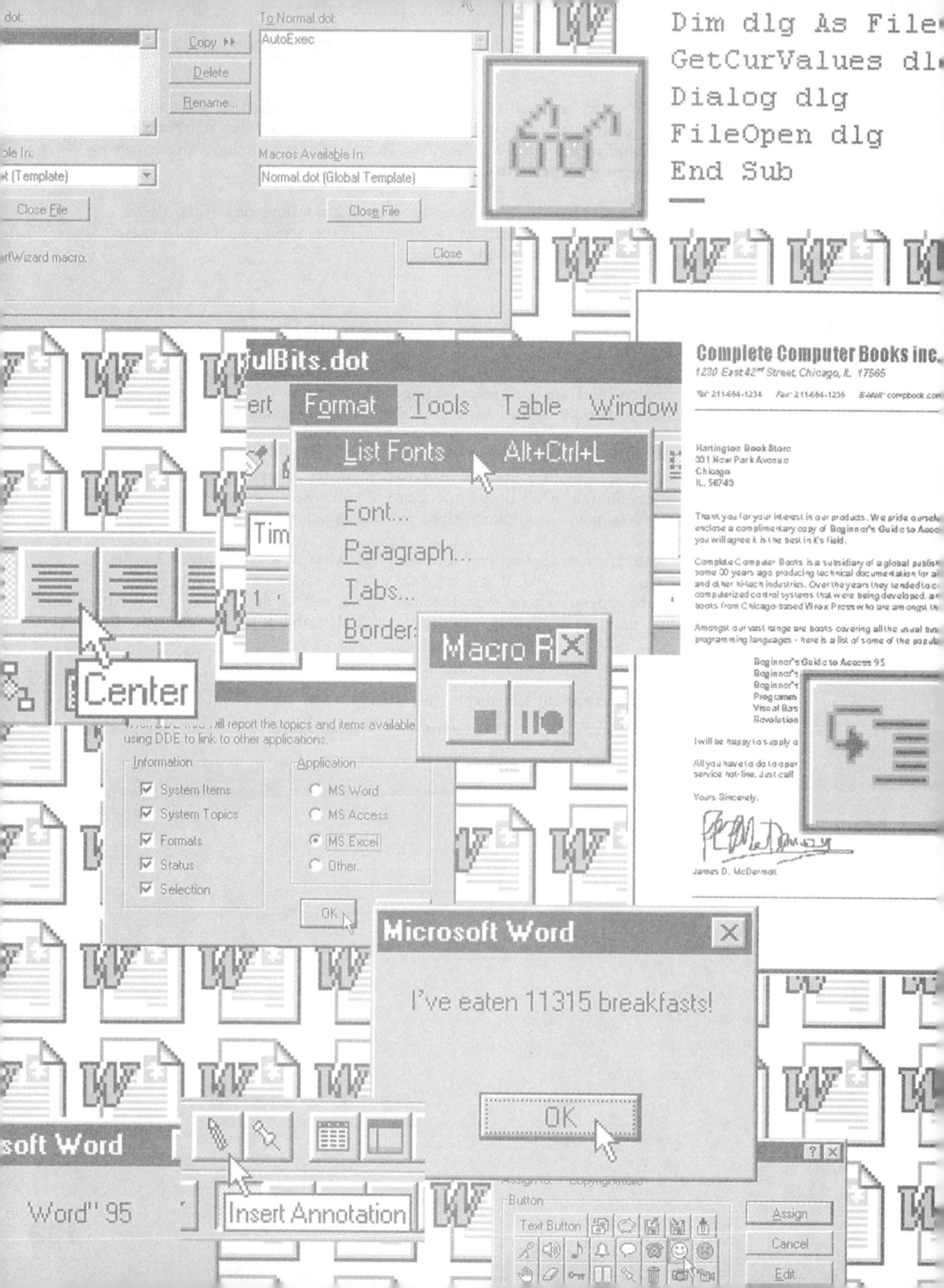

```
Dim dlg As File
GetCurValues dl
Dialog dlg
FileOpen dlg
End Sub
```

I've eaten 11315 breakfasts!

Working with Documents

Introduction

In previous chapters, we've learned a lot about the way WordBasic works, but we haven't gone into much detail about how you can use it to manipulate a document. In this chapter, you'll see some of the ways that we use WordBasic to process the actual text and other items within a document. For example, we need to know how to automate the simple tasks, like finding and selecting text, or just moving the insertion point around in the document. Covering ways to do this will take up the bulk of this chapter, and will introduce you to some new techniques along the way.

Word also allows you to store information 'inside' documents and templates, so that it isn't visible to the user. You can also store information outside Word altogether, on disk in `.ini` files and in the Windows registry.

We'll also take a more detailed look at how you make your macros available to users, by adding them to Word's menus and toolbars or by creating special key combinations to activate them.

This is the last chapter in Part 1, *Introducing WordBasic*, and you'll see a lot of different techniques in use as we gather up the 'loose ends' ready to start some real Word development in Part 2. In particular, we'll cover:

- Editing, finding and selecting text within individual documents
- Saving information globally, in a template and in a document

Editing, Finding and Selecting in a Document

When you're using Word, one of your most basic tasks is to edit the text you've entered to 'fine-tune' it. In fact, you often spend as long doing this as you did actually entering the text in the first place. As you've seen in earlier chapters, we can create WordBasic macros that help to automate this. In Chapter 1, we used the `CopyrightItalic` macro to automatically insert text that was formatted in a particular way.

The purpose of this section is to collect together the principle ways you can use WordBasic to change the look of a document. We'll look at:

- Moving and selecting text and other objects in a document
- Inserting and deleting text and other objects in a document
- Formatting the existing text in a document
- Inserting, modifying and formatting tables
- Searching for text and other objects, and using Find and Replace
- What bookmarks are and how they can be used in WordBasic

Moving and Selecting

When we were looking at what WordBasic actually is, back in Chapter 1, we used the example of one of Word's simplest commands, **CharLeft**. We then went on to introduce the concept that WordBasic is just another way of accessing the standard routines which form the fundamentals of Word itself.

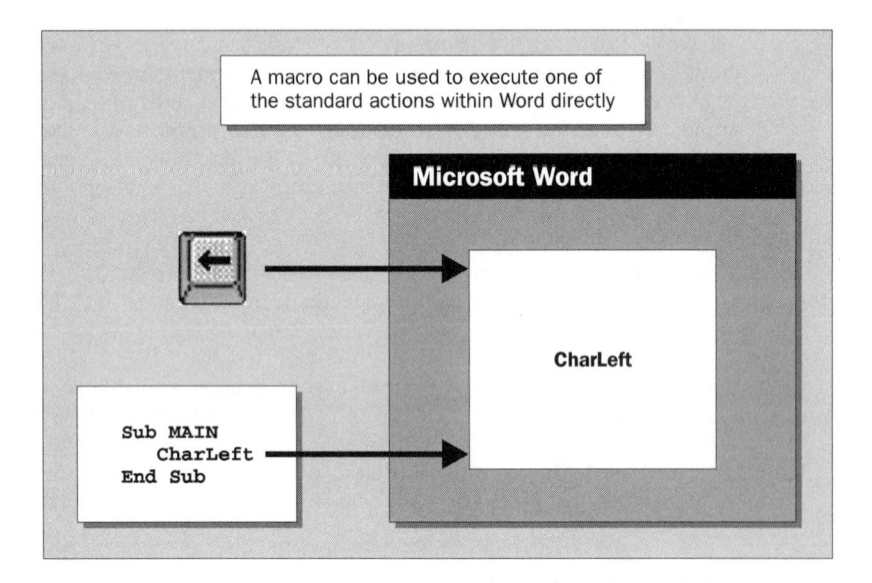

A macro can be used to execute one of the standard actions within Word directly

Microsoft Word

CharLeft

```
Sub MAIN
    CharLeft
End Sub
```

WordBasic provides a set of procedures that almost exactly mirror the normal keyboard action that you use to manipulate text and other objects, such as pictures and tables, in your documents. **CharLeft** moves the insertion point (the flashing cursor) left by one character, the same as pressing the left arrow key on the keyboard. However, WordBasic also allows you to move several characters at a time. The statement **CharLeft 4** moves the insertion point left by four characters—you don't need to use four separate **CharLeft** commands.

When you hold down the *Shift* key and press the left arrow, Word highlights (or selects) the text that the cursor moves over. In WordBasic, you can do the same by adding another argument. **CharLeft 4, 1** moves the insertion point left four characters, selecting the characters as it goes. Note that you have to include the 'number of characters to move' argument if you want to use the 'select' argument. If you only want to move one character and select it, you have to use **CharLeft 1, 1**.

This is the *statement* form of the **CharLeft** command. If the cursor can't be moved the number of characters you specify, it just moves as far as it can and stops. If the insertion point is at the beginning of the document, for example, **CharLeft** has no effect.

WordBasic also supplies the *function* form of the **CharLeft** statement. The syntax is identical, except that you have to enclose the arguments in brackets (because it's a function), and you get a return value which tells you how successful the operation was.

```
Result = CharLeft(3, 1)
```

does the same as

```
CharLeft 3, 1
```

but sets the value of **Result** to either **True** (**-1**) or **False** (**0**). If the insertion point was moved *at all* (not necessarily all three characters), **Response** is set to **True**. If the insertion point can't be moved, **Response** is **False**.

You can select objects in your document in the same way as you select text. If the **CharLeft 3, 1** command causes the insertion point to move over a picture inserted in your document, it's selected as well, just as if you used the keyboard or mouse.

Here's a selection of the function versions of the commands for moving the insertion point and selecting, repeated from Chapter 1. Remember that each has an equivalent statement version which doesn't return a value.

Function	What It Does	Example
CharLeft(*move, select*) **CharRight**(*move, select*) **WordLeft**(*move, select*) **WordRight**(*move, select*) **SentLeft**(*move, select*) **SentRight**(*move, select*) **LineUp**(*move, select*) **LineDown**(*move, select*) **ParaUp**(*move, select*) **ParaDown**(*move, select*) **PageUp**(*move, select*) **PageDown**(*move, select*)	Moves the insertion point and returns a value: **0** if the action can't be carried out at all; **-1** if it can be partly or wholly carried out. *move* is the number of characters, words, sentences, lines, paragraphs or pages to move. If *select* = **1**, the text moved over is selected.	**CharLeft(3)** moves three characters to the left. Returns **-1** if it can move any *(not necessarily all 3)* characters. Returns **0** if it can't move at all. **CharLeft(3, 1)** does the same, but also selects the text. **0** is equivalent to **False** **-1** is equivalent to **True**

You can use all of these functions to move progressively through a document. To move to the end of a document, we can call the **SentRight()** function repeatedly, until it returns **False**.

```
    While SentRight()
    Wend
```

This isn't a lot of use, except as a way to get the end of a document, and there are better ways to do that anyway. But if we wanted to count the number of sentences, we could build a macro based around the code:

```
        Count = 0
        While SentRight()
            Count = Count + 1
        Wend
```

We'll see how this kind of macro is developed in stages, and look at some of the problems you're likely to encounter as you develop your own macros.

Try It Out - Counting Sentences in a Document, Step 1

We can count the number of sentences in a document by counting how many times the **SentRight()** function returns **True**. You'll need to have created your own UsefulBits template to try this out. If you haven't already done so, create it now. Select File | New..., select the Template option in the bottom right of the New window and click OK. Call it **UsefulBits.dot**, then click OK again.

1 With your own UsefulBits template open, select Tools | Macro... and set the Macros Available In: option to UsefulBits.dot. Enter the name **CountSentences** and a short description. Then click Cre*a*te.

2 Enter the code that will count the number of sentences. Add a **MsgBox** statement to display the result:

```
Sub MAIN
REM CountSentences
    Count = 0
    While SentRight()
        Count = Count + 1
    Wend
    MsgBox "There are " + Str$(Count) _ " sentences""
End Sub
```

3 Open an existing document for the macro to work on—any one will do. Then click the Start button on the Macro toolbar. The number of sentences in the document is displayed.

> **Microsoft Word**
> There are 151 sentences
> [OK]

4 You'll have seen the document rush past as the macro moved the insertion point over the sentences. Click the Start button again. This time, there appears to be no sentences in the document.

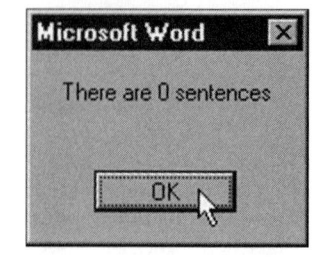

> **Microsoft Word**
> There are 0 sentences
> [OK]

Of course, the reason is obvious: the insertion point is now at the end of the document and there are no more sentences to count. This time, the **SentRight()** function returns **False** the first time it's called because it can't move the insertion point. So here's the first question that you must ask yourself when you write macros that use the text in a document: **where will the insertion point be when my macro starts?**

In our case, it needs to be at the very beginning. We can use WordBasic to handle this situation nicely. There are statements which place the insertion point at the start or end of a document, and functions which tell you if it's already there. There are also other 'start' and 'end' procedures which refer to other parts of a document:

Procedure	What It Does
AtStartOfDocument() **AtEndOfDocument()**	Checks whether the insertion point is at the start or end of the document. Returns **0** (**False**) or **-1** (**True**).
StartOfDocument **EndOfDocument**	Moves the insertion point to the start or end of the document.
StartOfDocument() **EndOfDocument()**	Moves the insertion point to the start or end of the document. Returns **0** (**False**) or **-1** (**True**).
StartOfLine **EndOfLine**	Moves the insertion point to the start or end of the line.
StartOfLine() **EndOfLine()**	Checks whether the insertion point is at the start or end of the line. . Returns **0** (**False**) or **-1** (**True**).
StartOfWindow **EndOfWindow**	Moves the insertion point to the start or end of the part of the document currently visible in window.
StartOfWindow() **EndOfWindow()**	Checks whether the insertion point is at the start or end of the window. Returns **0** (**False**) or **-1** (**True**).

Notice that the **AtStartOfDocument()** and **AtEndOfDocument()** functions do *not* move the insertion point, whereas the **StartOfDocument()** and **EndOfDocument()** functions do. You can also add a '*select*' argument to the **StartOfDocument** and **EndOfDocument** statements, and to the **StartOfDocument()** and **EndOfDocument()** functions, to select the text between the current insertion point and the start or end of the document, as you do with **CharLeft**. For example:

```
StartOfDocument         'Moves to the start of the document
StartOfDocument 1       'Moves and selects text to the start of the document

Result = StartOfDocument(1)   'Moves and selects text to the start of the
                              'document. Result is True if insertion point
                              'moved, False if it could not be moved.
```

So, now it's easy to make sure that we start at the beginning of the document.

Try It Out - Counting Sentences in a Document, Step 2

You'll need to open the **CountSentences** macro that we created earlier in this section. If you've closed it, open your own UsefulBits template, select Tools | Macro..., and in the Macro dialog select **CountSentences** and click Edit.

1 Modify the code that counts the number of sentences by adding the **StartOfDocument** statement to the beginning:

```
Sub MAIN
REM CountSentences
StartOfDocument
    Count = 0
    While SentRight()
        Count = Count + 1
    Wend
    MsgBox "There are " + Str$(Count) _ " sentences""
End Sub
```

2 Switch to an existing document and run the macro a couple of times. You'll see the insertion point fly back to the start of the document each time, and the results are the same each time it runs.

3 The sight of the document streaming past the window as the macro runs isn't very professional. Go back to the macro window and add the following highlighted lines to the code:

```
Sub MAIN
    WaitCursor 1
    ScreenUpdating 0
    StartOfDocument
    Count = 0
    While SentRight()
        Count = Count + 1
        Print "Counting sentences - found"; Count; " so far..."
    Wend
    MsgBox "There are" + Str$(Count) + " sentences"
    WaitCursor 0
    ScreenUpdating 1
End Sub
```

4 Switch back to your document window and run the macro again. Now it looks better. The document doesn't flash past on the screen and we get information in the status bar instead.

How It Works

We've made some simple additions to the macro, but they've made a terrific difference to the way it runs. We've changed the mouse-pointer from an arrow to an hourglass, and turned off screen updating:

```
            WaitCursor     1
            ScreenUpdating 0
```

For each pass round the loop, we print the current count into the status bar so that the user knows something is happening:

```
            Print "Counting sentences - found"; Count; " so far..."
```

Finally, we change the mouse-pointer back to an arrow and turn on screen updating again.

```
            WaitCursor     0
            ScreenUpdating 1
```

> **FYI** You don't actually need the final `ScreenUpdating 1` line here, because Word automatically turns screen updating back on when a macro ends or an error occurs. Having said that, it's good practice, because you may forget to turn it back on if you add code to the end of the macro

OK, so there are still a few problems with our macro. For example, it would be nice if it didn't leave the insertion point at the end of the document. We'll come back to this a little later. For the time being, just close and save the macro, and your UsefulBits template.

Where Is the End of a Document?

It's probably quite obvious that the start of a document is the position immediately before the first character, i.e. where the cursor is when you first open it. But where exactly is the end? Word defines the end of the document as being the point immediately *before* the final paragraph mark.

If you want to see this, open the Options... dialog from the Tools menu and, in the View tab, turn on All for the Nonprinting Characters options.

> ¶
> immediately before the first character - where the cursor is when you first open it. But where exactly is the end? In fact Word defines the end of the document as being the point immediately *before* the final paragraph mark ¶

If you use **LineDown**, **ParaDown** or **PageDown** to move to the last line, the **AtEndOfDocument()** function will *not* return **True** just because you're on the last line. You must be at the point before the final paragraph mark. Conversely, **AtStartOfDocument()** only returns **True** when the insertion point is before the first character in the document, not just on the first line.

Selecting the Current Word or Sentence

Word also provides statements which will select the current word or sentence in one operation:

```
SelectCurWord       'select the word containing the current insertion point
SelectCurSentence   'select the sentence containing the current insertion point
```

The **SelectCurWord** statement behaves slightly differently to the **WordLeft** and **WordRight** statements and functions. **SelectCurWord** only selects the word itself, while **WordLeft** and **WordRight** select the word, plus any trailing spaces. When you use **SelectCurWord** or **SelectCurSentence**, you must make sure that the current selection doesn't include more than one word or sentence, otherwise an error will occur.

There are other 'select current' statements which allow you to select everything from the current insertion point, or extend the current selection, up to a change in formatting. For example:

```
'extend the selection up to a different:
SelectCurAlignment    'text alignment
SelectCurColor        'font color
SelectCurFont         'font or size
SlectCurIndent        'paragraph indent
SelectCurSpacing      'text spacing
SelectCurTabs         'paragraph tab setting
```

Inserting and Deleting

In Chapter 1, we used the **Insert** and **InsertPara** statements to place text in our document. You can also insert a range of other objects, using the equivalent **Insert** statements. These include captions, addresses, date time fields, equations, footnotes, indexes, pictures, tables of contents, etc. For a full list, search the Word Help file on *Insert*—all the WordBasic **Insert** statements are listed here. Of course, you can insert other objects using OLE (Object Linking and Embedding). We'll be looking at this is detail in Part 3.

One thing we haven't considered, though, is how you delete text and other objects from a document. Again, WordBasic mirrors the Word keyboard methods. The **EditClear** statement is the closest relation to the *Delete* and *Backspace* keys:

EditClear	is equivalent to pressing the *Delete* key.
EditClear -1	is equivalent to pressing the *Backspace* key.
EditClear 4	deletes four characters to the right of the insertion point.
EditClear -3	deletes three characters to the left of the insertion point.

You can also delete text and objects by selecting them first. If you select existing text using one of the 'move' statements, then execute an **EditClear** statement, it's equivalent again to pressing *Delete*: the selected text is deleted. However, if you've selected some text and use **EditClear 4**, for example, Word will delete your text and count this as one press of the *Delete* key, then delete the next three characters to the right of the insertion point, like pressing *Delete* three more times. You can also use the **EditCut** or **Spike** statements to delete selected text or other objects.

EditCut   deletes selected text and other objects from the document and pastes them into the clipboard. This is equivalent to pressing Ctrl-X.

Spike   deletes selected text and other objects from the document and pastes them into an AutoText entry. This is equivalent to pressing Ctrl-F3.

Formatting Text

Again, in Chapter 1, we saw how to use the simple text-formatting statements, like **Bold** and **Italic**. You can use them to change the format of the currently selected text, or to change the attributes of text as you insert it. For example, the statement **Bold 1** changes all the text that is currently selected to bold format. If there's no text selected, it simply 'switches on' bold so that the text you type or insert next will be in bold format.

We also saw the function equivalent: **Bold()** and **Italic()**. These return a value which depends on the formatting of the currently selected text, or the text where the insertion point is if there's o selection. Remember that they can sometimes produce unexpected results: they return **1** if *all* the selected text matches the attribute (such as bold), **0** if none of it does and **-1** if *some* of it does. So, a result of **True** doesn't actually mean that it's all bold, but it could be...

We've supplied you with a sample utility which manipulates the format of text in a document. It's in a template called **QuickFmt.dot**, which will have been installed with the other sample files.

Try It Out - The Sample 'QuickFormat' Utility

You'll need the sample **QuickFmt.dot** template for this example. It will be in the folder **C:\BegWord** unless you changed it as you installed the samples.

1 Open the **QuickFmt.dot** template from your samples folder. Select Macro... from the Tools menu. Select the macro QuickFormat and click Edit.

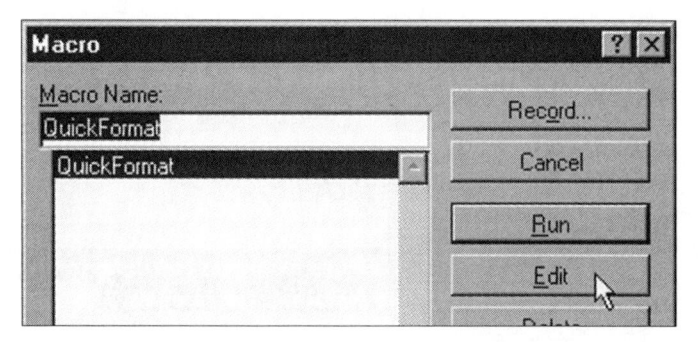

2 Open the template's document window by selecting QuickFmt from the Window menu. You'll see that we've included some sample text for you to experiment with. Place the cursor anywhere in the text and click the Start button on the Macro toolbar.

3 The QuickFormat dialog opens. This is a dynamic Word dialog that you'll be seeing more of later in the book. For the moment, we want to focus on how the formatting parts work.

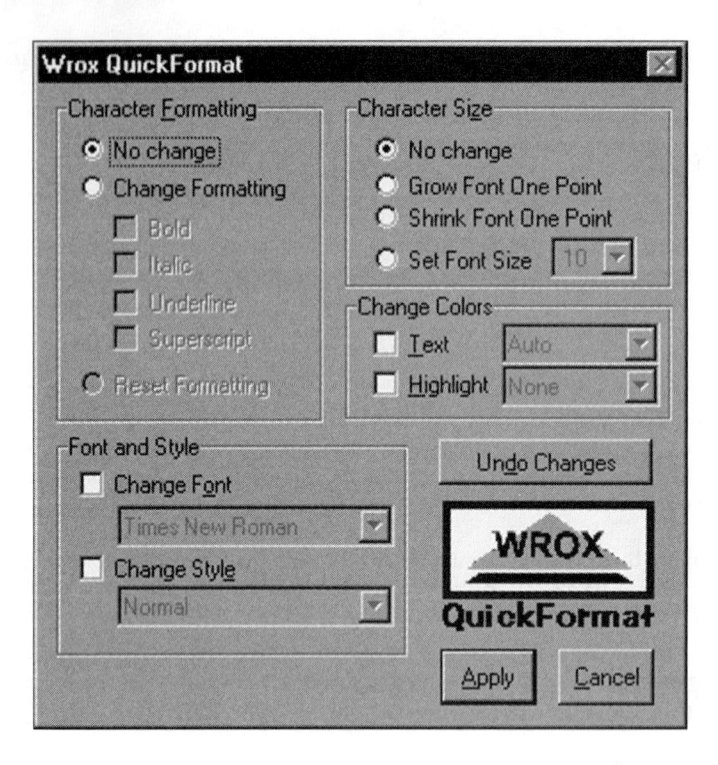

4 The settings of the various options will reflect the settings of the text at the point you placed the cursor, or the text that's currently selected. Click Cancel to close the QuickFormat dialog, then try it again with the insertion point in different places in the document and with different parts of the text selected.

5 Select some of the text with the red highlight and click the Start button again to open QuickFormat. You'll see that, although they're disabled, the Text and Highlight lists show the current colors.

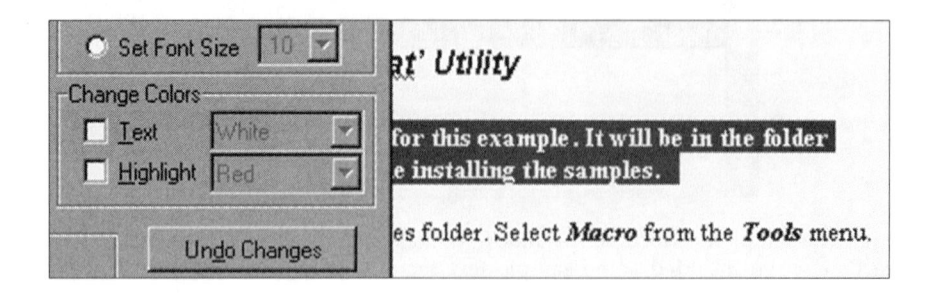

6 Turn on the Text and Highlight options, and the color lists are enabled, ready for use. Change the settings to Auto and None.

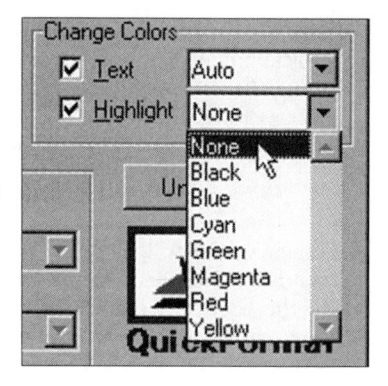

7 Click OK, and the selected text is changed to the new colors. Here, that's black text with no highlight, the default for Word.

8 Experiment with QuickFormat, then, when you're finished, close the template and macro windows, selecting No when Word prompts you to save the changes.

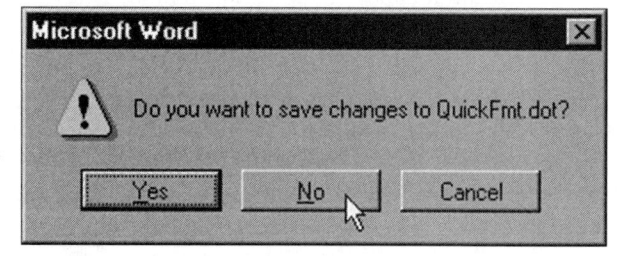

How It Works

We won't go into all the intricacies of this macro here—we'll just show you how the formatting parts work. We use many of the functions you've met before to retrieve the current formatting of the selection. If it's all bold, for example, the `Bold()` function returns `1`. So we can then set the check box in the dialog so that it's ticked when the dialog opens. `ChkBold` is the name of the Bold check box in the dialog, and the statement `DlgValue` is used to set its value to `1` (ticked).

```
If Bold() = 1 Then DlgValue "chkBold", 1
If Italic() = 1 Then DlgValue "chkItalic", 1
If Superscript() = 1 Then DlgValue "chkSuper", 1
If Underline() = 1 Then DlgValue "chkUnder", 1
```

We then use the `FontSize()` function to retrieve the current font size. If the selected font is in different sizes, it returns `0`. So, as long as we get a non-zero value, we can set the font size list (which is an array of strings containing the sizes) to the current size. To retrieve the name of the current font, we use the `Font$()` function. It returns an empty string if there are different fonts in the selection. The `StyleName$()` function works the same way to retrieve the current paragraph style.

```
If FontSize() > 0 Then DlgText "lstFontSize", Str$(FontSize())
If Font$() <> "" Then DlgText "lstFonts", Font$()
If StyleName$() <> "" Then DlgText "lstStyles", StyleName$()
```

To get the colors of the currently selected text, we use the `CharColor()` and `HighlightColor()` functions. These return the color number, between 0 and 16. If the text has different colors, they return `-1`. We've previously stored the names of the colors in two arrays,

`TextColor$()` and `Highlights$()`, so that we can display them in the lists in our QuickFormat dialog. Once we know the color number, we can set the list to the correct color using the `DlgText` statements again:

```
If CharColor() >= 0 Then DlgText "lstTextColor", TextColors$(CharColor())
If HighlightColor() >= 0 Then DlgText "lstHighLight", _
                                     Highlights$(HighlightColor())
```

When you click the Apply button, a separate subroutine in the macro is run. It uses a series of conditions to check the current settings in the dialog, then applies the corresponding formatting to the text. We could have used the **FormatFont** statement by setting all the arguments and then calling it, like we did in Chapter 1, but this method shows you the different statements at work.

The dialog option group **optFormat** is the setting for the Character Formatting option, and **optSize** is the setting for the Character Size option. In each case, the **DlgValue()** function returns the number of the option button which is set, the first being zero. The final few lines use the **DlgValue()** function to retrieve the settings of the Text and Highlight color check boxes, and the Font and Style check boxes. These return **True** if they're ticked.

```
Sub SetFormatValues       'carry out the format settings
 On Error Resume Next
 Select Case DlgValue("optFormat")
    Case 0   'No Change
        'do nothing
    Case 1   'Change Character Formatting
        Bold DlgValue("chkBold")
        Italic DlgValue("chkItalic")
        Underline DlgValue("chkUnder")
        Superscript DlgValue("chkSuper")
    Case 2   'Reset Character Formatting
        ResetChar
 End Select
 Select Case DlgValue("optSize")
    Case 0   'No Change
        'do nothing
    Case 1   'Grow Font One Point
        GrowFontOnePoint
    Case 2   'Shrink Font One Point
        ShrinkFontOnePoint
    Case 3   'Set Font Size To..
        FontSize Val(DlgText$("lstFontSize"))
 End Select
 If DlgValue("chkTextColor") Then CharColor DlgValue("lstTextColor")
 If DlgValue("chkHighLight") Then HighlightColor DlgValue("lstHighLight")
 If DlgValue("chkStyle") Then Style DlgText$("lstStyles")
 If DlgValue("chkFont") Then Font DlgText$("lstFonts")
 If ResetChar() Then DlgEnable "optCF2", 0
End Sub
```

So, *setting* the formatting of the text is a similar process to *retrieving* it. When the dialog loads, we use the *function* version of the procedures to retrieve the current format. Then, when the user clicks the Apply button, we use the equivalent statement versions to set the new formatting.

> **FYI** The `ResetChar` statement we used in the `SetFormatValues` subroutine simply removes any extra formatting attributes that may have been added to the selected text, such as bold, italic, etc., and returns it to the standard formatting of the paragraph style.

Working with Tables

Depending on your working environment, many of the tasks for which you use Word may involve **tables**. There are a full set of WordBasic procedures for manipulating tables, including ones to insert them, change the number and size of the rows and columns, sort and format the columns, and move around in the table. Here's a list of the common ones, but, for a full list, search the Word Help file on *Table*.

Procedure	What It Does
`NextCell` `PrevCell`	Moves to the next or previous cell in a table. This is equivalent to pressing the *Tab* key.
`NextCell()` `PrevCell()`	Moves to the next or previous cell in a table. Returns **True** if the move was possible, or **False** if not.
`TableInsertTable`	Inserts a table into a document.

`TableSelectTable`
`TableSelectColumn`
`TableSelectRow`
	Selects the complete table, or just the current column or row containing the insertion point.

`TableColumnWidth` `TableRowHeight`	Sets the column width or row height, including several option for indents and line spacing.
`TableInsertColumn` `TableInsertRow`	Inserts one or more columns or rows at the selected column or row, or at the current insertion point.
`BorderLineStyle`	Sets line style for the following border commands.

`BorderLeft`
`BorderRight`
`BorderTop`
`BorderBottom`
	Applies or removes a border. For the statement version, an argument of **1** adds the border, and **0** removes it. The function version returns the current setting of the border, as **1** (on) or **0** (off)

`ShadingPattern`	Sets or retrieves the current shading pattern.

Here's a refresher of some code we used in a macro in Chapter 2. It inserts and formats a table:

```
TableInsertTable .NumColumns = 3, .NumRows = 6
TableSelectTable       'select all the table
BorderLineStyle 8      'set border style to double border
BorderOutside          'make outside borders current line style
BorderLineStyle 1      'set border style to single border
BorderInside           'make outside borders current line style
CenterPara             'make all the cells center text-aligned
NextCell               'move to first cell and clear table selection
TableSelectRow         'select the current row
```

```
TableMergeCells         'merge all the cells in this row into one
ShadingPattern 4        'set the row to 20% gray shading pattern
Bold 1                  'turn on Bold formatting
Insert "Title Here"     'insert the text for the title
Bold 0                  'turn off Bold formatting
```

Getting Information about the Current Insertion Point

Many of the commands you use in a table will produce an error if you try and use them outside a table, in a normal document. Conversely, some operations you perform on a document aren't valid when the insertion point is in a table. For example, you can't insert a table into an existing table, neither can you use `NextCell()` if the insertion point isn't currently in a table.

To find out about where the current insertion point is, you use three special functions: `SelType()`, `SelInfo` and `Selection$()`.

Function	What It Does
`Selection$()`	Returns the text currently selected, without character formatting. Must be less than 65,280 chars. If no text is selected, it returns the character after the insertion point.
`SelType()`	Retrieves the way the insertion point is shown. **1** is a single point and **2** is a multicharacter selection. Can also be used to set and retrieve the way the insertion point or selection is displayed, i.e. as a dotted rather than solid format.
`SelType 1`	This particular statement form sets the insertion point to a single point at the beginning of the current selection and removes any selection.
`SelInfo()`	Returns up to 37 different types of information about the current selection or insertion point. You specify the information you want as a number argument. See some examples below.

To simply retrieve the currently selected text, you use `Selection$()`—easy enough. To tell if any is selected, you use `SelType()`.

```
If SelType() = 2 then MySelectedText$ = Selection$()
```

gets the currently selected text into `MySelectedText$` if the current selection isn't a single insertion point.

The `SelInfo()` statement is very versatile. Here are a few examples, but, for a full list, search the Help file on SelInfo.

```
SelInfo(1)      ' returns the current page number
SelInfo(3)      ' page number ignoring changes to starting page number
SelInfo(5)      ' total number of pages
SelInfo(12)     ' True if insertion point is in a Table
SelInfo(15)     ' number of rows in Table, or -1 if not in a Table
SelInfo(18)     ' number of columns in Table, or -1 if not in a Table
SelInfo(21)     ' returns -1 if Caps Lock is on
SelInfo(22)     ' returns -1 if Num Lock is on
SelInfo(23)     ' returns -1 if Overtype Mode is on
```

So we can use the `SelInfo()` function to check whether we're in a table. Using it with the value **14** returns the number of the row containing the end of the current selection, or the insertion point if there's no selection. If it's not in a table, it returns **-1**.

```
If SelInfo (14)  >= 0 Then MsgBox "You are in a table"
```

Searching and Replacing

WordBasic provides you with a full set of commands to perform searching and replacing, which mirror the options and settings in the Find and Replace dialogs. Because there are so many different options available, including searching for different text formats and special characters, there are several different statements that you can use.

Consider Word's normal Find dialog, shown below. This contains check boxes where you can select different ways of matching your text with the string in the Find What: box, such as matching case or finding whole words only. There are also buttons which open further windows where you can specify the format or style of the text that will match, select a special character such as a *Tab* or *Page Break*, and a Replace... button where you enter the string with which you want to replace what you find.

The equivalent WordBasic statement for this dialog is **EditFind** which has optional arguments for all the options in the Find dialog:

```
EditFind  .Find,  .Replace,  .MatchCase,  .WholeWord,   .PatternMatch,
.SoundsLike,  .FindAllWordForms,  .Direction,  .Wrap,  .Format
```

Notice that there's a **.Replace** argument. You would normally set this to an empty string to prevent an error if **.PatternMatch** is set to **1**. The final three arguments deserve special mention:

.Direction is the direction of the search, **zero** or omitted to search downwards and **1** to search upwards.

.Wrap defines what happens when the end (or start, if searching upwards) of the document or the current selection is reached. Set it to **zero** if you want the search to stop when the end or start is reached. Set it to **1** if you want it to continue from the other end of the document and stop when the whole document has been searched. Set it to **2** if you want it to search just the selection first, then prompt the user before searching the rest of the document.

You must set **.Format** to **1** if you've specified any formatting options which would limit the search. To specify formatting options, you use one of the other WordBasic **Find** or **Replace** commands.

> **FYI** Note that if there's any selected text in the document, **EditFind** searches it first. You may need to remove the selection if you want to search the whole document—otherwise you may not get the result you expect. You can remove a selection with **SelType(1)**, or by moving the insertion point. **CharRight** on its own moves the insertion point to the end of a selection and then removes the selection.

Specifying a Format when Searching

When you execute an **EditFind** statement, Word uses the last settings that were specified for all the Find options, including the format of the text. You can see this behavior if you open the Find or Replace dialogs after you've executed a search. They still show the last settings. You can set just the options in the various formatting dialogs that open when you select different options in the Find and Replace dialogs by using **EditFindFont**, **EditFindLang**, **EditFindPara** and **EditFindStyle**.

So, to carry out a search using **EditFind**, we have to follow a series of steps:

1 Use **EditFindClearFormatting** to clear any existing formatting options that users could have set in the Find dialog.

2 Set any formatting options we want for our search, using **EditFindFont**, **EditFindLang**, **EditFindPara** and **EditFindStyle**.

3 Execute the **EditFind** statement.

4 Check whether we found anything, using the **EditFindFound()** function, which returns **True (-1)** or **False (0)**.

Here's an example:

```
Sub MAIN
   EditFindClearFormatting
   EditFindStyle .Style = "Normal"
   EditFind .Find = "WordBasic", .Direction = 0, .MatchCase = 0, \
           .WholeWord = 1, .PatternMatch = 0, .SoundsLike = 0, \
           .Format = 1, .Wrap = 2, .FindAllWordForms = 0
   If EditFindFound() Then MsgBox "Found It !", "Yes", 64
End Sub
```

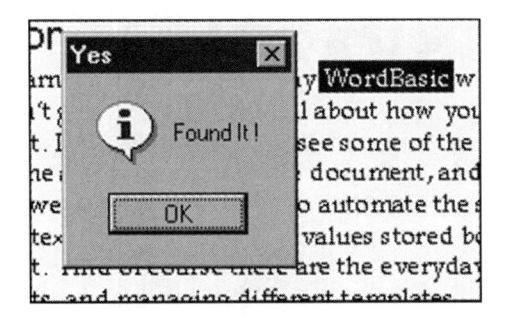

This looks for the word WordBasic, but only in text which has the Normal style applied. If it finds it, it displays a message. If you just want to search for a particular style, irrespective of the text itself, you set the `.Find` argument to an empty string.

Finding All the Instances in a Document

`EditFindFound()` returns **True** or **False**, depending on whether it found the particular text, font, style, etc. that you're searching for. So we can use a **While-Wend** loop to repeat the last find operation again, until all instances have been found. Remember that the search stops either at the end of the document, or after the whole document has been searched, depending on the setting of the `.Wrap` argument.

To repeat the last **Find** operation, we use the single statement **RepeatFind**. So we can look for all instances of the word WordBasic and count how many times it appears, using the code:

```
Sub MAIN
    Count = 0
    EditFindClearFormatting
    EditFindStyle .Style = "Normal"
    EditFind .Find = "WordBasic", .Direction = 0, .MatchCase = 0, \
            .WholeWord = 1, .PatternMatch = 0, .SoundsLike = 0, \
            .Format = 1, .Wrap = 1, .FindAllWordForms = 0
    While EditFindFound()
        Count = Count + 1
        RepeatFind
    Wend
    MsgBox "Found it" + Str$(Count) + " times !", "Yes", 64
End Sub
```

This increments a variable **Count** each time `EditFindFound()` returns **True**, and then repeats the last find. After searching the whole document, if it can't find the word, `EditFindFound()` returns **False** and we exit from the **While-Wend** loop and display the result. And to be really smart, we could include **ScreenUpdating** statements to turn off screen updating as the macro runs, which would mean that you won't see the document scrolling and the whole operation will work a lot quicker.

Replacing Text

Just as the **EditFind** statement contains arguments for all the options in the Find dialog, there's a corresponding statement to the Replace dialog. In fact, the Replace dialog is just an extended form of the Find dialog, with the added Re*p*lace With and Replace *A*ll buttons.

So, the **EditReplace** statement is similar to the **EditFind** statement, but with extra arguments for these buttons:

```
EditReplace  .Find, .Replace, .MatchCase, .WholeWord, .PatternMatch,
.SoundsLike, .FindAllWordForms, .Direction, .Wrap, .Format, FindNext,
ReplaceOne, ReplaceAll
```

Of course, in this statement, we use the **.Replace** argument for the text that we want to use as the replacement. The Replace dialog not only remembers the options you selected for the text you wanted to find the last time you used it, but also the options for the text that replaced it. Because you can specify different font, language, paragraph format and style options for the Find What text and the Replace With text, Word stores both sets.

To set the formatting of the replacement text, there are equivalent statements to those that specify the format of the text you want to find: **EditReplaceFont**, **EditReplaceLang**, **EditReplacePara** and **EditReplaceStyle**. And to clear the current settings, there's an equivalent **EditReplaceClearFormatting** statement.

So, to replace all occurrences of WordBasic with Word's macro language we could use:

```
Sub MAIN
    Count = 0
    EditFindClearFormatting
    EditReplaceClearFormatting
    EditFindStyle .Style = "Normal"
    EditReplaceFont .Font = "Courier", .Bold = 1
    EditReplace .Find = "WordBasic", .Direction = 0, .MatchCase = 0, \
            .Replace = "Word's macro language", .WholeWord = 1, \
            .PatternMatch = 0, .SoundsLike = 0, .Format = 1, \
            .Wrap = 1, .FindAllWordForms = 0, .ReplaceAll = 1
End Sub
```

This first clears any current formatting settings in both the Find and Replace dialogs. Next, it sets the format of the text we want to find to Normal style only, and the format of the text that will replace it to bold Courier font. Finally, it executes the **EditReplace** statement using `.Wrap = 1` and `.ReplaceAll = 1` to replace all the occurrences.

Using Bookmarks

One final aspect of text manipulation is the use of **bookmarks**. Many people shy away from using them because they feel that they are difficult to manage. In fact, this isn't true, as we'll show you.

What Are Bookmarks?

Word allows you to set bookmarks in a document. They can be a single point, or encompass whole areas of a document. A bookmark has a start point and an end point, and, if it's empty (i.e. a single point), the start and end points are the same. You can see a list of the bookmarks in a document and manipulate them yourself by opening the Bookmark dialog. Select Bookmark... from the Edit menu.

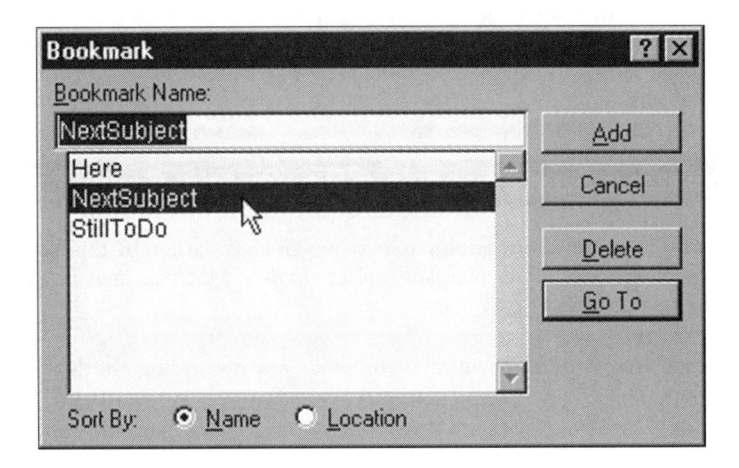

Bookmarks are saved in the document and can be retrieved and manipulated using WordBasic. The **EditBookmark** statement carries out the same tasks as the Bookmark dialog; you can use it to add, delete, or go to a bookmark. For example:

```
EditBookmark .Name = "Here", .Add       'adds the bookmark 'Here'
EditBookmark .Name = "Here", .Goto      'goes to the bookmark 'Here'
EditBookmark .Name = "Here", .Delete    'deletes the bookmark 'Here'
```

Since the `.Add` argument is the default:

```
EditBookmark .Name = "Another"          'adds the bookmark 'Another'
```

If you want to display the Bookmark dialog, you can also include the argument `.SortBy = 1` to sort the list by Location rather than the default, by Name.

Retrieving Bookmark Names and Details

To retrieve the list of bookmark names with WordBasic, we use the `CountBookmarks()` and `BookmarkName$()` functions. The following code displays each one in turn in a message box:

```
Sub MAIN
    For Loop = 1 To CountBookmarks()
        MsgBox BookmarkName$(Loop)
    Next
End Sub
```

You can also check whether a particular bookmark exists in the document, and whether it's empty, i.e. marks only a point and contains no text:

```
ExistingBookmark("Here")    'returns True if the bookmark 'Here' exists
EmptyBookmark("Here")       'returns True if the bookmark 'Here' is empty
```

Adding, Deleting and Going to Bookmarks

Bookmarks are especially useful for several tasks. They're an ideal way of marking a point in a document, so that you can refer to it later. For example, the `CountSentences` macro we created earlier in the chapter always left the insertion point at the end of the document. It would be nice if it moved it back to the original position once it had finished. We'll add the extra code required to achieve this.

Try It Out - Counting Sentences in a Document, Step 3

You'll need to open the `CountSentences` macro we created earlier in this section. If you've closed it, open your own UsefulBits template, select Tools | Macro..., and, in the Macro dialog, select CountSentences and click Edit.

1 Modify the code that counts the number of sentences by adding the lines shown highlighted below to the macro:

```
Sub MAIN
    WaitCursor 1
    ScreenUpdating 0
    EditBookmark "Here", .Add
    StartOfDocument
    Count = 0
    While SentRight()
        Count = Count + 1
        Print "Counting sentences - found"; Count; " so far..."
    Wend
    EditBookmark "Here", .Goto
    EditBookmark "Here", .Delete
    MsgBox "There are" + Str$(Count) + " sentences"
    WaitCursor 0
    ScreenUpdating 1
End Sub
```

2 Switch to a document window and place the insertion point somewhere in the body of the text.

3 Click the Start button on the Macro toolbar. The status bar shows the sentences being counted and, when it's finished, a message box shows the results:

> Microsoft Word
> There are 1406 sentences
> OK

4 Click OK to close the message box, and the document is shown with the insertion point back in the same place that it started from. (The window may have been moved up or down a few lines, but the current insertion point will be visible in the correct position).

How It Works

The **EditBookmark** statement can achieve the three actions we require. First, we add a bookmark at the current position in the document by specifying the name and the **.Add** argument:

```
EditBookmark "Here", .Add
```

Once we've finished moving the insertion point around, we go back to the bookmark we added by specifying the **.Goto** argument:

```
EditBookmark "Here", .Goto
```

It's good manners to clear up after you've modified a document. To remove the new bookmark, we specify the **.Delete** argument:

```
EditBookmark "Here", .Delete
```

If you don't want to type it in yourself, you'll find the complete **CountSentences** macro in the sample UsefulBits template we've supplied.

> **FYI**
>
> Adding a bookmark with the same name as an existing one replaces it with the new one. To be sure that the bookmark didn't already exist, we could have included a check first:
>
> ```
> If ExistingBookmark("Here") Then MsgBox "Bookmark Already Exists"
> ```

In this example, we've seen two more things that you need to keep in mind while designing macros. You should aim to leave the document, and the environment itself, in the same condition as when your macro started. Return the insertion point to the place it started (unless the macro is actually designed to move it somewhere else!). When your macro is complete, remove any bookmarks or other items that you've added.

Copying and Editing Bookmarks

As well as adding and deleting bookmarks, we can copy one to another. We can also compare two bookmarks, and set or change the start and end points. The statement,

```
CopyBookmark "Bookmark1", "Bookmark2"
```

copies the bookmark **Bookmark1** to **Bookmark2**. It doesn't copy the *contents* of the bookmarks (the text between the start and end points), but makes their start and end points refer to the same places. Both must already exist and, of course, the existing start and end points of **Bookmark2** are lost.

Word's Predefined Bookmarks

Word maintains a set of bookmarks that are updated automatically, whenever you have a document open.

The bookmark:	Refers to:
\Sel	The current insertion point or selection.
\PrevSel1	The last point where editing occurred.
\PrevSel2	The last but one point where editing occurred.
\StartOfSel	The start of the current selection.
\EndOfSel	The end of the current selection.
\Line	The current line or the first line of the current selection.
\Char	The first character after the insertion point, or the first character of the selection.
\Para	The current paragraph, or the first paragraph of the current selection.
\Section	The current section, or the first section in the selection.
\Doc	The entire contents of the active document.
\Page	The current page, or the first page of the selection.
\StartOfDoc	The beginning of the document.
\EndOfDoc	The end of the document.
\Cell	The current cell in a table, or the first cell in the selection.
\Table	The current table, or, if the selection includes more than one table, the entire first table of the selection.
\HeadingLevel	The heading containing the insertion point or selection, plus any subheadings and text below it.

Therefore, the following two statements are equivalent (providing the bookmark **Here** already exists):

```
CopyBookmark "\Sel", "Here"
EditBookmark "Here", .Add
```

Both set the bookmark **Here** to refer to the current selection, or the current insertion point if there's no selection. To set the start and end of a bookmark, we can also use the **SetStartOfBookmark** and **SetEndOfBookmark** statements. The next two lines achieve the same result as the previous two:

```
SetStartOfBookmark "\StartOfSel", "Here"
SetEndOfBookmark "\EndOfSel", "Here"
```

So, by moving the insertion point, or using the predefined bookmarks, we can create our own bookmarks to refer to any point or block of text in a document, which can include tables, pictures, or other objects. Once we've marked the document with a bookmark, we can get the text that it refers to quite easily, using the function **GetBookmark$()**. This returns the unformatted text contained between the start and end points of a bookmark:

```
ThisText$ = GetBookmark$("Here")
```

This function places the text referred to by *the contents of* the bookmark **Here** into the string variable **ThisText$**. Bear in mind that *only* unformatted text is returned. All special formatting is lost, and any graphics included in the bookmark will be ignored. For tables, only the contents of the cells will be returned; any column or row separation will also be ignored.

Comparing Bookmarks

Comparing bookmarks is the area that people find most confusing. If you think about the possibilities, you can soon see why this isn't as simple a task as you might first think. A bookmark contains a start and end point, so, when you compare two bookmarks, what exactly are you comparing?

Well, there are many possibilities. For example, one bookmark could be a single point inside another which covers two pages, or both could start at the same place with one being 'longer' than the other.

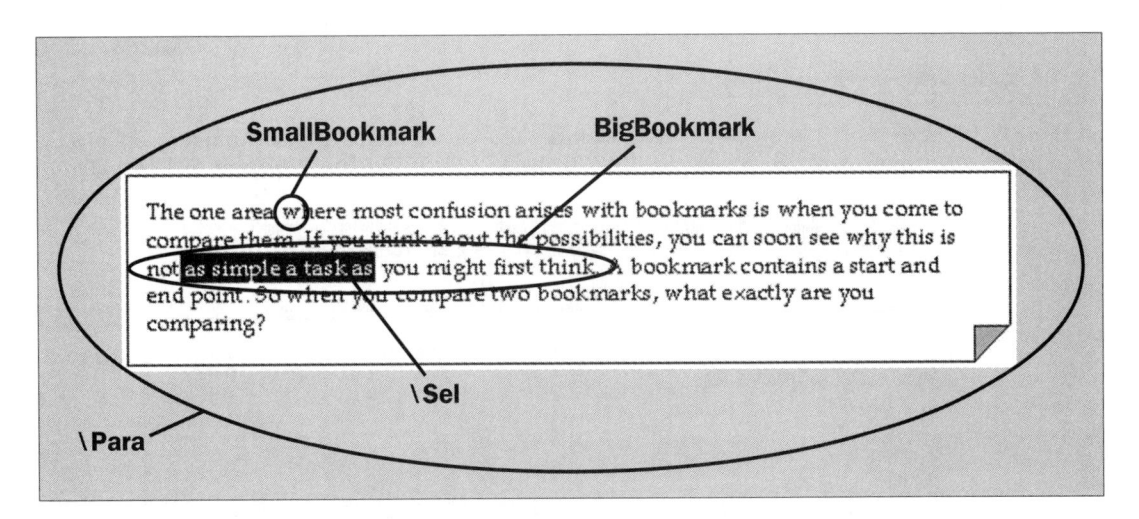

The `CmpBookmarks` function returns a value between 0 and 13, which tells you exactly how the two compare. For almost all our requirements, the only return value we're interested in is zero meaning they are equivalent, i.e. they have start and end points which are the same, or both refer to the same single point. So, we can treat the result as **True** (they *are* equivalent) or **False** (they're different). This isn't really the correct way to think about **True** and **False**, but it does allow us to use it in an **If-Then** or **While-Wend** construct:

```
While CmpBookmarks("Here", "There") Then
   . . .     'only True if Here is not the same as There
Wend
```

Of course, if you want to know more about the comparison, you can't use this form, you have to explicitly test the value:

```
If CmpBookmarks("Here", "There") = 5 Then
   . . .     'bookmark Here entirely encloses bookmark There
Wend
```

For a full list of the return values, search the Word Help file on CmpBookmarks().

Going to a Point in a Document

Now that we know about bookmarks, we can use them for another common task. Word allows you to move around a document using the **EditGoto** statement:

```
EditGoto .Destination = "Here"
```

This moves the insertion point to the place refereed to by the bookmark **Here**. If **Here** refers to more than a single point, the contents of the bookmark are also selected. You can, in fact, use the shorthand form,

```
EditGoto "Here"
```

because we are specifying all the arguments for the statement (there's only one). Of course, this is equivalent to the statement we used before to move the insertion point:

```
EditBookmark "Here", .Goto
```

But **EditGoto** is a lot more versatile than this. You can combine it with different options, equivalent to those you can set in the Go To dialog (select Go To... from the Edit menu):

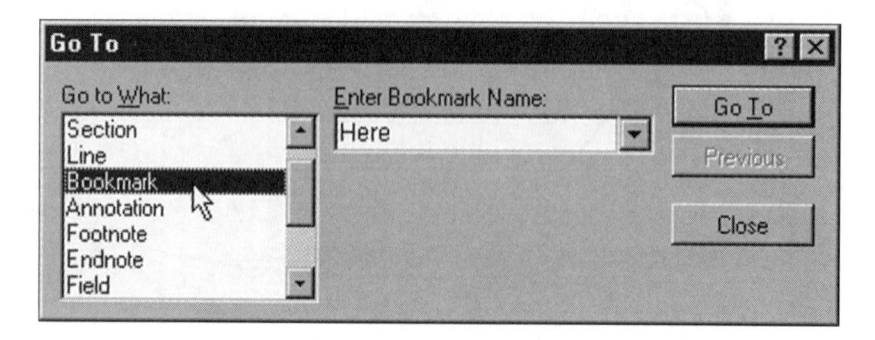

You can use an argument which moves the insertion point to all kinds of different items in a document. For example, we can move to the next table by using just `"t"` as the argument, or a particular page by using a number. Here's a list of the possibilities:

The symbol:	Means:	Example:
`"p"`, or a number	Page	`"p2"` or `"2"` goes to the second page.
`"s"`	Section	`"s3"` goes to the third section.
`"l"`	Line	`"l45"` goes to the 45th line.
(none)	Bookmark	`"Here"` goes to the bookmark Here.
`"a"`	Annotation	`"a'AH'"` goes to the next annotation by AH.
`"f"`	Footnote	`"f3"` goes to the third footnote reference mark.
`"e"`	Endnote	`"e5"` goes to the fifth endnote reference mark.
`"d"`	Field	`"d'TIME'"` goes to the next TIME field.
`"t"`	Table	`"t"` goes to the next table.
`"g"`	Graphic	`"g3"` goes to the third graphic in the document.
`"q"`	Equation	`"q"` goes to the next equation.
`"o"`	Object	`"o'WordArt'"` goes to the next WordArt object.

Notice that apostrophes are used around the relevant annotation text, field name or object type. To move relative to the current insertion point, we include a plus or minus sign. For example:

```
EditGoto "p"       'goes to the next page
EditGoto "p5"      'goes to actual page number five
EditGoto "p+5"     'goes to the fifth page after the insertion point
EditGoto "p-5"     'goes to the fifth page before the insertion point
```

Stepping through a Document

You often find that the task in hand involves stepping through a document. You may need to perform an operation on each paragraph, or collect a list of picture captions. We now have several techniques we can use to step through a document. In the **CountSentences** macro, we used the **SentRight()** function and stopped when it returned **False**:

```
While SentRight()
   Count = Count + 1
   Print "Counting sentences - found"; Count; " so far..."
Wend
```

Of course, we can use any of the other functions that move the insertion point, such as **ParaDown()** or **WordRight()**.

Another way is to use **EditFind** to locate a particular item, then look for the next occurrence using **RepeatFind**. The function **EditFindFound()** returns **False** when there are no more occurrences:

```
EditFind .Find = "WordBasic", .Direction = 0, .MatchCase = 0, \
        .WholeWord = 1, .PatternMatch = 0, .SoundsLike = 0, \
        .Format = 1, .Wrap = 2, .FindAllWordForms = 0
While EditFindFound()
    Count = Count + 1
    RepeatFind
Wend
```

A third way is to use **EditGoto**. This allows us to step through a document by going to each one of a particular type of item (pictures, graphics, tables or sections) it contains in turn. To do this we make use of bookmarks to check whether there are any more items to go to. (**EditGoto** doesn't return a value to indicate if it succeeded in moving the insertion point). Here's an example which counts the number of pictures in a document.

Try It Out - Counting the Number of Pictures in a Document

You'll need the sample UsefulBits template open for this. You'll also need a document that contains some pictures. If you don't have one on file, create one now by entering some text and using the Insert | Picture command to add some pictures to it. Alternatively, you can use one of the sample files that are supplied with Windows 95, Word 95 or Office 95.

1 Open the UsefulBits template from your samples folder. This will be `C:\BegWord` unless you changed it when you installed the samples. Select Macro... form the Tools menu. Select the macro CountPictures, then click Edit.

2 Switch to or open a document containing some pictures. Click the Start button on the Macro toolbar to run the **CountPictures** macro. The status bar displays the number of pictures found so far, though you'll also see messages that the document is being repaginated as it runs.

3 A message box displays the number of pictures found.

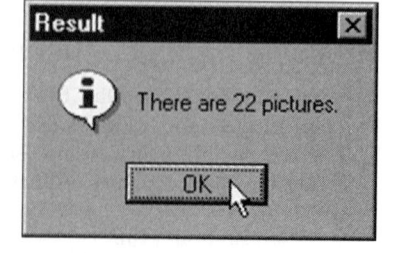

4 Click OK to close the message box and select Bookmark... from the Edit menu. The Bookmark dialog shows that two new bookmarks have crept into our document:

[Bookmark dialog screenshot]

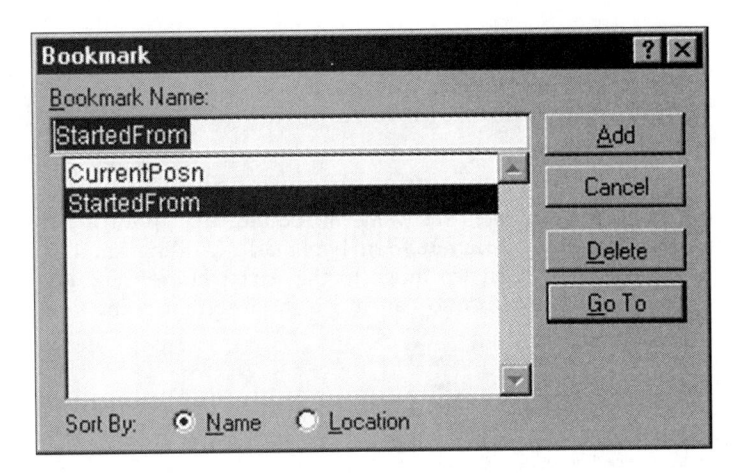

5 Select each one in turn and click Delete to remove them. Then switch to the macro editing window and add the lines shown highlighted below to the macro:

```
        Wend
        EditBookmark "CurrentPosn", .Delete
        EditBookmark "StartedFrom", .Goto
        EditBookmark "StartedFrom", .Delete
        ScreenUpdating 1
        MsgBox "There are" + Str$(Count) + " pictures.", "Result", 64
```

6 Run the macro again and open the Bookmark dialog afterwards. This time, the two rogue bookmarks aren't there.

How It Works

This example uses bookmarks to store the position of the insertion point as the macro runs. Once it has turned off screen updating, it adds a bookmark at the current insertion point called **"StartedFrom"**, because we want to come back to this point when the macro ends.

```
    Sub MAIN
        ScreenUpdating 0
        EditBookmark "StartedFrom", .Add
```

Now we move to the start of the document and create another bookmark **CurrentPosn**. We set **Count** to **zero**, then execute an **EditGoto** statement with the argument **"g"**. This moves us to the next graphic or picture.

```
        StartOfDocument
        EditBookmark "CurrentPosn", .Add
        Count = 0
        EditGoTo "g"
```

Now we can check whether **EditGoto** moved the insertion point. If there are no more pictures, it will still be in the same place. The current insertion point is held in the predefined bookmark **\Sel**, so we can compare this with the bookmark **CurrentPosn** we added before executing **EditGoto**. If they are the same, the result is **0 (False)**, if not, we get a non-zero (**True**) result.

```
    While CmpBookmarks("\Sel", "CurrentPosn")
        Count = Count + 1
        Print "Found"; Count; " pictures so far.."
        EditBookmark "CurrentPosn", .Add
        EditGoTo "g"
    Wend
```

In the **While-Wend** loop, we increment the value of **Count**, then print a message in the status bar. Next, we need to update our **CurrentPosn** bookmark. (Adding another with the same name replaces the original one.) Then we move to the next picture using **EditGoto** again. The loop continues to execute while **EditGoto** can move the insertion point to a new picture.

```
    EditBookmark "CurrentPosn", .Delete
    EditBookmark "StartedFrom", .Goto
    EditBookmark "StartedFrom", .Delete
    ScreenUpdating 1
    MsgBox "There are" + Str$(Count) + " pictures.", "Result", 64
End Sub
```

Once the loop ends, we can clean up. We move the insertion point back to its original position using **EditGoto** with the **.Destination** argument. In the first version of the macro, before you added the extra lines, there were no statements to delete the new bookmarks our code created, so they were still in the document. The extra lines just delete these two bookmarks once we've finished with them.

> **FYI** If you have a graphic inserted directly at the beginning of your document, this macro gives the wrong answer, When the first **EditGoto** statement is executed, it moves to the *next* graphic, even if there's a graphic at the current insertion point. So, in this case, your result is one less than it should be.

Saving Information Globally and in Documents

As well as storing text, graphics and other items in a document in the normal way (by typing or inserting them), we can also store information actually 'inside' a document or template so that it's not visible on screen. You've already seen one example of this, in Chapter 1, where we used the Organizer dialog to examine the AutoText entries in a template.

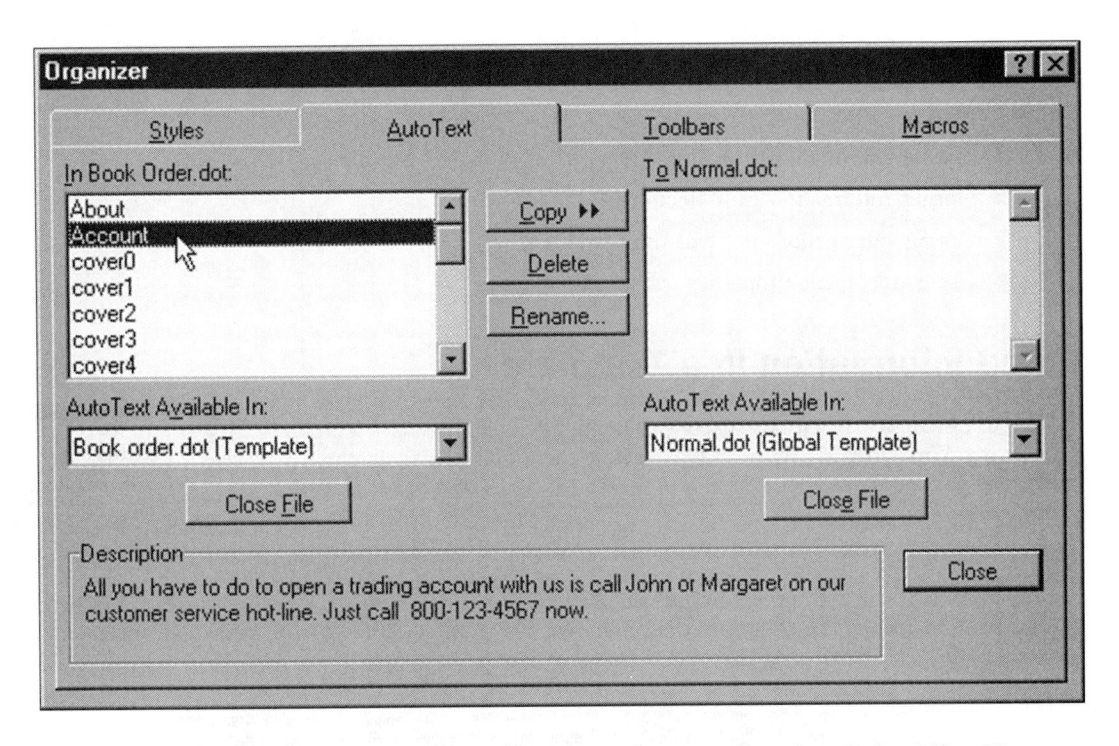

We can also use the document properties that Windows now stores for all the Office 95 applications' documents. These can be the normal built-in properties, such as the **Author**, **Company** and **Title**, or custom properties that you've added to the document. To see a document's properties, select Properties from the File menu while it's open, or right-click on it in Explorer or My Computer and select Properties.

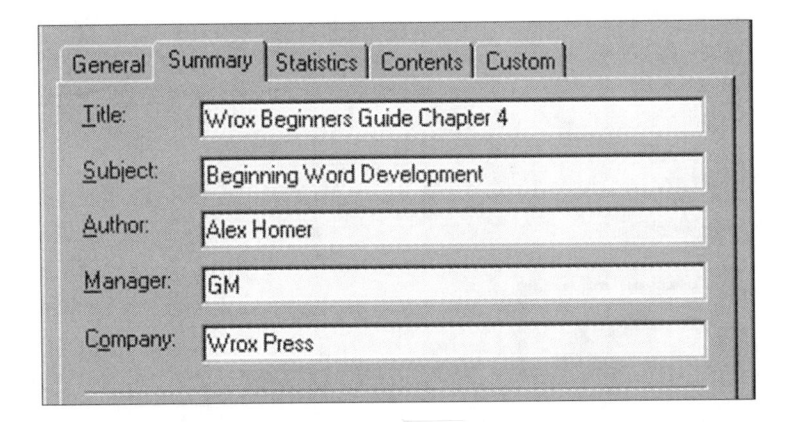

Word also allows us to use document variables. These can store information in a document so that it's saved with the document, and is available whenever that document is open. You can only manipulate document properties in WordBasic, so they can't be changed by the user in any of the standard Word dialogs.

Finally, you can store values outside Word altogether. You can manipulate `.ini` files (special format text files on disk) or access settings in the Windows **registry**. So, in this section we'll be looking at:

- Storing information in a template
- Storing information in a document
- Storing information in `.ini` files and the registry
- Using document properties

Storing Information in a Template

The `QuickFormat` macro we used earlier in this chapter has a graphic on it: our Wrox logo. So how did we get it there? It's stored in the template that contains the macro, and displayed in a `Picture` control in the dialog.

To see where it's stored, open `QuickFmt.dot` from your samples folder, and select AutoText... from the Edit menu. The AutoText dialog shows the graphic stored as an AutoText entry. AutoText entries are always stored in a *template*, not a document.

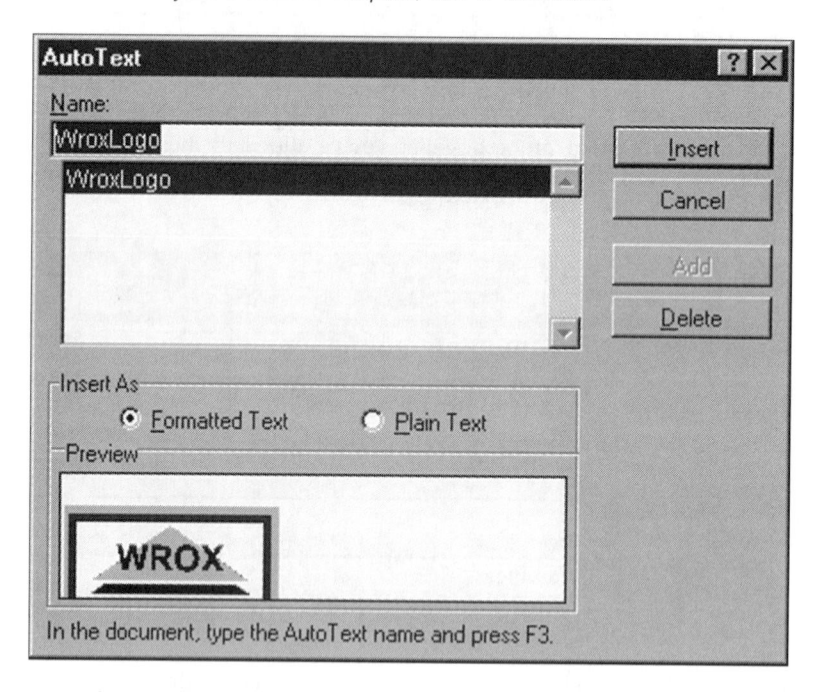

You can store graphics or text as AutoText entries, and text can be stored with or without its formatting. The two option buttons in this dialog allow you to select Plain Text or Formatted Text.

We can manipulate the AutoText entries using WordBasic. The statement **EditAutoText** is equivalent to the options in the AutoText dialog:

EditAutoText .Name, .Context, InsertAs, [.Insert | .Delete | .Add]

.Name is the name of the AutoText entry.
.Context is **zero** for the Normal template, or **1** for the active template.
.InsertAs is **0** for formatted text, and **1** for plain text.

You can supply only one of the other arguments at a time: either **.Insert** to insert the entry into the document at the current insertion point, **.Delete** to remove the AutoText entry from the template, or **.Add** to make the currently selected items in the document an AutoText entry.

There's also a statement, **AutoText**, which mirrors the AutoText button on Word's toolbar. It creates a new AutoText entry for any selected text in the document, or, if none is selected, it tries to match the text around the insertion point with an existing entry's name and insert that into the document.

However, you can be more precise than this. To insert the contents of an AutoText entry into your document, you place the insertion point in a word that's the name of an AutoText entry, and execute the **InsertAutoText** statement. To create a new AutoText entry, you execute the **SetAutoText** statement. For example,

```
SetAutoText .Name = "MyText", .Text = "This is my text", Context = 1
```

creates an entry named, MyText, containing the text, This is my text, in the active template.

To see what AutoText entries are available in a template, you use the now time-honored method of looping through them:

```
Sub MAIN
    For Loop = 1 To CountAutoTextEntries()
        ThisOne$ = AutoTextName$(Loop)
        Msg$ = "The entry '" + ThisOne$ + "' contains:" + Chr$(10)
        Msg$ = Msg$ + "'" + GetAutoText$(ThisOne$) + "'."
        MsgBox Msg$
    Next
End Sub
```

We loop from **1** to **CountAutoTextEntries()**. For each one, we use **AutoTextName$()** to retrieve the name of the entry, and **GetAutoText$()** to retrieve its contents. AutoText entries are useful if you have to allocate different numbers to each document created from a template, when you're creating invoices, for example. You just store the last number you used in an AutoText entry and update it each time a new document is created. You'll see more of this later on in the book.

Storing Information in a Document

While AutoText entries can be used to store information in a template, we use document variables to store values actually 'inside' a document. They're out of harm's way here, because there's no Word dialog with which the user can change them. They can only be manipulated using WordBasic.

Because they are saved with a document, they're portable, i.e. wherever the document is open, the values are available. AutoText entries are only available if you have access to the template that contains them, because they aren't stored in the document.

Working with document variables is very easy and you'll see more examples of them in use in later chapters. For the meantime, here's all the theory you need to know. Manipulating them in WordBasic is very similar to working with the AutoText entries that you saw in the previous section. To list all the document variables in a document, we can use this code:

```
Sub MAIN
    For Loop = 1 To CountDocumentVars()
        ThisOne$ = GetDocumentVarName$(Loop)
        Msg$ = "The doc variable '" + ThisOne$ + "' contains:" + Chr$(10)
        Msg$ = Msg$ + "'" + GetDocumentVar$(ThisOne$) + "'."
        MsgBox Msg$
    Next
End Sub
```

We loop from **1** to **CountDocumentVar$()**. For each one, we use **GetDocumentVarName$()** to retrieve the name of the entry, and **GetDocumentVar$()** to retrieve its contents.

To set the value of an existing document variable, or create a new one, we use either the **SetDocumentVar** statement or the **SetDocumentVar()** function. The only difference is that the function version returns **True** or **False**, depending on whether it could successfully set the value:

```
SetDocumentVar "MyVar", "ThisValue"
SetDocumentVar ("MyVar", "ThisValue")    'returns True or False
```

Both these set the document variable named **MyVar** to the value **ThisValue**. Notice that you can only store **string** values in document variables. If you want to store a number, you have to convert it to a string with **Str$()** first, then convert it back to a number with **Val()** when you retrieve it. To delete an existing document property you just set its value to an empty string.

Storing Information in .ini Files and the Registry

If you want to store values which must be available to any open document, you can store it in the Normal template. This is always loaded when Word is running. However, you have another option: you can use WordBasic to read and write values in either an `.ini` file, like those used in earlier versions of Windows, or directly into Windows registry.

The **registry** is where all the application and operating system settings are stored that keep your computer running smoothly. It consists of the files **USER.DAT** and **SYSTEM.DAT**, generally stored in your `Windows\System` folder. If you've ever seen what happens when the registry becomes corrupted, you're probably still recovering from shock—you need to be *very* careful what you do with it.

There are only two different procedures to manipulate the registry or an `.ini` file, though one of these is available both in statement and function form:

Procedure:	What It Does:
`GetPrivateProfileString$()`	Returns a value from the registry or an `.ini` file.
`SetPrivateProfileString` `SetPrivateProfileString()`	Sets a value in the registry or an `.ini` file. The function form returns **True** if it was successful.

To set a value, you must specify the full path, or name, of the section you want, the name of the key that refers to that item, the new value for the item, and the name of the file that contains the settings. If the settings are in a file `Wrox.ini`, and you want to set the value of the `ListSize` key in the `Options` section to `10`, you can use either of these statements:

```
SetPrivateProfileString "Options", "ListSize", "10", "C:\WORD\WROX.INI"
SetPrivateProfileString("Options", "ListSize", "10", "C:\WORD\WROX.INI")
```

The second version returns **True** or **False** depending on whether the setting was made. If the file is read-only, for example, your code may fail to set the new value. If the file, section or key you specify doesn't exist, they're created automatically. The file can be opened in a text editor to view the contents.

```
[Options]
ListSize=10
```

To retrieve this setting, you use the `GetPrivateProfileString$()` function:

```
My$ = GetPrivateProfileString("Options", "ListSize", "C:\WORD\WROX.INI")
MyValue = Val(My$)
```

This sets `My$` to the value of the `ListSize` key in the `Options` section of `Wrox.ini`. Notice that you have to store numbers as their string representation, and convert them back to numbers afterwards using the `Val()` function.

To store and retrieve values in the registry, you omit the name of the file, i.e. the last argument. Each registry entry has its own path, and the path to the options for Word is `HKEY_CURRENT_USER\Software\Microsoft\Word\7.0\Options`. So, to retrieve the settings for the current `\Startup` folder you would use:

```
Path$ = "HKEY_CURRENT_USER\Software\Microsoft\Word\7.0\Options"
StartupFolder$ = GetPrivateProfileString(Path$, "STARTUP-PATH", "")
```

Microsoft recommend you only use the registry to retrieve settings, such as the current Word options. If you want to store settings for your own use, you should use a separate **.ini** file to avoid any danger of corrupting the registry or overwriting existing settings. If you do decide to use the registry to store your own information, Microsoft recommend you create a key of the form:

HKEY_CURRENT_USER\Software\<Company_Name>\<Product>\<Settings>

You can view the contents of the registry by running the program **REGEDIT.EXE**. Select Run... from Windows Start menu, enter **regedit.exe** and click OK. Registry Editor opens, showing a list of the top-level keys. Click on the plus sign to open the branch for **HKEY_CURRENT_USER**, then on the entries for Software, Microsoft, Word, 7.0 and Options. The full path to the selected key is shown in the status bar, though you don't need to include My Computer in the paths you specify.

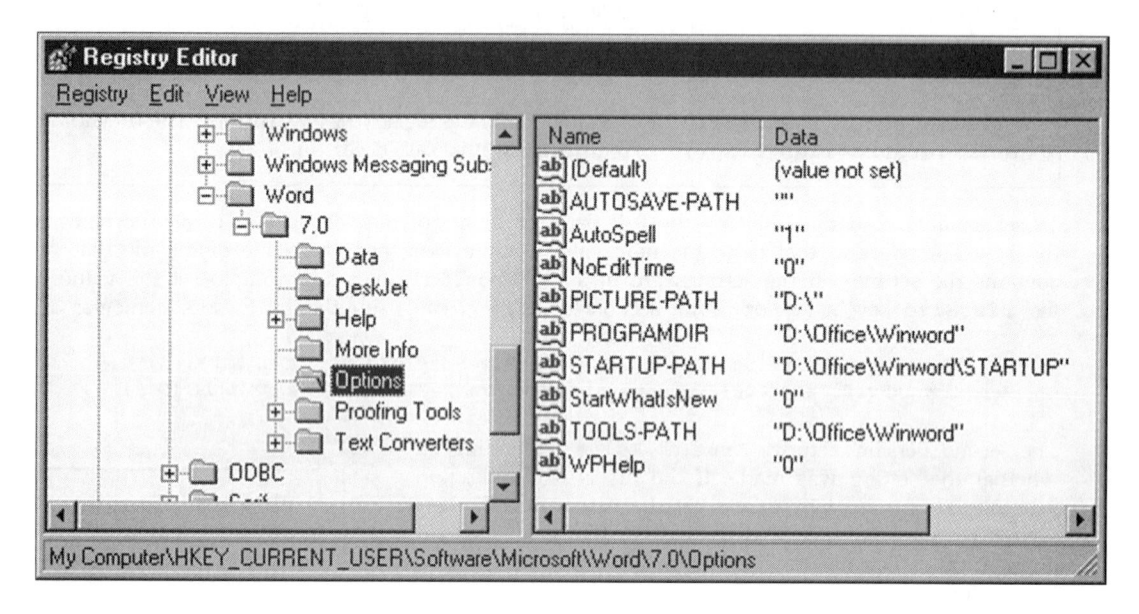

Using Document Properties

Manipulating document properties in WordBasic is a little more complicated than the other ways of storing values that we've seen. Because you can create your own custom document properties, there are functions which tell you what type of entry you're dealing with: they can be numbers, strings, dates or yes/no values. Remember that some properties, such as the number of pages, are also read-only.

On top of this, you can create a custom property and link it to a value in your document, so that it's automatically updated. This involves the use of fields which we'll meet in Part 2. We won't be doing a lot with document properties in this book, but here's a list of the functions that you can use:

Document Property Procedure:	What It Does:
`CountDocumentProperties()`	Returns the number of properties.
`DocumentPropertyName$()`	Returns the name of a property.
`DocumentPropertyType()`	Returns the type of a property.
`GetDocumentProperty()`	Retrieves a non-string property value.
`GetDocumentProperty$()`	Retrieves a string-type property value.
`DocumentPropertyExists()`	Checks if a named property exists.
`IsCustomDocumentProperty()`	Checks if a property is a custom one.
`IsDocumentPropertyReadOnly()`	Checks if a property is read-only.
`SetDocumentProperty`	Sets the value of a property.
`SetDocumentPropertyLink`	Sets the property link to a bookmark.
`DeleteDocumentProperty`	Deletes an existing property.

Making Macros Available to Your Users

Towards the end of Chapter 1, we showed you how a macro can be attached to a toolbar button when you record the macro. However, this isn't your only option; Word lets you attach macros to a toolbar button, a key combination (such as *Ctrl-Q*), or place them in a menu. We can do all of these things with our macros, whether we record them or create them from scratch. In this section, we'll take you through the process of adding the `ListFonts` macro that we saw earlier to Word's interface. You'll need the sample UsefulBits template we've supplied.

Setting a Key Combination for a Macro

Word contains many keyboard shortcuts which allow you to execute the various operations of Word without using the mouse. For example, pressing *Ctrl-B* toggles selected text to bold and back, and is equivalent to clicking the Bold button on the Formatting toolbar. We can add key combinations to run our macros in the same way.

Try It Out - Setting Up the ListFonts Key Combination

We'll customize Word's interface, so that pressing *Ctrl-Alt-L* starts the `ListFonts` macro running. This saves you having to open the Macro dialog and select it each time you want to use it. You'll need the sample UsefulBits template from your `C:\BegWord` folder, or wherever you installed the samples that accompany this book.

1 Open the sample UsefulBits template and select Customize... from the Tools menu. The Customize window opens. Click the KeyBoard tab in the dialog and make sure that the Save Changes In: option at the bottom right of the dialog is set to Usefulbits.dot. This is where the changes we make will be stored.

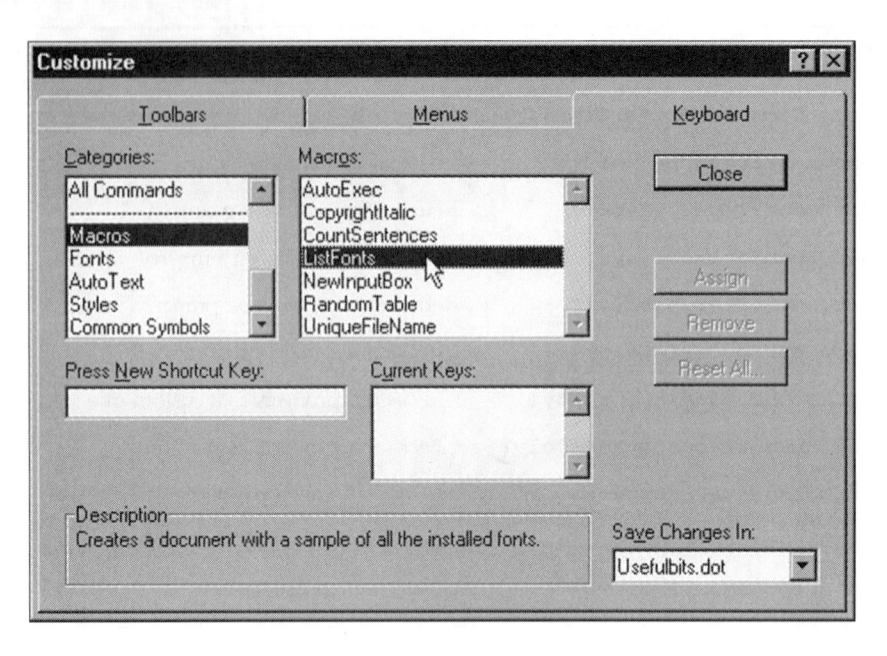

2 In the left-hand list of Categories, scroll down to near the bottom and select Macros. In the middle window, select our ListFonts macro.

3 Click in the Press New Shortcut Key: box and press *Ctrl-Alt-L*. You'll see it appear in the box, and underneath a description of any function that already uses that key. In our case, it's currently unassigned to any other function of Word.

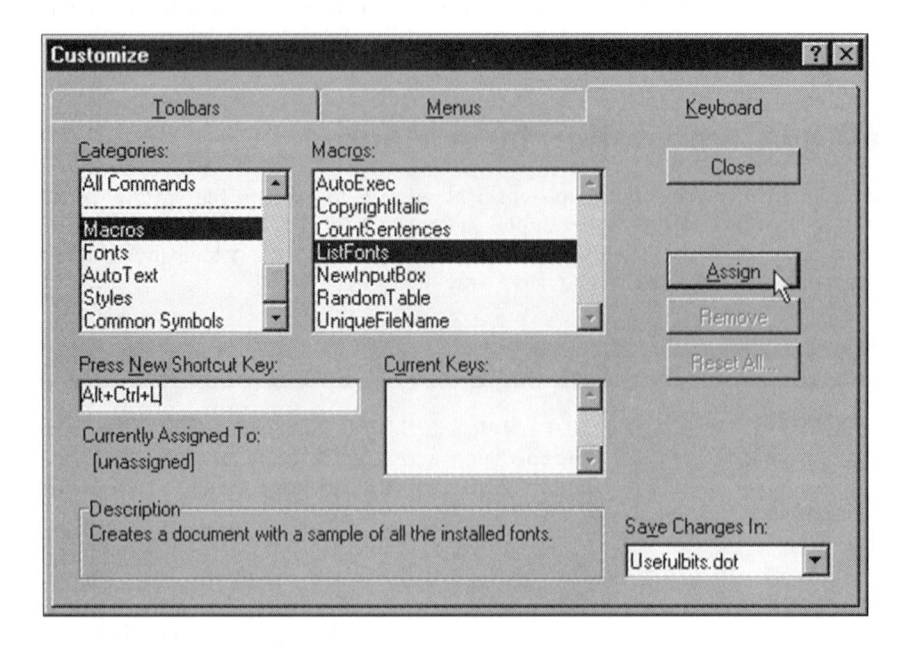

4 Click the Assign button to set the new shortcut key, then click Close. Back in the template's document window, press *Ctrl-Alt-L* to start the `ListFonts` macro.

Adding Macros to Your Toolbars

Shortcut keys are OK, but you have to remember what they are. The ones you use regularly, such as *Ctrl-B* for bold, are no problem, but for functions that you don't use so often, a toolbar button is your best bet. Because it has a ToolTip which tells you what it does when you hold the mouse-pointer over it for a few seconds, you can always find it in the future—long after you've forgotten the key combination that starts it.

Try It Out - Creating a Toolbar Button for the ListFonts Macro

We'll add a toolbar button which starts our `ListFonts` macro to one of Word's existing toolbars. We'll also show you how you can create a new toolbar for your macros if you wish.

1 With the UsefulBits template open, select Customize... from the Tools menu and click the Toolbars tab. Make sure the Save Changes In: option at the bottom right of the dialog is set to Usefulbits.dot. Scroll to the bottom of the Categories: list and select Macro, then, in the middle window, click on ListFonts and drag it onto an existing toolbar. You'll see it appear as a gray square.

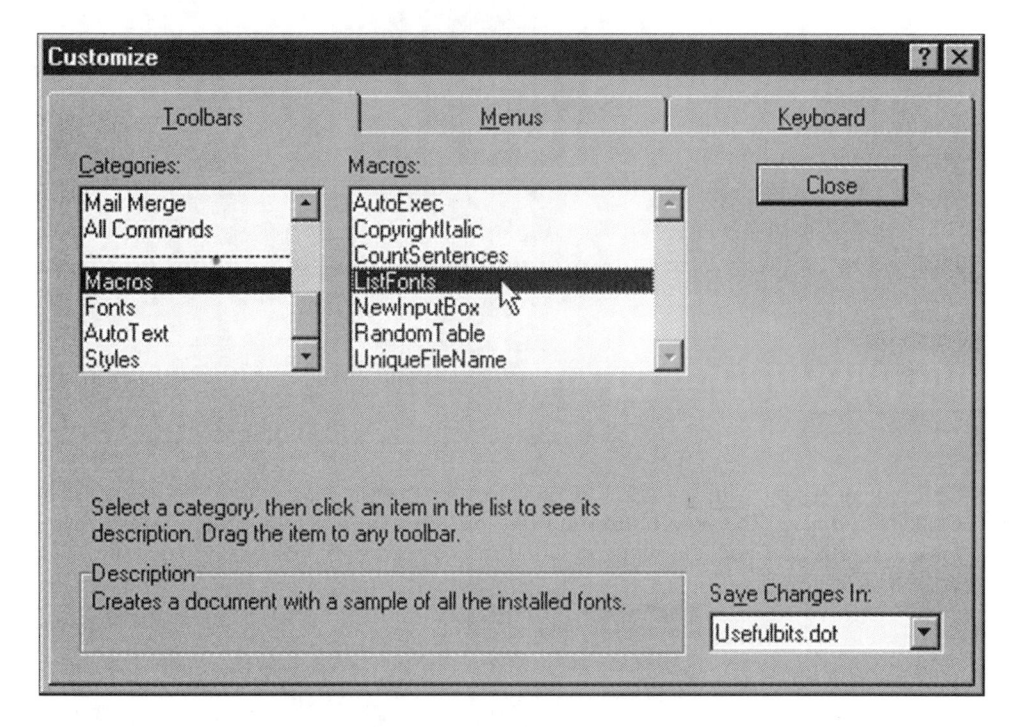

2 Drop it between the drop-down selector lists for the font and size, on the formatting toolbar. As soon as you let go of the mouse button, the Custom Button window opens. Select a picture for the button.

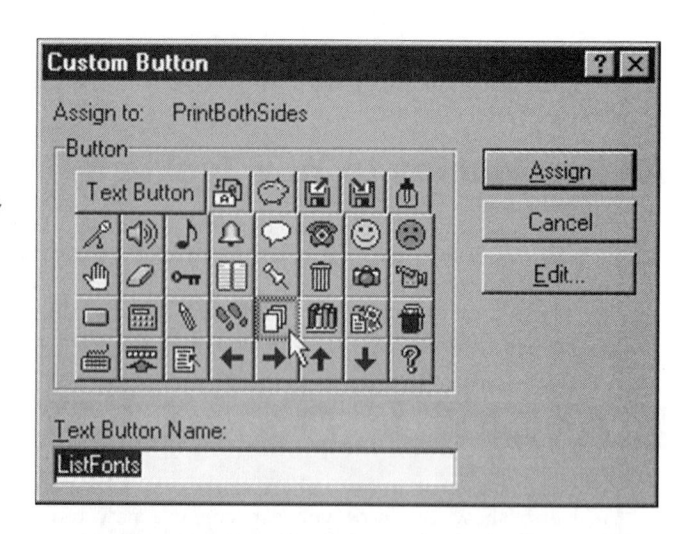

3 None of them are particularly suitable, but it doesn't matter. Click the Edit button and you can design your own button face.

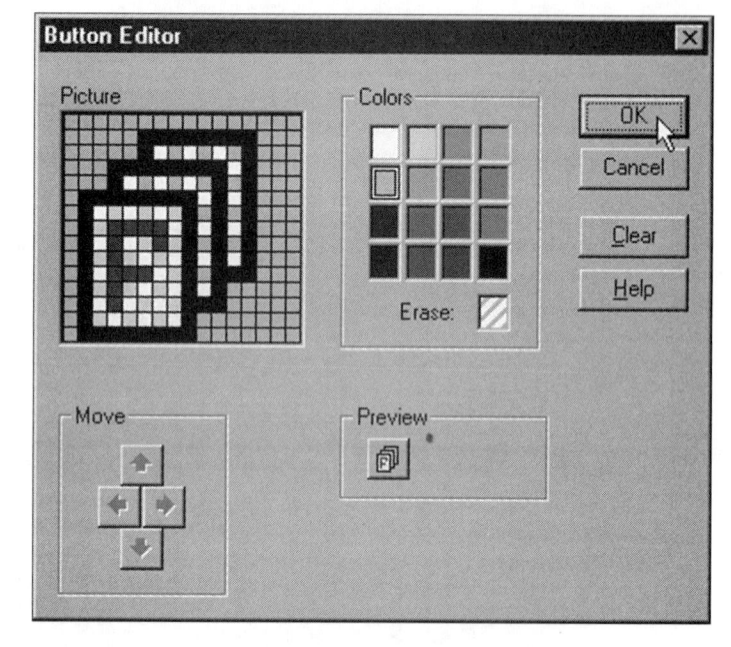

4 Once you're happy with it, click OK to close the Button Editor, then OK again to close the Customize dialog. The new button appears on the toolbar. Hold your mouse-pointer over it for a few seconds; and the name of our macro appears. It looks quite at home in the Word interface.

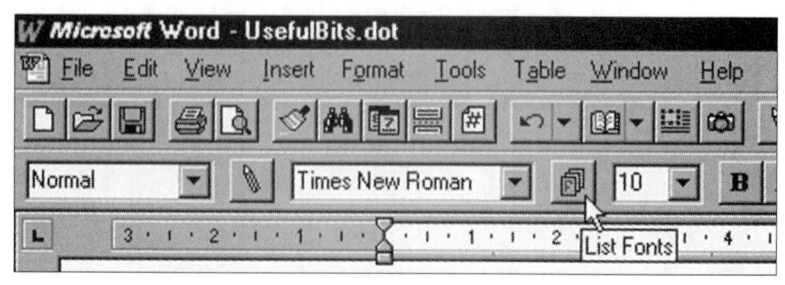

> **FYI** You can always change the position and layout of the buttons on the toolbar by opening the **Toolbars** tab of the **Customize** dialog again and dragging buttons around. To make a space between them, drag the one on the right a little towards the right. To remove a button, drag it off the toolbar altogether.

To create a new toolbar, select <u>T</u>oolbars... from the <u>V</u>iew menu to open the Toolbars dialog and click the <u>N</u>ew... button. Word prompts you for the name of the new toolbar, and the context where it will be available. Here, we're only making it available in documents that are based on our UsefulBits template.

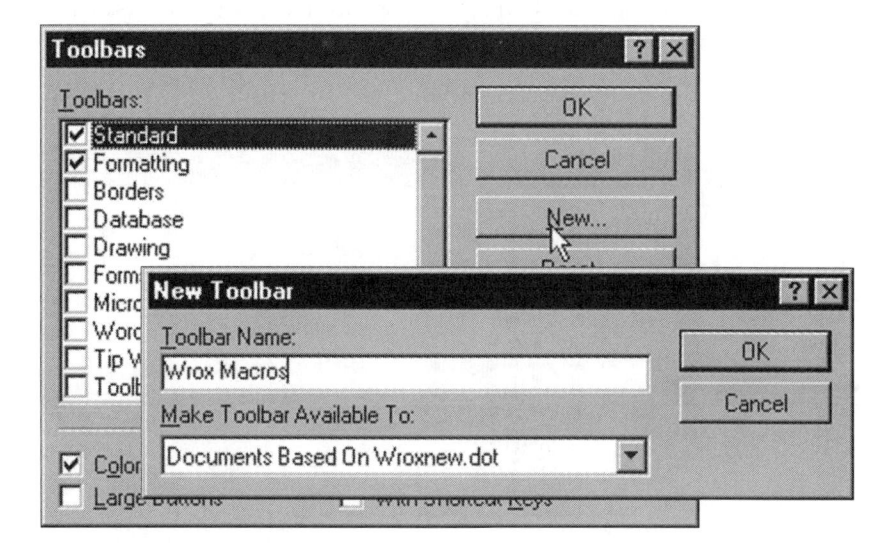

The new toolbar is created, and you can drag buttons onto it in the usual way. It behaves just like a standard Word toolbar: you can show or hide it with the Toolbars dialog and dock it at the edge of your screen.

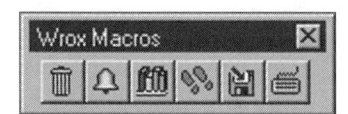

Adding Macros to Your Menus

Even toolbars can become confusing if they contain too many buttons, and, as the buttons are so small, it's not always immediately obvious what each one does. One of the best ways to add your macros to Word's interface is to use the standard menus that Word includes. We'll add our **ListFonts** macro to the Format menu.

Try It Out - Adding the ListFonts Macro to the Format Menu

This example assumes you've completed the previous two Try It Outs. If you haven't, you won't see the shortcut key combination appear on the menu when you carry out this example.

1 With the UsefulBits template open, select Customize... from the Tools menu and click the Menus tab. Make sure the Save Changes In: option at the bottom right of the dialog is set to Usefulbits.dot. Scroll to the bottom of the Categories: list and select Macros, then, in the middle window, select ListFonts.

2 Below the two list boxes are boxes where you specify the menu and position where your new entry will appear. Select the F&ormat menu in the top one, and (At Top) from the second one. Add a space to the macro name. Word has already suggested L as the hot-key which will suit us fine, as it's not already used on this menu.

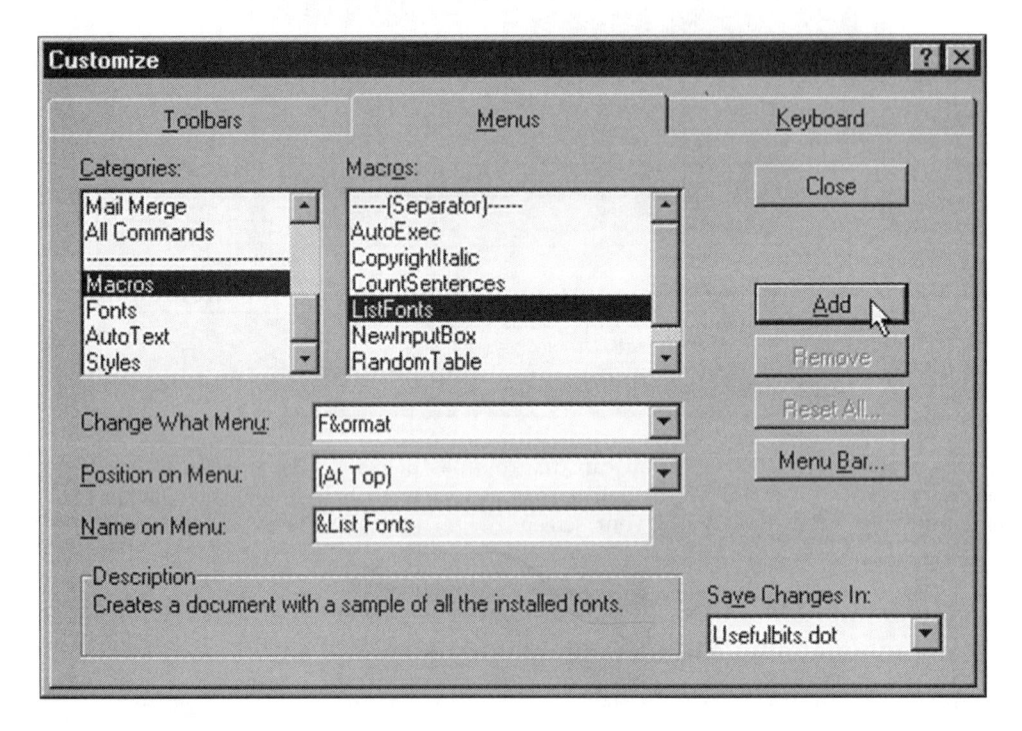

3 Click the Add button, then, in the middle list, select the (Separator) entry and change the Position On Menu: setting to our new List Fonts entry. Word will add a separator bar below the entry selected here.

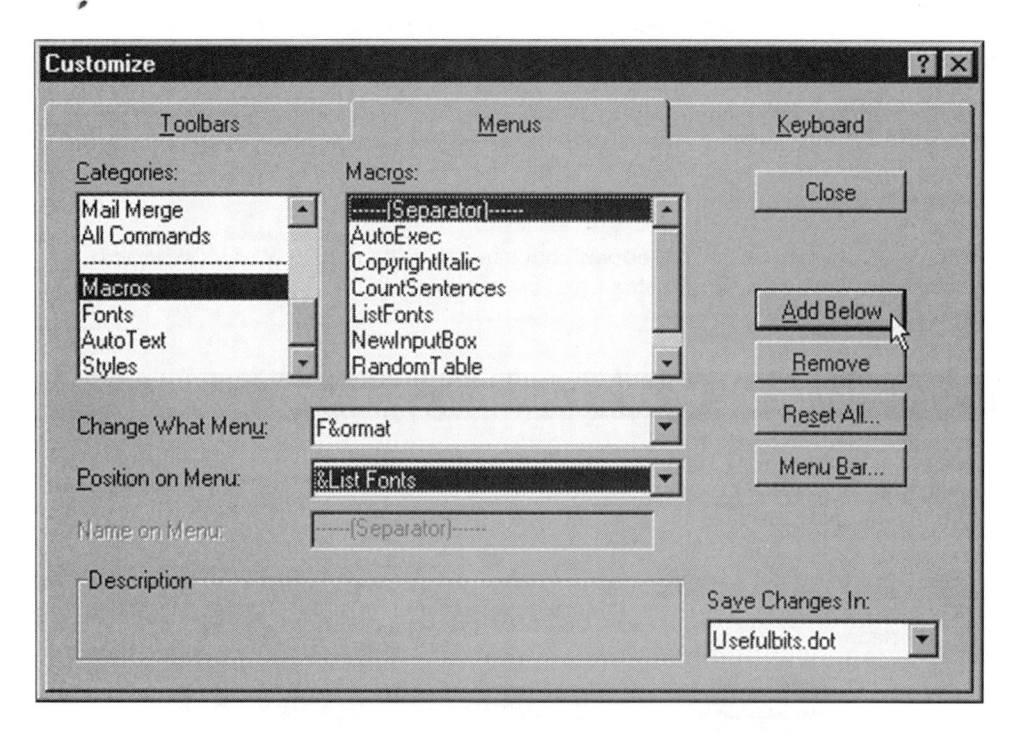

4   Click the Add Below button, then Close to close the Customize dialog.

5   Open the Format menu. It contains our new command and you'll see that Word has also added the shortcut key combination we created earlier. If you select it, our **ListFonts** macro will run.

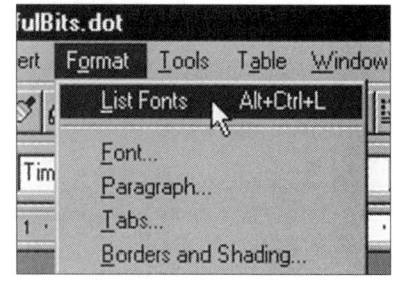

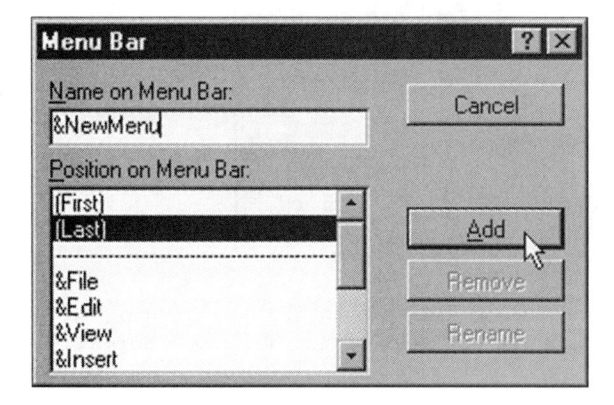

You can also add new 'top level' menus to Word. In the Customize dialog, click the Menu Bar button and enter the name for the new top-level menu. You can position it anywhere in the menu bar. Here, we're placing at the end, after the Help menu.

Once you've created the new top-level menu, you use the Customize dialog to add items to it, just as we did with the Format menu earlier.

175

Replacing Word Commands

As well as adding new commands to Word's interface, we can actually modify the existing ones. For example, if you regularly use a particular type of document that doesn't have the file extension **.doc**, it can be annoying to always have to change the Files of type: entry in the Open dialog every time you want to open that kind of file.

Instead, you can replace the **FileOpen** command with your own WordBasic macro, which will run whenever you select Open... from the File menu, click the Open button on the toolbar, or press Ctrl-O.

Try It Out - Replacing Word's FileOpen Command

To replace a built-in Word command, we just create a macro with the same name as the command, in this case **FileOpen**. We want the Open dialog to have our new file type **.txt**, as well as the normal **.doc**, as the Files of type: setting.

1 Select Macro... from the Tools menu. Change the Macros Available In: to Word Commands and select FileOpen. You'll see that the create button is disabled whenever Word Commands is selected.

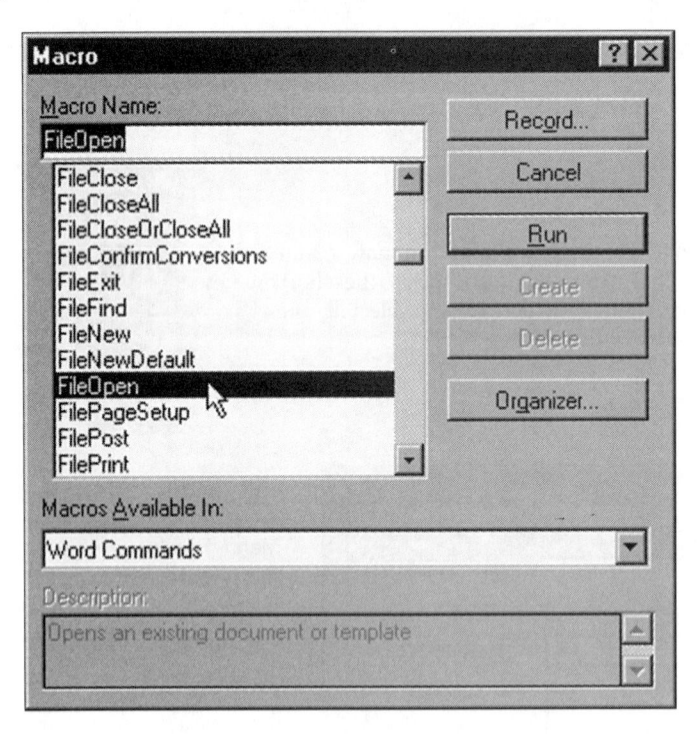

2 Change the Macros Available In: to Normal.dot. Because we want the new command to be available when no document is open, this is the best place to store it because **Normal.dot** is always loaded. (We could, of course, store it in a global template instead.) Now the Create button is available. Word has even filled in a description for us.

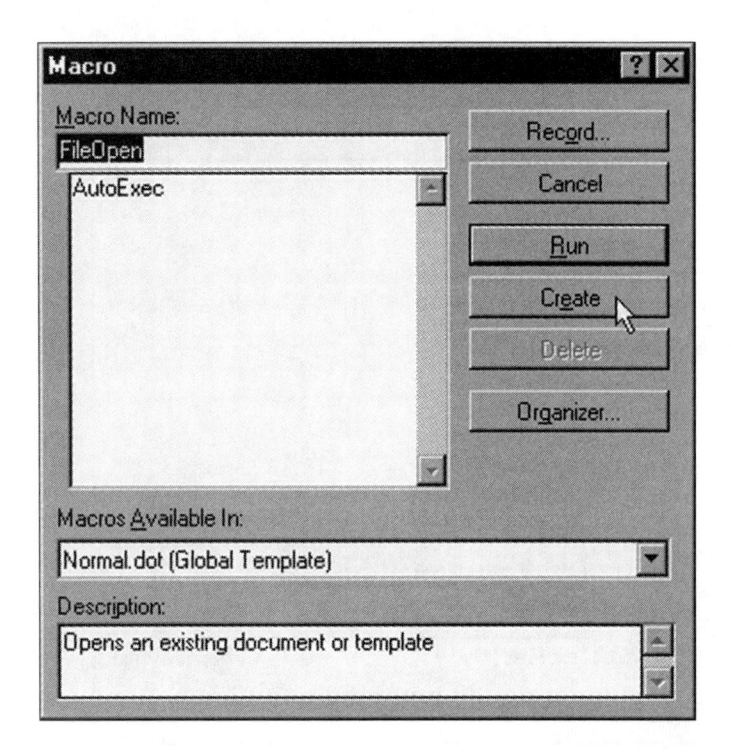

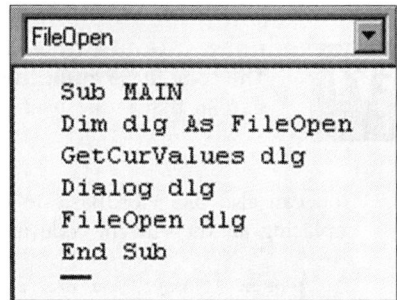

3 Click Create, and the macro editing window opens. Word has filled in statements which mimic the actions of the **FileOpen** command.

```
FileOpen
Sub MAIN
    Dim dlg As FileOpen
    GetCurValues dlg
    Dialog dlg
    FileOpen dlg
End Sub
```

4 The current code declares a dialog record for the **FileOpen** dialog and fills it with the current values, which include the current folder. However, the file name will be empty. We need to set this so that our new file type is shown. Add the line that is highlighted below to the macro:

```
Sub MAIN
    Dim dlg As FileOpen
    GetCurValues dlg
    dlg.Name = "*.doc; *.txt"
    Dialog dlg
    FileOpen dlg
End Sub
```

5 To try the macro, select Open... from the File menu, click the Open toolbar button, or press Ctrl-O. In all cases, the new version of the Open dialog appears, showing our **.txt** files as well as the standard **.doc** files.

177

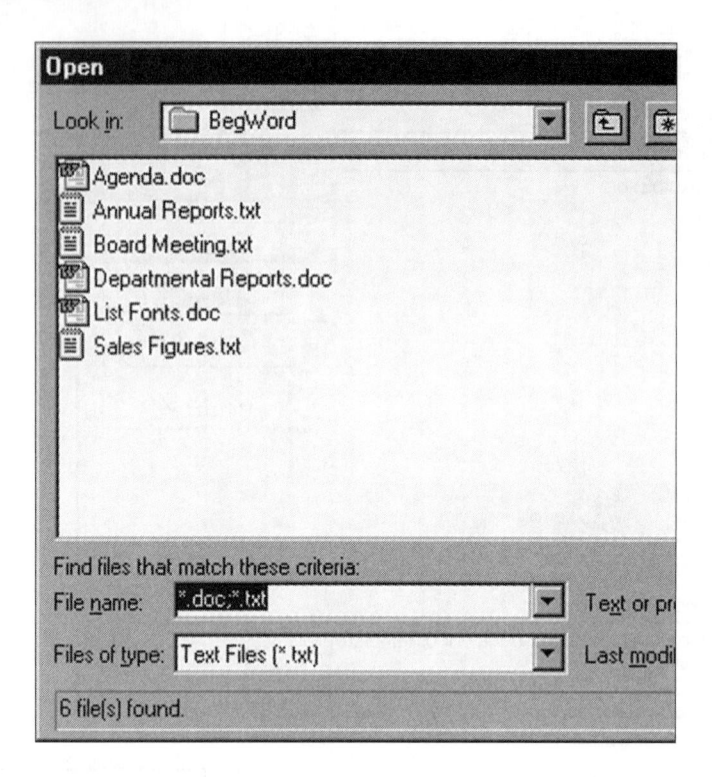

> **FYI** The code that Word generated for us isn't ideal. We could improve it by adding an error trap so that if the user presses the **Cancel** button, they don't get an error message.

You can also use WordBasic to completely change what a Word command does. For example, replacing all the current code in the new `FileOpen` macro with just the statement,

```
MsgBox "Sorry, you can't open any documents"
```

will prevent the `FileOpen` command being used at all—though whether you think that's a good idea is debatable. It could reduce your productivity!

Executing the Original Command

OK, so you've created the new `FileOpen` macro in your Normal template. But what happens if you just want the normal `.doc` files to be displayed in the Open dialog when another type of document is open?

You can restore the original command by creating a `FileOpen` macro in the template for the other document, which simply carries out the default actions of the `FileOpen` command. If this is the active template when the `FileOpen` command is selected, the second version of the macro will be run. You can have several `FileOpen` macros, as long as each is in a different template.

Remember that Word searches for a macro first in the active template, then in your Normal template and, finally, in any loaded 'global' templates. It's only if none of these contain a `FileOpen` macro that the original Word command will be executed.

Macros that Run Automatically

There are often occasions when you would like a particular macro to run automatically, for instance when a user opens or closes a document. If you give a macro a specific name, Word will run it for you whenever the relevant event occurs. There are five special names you can use:

`AutoExec`	Runs when you first start Word.
`AutoNew`	Runs each time you create a new document.
`AutoOpen`	Runs each time you open an existing document.
`AutoClose`	Runs each time you close a document.
`AutoExit`	Runs when you exit from Word.

So, it's as easy as creating a new macro and giving it the correct name. As an example of how useful these can be, consider the possibilities:

- You can use an `AutoExec` macro to load templates globally, prompt the user for a particular document, or just load and start a Word application, like the Book Order application we saw in Chapter 1. `AutoExec` only runs if it's in your Normal template or a globally loaded template.

- You can use an `AutoNew` macro to calculate a unique invoice or reference number for a new document using an AutoText entry in the template. You'll see how easy this is in Part 2.

- You can use an `AutoOpen` macro to modify the Word interface when particular technical reference documents are opened. It could add a toolbar with special buttons for managing the document, and remove others to control changes the user can make to the document.

- You can use an `AutoClose` macro to clean up any changes you've made to Word's interface, or the Normal and Add-in templates, when a document is closed.

- You can use an `AutoExit` macro to make sure files are backed up, by copying them to another drive or automatically starting a back-up program.

These are only some of the possibilities, and you'll find that others suggest themselves regularly as you continue to develop in WordBasic.

The Order of Execution of Auto Macros

Because the Normal template is always loaded, and is loaded first as soon as Word starts, it's `AutoExec` macro will always execute first. This is followed by any `AutoExec` macros in global templates. Once Word is running, execution order follows the normal hierarchy: the active template first, followed by the Normal template, then any globally loaded templates.

The default document that Word creates from the Normal template doesn't execute an `AutoNew` macro, but globally loaded templates do, so you can use this to carry out any initialization required.

Running a Macro as Word Starts

When you start Word, you can specify a particular macro that you want to run, not necessarily `AutoExec` or `AutoNew`. Adding `/m` plus the name of a macro to the end of the command line that starts Word will run that macro automatically and prevent the `AutoExec` macro running.

From Windows Start menu, select Settings, then TaskBar. In the Taskbar Properties dialog, select the Start Menu Programs tab and click the Advanced button. In the window that appears, open the directories in the left-hand pane until you find the shortcut to Microsoft Word.

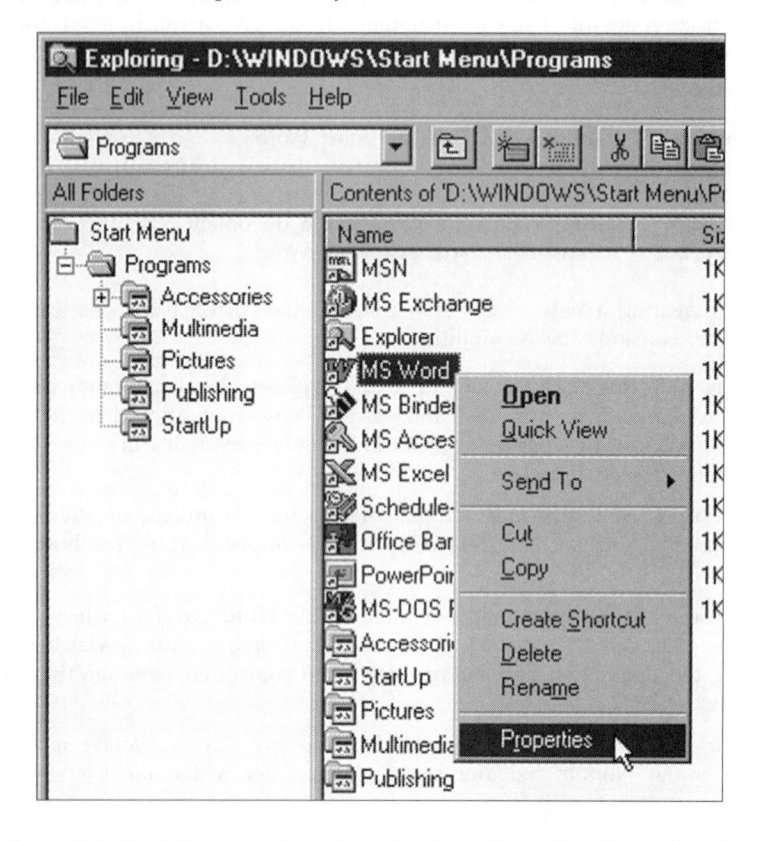

Click on it, then click the left mouse button and select Properties from the shortcut menu. In the Shortcut tab of the MS Word Properties window, add the command switch you want to the Target: box.

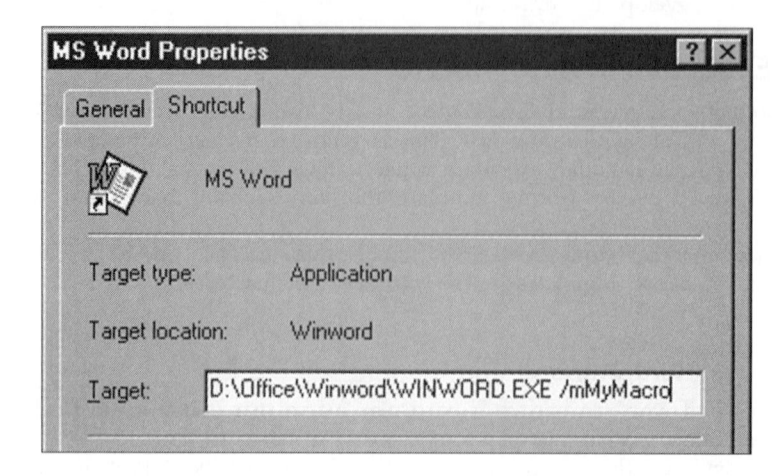

There are other command switches you can use.

/l*addinpath*	Loads the Word template or add-in globally. You must specify the full path to it. Equivalent to placing the template or add-in in your **\Startup** folder.
/t*templatename*	Creates a new document based on the specified template.
/a	Prevents add-ins and global templates, including the Normal template, from loading automatically and prevents the Windows' registry from being read and modified.
/n	Starts Word with no documents. Just the File and Help menus are shown.

Controlling Auto Macro Execution

However, there's one downside to all this. The auto macros can be used to run macros in the background, so that you don't see what's happening. WordBasic contains procedures that can damage the data on your system if they're used maliciously, and there have already been reports of this occurring. The increasing power of application programming languages, such as WordBasic and Visual Basic, makes the threat of document viruses more real.

Word contains a statement which will switch auto macros off and back on again. If you omit the argument, then *off* is assumed:

```
DisableAutoMacros          'prevent all auto-macros running
DisableAutoMacros 1        'prevent all auto-macros running
DisableAutoMacros 0        'Allow automacros to run normally
```

Remember that the **AutoExec** macro in the Normal template is always executed first, irrespective of how you start Word. So, by adding the **DisableAutoMacros** statement to it, we prevent any other auto macro from being executed automatically:.

```
Sub MAIN                       'AutoExec macro in Normal template
    DisableAutoMacros
    Print "Turned Off Auto Macros"
End Sub
```

However, this prevents any applications that require auto macros from working properly. For example, our Book Order application doesn't start running if you have this macro in your Normal template. In later chapters, we'll be looking at how you can overcome this problem.

Summary

In this chapter, we've looked broadly at how you use WordBasic to manipulate the contents of your documents, in fact we spent most of the chapter on this subject. We showed you how to move around in a document and select text and other objects. We also saw how you insert, delete, and format text, and work with tables. We also looked at searching and replacing, and how bookmarks are used in WordBasic.

As well as manipulating text in a document you've also seen other ways that Word can store information. We used document variables and properties, AutoText entries, and saw how to work with settings files and the Windows' registry.

We finished off looking at how you make your macros available to your users, on toolbars, menus and with shortcut keys. We also investigated how auto macros are used, and saw some of the problems they can bring.

With this chapter, we've come to the end of Part 1, so, by now, you should be fairly familiar with what WordBasic can do, and how we use it. There are hundreds of different statements and procedures available in WordBasic, and as many different ways of using them. But don't worry, if you feel comfortable with what we've covered in these four chapters, you are well on your way to mastering WordBasic.

So where do we go next? Well, it's time we looked in more depth at how WordBasic can be used in particular environments. So far we've only picked up the basics, but, in the rest of the book, you'll be learning new techniques and applying these to more complex and useful tasks.

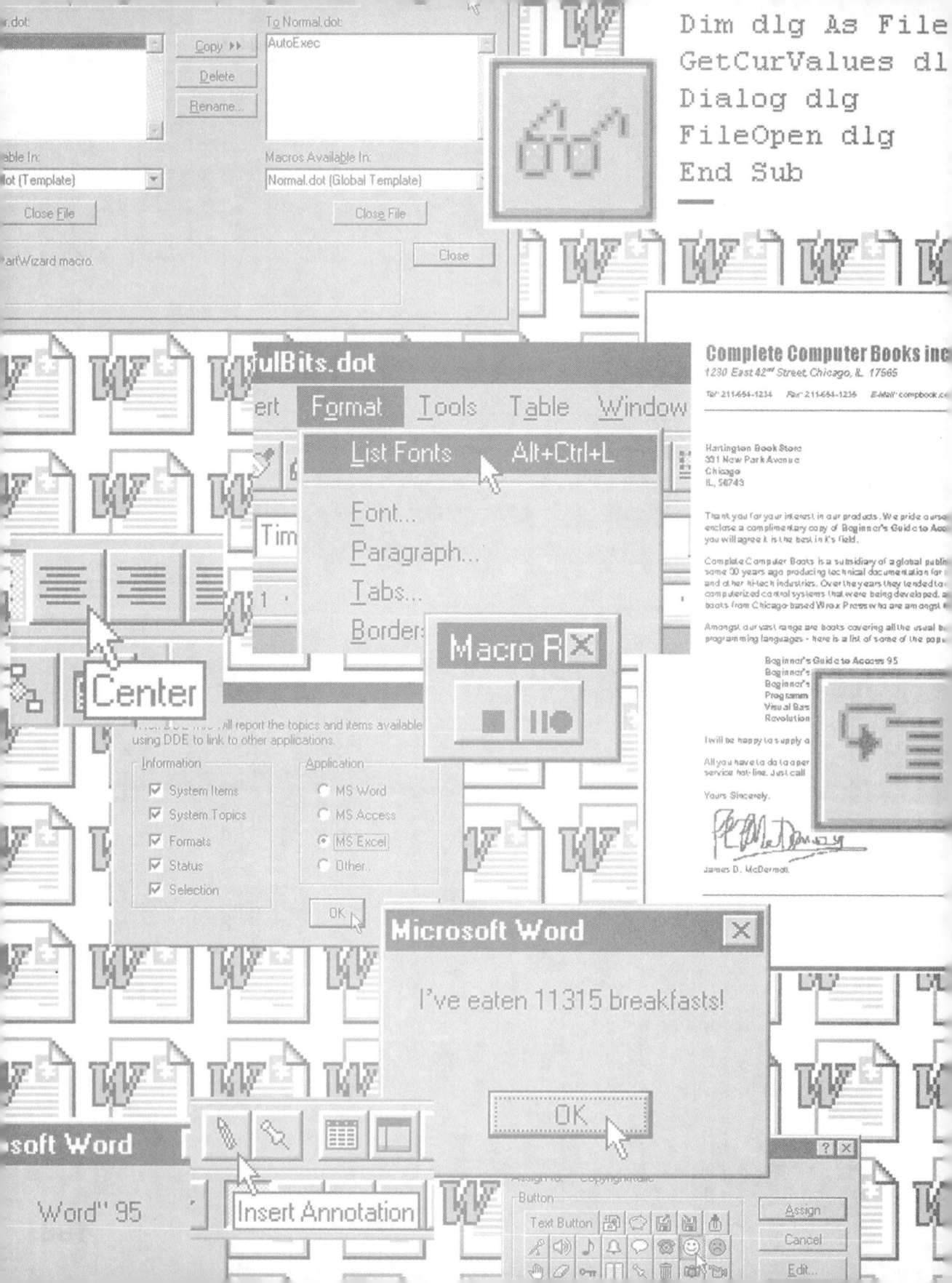

```
Dim dlg As File
GetCurValues dl
Dialog dlg
FileOpen dlg
End Sub
```

Part 2

Word in the Workplace

In Part 1 we walked through the fundamentals of WordBasic, examining the different ways it can be used to build procedures that will make you more productive in your everyday activities. We also looked at how WordBasic could be used to build a Word application - as a tool for a single highly-focused task. By now you should be comfortable with how simple WordBasic routines are created, and how you can put them to use in your own working environment.

You'll notice a difference in style in Parts 2 and 3. Starting from here, we won't be trying to give you a broad understanding of a whole range of different topics in one chapter. Instead, we'll be concentrating directly on focused sets of techniques which are aimed at particular activities or environments. In this part of the book we'll be examining ways that you can use Word in your workplace, and you may be surprised to see just how versatile Word actually is. We'll be looking at:

- Building your own wizards and add-in utilities
- Ways that Word can improve productivity in publishing environments
- Using Word's form capabilities to collect and process information
- Producing Windows 95 Help files in Word, and using Help Compiler

So read on, and let us widen your horizons by seeing some applications of Word that are really nothing to do with word-processing.

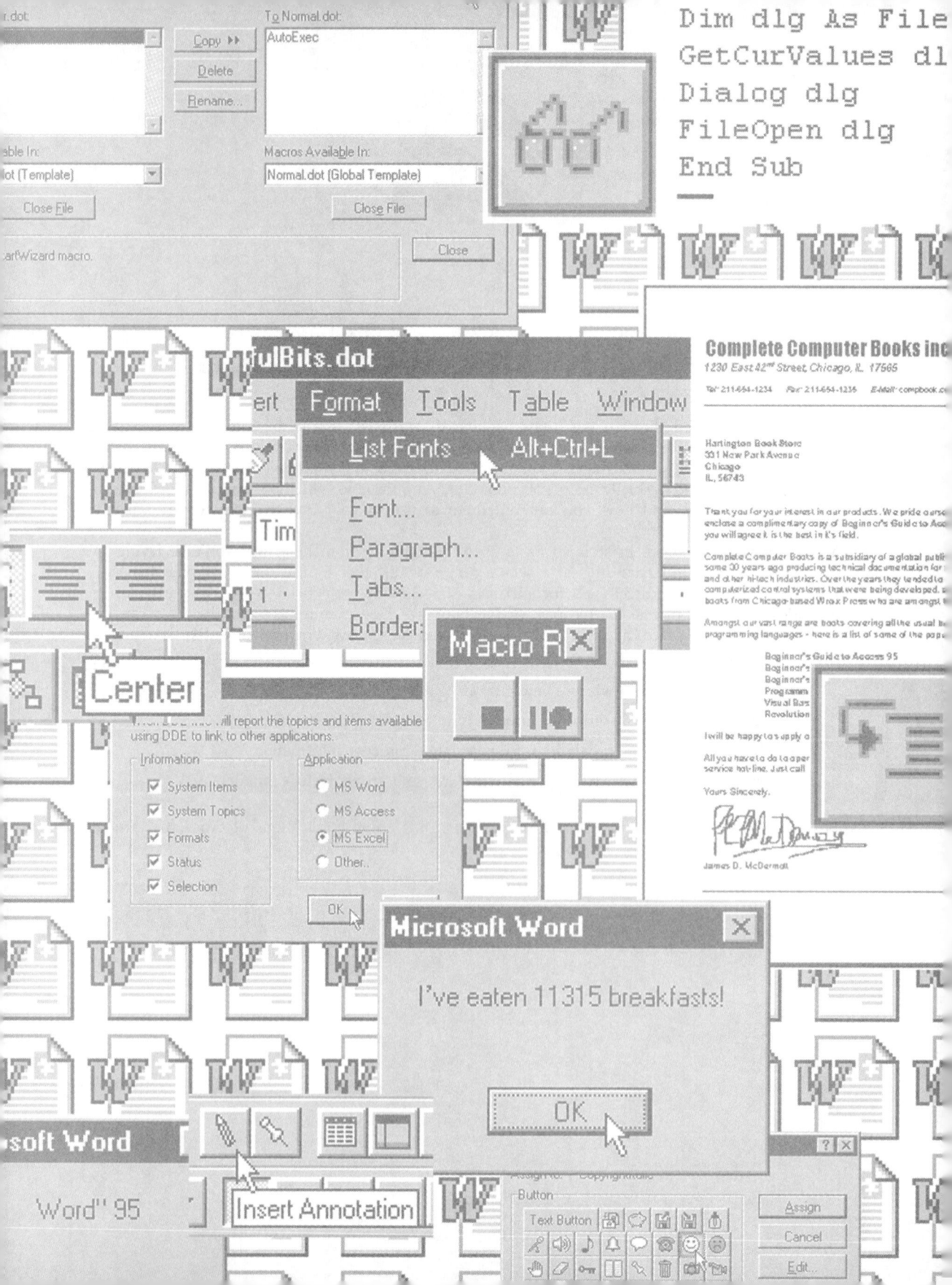

```
Dim dlg As File
GetCurValues dl
Dialog dlg
FileOpen dlg
End Sub
```

5

Wizards and Add-in Utilities

Introduction

Right at the start of Chapter 1, we asked the question, "What is a Word application?" In light of what we've learned in Part 1, let's see if that question makes any more sense. We said that an application is a way of utilizing Word for a single, highly focused task. In fact, the sample **Book Order** application that you used in Chapter 1 is so focused that when you start it, it goes straight into the process of collecting the information it needs for the letter. Once it has printed the letter, you end up back at the Windows desktop.

Compare this with the **QuickFormat** utility we saw. Until you open the F**o**rmat menu and see the entry for **QuickFormat**, you probably won't be aware it's there at all. It's only used as an extra function within Word, to help you format your text more quickly.

Despite this big difference in how they operate, both of these are created with the same building blocks. Both are dynamic dialogs supported by WordBasic code that carries out the tasks you select. The big difference is the approach taken during their design. In this chapter, we'll take a detailed look at how the **Book Order** application is put together and introduce you to another one of the sample files which is designed as a utility rather than an application. Along the way, you'll see how to use more advanced code techniques, and we'll examine how you can use other procedures that aren't actually part of Word, but exist within Windows 95 itself.

We'll be looking at:

- How to create a wizard-type application
- How to use WordBasic to produce add-in utilities
- How to add extra functionality using operating system procedures

We'll see some other uses of dynamic dialogs which should suggest to you not only how versatile they can be, but also give you some ideas about the ones you should be building now to solve your own particular workplace problems. So, first, let's go back to the **Book Order** application. If you're ready, we're off to meet the Wizard ...

Creating WordBasic Wizards

This part of the chapter is predominantly about a particular type of WordBasic application, usually referred to as a **wizard**. We'll look at the basics of creating them, then see more of how the sample Book Order application works.

What is a Wizard?

As applications have become more powerful and more complicated, software companies have discovered that users often don't benefit from these extra features because they just can't find the time to learn about them. In an attempt to make their applications easier to use, they regularly include **wizards**, which guide you through each step of the process, gathering all the information they need to carry out the task.

One example of a Word wizard is Table Wizard, which allows you create a formatted table in a document. Many of these wizards are written in WordBasic, but you can quite easily create your own.

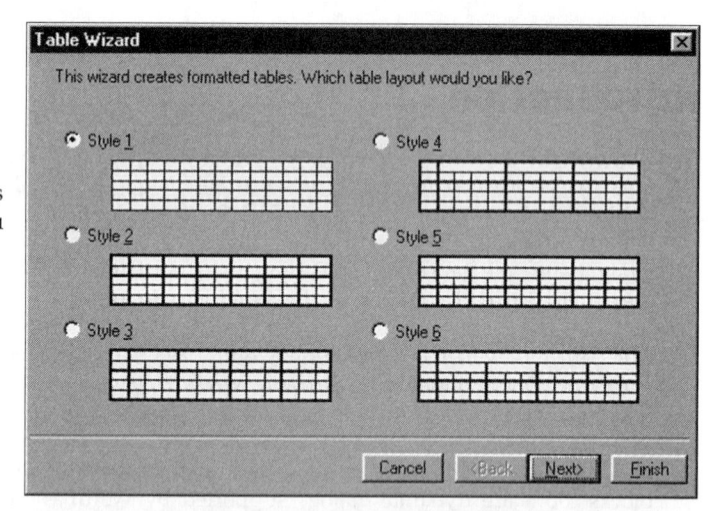

Of course, the Book Order application that we used in Chapter 1 is quite obviously also a wizard. The terminology here is flexible: we've called our Book Order template an *application* because it carries out the complete task of creating a document, while Table Wizard only helps you carry out a task that is part of a larger document.

A wizard appears to show a series of different windows, each with its own set of controls. Each window is aimed at a particular part of the overall task. For example, in this first window in the **Book Order** application, you tell it whether you want to create an inquiry or order acknowledgment letter, and how you want to send it. Subsequent windows collect the customer's name and address and all the other details the application requires.

This is a very different approach to the other dialogs we've used in Part 1. If you remember, the **QuickFormat** utility has only one set of controls, all in the one single window that you see when you start it:

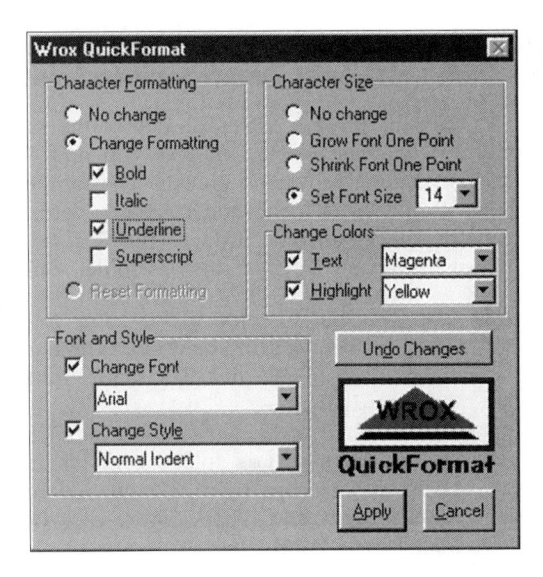

To see how a wizard works, and how you can create your own, we'll take an overall view of the structure, then look at each of the different parts in turn. We'll show you examples from our **Book Order** application and, at the same time, go through the stages of creating a new one.

The Overall Structure of a Wizard

To create a wizard, we use a macro which follows the same form as those we saw in dynamic dialogs, in Part 1. There's the usual **Sub MAIN** which defines the dialog and declares a dialog record based on it. To make the dialog dynamic, we include a dialog function. There is also a set of support procedures that can be called either from the main subroutine or from the dialog function. Because we need to be able to access certain variables from within different procedures, we have to declare these as **Shared** variables.

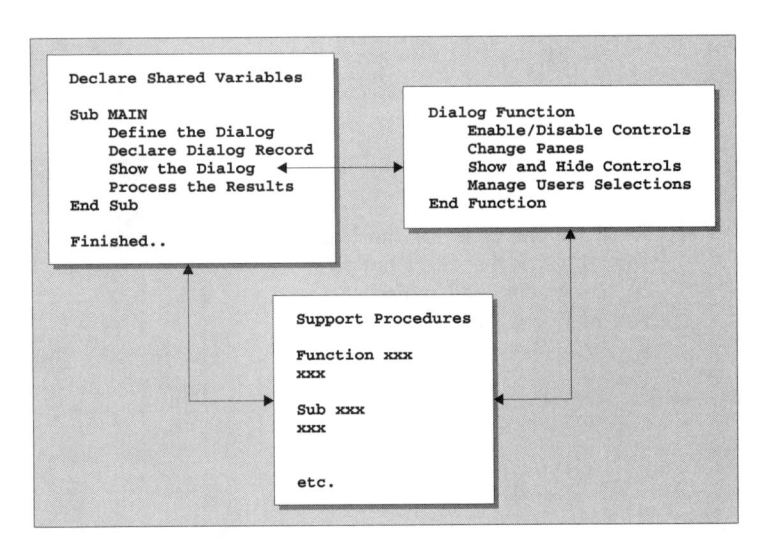

```
Declare Shared Variables

Sub MAIN
    Define the Dialog
    Declare Dialog Record
    Show the Dialog
    Process the Results
End Sub

Finished..
```

```
Dialog Function
    Enable/Disable Controls
    Change Panes
    Show and Hide Controls
    Manage Users Selections
End Function
```

```
Support Procedures

Function xxx
xxx

Sub xxx
xxx

etc.
```

To show you the actual process of creating a wizard, we're going to build one which prints out a list of files from your disk which you select in a variety of ways. This is a fairly simple wizard, designed purely to help you understand how the parts fit together. In the real world, of course, you would probably design and build one that has a lot more going on and that will perform a task far more complex than ours.

Try It Out - Using the Sample Blank Wizard Template

To start the process, we'll use one of the sample files supplied with this book. This is a blank wizard template which can save you time when you start creating any wizard, allowing you to get something on screen quickly. The sample files will be in `C:\BegWord` unless you changed this during installation. You'll need to complete each of the Try It Outs in this section in order because, together, they produce the final wizard. If you just want to see it working, you'll find a finished version in your samples folder, called **FileList.dot**.

1 Copy the file **BlankWiz.dot** from your samples folder to your default **\Templates** folder. This will be **\MSOffice\Templates** or **\Winword\Templates** unless you changed the defaults when you installed Word. You'll find it shown in the File Locations tab of Word's Options dialog.

2 In your **\Templates** folder, click on the copy of **BlankWiz.dot** twice, slowly, and rename it **FileList.dot**. Then, double-click on it to load it into Word.

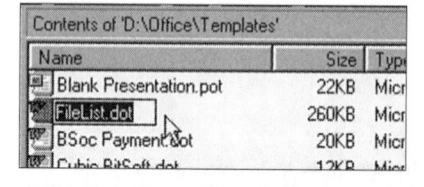

3 Select Macro... from the Tools menu, select the macro called Application and click Edit.

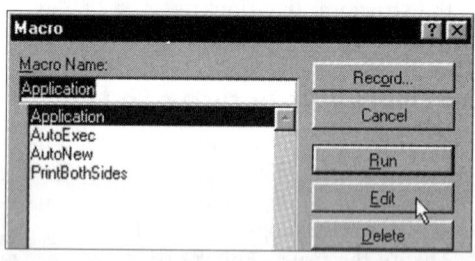

4 You'll see the code for the blank wizard. Click the Start button on the Macro toolbar and the wizard opens up:

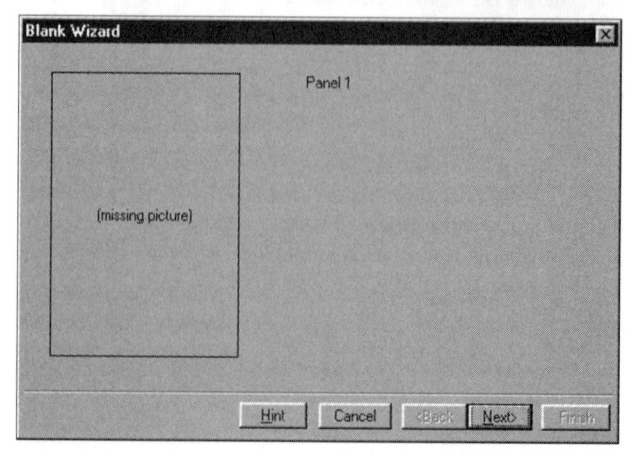

5 Click the <u>N</u>ext button to step through the panels. When you get to the last one, the picture control displays the normal 'Finished' graphic:

How It Works

OK, so it's not exactly an earth-shattering application as it stands, but all the elements are already there for you to create a useful wizard with the minimum of effort. The code looks after displaying the dialog and managing the navigation buttons. All we have to do now is to add the controls we want for each panel and the code that manages them and carries out the tasks required when the user clicks the <u>F</u>inish button.

Have a look through the code in the **Application** macro. It's grouped into three sections, like the diagram you saw earlier. First come the **Shared** variable declarations and the **Sub MAIN** containing the dialog definition. Next is the dialog function and, finally, the support procedures:

```
'---------- Blank Wizard Starter Code ----------------

Dim Shared WizName$
Dim Shared CurrPanel
Dim Shared LastPanel
Dim Shared PanelItems(10)

'---- The Dialog Definition and Sub MAIN --------------

Sub MAIN
On Error Goto WizError

WizName$ = "Blank Wizard"

Info1$ = "Panel 1"
Info2$ = "Panel 2"
Info3$ = "Panel 3"
Info4$ = "Panel 4"

Begin Dialog UserDialog 628, 276, WizName$, .WizFunction
    ...     'the dialog definition is here
End Dialog

REM ScreenUpdating 0
REM DisableInput 1 'Set the Escape Key to Cancel Dialog

Dim dlg As UserDialog

If Dialog(dlg, - 2) Then           'show the dialog, No default button
    'carry out the actions
EndIf

DisableInput 0
ScreenUpdating 1
```

```
        Goto WizExit

    WizError:
        MsgBox "Error starting application - " + Str$(Err), WizName$

    WizExit:
    End Sub


    '------ The Dialog Function ------------------

    Function WizFunction(Ctrl$, Action, SupValue)
        ...     'the dialog function is here
    End Function

    '------ Support Procedures --------------------

    Sub ChangePanel(Old, New)
        ...
    Function NextPanel(ThisPanel)
        ...
    Function PrevPanel(ThisPanel)
        ...
    Sub ItemsInPanel(Count)
        ...
    Sub EnableControls
        ...
    Sub DisplayHint
        ...
    '---------------------------------------------
```

There's nothing unusual in **Sub MAIN**; we simply define the dialog and then show it in the normal way. The four string variables, **Info1$** to **Info4$**, are used to fill the text labels on each panel. Finally, as long as the user clicks the Finish button to close the dialog, rather than the Cancel button which returns zero, we can carry out the actions required for the wizard.

Using Panels of Controls

Although it looks as though a wizard uses several dialog windows, we know this isn't really possible in WordBasic. We can only have one user-defined dialog active at any time, so we would have to keep creating new ones for each window. The process certainly wouldn't be as smooth as the wizards we've seen.

In fact, a wizard is just one single, complex dialog. All the controls for all the panels are in one dialog. To give the impression of several windows, we hide them all, except the ones that we want on that panel. When you click Next or Back, the wizard hides the controls that are currently visible and shows the set for the next (or previous) panel.

One difficulty is creating and managing the multitude of controls in the dialog. It's not easy using Dialog Editor to create a wizard dialog because you have many different controls overlaying each other, so, instead, we take a different approach. We lay out the dialog definition as separate panels so that the controls for each panel are together. Generally, we add the controls for each panel by typing their definition directly into the macro definition, so you need to be able to get your head round **X**, **Y**, **Width** and **Height** values...

```
                Text 25, 100, 275, 18, "Caption Goes Here", .MyCaption
```

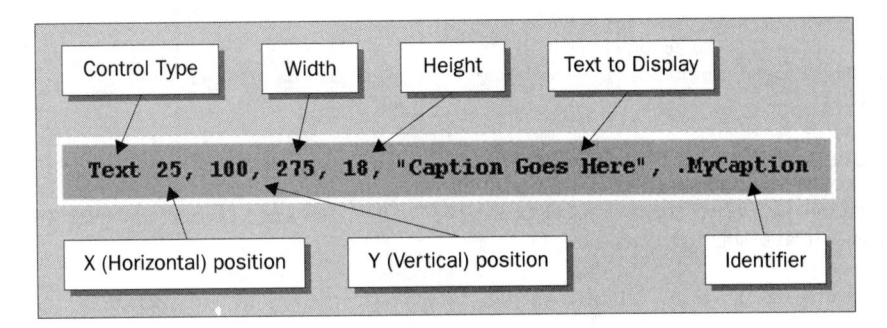

Diagram annotations: Control Type, Width, Height, Text to Display, X (Horizontal) position, Y (Vertical) position, Identifier

There are 51 controls altogether in the definition of the dialog, so this makes the dialog definition for the Book Order application pretty involved. Here's what part of it looks like:

```
'Panel 1
    Text 275, 10, 325, 40, "Welcome to the Customer Enquiry system. This
        will automatically create a letter in response to an order or
        enquiry for one of our books."                                  '8
    Picture 0, 6, 283, 226, "LogoPic", 1, .logo1                        '9
    Text 285, 60, 200, 13, "Is this an order or an enquiry?"            '10
    GroupBox 285, 75, 300, 100, ""                                      '11
    OptionGroup .Order                                                  '12
        OptionButton 315, 95, 250, 15, "An &Order for"                  '13
        OptionButton 315, 125, 250, 15, "This is an &Inquiry about
                                                    our books"         '14
    Text 480, 96, 50, 15, "copies"                                      '15
    TextBox 430, 95, 40, 16, .Quantity                                  '16
    CheckBox 335, 145, 230, 15, "Enclose &Complimentary copy", .Sample  '17
    GroupBox 285, 185, 300, 38, ""                                      '18
    Text 310, 200, 90, 15, "Send by:"                                   '19
    OptionGroup .Sendby                                                 '20
        OptionButton 380, 200, 100, 15, "&Post/Fax"                     '21
        OptionButton 480, 200, 100, 15, "E-&Mail"                       '22
    ItemsInPanel 15    'The number of controls in panel 1
```

This defines the first panel of the wizard, the one that you saw earlier. Notice that we've added a number as a comment after each control. This is because, in the dialog function, we need to be able to refer to the controls using their positional value, as well as their identifier name. Remember that, in Part 1, we told you that Word automatically numbers each control in a dialog and these comments help to identify the controls we're interested in. You'll see more of this when we come to look at the dialog function.

The last line of the definition for panel **1** is a call to a user-defined support procedure, **ItemsInPanel**. We send as the argument the number of controls we've defined for that panel. To manage the different panels and make the correct controls visible for each one, we maintain a set of **Shared** variables, i.e. the number of the currently displayed panel, the number of the last panel and an array holding information on which controls belong to each panel.

```
    Dim Shared Panel, LastPanel
    Dim Shared PanelItems(10)    'default for 11 panels - change if more needed
```

The **ItemsInPanel** routine is called at the end of the definition for each panel. It increments the value in **LastPanel** and sets the value in the **PanelItems** array for that panel to the number of the last control in that panel.

```
Sub ItemsInPanel(howMany)
    LastPanel = LastPanel + 1
    PanelItems(LastPanel) = howMany + PanelItems(LastPanel - 1)
End Sub
```

So, we can always tell which controls belong to a panel by looking at the numeric identifiers of the last control in the previous panel and the last one in this panel. In the case of the panel in the definition above, we have **PanelItems(0) = 8** and **PanelItems(1) = 23** (remember that WordBasic arrays start at zero, not **1**).

Every wizard has a set of default controls, which are referred to as panel **0**:

```
'Controls shown in every panel:
    Picture 3, 238, 500, 11, "LinePic", 1, .LinePicA        '0
    Picture 128, 238, 500, 11, "LinePic", 1, .LinePicB      '1
    Picture 30, 20, 200, 200, "", 1, .WizPic                '2
    PushButton 229, 250, 73, 19, "&Hint", .Hint             '3
    CancelButton 313, 250, 80, 19                           '4
    PushButton 401, 250, 71, 19, "<&Back", .Back            '5
    PushButton 471, 250, 71, 19, "&Next>", .Next            '6
    PushButton 550, 250, 75, 19, "&Finish", .FastForward    '7
    PanelItems(0) = 8
```

These are always visible and include the navigation buttons and the **Picture** controls which display the line across the bottom of the dialog and the picture on the left-hand side. The pictures are stored in the template as AutoText entries, rather than as separate files on disk. This makes the template more transportable; you don't have to include the picture files when you move it.

Because the main **Picture** control is in panel **0**, it's visible in every panel. However, as you change panels, you can change the picture it displays, just like in a real wizard. If you don't want it to be visible all the time, you can place individual **Picture** controls in the panels where you want a picture displayed. This is what we've done in the Book Order application.
Alternatively, you can add code to the wizard which shows and hides it as you change panels.

However, if you want to use a **FilePreview** control, you should include it in the definition of panel **0** and show or hide it as required. You can only use one **FilePreview** control in a dialog. You can't include individual ones in different panels.

Adding and Removing Controls

As you design the dialog, you often have to make adjustments to it by adding controls or moving them from one panel to another. It's important to complete the dialog definition before you write any other parts of the code. If you add or remove controls in one panel, the numeric identifiers of all the controls that follow will automatically change and probably stop your code from working. Of course, you must remember to keep the **ItemsInPanel** argument updated. If you don't, you'll find that controls from other panels become visible, or that you 'lose' one that was there before!

If you need to remove a control, you can always replace it with a **Text** control, which takes up few resources and make it invisible in the initialization section of the dialog function. This saves you from renumbering controls afterwards. Of course, if you think that you may need to add controls later, you can drop extra **Text** controls into the definition as you create it ready to be replaced at a later development stage.

> **FYI** You should make a point of adding the numeric identifiers as comments to the end of each line in your definition. It makes it a lot easier to work with the controls when you're writing the dialog function or other procedures later. In fact, once the dialog definition is complete, it's worth printing it out as hard-copy to refer to.

Try It Out - Defining Our File List Wizard Dialog

We'll add the controls we need to the blank wizard definition from the previous example. At the same time, we can fill in the wizard name and set the other variables we'll need later on. To save a lot of error-prone typing, we'll copy the code we need from the complete `FileList.dot` template in your samples folder. You'll need to open this and the new copy of FileList that you're creating.

1 Switch to, or open, the sample copy of `FileList.dot` that we've supplied. Open the **Application** macro by selecting Macro... from the Tools menu, selecting Application and clicking Edit.

2 Copy the code from the line `WizName$ = "File List Wizard"` to the line **End Dialog** to the clipboard:

```
            CheckBox 300, 145, 300, 18, "I only want to list files containing
this text:", .chkFText                                              '14
            TextBox 325, 168, 250, 51, .txtToFind, 1                '15
        ItemsInPanel 5   'The number of controls in the 2nd panel
    'Panel 3
        'Controls for the third panel go here
        Text 300, 15, 300, 42, Info5$, .lblInfo5                    '16
        TextBox 300, 70, 290, 17, .txtStart                         '17
        GroupBox 300, 100, 290, 70, "", .box1                       '18
        OptionGroup .grpSubFolder                                   '19
            OptionButton 335, 118, 240, 17, "Only search in this folder",
.optF0                                                              '20
            OptionButton 335, 140, 240, 17, "Search all the sub-folders",
.optF1                                                              '21
        Text 300, 200, 300, 42, Info6$, .lblInfo6                   '22
        ItemsInPanel 7   'The number of controls in the 3rd panel
End Dialog
```

3 Switch to, or open, your new copy of `FileList.dot` from your `\Templates` folder. Open the **Application** macro and select all the code from `WizName$ = "Blank Wizard"` to the **End Dialog** line, just as you did in Step 2. Then paste the new code from the clipboard.

4 Click the Start button on the Macro toolbar and the wizard now has controls on each panel. Panel **2** is shown on the next page.

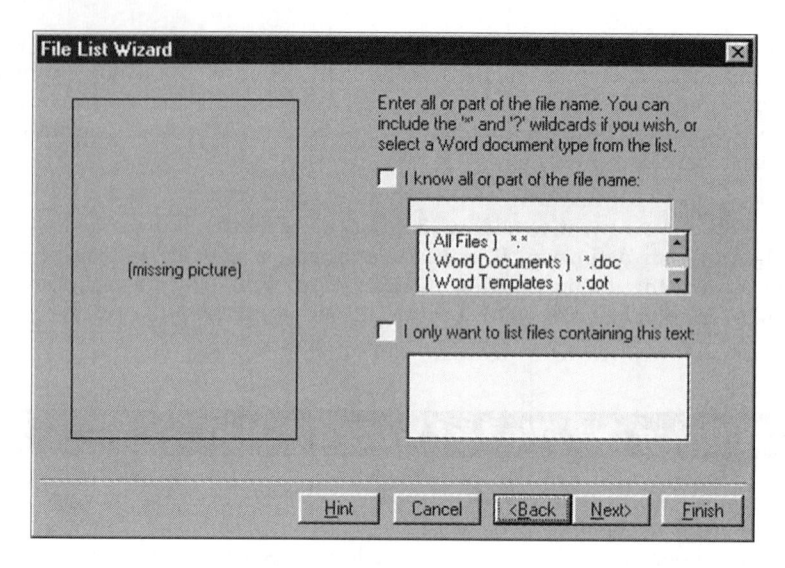

[Screenshot of the "File List Wizard" dialog box with a missing picture placeholder on the left, and on the right: instructions, an "I know all or part of the file name:" checkbox with text field, a list box containing "{All Files} *.*", "{Word Documents} *.doc", "{Word Templates} *.dot", an "I only want to list files containing this text:" checkbox with text area, and Hint, Cancel, <Back, Next>, Finish buttons.]

How It Works

We've replaced the blank dialog definition with a new one, with only three panels. We've tried to keep it fairly simple so that it's easier for you to see what's going on:

```
Begin Dialog UserDialog 628, 276, WizName$, .WizFunction

'Controls shown in every panel:
    Picture 3, 238, 500, 11, "WizLine", 1, .Line1              '0
    Picture 128, 238, 500, 11, "WizLine", 1, .Line2            '1
    Picture 30, 20, 200, 200, "", 1, .WizPic                   '2
    PushButton 229, 250, 73, 19, "&Hint", .cmdHint             '3
    CancelButton 313, 250, 80, 19, .cmdCancel                  '4
    PushButton 401, 250, 71, 19, "<&Back", .cmdBack            '5
    PushButton 471, 250, 71, 19, "&Next>", .cmdNext            '6
    PushButton 550, 250, 75, 19, "&Finish", .cmdFinish         '7
    PanelItems(0) = 8

'Panel 1
    'Controls for the first panel go here
    Text 300, 20, 300, 51, Info1$, .lblInfo1                   '8
    Text 300, 90, 300, 51, Info2$, .lblInfo2                   '9
    Text 300, 205, 300, 17, Info3$, .lblInfo3                  '10
    ItemsInPanel 3     'The number of controls in the 1st panel

'Panel 2
    'Controls for the second panel go here
    Text 300, 15, 300, 42, Info4$, .lblInfo4                   '11
    CheckBox 300, 55, 300, 18, "I know all or part of the file
                                name:", .chkFName              '12
    ComboBox 325, 77, 250, 60, FTypes$(), .cboFType            '13
    CheckBox 300, 145, 300, 18, "I only want to list files
                                containing this text:", .chkFText  '14
    TextBox 325, 168, 250, 51, .txtToFind, 1                   '15
    ItemsInPanel 5     'The number of controls in the 2nd panel
```

```
'Panel 3
   'Controls for the third panel go here
   Text 300, 15, 300, 42, Info5$, .lblInfo5                '16
   TextBox 300, 70, 290, 17, .txtStart                      '17
   GroupBox 300, 100, 290, 70, "", .box1                    '18
   OptionGroup .grpSubFolder                                '19
      OptionButton 335, 118, 240, 17, "Only search in this
                                     directory", .optF0    '20
      OptionButton 335, 140, 240, 17, "Search all the
                                     sub-directories", .optF1   '21
   Text 300, 200, 300, 42, Info6$, .lblInfo6               '22
   ItemsInPanel 7   'The number of controls in the 3rd panel

End Dialog
```

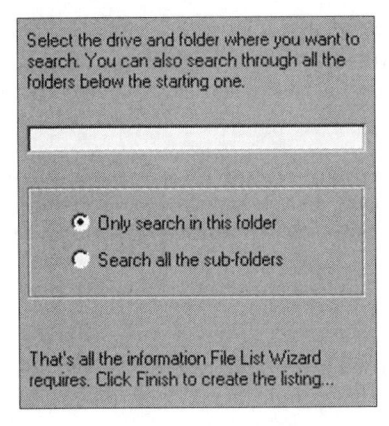

The standard controls for the navigation buttons and pictures appear in panel **0**, and panel **1** is just three text labels to introduce the wizard. Panel **2** contains the two check boxes, combo box and text box where the user enters details about the files they want to find. The third panel has a text box for the search path and a group box with two options buttons where the user selects whether to include subfolders in the search.

> **FYI**
>
> You may notice that we've used a naming convention for the controls in the dialog. This convention is the one commonly adopted for Visual Basic and the other MS Office macro languages. Essentially, the convention is to use a descriptive name for the control, prefixed with a three letter code for the type of control. These codes are summarized in the table that follows.

Prefix	Control Type	Comment
cmd	PushButton	The purpose of a push button is to do some action, so **cmd** represents *command*.
txt	TextBox	
lbl	Text	**lbl** stands for *label*, since this is the main purpose of a text control.
opt	OptionButton	
chk	CheckBox	
cbo	ComboBox	

The combo box in panel **2** shows a list of common Word file types. We create this in the usual way, by declaring an array and filling it with the values for the list before we define the dialog:

```
Dim FTypes$(4)
FTypes$(0) = " ( All Files )    *.*"
FTypes$(1) = " ( Word Documents )    *.doc"
FTypes$(2) = " ( Word Templates )    *.dot"
FTypes$(3) = " ( Text Files )    *.txt"
FTypes$(4) = " ( Rich Text Format )    *.rtf"
```

Then, in the dialog definition, we specify this array as the source which will provide the drop down list part of the combo box with entries:

```
ComboBox 325, 77, 250, 60, FTypes$(), .cboFType
```

Except for the last panel, the **Picture** control still reports that the picture is missing. We've included the two pictures in the BlankWiz template as AutoText entries, so all we need to do is tell the **Picture** control what they are called. We'll be doing this when we come to modify the support functions.

Apart from the missing pictures, we now have a fully working wizard interface, but there are other things we must consider. For example, we could place default values in the controls, or selectively enable and disable them to make using the wizard more intuitive. We'll come to all these as we continue to develop the new wizard.

Displaying the Dialog

Once we've created the dialog definition, we can add the code to display the dialog. This is the same as an ordinary dynamic dialog, and it's already in the sample blank wizard template:

```
REM ScreenUpdating 0
REM DisableInput 1
Dim dlg As UserDialog
If Dialog(dlg, - 2) Then                'show the dialog, No default button
    'carry out the actions
EndIf
DisableInput 0
ScreenUpdating 1
```

So that you can see what's going on, we've left a **REM** in front of the statements that switch off screen updating and disable the *Escape* key. If your macro gets stuck in a loop while executing, it's nice to be able to stop it without the three-fingered salute (*Ctrl-Alt-Del*). This can save a lot of frustration, and once you've lost a couple of hours work, you'll agree it's a good idea! Once everything is tested and ready to ship, you just remove the two **REM**s.

You can also add statements to preset any of the control's contents before the dialog is shown. For example, if you wanted the text box named **.txtQuantity** to have the value **5**, you just add:

```
dlg.txtQuantity = 5
```

Normally, when you display a dialog, the default button is the first button listed in the dialog definition. Setting the **DefaultButton** argument to **-2** means there will be no default button. We'll be setting the focus in the dialog ourselves to make it easier for the user to navigate through the panels.

Controlling the User's Options

Once the dialog opens, the dialog function takes over the work of manipulating it. All the usual tasks, like enabling and disabling controls, moving the focus and checking the user's input, operate just as any normal dynamic dialog. In the first panel of the Book Order application, for example, the user can select whether to send a complimentary copy of a book (using the Sample check box). We only want this to be enabled when they select Inquiry rather than Order.

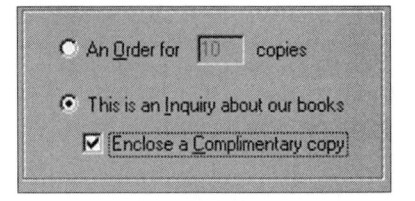

In the dialog function's initialization section, where the **Action** has a value of **1**, we disable the Enclose a Complimentary copy check box (the control identifier is **"Sample"**):

```
DlgEnable "Sample", 0
```

Then, when they click the Inquiry option button, we can enable the Enclose a Complimentary copy check box and move the focus to it:

```
Case 14              'An inquiry
   DlgEnable 17, 1
   DlgFocus 17
   DlgEnable 16, 0
   DlgValue "TAccount", 1
```

Here, you can see we've used the numeric identifier of the option button (**14**) in the case statement, and the numeric identifiers of the **Quantity** (**16**) and **Sample** (**17**) controls. The final line sets the value of a check box in a different panel. The **TAccount** control is in panel **2**, and is used to control if the letter contains information about opening an account. If it's an inquiry, we set the default value for this control to Yes (ticked). Notice also that, in this situation, we can quite freely use the text name of the control, as well as the numeric identifier.

Finding the Numeric Identifier of a Control

So how does the dialog function know the numeric identifier of each control? Remember, the dialog function takes the name of the control as a text-type argument:

```
Function DlgControl(id$, iaction, wvalue)
```

We can retrieve the numeric identifier for a control using the **DlgControlID()** function:

```
idnum = DlgControlId(id$)
```

In our example above, the numeric identifier of the **Quantity** text box is **16**, so the value of **idnum** would be **16**.

Showing and Hiding Panels

The theory behind showing different panels of controls is dead easy: we just make the right ones visible at the right time. The difficult part is keeping track of which are the right ones. You've seen how we created and set the values of several shared variables before we displayed the dialog. These variables contain information about which controls belong in each panel, and, since they were declared as **Shared**, they are available within the dialog function.

`Panel` is the number of the currently displayed panel, starting from `1` and going up to `LastPanel`. The array `PanelItems()` contains the numeric identifier of the last control in each panel. The first step is to decide which is the next panel to be displayed when the user clicks a button. In the dialog function, we can detect a button click:

```
Select Case idnum
   ...
   Case 5              '<Back
       ChangePanel(Panel, PrevPanel(Panel))
   Case 6              'Next>
       ChangePanel(Panel, NextPanel(Panel))
   ...
```

Clicking the Back button calls the `PrevPanel()` function to get the number of the previous panel and passes this and the number of the current panel to our `ChangePanel` subroutine. Similarly, clicking Next sends this routine the number of the current and next panels. The `NextPanel()` and `PrevPanel()` functions are simple enough; they just increment or decrement the current panel number (unless it's the first or last one, of course):

```
Function NextPanel(oldPanel)
    If oldPanel = LastPanel Then
        NextPanel = oldPanel
    Else
        NextPanel = oldPanel + 1
    EndIf
End Function

Function PrevPanel(oldPanel)
    If oldPanel = 1 Then
        PrevPanel = oldPanel
    Else
        PrevPanel = oldPanel - 1
    EndIf
End Function
```

Obviously, we're not forced to always show the panels in numerical order. In some cases, you may want to skip a panel, depending on the options that the user selects in other panels. You can modify these functions to return the next or previous panel in a nonlinear order, like this:

```
...
If (oldPanel = 2) And (DlgValue("Skip") = 1) Then
    NextPanel = 5
Else
    NextPanel = 3
EndIf
...
```

Once we know what the next panel is, we can hide all the controls on the other ones and show only the controls on this panel. We use a special form of the `DlgVisible` statement, which accepts two control identifiers. It operates on all the controls in numeric identifier order, from the first to the last. For example:

```
DlgVisible 12, 19, 0     'hide all the controls with IDs from 12 to 19
DlgVisible 12, 19, 1     'show them all again
```

Our **PanelItems** array holds the numeric identifier of the last control in each pane, so if we are currently on panel **1** and want to move to panel **2**, we can hide all the controls on the current panel with:

```
DlgVisible PanelItems(old - 1), PanelItems(old) - 1, 0
```

In our case, this is evaluated as:

```
PanelItems(1 - 1) = 8     'the ID of the first control in panel 1
PanelItems(1) - 1 = 22    'the ID of the last control in panel 1
DlgVisible 8, 22, 0
```

Similarly, we make all the controls on the new panel visible. This is the complete subroutine:

```
Sub ChangePanel(old, new)
    DlgVisible PanelItems(old - 1), PanelItems(old) - 1, 0
    DlgVisible PanelItems(new - 1), PanelItems(new) - 1, 1
    Panel = new
    EnableControls
End Sub
```

Once we've got the right controls displayed, we update the current panel variable, **Panel**, and execute a subroutine which sets the enabled state of the navigation buttons at the bottom of the dialog to reflect our new panel.

Enabling the Navigation Buttons

Each time we change panel, we need to update the state of the navigation buttons. If we're on the first panel, we want the <u>B</u>ack button disabled, and if we're on the last panel we must disable the <u>N</u>ext button. The Cancel and <u>H</u>int buttons (if included) are always enabled. The <u>F</u>inish button can be enabled at the point where the wizard has collected enough information to complete the task, even if there are more panels the user hasn't visited yet.

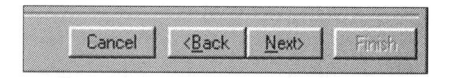

In our Book Order application, we don't use a <u>H</u>int button because all the options are obvious enough. We've also disabled the <u>F</u>inish button until the last panel is displayed. Here's the **EnableControls** routine from the Book Order application:

```
Sub EnableControls
    Select Case Panel
        Case 1
            If DlgValue("Order") = 0 Then
                DlgFocus("Quantity")
            Else
                DlgFocus("Sample")
            EndIf
            DlgEnable 6, 1          'Enable the Next> button
            DlgEnable 5, 0          'Disable the <Back button
            DlgEnable 7, 0          'Disable the Finish button
        Case 2
            DlgFocus "CName"
            DlgEnable 5, 1          'Enable the <Back button
            DlgEnable 6, 1          'Enable the Next> button
```

```
                DlgEnable 7, 0              'Disable the Finish button
            Case 3
                DlgFocus "TAbout"
                DlgEnable 5, 1              'Enable the <Back button
                DlgEnable 6, 1              'Enable the Next> button
                DlgEnable 7, 0              'Disable the Finish button
            Case 4
                DlgFocus "FName"
                DlgEnable 7, 1              'Enable the Finish button
                DlgEnable 6, 0              'Disable the Next> button
        End Select
    End Sub
```

This uses a **Select-Case** construct to decide which panel is being displayed. For each panel, it moves the focus to a particular control and enables or disables the Back, Next and Finish buttons as appropriate. However, in the File List Wizard that we're building, we'll include a Hint button and allow users to select Finish in the second panel.

Checking the User's Selections

One of the best ways to control what the user enters in a dialog is to enable and disable appropriate controls and monitor the values they select, using the **Action 5** (idle) events that occur while the dialog is displayed. We saw plenty of examples of this in Part 1. However, it's usual practice to allow the user to roam backwards and forwards in a wizard, filling in values as they wish, so disabling the Next or Finish buttons may restrict her unreasonably.

Instead, we check the values the user has entered only when they click the Finish button. And because it's so easy to change the display to any panel, we can switch to the panel with the error and highlight the particular control they need to change.

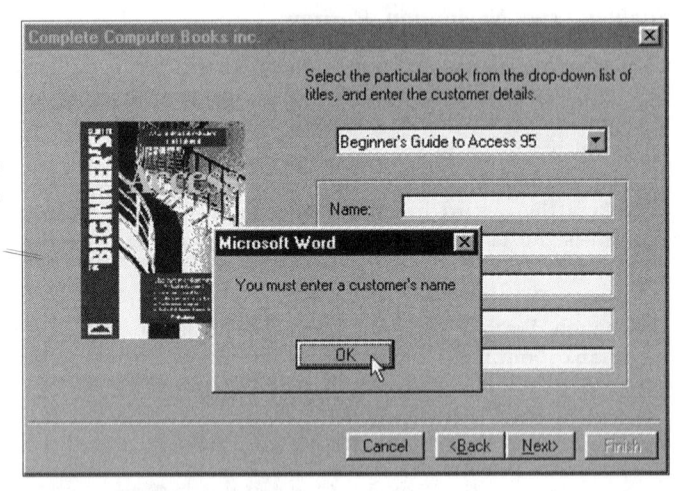

```
    fRet = 1                        'keep the dialog open
    ...
    Select Case idnum
        ...
        Case 7                  'Finish button clicked, so exit dialog box
            ErrPane = 0
            If Len(DlgText$("CName")) < 1 Then
                ErrM$ = "You must enter a customer's name"
                ErrC$ = "CName"
                ErrPane = 2
            EndIf
```

```
            If DlgValue("Order") = 0 And Val(DlgText$("Quantity")) < 1 Then
                ErrM$ = "You must enter an order quantity of 1 or more"
                ErrC$ = "Quantity"
                ErrPane = 1
            EndIf
            ...
            If ErrPane > 0 Then
                ChangePanel(Panel, ErrPane)    'go to the panel with the error
                DlgFocus ErrC$                 'Set the focus to that control
                MsgBox ErrM$                   'display a message
            Else
                fRet = 0                       'allow the dialog to close
            EndIf
```

This shows you how we've done it in the Book Order application. When the user clicks the Finish button, we perform a series of checks on the values in the various controls, in any of the panels. (This is just a selection from our application.) If any of the checks fail, we set a variable **ErrM$** to the message we want to display, **ErrC$** to the name of the control with the error and **ErrPane** to the number of the panel it's on.

Once we've checked everything, if the value of **ErrPane** is still zero we know there are no errors, so we return a value of zero in **fRet**. This is assigned to the function name when it ends, so allowing the dialog to close. Otherwise, we leave it set to **1** to keep the dialog open, move back to the panel and control with the error, and display a message.

Try It Out - Creating the File List Dialog Function

Now we'll catch up with our File List Wizard, adding the code for the new dialog function. You'll need the FileList template from the previous Try It Out open for this next stage.

1 Switch to, or open, the sample copy of **FileList.dot** we've supplied. Open the **Application** macro by selecting Macro... from the Tools menu, selecting Application and clicking Edit.

2 Highlight (select) all the code from the line **Function WizFunction (Ctrl$, Action, SupValue)** to the line **End Function**, by dragging over it with the mouse. Copy the selected code to the clipboard.

3 Switch to, or open, your new copy of **FileList.dot** from your **\Templates** folder. Open the **Application** macro, select the dialog function code and paste the new code from the clipboard. Word prompts you to confirm the replacement.

4 Click the Start button on the Macro toolbar. Now you'll see some subtle differences in the way that the wizard's controls work. In panel **2**, the combo box and text box are disabled until you click the appropriate check box. When you do, the focus moves to that control.

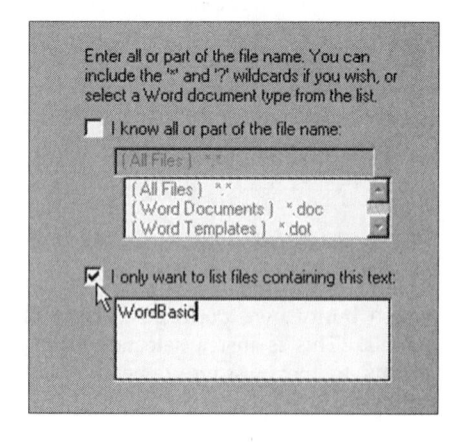

How It Works

As we've seen in other dynamic dialogs, it's the dialog function that makes it 'come alive'. We'll work through our dialog function, showing you what each part does. First, we set the return value **RetVal** to **1**, to keep the dialog open:

```
Function WizFunction(Ctrl$, Action, SupValue)
    RetVal = 1
    If Len(Ctrl$) Then IDNum = DlgControlId(Ctrl$)
```

We'll be using the numeric identifier of each control, rather than the text name that is contained in the **Ctrl$** argument, so we have to convert this first. The last line converts the text control identifier into its numeric equivalent, but, because the dialog function is regularly called with **Ctrl$** empty, such as in **Action 5** 'idle' events, we have to check that it's not an empty string before we try to convert it.

So what's going on in the rest of the dialog function? By now, you should be familiar with how dialog functions work, and this one follows the usual format. For the **Action 1** event, which occurs when the dialog is being initialized, we set the current panel to **1**, hide all the controls in the rest of the panels and run the **EnableControls** subroutine which sets the state of the navigation buttons, so that the Back and Finish buttons are disabled. Finally, we disable the combo box and text box in panel **2**:

```
Select Case Action
Case 1    'Initialization
    CurrPanel = 1
    ' Hide all except first panel and enable control buttons
    DlgVisible PanelItems(CurrPanel), PanelItems(LastPanel) - 1, 0
    EnableControls
    DlgEnable "cboFType", 0
    DlgEnable "txtToFind", 0
```

The remainder of the function is concerned with **Action 2** events, which occur when the user clicks a button or other control. For the Hint button, we run the **DisplayHint** subroutine, which just displays the appropriate hint. For the Back and Next buttons, we run the **ChangePanel** subroutine to change to the next or previous panel:

```
        Case 2     'Button or control clicked
            Select Case IDNum
                Case 3                  'Hint
                    DisplayHint
                Case 4                  'Cancel, so exit dialog box
                    RetVal = 0
                Case 5                  '<Back
                    ChangePanel(CurrPanel, PrevPanel(CurrPanel))
                Case 6                  'Next>
                    ChangePanel(CurrPanel, NextPanel(CurrPanel))
```

If the user clicks the Finish button, we carry out a check to ensure that there's a start path in the **txtStart** control on panel **3**. If there isn't, we change to that panel, set the focus to the **txtStart** control and display a message. If they have entered a path, we just set **RetVal** to zero, which allows the dialog to close:

```
                Case 7                  'Finish, so exit dialog box
                    If Len(DlgText$("txtStart")) = 0 Then
                        ChangePanel(CurrPanel, 3)
                        DlgFocus "txtStart"
                        Msg$ = "You must enter a start path for the search."
                        MsgBox Msg$, "File List Wizard", 48
                    Else
                        RetVal = 0
                    EndIf
```

The only other situation we're interested in is when they click either of the check boxes on the second panel, to enter a file name or the text they want to find in a document. The **SupValue** argument contains the value of the check box in this case, so we can use an **If-Then** construct to decide whether to enable the appropriate control and set the focus to it, or disable it and set it back to its default value:

```
                Case 12                 'file name check box
                    If SupValue = 1 Then
                        DlgEnable 13, 1   'file name combo box
                        DlgFocus 13
                    Else
                        DlgEnable 13, 0
                        DlgText 13, " ( All Files )    *.*"
                    EndIf
                Case 14                 'text to find check box
                    If SupValue = 1 Then
                        DlgEnable 15, 1   'text to find textbox
                        DlgFocus 15
                    Else
                        DlgEnable 15, 0
                        DlgText 15, ""
                    EndIf
                Case Else     'do nothing
            End Select        'for IDNum
        Case Else             'do nothing
    End Select                'for Action
```

Finally, we assign the current return value, **RetVal**, to the function name, and exit.

```
    WizFunction = RetVal
End Function
```

Processing the Results

Once the dialog has closed, we can carry out the actions needed to complete the task. All the values in the controls of the dialog are still accessible, as they're stored in the dialog record. To retrieve the value from the **Quantity** control in our Book Order application, for example, we would use:

```
BooksToSend = dlg.Quantity
```

In fact, in principle, this part of a wizard is exactly the same as any other dialog macro. It's likely, though, that the code to complete the task will be more complex than you would normally find in a simple macro that uses Word's built-in dialogs.

Our Book Order application contains a lot of code which builds up the letter using a series of AutoText entries, both text and pictures. We've commented the code fully, so that you can examine it and see how it works. Hopefully, you'll see that, apart from some text manipulation, it's not a very complicated application.

So, let's finish off our sample File List Wizard. You'll need the FileList template from the previous Try It Out open for this next stage. If you don't want to create it yourself, you can open the finished version. It's in the samples folder and is called **FileList.dot**.

Try It Out - Finishing off Our File List Wizard

We've got a few things to do. We need to update the **EnableControls** procedure to insert the correct picture into the **Picture** control in the dialog, and arrange to display hints for the last two panels of the wizard. We also need to add the code that sets the default values for the wizard's controls, and produces the results.

1 Switch to, or open, your new FileList template from your **\Templates** folder, and open the **Application** macro. Scroll down to the **EnableControls** procedure near the end and edit the lines highlighted below, by adding the name of the picture we want to display. In the third **If-Then** construct, remove the line that sets the picture. In our case, it's handled by the case where **CurrPanel = 2**.

```
Sub EnableControls
   If CurrPanel = 1 Then
      DlgFocus 6              'Give the Next> button the focus
      DlgEnable 5, 0          'Disable the <Back button
      DlgEnable 7, 0          'Disable the Finish button
      DlgSetPicture "WizPic", "FLWTextPic", 1
   EndIf
   If CurrPanel = 2 Then
      DlgEnable 5, 1          'Enable the <Back button
      DlgEnable 7, 1          'Enable the Finish button
      DlgSetPicture "WizPic", "FLWDrivePic", 1
   EndIf
   If CurrPanel = LastPanel - 1 Then
      DlgEnable 6, 1                  'Enable the Next> button
   >> Remove this line :   DlgSetPicture "WizPic", "", 1
   EndIf
```

Chapter 5 - Wizards and Add-in Utilities

2 Switch to, or open, the final version of FileList we've supplied from your samples folder. Open the **Application** macro and highlight all the code from **dlg.txtStart = UCase$(Files$("."))** to **EndIf** in the **Sub MAIN** section. Copy this to the clipboard.

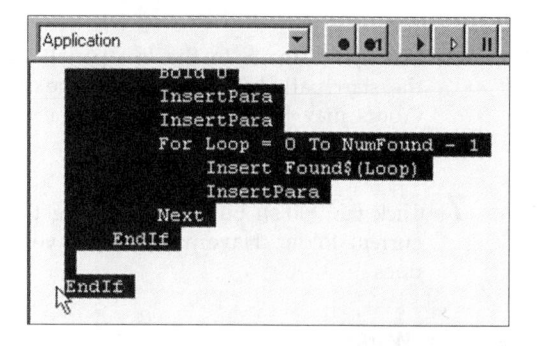

3 Switch back to your new copy of FileList and select the three lines from **If Dialog(dlg, -2) Then** to **EndIf**.

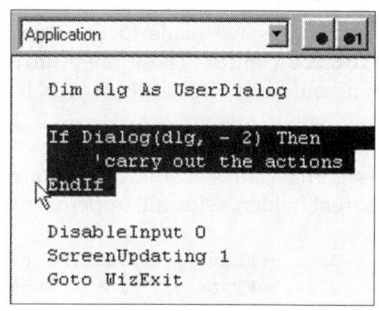

4 Paste over these lines to replace them with the code from the final version. Then click the Start button on the Macro toolbar. You see the first of our new pictures in the first panel:

5 Click Next, and you'll see the second new picture. In the combo box, the default entry is (All files) *.*:

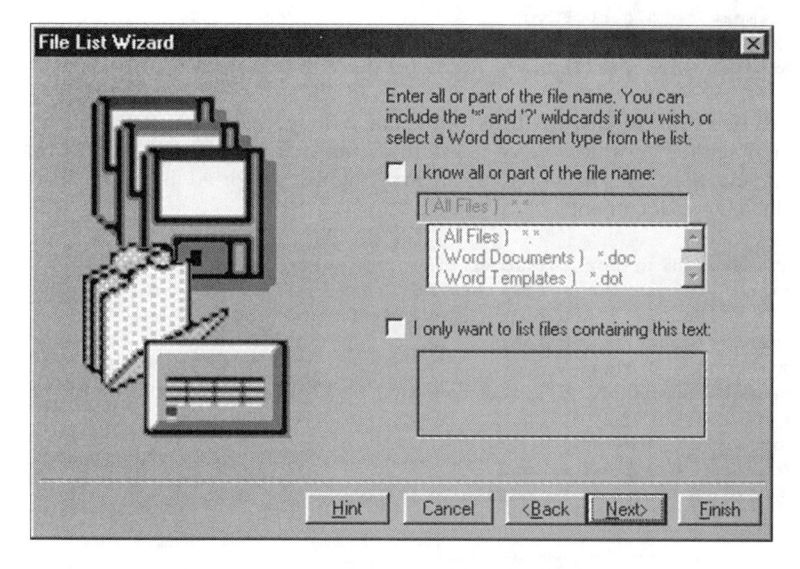

6 Click Next again. In the last panel, you can see that the start path has defaulted to the current folder. (Yours may be different to the one shown.)

> Select the drive and directory where you want to search. You can also search through all the directories below the starting one.
>
> C:\Msoffice\Templates\

7 Click the Finish button and you get a new document containing a list of all the files in the current folder. Have a play with your new wizard, to make sure you understand what it does.

How It Works

The changes we made to the **EnableControls** routine simply display our graphics in the **Picture** control. These are AutoText entries which we've supplied in the BlankWiz template, but you can easily create your own if you wish.

The changes to **Sub MAIN** do two things. First, they set the defaults for our wizard's controls by assigning values to the dialog record. The expression **UCase$(Files$("."))** returns the current folder, with all uppercase letters:

```
dlg.txtStart = UCase$(Files$("."))
dlg.cboFType = "  ( All Files )     *.*"
```

Next, we show the dialog. If the result is **True** (i.e. the user pressed Finish, not Cancel), we can process the results. We can pull the values for the start path, include subfolders, and text to find straight out of the dialog record. The file name is a little more difficult, because we've allowed it to contain a description, just like in Word's Open dialog. We strip off just the file name by looking for a closing bracket, and use the **LTrim$()** function to remove any extra spaces:

```
If Dialog(dlg, - 2) Then                    'show the dialog
    ffFilePath$ = dlg.txtStart
    ffSubDir = dlg.grpSubDirectory
    ffText$ = dlg.txtToFind
    ffFileName$ = dlg.cboFType
    bracket = InStr(ffFileName$, ")")
    If bracket Then ffFileName$ = LTrim$(Mid$(ffFileName$, bracket + 1))
```

Now we're ready to go. In case it turns out to be a long operation, we print a message in the status bar, then send the values we've lifted from the dialog record to the **FileFind** procedure. If we do find any files, they're stored in an array which is sorted into alphabetical order, then printed out in a new document:

```
Print "Searching for matching files, please wait..."
FileFind .SearchPath = ffFilePath$, .Name = ffFileName$, \
        .SubDir = ffSubDir, .Text = ffText$
NumFound = CountFoundFiles()
If NumFound = 0 Then
    MsgBox "No matching files found.", "FileList Wizard", 64
Else
    Dim Found$(NumFound - 1)
    For Loop = 0 To NumFound - 1
        Found$(Loop) = FoundFileName$(Loop + 1)
```

```
            Next
            SortArray Found$()
            FileNew
            For Loop = 0 To NumFound - 1
                Insert Found$(Loop)
                InsertPara
            Next
        EndIf
    EndIf
```

All standard stuff. If you want to know more about how **FileFile** (or any other procedure) works, just place the insertion point in the name of the procedure in the macro window and press *F1*. The Word Help file opens automatically in the relevant place.

Displaying Hints in a Wizard

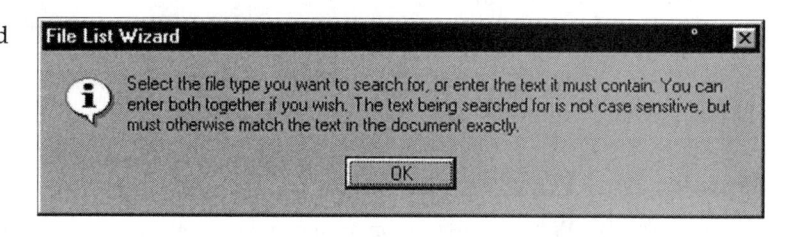

One final part we need to look at is how to create and display hints in a wizard. You're not obliged to include them, (we don't in our Book Order application), and you can hide the Hint button in the initialization event of your dialog function. However, hints are easy enough to implement. Run the File List Wizard again, go to panel 2, and click the Hint button. You get a standard message box giving you more information about that panel.

Right at the end of the **Application** macro is the subroutine **DisplayHint**. It takes the value of the current panel and builds it into a string which is the name of an AutoText entry, in our case **WizHint1**, **WizHint2**, etc.

```
    Sub DisplayHint
        HintName$ = "WizHint" + LTrim$(Str$(CurrPanel))
        Msg$ = GetAutoText$(HintName$, 1)
        If Msg$ = "" Then Msg$ = "No hint available."
        MsgBox Msg$, WizName$, 64
    End Sub
```

If it can't find an AutoText entry with that name, it displays a message telling you that there's no hint. All you need to do, then, is supply the text for the hints as AutoText entries with the correct name.

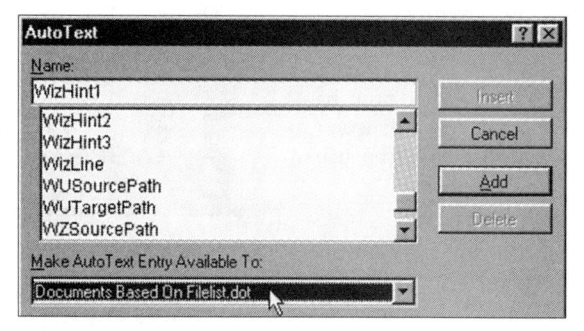

You can create an AutoText entry by typing it into a document, highlighting it, and selecting AutoText from the Edit menu. The AutoText dialog allows you to enter the name for the entry and select which of the currently loaded templates it's stored in. Remember to put in your wizard template, not **Normal.dot**. You can copy AutoText entries between templates using the Organizer dialog that we met in Part 1.

Coping with Coordinates

If you start with the **BlankWiz** template, it's not such a great task to build your own wizards. One of the hardest parts is positioning the controls exactly where you want them. To help you out, we've included a scale diagram of the standard wizard dialog in the BlankWiz template for you to use. Print off a few copies and design your control layout on them. Then you can just read off the **X** and **Y** coordinates and size for each control, ready for when you come to create the dialog definition in Word.

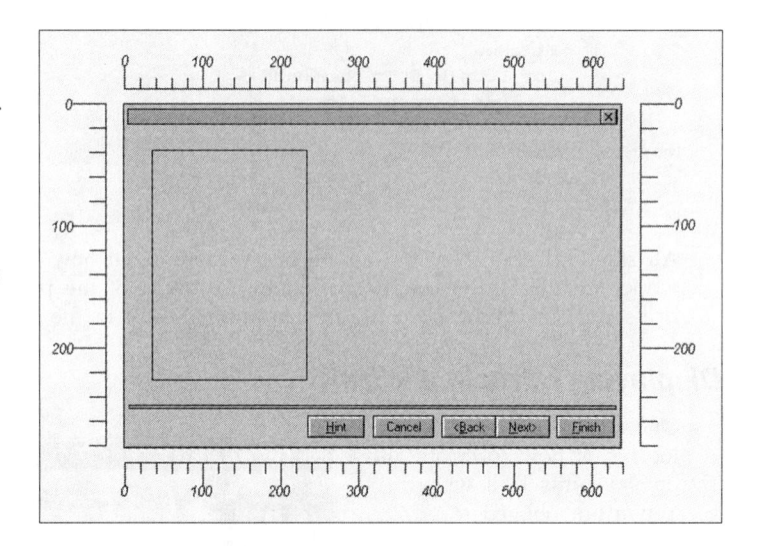

Making Your Wizards Available

Our File List Wizard starts automatically when you open the FileList template, because the template already contains an `AutoOpen` macro which just starts the `Application` macro. However, your users may want the wizards you create to be permanently available, like those in other applications. If your wizard helps the user to perform a particular task as they are writing in Word, it would be nice to have it available on a menu, or even start automatically when the user selects an existing Word command. You'll see both of these techniques in use in the next section, where we look at add-ins and utilities.

One point worth considering, though, is renaming your wizard so that is has the file extension **.wiz** rather than **.dot**. If you do this, and place it in your **\Templates** folder, it appears just like one of the wizards that are supplied with Word. Here, we've done just this, and it now has a 'magic wand' icon rather than the usual Word one.

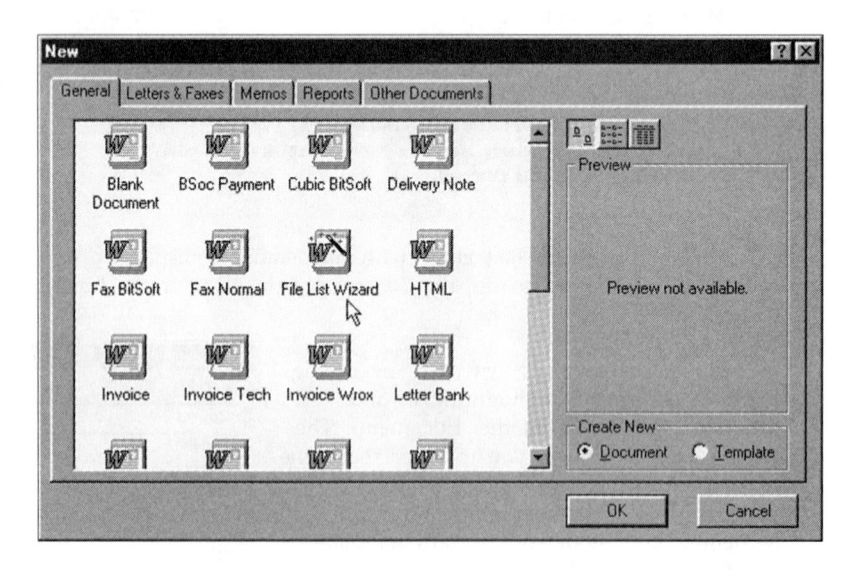

> **FYI** If you don't have the **Hide MS-DOS file extensions** option set in the **View** tab of the **Options** dialog that's available in **My Computer** or **Explorer**, you'll also see the **.wiz** file extension, together with the file extensions for all the other templates.

Word Add-in Utilities

In this part of the chapter, we'll look at another type of WordBasic macro, this time one that is used as an add-in, rather than as a separate application. You'll find the sample we've supplied very useful, and it will help you to appreciate just how easy it is to integrate your own add-ins into Word. You'll see how we can add extra functionality by making our code available on Word's standard menus and toolbars, even by replacing or modify existing Word functions.

What are Add-ins?

Unlike a Word application, which often remains very much aloof from Word itself, an **add-in utility** actually knits itself deep into the Word interface. To start an application, you usually open its template, or create a new document based on it. To start the Book Order application, for example, you simply opened the template `Book Order.dot` and the application started automatically.

An add-in, on the other hand, doesn't make itself known until you perform a certain action, then it springs into life. In this part of the chapter, you'll see an add-in which replaces one of Word's standard commands to save you time and effort if the file you want is compressed as a **zip file**.

Introducing Wrox Zip

Wrox Zip was produced especially for this book, both to demonstrate how you can use WordBasic to create utilities and as a useful tool for you to use in the course of your work. Because it contains commercial code and uses routines which are part of another company's tool set, we've had to supply it in executable (encrypted) form. You won't be able to open the macros to view them, but we'll give you some pointers to how they work.

Before you can use Wrox Zip, you have to install it. The WordBasic code is all held in one template that you install as a global template in Word, but there are several other support files that it requires, which must be installed in the correct directories first.

Try It Out - Installing Wrox Zip

You'll find the files required for Wrox Zip in a separate subfolder called `Wroxzip`, in your samples folder. This will be `C:\BegWord` unless you changed the defaults when you installed the samples.

1 Copy these files to your Windows 95 `\System` folder: `Dz_ez32.dll`, `Dzip32.dll`, `Dunzip32.dll` and `Dzprog32.exe`. Unless you changed the default folder when you first installed Windows 95, your `\System` folder will be `\Windows\System`

2 Copy the files `Wroxzip.hlp` and `Wroxzip.cnt` to your Windows `\Help` folder. Unless you changed the default folder when you first installed Windows 95, your `\Help` folder will be `\Windows\Help`

3 Copy the file `Wroxzip.dot` to your Word 95 `\Startup` folder. Unless you changed the default when you first installed Word 95, your `\Startup` folder will be `\Winword\Startup`. If you installed Word as part of Office 95, your default `\Startup` folder will be `\Msoffice\Winword\Startup`

4 Start Word 95. Wrox Zip will be loaded automatically as a global template. To unload it and load it again, select File | Templates... and set or clear the check box marked Wroxzip.dot.

> **FYI** If you don't want **Wrox Zip** to be loaded automatically each time you start Word, place it in a different folder, such as your Word `\Templates` folder, and use the **Templates** dialog to load and unload it.

What are Zip Files?

Ordinary files contain information laid out consecutively. A text file may contain many instances of the word **because**. In each case, it's is stored as seven characters. When you **zip** a file, you replace each occurrence of repeated words or characters with a single symbol that only uses one location in memory or on your disk.

A table of all the symbols is included in the zip file, so that when it's **unzipped** each one can be replaced with the original contents. So, if the word **because** appeared 20 times in your document, it would take up 140 locations of storage. If you zip your file, it only needs 21, taking up 85% less space. In actual fact, there is some overhead in a zip file for the storage of the file names and other information, but the principle of the compression is as we've described.

The same method works with files that don't contain text. For example, graphic files often contain whole areas of the same color. Files created in the Windows **.bmp** format can often compress to only 5% of their original size.

Wrox Zip uses the **DynaZIP**© compression system to create and read zip files. These tools are fully 32-bit and support Windows 95 long file names. However, you may wish to disable this feature if you intend to exchange files with users who do not have Windows 95 or Windows NT installed. We'll tell you more about this as we look at Wrox Zip in more detail.

> **FYI** If you want to know more about DynaZIP, contact:
>
> Inner Media Inc., 60 Plain Road, Hollis, NH 03049, USA
> Tel: +1 (603) 465 2696   Fax: +1 (603) 465 7195
> E-mail: 70444.31@compuserve.com

Opening and Saving Files

Once you've installed **Wrox Zip** you'll find some subtle changes to the Word interface. We'll go through how you can use **Wrox Zip**, and show you just how neatly it fits into Word.

Try It Out - Saving and Opening a Zip File

You'll need to have the **Wrox Zip** add-in loaded as a global template to carry out this example. If you haven't installed it yet, do so now by following the steps in the previous Try It Out. Once installed, you'll see it listed and ticked in the **Templates** dialog. Select **Templates...** from the **File** menu.

1 Select **Open...** from the **File** menu to show the normal Word **Open** dialog. However, you'll see that the file name is set to show files with the **.zip** extension, as well as the usual **.doc** and **.dot** files.

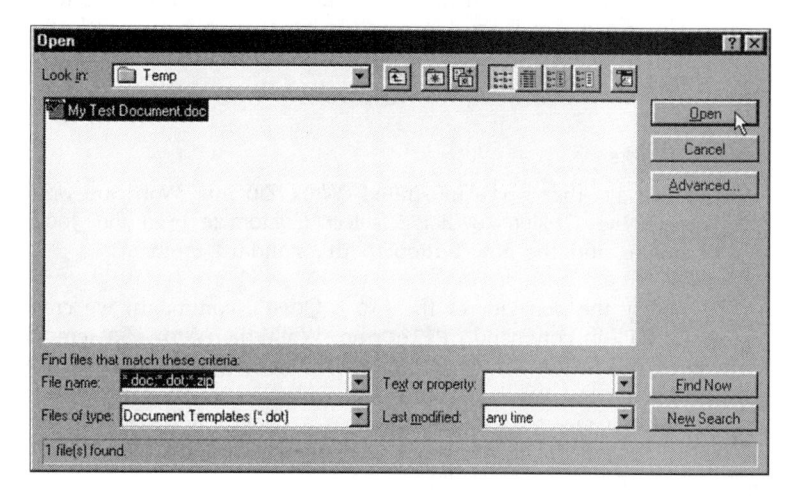

2 Select an existing Word document file and click the **Open** button to open it in Word. Now we'll save it as a zip file. Select the new **Save As Zip** command from the **File** menu, or click the new **Save As Zip** toolbar button.

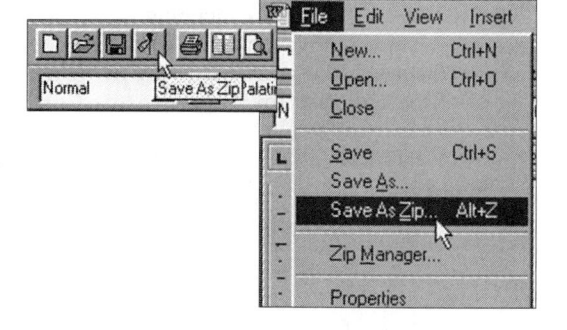

3 Word saves the document as a normal **.doc** file, then starts **Wrox Zip**. You'll see a progress gauge showing you the file being compressed.

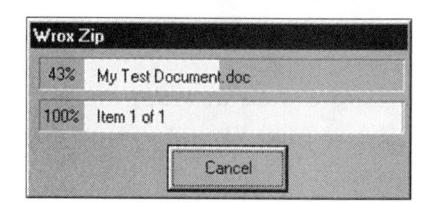

4 Using My Computer or Explorer, look at the files in the folder you originally opened the document. You'll see the new zip file, with the same name as the document, but with a `.zip` extension. Look at the difference in the size!

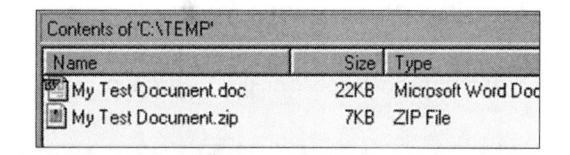

> **FYI** If you can't see the file sizes in **My Computer** or **Explorer**, select **Details** from the **View** menu.

5 Switch back to Word and click the Open button on the toolbar, or select Open... from the File menu. You'll see the new zip file. Select it and click Open. You'll be asked to confirm that you want to overwrite the existing file. Select Yes. The file is extracted (unzipped) and loaded back into Word.

How It Works

All the ways that we've integrated Wrox Zip into Word are ones you've already seen in Part 1. We used the Customize dialog (select Customize from the Tools menu) to add the new items to the menus and the new button to the standard toolbar.

To modify the behavior of the File | Open... command, we created a macro with the same name as the built-in command, `FileOpen`. While the Wrox Zip template is loaded, this macro runs instead of the normal Word command. You saw this done in Chapter 4, when we changed the Open command to display text files as well as document files. The code in the `FileOpen` and `SaveAsZip` macros just has to act as a communication layer between Word and the DynaZIP modules; they do all the work of managing the zip file.

If you have a zip file containing more than one document, Wrox Zip will display a list and allow you to select the one that you want. Alternatively, if you want, you can unzip and load all of the files into Word.

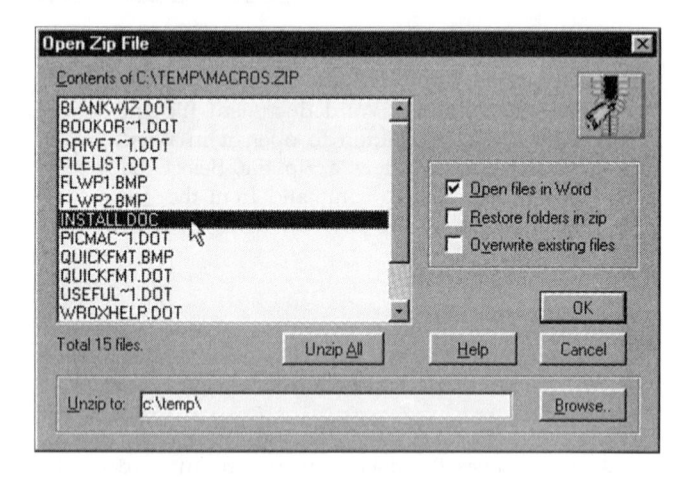

Setting the Default Options for Wrox Zip

By default, Wrox Zip places the new zip files in the same folder as the document that is creating them. When you unzip an existing zip file, the document is placed in the same folder as the zip file. If you always want the zip files or documents to be placed in one particular folder, you can change the default options for Wrox Zip.

You can also automatically delete the original document file after it's been successfully zipped, or delete the zip file after the document has been extracted.

Chapter 5 - Wizards and Add-in Utilities

Try It Out - Setting Wrox Zip's Defaults

You'll need to have the Wrox Zip add-in loaded as a global template to carry out this example. If you haven't installed it yet, do so now by following the instructions given earlier in this section.

1 Select Zip Options from the Tools menu. The Wrox Zip Options dialog opens.

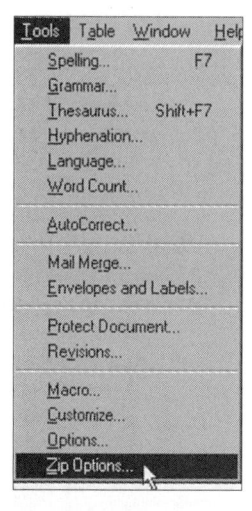

2 Here you can change the directories where you want the zip files and extracted files to be placed either by typing in a new path, or by clicking the Browse... buttons. If you prefer, leave the options set to using the same folder.

3 Decide if you want to automatically delete the zip file or document when the operation is complete, and set the relevant options.

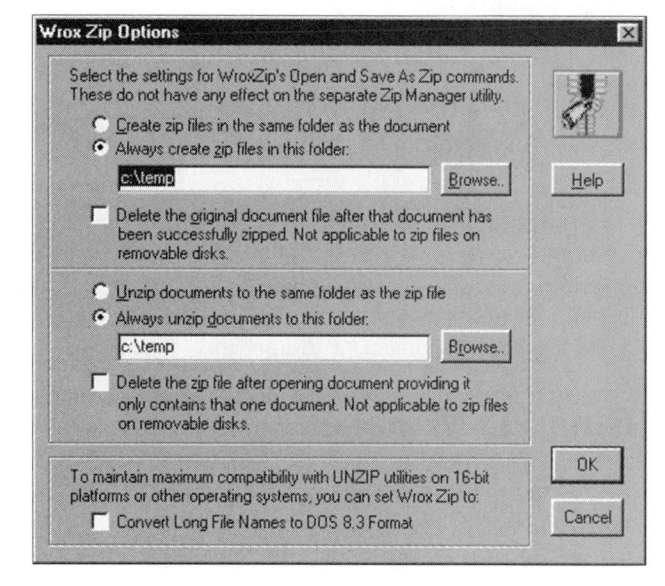

4 If you intend to send your zipped documents to other users whose system can't handle Windows 95 style long file names, make sure you set the Convert Long File Names option. Otherwise, they may not be able to unzip the files.

215

Saving and Using Values in a Template

Wrox Zip stores the settings from the Options dialog as AutoText entries in your Normal template. If you open the AutoText dialog, you'll see these listed:

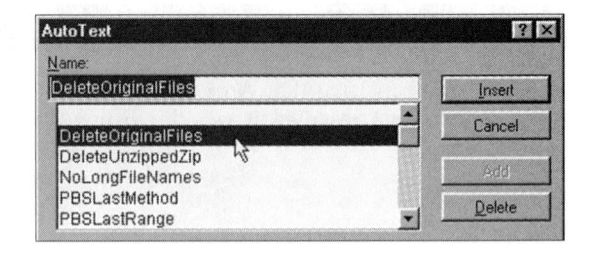

Because your Normal template is always loaded, these values should always be available. However, there's one wrinkle that you should be aware of. If you have no document loaded, i.e. when just the File and Help menus are shown in Word, your Normal template isn't loaded either. So, when you select Open... from the File menu, the AutoText entries are not available.

Wrox Zip needs to use these when you open a file, so how do we get round it? Simple. The **FileOpen** macro first creates a new temporary document, which forces the loading of **Normal.dot**. Once the user has selected the file they want and we've unzipped it if necessary, we load it into Word, then unload the temporary document again. By turning off screen updating while we switch to it and close it, the user doesn't realize that this is happening.

```
        TempWindow$ = ""
        If CountWindows() = 0 Then        'no documents open
           FileNewDefault                 'create a new one
           TempWindow$ = WindowName$()    'save it's name (ie 'Document 6')
        EndIf
        ...
        'rest of FileOpen code
        ...
        If Len(TempWindow$) Then          'we've got a temporary document
           ScreenUpdating 0               'turn off screen updating
           Activate TempWindow$           'switch to the temporary document
           FileClose                      'close it
           ScreenUpdating 1               'and turn screen updating back on
        EndIf
```

If you close all the documents you have open and then select the Open... command, you'll see this temporary document being opened first, before the Open dialog appears. Once you've loaded your document, it disappears.

Using Zip Manager

As well as allowing you to save and load documents as zip files, Wrox Zip also contains a utility to manipulate zip files directly, called Zip Manager. To start it, select Zip Manager from the File menu.

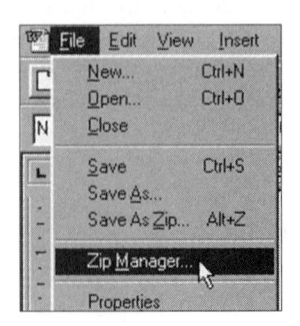

Zip Manager allows you to create new zip files and extract files from existing ones. Although it perhaps isn't up to commercial C++ application usability standards, it's not bad for WordBasic! There are many things that WordBasic doesn't yet support, but you'll find that Zip Manager can quite easily cope with all your everyday 'zipping' needs.

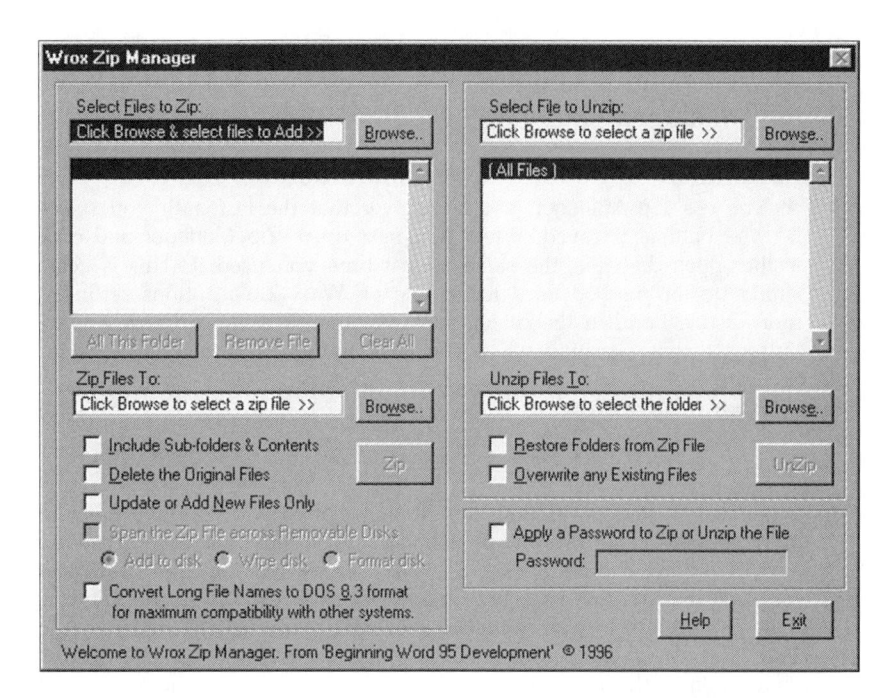

We don't intend to go through a tutorial on using Zip Manager; it's quite self-explanatory, and there's a Help file provided for you to read about it. However, before you start working with multivolume zip files (that span several floppy discs), we recommend you read the relevant Help file sections.

To get Help on any aspects of Wrox Zip or Zip Manager, you can click the Help buttons that appear in most of the dialogs, or select Zip Manager Help from Word's Help menu.

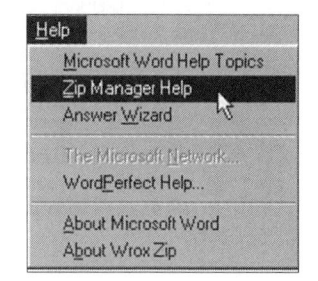

Getting File Names and Paths in WordBasic

As you use Zip Manager, you'll soon discover that it can be difficult to select a folder by browsing. If you click the Browse button next to the Unzip Files To: text box and try to select an empty folder, you can't do it. This is because we've used Word's File Open dialog, which only allows you to close it when a file is selected. If you select a folder and click Open, it displays the contents of the folder and the dialog remains on screen.

The obvious solution is to use the File Save As dialog, but this has its own problems. Yes, it allows you to select an empty folder, but it won't allow you to leave the name empty (for obvious reasons). If you send it a file type, such as `"*.zip"` for the **Name** argument, it's ignored. Word forces it to be one of the types it supports, such as **.doc**, **.do**, **.txt** etc.

The only other solution is to create a custom dialog to get the path we want, using list boxes to display the drives and directories available. But we can't do this if we already have a custom dialog in use. Remember, Word only allows one custom dialog record to exist at a time. You can display standard Word dialogs while your custom dialog is open, as we are doing with the File Open dialog, but you can't use one you've designed yourself.

Saving Paths as AutoText Entries

As you use Zip Manager, you'll discover that the last path you selected with each of the four Browse buttons is saved. When you next open Zip Manager and click Browse, the folder shown in the Open dialog is the same as last time you used it. This is achieved with AutoText entries, similar to the method used for saving of Wrox Zip's options settings. However, we've been a bit more astute here. In the dialog function, there's is an **Action 2** entry for each of the Browse buttons that is executed when you click them.

```
Case "WZTargetPath"
    Add$ = GetFile$(Ctrl$, "*.zip")
    If Len(Add$) Then DlgText "txtZTarget", Add$
```

When we created the dialog definition, we used a descriptive name for the Browse button: **WZTargetPath** for the button you click to specify the target path and name when creating a zip file. To get the path and file name, we use the function **GetFile$()**, which is included in the same macro, and pass two arguments to it. **Ctrl$** is the value that Word sends to the dialog function when an **Action 2** event occurs, i.e. the name of the control that was clicked. The other argument is the name we want for the new file. By sending **"*.zip"**, the File Open dialog allows the user to select any existing zip file as the target and add the new documents to it.

```
Function GetFile$(CID$, Pattern$)
    On Error Resume Next
    ChDir GetAutoText$(CID$)
    On Error Goto GFExit
    Dim FORec As FileOpen
    GetCurValues FORec
    FORec.Name = Pattern$
    Dialog FORec
    SavePath$ = Files$(".")
    SetAutoText CID$, SavePath$
    GetFile$ = FORec.Name
GFExit:
End Function
```

The function uses the control name as the name of the AutoText entry. It looks to see if there's one already, and, if there is, it changes to that folder. Once the user has selected a file, it uses **Files$(".")** to find the current folder (where the file came from) and stores this back in the AutoText entry.

Extending the Power of WordBasic

If you've been involved in any programming before, you'll almost certainly have come across the term **API**, or **Application Programming Interface**. One of the advantages that Windows has brought is a set of procedures which are part of the operating system, yet are fully documented and available to you as a programmer. Unlike early operating systems, these work at a very high level. You can get a lot done in one line of code using an API procedure.

Windows 95 provides a set of procedures collectively known as the **Win32 API**. There are close to a thousand of these, so we won't be providing you with a list! We will, though, take a brief look at how they are used and point you in the right direction for finding out more.

The API procedures are held in a set of libraries that is installed with Windows and form part of the operating system. The main ones are in three files, `User32.dll`, `Gdi32.dll`, and `Kernel32.dll`. These are **dynamic-link library** files, or **DLLs**, and each contains several hundred procedures.

You can also use procedures in other DLLs. `Shell32.dll` contains procedures connected with drag and drop and manipulating the registry. `Winmm.dll` has procedures which provide Windows multimedia capabilities. You can even buy in DLLs for special tasks. The DynaZIP system, which is used by our Wrox Zip add-in, is supplied as a set of special DLLs.

What are DLLs?

There are many functions that your applications need, which are the same as those required in every other application. Instead of including all these functions in every application, you can use code that achieves the same task but is available to them all.

For example, your program needs to translate its results into a display on screen, using display driver code. You could write your own and use it in every application you create, but you would have to create versions for each different type of display card your users have installed.

Windows' DLLs contain the code that is needed to drive the display that the user selected when they installed Windows originally, so it's a far better idea for your program to use this 'common' code, together with every other supplier's applications.

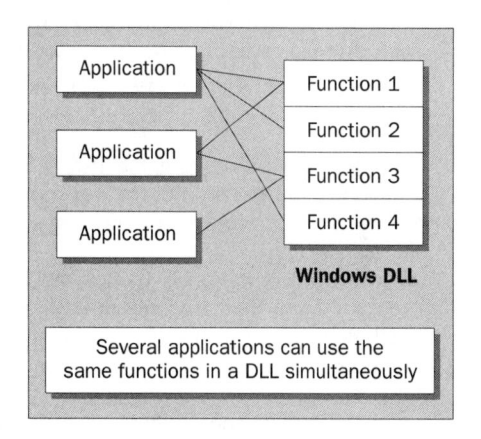

```
Application ──┐         ┌── Function 1
              ├─────────┤── Function 2
Application ──┤         ├── Function 3
              ├─────────┤
Application ──┘         └── Function 4
                           Windows DLL

Several applications can use the
same functions in a DLL simultaneously
```

The actual workings behind DLLs, and the way their functions are linked to applications, is beyond the scope of this book. What we need to know is how we can use them to get results.

Using a DLL Function in Word

Using DLL functions is often considered a 'black art', and it's the quickest way to create your own personal General Protection Faults and Illegal Operation messages. The reason is that there's no insulating layer between you and the Windows operating system, like there is when you run a WordBasic macro. If an error occurs, it can scramble whole blocks of memory, leaving your application as just a heap of meaningless numbers. You need to be careful and *always* save your work before you run any code that includes a call to a DLL function, until you're sure that everything is working correctly.

To use an API DLL function, we just have to tell Word about it by declaring it outside the normal **Sub MAIN** section of our macro, just like we do with **Shared** variables. For example, here's an API function which is stored in **Kernel32.dll**, which shows how it's defined in Windows documentation:

```
Declare Function GetDriveType Lib "kernel32" Alias "GetDriveTypeA"(lpDrive As
    String) As Long
```

We can break this function declaration down so that it makes more sense:

```
Declare Function GetDriveType      'the name we'll be using to refer to it
Lib "kernel32"                     'the DLL that contains the function
Alias "GetDriveTypeA"              'the function's real name in the DLL
(lpDrive As String)                'the arguments we have to supply
As Long                            'the return value data type
```

WordBasic doesn't support the **Long** data type directly, but it's clever enough to convert any values we send to the function, and those it returns, between WordBasic's **Double** type and the DLLs **Long** type as required. DLL functions mainly only use **String** and **Long** data types as arguments and return **Long** data types (although there are many exceptions to this, as you'll see).

Getting Information about Hard Drives

So let's look at a particular case where a DLL function could be useful. In the File List Wizard that we created earlier in this chapter, you had to type in a path for the start of the search; you couldn't select it like you do in a Windows Open dialog. In Zip Manager, we improved on this, but we still found problems. The only solution seems to be to create our own folder selector dialog.

But where would we get a list of drives from? Word doesn't offer this kind of information in its standard functions, and we can't just guess because one user could have **A:**, **B:** and **C:** only, while another has a networked system with **A:**, **C:**, **F:** and **H:**

The obvious solution is to use the **GetDriveType()** function. This takes a string containing the root folder of a drive and returns a value depending on what type of drive it is, or **1** if it isn't installed. So we can quite simply loop through the 26 available drive letters and check the type of each one.

However, that's not a very scientific approach. To make a list of drives for a list box, we need to place the results in an array. We've supplied you with a sample template that contains a useful set of procedures for managing disk drives.

Try It Out - Getting Drive Information Using the API

You'll need the **DrivInfo.dot** template for this example. It will be in the folder where you installed the sample files. The default is **C:\BegWord**.

1 Open the file **DrivInfo.dot** from your samples folder. Select Macro... from the Tools menu, select the DriveType macro and click Edit to open it.

2 Click the Start button on the Macro toolbar. The macro first tells you how many drives you've installed:

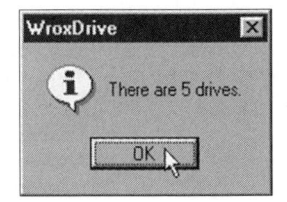

3 Click OK. For each drive, it gives you the drive letter, volume label and type.

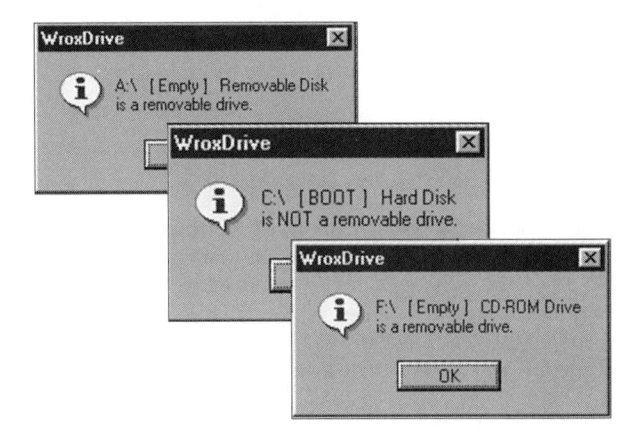

How It Works

The procedure you've just run is a demonstration, of both the user-defined functions we've created in the macro and the API functions that they use to get information from Windows.

```
Sub MAIN
    REM Demonstrates the functions...
    NumDrives = CountDrives
    MsgBox "There are" + Str$(NumDrives) + " drives.", "WroxDrive", 64
    Dim DrvArray$(NumDrives - 1)
    NumDrives = MakeDriveList(DrvArray$())
    For ThisDrive = 0 To NumDrives - 1
        Msg$ = DrvArray$(ThisDrive) + Chr$(10)
        If IsFixedDrive(DrvArray$(ThisDrive)) Then
            Msg$ = Msg$ + "is NOT a removable drive."
        Else
            Msg$ = Msg$ + "is a removable drive."
        EndIf
        MsgBox Msg$, "WroxDrive", 64
    Next
End Sub
```

The core of this code is three function calls: **CountDrives**, **MakeDriveList()** and **IsFixedDrive()**. These are user-defined functions, included in the macro. The demonstration simply calls these functions and presents the results.

You'll see that it uses **CountDrives** to find out how many drives there are, then uses this to create an array of the correct size, **NumDrives - 1** because the first array element is indexed zero, remember. Then it sends this array as an argument to the **MakeDriveList()** function, which fills it with a list of drive descriptions. Finally, it loops through the array, sending each drive description to the **IsFixedDrive()** function to see whether it's a fixed or removable disc, and prints a message about that drive.

Here's the `CountDrives` function. It creates a string containing the root path for all the possible drive letters from `A:\` to `Z:\` in turn, and checks the return value of Windows' `GetDriveType()` function. If it's greater that `1`, the drive exists:

```
Function CountDrives
    CountDrives = - 1
    On Error Goto CDError
    DrvCount = 0
    For Drv = 1 To 26
        DLetter$ = Chr$(64 + Drv) + ":\"
        If GetDriveType(DLetter$) > 1 Then DrvCount = DrvCount + 1
    Next
    CountDrives = DrvCount
CDError:
End Function
```

That's how easy using API functions can be. And if we just want to find out if a particular drive is a fixed or removable disc, it's even easier. Windows defines the constant `DRIVE_FIXED = 3` for the return values of `GetDriveType()`, so all we need to do is to check the return value for the drive letter we've got. Because we're allowing any length of path argument to be sent to the `IsFixedDrive()` function, we make sure it's suitable for the `GetDriveType()` function by adding on the colon and backslash within the function if required:

```
Function IsFixedDrive(DrvLetter$)
    IsFixedDrive = 0
    On Error Goto IFDError
    Letter$ = Left$(DrvLetter$, 1) + ":\"
    If GetDriveType(Letter$) = 3 Then IsFixedDrive = - 1
IFDError:
End Function
```

Identifying the Type of Drive

So what about creating the list of drives? This should be easy now because we can use `GetDriveType()` to tell us what kind of drive each one is. Within the function, we've declared the Windows return values for `GetDriveType()` so that you can see what they mean. It makes the code a bit more cumbersome, but easier to understand...

```
Function MakeDriveList(Drv$())
    DRIVE_REMOVABLE = 2
    DRIVE_FIXED = 3
    DRIVE_REMOTE = 4
    DRIVE_CDROM = 5
    DRIVE_RAMDISK = 6
    MakeDriveList = 0
    On Error Goto MDLError
    DrvCount = 0
    For Drv = 1 To 26
       DLetter$ = Chr$(64 + Drv) + ":\"
       DrvType = GetDriveType(DLetter$)
       If DrvType > 1 Then
           DLabel$ = DLetter$ + "   " + GetDriveLabel$(DLetter$)
           Select Case DrvType
              Case DRIVE_REMOVABLE
                 DLabel$ = DLabel$ + "    Removable Disk"
              Case DRIVE_FIXED
```

```
                    DLabel$ = DLabel$ + "    Hard Disk"
                Case DRIVE_REMOTE
                    DLabel$ = DLabel$ + "    Network Drive"
                Case DRIVE_CDROM
                    DLabel$ = DLabel$ + "    CD-ROM Drive"
                Case DRIVE_RAMDISK
                    DLabel$ = DLabel$ + "    RAM Disk"
            End Select
            Drv$(DrvCount) = DLabel$
            DrvCount = DrvCount + 1
        EndIf
    Next
    MakeDriveList = DrvCount
MDLError:
End Function
```

Again, this is fairly simple stuff. We loop through all the possible drive letters and apply them to **GetDriveType()**. A result greater than **1** means that we've got a drive, so we get the drive's volume label and add it to the string **DLabel$**, together with the drive letter. Next, a **Select-Case** statement decides what type of drive it is, and adds the description to the **DLabel$** string.

Now we can place the string in the **Drv$** array, increment the 'number of drives found' counter **DrvCount**, and go to the next drive letter. Finally, we return the number of drives by assigning it to the function's name.

Before you get too carried away, though, we haven't explored where the drive's volume label comes from; we just used another function, **GetDriveLabel$()**. This isn't a Windows function, but another of our own user-defined ones. It uses a Windows API function called **GetVolumeInformation()**, which provides (amongst other things) the volume name of the drive:

```
Declare Function GetVolumeInfo Lib "kernel32" Alias "GetVolumeInformationA"(lpPath
    As String, lpNameBuffer As String, nNameBuffLen As Long, lpSerialNumber As Long,
    lpMaxComponent As Long, lpSystemFlags As Long, lpSystemBuffer As String,
    nSystemBuffLen As Long) As Long
```

Returning String Values from a DLL

We have a problem here. The **GetDriveType()** function took a string-type argument and returned a long-type value. To get the volume label, we need the function to return a string type, hopefully containing the volume label! But Windows DLLs can't return strings, only numbers.

The way that the API functions get round this is to use a **buffer**. This is an area of memory which is specially set aside, and that both the DLL and the application know about. The application, in our case WordBasic, creates the area of memory and tells the DLL where it is, and how big it is. The DLL then fills it with characters, terminating it with a **Chr$(0)** null character, and returns a value indicating how successful the operation was. This value may be the number of characters in the buffer, or it may have some entirely different meaning. However, that's not so important, because Word automatically adjusts the length of the string after the DLL returns by using the null-terminating character.

So here's the function declaration again:

```
Declare Function GetVolumeInformation          'our name for the function
    Lib "kernel32" Alias "GetVolumeInformationA"  'the real name and location
    (lpPath As String,                          'drive we want to know about
    lpNameBuffer As String,                     'buffer for volume label
    nNameBuffLen As Long,                       'length of vol.label buffer
    lpSerialNumber As Long,                     'drive's serial number
    lpMaxComponent As Long,                     'max file name length
    lpSystemFlags As Long,                      'file system properties
    lpSystemBuffer As String,                   'buffer for file system name
    nSystemBuffLen As Long)                     'length of system buffer
    As Long                                     '0 if error or 1 if success
```

To create a buffer in WordBasic, we build a string with the **String$()** function:

```
LabelBuff$ = String$(255, " ")
```

This creates a string of 255 spaces. When we use the variable's name in our DLL call, WordBasic will automatically pass the string by reference. In other words, it tells the DLL the memory address of the string. The DLL can then modify it as required. You should always use strings of 255 characters or more with API functions, to give Windows plenty of room to write information, without trying to write over other programs memory space, even in this case where we only expect eleven characters.

So here's the complete **GetDriveLabel$()** function. It creates the two buffer strings, **LabelBuff$** and **SystemBuff$**, and sends these to the **GetVolumeInformation()** function, remembering to include the maximum number of characters we can fit in the two buffers. Notice that we use a number one less than the length of the string, to allow for the terminating null character.

```
Function GetDriveLabel$(GDrv$)
    GetDriveLabel$ = "[ Empty ]"
    On Error Goto GDLError
    GDrv$ = Left$((GDrv$ + ":\"), 3)
    LabelBuff$ = String$(255, " ")
    SystemBuff$ = String$(255, " ")
    Result = GetVolumeInformation(GDrv$, LabelBuff$, 254, SerialNo, \
            MaxComp, 0, SystemBuff$, 254)
    If Result = 1 Then GetDriveLabel$ = "[ " + LabelBuff$ + " ]"
GDLError:
End Function
```

If we get a result of **1**, we know that the function succeeded, so we can build up the volume label string, then return it to the calling routine by assigning it to the function name.

The **GetVolumeInformation()** function returns more information that we need here, but you can also use it to find out more about the operating system your application is running on. For example, the **lpMaxComponent** argument is set to the maximum length of a file name. In Windows 95, it returns **255**.

> **FYI**
>
> We've included two other functions in the `DriveType` macro that you may find useful in your code:
> `Function GetPathOnly$(FullName$)` takes a full path and file name string and returns just the path, with the file name removed.
> `Function GetNameOnly$(FullName$)` takes a full path and file name string, and returns just the file name.

Finding out about API Procedures

One of the hardest things about using API procedures is finding out if there's one that does what you want, and if there is, what it's called. Then, even after you've found the declaration, you may not know what values the arguments expect, or what the return values mean.

None of the normal Windows Help files list the API procedures, but if you have any other programming languages available, you might find some details supplied with them. Visual Basic, Visual C++, Visual Foxpro, Delphi and other packages all contain good references to most of the API procedures.

You can also buy books which give you all the information you need, and if you are seriously into API programming you will need all the help you can get. However, if you keep your eyes open as you read computing magazines, and when you are viewing sample code for WordBasic and other languages, you'll often pick up details of some of the popular procedures. We'll show you a few more as you work through the book.

An Example of the Drive List Functions

To show you these functions in action in a dialog, we've included a simple utility in the DrivInfo template for you to try. With `DrivInfo.dot` open, select Macro from the Tools menu, select the macro, DriveExample, and click the Run button. You'll see a dialog with a drive selector list box, and lists of all the subdirectories and files in the current folder. You can change the drive or folder by selecting the one you want from the lists, and click any Word document file (.doc, .dot, .rtf, .txt, .wbk) to see a preview of it.

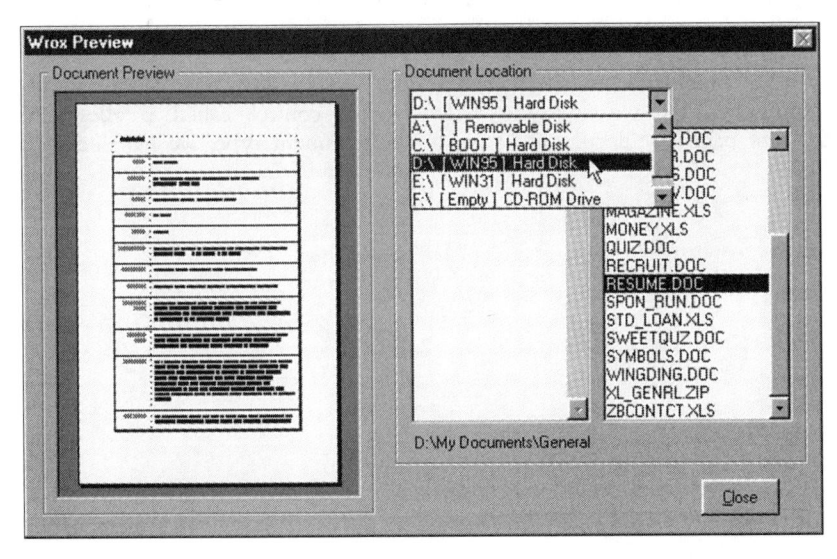

We've used the `MakeDriveList()` function to fill the drop-down list containing the drives. The rest of the macro is concerned with filling the lists of subdirectories and files, and changing to another folder. If you want to see how this is done, open the macro by clicking the Edit button in the Macro dialog. We've commented the code for you so that you can follow it easily.

Displaying a Preview of a Document

The previewing of the file is done with a `FilePreview` control, which is manipulated in a similar way to a normal `Picture` control. The only real difference is that you can't set it to 'empty' like you can with a picture. If you set a picture control's source to an empty string, it displays the 'Missing Picture' message. If you do the same with a `FilePreview` control, you get an error.

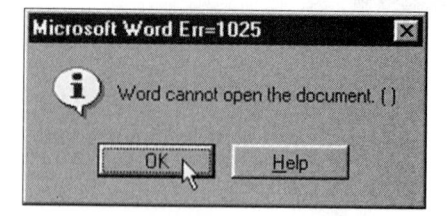

So, to keep it looking neat, we hide the `FilePreview` when there's no document to display. The procedure, `DisplayPreview`, is called each time the user selects a file:

```
Sub DisplayPreview
    FName$ = CurrPath$                           'get path, and add file name
    If Right$(FName$, 1) <> "\" Then FName$ = FName$ + "\"
    FName$ = FName$ + DlgText$("lstFiles")
    DocTypes$ = ".doc.dot.rtf.txt.wbk"           'check if it's a document type
    If InStr(DocTypes$, LCase$(Right$(FName$, 4))) Then
        DlgVisible "prvDoc", 1                   'show the preview control
        DlgFilePreview "prvDoc", FName$          'and show the preview
    Else
        DlgVisible "prvDoc", 0                   'hide the preview control
    EndIf
End Sub
```

The variable, `CurrPath$`, already holds the current folder when the procedure is called, and we build up the full name of the file we want to preview in another variable `FName$`. Notice that we have to check if it's already terminated with a backslash before adding another one (if the current folder is the root of a drive, it will already have a backslash on the end). The name of the file is retrieved from the `lstFiles` list box in the dialog.

We set a variable `DocTypes$` to hold the Word document types, so we can see if the current file is a document. If it is we make the `FilePreview` control, called `prvDoc`, visible and set it to show the first page our document. If it's not a document type, we just hide the control.

Summary

In this chapter we've explored how you can use WordBasic to build wizards, a special kind of application that walks the user through all the steps of completing a complex task. We looked in detail at the Book Order application that you first met in Chapter 1 and saw how the same techniques could be used to build another one which created a list of files which matched certain parameters.

We also saw how WordBasic can be used to build add-in utilities, such as the Wrox Zip add-in that we created especially for this book. If you use e-mail or the Internet to any great extent, Wrox Zip can save you a lot of time.

We also started to come up against the limitations of WordBasic when handling files and folders; we couldn't get the Open and Save dialogs to do exactly what we wanted. So, in the last part of the chapter we looked at how you can use procedures that are part of the operating system itself, rather than built into Word and WordBasic.

In this chapter, we've covered:

- How to create a wizard type of application
- How to use WordBasic to produce add-in utilities
- How to add extra functionality using operating system procedures

In the next chapter, we'll move on to more specific uses of WordBasic and look at how you can build macros that are aimed at one particular working environment.

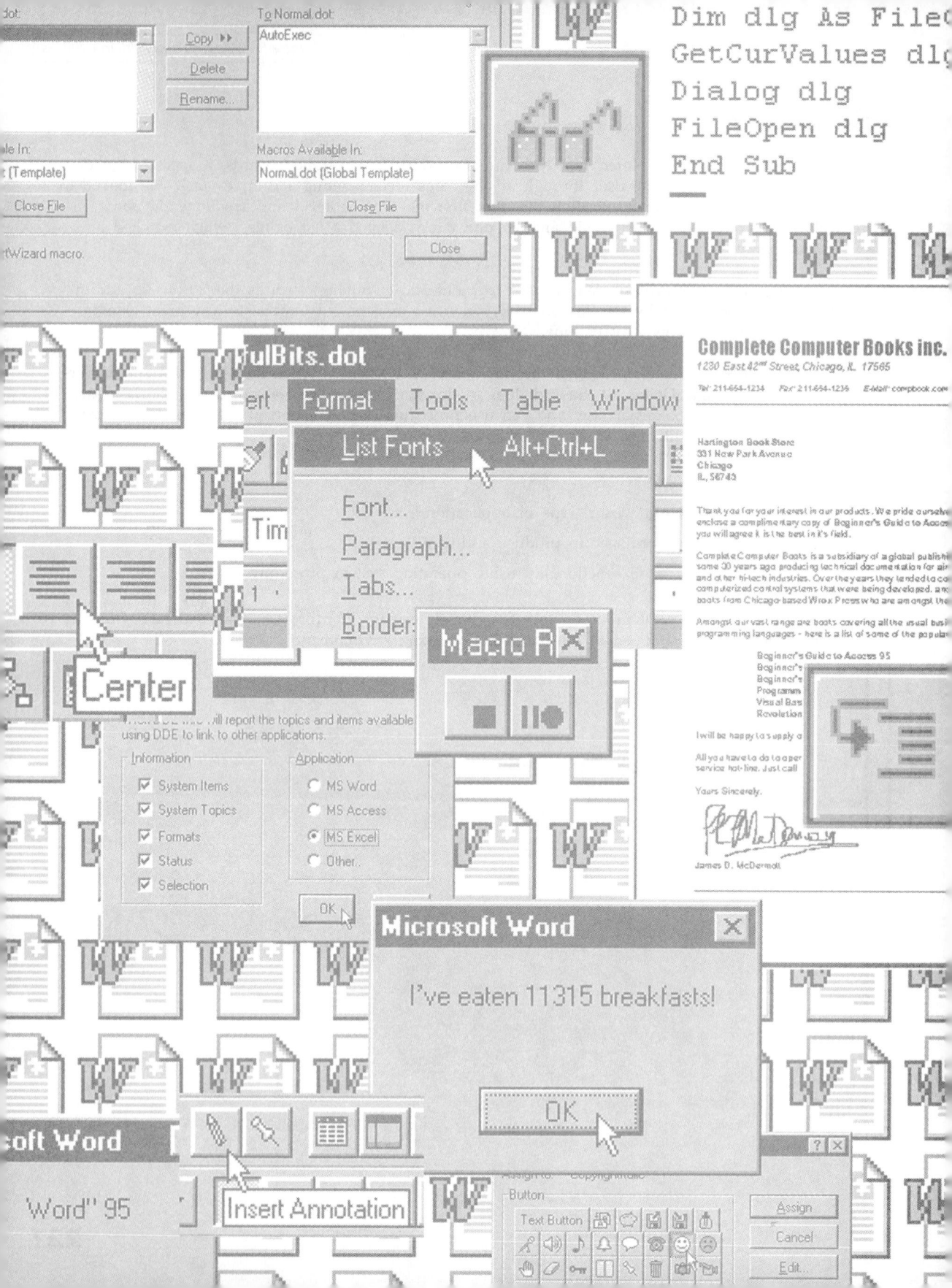

```
Dim dlg As File
GetCurValues dlg
Dialog dlg
FileOpen dlg
End Sub
```

6

Word in a Publishing Environment

Introduction

In this chapter, we'll be getting back to using Word as it was originally intended, as a word processor rather than a programming language. One of the reasons for choosing a powerful application like Word is that you need to work with documents too complex for a more basic word-processing package to manage, say when you are publishing material for a particular audience.

To regard yourself as a publisher, you don't have to be writing a novel or a computer manual. You may have to produce technical documentation for a product manufactured by your company, or sales and marketing reports for your board of directors. Even if you're only producing a weekly newsletter, it's still publishing!

While we don't intend this book to be a primer for using Word, we hope to increase your awareness of the issues involved in managing large documents. Our approach here is not to teach you how to use the basic functions of Word, but how to automate those tasks that take up your time.

In this chapter, we'll be looking at:

- How you can build and manage large documents
- How you can control changes made to a document
- How to make creating indexes easier
- Ways to manage pictures inserted into documents
- Using WordBasic to make printing easier

Managing Large Documents

As your documents grow, you start to notice several side effects. They take longer to save, even if you make only minor amendments, and it's a lot harder to find your way around as you're editing them. Also, if several people are working on a document, you soon find that it's difficult to keep track of who altered what, and when.

In many cases, a large document is built up of several sections. If you're producing a book, you're most likely to divide your manuscript into different chapters, while a technical document or report could be divided up by topic. For example, your work on developing an aircraft engine could be broken down into chapters on rotor design, fuel subsystems, mounting components, etc., or you could divide up your monthly sales report to the board by product and region.

You may often find that different people are responsible for producing the different sections of a document, so it makes sense to assemble the final product from several smaller documents. That way, each person can work on their own section, following your style and layout guidelines. Then, when all the parts are complete, you can merge them into one document, or even keep them as separate parts and just combine them each time you want to print the full result. The easiest way to manage a large document like this is to use Word's **master document** feature.

Using Master Documents and Subdocuments

Word has a built in system for creating and managing a document which is composed of individual files. You create one document as the master document, then one or more subdocuments which are stored in separate files on disk. But while you're editing or printing the master document, you can see the whole thing.

This is an excellent way to manage a large and complicated document, whether you're the single author or you have different people working on each subdocument. Because each part is a separate entity, you can open a subdocument to edit it without having to open the whole (master) document. In the same way, you can assemble individual Word documents from different authors and combine them in a master document once they are all complete.

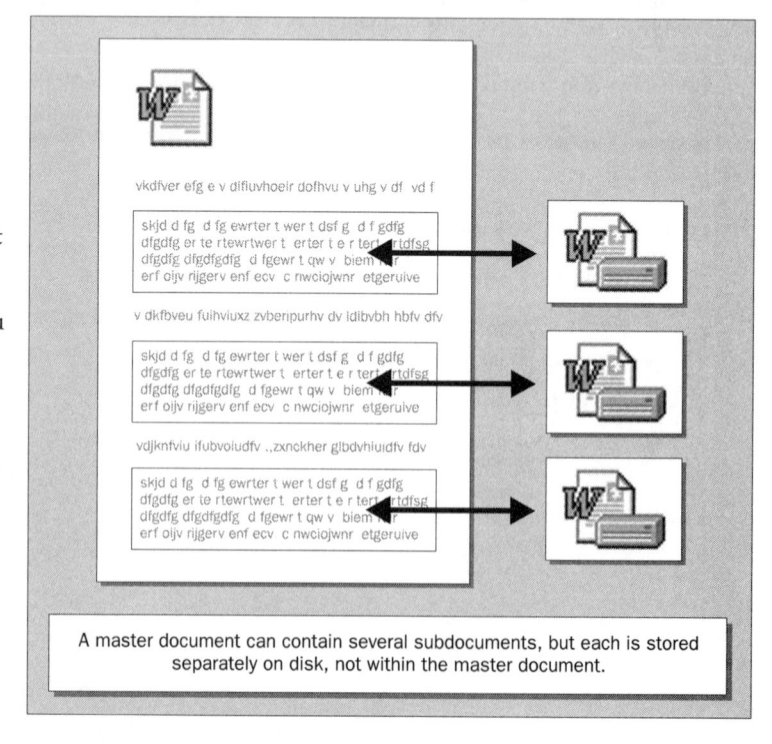

A master document can contain several subdocuments, but each is stored separately on disk, not within the master document.

The Ups and Downs of Master Documents

Before you start working with master documents, it's worth looking at some of their good and bad points. On the down side, unless you create each subdocument from within the master document first, you'll find that you may have problems when you come to include them. In particular, all subdocuments must have the same template and document styles as the master document; mixing styles across subdocuments just doesn't work. Of course, you want all the subdocuments to match, so you need to lay down the overall styles for them all. If you don't, instead of appearing as a complete document, the final product will look as if it's been built of disparate parts.

On the plus side, though, using master documents does mean that you can create an index and table of contents automatically for the entire document. Word will also number the pages correctly for you.

The way that Word handles the file names of subdocuments is, however, a little less than ideal. If you create new subdocuments from within your master document, Word uses a file name based on the first line of text it contains. If there's no text on the first line, it resorts to the rather uninformative **M1.doc**, **M2.doc**, etc. As an alternative, you can import existing subdocuments into a master document and use the file names you want.

Bear in mind that if you move a subdocument to another location on disk, you break the link to the master document. So, if you intend to distribute your completed documents, you probably need to combine them into a single file first. Word contains a command to merge one or more of the subdocuments into the master document, so that it no longer exists as a separate file on disk.

Controlling Updates to Subdocuments

Once you have inserted a subdocument, you can lock it to protect it from being changed. You can also lock the master document so that users can only edit unlocked subdocuments.

To lock a master or subdocument you must be in Master Document view. Simply place the insertion point anywhere in the document and click the Lock Document button on the Master Document toolbar. A padlock symbol appears in the left margin to indicate that the document is locked.

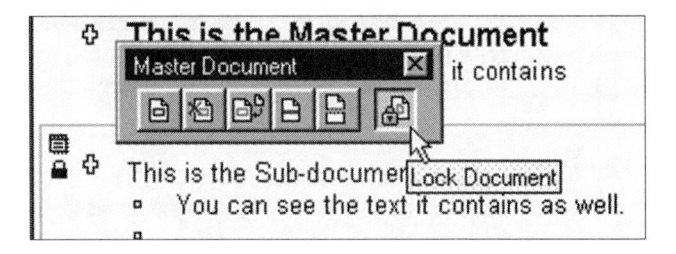

Now, if anyone attempts to change the subdocument, Word displays a message. They can only save the changes by using a different file name. This is a relatively simple way of controlling updates to the documents, but if you want to protect them more thoroughly, you have to use the normal Protect Document... command (on the Tools menu) or document passwords. We'll be looking at these later.

You can tell from this dialog that we don't get much control over how a new subdocument is named. As we suggested earlier, it's often better to create all the documents first, then build the master document by inserting them individually. But, of course, you can't prepare a template which already contains the necessary information to link to the empty subdocuments, because each subdocument is a different file. So each master document has to use unique names for its subdocuments. If you have a regular report to produce, you end up creating each master document from scratch, then inserting all new subdocuments.

Word's Master Document Commands

To turn a document into a master document, you just change the view. Select **Master Document** from the **View** menu and Word displays the **Master Document** toolbar, which makes it easy to create and manipulate subdocuments. The master document is shown with a series of levels, rather like you see in **Outline View**.

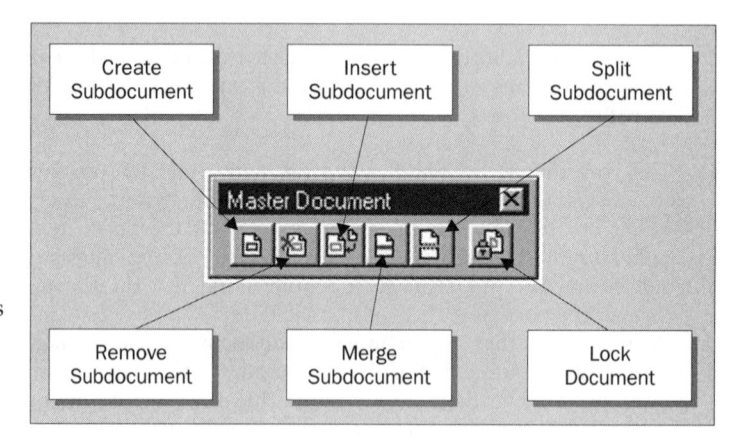

As you create a new subdocument or insert an existing one, you see it appear in the master document. You can activate a subdocument by double-clicking on the subdocument symbol in the margin of the master document. If it's already open, the subdocument is brought to the front; if not, Word opens it in a new window.

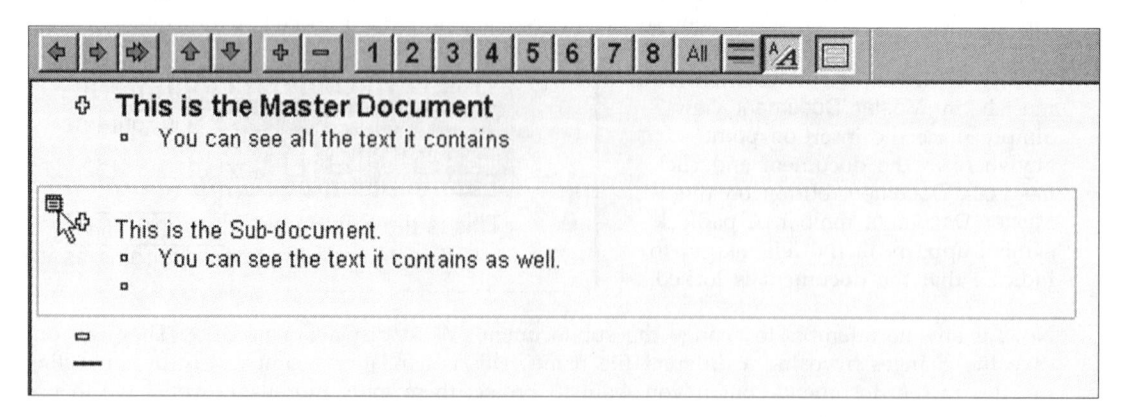

> ⊕ **This is the Master Document**
> ▫ You can see all the text it contains
>
> This is the Sub-document.
> ▫ You can see the text it contains as well.

You can also switch the master document to **Normal** and **Page Layout** views, which will show the subdocuments just as they appear in the final document. For example, here's the same master document, but viewed in **Page Layout** view (select **Page Layout** from the **View** menu, or click the button at the bottom left of the Word window):

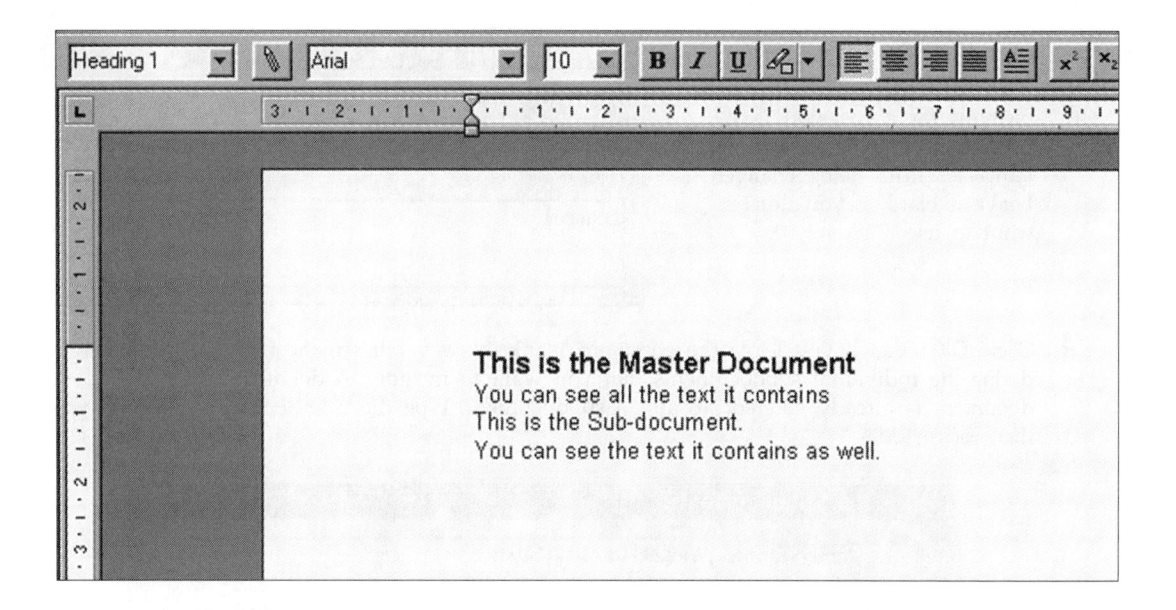

> **This is the Master Document**
> You can see all the text it contains
> This is the Sub-document.
> You can see the text it contains as well.

Creating the Master and Subdocuments Automatically

We can make life easier by preparing a template for the master document, then using a macro to get a list of the subdocuments we want. We can then create these, based on this template (remember, they all have to use the same template) and insert them into the master document.

You'll need the template MasterDoc, which will be in the folder where you installed the samples from the disk that accompanies this book. Unless you changed the defaults, this will be `C:\BegWord`.

Try It Out - Creating a Master Document with Wrox MasterDoc

Before you start, you must copy the file `MasterDoc.dot` into your `\Templates` folder. This will be `\Winword\Template` or `\Msoffice\Templates` unless you changed the defaults when you installed Word 95 or Office 95.

1 Select New... from the File menu to create a new document. (Don't use the New button on the toolbar because this uses the Normal template.) In the New dialog, select the template MasterDoc and click OK.

2 A new document is created and the normal Save As dialog opens. The default file name is New Master Document.doc, but you can change this if you want to.

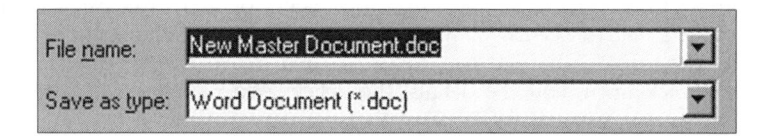

233

3 Click Save and the next dialog prompts for a password to protect the subdocument templates from being changed. Leave it blank if you don't want to use a password.

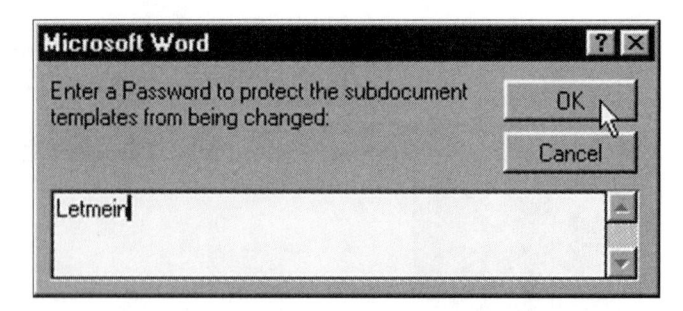

4 Click OK, even if you leave the password blank. Now you'll see the main dialog, where you define the individual subdocuments that you want to include. A default title for the document is already entered. To add a subdocument, type the title and file name you want, then click Add.

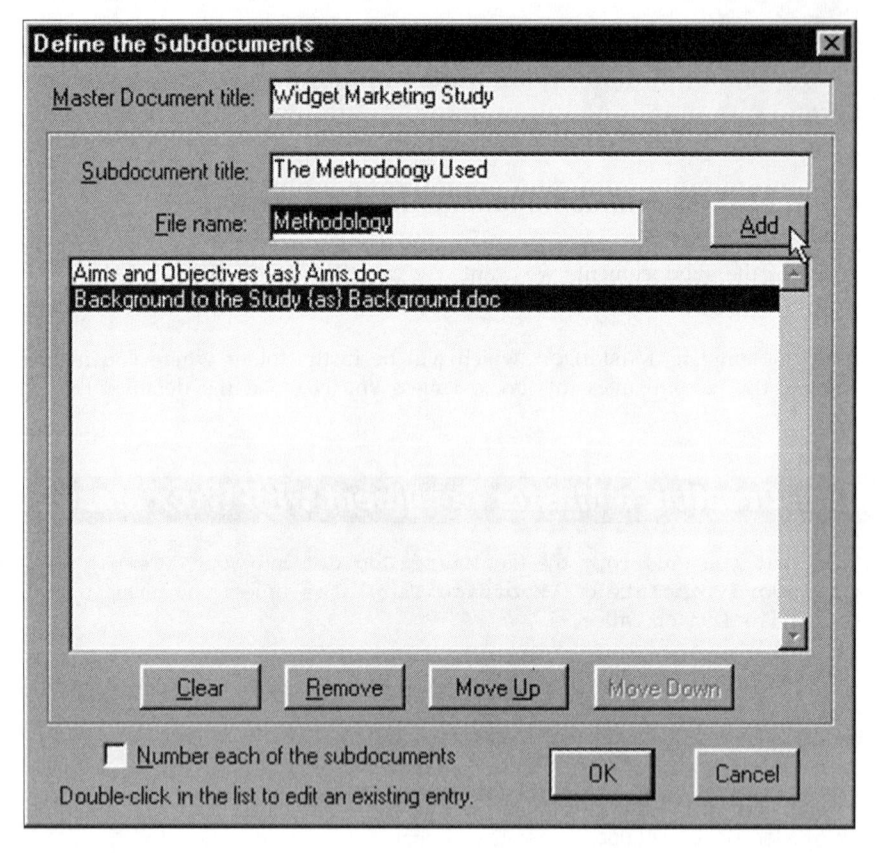

5 Notice how Word automatically suggests a file name for you. You can edit this if you want, as we've done. You'll see a list of the currently defined subdocuments, which you can manipulate using the Clear, Remove, Move Up and Move Down buttons below. To change an entry, double-click on it, edit the details, then click Add to replace it in the list.

6 Turn on the Number each of the subdocuments check box at the bottom of the dialog. You'll see the subdocument numbers appear in the list:

```
1 : Aims and Objectives {as} Aims.doc
2 : Background to the Study {as} Background.doc
3 : The Methodology Used {as} Methodology.doc
4 : Producing the Results {as} Results.doc
```

7 Once you've prepared the list of subdocuments, click OK. The new document is created for you and, again, you're prompted to save it when it's complete.

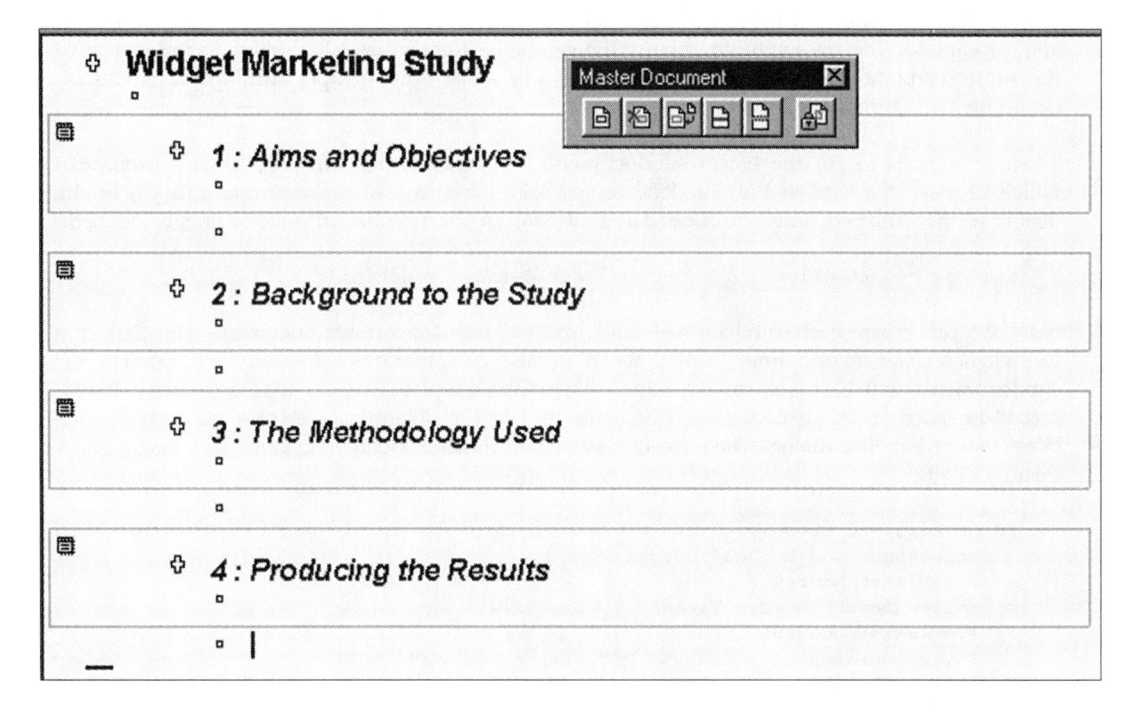

How It Works

The macro that creates the master document is reasonably trivial. Word includes a set of macro commands that can be used to switch to Master Document view and insert subdocuments. You can also create new subdocuments, or open, merge or split existing ones, just like using the buttons on the Master Document toolbar.

Our `CreateMasterDocument` macro runs as soon as a new document is created based on the MasterDoc template, because we've included an `AutoNew` macro which starts it. Here's the beginning of the `MAIN` procedure in our `CreateMasterDocument` macro, and the declaration of the `Shared` variables:

```
Dim Shared SubDocList$(0)     'subdocument details
Dim Shared DocTitle$          'title of main document
Dim Shared ListMax            'maximum number of subdocuments
Dim Shared DList$(0)          'list of sub documents for use in dialog
Dim Shared DCount             'actual number of documents

Sub MAIN
DocTitle$ = GetDocumentProperty$("Title")
```

```
    DocTemplate$ = GetDocumentProperty$("Template")
    On Error Goto CMDExit
    Dim FSA As FileSaveAs          'save the master document first,
    Dialog FSA                     'then get the Template password
    Prompt$ = "Enter a Password to protect the subdocument templates from being
    changed:"
    TemplatePW$ = InputBox$(Prompt$)
```

We can get the title of a document and the file name of its template using the **GetDocumentProperty$()** function we looked at in Part 1. Then, we save the new document and prompt for the password to protect the template. Remember, all the subdocuments must use the same template as the master document, so this stops other people adding new styles or changing the settings stored in it.

The next step is to get the list of subdocuments. We've created a function, called **GetDocList**, which displays the Define the Subdocuments dialog you saw in the example and places the details in the **Shared** array **SubDocList$**. It returns the number of subdocuments defined:

```
    NumDocs = GetDocList            'our user-defined function
```

Now we can create each subdocument and insert it into the master document. The first step is to switch off screen updating, display the hourglass cursor and disable auto macros. The new subdocuments will be based on the same MasterDoc template, so we need to prevent the **AutoNew** macro running each time. Next, we update the document's Title property in case it's been changed in the dialog. Then we can switch to Master Document view and insert the master document title:

```
    If NumDocs > 0 Then
       ScreenUpdating 0 : WaitCursor 1
       DisableAutoMacros 1
       SetDocumentProperty "Title", 0, DocTitle$, 1
       ViewMasterDocument
       Style "Heading 1" : Insert DocTitle$ : InsertPara
       Style "Normal" : InsertPara
```

We're ready create each subdocument. We get the file name and title from the array **SubDocList$** using string-handling commands to split it up in the correct places. If the file name contains any spaces, we have to enclose it in inverted commas first. Then we print a message in the status bar, create a new document based on the correct template and insert the subdocument title into it. Then we can save and close it:

```
       For CurrentDoc = 1 To NumDocs
          SubTitle$ = SubDocList$(CurrentDoc - 1)
          TPos = InStr(SubTitle$, " {as} ")
          SubName$ = Mid$(SubTitle$, TPos + 6)
          If InStr(SubName$, " ") Then SubName$ = Chr$(34) + \
             SubName$ + Chr$(34)
          SubTitle$ = Left$(SubTitle$, TPos - 1)
          Print "Inserting subdocument "; SubTitle$
          FileNew .Template = DocTemplate$
          Style "Heading 2" : Insert SubTitle$ : InsertPara
          Style "Normal" : InsertPara
          FileSaveAs .Name = SubName$
          FileClose
```

Back in the master document, we go to the end and insert the new subdocument, specifying the password to protect the template. Then we go round the loop again, repeating the process for the next subdocument. Once they're all inserted, we go back to the start of the master document and save it. The rest is just clearing up, error messages, and turning auto macros back on:

```
        EndOfDocument
        InsertSubdocument .Name = SubName$, .PasswordDot = TemplatePW$
    Next
    StartOfDocument
    WaitCursor 0 : ScreenUpdating 1
    On Error Goto CMDExit
    FileSave
Else
    MsgBox "No subdocuments to create", "Wrox MasterDoc", 48
EndIf
Goto CMDExit
CMDError:
WaitCursor 0
Msg$ = "Can't create document. (" + Str$(Err) + " )"
MsgBox Msg$, "Wrox MasterDoc", 48
CMDExit:
WaitCursor 0 : DisableAutoMacros 0
End Sub
```

So, all in all, building the master document isn't difficult. The complicated part of our macro is, in fact, the Define the Subdocuments dynamic dialog. This uses many of the techniques you've seen in earlier chapters to maintain a list of entries which can be manipulated.

Using 'Dynamic Lists' in a Dialog

One of the failings of WordBasic is that when you use **ReDim** to change the size of an array, you lose all the existing values. In a dialog **List** control, you have to supply an array containing the values for the list. Any empty array elements are shown as blanks in the dialog.

To get round this, we've used two arrays. One is sized to the maximum number of entries allowed. You can see these as the **Shared** variable **ListMax** and the shared array **DList$** in the code above. To keep count of how many elements are used, we have another **Shared** variable, **Dcount**, the number of items in the list. We actually maintain the list of entries in **DList$()**, then **ReDim** the array **SubDocList$** to the correct size and copy the entries across to it each time there's a change in the list. Remember that arrays start at zero, so we have to use **DCount - 1** as the size:

```
Sub CopyDList(NewPos)
    Redim SubDocList$(DCount - 1)
    For i = 0 To DCount - 1
        SubDocList$(i) = DList$(i)
    Next
    DlgListBoxArray "SDList", SubDocList$()
    If NewPos > (DCount - 1) Then NewPos = DCount - 1
    DlgValue "SDList", NewPos
End Sub
```

Notice that we have to issue the **DlgListBoxArray** command to update the list box in the dialog when the content of the array changes. This places the highlight (the currently selected item in the list) back on the first entry again, so we then have to reset it using the **DlgValue** command. This is why we use the **NewPos** argument in the routine; it holds the current position (or the new position required) of the highlight.

Once you've grasped this technique, you can see how easy it is to manipulate the contents of the list. To add an item at the end (when the highlight is already at the end of the list) we just set the value of **DList$(DCount)** to the new entry, and increment **DCount**. Because the list could be empty, we have to test for the current position (**APos**) being less than or equal to **DCount - 1**. To add a new entry in the middle of the list, we use a loop to shuffle everything else up one place and add it in the vacant slot. Of course, before we add any items, we have to check that we haven't exceeded the limits of the array:

```
Sub AddEntry(APos)
If DCount < (ListMax - 1) Then                  'room for another entry
    If APos >= (DCount - 1) Then                'add at end of the list
        DList$(DCount) = NewDoc$
        DCount = DCount + 1                     'increment number in list
        CopyDList(DCount - 1)                   'update the dialog list
    Else
        For i = DCount To APos + 1 Step - 1     'move all the entries
            DList$(i) = DList$(i - 1)           'above up one place
        Next
        DList$(APos) = NewDoc$                  'add it within the list
        DCount = DCount + 1                     'increment number in list
        CopyDList APos                          'update the dialog list
    EndIf
Else
    MsgBox "No more room for subdocuments", "Wrox MasterDoc", 48
EndIf
End Sub
```

Similarly, we can delete items, or move one up or down in the list. Clearing the list is also easy; we set **DCount** to zero, **ReDim** the list box array **SubDocList$** to zero to clear it, and update the dialog display:

```
Sub ClearDList
DCount = 0
Redim SubDocList$(0)
DlgListBoxArray "SDList", SubDocList$()
End Sub
```

The rest of the code in the macro deals with the dialog function and manages, the other 'niceties', enabling the various controls and looking after numbering the entries in the list. If you want to implement this type of dialog, you can use the sample macros as a starting point.

Other Ways to Build a Master Document

If you don't want to use the built-in master document system, you can manage your own multifile documents using **fields**. We'll be looking at fields in more detail in Part 3 of this book, but, in essence, a Word field is simply a way of inserting information, other than as text, into a document. Word supports many types of field, but, for managing documents, we're only interested in two: the {INCLUDETEXT} and {RD} fields.

Using {INCLUDETEXT} Fields to Insert Subdocuments

When you use an {INCLUDETEXT} field in your document and specify the name of the other file, you effectively tell Word to place a copy of the file (or a part of it) at that point in the document. Despite the name of the field, you can include other types of object, not just text from a Word document. Word doesn't use OLE (Object Linking and Embedding) for this. Instead, the objects you can use are those for which Word has filters installed, such as Excel spreadsheets, graphics and text files of various types, and other word processor application's files.

To insert an {INCLUDETEXT} field, you use the Field... command on the Insert menu. Word displays the Field dialog, where you select the type of field you want. You have to add the name of the file you want to include to the field, which you type into the Field Codes: box in the dialog. Rather than including the whole file, you can also add the name of a Bookmark that contains the text you want.

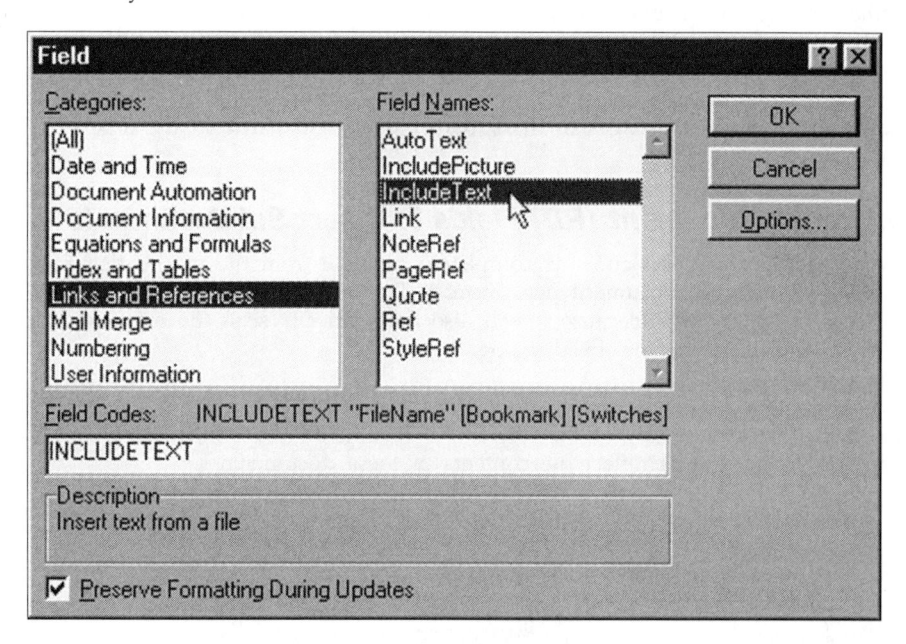

You can use two switches with the {INCLUDETEXT} field. If you want to specify the filter to be used with the file, you include **\c <classname>** where **<classname>** is the name of the filter. To use the Excel converter for example, you specify **MSBiff**. There's a list of all the possible filters in Word's Help file, but remember that your users may not have installed all the filters when they first installed Word.

When you update the text which is inserted in the document by an {INCLUDETEXT} field, you can pass the changes back to the original file on disk. Some file types may not support this, but it does work with Excel and other Word documents. It depends on the filters that are installed. If you want to prevent the changes being passed back to the original file, you add the **\!** switch to the {INCLUDETEXT} field. For example,

```
{ INCLUDETEXT "C:\\MyDocs\\Sales.xls" R1C1:R10C5 \cMSBiff \! }
```

could include the sales figures for March which are in the Excel file **Sales.xls**, but prevent them being changed. The Bookmark in this case is an Excel range (not a bookmark in the Word sense), and we've specified the Excel file converter. You'll also notice that we have to use double backslash characters in the file name, so that Word can tell they're not switches.

If the original file is edited and changed in Excel, we can update the contents of the {INCLUDETEXT} field in our document just like with any other field. We highlight it and press F9.

Having said all this, {INCLUDETEXT} fields are really only included to maintain backward compatibility with earlier versions of Word, though you may find that this method suits your needs better than the built-in master document system. To insert parts of a file into your document, you can use the **InsertFile** macro statement with the **.Link** argument set to **1**, which is broadly equivalent to the Word Field dialog.

This method allows you to build your own master documents system if you wish, and maintain more control over the individual documents within it. You can also use non-Word documents as the subdocuments, while avoiding the overheads of OLE. However, this does make your master document very large, because the subdocuments are still inserted into it. The main advantage is that it correctly numbers the pages in the subdocuments, and hence in the indexes and tables of contents.

Using Reference Document {RD} Fields to Insert Subdocuments

If you want to keep the subdocuments completely separate from the master document, you can use the {RD} or **reference document** field instead. This is very useful if you need to create tables of contents or indexes, because it will also automatically scan the referenced documents. You insert {RD} fields using the Field dialog.

This also keeps your master document down to a reasonable size, because the original document doesn't contain (or display) any of the referenced document. However, the big disadvantage is that page numbering doesn't reflect the contents of these documents.

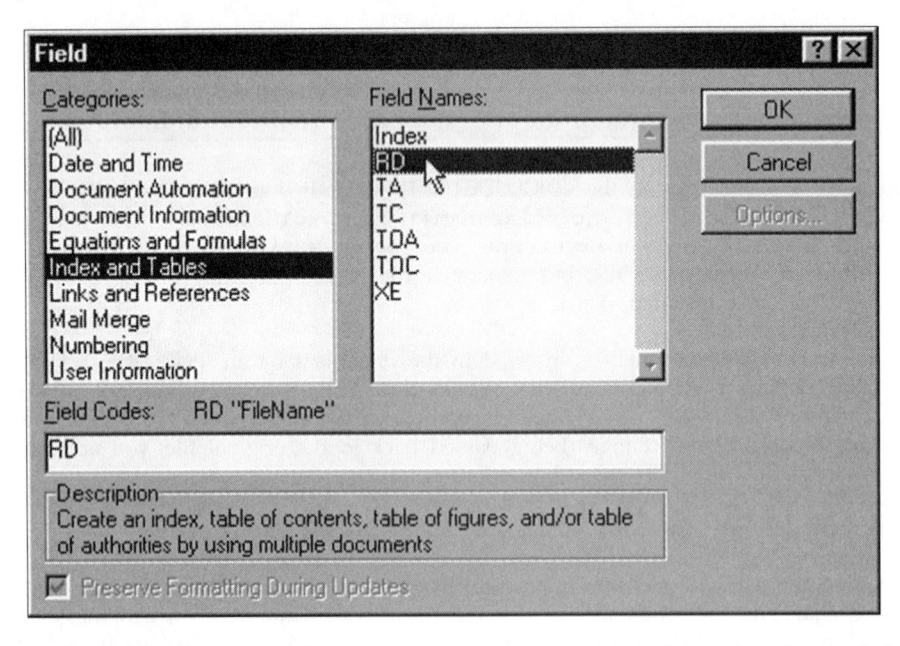

To get round this problem, you have to change the starting page for each referenced document. You insert a section break in the document, select Insert | Page Numbers..., click Format... and change the Start At: setting for Page Numbering. The only difficulty now is that you must update this manually, every time the number of pages in a previous referenced document changes. Alternatively, you can format the page numbers to start from one in each section and use the section number as part of the page number, for example 4 – 13.

To insert {RD} fields from a macro, use the **InsertField** statement. The only argument you need in the field is the name of the referenced document, so the statement,

```
InsertField .Field = "RD C:\\MyDocs\\Section1.doc"
```

will insert an {RD} field to reference the document **Section1.doc**. Notice that we have to use two backslash characters again, so that Word doesn't translate them as switches.

So, there are several ways to create large documents, but unless you're reaching the limits of master documents, or need to include some features that they can't support, you're probably better off sticking to Word's master document system. It's only when you need to include other application's data files, or have huge documents running into hundreds of pages that you may find using fields a useful technique to have under your belt. We'll see a lot more about using fields in Part 3.

Protecting Your Documents

Whether your document consists of a master and subdocuments, or is just a single document, you often need to protect it from being changed, particularly when several people are working on it. One option is to apply a password, so that the document can only be opened by those who know it. You can also allow other users to open a document to review it, but have any recommendations they make for changing details stored within the document without affecting the original text. One method is to force them to use **annotations**, where a field is inserted in the document and their comments appear in a separate pane, similar to a footnote. Alternatively, you can force them to use **revisions**. In this case, the changes they make appear in the original document, but as alterations to the text. Things they delete appear with a line through them, and text they add appears in a different color.

Several people can review the same document. Their annotations appear with their initials, and their revisions can be set up to appear in different colors. Once you get the document back, you can accept or reject each one individually.

Applying a Password to a Document

To prevent users opening your document at all, you apply a Protection Password to it in the Save tab of the Options dialog (select Options... from the Tools menu). Other people can only open the document by supplying this password. If you use this method, be sure to keep a record of the password, because you won't be able to open it again if you forget it. The passwords are case-sensitive, so **MyPassword** is different from **Mypassword**.

To control alterations to a document you use the Write Reservation Password instead. When this is set, users can only save changes to the document if they know the password, although they can still open the document to view it in Read only mode. Of course, you can use both together, with different passwords, to allow some users to view your documents, some to edit them, while others are locked out completely.

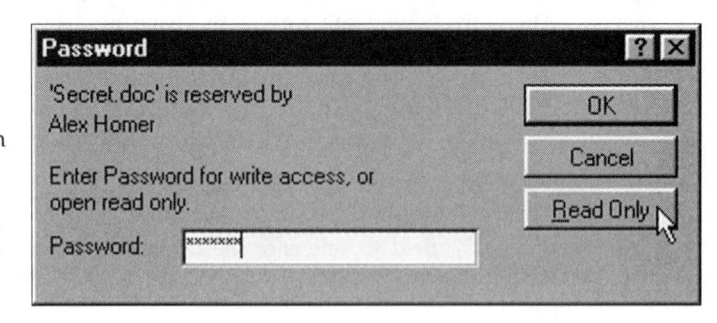

You can also set the Read-Only Recommended option in this dialog, with or without a password. When this is set, Word displays a message suggesting that the user opens it in Read-only mode, so that they can't make changes to it. This is only a suggestion, though. If you haven't specified a password and they click No, the user can open and edit the document as normal.

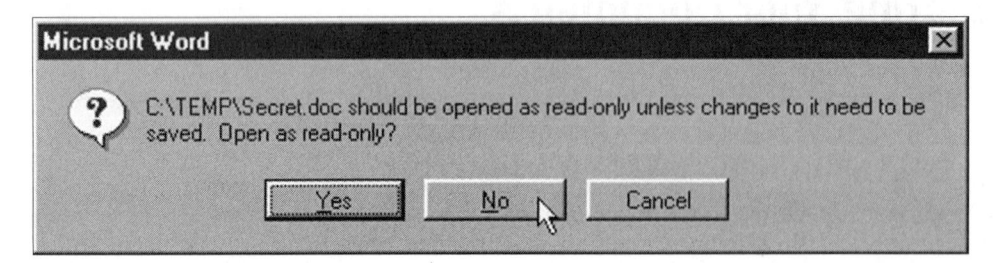

You can set all of these options when you save a file, using a macro, with the normal **FileSaveAs** statement. There's also an extra argument available. You can lock the document for annotations, so that users can still comment on a document which has a Write Reservation Password by inserting annotations in it.

Argument	What It Does
.LockAnnot	Sets to 1 to lock the document for annotations only.
.Password	Requires the password to open the document.
.WritePassword	Requires the password to save changes to the document.
.RecommendReadOnly	Displays the Recommend Open Read-only dialog.

For example,

```
FileSaveAs .Name = "MyDoc.doc", .Password = "Letmein"
```

will save the current document so that it can only be opened by specifying the password. To allow any user to open the document, but only to add annotations unless they know the Write Reservation password, we would use:

```
FileSaveAs .Name = "MyDoc.doc", .LockAnnot = 1, .WritePassword = "Letmein"
```

Preventing Changes to the Original Text

You can choose to protect the document so that others can only add annotations, revisions, or change the contents of fields in the document. Select Protect Document... from the Tools menu to open the Protect Document dialog. If you don't add a password, the user can turn off the protection themselves and make changes directly to the document.

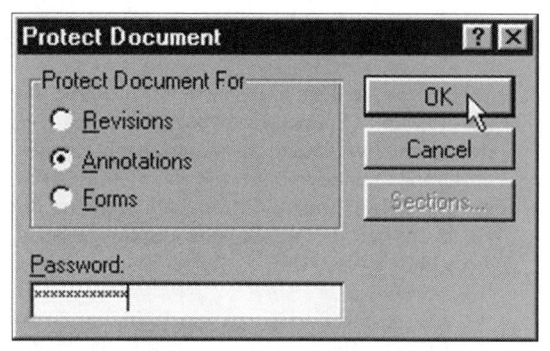

You can also use macros like this to protect and unprotect a document. There are three statements available:

Argument	What It Does
`DocumentProtection()`	Tells you the current state of the protection. Returns **0** if there is no protection, **1** if the document is protected for **Fields**, **2** if protected for **Annotations** and **3** if protected for **Revisions**.
`ToolsProtectDocument`	Protects the currently active document. Takes three arguments: `.DocumentPassword` is the password to apply, `.NoReset` prevents any fields in the document being set back to their default values, and `.Type` is the type of protection to apply, using the same values as the `DocumentProtection()` function.
`ToolsUnprotectDocument`	Removes protection from the currently active document. The only argument required is `.DocumentPassword`—the password to apply.

If you try and protect a document that's already protected, or unprotect one that isn't protected, you'll get an error message. To prevent this, use the `DocumentProtection()` function first:

```
If DocumentProtection() > 0 then ToolsUnprotectDocument \
                                 .DocumentPassword = "Letmein"
```

> **FYI** Don't worry about the **Fields** options in the **Document Protection** dialogs and statements for the time being. We'll be looking at fields, and how they are used, in more detail in Part 3.

Controlling Changes to Your Documents

If you have to manage documents which are reviewed by several people, you can find it difficult to keep track of the process. The usual way, and probably the least effective and most time consuming, is to get each reviewer to make changes and then return it to you so that you can accept or reject them. But trying to compile all the changes into a final version can be a nightmare. Instead, you can make use of Word's revisions and annotations features.

Using Revisions in a Document

When you protect a document for revisions, Word automatically marks changes to the text within the document by placing a line through deleted items and inserting new items in a different color. You can set the colors and style for each type in the Revisions tab of the Options dialog. Select Options... from the Tools menu.

As you edit a document which has revisions turned on, you can use the Revisions dialog to choose how they appear. To open the Revisions dialog, select Revisions from the Tools menu. The top check box allows you to turn revisions on and off. If you have specified a password in the Protect Document dialog, the check box will be set and disabled so that the user can't turn off revisions.

Rather than having them appear on screen as you type, you can hide the revisions so that the document looks quite normal and your changes appear to be made directly to it. This makes working on the document a lot easier, but still means that your changes are entered as revisions, which you can choose to look at when you've finished. You can also opt to show or hide the revisions when the document is printed.

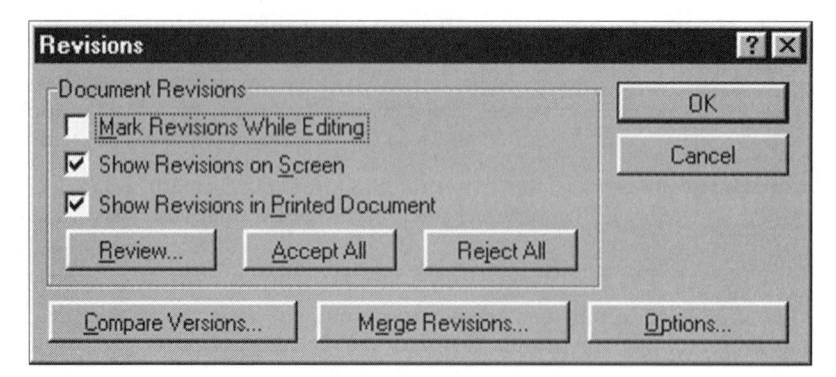

Once you get your document back from all the reviewers, you compile a final version. If you have several copies which have been edited by different reviewers, you can compare them and merge all of the revisions into one document. Then, you use the other three buttons in the dialog to review each revision, or accept or reject them all.

Using Annotations in a Document

You normally use annotations when you want reviewers to make separate comments on a document, rather than edit it directly. They can't type in the main document window. Instead, they click the Insert Annotation button, or select Annotation from the Insert menu.

An annotation field is placed in the document at the current insertion point (cursor position), and the Annotations pane opens at the bottom of the window, rather like a footnote window. The reviewer's comments appear here, instead of in the document itself.

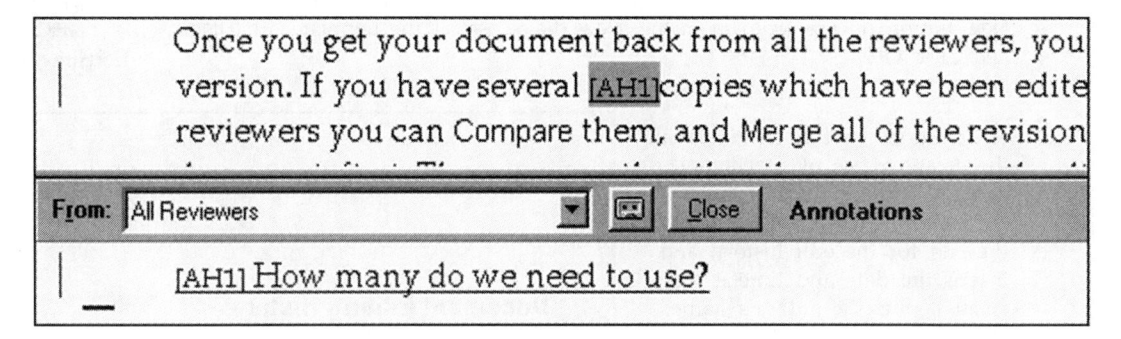

Once you get the document back, you turn off the document protection. Select Unprotect Document from the Tools menu. Now you can read and act upon the comments made by each reviewer, by selecting View | Annotations to open the Annotations pane.

In Normal view, clicking on an annotation field scrolls the Annotations pane to show the appropriate annotation. Similarly, clicking on an annotation in the Annotations pane scrolls the document to show where it refers to. You can also use the From: drop-down list to show just the annotations from one reviewer. Once you're happy with the final version of the document, you can remove them. If you ensured that Mark Revisions While Editing is selected when the annotations were added then this would simply be a case of using the Reject All button in the Revisions dialog. Otherwise, you'll need to process the annotation marks individually, probably by creating a small macro to search through the document looking for the marks. A ^a string for the **Find** parameter of an **EditFind** statement would be sufficient for this. There's a macro called **GrabAnnotation** in the **Usefulbits.dot** template for you to look at and modify if you'd like to try this.

Adding Edit History to a Document

One thing that these features don't offer is a way to track the progress of a document through different editing stages. For example, you may have several people working in turn on a document, each making particular changes to it. It would be nice to know at any point which stage of the editing process it had reached.

We've included a sample template which uses auto macros to keep track of the way documents based on it are edited. These macros maintain a list of the editing sessions that the document has been through, added to the end of it. You can copy them into any template and modify them as you wish.

You'll need the EditHistory template, which will be wherever you installed the samples from the disk that accompanies this book. Unless you changed the defaults, this will be `C:\BegWord`.

Try It Out - Using the Wrox EditHistory Template

Before you start, you must copy the file **EditHistory.dot** into your **\Templates** folder. This will be **\Winword\Template** or **\Msoffice\Templates** unless you changed the defaults when you installed Word 95 or Office 95. Don't open the original copy of the template.

1 Select New... from the File menu to create a new document. (Don't use the New button on the toolbar.) In the New dialog, select the template EditHistory and click OK.

2 A new document is created, with the default name of Document1 or similar. Our macro automatically adds a heading at the end for the edit history, and inserts the date and time it was created, plus the author's name. Type some text into the new document.

> This is a test document for Chapter 6.
>
> **Document Editing History:**
> Created 03/30/96 9:43 AM by Alex Homer.

3 Now close the document, using the Close button at the top right of the window, or the Close command on the File menu. A dialog appears where you need to enter a comment of at least ten characters before you can click Save. Enter a suitable comment in the dialog:

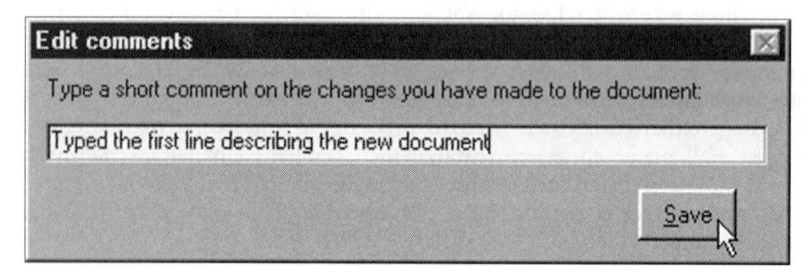

> **Edit comments**
> Type a short comment on the changes you have made to the document:
> Typed the first line describing the new document
> Save

4 Click Save, and the usual Save As dialog opens. Unless you've previously saved a new document, this always appears when you close it.

5 Now open the new document again by selecting it in the list of most recently used files in the File menu, or with the normal Open dialog. You'll see your comment, together with the date and time you last saved it:

> This is a test document for Chapter 6.
>
> **Document Editing History:**
> Created 03/30/96 9:43 AM by Alex Homer.
> 03/30/96 9:46 AM by Alex Homer. Typed the first line describing the new document.

6 Repeat the process, and each comment is added to the end of the list automatically:

> This is a test document for Chapter 6.
> This is a second line of text.
>
> **Document Editing History:**
> Created 03/30/96 9:43 AM by Alex Homer.
> 03/30/96 9:46 AM by Alex Homer. Typed the first line describing the new document.
> 03/31/96 3:24 PM by Alex Homer. Added another line.
> 03/31/96 4:08 PM by Alex Homer. Corrected the spelling.

How It Works

You've seen how all Word documents contain document properties. These can be built-in properties, such as the **Title** and **Author**, or custom properties which you create yourself. We're using macros to manipulate various document properties and create the history entries in the document. There are three macros in the EditHistory template: **AutoNew**, **AutoOpen** and **AutoClose**.

The **AutoNew** macro runs when a new document is created, based on the EditHistory template. It inserts the heading for the edit history entries, and a line showing when the document was created. It gets the author's name from the built-in document property Author, and uses WordBasic's **Date()** and **Time()** functions to get the current date and time.

```
Sub MAIN      'The AutoNew macro
For i = 1 To 5
    InsertPara
Next
LastEditor$ = GetDocumentProperty$("Author")
LastEditDate$ = Date$() + " " + Time$()
EndOfDocument : InsertPara : InsertPara
Bold 1 : Insert "Document Editing History:"
Bold 0 : InsertPara
Insert "Created " + LastEditDate$ + " by " + LastEditor$ + "."
InsertPara
StartOfDocument
End Sub
```

Once the document has been saved, it's the `AutoOpen` macro that runs whenever it's opened. The `AutoNew` macro doesn't run again for that document. In the `AutoOpen` macro, we get the name of the last person who edited it, and the date and time is was last saved. Word stores these in two built-in document properties, `LastSavedBy` and `LastSavedTime`. The only other thing we need is the comment that the user entered last time they closed the document. The `AutoClose` macro stores this in a custom document property, `WroxUsrLastEdit`:

```
Sub MAIN    'The AutoOpen macro
LastEditor$ = GetDocumentProperty$("LastSavedBy")
LastEditDate$ = GetDocumentProperty$("LastSavedTime")
LastComment$ = GetDocumentProperty$("WroxUsrLastEdit")
EditEntry$ = LastEditDate$ + " by " + LastEditor$ + ". " + LastComment$
EndOfDocument
Insert EditEntry$ : InsertPara
StartOfDocument
End Sub
```

We use the `AutoClose` macro to gather information about the editing that was done while the document was open, using a dynamic dialog which forces the user to enter at least ten characters. We haven't included details of this dialog because, in many ways, it's the same as those we created in Part 1.

```
Sub MAIN    'The AutoClose macro
...
'Declare the custom UserDialog
...
Dim UD As UserDialog
DisableInput 1
Dialog UD
DisableInput 0
SetDocumentProperty "WroxUsrLastEdit", 0, UD.txtComment + ".", 2
FileSave
End Sub
```

Once we've got the comment, we can update the `WroxUsrLastEdit` document property, ready for the `AutoOpen` macro to insert in the document the next time it's opened. Notice that we have to use `FileSave` to save the document again, because we've changed the value of a document property in it.

To create a new document property, or change the value of an existing one, we use the `SetDocumentProperty` statement. It takes four arguments:

> **SetDocumentProperty** *Name$, Type, Value($), CustomOrBuiltin*

Name$	The text name of the property, which can be either a custom or built-in property.
Type	**0** for a string, **1** for a number, **2** for a date, and **3** for a yes/no type.
Value($)	The value to set. This can be a string or number, but must match the type of that property.
CustomOrBuiltin	**0** to let Word decide if it's a custom or built-in property, **1** if you want to specify a built-in property, or **2** if you want it to be stored as a custom property.

So, the line in our `AutoClose` macro,

```
SetDocumentProperty "WroxUsrLastEdit", 0, UD.txtComment + ".", 2
```

sets the `WroxUsrLastEdit` custom document property to a string which is the value in the `txtComment` field of our `UD` dialog record, adding a full stop.

OK, so there are other ways of achieving the same effect, but you can see from this example how simple it is to manipulate document properties and store information in them. It also demonstrates how you can use the `AutoNew`, `AutoOpen` and `AutoClose` macros.

Creating Indexes and Tables of Contents

One you've finished writing your document, you may need to include an index and/or a table of contents. While creating tables of contents is easy (providing you've used the correct Word styles for your headings), indexing is usually a major task that no-one looks forward to. In this section, we'll show you how you can make both of these jobs less of a chore.

Creating a Table of Contents

As long as you use Word's heading styles for the headings in your documents, creating a table of contents is easy. By default, Word shows four heading styles, Heading 1 to Heading 4, but you can actually define your own, up to Heading 9, and they will still be included in the table of contents.

Once your document is complete, place the insertion point where you want the table of contents to be created and select Index and Tables... from the Insert menu. Open the Table of Contents tab and set the options you want to use:

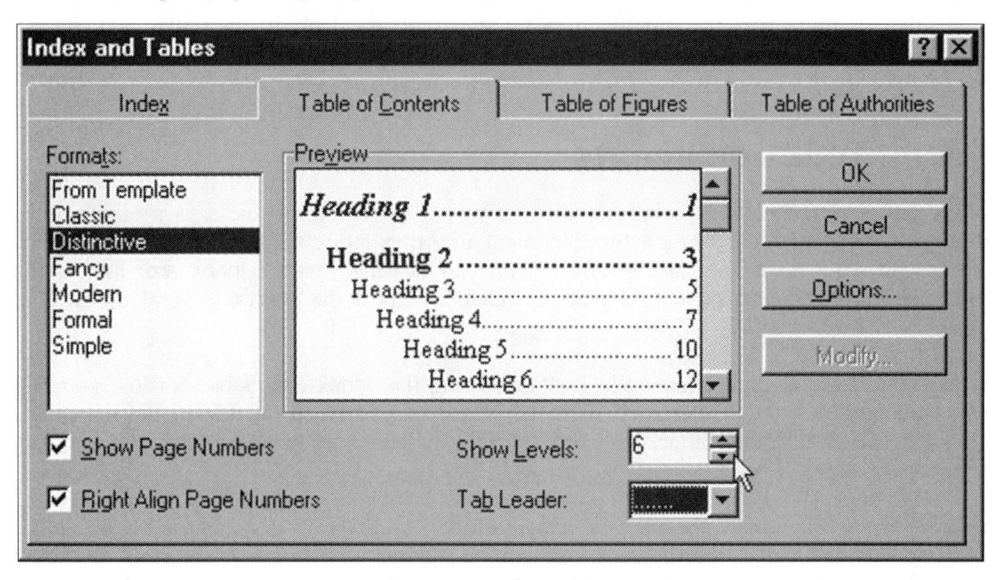

There are several built-in formats available, and you can also control the way the page numbers appear and select the Tab Leader, the line between the text and page number. The important setting is Show Levels. Here, you tell Word how many levels of heading you want to include. If you have used headings up to Heading 5 in your document, but only want to include the first three in the table of contents, you set this value to 3. To see a sample of a table of contents, look in the front of this book. This is how we create them!

Your table of contents can also include text which is formatted in a style that isn't one of the heading styles. Click Options..., and the dialog allows you to select other styles and specify at which level you want them to appear. For example, you could set the Show Levels option in the main dialog to 3, then set the headings for Annotation Text to 4 and Footer style text to 5.

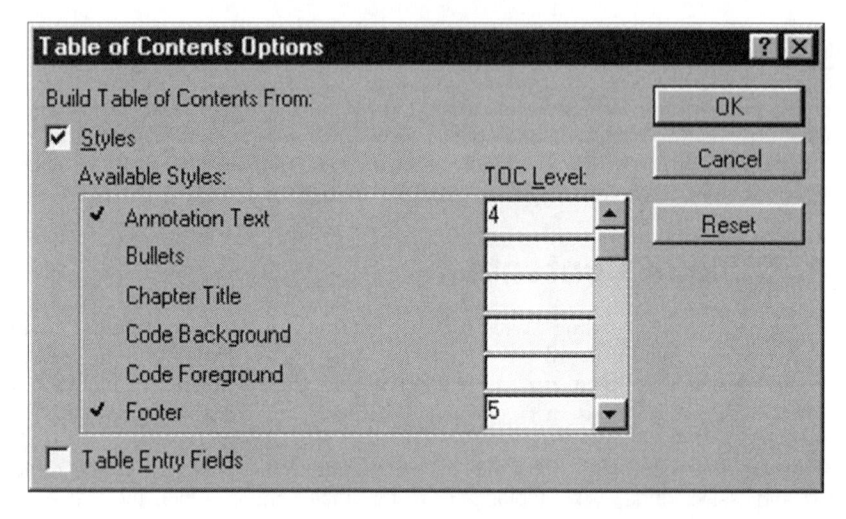

To create a table of contents using a macro, you use the **InsertTableOfContents** statement. This takes arguments which broadly mirror the settings available in the Index and Table and Options dialogs. The Word Help file contains more information about this statement and its arguments.

Indexing Your Documents

While tables of contents are relatively easy to manage, creating an index is a real headache. The traditional way is to go through the document inserting index fields after each occurrence of the words you want to include in the index. Then you use the Insert | Index and Table... command to create the index. You often find that you have to repeat the process several times to get it right.

When you create an index manually in Word, using the Index and Tables dialog, you insert {XE} fields into the document after each word or phrase you want to include in the index. Inserting the field {XE "templates"} after the word *templates* will add an entry in the index for it, pointing to the page where it occurs.

So how can we automate the process? One method would be to assemble a list of all the words in the document and choose the ones we want to index. Then we can get Word to automatically mark all the occurrences of these words using the **MarkIndexEntry** macro statement with the **.MarkAll** argument set to 1.

But this isn't entirely useful. If you include a common word, like *templates*, when you are indexing a book about Word, you'll end up with hundreds of references in the index, one for each occurrence of the word. What we really need is a method of selecting the main references for each word, so that the index entry for *templates* would look something like this:

```
templates
    creating    145
    explained   288
    macros      72, 168, 296
    saving      335, 421
```

To create a two-level index, we add {XE} fields which show the first and second level words, separated by a colon (:). For example, placing the field
{XE "templates:creating"} on page 145 of the document will produce the first two lines of the index shown above.

Indexing with a Concordance File

We've included some WordBasic routines which at least partly automate the process for you, and make it easier to see which words have been indexed when you look through the document. Instead of inserting index entries into the document directly, we'll take advantage of the WordBasic statement **AutoMarkIndexEntries**. This uses a concordance file to automatically insert the correct {XE} fields into your document.

A **concordance file** is a Word document containing a two column table. The first column contains the words or phrases we want to index, and the second contains the entries, either as single- or two-level, that we want to be shown in the index. Our approach takes us through four steps:

- Create a concordance file from words highlighted in the document.
- Edit the concordance file entries to make the index two-level.
- Insert {XE} index fields in the document with **AutoMarkIndexEntries**.
- Build the index from the {XE} fields.

To select the words and phrases in the document we want to index, we'll use one of Word 95's new features: **highlights**. This is the computing equivalent of the pink, green and yellow highlighter pens, and is very easy to use. It also makes it easy to see later where the indexed words are. Then we can use a macro to create the concordance file, and keep on editing it and rebuilding the index until it's correct.

Try It Out - Auto Indexing with WroxIndex

You'll need the template WroxIndex which will be in the folder where you installed the samples from the disk that accompanies this book. Unless you changed the defaults, this will be **C:\BegWord**. You'll also need a document to index. We've supplied one for you called **IndexMe.doc**, and it's in the samples folder as well. It's part of one of the Help files that you'll be seeing in a later chapter.

1 Copy the file **WroxIndex.dot** into your **\Templates** folder. Unless you changed the defaults when you installed Word 95 or Office 95, this will be **\Winword\Template** or **\Msoffice\Templates**. Then, open the file **IndexMe.doc**. You might like to make a copy first and open this, to avoid changing the original.

2 You'll see the Wrox Index toolbar displayed. If you can't see it, select Toolbars... from the View menu and put a check by it in the list. You can dock the toolbar at any edge of the screen to get it out of the way—try the right-hand side. The text on the buttons is rotated through 90 degrees automatically.

> **FYI** If the **Wrox Index** toolbar isn't shown in the list in the **Toolbars** dialog, select **Templates...** from the **File** menu and make sure the document is attached to the **WroxIndex** template. If it isn't, click **Attach...** and select this template in your \Templates folder.

3 First, we need to highlight the words we want to index. The Highlight button is on the Formatting toolbar. Click the down arrow next to it to choose a color you like—yellow is probably the best bet, so you can still read the text. The main button part remains depressed, ready to use:

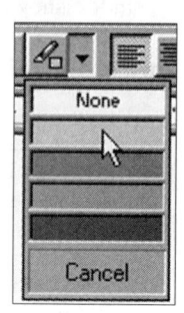

4 Now go through the document, highlighting the words and phrases you want to index. Try not to include single words—go for definite phrases. That way, you avoid too much duplication appearing in the index. Double-clicking selects a whole word. To remove the highlight, just go over it again.

WroxPBS Duplex Print is Word add-in macro that allows you to print on both sides of the paper with printers that do not support duplex printing directly. It allows you to print the currently selected parts of the document, or a range of pages by specifying the start and finish page numbers.

You can also print normally (one-sided) with it, open the Print Setup dialog, or switch to the normal Windows 95 Print dialog. WroxPBS is a sample from Wrox Press

Installing WroxPBS

To install the **WroxPBS Duplex Print** macro on your system, follow these steps:

1 Open the File menu in Word and select Templates. In the Templates dialog click the Organizer button

2 Select the Macros tab. In the left-hand pane, under the list of macros, your Normal template should be shown. If it isn't, click the Close File button - the caption changes to Open File. Click it again and move to your Templates folder and open the file `Normal.dot`.

3 In the right-hand part of the window click the Close File button under the list of macros. Click it again and move to the samples folder or wherever the `UsefulBits.dot` template is stored. Open it in the right-hand pane.

5 Now we can create the concordance file. Click the Collect Index Terms button on the toolbar. The macro creates a new document containing the two column concordance table. Here's part of it:

attach the new macro to a menu and toolbar button	attach the new macro to a menu and toolbar button
AutoText	AutoText
Beginning Word 95 Development,	Beginning Word 95 Development,
curved paper path	curved paper path
duplex printing	duplex printing
How It Works	How It Works
Installing WroxPBS	Installing WroxPBS
Normal template	Normal template
Normal.dot	Normal.dot
Organizer	Organizer
print part of a document	print part of a document
print the whole document	print the whole document

6 Now the hard part. You need to go through the table changing the text in the right-hand column to create the index entries you want. Don't change anything in the left-hand column, or Word won't be able to find the text in the document. You can sort the table using the Sort text...command on the Table menu, and setting the Sort By to Column 2. This makes it easier to see what the final index will look like.

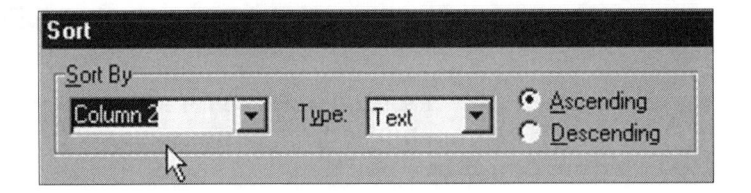

AutoText	AutoText
Beginning Word 95 Development,	Beginning Word 95 Development
How It Works	How WroxPBS Works
Installing WroxPBS	Installation
attach the new macro to a menu and toolbar button	macro:attach to menus and toolbar buttons
replace the print command	macro:replace Print command
Normal.dot	Normal.dot
Organizer	Organizer
PBSPaperPath	PBSPaperPath
Using Print Manager	Print Manager
Setting the Print Range	print range:setting
curved paper path	printers:curved paper path
duplex printing	printers:duplex
straight paper path	printers:straight paper path
Print Both Sides	printing:both sides
Print One Sided	printing:one-sided
Print Options setting	printing:options

7 Save the concordance file by clicking the Save button on the toolbar—you don't have to close it. It was automatically named `CCTIndex.doc` when it was first created. Then go back to the IndexMe document and click the Create Index Entries button on the Wrox Index toolbar. You'll see the {XE} fields appear in the document:

WroxPBS DuplexPrint is Word add-in macro that allows you to print on both sides of the paper with printers that do not support duplex printing{ XE "printers:duplex" } directly. It allows you to print the currently selected parts of the document, or a range of pages by specifying the start and finish page numbers.

You can also print normally (one-sided) with it, open the Print Setup dialog, or switch to the normal Windows 95 Print dialog. WroxPBS is a sample from Wrox Press{ XE "Wrox Press" }.

Installing WroxPBS{ XE "Installation" }

To install the **WroxPBS Duplex Print** macro on your system, follow these steps:

1. Open the File menu in Word and select Templates. In the Templates dialog click the Organizer{ XE "Organizer" } button

2. Select the Macros tab. In the left-hand pane, under the list of macros, your Normal template{ XE "templates:Normal" } should be shown. If it isn't, click the Close File button - the caption changes to Open File. Click it again and move to your Templates folder and open the file `Normal.dot`{ XE "Normal.dot" }.

3. In the right-hand part of the window click the Close File button under the list of macros. Click it again and move to the samples folder or wherever the `UsefulBits.dot`{ XE "UsefulBits.dot" } template is stored. Open it in the right-hand pane.

---

8 Now the magic part. Click the Build Document Index button, and the new index appears at the end of the document. To see it more clearly, select Options... from the Tools menu and turn off the display of all Nonprinting Characters. (This was turned on automatically when the index entries were added to the document.)

```
┌─Nonprinting Characters─────┐
│  ☐ Tab Characters          │
│  ☐ Spaces                  │
│  ☐ Paragraph Marks         │
│  ☐ Optional Hyphens        │
│  ☐ Hidden Text             │
│  ☑ All                     │
└────────────────────────────┘
```

```
A                                        curved paper path, 3
AutoText, 3                              duplex, 1
B                                        straight paper path, 3
Beginning Word 95 Development, 2         printing
H                                            both sides, 2
How WroxPBS Works, 2                         one-sided, 2
I                                            options, 2
Installation, 1                              part of a document, 2
M                                            reloading pages, 3
macro                                        start and end pages, 2
    attach to menus and toolbar buttons, 1   whole document, 2
    replace Print command, 1             S
N                                        saved settings, 3
Normal.dot, 1                            T
O                                        templates
Organizer, 1                                 Normal, 1
P                                        U
PBSPaperPath, 3                          UsefulBits.dot, 1
Print Manager, 2                         W
print range                              Wrox Press, 1, 2, 3
    setting, 2                           WroxPBS.cnt, 1
printers                                 WroxPBS.hlp, 1
```

9 Click the Remove Index Entries button. This removes all the {XE} fields from the document.

10 Click the Un-Highlight Index button. This removes all the highlights from the document, and it's ready to print or distribute.

Editing Your New Index

If you've never had to index a document before, the example you've just seen may seem like hard work, but if you do it regularly, this method should be like a breath of fresh air. If you're not completely happy with the index, just go back to the concordance file and edit any index entries in the right-hand column that don't look right. You can even add your own entries to the end if you want something to appear in two places in the index.

Once you've edited the concordance document, remember to save it. Then click the Create Index Entries button. This removes any existing entries and automatically replaces them with the new ones. Finally, click Build Document Index to replace the index with the new version.

When you're happy with your index, you can remove the {XE} index fields and highlighting from the document, as we did above. As long as you have the concordance file, you can always re-insert them again to rebuild the index. However, if you edit the document later, you'll have to add new terms to the concordance table manually to include them in a new index.

How It Works

The most complicated part is the `CollectIndexTerms` macro. This steps through the document, collecting the words and phrases that are highlighted, and storing them in an array. It then sorts the array, creates a new document with a two column table and fills it with the highlighted text. We've set the array to hold 1001 items. If you get an error message as the macro is running, you can increase this to make room for more entries.

```
Sub MAIN
Dim Words$(1000)
StartOfDocument : ScreenUpdating 0 : WaitCursor 1
WCount = 0
```

To find text that is highlighted, we first clear any existing values in the Find Formatting dialog. Next we use the `EditFindHighlight` statement immediately followed by `EditFind`, with the `.Format` argument set to `1`. Then we can check to see whether we found anything with `EditFindFound()`. If we have, we pull it from the text with `Selection$()` and see if it's already in the array. We only want to add it once for each occurrence. To avoid problems with different cases, we compare each phrase as lower case. Then we do another `EditFind`, and go round the loop again.

```
EditFindClearFormatting
EditFindHighlight
EditFind .Format = 1, .Find = "", .Replace = "", .Direction = 0
While EditFindFound()
    WFound$ = LTrim$(RTrim$(Selection$()))
    Exist = 0
    For i = 0 To WCount - 1
        If LCase$(Words$(i)) = LCase$(WFound$) Then Exist = 1
    Next
    If Not Exist Then
        Words$(WCount) = WFound$
        WCount = WCount + 1
    EndIf
    CharRight
    EditFindHighlight
    EditFind .Format = 1
Wend
```

Once we've built the list of phrases, we sort it up to and including the last element we used, `WCount - 1`. (If we sorted the whole array, all the blank elements would appear at the beginning.) Then we can create a new document, insert the table and fill it from our array. Finally, we save the document as `CCTIndex.doc`.

```
StartOfDocument
If WCount > 0 Then
    SortArray Words$(), 0, 0, WCount - 1
    FileNewDefault
    TableInsertTable  .NumColumns = 2, .NumRows = WCount
    For i = 0 To WCount - 1
        Insert Words$(i) : CharRight
        Insert Words$(i) : LineDown : CharLeft
    Next
    FileSaveAs .Name = "CCTIndex.doc"
EndIf
WaitCursor 0
End Sub
```

So, we've got our concordance file, and it's ready for editing. Once that's done, we run the **CreateIndexEntries** macro. This is a nice easy one. It uses the **RemoveIndexEntries** macro to remove the existing {XE} fields, then Word's **AutoMarkIndexEntries** statement to insert the new ones. All we need do is to supply the name of our concordance file.

```
Sub MAIN
RemoveIndexEntries
StartOfDocument
AutoMarkIndexEntries "CCTIndex.doc"
ScreenUpdating 1
WaitCursor 0
End Sub
```

Removing the existing {XE} fields isn't difficult either; you saw **EditGoTo** used in Part 1 of the book. We set a bookmark where we are at the moment, then go to the next {XE} field, using **EditGoTo "d'XE'"**. We can tell whether we found one by comparing the bookmarks **"\Sel"** (the current insertion point) and **"WI_Temp"** (the one we planted before we used **EditGoTo**). Once **EditGoTo** stops moving the insertion point, we know that there are no more {XE} fields left.

```
Sub MAIN
    StartOfDocument
    ScreenUpdating 0 : WaitCursor 1
    EditBookmark "WI_Temp", .Add
    EditGoTo "d'XE'"
    While CmpBookmarks("WI_Temp", "\Sel") <> 0
        CharRight 1, 1
        EditClear : CharLeft
        EditBookmark "WI_Temp", .Add
        EditGoTo "d'XE'"
    Wend
    EditBookmark "WI_Temp", .Delete
    StartOfDocument
End Sub
```

Now we've got the index entries into the document, we can build the index. The **Build Document Index** macro goes to the end of the document, adds some blank lines and uses Word's **InsertIndex** statement. It does all the hard work for us. If you want your index to look different, you can change the **.HeadingSeparator** argument to give a blank line (**1**) or none at all (**0**). We liked the version with the initial letter as a heading separator. You can also change the number of columns and right-align the page numbers. See Word's Help file for more details.

```
Sub MAIN
    EndOfDocument : InsertPara : InsertPara
    InsertIndex .Replace = 1, .Columns = 2, .HeadingSeparator = 2
End Sub
```

The **AutoMarkIndexEntries** statement automatically turns on the view of paragraph marks and other non-printing characters. We chose to leave these in view when the macro finishes, but you may want to add code to hide them again. The **ToolsOptionsView** statement has arguments which will turn the different settings off.

The only other macro that we need is one to remove the highlighting from the document and, surprisingly, this is the most awkward to get working correctly. In theory, the **Highlight** statement toggles highlighting on and off, in the same way that the **Bold** statement toggles bold format on and off. But, unlike with the **Bold** statement, there's no optional argument; you can't use **Highlight 0** to force it to be turned off. We found that this works, as long as the first character in the document isn't highlighted:

```
Sub MAIN
    ScreenUpdating 0
    EditSelectAll
    Highlight : Highlight : Highlight : SelType 1
    ScreenUpdating 1
End Sub
```

Managing Pictures in a Document

In some types of document, like the manuscripts for this book, there are many pictures and graphics inserted into the text. Word is quite capable in this area, and makes it easy to size and position the pictures wherever you want them, using frames. However, once you've inserted a few large pictures, you soon find your document is growing into a multi-megabyte monster. For example, even using 16 color pictures, each chapter of this book is over 3MB in size.

One way to make your documents easier to work with is to leave adding the pictures until you're ready to print them. And if you transfer your documents to another application for pre-press treatment, such as PageMaker® or similar, you usually have to strip out the pictures and re-insert them later.

So how can you be sure of getting the right picture in the right place? And if you want to preview or print the documents before they go to pre-press, you need to include the pictures anyway, so that you can check the whole thing makes sense and fits together properly. We get round this problem by using macros which automatically strip the pictures out of a document and re-insert them again as required. That way, you can work with just the text for editing and pre-press tasks, but preview and print the whole thing whenever you need to.

Using WroxPic to Manage Pictures in a Document

WroxPic is a series of macros which can insert single pictures, strip and re-insert all the pictures, and list the file names of the pictures in a document. We designed it to work the way that we find most useful, but you're welcome to change and adapt it to suit your own needs. It works by adding text directly below each picture, which contains the name of the picture file on disk. It doesn't contain the path, so you may need to reload the pictures from a different folder if they've been moved.

To give you some idea of how it works, here's the way a picture inserted into one of our manuscripts looks. We use the text *** *Insert picture:* to identify where a picture goes when it comes to pre-press time. Underneath that, a caption contains any other details about how it should be positioned or annotated:

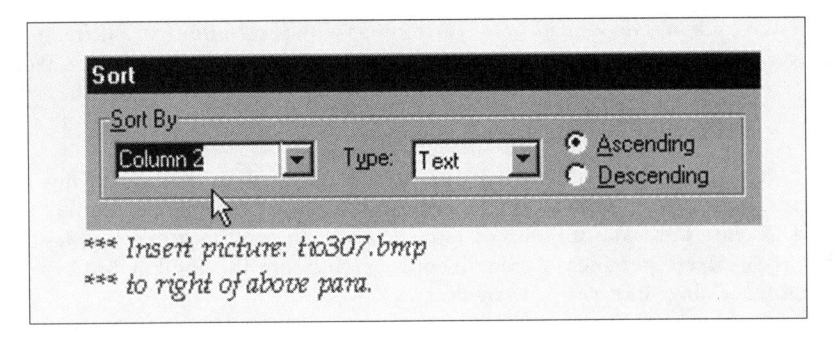

> *** Insert picture: tio307.bmp
> *** to right of above para.

All the text is formatted in a style we call Layout Style, which is large red italics that are obvious on screen. The macros can then find a picture by searching for the text and style used in the caption. We'll show you how it works.

Try It Out - Inserting, Listing and Removing Pictures

You'll need the template **WroxPic**, which will be in the folder where you installed the samples from the disk that accompanies this book. Unless you changed the defaults, this will be `C:\BegWord`. We've also supplied a document and some picture files you can use for this example. You'll find them in the `\Pictures` subfolder of your samples folder.

1 Copy the file `WroxPic.dot` into your `\Templates` folder. Unless you changed the defaults when you installed Word 95 or Office 95, this will be `\Winword\Template` or `\Msoffice\Templates`. Then open the file `PicDemo.doc` from the `\Pictures` subfolder of your samples folder. You may like to make a copy of it first and open that, to avoid changing the original.

2 You'll see the Wrox Pictures toolbar displayed. If you can't see it, select Toolbars... from the View menu, and put a check by it in the list. You can dock the toolbar at any edge of the screen to get it out of the way—try the right-hand side.

> **FYI** If the Wrox Pictures toolbar isn't shown in the list in the Toolbars dialog, select Templates... from the File menu and make sure the document is attached to the WroxPic template. If it isn't, click Attach... and select this template in your `\Templates` folder.

> **FYI** If you move a template which contains a toolbar with text buttons to a different machine, you occasionally find that the text doesn't fit on the buttons correctly. When Word creates toolbar text buttons, it calculates the size based on the proportions of the system font that is installed on that computer. You have no control over the process.
>
> Different machines can use system fonts with different proportions. They may have been installed by the graphic card software, or changed in Window's **Display Properties** dialog. To cure this, you can either change the system font back to a standard one, 10pt Arial at 96 pixels per inch or Small Fonts, or recreate the toolbar buttons using the **Customize** dialog, like you saw in Part 1.

3 First, we need to set the default values for the macros to use. Click the Set Defaults button on the toolbar. (If you don't do it first, you'll find the dialog opens automatically when you use a different command.) The Picture Default Settings dialog opens:

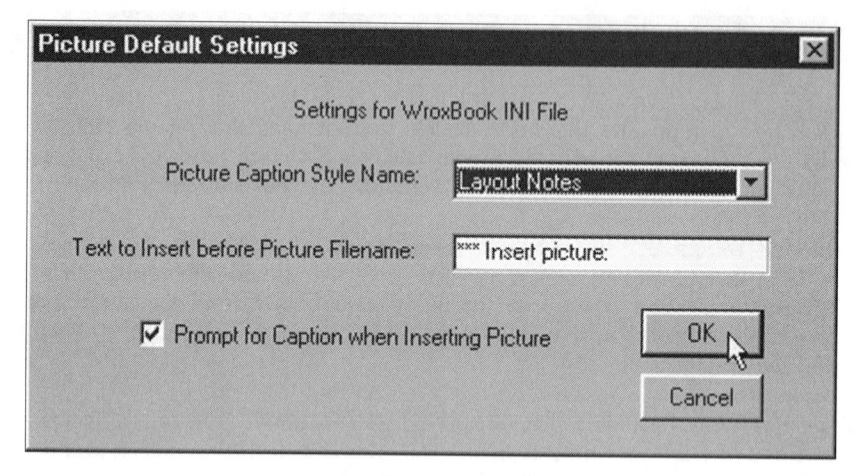

4 Select the Layout Notes style, which we've included in the template. Fill in the text you want to place under each picture and set the Prompt for Caption when Inserting Picture option. Then click OK.

5 The document we've supplied gives you an overview of how WroxPic works. We'll add another picture to it. Scroll down to the bottom of page two, below the text that tells you about the Load Pictures command. Click the Insert Picture button on the Wrox Pictures toolbar to open the normal Insert Picture dialog.

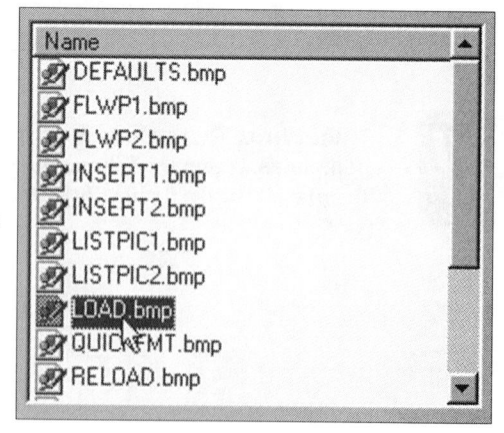

Chapter 6 – Word in a Publishing Environment

6 Select the file **Load.bmp** from the samples **\Pictures** folder and click OK. The picture is inserted in the document, and the Insert Picture Caption dialog opens. Enter a caption for your new picture:

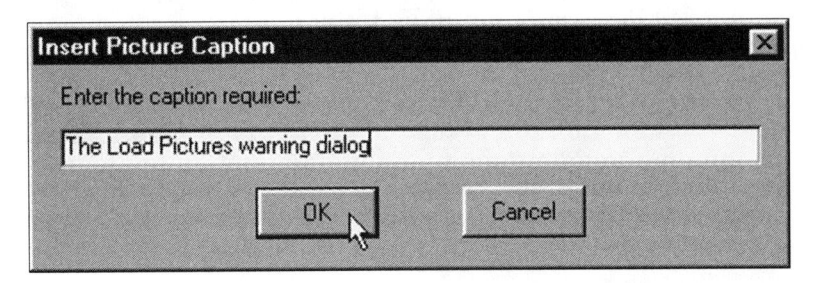

7 Click OK and the caption is added.

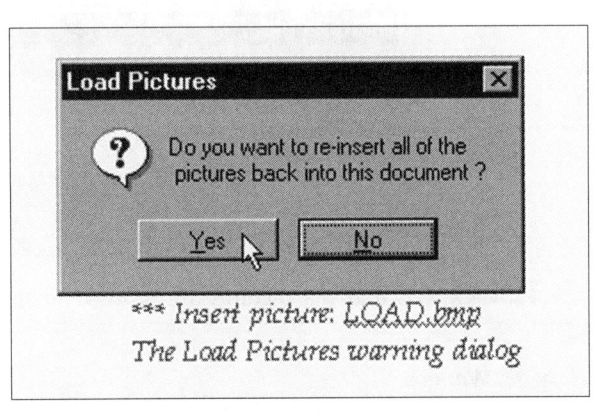

8 Now we'll make a list of the pictures. Click the List Pictures button and the Print Picture List message box allows you to include the page numbers, or just list them all in alphabetical order.

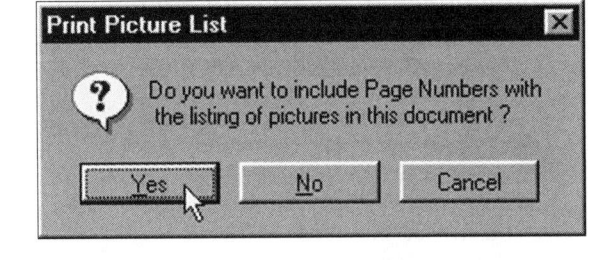

9 Click Yes and a new document opens, containing the list:

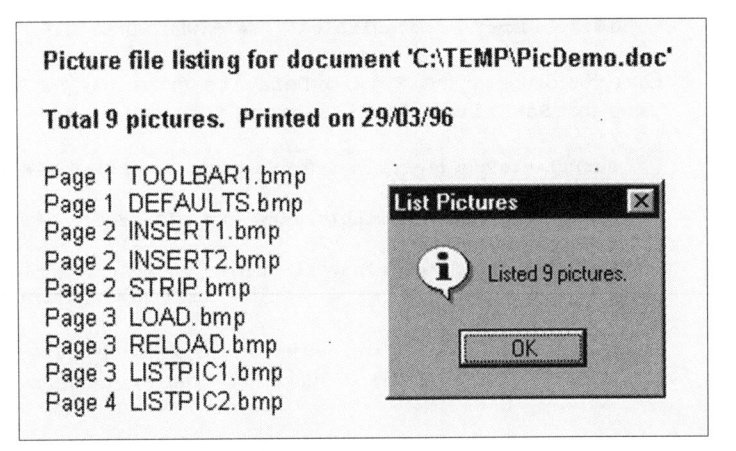

261

10 Next, we'll strip out the pictures. Click the Strip Pictures button on the Wrox Pictures toolbar and click Yes in the warning dialog. All the pictures are removed, leaving just the captions. The macro tells you that it's removed nine pictures:

11 Putting them back is just as easy. Click the Load Pictures button and answer Yes to the prompt. A dialog appears asking for the folder where the pictures are stored. Enter the path to your **\Pictures** subfolder.

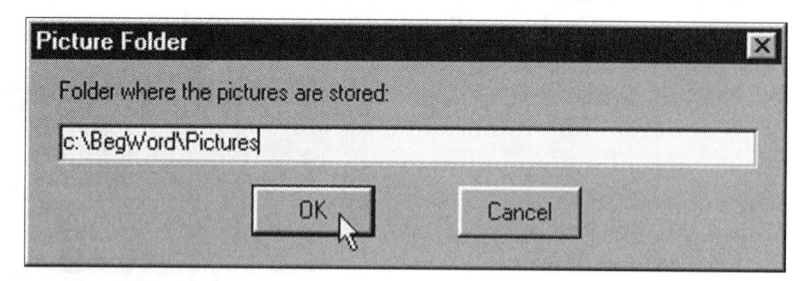

12 Click OK, and the pictures are restored to their previous positions.

How It Works

There's not a lot in the WroxPic macros that you haven't seen before. Instead of printing all the code, we'll show you the parts that demonstrate new techniques. One of these is the problem of storing values so that they're available to different macros. There's a set of defaults that you entered when you first ran WroxPic, which are used in all the macros.

Each macro has to be able to get the text and style for the picture captions and the setting of the Prompt for Caption option. These values are set by the user in the **SetWroxDefaults** macro, and we store them in an **.ini** file in the Word application folder. The function **DefaultDir$()** with an argument of **9** returns the path to your Word folder, so we can create the name for the **.ini** file with:

```
INIFileName$ = DefaultDir$(9) + "\WROXWORD.INI"
```

Once the dialog in the **SetWroxDefaults** macro has got the values, it stores them in this file using the **SetPrivateProfileString** statement:

```
SetPrivateProfileString("Pictures", "CaptionStyle", CaptionStyle$, \
                                                    INIFileName$)
SetPrivateProfileString("Pictures", "InsertText", DRec.txtInsert, \
                                                    INIFileName$)
SetPrivateProfileString("Pictures", "IncludeCaption", \
                        Str$(DRec.chkPrompt), INIFileName$)
```

Then, each of the macros can retrieve them with the **GetPrivateProfileString()** function. Notice that the code checks to make sure that the defaults have already been set. If the style is returned as an empty string, it runs the **SetWroxDefaults** macro so that the user can set the defaults. Then it retrieves them again. This time, if it can't find the style (i.e. the user clicked Cancel) the macro exits:

```
PicCaptionStyle$ = GetPrivateProfileString$("Pictures", \
                                "CaptionStyle", INIFileName$)
If PicCaptionStyle$ = "" Then SetWroxDefaults
PicCaptionStyle$ = GetPrivateProfileString$("Pictures", \
                                "CaptionStyle", INIFileName$)
If PicCaptionStyle$ = "" Then Goto Pic_Exit
PicInsertText$ = GetPrivateProfileString$("Pictures", \
                                "InsertText", INIFileName$)
IncludeCaption = Val(GetPrivateProfileString$("Pictures", \
                                "IncludeCaption", INIFileName$))
```

We've purposely named the macro that inserts pictures with the same name as the built-in Word command, **InsertPicture**. That way, it runs when you select Picture... from the Insert menu, as well as when you click the Wrox Pictures toolbar button. While you're creating a document, this is the only macro that you'll need to use regularly, so you can hide the Wrox Pictures toolbar and use the menu command instead.

We don't store the path where the pictures come from in the **.ini** file, because the folder will probably be different for each document. Instead, every time you insert a picture, the **InsertPicture** macro stores the current folder (where the picture came from) in the document as a document variable, called **LastPictureFolder**. The Word function **DefaultDir$()** with an argument of **1** returns the current folder:

```
SetDocumentVar("LastPictureFolder", DefaultDir$(1))
```

Then, when we come to reload the pictures, we can look in this folder first. If we can't find a value, we call another of the macros in the WroxPic template which asks the user to enter it. This macro is also used if the pictures themselves can't be found in the folder contained in **LastPictureFolder**; in other words, if they (or the document) have been moved.

```
OldFolder$ = GetDocumentVar$("LastPictureFolder")   'get the picture folder
If OldFolder$ = "" Then OldFolder$ = DefaultDir$(1)
PicFolder$ = GetPicFolder$(OldFolder$)        'display Picture Folder dialog
```

Because the document contains our standard text directly under each picture, we can use **EditFind** to step through the document and reload the pictures, or just collect a list of the picture file names. The only other task is to strip out the pictures. To do this, we use the **EditGoTo** statement, just like we did in the section on indexes. This time, we search for a graphic using:

```
EditGoTo .Destination = "g"
```

The only thing that you have to watch out for when you use WroxPic is if you change the default settings after creating a document (or even worse, part way through it). If you do, to make the macros work correctly, you'll need to change them back to suit that document. This beats having to remove or re-insert all the pictures by hand, and your pre-press department will love the list of picture files you can give them with your document!

Better Printing with WordBasic

Finally, to end this chapter, we'll show you how you can take over the task of printing documents in Word. This allows you to manipulate the output to meet your own special needs. One way that you may find useful is shown in the **WroxPBS** macro we've included with the samples for this chapter. This allows you to print on both sides of the paper with printers which only support one-sided printing.

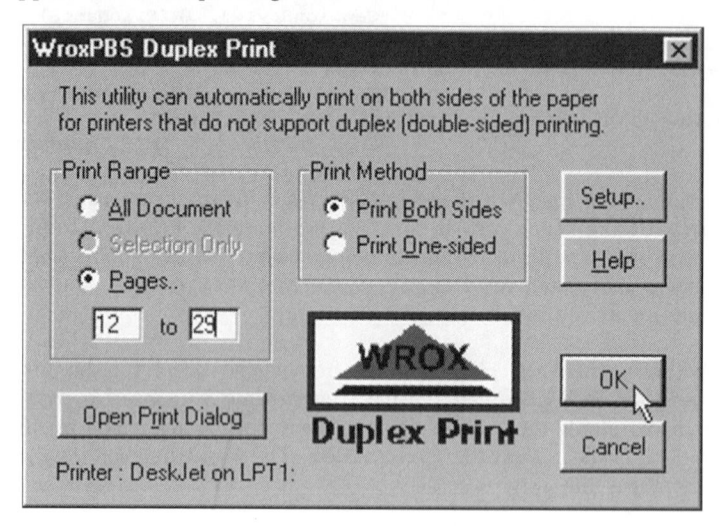

Taking Over Word's Printing Commands

We've seen before how easy it is to replace a Word command with our own macro. We did this with the **InsertPicture** macro in the previous section. In the final part of this chapter, we'll see how you can completely replace part of the Word interface. If you already have a printer capable of printing on both sides of the paper, this particular example may not be of much relevance. However, if you're one of the millions who rely on a normal single-sided printer, you could find **WroxPBS** becoming a permanent part of your setup.

To replace a Word function with one of your own, you simply create a macro with the same name as the Word built-in one. In our case, it's **FilePrint()**, the code which runs when you select Print... from the File menu. However, the Print toolbar button on Word's Standard toolbar calls a different function: **FilePrintDefault()**. So we need to take over both of these.

The macro we've supplied is called **PrintBothSides**, and is in the UsefulBits template in your samples folder. The easiest way to integrate it into Word's interface is to copy it into your Normal template using the Organizer dialog and arrange for it to be run instead of the built-in **FilePrint** and **FilePrintDefault** macros. How? Create new macros for both of these and enter code in each one which calls **PrintBothSides**. Now, each time you select File | Print... from the menus, or click the Print toolbar button, the new macro runs instead.

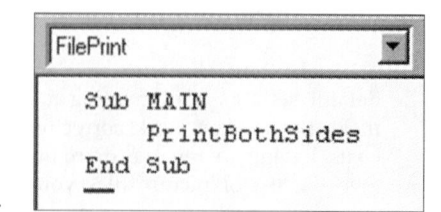

Creating Your Own Print Dialog

If you're taking over a Word function completely, you must make sure your macro can manage all the tasks that the Word function includes. Otherwise, you'll have to uninstall your macro before you can access these extra functions. In our case, there are several functions in both the Print Setup and the normal Print dialog which we don't want to have to duplicate, such as setting the default printer or changing the specific printer options.

So, we must design our new Print dialog with the capabilities to access the original Print and Print Setup dialogs. This is easy enough, because we can call the original Word function from within the macro that replaces it. To open the original Print dialog from within out **PrintBothSides** macro, we've used the following code in the dialog function:

```
        Case "cmdPrint"           'the Open Print Dialog button was clicked
            Dim FP As FilePrint   'declare a FilePrint dialog record
            GetCurValues FP       'get the current settings, if any
            If Dialog(FP) Then    'show the dialog, returns true for OK
                RetVal = 0        'close our own Print dialog
                FilePrint(FP)     'start the normal print process
            EndIf
```

To open the Print Setup dialog, we use:

```
        Case "cmdSetup"
            ToolsMacro .Name = "FilePrintSetup", .Run
            DlgText "lblPrinter", "Printer : " + GetPrtName$
```

This method uses the **ToolsMacro** command to run the original Word code. In this case, we don't want to close our own Print dialog, but instead we use another function in our macro which updates the printer name displayed in the dialog. Notice that we can't use the **ToolsMacro** command to run the original **FilePrint** code. If you try this, Word reports an error: The code is already running.

Installing the WroxPBS Duplex Print Utility

You can install **WroxPBS** by copying it into your Normal template with Organizer. Select File | Templates... and click the Organizer... button. Copy the macro **PrintBothSides** from the sample **UsefulBits.dot** template into **Normal.dot** in your **\Templates** folder. Then create the two macros **FilePrint** and **FilePrintDefault** as described above if you want to take over Words printing functions completely.

```
    Sub MAIN              'This is all the code you need for the
        PrintBothSides    'FilePrint and FilePrintDefault macros
    End Sub               'in your Normal template.
```

We've also supplied a help file for **WroxPBS**. Copy the two files **WroxPBS.hlp** and **WroxPBS.cnt** from the **\WroxHelp** subfolder of your samples folder into Windows own **\Help** folder. Unless you changed the defaults when you installed Windows, this will be **\Windows\Help**. You also need to set it up for your printer, which is easy enough...

Try It Out - Printing on Both Sides with a Single-side Printer.

To try this out, you'll need to have installed **WroxPBS** as shown above. We'll set it up and see it working. First, you need to establish how your printer handles the paper. If it's rolled through 180 degrees before or after printing, so that the pages are stacked in reverse order afterwards, you are ready to go—start at Step 3. You only need to follow Steps 1 and 2 first if your printer stacks the paper in the same order as it prints it

1 In any document, type the number 1 and select (highlight) it by holding the *Shift* key and pressing the left arrow key.

2 Select AutoText from the Edit menu and in the Name: box enter PBSPaperPath. Then click the Add button.

▶ Start here if you don't need to set up **WroxPBS** for your printer.

3 Click the Print button, or select Print... from the File menu. Instead of the normal Print dialog, the WroxPBS dialog opens. Make sure you select Print Both Sides in the Print Method section, and All Document in the Print Range section:

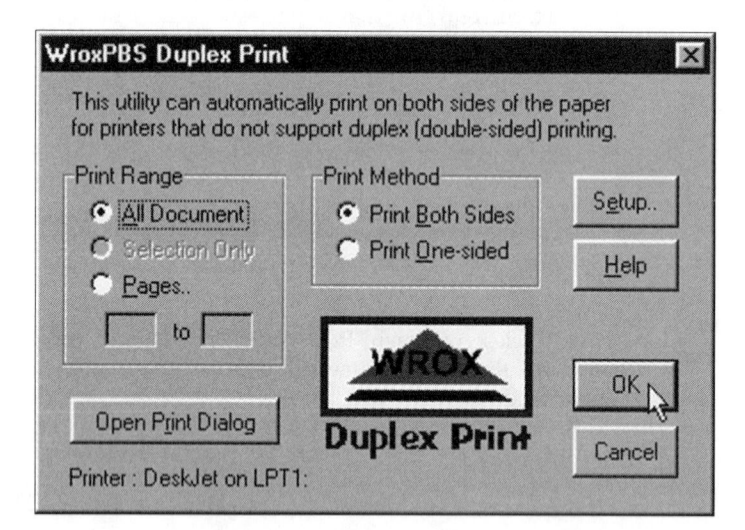

4 Click OK to start printing. You'll see Word's own Printing status dialog showing you the odd pages being printed. If you have a curved-path printer, they'll be printed in reverse order.

5 Next, the WroxPBS message box opens. You can either wait till the first set of pages have finished printing, and place them back in the paper-in tray, or spool the rest to Print Manager.

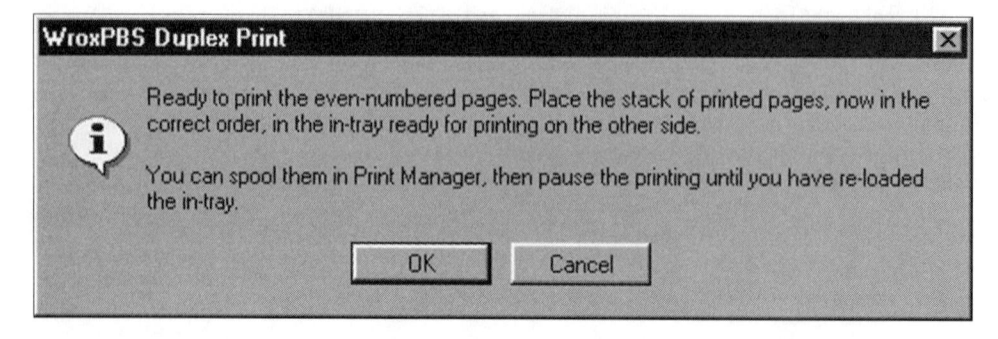

> **FYI** To pause printing in **Print Manager**, right-click on the spooled pages entry and select **Pause Printing** from the short-cut menu. It appears ticked. To resume printing, right-click it and select **Pause Printing** again.

6 Make sure you reload the printed pages so that they will be printed on the other side. Then click OK, or resume printing from Print Manager.

7 The pages are printed on the other side, and all you have to do is pick up the stack and staple or bind it.

Using the other Features of WroxPBS

If you need to use Word's own Print dialog, just click Open Print Dialog instead of OK while WroxPBS is displayed. To open Word's Print Setup dialog, click the Setup button. You can also print part of a document if you wish. Either select the area you want to print before you open WroxPBS and click Selection in the Print Range section, or click Pages and enter the start and end page numbers.

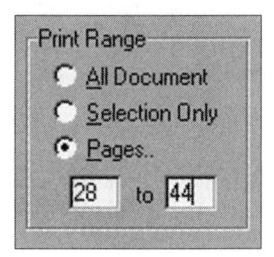

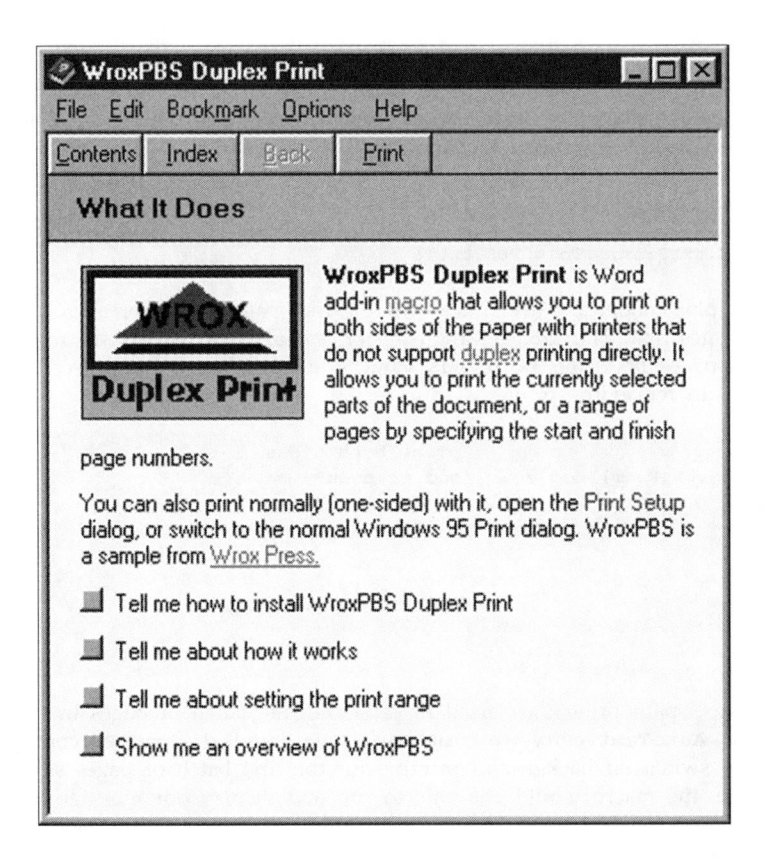

There's a full help file with `WroxPBS`, though we haven't actually installed it here. You'll be creating this Help file yourself in a later chapter, but if you want to explore now, you can copy the files `WroxPBS.hlp` and `WroxPBS.cnt` into your `\Windows\Help` folder from the `\WroxHelp` samples subfolder. Then, click the Help button in the dialog and explore.

How It Works

Much of the `PrintBothSides` macro is concerned with creating the dynamic dialog and managing the controls in it, such as enabling them at the correct time. Again, we've covered all this in earlier chapters, so we won't be talking about it again here.

The actual printing is done with the section of code you can see below. First, we collect the settings of the controls in the dialog. They're stored in the fields of the dialog record `PBS`, and `PBS.grpRange` is the setting chosen in the Print Range section. We have a problem if the user chooses Selection, because we can't easily determine the first page number. However, this only affects things when we're using Print Both Sides mode. If you're printing a selection, you probably won't expect the resulting print to be laid out with the correct left- and right-hand page margins.

```
    If PBS.grpRange = 2 Then                'print selected pages
        PrintRange = 3                      'use From and To arguments
        PBS.txtFrom = LTrim$(PBS.txtFrom)
        PBS.txtTo = LTrim$(PBS.txtTo)
    Else                                    'all pages in doc/selection
        PrintRange = PBS.grpRange
        PBS.txtFrom = "1"                   'first page is 1
        'In PrintBothSides mode this falls down when printing
        'a selection, because the first page may not be page
        'one - it could be anything..
    EndIf
```

Now we check to see which print method is selected. If `grpMethod` is `1`, the user selected single-sided printing, so we print the document normally, in background printing mode so that they can continue to work as it's spooling in Print Manager.

```
    If PBS.grpMethod = 1 Then                'normal printing method
        FilePrint .Background = 1, .Range = PrintRange, \
                  .From = PBS.txtFrom, .To = PBS.txtTo
```

If `grpMethod` is `0` we're in duplex mode, and we find out if the first page is odd or even. If it's odd we print all the odd pages first. The `Order` argument for `FilePrint` will be set to `1`. Otherwise, we'll print the even pages first. The `OddEven$` value is used in the text displayed in the message box when it's time to reload the printer.

```
    Else                                    'print both sides
        FirstPageOdd = Val(PBS.txtFrom) Mod 2   'odd or even?
        If FirstPageOdd Then
            PageOrder = 1                   'print only odd pages
            OddEven$ = "even"
        Else
            PageOrder = 2                   'print only even pages
            OddEven$ = "odd"
        EndIf
```

If we have a normal curved paper-path printer, we need to print the first batch of pages in reverse order. This is where the `AutoText` entry we created when we installed `WroxPBS` comes in. Also notice that we have to switch off background printing for the first batch of pages so that we keep control. Otherwise, the macro would continue to run and display our message box before printing of the first half was finished, probably causing confusion. However, the pages are still spooled in Print Manager, so the process is fairly quick.

```
        'reverse printing if not straight paper path
        If StraightPath = 0 Then ToolsOptionsPrint .Reverse = 1
        FilePrint .Background = 0, .Range = PrintRange, \
            .Order = PageOrder, .From = PBS.txtFrom, \
            .To = PBS.txtTo
        ToolsOptionsPrint .Reverse = 0   'forward printing
        PageOrder = PageOrder Mod 2 + 1              'switch to the opposite mode
        … 'create message for message box …
        If MsgBox(Msg$, "WroxPBS Duplex Print", 65) Then
            FilePrint .Background = 1, .Range = PrintRange, \
                .Order = PageOrder, .From = PBS.txtFrom, \
                .To = PBS.txtTo
        EndIf
    EndIf
```

Once you respond to the message box, the second batch is printed. This time, we can use background printing so that the user can continue to work while the pages are being spooled.

Another part of the macro that you may find useful is a function that gets the name of the current default printer, so it can be displayed in the dialog. This declares a dialog record of type **FilePrintSetup**, gets the current values, and returns the printer name from the **.Printer** field:

```
Function GetPrtName$
    Dim FPSRec As FilePrintSetup
    GetCurValues FPSRec
    GetPrtName$ = FPSRec.Printer
End Function
```

The settings in the WroxPBS dialog are saved and reinstated the next time you use it. We store them in AutoText entries when the macro ends, and read them back when it's run again:

```
REM Get last values used from AutoText entries
Sub GetLastATEntries
    On Error Resume Next
    StraightPath = Val(GetAutoText$("PBSPaperPath"))
    LastRange = Val(GetAutoText$("PBSLastRange"))
    If LastRange < 0 Or LastRenge > 2 Then LastRange = 0
    LastMethod = Val(GetAutoText$("PBSLastMethod"))
    If LastMethod < 0 Or LastMethod > 1 Then LastMethod = 0
End Sub

REM Save last values used in AutoText entries
Sub SetLastATEntries
    On Error Resume Next
    SetAutoText "PBSLastRange",  Str$(DlgValue("grpRange"))
    SetAutoText "PBSLastMethod", Str$(DlgValue("grpMethod"))
End Sub
```

Summary

You've seen a lot of different parts of Word in this chapter and, unless you're regularly involved in publishing, some of them may well have been new to you. Remember, the simple act of typing and printing a document means that you are, technically, involved in the world of publishing. Just because the only person to see your document is the marketing director doesn't mean the task is any less significant than producing a best-selling novel.

In particular, producing large or complex documents is easier if you plan the task out first, and break it down into manageable chunks. This makes it easy for you to combine each part into a single master document. You've also seen other ways to make creating indexes, manipulating pictures and printing much easier. In this chapter, we've looked at:

- How you can build and manage large documents
- How you can control changes made to a document
- Techniques to make creating indexes easier
- Ways to manage pictures inserted into documents
- Using WordBasic to make printing easier

In the next chapter, we'll move on to looking at how you can produce documents in other formats. Rather than just printing your text and pictures on paper, you can create them in different ways that are designed for viewing on screen. The two most obvious examples of this are Help files and the exciting new opportunities of the Internet's World Wide Web.

At the end of Part 2 of the book, we'll be taking a detailed look at how you create Windows Help files, but, first, in the next chapter, you'll see how Word can easily be adapted to design pages in the special HTML format that is used on the Internet. You can't have failed to see the impact this medium has already had, and it's quite likely that every Word user will at some stage have to come to terms with the way it works, as companies fall over themselves to establish a presence on 'The Net'. So, turn the page, and don't get left behind...

Chapter 6 – Word in a Publishing Environment

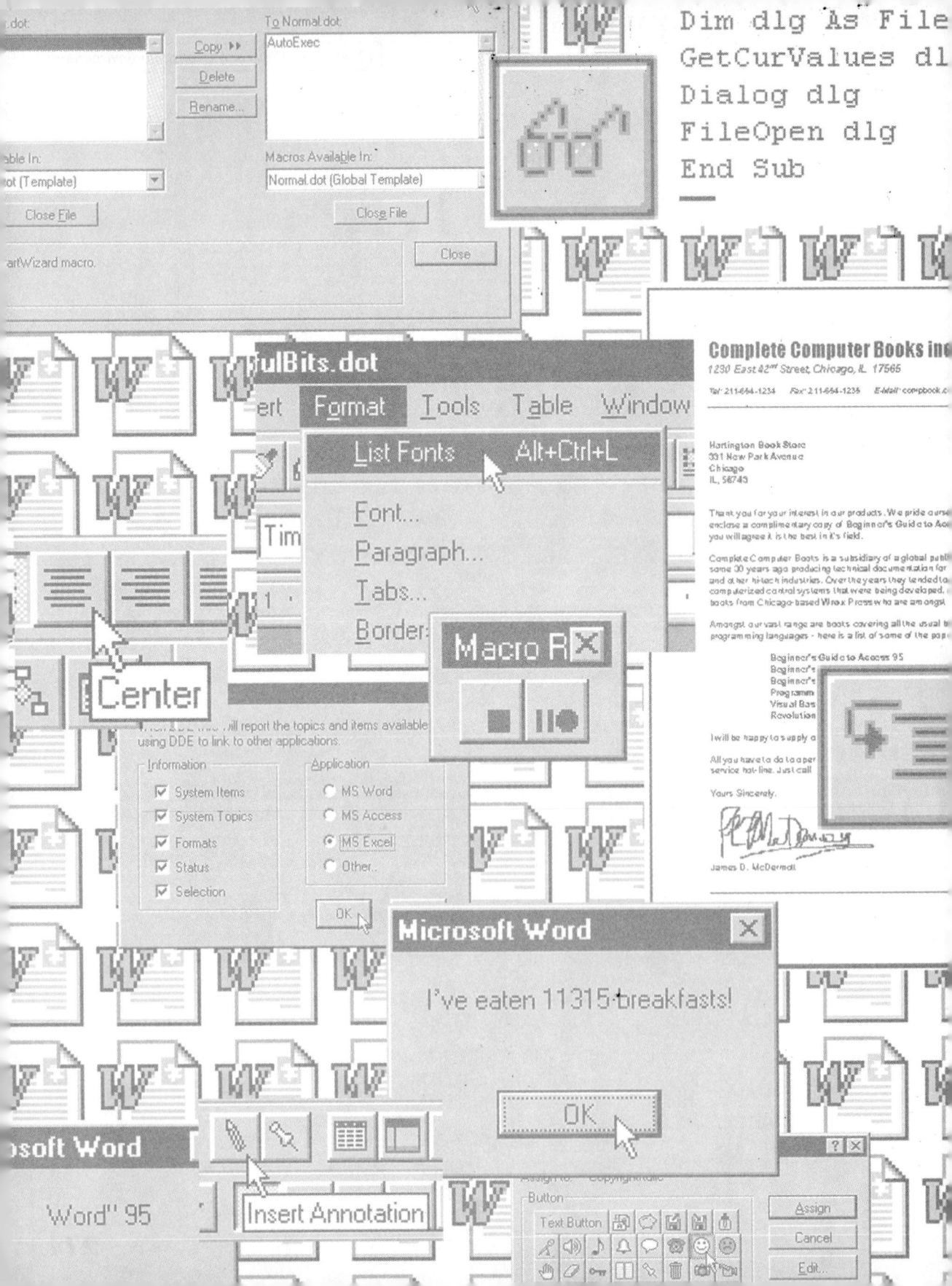

```
Dim dlg As File
GetCurValues dl
Dialog dlg
FileOpen dlg
End Sub
```

Creating Web Pages for the Internet

Introduction

In this chapter, you'll see how to create documents that can be displayed on the Internet's World Wide Web. There are hundreds of books dedicated entirely to the Net, but we'll show you everything you need to get started in just one chapter. We won't be going into detail about what the Internet is, or how you use it—you don't need us to tell you what you've probably already picked up from all the hype and fuss that surrounds it!

We'll be concentrating on why you should be getting involved now, and the ways you can benefit from learning more. You don't have to have a permanent ISDN connection to the Net, or be trying to make money out of it. Even if you only have a simple dial-up account with a service provider, you'll be able to take advantage of the techniques that we use in this chapter.

The basis of all web pages is a special language called **Hypertext Markup Language** (HTML). Basic pages are generally called **hypertext documents**, but if they include multimedia elements, such as pictures, sound or video, they're often called **hypermedia documents**. You'll meet more examples of hypertext documents later in the book, such as Window's own Help Files that we'll look at in the next couple of chapters.

You may be surprised to find out that web pages can be useful even if you're not connected to the Net at all. Many companies are using them to manage and distribute internal information across their own networks. This is seen to be a major growth area for the future and has already been christened with 'it's own special term—**Intranet**. We'll see how this works when we create a few of our own pages.

So, in this chapter we'll show you:

- Why you need to know about web pages and HTML documents
- The basic structure of a web page and the various HTML commands
- How to create web pages using HTML directly in Word

Why do I Need to Know about the Internet?

So why is the Net so important? Is it just all hype? Whatever your opinion, there's no doubt that the Internet is going to be a decisive factor in the development of computing over the next decade. For example, here's what your own environment probably looks like today:

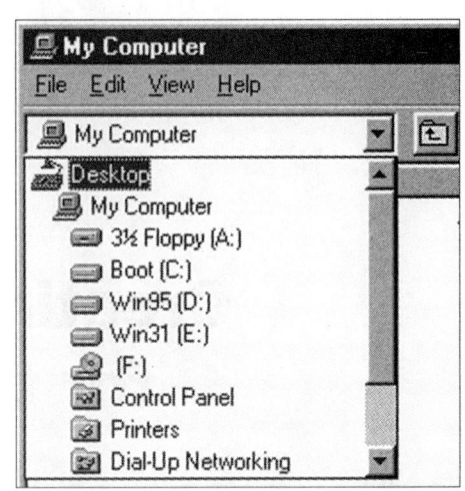

In a few years time, if not sooner, this will have changed. If the big names in the business get their way (and there's no reason to suppose that they won't), your environment could well look more like this:

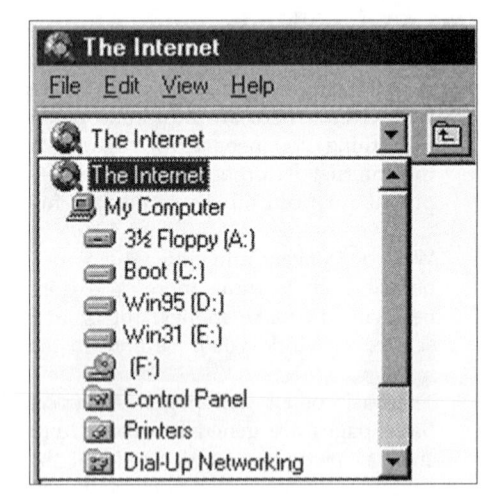

You might be able to remember when tank-tops and flared trousers were the height of fashion. Don't laugh, because, by the start of the new millennium, people will laugh at the thought of using a computer that didn't have a modem, or access to the global information resource.

How does the World Wide Web Work?

The Web is only a part of the global Internet structure. You can, of course, use it to send e-mail or transfer files in various ways, but the real success of the Web has come from its highly attractive and graphical capabilities. However, despite all the hype that currently surrounds it, and its phenomenal growth rate, there are a few problems. Putting aside the usual complaints of insufficient bandwidth, overcrowding and lack of organization, there are two fundamental difficulties.

Firstly, the Internet was originally designed to be a system for passing information between geographically scattered scientific and academic sites, not as a graphical entertainment medium. It handles information in what is, basically, a simple ASCII text form. Each individual byte of information can only be a number between 0 and 127, so even the copyright symbol ©, which has an ASCII code of 169, can't be transmitted as a single character.

Secondly, there is no standard application for viewing the information. When you create a macro in Word 95, you can be fairly sure that it will appear and work in exactly the same way on every other user's machine, because you can safely assume that they will be running the same software as you. However, if you've got used to the excellent new highlighter facility in Word 95 and pass a document containing this to someone who is using Word 6, the highlighting disappears because the older version doesn't support it.

With the World Wide Web, things are even worse. The people who view your web pages *may* be using one of the mainline browsers, like Netscape or Internet Explorer, under Windows 95 (**browser** is the usual term given to the software that displays web pages). But you don't know if this is the latest version that supports all the new functionality. And they may not even be using Windows at all. Because of its roots, the majority of Internet server sites still use Unix or one of its variants. They could even be viewing your pages on a terminal that only supports monochrome 80-column text!

What is HTML?

To get round these problems, the Web uses a system called **Hypertext Markup Language** (HTML), which allows the browser software to display as much of the original formatting and layout of the information as it can on the particular hardware where it resides.

HTML is a **page description language**. This means that instead of specifying exactly how the information should appear on screen, you send a set of instructions about the logical format of the text and any included graphics. If you imagine the way a normal laser or ink-jet printer handles information, you can see why this method is so efficient. To print the single word Hello, a 300 dpi printer has to map out over 10,000 points on the paper, yet the document that produces it is only a few bytes long. The printer driver is responsible for converting these into the individual points on the paper.

In HTML, as used on the Web, the browser itself is responsible for this conversion. With a few simple instructions, we can tell it what to display and how to lay it out, including the size of the text and its position on the page.

What is a Web Page?

It's time we looked at some real web pages. We've supplied samples for you to view in your own browser which use fairly standard methods to provide an attractive layout and help you to see how pages are created. To view them, you'll need to have a browser of some type installed. It doesn't really matter which one, because these pages only use features that are supported by most of the common Windows-based browsers. We're using Internet Assistant from Microsoft, which is included in the Windows 95 Plus! pack, or can be downloaded from Microsoft's own Internet site at **http://www.microsoft.com**.

Try It Out - Viewing the Sample Web Pages

Because you may be using a different web browser from us, we can't include specific instructions on how you load a page, or move back and forth between them. However, most browsers operate in much the same way as Internet Assistant, so you should have no problems following the example.

1 Start you web browser and load the sample page **WroxHome.htm** from the **\WroxPage** subfolder of your samples folder. Unless you changed the defaults when you installed the samples, this will be **C:\BegWord\WroxPage**. You don't need to be connected to your Internet provider; if you're prompted to connect, just click Cancel.

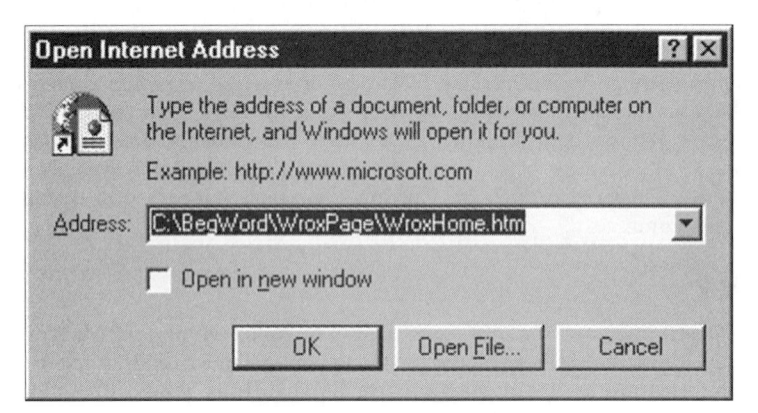

2 The page you see shows you some of the ways you can use web pages. If you've ever 'surfed the Net' (used a web browser), you'll recognize the blue underlined text as being a hot link which leads to another page. To liven up the page, we've also added some graphics, including the black 'blobs' for each topic. Finally, at the bottom of the page, notice that there are links to send e-mail to the page creator, or to jump to their home page.

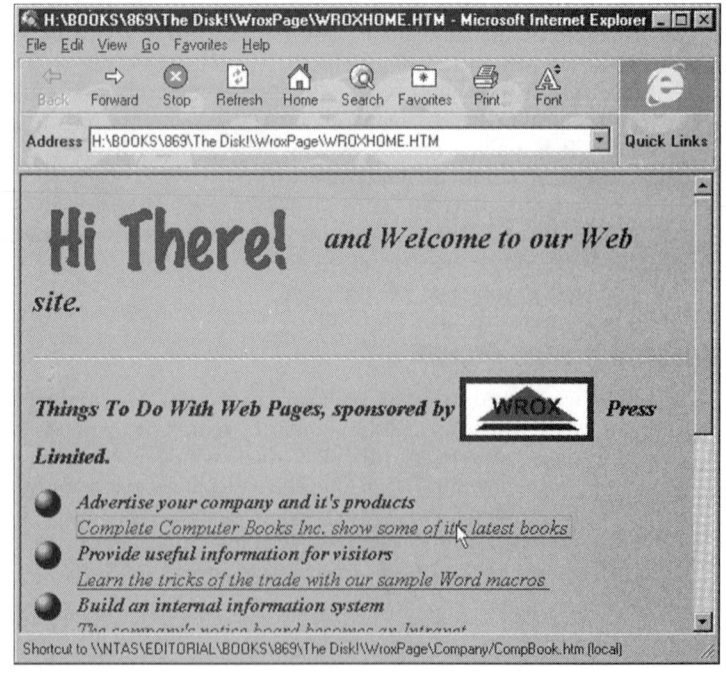

Chapter 7 - Creating Web Pages for the Internet

3 There are around fifteen pages that you can view from here. As you do so, you'll notice that there's no easy way to get back to this page. This is often the case with the Web because if you jump to another site, rather than just to another page at the same site, the new site has no way of knowing where you came from. To get back, you have to click the Go Back button on your browser's toolbar.

4 To take a quick look at some of the pages, click the hot link in the third option, The company's notice board becomes an Intranet. This shows you how the main home page of a company's internal information system might look. You'll notice in this case that we've gone for a smoother corporate look, using 3D images. This time, to jump to another page, you have to click the ball itself, because the text isn't part of the hot link.

5 Click the Back button to return to the first page, then select the fifth option, Tell us what you want us to write about. This shows a page that has controls similar to those we used in a Word dialog in Part 1. You can set the various options and choose from the drop-down lists. Towards the end of the page, you'll see some radio buttons and text boxes.

277

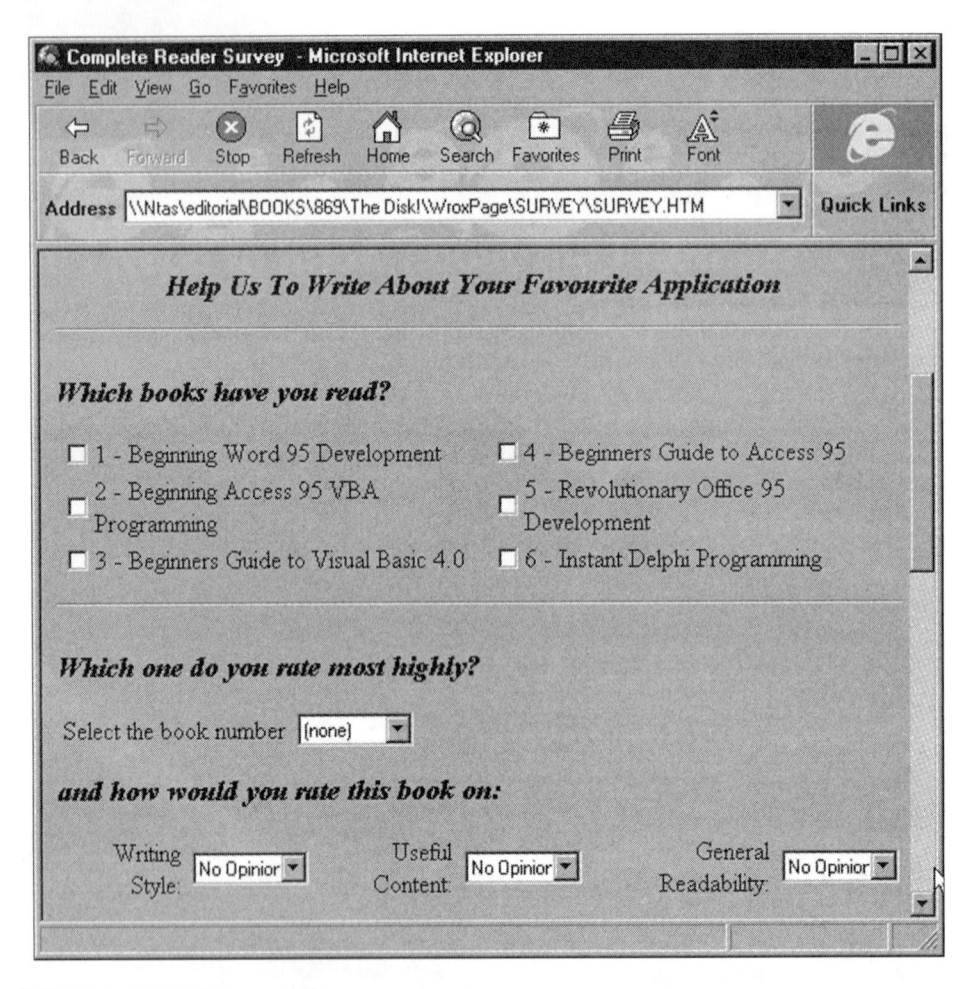

6 Scroll to the bottom of the page, where you'll find the Wrox logo and a hot link where you can send e-mail directly. When you move the mouse pointer over the Wrox logo, it changes to a pointing finger to show that the graphic is also a hot link. You should see the address of the page to which it links in the status bar. If you clicked here, you'd go straight to our home page, but, just for the minute, don't!

7 Instead, click on the feedback@compbook.com hot link and, providing that your browser is mail-enabled, a normal e-mail message window opens (you may have to log into your e-mail application first). Because compbook.com is a fictitious site, your mail won't actually go anywhere, but at least you can see how easy it is to let people send you mail this way.

8 Continue to explore. Remember that you have to use the Back button in your browser's toolbar, to get back to the first page. In the following pages of this chapter, you'll see how we created some of these pages and learn more about the general techniques of HTML.

What We've Seen

You'll find that many of the links in these pages don't actually take you anywhere. We've just supplied some examples of pages for you to try out. However, you can see how useful a well-designed site can be for displaying information, collecting opinions, or selling your company and its products.

You can also see how easy it is to provide a path for your reader to jump to other sites. When you click on a link to Wrox Press, for example, your browser will load the Wrox Press home page, dialing into your Internet provider if you aren't already connected. If your browser software has e-mail functionality built in, clicking on a 'feedback' or an e-mail address link opens a new message window where you can send mail directly.

The pages you've seen may not be as exciting as many you come across on the Web itself, because page design is as much an art as a science. On top of this, we've tried to stick to common functions in our pages so that they'll work broadly the same way on different types of browser. There's no surer way of irritating a viewer that to tell them that their browser is no good for displaying your pages and that they need to immediately go out and buy browser X. They're more likely to consider that it's your pages that are the problem and go elsewhere. Also, you should be aware that how the page looks will vary across systems with different screen resolutions. What may look great on a system running at 1024x780 pixels may look awful to someone with a VGA screen running at 640x480. Giving a little consideration to your wider audience is well worth the effort.

Creating Web Pages as HTML Text Files

There a many different applications, add-ins and other support materials that can help you to create web pages. They often do this by hiding the basic structure of the page, so you only see the results, in a kind of 'What You See Is Nearly What You Get' mode. Why *nearly*? Well, the big problem is that, although there's a standard definition for HTML, the browser manufacturers are all falling over themselves in the race to add proprietary extensions.

You often see web pages with the line Optimized for use with Netscape, or something similar. In this book, we're aiming to build web pages that will work with *all* the common web browsers. Our philosophy is that everyone is welcome, so by sticking as near as possible to standard HTML, we'll try to make sure that almost everyone who visits our site can actually read our pages.

Besides, you really ought to know what makes HTML work. By learning something about the basics of the language, you'll be more capable of solving problems than the design software that you're using. You can also make the most of the opportunities that the new versions of HTML offer, without waiting for someone else to update the web page design software that you use. In fact, as you'll see later on, we've supplied you with a simple tool that both requires you to understand how HTML works *and* allows you to add new functions to it or modify the existing ones that it contains.

The Structure of a Web Page

A web page is basically just simple text, plus the instructions about how it should be formatted. If you include graphics, they're sent to the browser separately in a specially encoded form. There are instructions to specify where they fit in the page. These instructions are called **tags**. Different types of tag control all aspects of the page format. Your browser reads the tags and translates them into a screen display that is best suited to your hardware and operating system. This means that the same tag may have different effects when it's executed by different browsers.

That's the big strength of HTML. All browsers are designed to ignore tags that they can't handle or don't recognize. So as the language expands and new tags are introduced, the pages can still be viewed on an older browser or non-graphical terminals. The only problem is that a user viewing your web pages with an older browser may not get all of the formatting that you intend them to see and so may well miss a lot of the information the page contained in the page. For example, if their browser can't display tables, all your carefully formatted information may become just a jumble of text.

HTML has grown up as a world-wide standard and is just reaching Version 3. However, a great many browsers still only support Version 2, plus extensions to the language that are specific to that browser. Having the ability to read tables is the main reason for moving to HTML 3, though, and most mainline browsers already support the emerging standard. All this, however, makes it more difficult to decide at which level you should pitch your pages. Should you go for all the latest effects, or stick with the traditional ones so that your pages are almost universal in appeal?

We'll start out using only the most commonly supported functions up to and including HTML 2, but in later sections we'll show you how some of the newer tags and some of the specific extensions work.

Defining the Areas of the Page

The simplest web page consists of a set of tags that define the **head** and **body** areas. When viewed in a normal text editor, the HTML codes to do this will look like the figure below. We've typed them into **NotePad** and saved the file as **MyPage.htm** on disk.

```
<HTML>
    <HEAD>
        <TITLE>
            My Document Title Here
        </TITLE>
    </HEAD>
    <BODY>
        This is the text for the body of the page
    </BODY>
</HTML>
```

Notice that each tag is enclosed in greater-than (<) and less-than (>) characters, and the closing tag is the same as the opening one, but with a forward slash included. In some ways, using HTML is similar to using a programming language. Here we've indented the tags to make it easier to see what's going on. You can include as many spaces, tabs and blank lines as you like. The browser will remove these when it displays the page.

So what does this page look like in a browser? Well, as you can see, it's pretty basic. The text enclosed in the `<TITLE>` tags is used as the browser's window title and in its various history lists. The text in the body area of the document is displayed on the page.

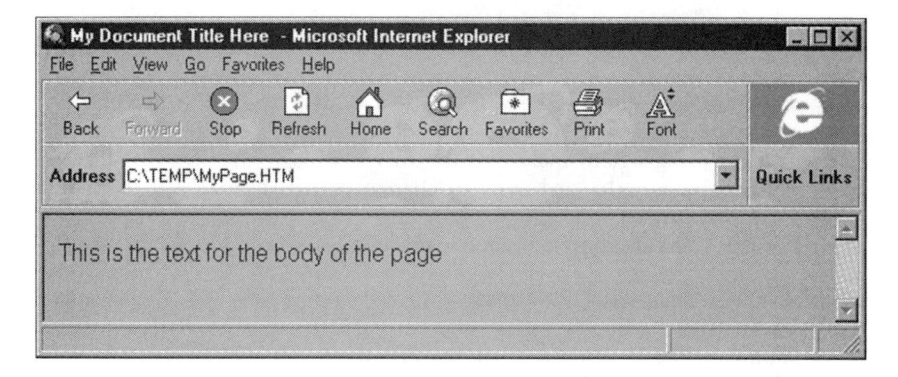

Later in this chapter you'll meet another tag that defines an area of the page. In the previous example, we saw how a web page can be used with controls, like a Word dialog. To do this, you define part of the body section of the page as a form, using the `<FORM>` and `</FORM>` tags. But more of this later.

FYI All web browsers expect the HTML page text file to have the extension `.htm` or `.html`. On Unix-based systems the four letter extension is often used, but, of course, this can't be used in Windows 3. In Windows 95 you can use either form.

Controlling the Formatting of Text

In the previous example, the text is displayed in the browser's default font and size, but HTML contains an ever-increasing range of tags that control all the individual elements of your page. Before we go into specifics, we'll have a look at an example of the simplest ones—tags which define the level of heading in the page and the actual formatting of the font. For example, here's our page as a text file in NotePad again, then displayed in Internet Explorer.

```
<HTML>
    <HEAD>
        <TITLE>
            My document Title
        </TITLE>
    </HEAD>
    <BODY>
        <H1> This is a heading </H1>
        This is normal default text, but you can
        also do <B> bold </B> and <I> italic </I>
        as well.
    </BODY>
</HTML>
```

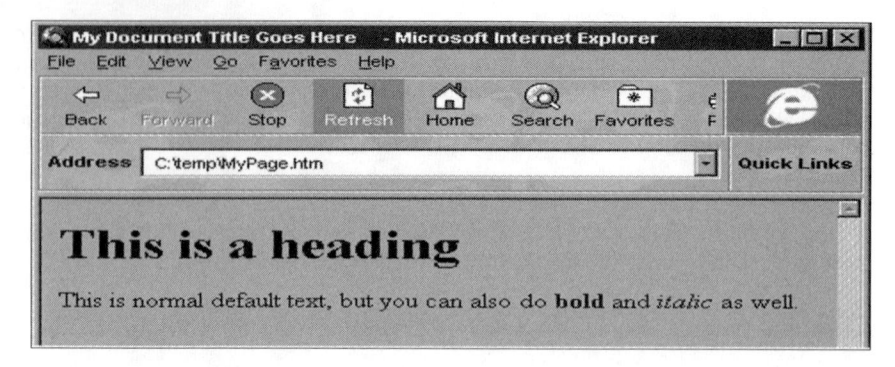

You can see how the tags can change the way the text is displayed. The heading tags `<H1>` and `</H1>` define a level-1 heading. You can use levels from 1 to 7. To indicate the end of the heading we use the same tag again, including the forward slash character. In the rest of the text, we've included two other tags, `<B>` and `<I>` to change particular words to bold or italic.

Formatting text is easy. You can combine some pairs of tags. For example, the line,

```
<H1> This is a <I> heading </I> </H1>
```

changes the formatting of the heading so that the last word is italic. Notice that the `<I>` and `</I>` tags are nested, or enclosed, within the `<H1>` and `</H1>` tags. However, the `<B>` and `</B>` tags will have no effect in this situation because the heading text is already displayed in bold format. You can also see how the browser ignores the carriage returns that we placed in the line in **NotePad**. It places all the text on one line and will only wrap it to the next line if the window is resized.

There are other differences between the way the heading tags and the bold and italic tags work. At the end of the heading line the browser automatically inserts a carriage return and a blank line, but, at the end of a section of bold or italic text, it continues on the same line. If we change the HTML code to read,

```
also do <STRONG> bold </STRONG> and <ADDRESS> italic </ADDRESS>
```

we get a different result again. Even though we've used a different tag, the browser displays the same bold part, but the italic part now appears on a different line. The browser has added a carriage return before and after it.

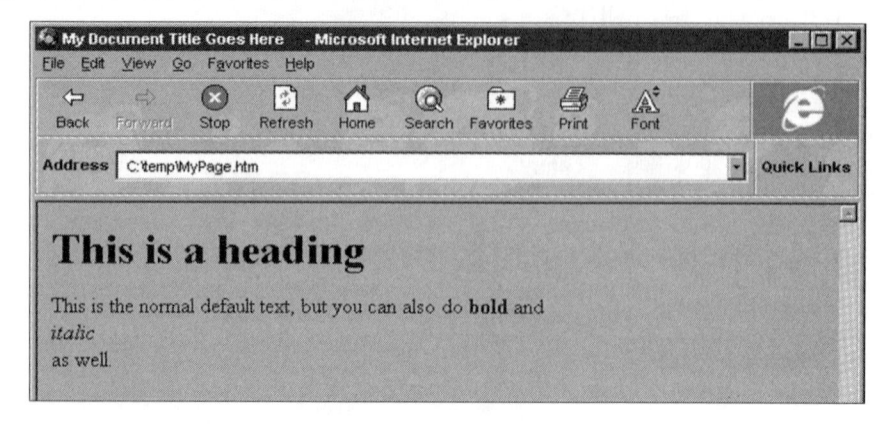

If all this seems very confusing, it's because there are different categories of tags. The HTML tags that affect formatting can be broken down into groups. You can use **logical** or **physical tags** to define the style of the text, and use tags which affect blocks of text or just individual groups of words.

Logical and Physical Formatting Tags

In the previous example, we displayed text as bold by using two different tags, `<B>` and `<STRONG>`. The latter is an example of a logical formatting tag where the browser itself decides how the text will actually be displayed. This is useful if the page is being viewed on a simple monochrome screen that may not support bold text. The browser will know that you want to draw attention to that text, so, instead of using bold, it will perhaps underline it or display it in reverse video.

The `<B>` tag, however, just tells the browser to display it as bold text. As you've seen, this has no effect if the text is already bold and may not affect the text at all on a simple terminal. So, unless you know that all of your audience will be using suitably equipped browsers, wherever possible you should consider using logical format tags than rather than physical ones.

Of course, because the browser itself chooses the actual format of the text for a logical tag, you can't be sure what it will look like. So, whereas the logical `<ADDRESS>` tag we used above produces italic text in Internet Explorer and most mainline browsers, it may not do so on others. However, it still gives you maximum compatibility overall.

The `<ADDRESS>` tag has the problem of breaking the line, rather than displaying the text as a continuous line. No matter. The `<CITE>` tag gives the same formatting effect to the text, but doesn't add carriage returns. Using,

```
also do <STRONG> bold </STRONG> and <CITE> italic </CITE>
```

will give the same display in our browser as the original, which used the bold and italic tags, but it might not do the same in others!

So, as we suggested earlier on, you can never be sure exactly what your page will look like in another browser unless you actually view it there. If you are doing a lot of web page design, it's worth obtaining a copy of the three or four mainline products to try your pages in. In general, though, you can expect them to look broadly similar in all browsers if you stick to the common tags. Here's a list of those that affect text formatting:

Tag	Format	Line Breaks?	Type
`<ADDRESS>`	Italic	Yes	Logical
`<B>`	Bold	No	Physical
`<CITE>`	Citation (Italic)	No	Logical
`<CODE>`	Code Sample (Fixed-width Text)	No	Logical
`<DFN>`	Definition (Italic)	No	Logical
`<EM>`	Emphasized (Italic)	No	Logical
`<H1> .. <H7>`	Bold Heading	Yes	Logical

Table Continued on Following Page

Tag	Format	Line Breaks?	Type
`<I>`	Italic	No	Physical
`<KBD>`	Keyboard (Bold Fixed-width Text)	No	Logical
`<LISTING>`	Code Listing (Fixed-width Text)	Yes	Logical
`<PRE>`	Pre-formatted (Fixed-width Text)	Yes	Logical
`<S>`	Strike-through Text	No	Physical
`<SAMP>`	Code Sample (Fixed-width Text)	No	Logical
`<STRIKE>`	Strike-through Text	No	Physical
`<STRONG>`	Bold	No	Logical
`<TT>`	Tele-type (Fixed-width Text)	No	Logical
`<U>`	Underlined	No	Physical
`<VAR>`	Small Font Fixed-width Text	No	Logical
`<XMP>`	Example (Fixed-width Text)	Yes	Logical

You'll find that many of the tags give the same effect in any browser. For example, in Internet Explorer the `<CODE>`, `<TT>` and `<SAMP>` tags all produce normal fixed-width font.

> **FYI** We've used uppercase for our tags, but you can use lowercase instead. The majority of browsers are not case-sensitive in any HTML tags, though there are minor exceptions with some of the new language extensions. We use uppercase because it makes the tags stand out in the page better during design.

Block Formatting HTML Tags

Rather than just formatting one or more words, or complete lines of text, you can use tags which affect a block of text. For example, you regularly see lists of items in a web page, or definitions of particular words. The sample pages we've supplied contain both types, so we'll look at these here. The common types of block formatting are lists, definitions, block quotes, directory lists and menu lists.

Block quotes are areas where the whole paragraph is indented from both margins. With all block formatting tags, you enclose the whole paragraph with the opening and closing tags. Here's an example, followed by how it looks in Internet Explorer:

```
This text is displayed in the default position, running right
to the edges of the page.
<BLOCKQUOTE>
    This is some text in a block quote which will be indented
    from both margins when displayed.
</BLOCKQUOTE>
```

[Screenshot: Internet Explorer window showing text "This text is displayed in the default poisition running right to the edges of the page." followed by an indented block quote "This is some text in a block quote which will be indented from both margins when displayed"]

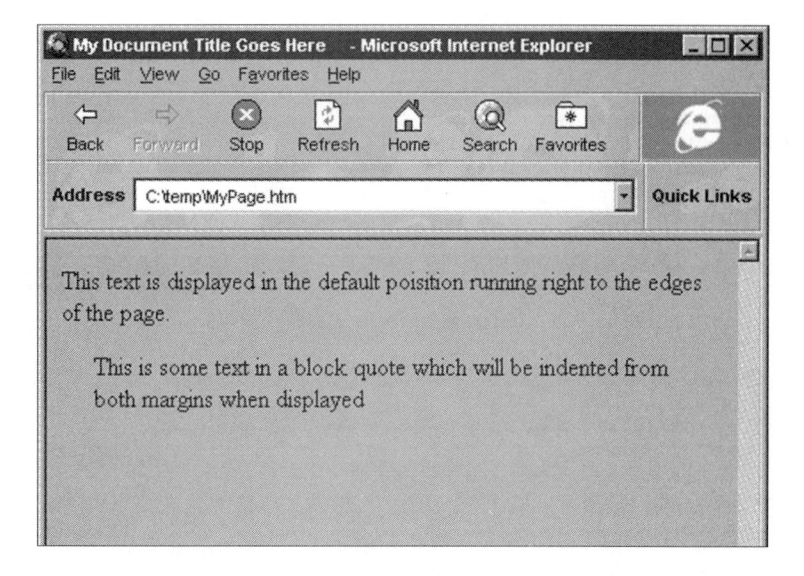

Using Lists in Your Web Pages

You can create several different types of list. The two basic ones are an **ordered** or an **unordered list**. The only real difference is that an ordered list numbers each item, whereas an unordered list uses bullet characters. All the indenting from the margin is done automatically for you.

An unordered list uses the `<UL>` and `</UL>` tags to enclose the whole list, and each list item is preceded by the `<LI>` tag. Notice that this is a single tag, not one of a pair of opening and closing tags like all those we've seen previously:

```
<UL>
   <LI> An unordered list item
   <LI> Another unordered list item
   <LI> And one more
</UL>
```

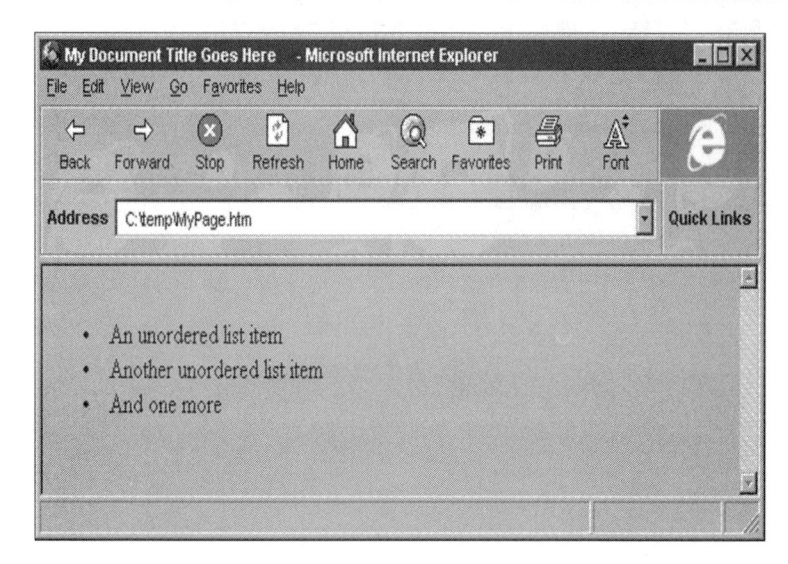

[Screenshot: Internet Explorer window displaying a bulleted list:
• An unordered list item
• Another unordered list item
• And one more]

To produce an ordered list, we just use the `<OL>` and `</OL>` tags instead:

```
<OL>
    <LI> Item one in an ordered list
    <LI> Item two in an ordered list
    <LI> Item three in an ordered list
</OL>
```

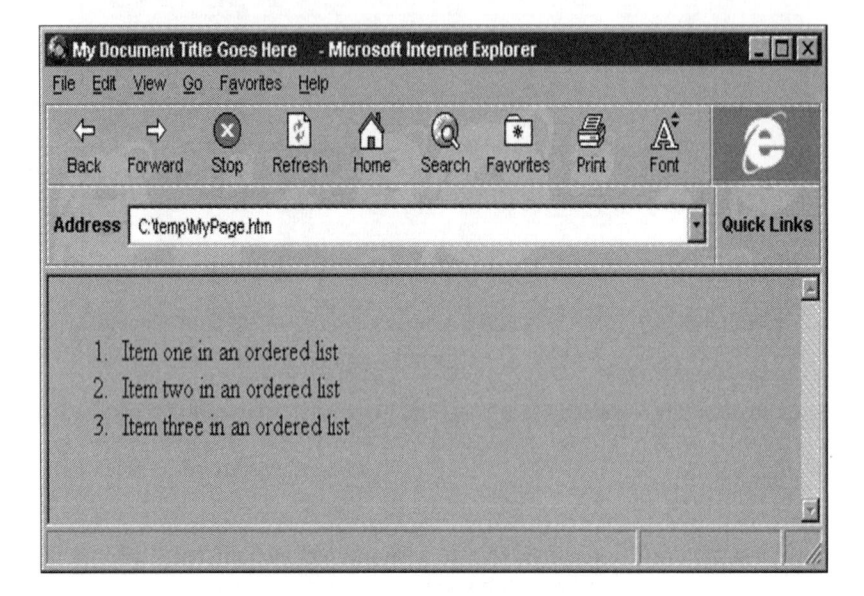

If you want to, you can also nest one list within another. Here's an example of a nested list from one of the sample pages, `WroxPage\Company\Book3.htm`. The code that produces it is:

```
<UL>
    <LI>Quick-start introduction to the main techniques.
    <LI>Easy to implement custom solutions described.
    <LI>Benefit from three ready-built network applications:
    <OL>
        <LI>Wrox KickStart helps you get it going.
        <LI>Wrox NetWatcher helps you maintain control.
        <LI>Wrox GateKeeper helps you stay secure.
    </OL>
    <LI>See how the experts have commissioned their systems.
    <LI>Make all your projects a success in future...
</UL>
```

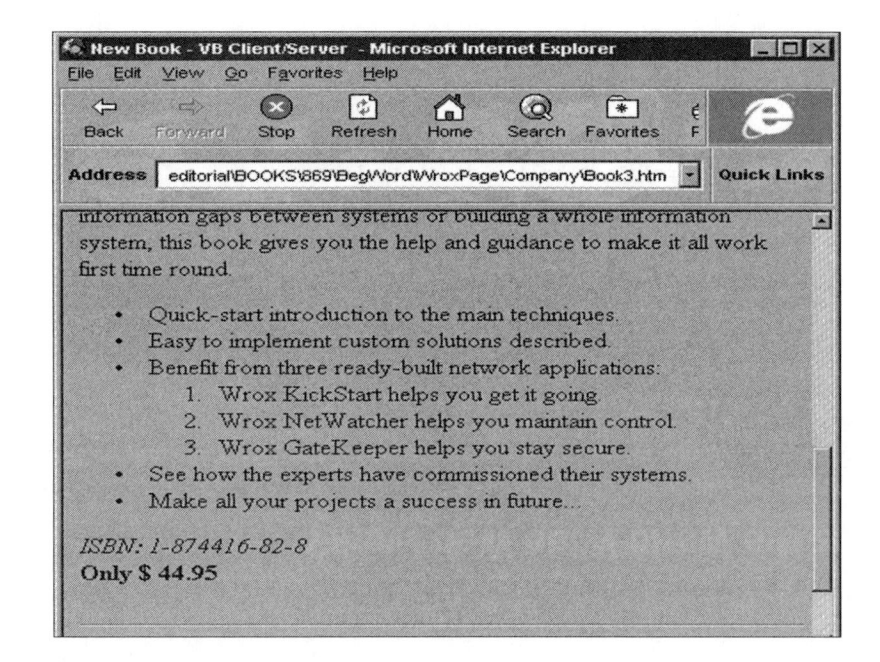

![Screenshot of New Book - VB Client/Server in Microsoft Internet Explorer showing text about an information system book, with bullet points and a numbered list of Wrox applications (KickStart, NetWatcher, GateKeeper), ISBN: 1-874416-82-8, Only $ 44.95]

You can also use two predefined list formats, directory lists and menu lists. In Internet Explorer, they both provide the same effect, though you are limited to 20 characters in a `<DIR>` list. You'll see in the browser that the items are indented from the left margin, but don't have any bullets or numbers.

```
<DIR>
   <LI> Directory list item
   <LI> Another item
   <LI> And one more
</DIR>
```

```
<MENU>
   <LI> A menu list item with more than 20 characters of text
   <LI> Another menu list item
   <LI> And one more
</MENU>
```

One of the popular extensions to HTML, which was first introduced in Netscape's browser, is the control over the bullet or number format. You can see from the screenshot that the first two examples here are supported by Internet Explorer, but the third isn't:

```
<OL>
   <LI TYPE=A > Capital Letters
   <LI TYPE=a > Lower-case Letters
   <LI TYPE=I > Roman Numerals
   <LI TYPE=i > Lower-case Roman Numerals
</OL>

<OL>
   <LI VALUE=5 > Item five
   <LI VALUE=8 > Item eight
```

287

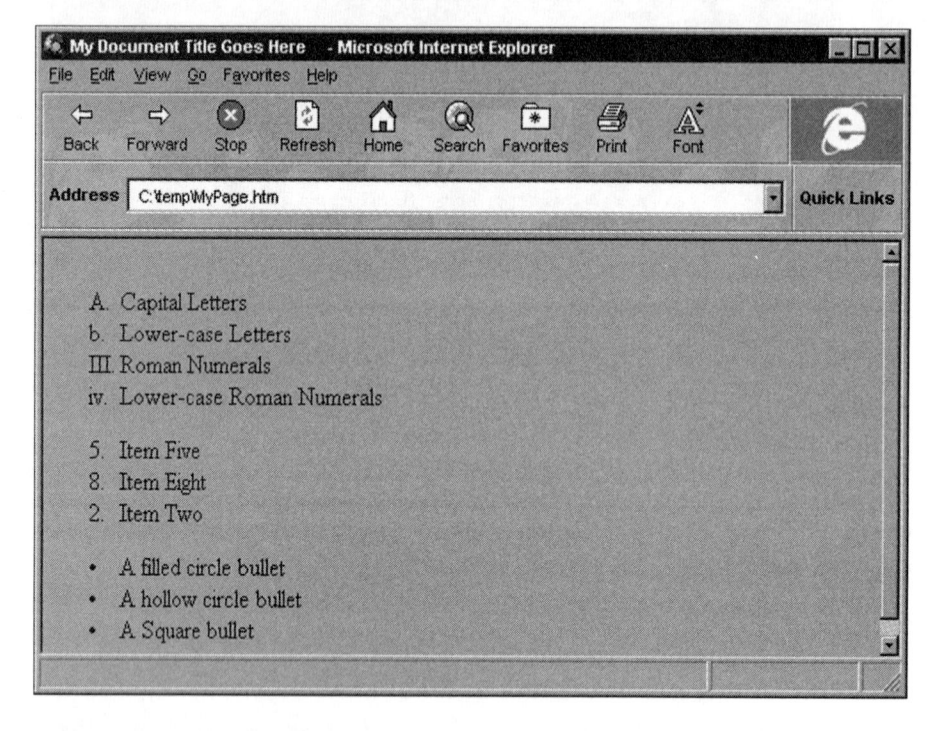

```
      <LI VALUE=2 > Item two
</OL>

<UL>
   <LI TYPE="disc" > A filled circle bullet
   <LI TYPE="circle"> A hollow circle bullet
   <LI TYPE="square" > A square bullet
</UL>
```

Using Definitions in Your Web Pages

The final type of block formatting that we'll cover here is the **definition list**. Again, it uses a pair of tags, `<DL>` and `</DL>` to enclose the list. Within the list, each item uses two single tags to specify the definition term and the definition itself:

```
<DL>
   <DT> The term to be defined
   <DD> The definition of it
</DL>
```

In the browser, the term is displayed flush with the left margin and the definition is indented. Here's an example from one of the sample pages we've supplied, with the result displayed in Internet Explorer. You can see that we've formatted the definition term to make it stand out:

```
<DL>
   <DT> <STRONG><CODE> AddAddress </CODE></STRONG>
   <DD> This is a very simple demonstration of how you can add . . .
</DL>
```

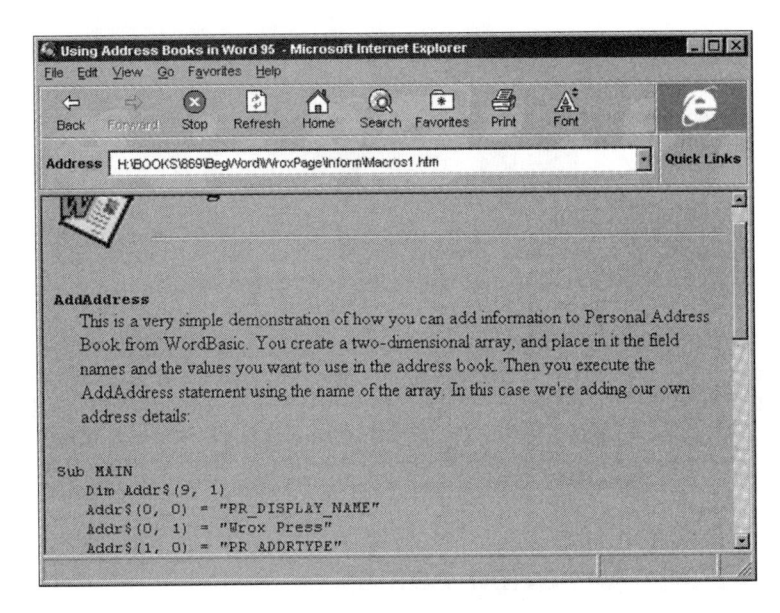

You'll also see some sample code below the definition. This is formatted using the **`<PRE>`** tag we met earlier. It makes it look like it would had we typed it into Word's macro editor.

> **FYI** Some browsers also support a **`<DL COMPACT>`** tag which produces a definition list with less space between the individual definitions.

Combining Different Tags

You saw earlier on how we can nest tags to give different effects. For example, we can format each item in a list differently. Here's an example, followed by the section of HTML code that produces it:

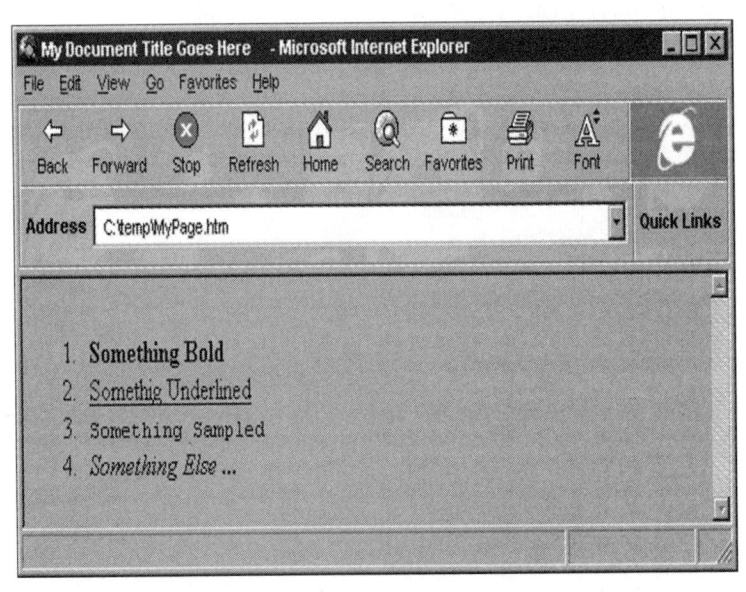

```
<OL>
    <LI> <B> Something Bold </B>
    <LI> <U> Something U </U>
    <LI> <SAMP> Something Sampled </SAMP>
    <LI> <CITE> Something else... </CITE>
</OL>
```

Remember, though, that some combinations, such as bold in a heading line, have no effect. And different browsers allow different combinations, so, where possible, you should try to stick to logical tags so that it looks correct to the majority of your viewers.

> **FYI** Because of the limitations of the Internet when it comes to transmitting text, you can't send characters with an ASCII code greater than 127 (the largest 7-bit value) directly. Instead, you use the & character to specify the one you want. There are special values for use with &, or you can use the ASCII code of the character instead. To send a copyright symbol, for instance, you can use `&copy` or `&#169`.

Making Web Page Creation Easier

Before we go any further, we should consider how you actually go about inserting tags into your HTML documents. It may be that you have existing Word documents that you want to convert into web pages, so you only need to insert the required tags and reformat them to suit the new medium. But even if you're creating the pages from scratch, it takes time to keep typing in all the tags, especially the longer ones. We've supplied a template that makes it easier to select the correct tag and insert it into your document.

Try It Out - The WroxWeb HTML Assistant

For this example, you'll need to have installed the samples from the disk that accompanies the book. If you installed them in a different folder from the default `C:\BegWord`, you'll have to change one line of the macro, as we'll show you in the example.

1 In Word, select New... from the File menu (don't click the New button on the toolbar), and in the New dialog double-click WroxWeb.dot to create a new document based on this template. Immediately, you're prompted to save it as a text file. Enter a name and click Save.

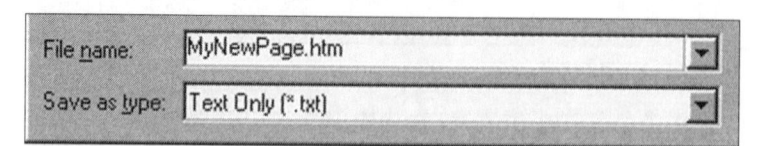

```
File name:     MyNewPage.htm
Save as type:  Text Only (*.txt)
```

> **FYI** If you've got **AutoMacros** switched off, the `AutoNew` macro in our template will not start running automatically and won't work correctly. In this case, open the Macro dialog and double-click on the **AutoNew** entry to run it once you have created the new document.

Chapter 7 - Creating Web Pages for the Internet

2 Now you have a blank HTML document page. It has a title and body section ready for you to complete. Ignore the other tags for the time being, we'll come back to them later.

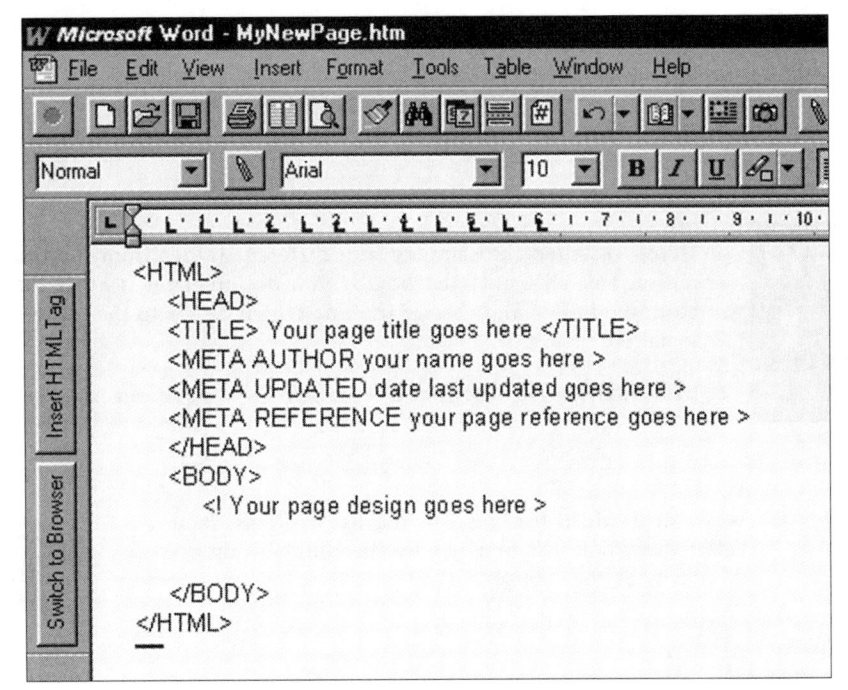

```
<HTML>
    <HEAD>
    <TITLE> Your page title goes here </TITLE>
    <META AUTHOR your name goes here >
    <META UPDATED date last updated goes here >
    <META REFERENCE your page reference goes here >
    </HEAD>
    <BODY>
        <! Your page design goes here >


    </BODY>
</HTML>
```

3 Enter your page title between the `<TITLE>` tags, and type some text in the body section. It doesn't matter what, because we're just going to see the way that tags are inserted. Once you've typed some text, select a word or two in the middle of it.

This is the text that **will be displayed** on my new Web page.

4 Now click the **Insert HTML Tag** button on the toolbar to open the **Select Tag** dialog. (If you can't see the toolbar, select **Toolbars** from the **View** menu, and place a tick next to **WroxWeb**.) Scroll down the list of tags and select `<STRONG>`, then click **OK**.

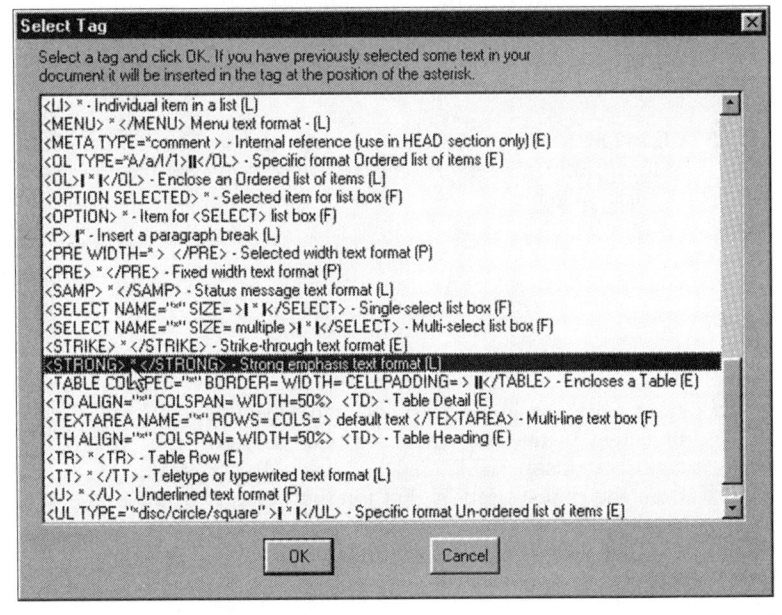

291

5 The `<STRONG>` and `</STRONG>` tags are automatically inserted into your document around the selected text.

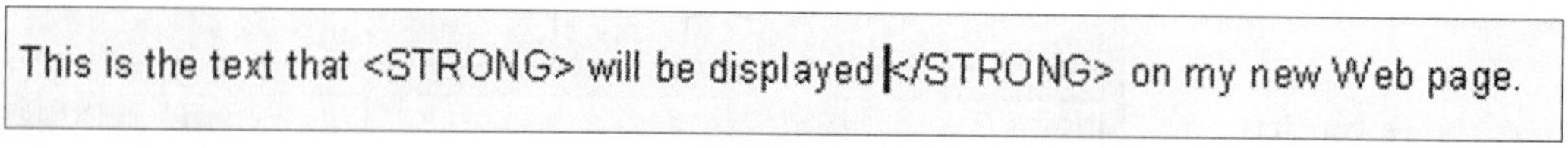

> This is the text that <STRONG> will be displayed </STRONG> on my new Web page.

> **FYI** If you installed the samples in a different folder from the default, you'll get an error message or an empty list box. If you do, open the `GetHTMLTag` macro in the macro editing window and change the line which points to the folder where the samples were installed:
>
> `ListPath$ = "C:\BegWord\WroxWeb\"   'location of Tag List document`

6 Next, we'll add a list. Type in the list of items, then select the whole list (but not the heading) by dragging over it with the mouse.

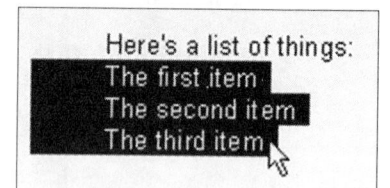

> Here's a list of things:
> The first item
> The second item
> The third item

7 Click Insert HTML Tag and select the `<OL>` entry. Notice that there's also an entry above it for the Netscape list extensions format, but we want the simple list form.

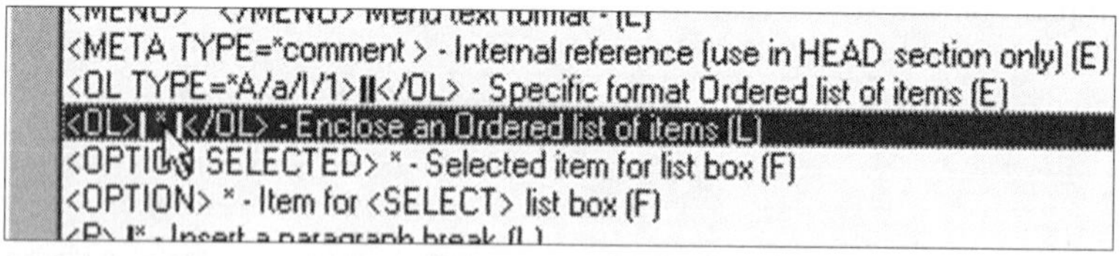

> `<MENU> </MENU>` Menu text format - (L)
> `<META TYPE="comment >` - Internal reference (use in HEAD section only) (E)
> `<OL TYPE="A/a/I/1>|</OL>` - Specific format Ordered list of items (E)
> `<OL>|*|</OL>` - Enclose an Ordered list of items (L)
> `<OPTION SELECTED>` * - Selected item for list box (F)
> `<OPTION>` * - Item for `<SELECT>` list box (F)
> `<P>` * - Insert a paragraph break (L)

8 Click OK to insert the tags around the list. They're automatically placed on separate lines above and below the list of items.

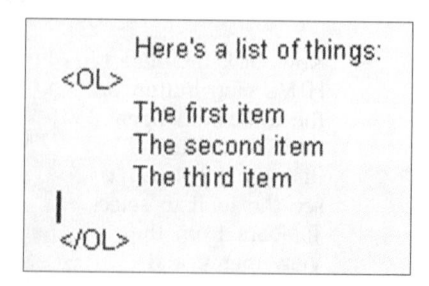

> Here's a list of things:
> `<OL>`
> The first item
> The second item
> The third item
>
> `</OL>`

9 Now place the insertion point at the beginning of the first item in the list, where we want to insert the `<LI>` tag. Click Insert HTML Tag and select the `<LI>` tag from the dialog. Repeat this for the other two items in the list. Because this is a single tag, it's just placed at the current insertion point.

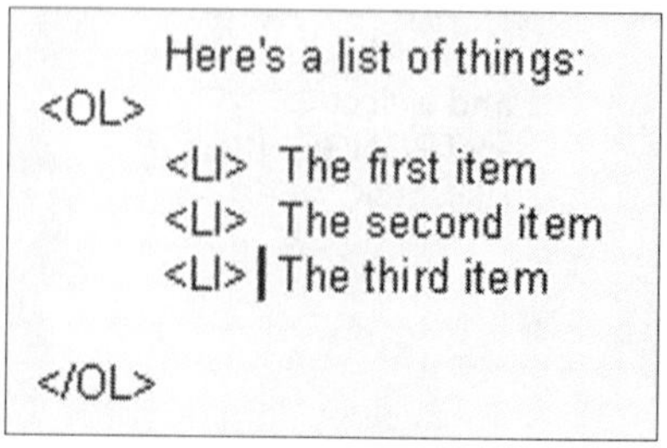

> Here's a list of things:
> `<OL>`
> `<LI>` The first item
> `<LI>` The second item
> `<LI>` The third item
>
> `</OL>`

10 Finally, we'll format the whole list. Place the insertion point before the `<OL>` tag and drag over the whole list to select it, including the `</OL>` tag. Then click Insert HTML Tag and double-click on the entry for `<CITE>`. The tags are placed around the table, though you may want to add a carriage return to tidy up the layout afterwards, like this:

```
Here's a list of things:
<CITE>
<OL>
    <LI> The first item
    <LI> The second item
    <LI> The third item
</OL>
</CITE>
```

How It Works

OK, so **WroxWeb** isn't the prettiest of web creation tools around, but it's home-made and uses just a few simple macros in WordBasic. What it will do is to help you understand just how a web page is constructed, while saving you time typing out the tags in full. It uses a method of storing information for a macro that we haven't met before: in a table in another document. We've created a document, called `TagList.doc`, which contains a single-column table including all the tags for the dialog. So you can edit the contents and easily add others when the standards change.

To manipulate our HTML document, we first have to open the `TagList.doc`. The `GetHTMLTag` macro first saves the name of the current window (our HTML page) and any selected text in it. Then we can try and activate the `TagList.doc` window (assuming it's already open) or, if not, we load it from disk.

```
. . .
    ScreenUpdating 0                            'turn off screen updating
    PrevWin$ = WindowName$()                    'save the active window title
    Existing$ = ""
    If SelType() <> 1 And SelType() <> 5 Then
        Existing$ = Selection$()                'save any currently selected text
        EditClear                               'and delete if in the document
    EndIf
    If Not SwitchToWindow(ListName$) Then       'try and activate TagList window
        FileOpen ListPath$ + ListName$          'if not then open it from disk
    EndIf
. . .
```

If we try and switch to a window that isn't open, WordBasic creates an error. By using a separate function for this, we can trap the error and tell whether it's already open or not:

```
Function SwitchToWindow(WinName$)               'return True if open, False if not
    On Error Goto NotFound
    SwitchToWindow = 0                          'set result to False
    Activate WinName$                           'activate the window
    SwitchToWindow = - 1                        'if we didn't get an error we must
NotFound:                                       'have opened it, so return True
End Function
```

Reading the Contents of a Table with WordBasic

Once we've activated the `TagList.doc` document window we can read the list of tags into an array. This is done with the `FillTagArray` function, which returns the number of tags. We've used `EditGoto` to make sure that we're in the table (in case there are any blank lines at the start of the document), and then called the **SelInfo()** function with an argument of **15**. This is just one of the dozens of arguments you can use with **SelInfo**, and this particular one returns the number of rows in the table where the insertion point currently resides.

To get the contents of the current cell, we use **EditGoTo** with the predefined bookmark **\Cell**. However, this selects the whole cell, not just the text in it, so we need a **CharLeft 1,1** to shrink the selection so that it only includes the text. After that we can store it in the array. When we've got all of them, we sort the array and return:

```
Function FillTagArray
    On Error Goto FTA_Err
    FillTagArray = 0                        'number of tags in table
    StartOfDocument                         'got to start of document
    EditGoTo "t"                            'go to first cell of table
    Count = SelInfo(15)                     'get number of rows in table
    Redim Tag$(Count - 1)                   'resize the array to suit
    For Loop = 0 To Count - 1               'loop for each row in the table
        EditGoTo .Destination = "\Cell"     'select the current cell
        CharLeft 1, 1                       'shrink the selection one char.
        Tag$(Loop) = Selection$()           'and read it into the array
        LineDown                            'go to the next row
    Next                                    'and loop again
    SortArray Tag$()                        'sort the array
    FillTagArray = Count                    'set the number of tags
    Goto FTA_Exit
FTA_Err:
    FillTagArray = 0
FTA_Exit:
End Function
```

The remainder of the macro is concerned with creating and displaying the dialog, and inserting the actual tag. Having got the list of tags in the array we switch back to the HTML page window and get the user's choice of tag. Then we only have to insert it into the document:

```
. . .
NumTags = FillTagArray                      'fill the array with the tags
Activate PrevWin$                           'and go back to the HTML page
. . .
'create the dialog
. . .
If Dialog(dlg) Then
    TheTag$ = Tag$(dlg.lstTag)              'get the selected tag text
    EndPos = InStr(TheTag$, "-") - 1        'chop off the description part
    TheTag$ = Left$(TheTag$, EndPos)
    IPos = InStr(TheTag$, "*")              'find the text insertion point
    Insert TheTag$                          'insert the tag
    CharLeft(EndPos - IPos + 1)
    EditClear                               'remove the insertion marker
    Insert Existing$                        'and insert the existing text
EndIf                                       'that we deleted previously
ScreenUpdating 1
End Sub
```

How WroxWeb Uses the Tag List Entries

If you look at the table in **TagList.doc**, you'll see that the entries follow the same form as the tags they produce. For example, the **<OL>** entry is:

```
<OL>
 *
</OL> - Enclose an Ordered list of items (L)
```

The asterisk character marks the point where any selected text will be placed. If there's no selected text the tags are just inserted as they stand. However, when the text is displayed in a list box, the carriage returns become vertical bars, as you can see in the previous example. We could hide these in the macro that creates the dialog, but this would considerably slow down the operation, so we haven't bothered.

All the tag entries we've used so far place the selected text between the tags, but there are tags that require extra arguments, as with the extensions to the list tags we saw earlier. In this case, the entry in **TagList.doc** looks like this:

```
<OL TYPE=*A/a/I/1>

</OL> - Specific format Ordered list of items (E)
```

When you insert this tag, the insertion point is left after the **TYPE=** part, where the asterisk is, and any selected text is inserted here. So, before you open the dialog, you have to remember to select the correct items in your HTML page. You can see the asterisks in the list, though, so you can tell where your selected text will be inserted.

```
<MENU>   </MENU> Menu text format - (L)
<META TYPE=*comment > - Internal reference (use in HEAD section only) (E)
<OL TYPE=*A/a/I/1>|</OL> - Specific format Ordered list of items (E)
<OL>|*|</OL> - Enclose an Ordered list of items (L)
<OPTION SELECTED> * - Selected item for list box (F)
<OPTION> * - Item for <SELECT> list box (F)
<P> |* - Insert a paragraph break (L)
```

If you want to change this behavior, you can easily edit the entries in the TagList table to suit the way you prefer to work. Notice that you must include the hyphen after the tags, even if you enter a description.

FYI We've tried to show which tags are standard and which extended by adding a letter to the end of the description. **(P)** and **(L)** are physical and logical formatting tags, **(L)** indicates tags used for lists, **(F)** shows tags used in forms, and **(E)** shows the tags that are generally extensions of the standard.

Saving the HTML Document as a Text File

The other macros in the WroxWeb template are concerned with saving the document as a text file, with the **.htm** file extension. The template contains the boiler-plate text that makes up the default HTML document and the narrow tab settings. When you create a new document based on it, the **AutoNew** macro uses the **FileSaveAs** dialog to force it to be saved in text format with the file extension **.htm**:

295

```
Sub MAIN         'the AutoNew macro
Dim dlg As FileSaveAs                   'declare the dialog
GetCurValues dlg                        'get the current values
dlg.Name = "*.htm;*.txt"                'set file name to .htm and .txt
dlg.Format = 2                          'set file type to Text file
If Dialog(dlg) Then
   TheName$ = dlg.Name
   'get the file name entered and change the extension to .htm
   If InStr(".txt.doc.rtf.dot", LCase$(Right$(TheName$, 4))) Then
      TheName$ = Left$(TheName$, Len(TheName$) - 4) + ".htm"
   EndIf
   dlg.Name = TheName$                  'set new name in the dialog record
   FileSaveAs dlg                       'and save the file
   EditFindClearFormatting
   EditFind .Find = "!", .Direction = 0, .WholeWord = 0, .Wrap = 0
   LineDown                             'go to the body of the document
   SetDocumentDirty 0                   'and clear the dirty flag
EndIf
End Sub
```

Then it simply moves the insertion point to the body of the document ready for you to start typing. It also executes the **SetDocumentDirty 0** statement to prevent Word displaying a message when you close the document. Otherwise, when you save a document in text format and then close it, Word tells you that all the formatting will be lost and asks if you want to save it as a Word document as well.

When we close the last HTML document, we also have to close the **TagList** document. We take over the **DocClose** and **FileClose** commands and add the following code:

```
. . .
ListName$ = "TagList.doc"               'name of Tag List document
On Error Goto FC_Err
If CountWindows() < 3 Then              'closing the last .htm document
   Activate ListName$                   'switch to the TagList window
   FileClose                            'and close it
EndIf
FC_Err:
. . .
```

When the HTML document is saved as a text file after being edited, Word doesn't clear the 'dirty' flag, so we also take over the **FileSave** command, and just add the **SetDocumentDirty 0** statement to it. Finally, we've included a modified **FileOpen** command that, as well as normal Word documents, also displays **.htm** documents in the Open dialog. If you install WroxWeb as a global macro while you're working with HTML documents, you can use this to open them quickly.

One problem that you'll come up against, though, is that Word doesn't save the template information when you save a document as a text file. So you have to use the Templates dialog to attach the WroxWeb template to each HTML document when you open it, or install WroxWeb as a global template from the same dialog. If you do this, make sure you unload it again before you work with normal Word documents.

Viewing Your Web Pages

So, we've designed our page. Now we're ready to display it in our browser and make sure it looks OK. The WroxWeb template can help you do this as well, though it does depend on which browser you're using. If you have Internet Explorer, it should work fine without any adjustments, but if you aren't we need to consider what changes you'll have to make to the macro so that it works on your setup. Try this example first and, if you have problems, read the section after it to see how you need to change the macro.

Try It Out - Activating Your Browser with WroxWeb HTML Assistant

This example uses the HTML document that we created in the previous Try It Out. If you're not using Internet Assistant, you may find that your browser doesn't respond correctly. In this case, we'll show you how to adjust the macro.

1 With your new HTML document open in Word, click the Switch to Browser button on the WroxWeb toolbar. You should see the page appear in your web browser. You can easily edit it in Word, then switch back and view the results directly in your browser.

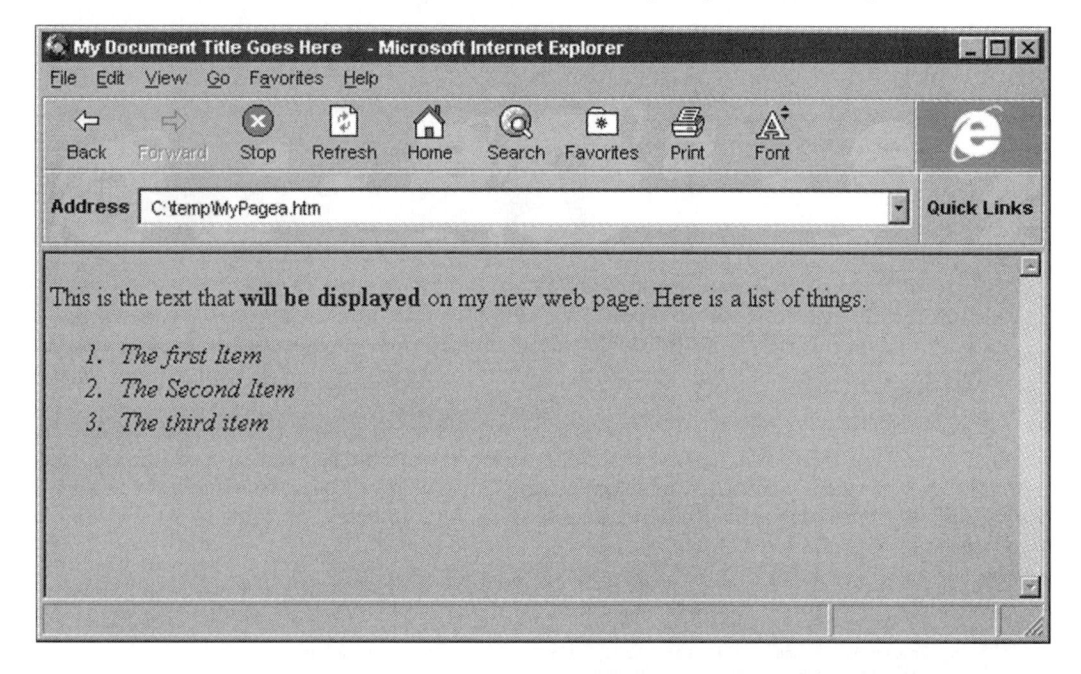

2 If the page doesn't appear, try starting your browser software from the Windows Start menu, then click the button again. If you get an error message, make a note of whether there's a problem actually finding your browser.

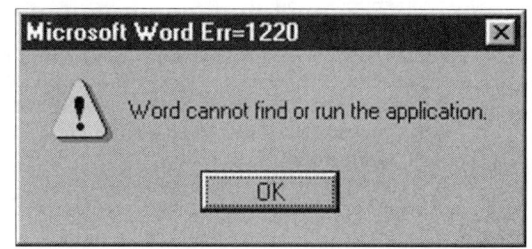

3 If it still doesn't work, open My Computer and select Options... from the View menu. In the File Types tab, make sure that the entry for Internet Document (HTML) is associated with your browser software.

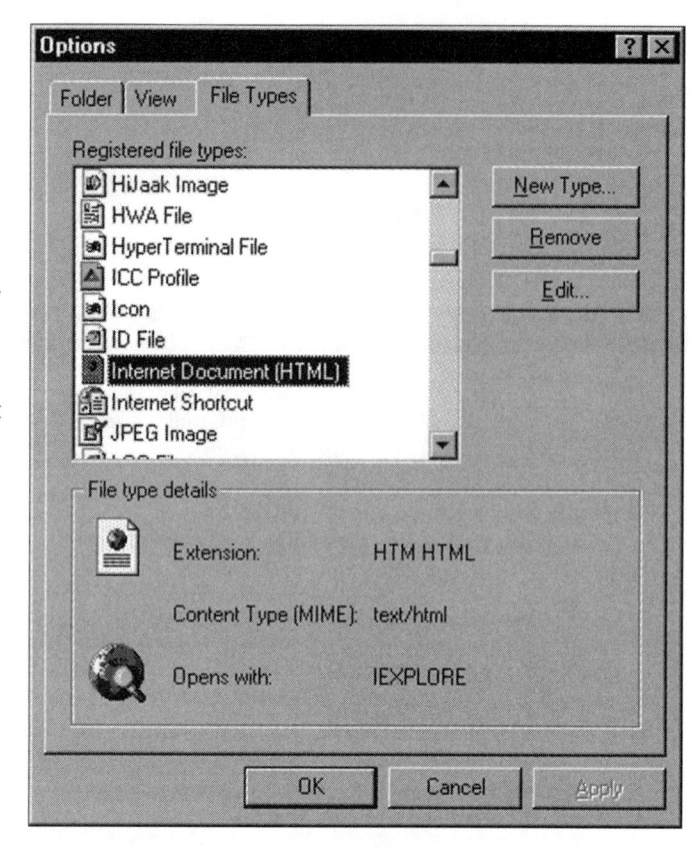

If none of these work, you need to edit the macro. The theory is that you get the title of the document and then look for an application window with that as the start of the window title. Internet Explorer displays the title of the current page first in its title bar, but, if your browser is different, you can modify this part of the code.

Here's the first part of the macro. We have to save the document first so that the browser can load it and we then pull the title out. This is done using **EditFind** to look for the opening **<TITLE>** tag, then extending the selection up to the next **<** character which is the start of the closing **</TITLE>** tag. We use a bookmark to return the insertion point to its previous location afterwards.

```
Sub MAIN
On Error Goto JB_Err
ToolsMacro .Name = "FileSave", .Run        'save the document
ScreenUpdating 0                            'turn off screen updating

'This assumes you browser displays the title of the page
'first in it's title bar. If not, change the code below
'to set the correct value in TheTitle$ to match it.
EditBookmark .Name = "temp", .Add           'current insertion point
StartOfDocument                             'goto start of document
EditFindClearFormatting                     'find the <TITLE> tag
EditFind .Find = "<TITLE>", .Direction = 0, .WholeWord = 0, .Wrap = 0
CharRight                                   'go right one, then extend the
```

```
    ExtendSelection "<"                              'selection up to </TITLE> tag
    CharLeft 1, 1                                    'and go back on character
    TheTitle$ = LTrim$(RTrim$(Selection$()))         'pull out the title
    EditBookmark .Name = "temp", .Goto               'go back to last position
    EditBookmark .Name = "temp", .Delete             'and remove bookmark
    SetDocumentDirty 0                               'then clear the dirty flag
    ScreenUpdating 1                                 'turn screen updating back on
```

Now we can switch to it if it's running, using the **AppActivate** statement. If it isn't already running, we need to start it. We build the file name of the current document using the **FileSummaryInfo** dialog record and add the obligatory quotation marks around it if it's a long file name including spaces. Then we get the browser to display it using the **Shell** statement with just the file name:

```
    If AppIsRunning(TheTitle$) Then                  'browser is running already
        AppActivate TheTitle$                        'just activate it
    Else
        Dim FSI As FileSummaryInfo                   'declare a dialog record
        GetCurValues FSI                             'get the current values
        TheFile$ = FSI.Directory + "\" + FSI.FileName    'build the file name
        If InStr(TheFile$, " ") Then
            TheFile$ = Chr$(34) + TheFile$ + Chr$(34)        'add quotes round it
        EndIf
        Shell TheFile$    'works with Internet Explorer    and start it up

        'you may have to use this form with your browser instead:
        'Browser$ = "C:\Netscape\Netscape.exe"        'set the browser name
        'Shell Browser$ + " " + TheFile$              'and send the file to it

    EndIf
    JB_Err:
    End Sub
```

If this doesn't work, you may have to use the alternative syntax, i.e. the full path and file name of your browser followed by a space and the document file name. Happy experimenting!

Paragraphs, Line Breaks, Centered Text and Ruled Lines

So far, our documents have been, to say the least, a little dull. In the rest of this chapter we'll look at ways of making them both more attractive and more functional. As a starter, though, look back at the page we've just created. You may well have expected a line break after the full stop and before the list heading, but HTML doesn't recognize carriage returns or extra spaces in your file, so it all ends up on one line.

> This is the text that **will be displayed** on my new web page. Here's a list of things:
>
> 1. The first item
> 2. The second item
> 3. The third item

We use special tags to get round this. **<P>** by itself inserts a paragraph mark so that the following text will start on a new line with a blank line before it. **
** just inserts a carriage return without a blank line. However, using several of these in a row has no effect. The browser accepts the first one, then ignores any that follow until it meets some more text.

Normally, your text will be wrapped to fit the browser window, but you can use the `<NOBR>` tag to prevent doing so. Then, within this text you can include a soft line break using the `<WBR>` tag. If the browser window is narrower than the text, the line will wrap, but only at this point.

If you want text to be centered on a line you use the `<CENTRE>` tag, and you can insert a horizontal line across the page with the `<HR>` tag. Here's how all these tags look in a browser, with the HTML code that produces them:

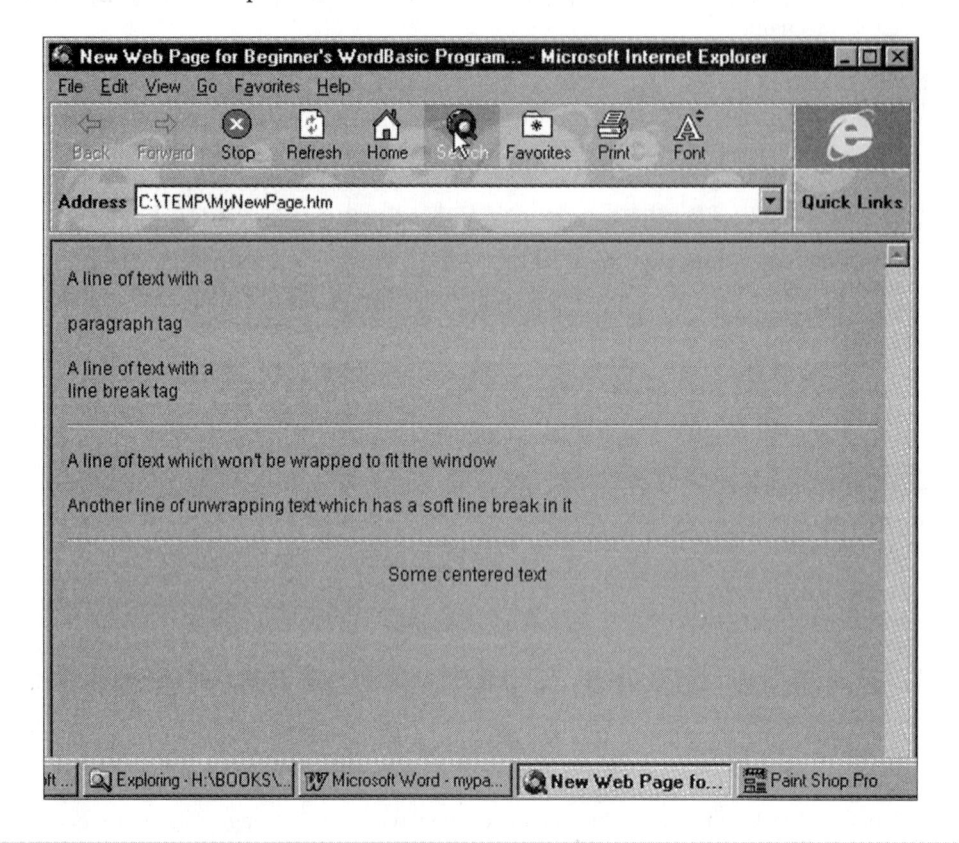

```
A line of text with a <P> paragraph tag
<P>
A line of text with a <BR> line break tag
<HR>
<NOBR>
    A line of text which won't be wrapped to fit the window
</NOBR>
<P>
<NOBR>
    Another line of unwrapping text which has a soft <WBR> line break in it
</NOBR>
<HR>
<CENTER> Some centered text </CENTER>
```

> **FYI** Amongst the extensions that are available in some browsers are the options to change the size of the horizontal ruled line. For example, the following produces a line half the browser window width, centered on the page and with a thickness of six pixels:
>
> ```
> <HR SIZE=6 ALIGN="Center" WIDTH="50%" >
> ```

Using Graphic Images in Your Web Pages

One of the things that really makes the Web come alive is the use of graphic images. Including them in your document is very easy, using just one tag: `<IMG>`. There are, though, a range of different arguments you can use with it to control how the image is displayed in the page.

To insert an image from the file `mypic.gif`, stored in the same folder as your `.htm` page file, you use `<IMG SRC="mypic.gif" >`. It's as easy as that. If it's in a different folder, you just use the relative path to it; for example `<IMG SRC="pics\mypic.gif">`. The image is displayed against the left margin and any text following it in the HTML document is displayed next to the image. If you want the image displayed in the center of the page, you just enclose it with the `<CENTER>` and `</CENTER>` tags.

Aligning Text with Images

To control how the text aligns with the image, you include an `ALIGN` argument in the tag. There are five possibilities: `TOP`, `MIDDLE`, `BOTTOM`, `LEFT` and `RIGHT`. The default is `BOTTOM`, with the text next to the image aligned with the bottom of the image. Not surprisingly, `TOP` and `MIDDLE` align the text to the top and middle of the image. However, `LEFT` and `RIGHT` are different. They align the image to the left or right margins, but also wrap text around the image. Here's some examples and the results they produce in Internet Explorer. You can see other examples in the sample pages—try `C:\BegWord\WroxPage\SiteLink\BitSoft.htm`.

```
<IMG SRC="wroxlogo.gif"> BOTTOM aligned. <P>
<IMG SRC="wroxlogo.gif" ALIGN=MIDDLE> MIDDLE aligned. <P>
<IMG SRC="wroxlogo.gif" ALIGN=TOP> TOP aligned. <HR>
<IMG SRC="wroxlogo.gif" ALIGN=LEFT> This is some text wrapped around a LEFT
aligned image <P>
<IMG SRC="wroxlogo.gif" ALIGN=RIGHT> and this is some text wrapped around a RIGHT
aligned image <P>
```

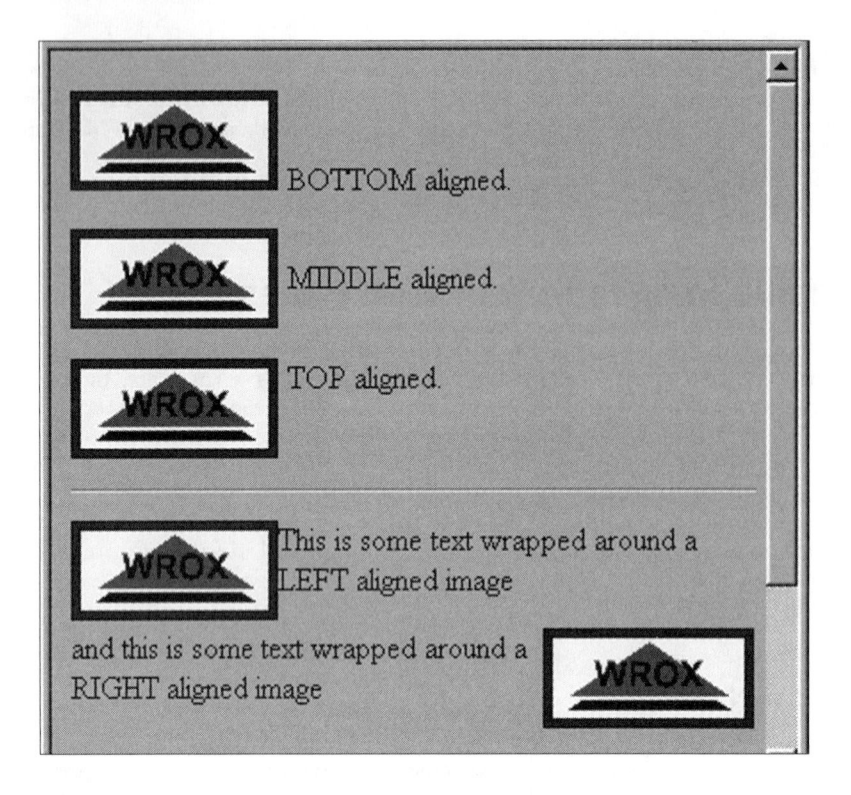

[Screenshot showing WROX logo images demonstrating BOTTOM aligned, MIDDLE aligned, TOP aligned, LEFT aligned (with wrapped text), and RIGHT aligned (with wrapped text) image placements.]

> **FYI** If you want to format the text next to an image, you generally need to enclose the image within the text formatting tags as well. For example:
>
> `<H2> <IMG SRC="wroxlogo.gif" > Wrox Press </H2>`

You can see that, by default, text next to a **LEFT** aligned image is often not displayed far enough away from it. Amongst the extensions to HTML are the **HSPACE**, **VSPACE**, and **BORDER** arguments which allow you more control over the placing of text around an image, and its appearance. To place a border that is five pixels wide around an image and space the text ten pixels away from it vertically and horizontally, we could use:

`<IMG SRC="wroxlogo.gif" ALIGN=LEFT BORDER=5 VSPACE=10 HSPACE=10 >`

Image Formats

There are only two image formats you can use with HTML pages, and the common Windows `.bmp` format isn't one of them. The options are GIF files (`.gif`) or JPEG (`.jpg`) formats, so you'll need a graphics program which can handle these if you want to create or modify images yourself. We use Paint Shop Pro®, but there are several others available.

The latest ones support a special version of GIF files called Version 89a, which allows you to use transparent backgrounds. While you might assume that the background of a web page is light gray, this isn't always true. In most browsers the user can change the default color and your images will look terrible if they still display on a light gray background. (You can also change the background color of the page in your HTML code, so transparent background images also save you having to keep different versions with different colored backgrounds.)

Alternative Text for Images

One thing you should always do is provide alternative text for images which contain information relevant to the page (rather than just decorative additions). Your viewers may not be able to follow your pages properly if they have turned off the display of images in their browser, to make loading of pages quicker, or are using a browser that doesn't support graphics. You specify the alternative text in the `ALT` argument of the `<IMG>` tag, like this:

```
<IMG SRC="wroxlogo.gif" ALT="Wrox Press">
```

If the image isn't being displayed, the viewer sees the alternative text instead. When you use graphic bullets, for instance, you can use "o" as the alternative text. Failing to provide alternative text for images should be an offense punishable by instant death!

Making Images Load More Quickly

The one thing that really slows down the loading of pages over the Web is including large graphics. Overdoing it will probably deter people from visiting your site regularly, so you should aim to minimize the delays while any images are loading. The obvious ways are to keep the size of the images as small as possible, and use fewer colors. Both the supported image formats compress the actual files, but the more complex the image is, the larger the file. If there are blocks of the same color in your image it will compress a lot better.

You should also try to use the same image in different positions and on different pages. Don't, for example, use a different one for each bullet in a list. The browser caches images as it loads them, so they only have to be loaded from the user's hard disk the next time they are referenced. The extensions for HTML also include the ability to specify the size of the image before it's actually downloaded to the browser. This means that space is left on the page for it and the page doesn't keep changing as each image is loaded and displayed. For an image 200 x 100 pixels, the syntax of these arguments is:

```
<IMG SRC="wroxlogo.gif" WIDTH=200 HEIGHT=100 >
```

Inserting Hypertext Links into Your Web Pages

The final major subject that we have to look at is how you provide jumps, or hot links, to other pages or other sites. If you've experimented with the sample pages, you'll have seen how we can provide jumps to another page or to a different place in the same page. We can also use hot links to send e-mail messages or download files. All hot links are defined using the `<A>` tag, and there are three main forms: links to another part of the same page, links to another page and links to another resource.

Understanding Web Addresses

In general, all web and Internet addresses have a similar format. The first part is the protocol type, which defines how the information is transmitted. This is followed by a colon and two slash characters, then the address itself. The Web uses the protocol `HTTP` (Hypertext Transfer Protocol), while `FTP` (File Transfer Protocol) is used to transfer binary files. Most mainline browsers will also accept another protocol type: **MAILTO**. This is used with a normal e-mail address and starts the browser's mail function so that you can send mail directly. There are other types of protocol, but these are the main ones that concern us here.

The complete address is called the **Uniform Resource Locator**, or **URL** for short, and defines the actual server site, plus the folder and file name of the document or file. There may also be the **WWW** (World Wide Web) prefix. For example, our web home page is at `http://www.wrox.com`. Normally, URLs are given in lowercase, though sometimes they are mixed case. Whereas file names are not case-sensitive on Windows-based servers, they often are on Unix servers. So, if you don't supply the correct combination of upper and lowercase, you may find you get a 'file not found' message.

'Local' Address Formats

When you're loading pages from a local server, you don't need to specify the full URL to the page. As you've seen from the first example in this chapter, you can load pages from disk and jump between them using the hot links. In this case, the URL is just the file name of the `.htm` page, together with the path if it's not in the same folder. When you build your company Intranet, this is the syntax you'll use to load your locally stored pages.

Like normal DOS commands, the URL can include the double-dot (`..`) syntax to refer to the parent folder. So, if the page you want to load is called `MyPage.htm` and its full path name is `C:\NewPage\MyPage.htm` and the page containing the link to it had a path of `C:\SomeFolder\ThisPage.htm`, the syntax for the link would use `"../NewPage/MyPage.htm"`

Links to a Different Page

So how do you define the hot link in a page? Here's an example taken from one of the sample pages. (Remember, you can load any of these into Word to see how they are constructed.) It displays the last two options in our sample home page `C:\BegWord\WroxPage\WroxHome.htm`.

```
<IMG SRC="blkbutn.gif" ALIGN="left" ALT="o">
<STRONG> Collect information from your visitors </STRONG> <BR>
<A HREF="Survey/Survey.htm">
   Tell us what you want us to write about <BR>
</A>
<IMG SRC="blkbutn.gif" ALIGN="left" ALT="o">
<STRONG> Just do it for fun! </STRONG> <BR>
<A HREF="ForFun/ForFun.htm">
   Well go on then, take a look
</A>
```

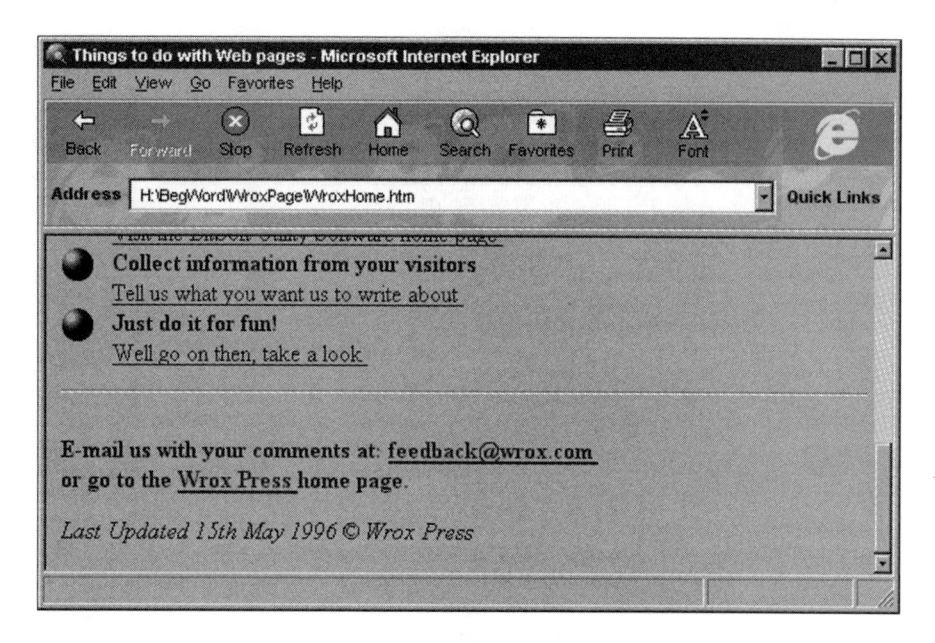

You can see the `<IMG>` tags that display the black 'blobs' and the text next to them. However, the HTML code in the shaded lines is what forms the hot links. The opening `<A>` tag includes the URL of the page we want to jump to, as the `HREF` argument to the tag, and in this case it's a local page in a subfolder. Everything between this tag and the closing `</A>` tag becomes 'hot'. When you click on it, the browser attempts to load the page referenced by `HREF`.

Graphics and Images that are 'Hot'

You aren't limited to using text as the hot link. Images work equally well and clicking on these has the same effect as clicking on the text. For example, at the top of the same page we used this HTML code to make our Wrox logo 'hot':

```
<H3>
    Things To Do With Web Pages, sponsored by
    <A HREF="http://www.wrox.com">
        <IMG SRC="wroxlogo.gif" BORDER=0 ALIGN="middle" ALT="Wrox">
    </A>
    Press Limited.
</H3>
```

This displays the text in Heading 3 format, aligned with the middle of our Wrox logo. When you display an image as a hot link, the browser generally places a border round it to show that it's hot. Although it's not obvious with our logo, we have removed this using `BORDER=0` in the `<IMG>` tag. And (of course) we've supplied alternative text so it still works on non-graphical browsers.

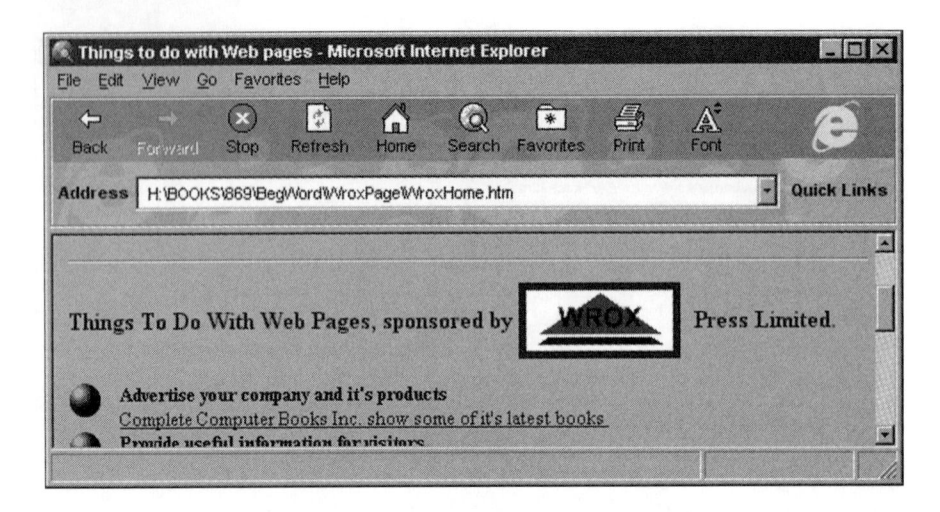

[Screenshot: Internet Explorer window showing "Things to do with Web pages" page at H:\BOOKS\869\BegWord\WroxPage\WroxHome.htm, with Wrox logo and bullet list including "Advertise your company and it's products", "Complete Computer Books Inc. show some of it's latest books", "Provide useful information for visitors".]

The URL of the page we want to jump to is **http://www.wrox.com** the Wrox Press home page. Notice that the text itself isn't a hot link, because it's outside the **<A>** and **</A>** tags.

Links to another Part of the Same Page

Jumping to another place on the same page uses the same syntax as jumping to a different page, but, instead of supplying a path and file name or a URL, we use a name that identifies a particular location on the same page. There's an example in the Just For Fun page: **C:\BegWord\WroxPage\ForFun\ForFun.htm**. Just under the image at the top of the page is a hot link Go to the list of other sites. If you click here, the display just jumps to the bottom of the same page, where there's a list of sites with better jokes than ours.

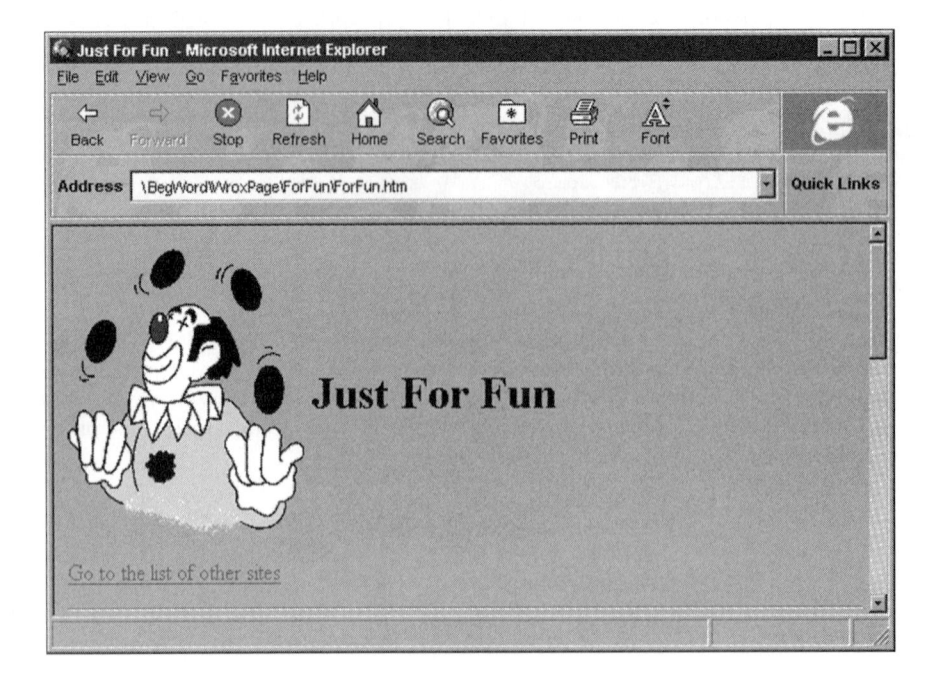

[Screenshot: Internet Explorer window showing "Just For Fun" page at \BegWord\WroxPage\ForFun\ForFun.htm, with a clown illustration and the heading "Just For Fun", plus a hot link "Go to the list of other sites".]

The code that creates this hot-link uses a URL that consists of a hash sign (#) followed by a name which identifies the new location:

```
<A HREF="#links"> Go to the list of other sites</A>
```

To identify the location itself, we use the `<A>` tag again, but this time without the closing `</A>` tag. Within it, the **NAME** argument specifies the name of that location. You don't use the hash character again in the **NAME** argument:

```
<A NAME="links">
```

Links to another Resource

The `<A>` tag can also cause the browser to load a resource that's not a web page. If you look back at the WroxHome page we saw at the beginning of this section, there's a hot link marked feedback@wrox.com at the bottom. If your browser supports e-mail, clicking here opens a message window with this e-mail address already filled in. The code that produces it is almost identical to the previous uses of the `<A>` tag you've seen:

```
<A HREF="mailto:feedback@wrox.com"> feedback@wrox.com </A>
```

The text between the tags is what you see on the page, and the **HREF** argument is the protocol **mailto:** followed by the e-mail address. It's as easy as that, though remember that not all browsers will support this particular use of the `<A>` tag.

In another page, we've implemented a hot link that would download a sample file if your were connected to the server. Again, this only works on browsers that support this protocol, but it's just as easy to set up in HTML. To provide a link which downloads the file **myfile.zip** from the **\apps** folder at the site named **ftp.compbook.com**, the code is:

```
<A HREF="ftp://ftp.compbook.com/apps/myfile.zip"> Download the file </A>
```

Adding Extra Features to Your Web Pages

Using just the techniques we've described so far, you can create very attractive and usable web pages. In fact, the tags we've been using represent the majority that are defined by the HTML standards up to Version 2. In Version 3, though, there are a number of new possibilities.

The most important of these is support for tables, which gives you much more control over the final appearance of your pages. We also need to look at how you create forms to gather information from visitors. Finally, we'll see some of the other techniques in use, such as graphics that respond differently depending on where you click on them, and how you can add sound, video and other effects.

Using Tables in Your Web Pages

Although defining a table looks complicated, with a jumble of tags to specify how it will appear, it really is quite easy to do. It uses four basic tags: `<TABLE>`, which defines the whole table, `<TR>`, which defines a complete row, `<TH>`, which defines a table heading cell, and `<TD>`, which defines the details of an individual cell. Here's a simple example. We've added the **BORDER=1** argument so that you can see the table borders (by default, they're not shown).

307

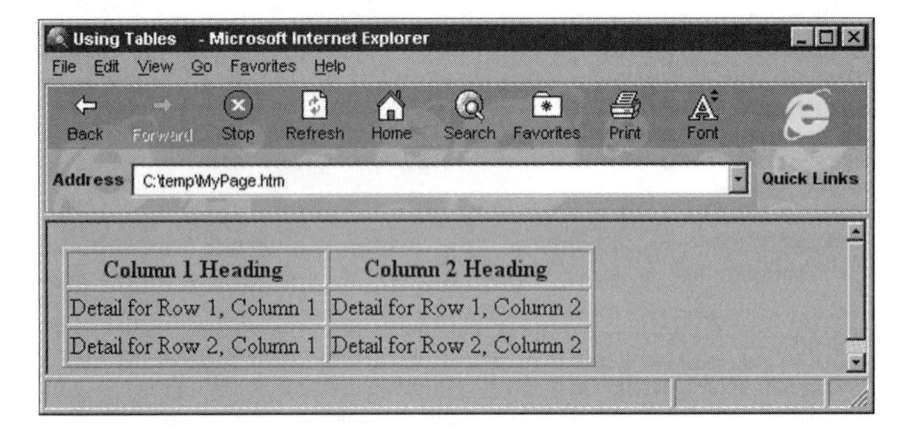

```
<TABLE BORDER=1 >
   <TR>
      <TH> Column 1 Heading </TH>
      <TH> Column 2 Heading </TH>
   </TR>
   <TR>
      <TD> Detail for Row 1, Column 1 </TD>
      <TD> Detail for Row 1, Column 2 </TD>
   </TR>
   <TR>
      <TD> Detail for Row 2, Column 1 </TD>
      <TD> Detail for Row 2, Column 2 </TD>
   </TR>
</TABLE>
```

[Screenshot of Internet Explorer showing "Using Tables" page with the rendered table containing Column 1 Heading, Column 2 Heading, and the four detail cells.]

The only difference between the `<TH>` tag and the `<TD>` tag is the way the result is formatted. `<TH>` generally makes the text bold and centers it in the cell. `<TD>` aligns text left, unless you add an `ALIGN` argument to change this.

Aligning Text in a Table Cell

In any cell you can align text `LEFT`, `RIGHT` or `CENTER`. You can also change the vertical alignment of text, which is useful if some cells have text that wraps over several lines. By default, text is aligned centrally in a cell, but you can add the `VALIGN` argument with the values `TOP` or `BOTTOM` to change this.

Changing the Appearance of a Table

Other arguments allow you to change the color of the cell background or the borders, and use a background image in the table. Of course, you can display images in the cells themselves, by placing the `<IMG>` tag within the `<TD>` and `</TD>` tags. With only a little effort you can create tables that either look really striking or unbelievably hideous.

Adding Captions to a Table

One other tag that's useful with tables is `<CAPTION>`. You can use this to display a text caption above or below a table. The two common arguments are `ALIGN` and `VALIGN`. `ALIGN` controls the horizontal alignment, and can be `LEFT` or `RIGHT`. Otherwise, the default is centered. `VALIGN` can be `TOP` or `BOTTOM`, to place the caption above or below the table. This code places a caption to the left and above a table:

```
<TABLE>
   <CAPTION ALIGN=LEFT VALIGN=TOP> Text of the caption </CAPTION>
   . . . rest of table definition . . .
</TABLE>
```

Here's an example of some of these various table tags used together, and the result displayed in Internet Explorer. It's called **UseTable.htm**, and we've supplied it with the other samples in the **C:\BegWord\WroxPage** folder.

```
<TABLE BORDER BORDERCOLORLIGHT=Black BORDERCOLORDARK=White>
   <TR >
      <TH ALIGN=LEFT> <IMG SRC="wroxlogo.gif"> </TH>
      <TH BGCOLOR=Red> <H2> Wrox Press Limited </H2> </TH>
   </TR>
   <TR>
      <TD ALIGN=RIGHT BGCOLOR=#EED6C6> <STRONG> Where? </STRONG> </TD>
      <TD ALIGN=CENTER>
         <STRONG> Chicago, USA <I> and </I> Birmingham, England </STRONG>
      </TD>
   </TR>
   <TR>
      <TD ALIGN=RIGHT BGCOLOR=#EED6C6> <STRONG> Why? </STRONG> </TD>
      <TD ALIGN=CENTER > Publishing the best computer books around. </TD>
   </TR>
   <TR>
      <TD ALIGN=RIGHT BGCOLOR=#EED6C6> <STRONG> Contact? </STRONG> </TD>
      <TD ALIGN=CENTER>
         <A HREF="http://www.wrox.com"> http://www.wrox.com</A> or e-mail
         to <A HREF="mailto:feedback@wrox.com"> feedback@wrox.com</A>
      </TD>
   </TR>
   <TR>
      <TD ALIGN=RIGHT VALIGN=TOP BGCOLOR=#EED6C6>
         <STRONG> More Info: </STRONG>
      </TD>
      <TD> Wrox are one of the <I> premier </I> publishers . . </TD>
   </TR>
</TABLE>
```

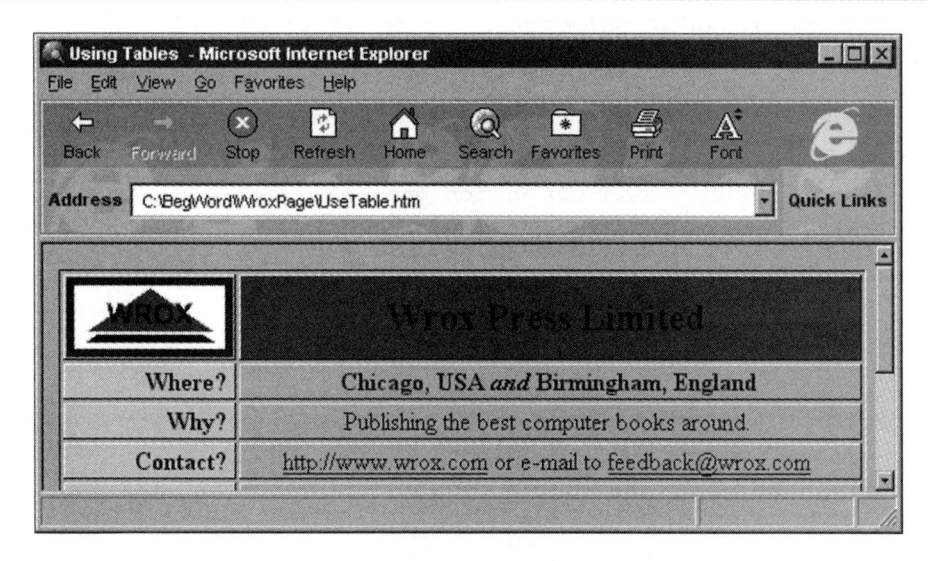

Here, we've used several arguments to change the color of the cell background and borders. The **BGCOLOR** argument can be set to a color name, such as **Black**, **Red**, etc., or to the **RGB triplet**, the values between 0 and 255 for each of the three primary colors, red, green and blue. It's usual to specify these in hexadecimal form, preceded by a hash sign. So **#EED6C6** gives a kind of light pink color. You can also change the color of the table borders using the **BORDERCOLOR** argument, together with a color name or RGB triplet.

In our example, though, we've taken advantage of two other arguments: **BORDERCOLORLIGHT** and **BORDERCOLORDARK**. These are the colors of the 3D-effect border lines. By reversing them from their normal colors we've got a table that appears to have etched lines between the cells—a lot nicer.

> **FYI** You can use the color (and other) arguments in any of the table tags. For example, you can set the background color of the table in the opening `<TABLE>` tag, then set individual cells to a different color in the `<TR>`, `<TH>` or `<TD>` tags. The settings in the `<TH>` and `<TD>` tags override those in the `<TR>` tag, which in turn overrides those in the `<TABLE>` tag.

Using Forms and Controls in Your Web Pages

Right at the start of this chapter, we talked about the sections of a web page: the head section and the body. We also mentioned that there's another section you use to create a form on the page. This uses the `<FORM>` and `</FORM>` tags to define the area in which the controls that make up the form are placed. The controls you can use are:

Control Type	HTML Code Example
Text Boxes	`<INPUT NAME="mytext" TYPE="text" VALUE="Type here" >`
Password Boxes	`<INPUT NAME="mypword" TYPE="password" >`
Check Boxes	`<INPUT NAME="mychk" TYPE="checkbox" CHECKED >`
Option Buttons	`<INPUT NAME="myopt" TYPE="radio" CHECKED >`
Submit Buttons	`<INPUT NAME="mybtn1" TYPE="submit" VALUE="Send Now" >`
Reset Buttons	`<INPUT NAME="mybtn2" TYPE="reset" VALUE="Clear" >`

Scrolling or Drop-down List Boxes	`<SELECT MULTIPLE>`
	    `<OPTION> Option one`
	    `<OPTION SELECTED> Option two`
	    `<OPTION> Option three`
	    `<OPTION> Option four`
	`</SELECT>`

Multi-line Text Areas	`<TEXTAREA NAME="myarea" SIZE="40,6" >Enter your address here </TEXTAREA>`

The `<INPUT>` tag creates the common control types, and you just have to specify the **TYPE** argument to tell the browser which type of control you want. The **VALUE** argument sets the default text for a text box and the caption of a button. Including the **CHECKED** argument means that you can set an option button or check box. The special kind of text box created when `TYPE="password"` displays asterisks as you type in it. It's designed for collecting a password from your users. The screenshot shows the controls that are created by the examples in the table opposite:

The final control in this is one of the new additions to the set: the `<TEXTAREA>` tag. This creates a multiline text box where the user can enter several rows of text, separating each with *Return*. The default text that will be displayed in the text box when the form is opened is placed between the `<TEXTAREA>` and `</TEXTAREA>` tags.

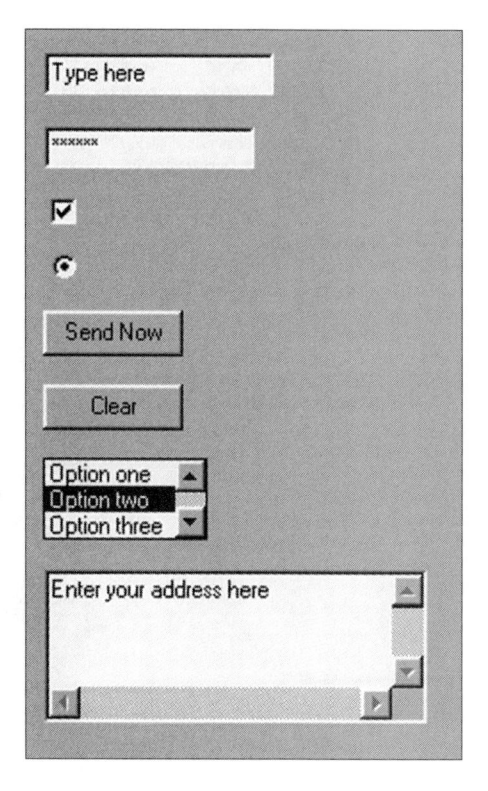

Setting the Size of a Text Box Control

You can specify the width of a single-line text or password box using the **SIZE** argument. **SIZE=20** creates a control wide enough for 20 characters. You control the size of a multiline text box by specifying values for the width and height (in characters) for the **SIZE** argument in the opening `<TEXTAREA>` tag as shown.

Creating a List Box Control

To create a scrolling or drop-down list you use the `<SELECT>` and `</SELECT>` tags, and inside them a set of `<OPTION>` tags. Each `<OPTION>` defines an entry for the list and including the **SELECTED** argument in the `<OPTION>` tag sets that as the default selection when the form is first displayed. If you want users to be able to select more than one item in a list, you include the **MULTIPLE** argument within the opening `<SELECT>` tag, as shown in the example in the table above. Generally, you'll get three items in the list displayed by default, but by adding the **SIZE** argument in the opening `<SELECT>` tag you can control the number yourself. If you set it to 1 and leave out the **MULTIPLE** argument, you get a drop-down list like this:

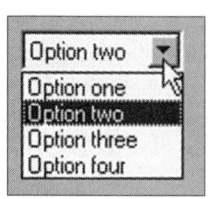

Creating Option Groups

As with a normal Word dialog, you can use groups of option buttons which allow the user to select only one. To do this you simply give the controls which are in the same group the same value for the **NAME** argument. This allows you to include more than one option group on a form, as you can see on the next page.

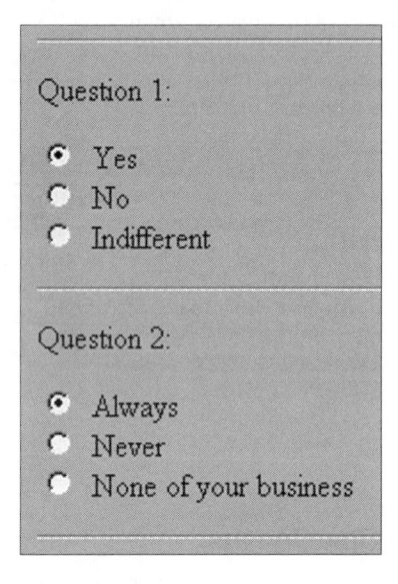

```
<HR> Question 1: <P>
   <INPUT NAME="question1" TYPE="radio" CHECKED > Yes <BR>
   <INPUT NAME="question1" TYPE="radio" > No <BR>
   <INPUT NAME="question1" TYPE="radio" > Indifferent
<HR> Question 2: <P>
   <INPUT NAME="question2" TYPE="radio" CHECKED > Always <BR>
   <INPUT NAME="question2" TYPE="radio" > Never <BR>
   <INPUT NAME="question2" TYPE="radio" > None of your business
<HR>
```

FYI We've included a sample page with a form on it for you to try. Load the file `C:\BegWord\WroxPage\Survey\Survey.htm`. This is the page we used in the first example at the start of this chapter.

Sending Information from a Form

As the user manipulates the controls on a form, they can change the values back to the defaults by clicking the Reset button (or whatever you have set its caption to in the **VALUE** argument). However, when they click the Submit button, the data is sent to the server for processing. Here, we hit a problem because the server must have a specially written program ready to handle this information. We won't be going into what are usually called *server-based interface applications* here, because it depends entirely on what type of server you're using. Normally, your service provider will provide the application and details of how you interface with it.

Including Clickable Image Maps in Your Pages

As they use graphics and images more and more, people have looked for ways to create images which react differently depending on where you click on them. An obvious example is a map, where clicking on any town or region displays more information about that specific item. This called an **image map**.

Of course, it doesn't have to be a map like you see in an atlas, it could just as easily be a map of your building showing the use of each office or part of the factory floor. And it might not be a map of anything physical. Often, image maps are used for toolbars or just as an attractive front-end menu for a web site.

Server-based Interface Applications

Until recently, image maps suffered from the same restriction as forms. When the user clicks on the map, the coordinates of the mouse-pointer are sent back to the server which is then responsible for displaying the correct page. Again, this is something that requires participation from your service provider to set up and needs a specially written application, plus a data file listing the URLs of the pages that the user can jump to.

If you only want to create a toolbar-type image map, it's probably easier to use a series of different images displayed in a row. Placing a series of **<IMG>** tags in your page displays the images next to each other across the page, and each one can reference a different URL. However, if your needs are more complex that this, help is at hand...

Client Side Image Maps

Now, thankfully, extensions to HTML allow you to control your own destiny with image maps. And it's incredibly easy to achieve. All you need to do is to add the argument **USEMAP** to the **<IMG>** tag that displays the image map. Then, elsewhere in the page, you create the map that defines which page will be displayed. Here's the HTML code of an alternative 'home page' for our samples. You can load it into your browser from **C:\BegWord\WroxPage\ImageMap.htm**. It may not work, though, if your browser doesn't support client-side image maps.

```
<CENTER>
   <H1> Things to do with Web Pages </H1>
   <H2>
      sponsored by
        <IMG SRC="wroxlogo.gif" ALIGN=MIDDLE WIDTH=108 HEIGHT=50>
      Press
   </H2>
   <HR SIZE=5>
   <IMG SRC="imgmap.gif" WIDTH=543 HEIGHT=263 USEMAP="#mymap">
</CENTER>

<MAP NAME="mymap">

   <AREA SHAPE=RECT COORDS="49,44,172,134"
      HREF="Intranet\Intranet.htm" ALT="The Company Intranet">

   <AREA SHAPE=RECT COORDS="55,138,203,213"
      HREF="ForFun\ForFun.htm" ALT="Just Do It For Fun">

   <AREA SHAPE=RECT COORDS="214,21,344,84"
      HREF="Survey\Survey.htm" ALT="Survey Your Visitors">

   <AREA SHAPE=RECT COORDS="278,82,336,128"
      HREF="Survey\Survey.htm" ALT="Survey Your Visitors">

   <AREA SHAPE=RECT COORDS="214,21,344,84"
      HREF="Survey\Survey.htm">

   <AREA SHAPE=RECT COORDS="347,52,506,147"
```

```
            HREF="Company\CompBook.htm" ALT="Advertise Your Company">

        <AREA SHAPE=RECT COORDS="331,146,484,233"
            HREF="Inform\Hints1.htm" ALT="Hints and Tips">

        <AREA SHAPE=RECT COORDS="210,136,303,221"
            HREF="SiteLink\BitSoft.htm" ALT="Link To Other Sites">

        <AREA SHAPE=CIRCLE COORDS="221,125,30"
            HREF="SiteLink\BitSoft.htm">

    </MAP>
```

The first part of the page is quite normal, using some introductory text and our Wrox logo. Under that is the image map, which is stored on disk as the file **imgmap.gif**. We display it just like a normal image, but include in the tag the argument **USEMAP="#mymap"**. This indicates that the image is, in fact, an image map, and that the coordinates of the various hot link areas are in a map definition within the same page. If it was in a different page, we would include the full URL to it here instead. In this respect, this argument behaves just like a normal **<A>** tag.

To create the map definition, we include the name of the map in the opening **<MAP>** tag, then list all the hot link areas in individual **<AREA>** tags. The **SHAPE** argument can be **RECTANGLE**, **RECT**, **CIRCLE**, **CIRC**, **POLYGON** or **POLY**. The **COORDS** argument indicates the position of the 'hot' area in pixels, with respect to the top left corner of the image For a rectangle, you specify the **X** and **Y** coordinates of the top left and bottom right corners, for a circle you specify the center **X** and **Y** positions and the radius, and for a polygon you list the **X** and **Y** coordinates of each vertex.

The **HREF** argument is simply the **URL** of the page you want to jump to, or the resource you want to load. You can even use the **NOHREF** argument in an **<AREA>** tag to define an area which isn't hot, overlapping an area which is. The **<AREA>** tag that appears first in the **<MAP>** definition takes precedence over later ones which define the same area or overlap.

Finally, the **ALT** argument defines the text that is displayed if the user has graphics switched off, or is using a non-graphic browser. Here's the result of the code sample shown above, which provides an alternative starting point for our sample web pages.

Chapter 7 - Creating Web Pages for the Internet

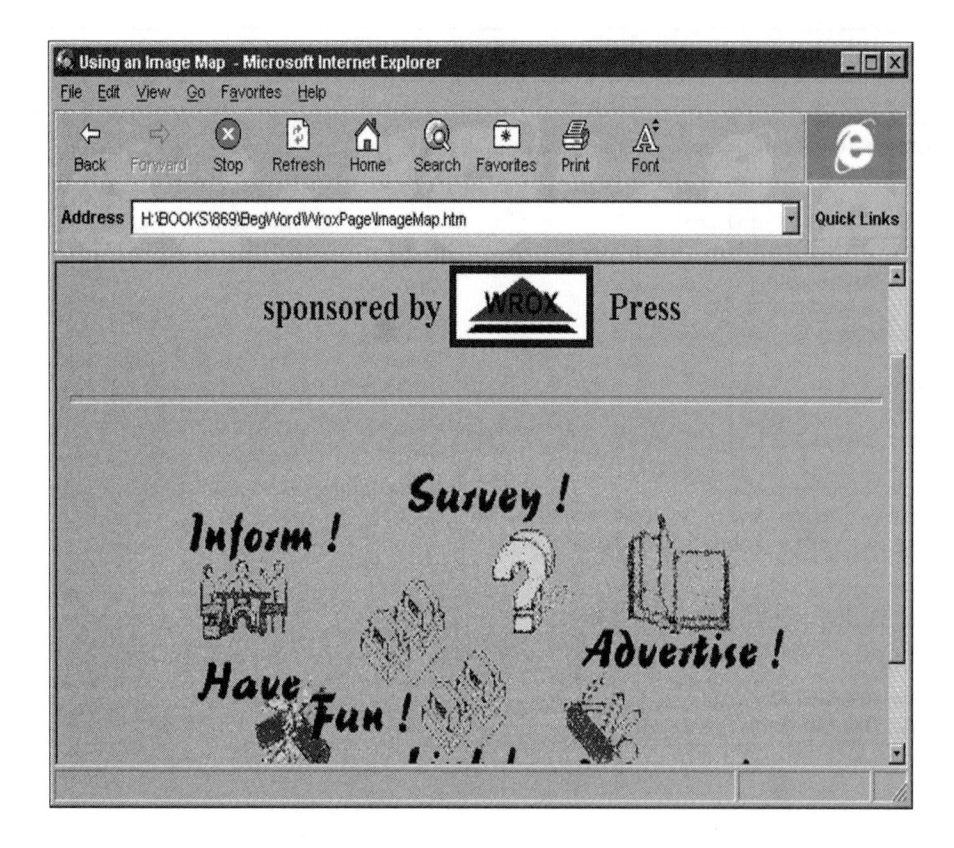

It's likely that server-based image maps will disappear in the near future, having been taken over by the client-side version we've seen here. In the meantime, though, remember that not every browser supports these, so, for now, you should consider implementing your image maps with both sorts of functionality.

Other Miscellaneous HTML Tags

We've covered a lot in this chapter, so, to finish off, we'll briefly show you some of the other tags and language extensions that you can use to liven up your pages. There are also completely new techniques coming out, such as Java and ActiveX which change your pages from being just a static display into a feast of moving images. Many of these are not yet supported by all browsers, but you can be sure that the extra features they offer will soon make them obligatory in all pages.

Fonts, Colors, Sound and Video

New browsers are adding extra effects which allow your pages to become more interactive, or just more decorative. On the next page you'll see a list of some of the HTML tags that can help to spice up your web pages.

HTML Tag and Example	Purpose

`<BODY BACKGROUND=URL>`
`<BODY BACKGROUND="grn_tile.gif >`
`... </BODY>`
	Sets the background image for the page. The image is tiled over the whole visible area of the browser window.

`<BODY BGCOLOR=color>`
`<BODY BACKGROUND=White >`
`... </BODY>`
`<BODY BACKGROUND=#FFFF00 >`
`... </BODY>`
	Sets the background color of the whole page.

`<BODY TEXT=color>`
`<BODY TEXT=Green> ... </BODY>`
`<BODY TEXT=#FFE450> ... </BODY>`
	Sets the color of the text for the whole page.

`<BODY LINK=color>`
`<BODY LINK=Yellow> ... </BODY>`
`<BODY LINK=#FFFF00> ... </BODY>`
	Sets the color of links that have not been visited.

`<BODY VLINK=color>`
`<BODY VLINK=Purple> ... </BODY>`
`<BODY VLINK=#C0C000> ... </BODY>`
	Sets the color of links that have been visited.

`<BODY BGPROPERTIES>`
`<BODY BGPROPERTIES=FIXED>`
`... </BODY>`
	Prevents the background image from scrolling as you scroll the browser window.

`<BODY LEFTMARGIN=size>` `<BODY LEFTMARGIN=20> ... </BODY>`	Sets the width of the left margin in pixels.
`<BODY TOPMARGIN=size>` `<BODY TOPMARGIN=10> ... </BODY>`	Sets the height of the top margin in pixels.
`<BASEFONT=size>` `<BASEFONT=5>`	Sets the base reference size of the font for the whole page, ready to be used with the `<FONT SIZE>` tag.

`<FONT COLOR=color>`
`<FONT COLOR=Red> This is red text`
`</FONT>`
`<FONT COLOR=#EED6C6> This is pinkish </FONT>`
	Sets the color of the font.

`<FONT FACE=name>` `<FONT FACE="Arial"> This is Arial font </FONT>`	Selects a font using the name. You can list more than one font, and the first one that is found on the viewer's system is used.

`<FONT SIZE=size>`
`<FONT SIZE=5> This is size 5 font </FONT>`
`<FONT SIZE=+3> Now 3 larger than base </FONT>`
	Sets the size of the font. The default is 3, and you can use 1 to 7. If specified with a + or – sign, it indicates a size relative to the `<BASEFONT>` setting.

`<BGSOUND>`
`<BGSOUND SRC="hello.wav" LOOP=3>`
`<BGSOUND SRC="hello.wav" LOOP=INFINITE>`
	Plays a sound when the page is opened and repeats it a number of times or until the page is closed again. Setting `LOOP=-1` is the same as `INFINITE`.

HTML Tag and Example	Purpose

`<IMG DYNSRC=URL>`
`<IMG DYNSRC="video.avi" LOOP=3>`
`<IMG DYNSRC="video.avi" LOOP=INFINITE>`
`<IMG DYNSRC="video.avi" CONTROLS>`
`<IMG DYNSRC="video.avi" START=FILEOPEN>`
`<IMG DYNSRC="video.avi" START=MOUSEOVER>`
	Plays a video clip in the page. Can loop a fixed number of times, or infinitely. To display the video control bar include the **CONTROLS** argument. The clip starts when the page is opened. To play it when clicked, include the **START=MOUSEOVER** argument. You can also use **START=MOUSEOVER**, **FILEOPEN** to achieve both effects.

Comments, <BASE> and <META> Tags

With the exception of the comment tags, the following tags are used in the `<TITLE>` section of the page only. There are tags which allow you to reload the current page automatically, or load another page. You can also specify the base address of your page, which is used when referencing the images or other pages that you provide links to as well.

HTML Tag and Example	Purpose
`<BASE=URL>` `<BASE="http://www.wrox.com">`	Specifies the document's full URL in case it's viewed out of context and the viewer wants to refer to the original page. Also sets the base address of the other files referred to. Used in the `<TITLE>` section of the page only.
`<META TYPE=attribute>` `<META AUTHOR=Alex Homer>`	Allows you to include information which can be read by a suitably equipped browser for reference purposes. Used in the `<TITLE>` section of the page only.
`<META HTTP-EQUIV>` `<META HTTP-EQUIV="REFRESH" CONTENT=10>`	Reloads the page after a number of seconds specified by **CONTENT**. Alternatively, you can load a different page instead. `CONTENT="10;URL=http:///www.wrox.com"` will load the Wrox home page after ten seconds. Used in the `<TITLE>` section of the page only.

`<COMMENT> and <!>`
`<COMMENT> This is a comment </COMMENT>`
`<! This is a comment>`
	Allows you to insert comments in the page which are not visible in the browser.

Summary

By now, you should be able to throw together a respectable web page and be ready for the global information system based future that's not so far away. If you start designing your company's web site now, you're sure to be ready to meet the pressures of the future. Let's face it, you don't want to be the only business in your industry that isn't 'on the Net' do you?

We've shown you how to build web pages by understanding the different elements that go to make them up. Of course, there are tools available to help. Microsoft produce an add-in for Word, called Internet Assistant, and a full-featured product called Front Page. On top of this there are many other templates and tools that you can buy or even download for free.

HTML is an ever-changing language and you'll find that many of the tags are browser-specific, or have different arguments for different browsers. The two front-runners, though, are gradually standardizing with HTML 3, so you should find the compatibility problems reducing as time goes on.

What this does mean is that you need to stay up to date with the new developments. In this chapter we have been using the beta product of Microsoft's Internet Explorer 3.0. This is improving all the time and currently supports Active Documents which will bring even more interactive features to the Web with pages full of ActiveX controls, but that is another story... To help you keep up to date, we've established a guide to the current HTML language and it's extensions on our own Web site. Check in to **http://www.wrox.com** and see how to add scrolling marquees of text to your pages now!

In this chapter we've seen:

- Why you need to know about web pages and HTML documents
- The basic structure of a web page and the various HTML commands
- How to create web pages using HTML directly in Word

In the next couple of chapters you'll meet a different type of hypertext document, the Windows Help file, and in Part 3 you'll see how we can create hypertext Word documents.

Chapter 7 - Creating Web Pages for the Internet

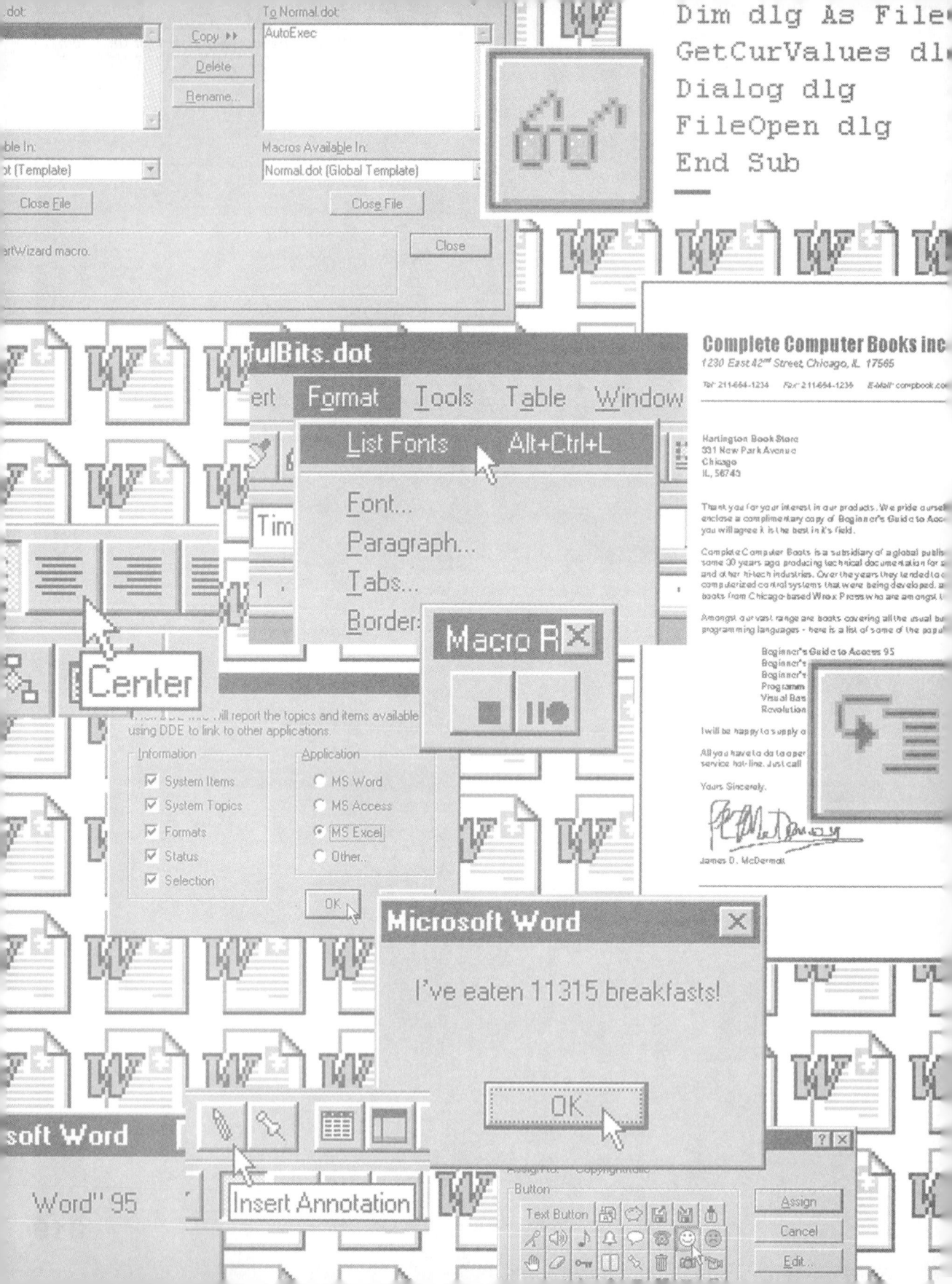

```
Dim dlg As File
GetCurValues dl
Dialog dlg
FileOpen dlg
End Sub
```

Creating Windows 95 Help

Introduction

If you're developing applications or add-ins for Microsoft Word, you'll want to be able to include **Help files** so that your users can gain the most benefit from them. It may also cut down your workload by reducing the number of support calls you get! In this chapter and the next, we'll be looking at how Windows 95 Help files are created, and you'll be building one for the Print Both Sides add-in you saw in Chapter 6.

Although building a Help file isn't that difficult, it *is* complicated. There are a lot of different parts that need to be properly linked together. This is why we've chosen to split the subject over two chapters. This chapter introduces Window 95 Help and shows you how to create the Word documents that form the main part of a Help file. The next chapter covers the other parts of a Help project and shows you how to compile and link your Help file.

So that you can get some practical experience, we've included all the components needed to create the **WroxPBS** (Print Both Sides) Help file. At each stage, you'll see how this changes from a normal Word document into a finished Help file. And to make your life even easier, you'll find that the samples supplied with the book include a Word template which automates many of the repetitive tasks.

In this chapter, we start the process of creating a Help file. You'll see:

- An overview of the Windows 95 Help system
- The different components that make up a Help file
- How the Word document forms the basis of a Help file
- The way the document is structured in a Help file

The bulk of this chapter deals with creating a Help file, but, first, we'll look at the Windows 95 Help system in general.

Introducing Windows 95 Help

A lot of people shy away from creating Help files. In fact, there's a totally separate section of the industry devoted to producing Help files for other companies. Why should this be? Well, having completed their wonderful new application, few programmers relish the task of writing the documentation for it, and building a good Help file is more difficult than simply writing out the instructions on how a program works. You are expected to include attractive graphics, striking design elements and lots of things that smack of being nothing to do with 'real' programming at all.

It's also becoming normal practice for software companies to reduce the amount of expensive printed documentation included with their products in favor of online documentation. While there are other ways it can be distributed, like the various portable document formats such as Adobe Acrobat™, the favorite method is to use Windows Help files. These have many advantages over the door-stop style books of the past. Help files are:

- Always ready to hand—at the click of a button
- Easier to use—you can search for topics and follow links
- Updatable—new sections can be added automatically
- Cheaper—that's why the software companies like them

And they don't suffer from coffee stains or being dropped in the bath! However, they do have their disadvantages. You have to be at the computer to use them. You can't read up on the product in any odd spare moments unless you've got a laptop handy. Some people find that reading text on screen is less productive than from a book, and on a small screen the Help windows just keep getting in the way.

On the positive side, though, the extra features supported in the Windows 95 Help system have made understanding your new applications easier. Things like contents pages, step-by-step tutorials and the ability to run programs under the control of the Help system gently ease a new user into a piece of software, but at the same time, when they've got a problem to solve, the Help system must also be able to supply the answer they need in enough detail, without keeping them waiting. Otherwise, the user spends ages cycling through the same topics and appears to be getting nowhere.

Different Kinds of Help

While it's safe to assume that you're familiar with using Windows Help files in general, we need to look a bit more closely at the various types. Windows 95 Help system supports different kinds of Help. The most usual is a single page covering one topic, with links to other pages. This is the system that has been used successfully under earlier versions of Windows, and is very similar to the pages you see displayed on the Internet's World Wide Web.

The technical name for this type of Help is a **hypertext** document. In a hypertext Help file, links to another topic (which are often referred to as **jumps**) are usually shown in green with a solid underline. The mouse pointer changes to a pointing finger when placed over one. Clicking on the jump displays the new topic.

```
folders that are used for the zip files, and delete t
setting the Default Options. And this menu is also
```

Also used in Help documents are **pop-up windows**. These are small windows which open on top of a page and usually provide some extra details or a definition of the term you click on. A word that has a pop-up window linked to it usually appears in green, but with a dotted rather than solid underline.

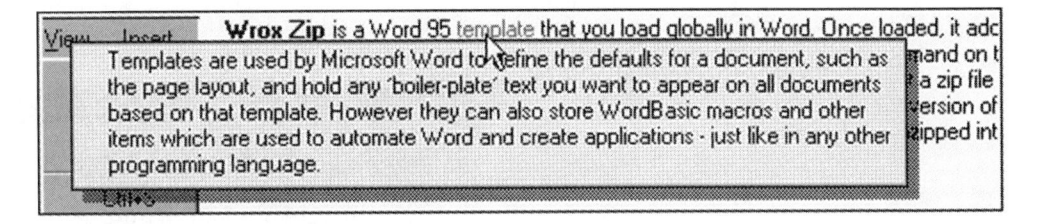

Pop-up windows are often used in conjunction with a graphic. For example, the Help file may contain a picture of a dialog, and clicking the various parts brings up information describing what each section of the dialog does. You'll see that we use this in our Help files, because it's easy to implement in WordBasic, but this technique isn't used a great deal in Windows 95 Help files, which tend to use context-sensitive help instead.

Context-sensitive Help

It's obvious that when a user needs help with part of your application, you should display the page that refers to the task they are currently trying to master. This is called **context-sensitive help**, and means that the user sees a page devoted to the context that they are in, which could be anything from a particular dialog to a complicated series of operations. Normally, the user presses *F1* (the standard Help key) or clicks the What's This? button, if there is one in the title bar, then clicks on the item they want help with.

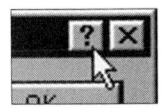

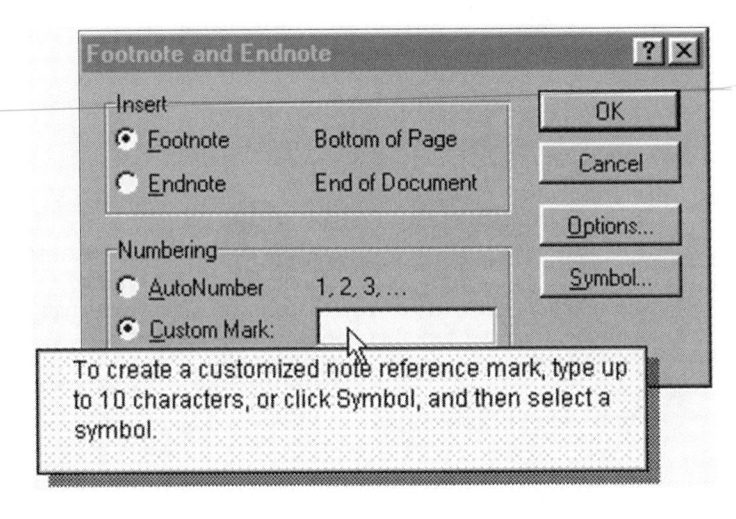

While the What's This? button generally produces a pop-up window, the *F1* key may open a page in the Help file, but this varies from application to application, depending (among other things) on how much information needs to be displayed.

WordBasic doesn't allow us to use context-sensitive help in quite the same way as other programming languages, but we can still achieve quite a lot. You'll see more when we try out the Wrox Zip Help file at the end of this section.

The Help Topics Window

If you just want to learn about an application, rather than get help with a specific topic, you can use the Help Topics window. This is new to Windows 95 Help, and provides a focal point where you can see a list of contents, look up items in the Index, or search for particular words in the Find window. Most applications, like Word, have a command on their Help menu which opens the Help Topics window.

The Contents tab displays a list of the main topics in the Help file, organized into 'books'. By double-clicking on a book, you open it to reveal the contents. A book can contain other books, so that you can quickly find the subject you want without being distracted by long lists of topics.

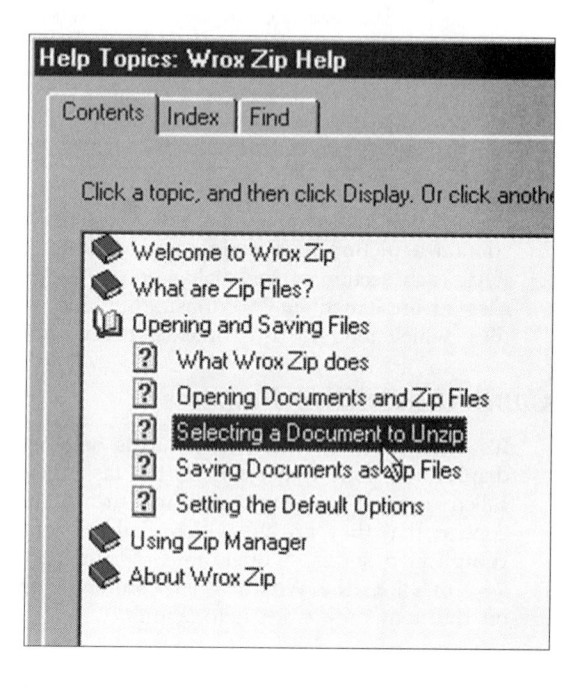

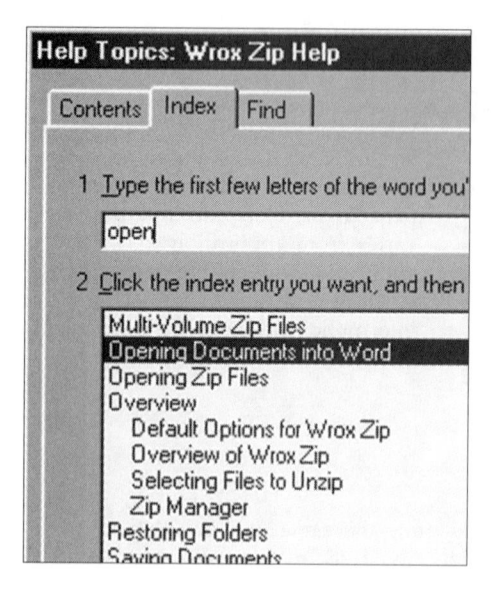

The Index tab is the equivalent to the old Windows 3.x Search dialog. It shows a series of subjects and keywords in alphabetical order, just like the index in a book. You can search for matching entries by typing part or all of the subject you want. Notice the two-level hierarchy that the index supports; you may find a subject listed under several keywords.

Selecting a topic may take you straight to it. If there are several topics that include that keyword, however, you see the **Topics Found** dialog. Here, you can refine your search by selecting which of the matching topics actually contains the information you want.

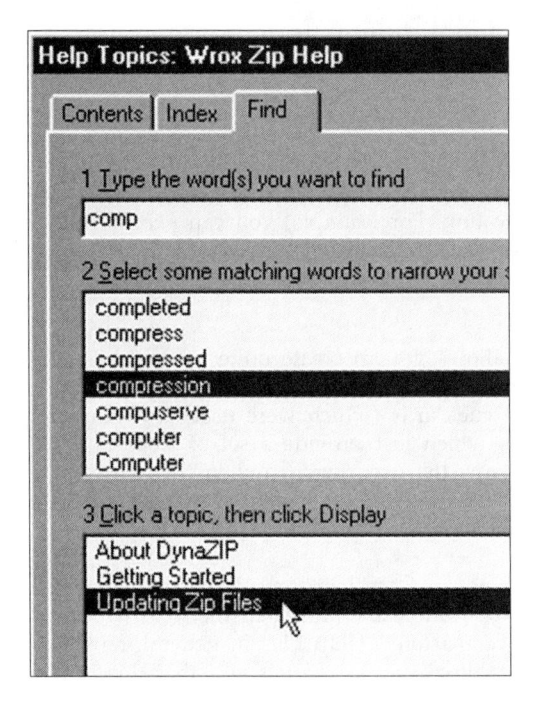

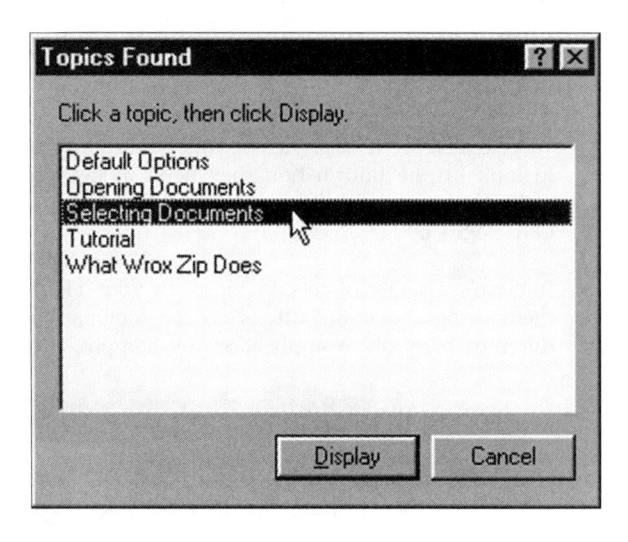

The **Find** tab allows you to search for a particular word or group of words. This can be useful if your user meets a term they are unfamiliar with, but there's no jump or pop-up window attached to it. They can select the word in the **Find** list and jump to any topic that contains that word.

It's also possible to add extra tabs to the **Help Topics** window. Microsoft Word has an **Answer Wizard** tab which allows you to enter a question and see a list of topics that are connected with that subject. This is a rather specialist implementation of Help, and not one we'll be considering here.

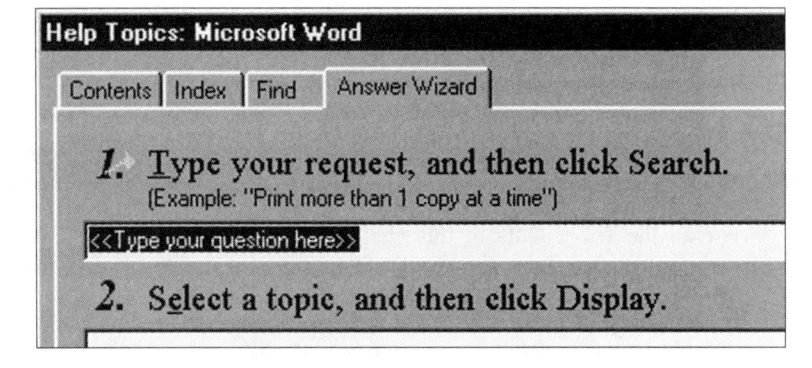

Help Contents, Browsing, and Running Applications

Some Help authors provide their own Contents window which displays the topic that the user has chosen, rather than the normal Help Topics dialog. This is quite easy to do and is a good way to give your users a controlled introduction to your application, rather than expecting them to look up the information they need to get started. If you have Microsoft Office, you'll see this technique used when you open the Getting Results Help file (in the **\Cdonline** folder of your Office 95 CD).

If there's a series of related topics in your Help file, you can also allow users to **browse** through them using a pair of buttons on the toolbar. This is another useful way to introduce them to the different parts of an application, by stepping through a set of topics in a predefined order.

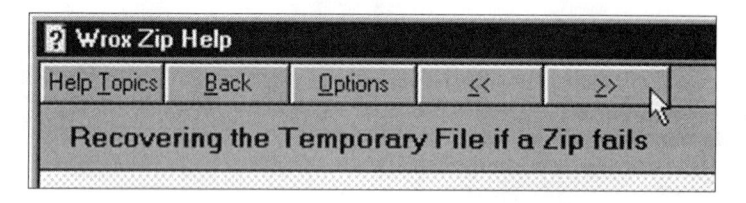

You can also start another application from within a Help file. You'll see a couple of examples of this in the Try It Out later in this section. And you can 'execute' a data file, just as though you had double-clicked on it. This loads the relevant application. For example, you can execute a **.wav** sound file or an **.avi** video file, and it's played automatically.

Training Card Help

The added functionality of the new Help system also allows you to create quite powerful tutorials which can interact with a user as they perform a series of tasks. You'll see it used in different ways by different software companies. Unlike cue cards (which were used as a training utility with some applications), or other Help windows which just provide a set of steps to follow, **training card Help** actually responds to the actions the user carries out in the application. When they follow a step, the next one is automatically displayed. Training card Help can even select options in the application automatically.

Again, this is a specialist implementation of Help, and not one we'll be considering in detail in this book. It requires a close association between the application and the Help file, one which can't be supported in Word Basic. However, once you've mastered Help files in general, and if you program in other languages, such as Visual Basic, Delphi or C++, you'll find that this is the next logical step in developing ever more powerful Help systems

Before we go on to create a Help system in more detail, we'll take a look at the Help file supplied with our sample Wrox Zip add-in. This contains several of the new features that Windows 95 Help supports.

Try It Out - Using the Wrox Zip Help File

For all the Try It Outs in this chapter, you'll need to have installed the sample files from the disk that accompanies this book. This one uses the Wrox Zip Help file, which is in the **\WroxZip** subfolder of your samples folder. Unless you changed the defaults during installation, the sample folder will be **C:\BegWord**. If you haven't installed the Wrox Zip add-in, as described in Chapter 5, you can run it from here.

1 If you haven't installed Wrox Zip as an add-in, you need to open the Wrox Zip template first. In My Computer or Explorer, go to your samples folder, open the **\WroxZip** subfolder and double-click on **WroxZip.dot**. If you *have* installed Wrox Zip as an add-in, you can skip this step.

2 Open the Help menu in Word and select Wrox Zip Help Topics. The Wrox Zip Help file opens with the Getting Started topic. Another window, an overview of Wrox Zip, is displayed over it.

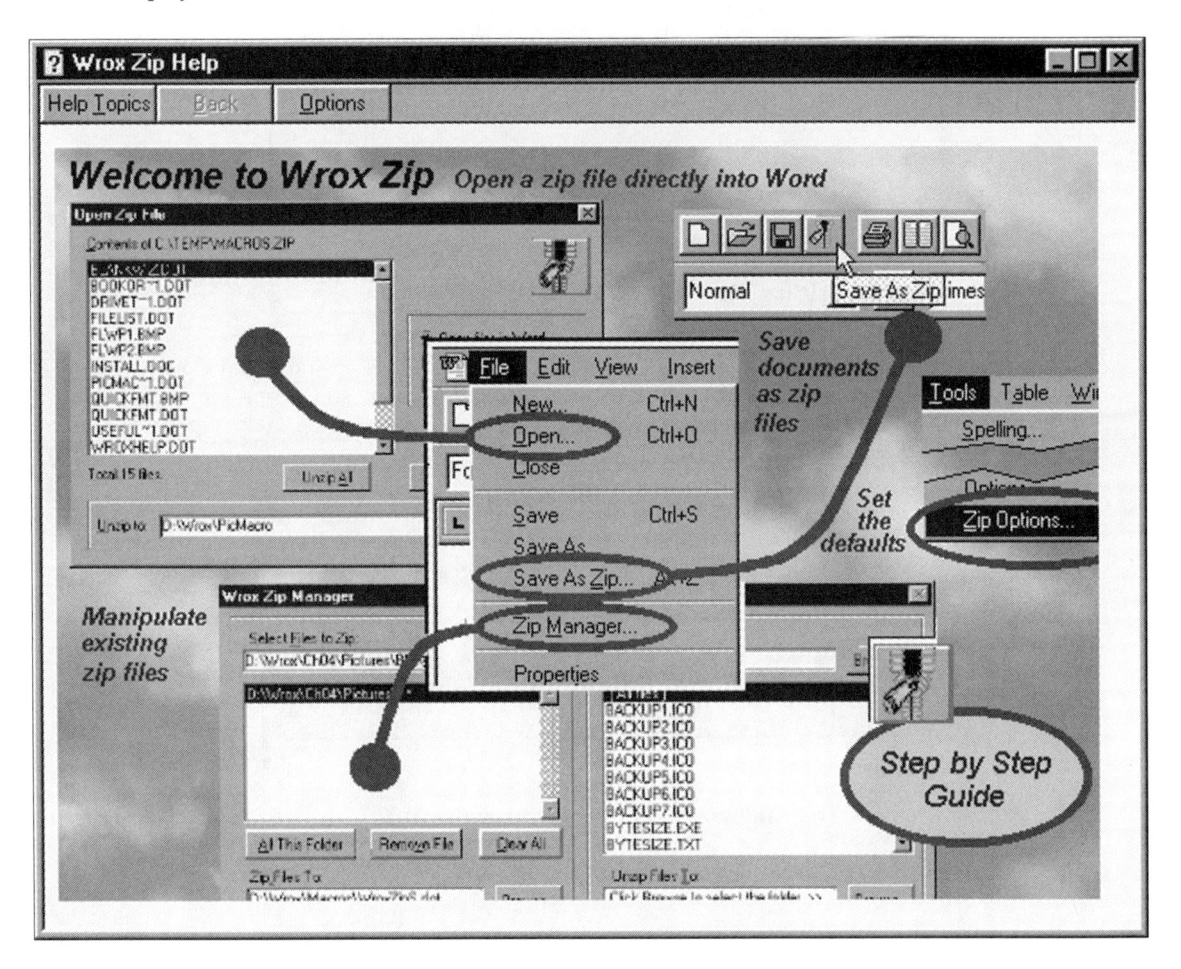

3 As you move the mouse pointer over the large Overview window, you'll see it changes to a pointing finger when it's over a hot spot. Close the Overview window and go to the Getting Started With Wrox Zip topic. Click the first button, Installing Wrox Zip on your computer.

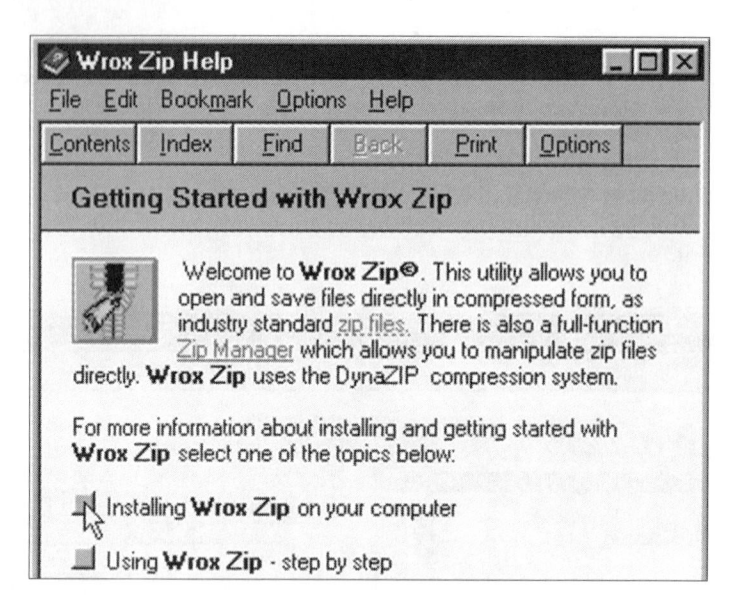

4 The Installing Wrox Zip topic appears in another window. This window stays on top of all the others. Clicking on the main Word window activates it, but still keeps the Help topic visible. This is ideal for a step-by-step topic, because you can see the Help topic while you work in other windows.

5 Near the top of the Installing Wrox Zip window is a button marked Open Explorer now so that I can copy the files. Click this and Explorer starts up. Notice that you can click on either the button or the text. The mouse pointer changes to let you know that the text is a hot spot.

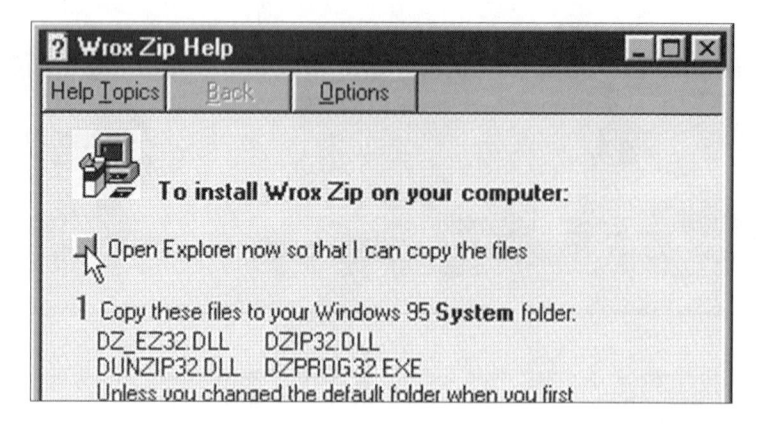

6 Close the Install topic with the normal Close button at the top right of the window, and the Getting Started topic is visible again. Click the Contents button at the top of the window. The familiar Help Topics window appears with the Contents tab open. Double-click the book, Using Zip Manager, to open it.

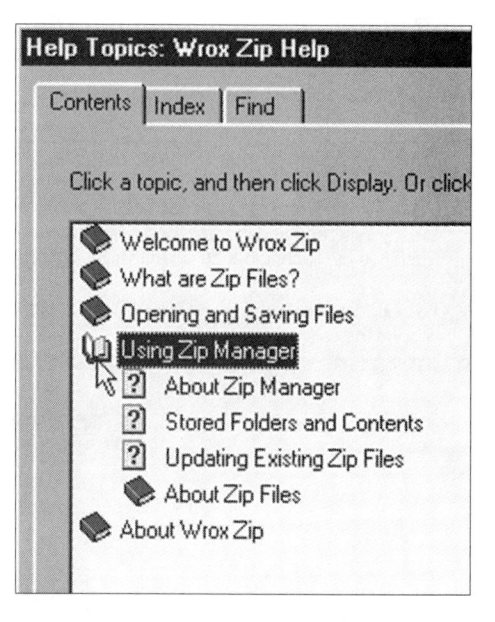

7 Double-click the topic About Zip Manager, and a different window opens, showing the Zip Manager dialog. You can click on different parts of the Zip Manger Help window and see information displayed in a pop-up window, describing what that control does.

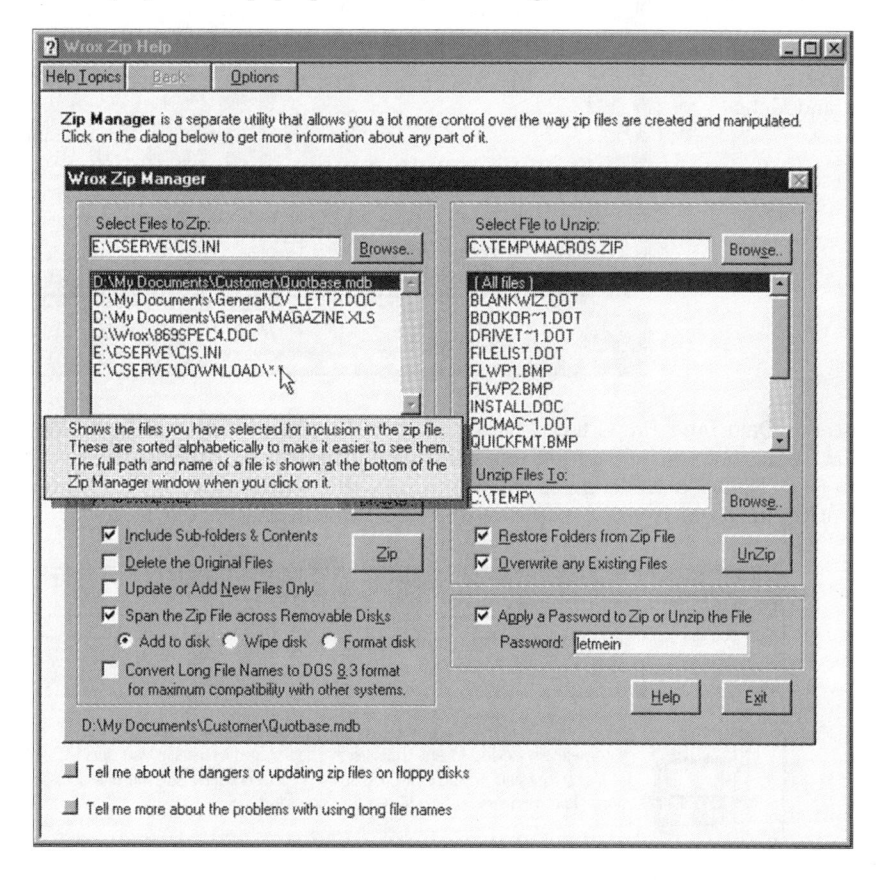

8 Click on the Update or Add New Files Only check box in the right-hand half of the dialog. A pop-up window tells you about updating zip files. In the pop-up window, is a 'short-cut' button, marked with an upward-pointing arrow:

> When you specify an existing zip file as the target, the new files you add will replace any in the zip file with the same name. Even if the existing file has the same date and time, it is replaced with a newly-compressed version. To save time zipping files which have not changed you can set this option. Wrox Zip will then only compress files which are newer, or which don't already exist, and add them to the zip file. If the zip file does not already exist this option has no effect, and you cannot use it when you are spanning a zip file across multiple floppy disks.
>
> To work correctly Update and Add depends on the settings of your system date and time. Click here 🔼 to check or change the settings on your computer.

9 Click on this short-cut button and Control Panel opens, allowing you to check and update the current settings for the time and date:

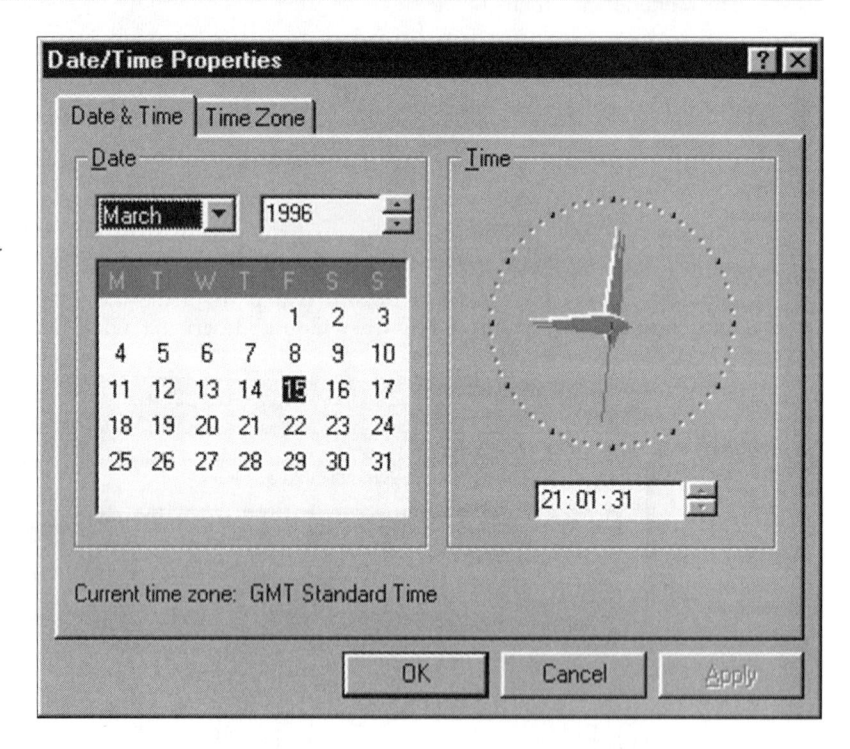

10 Close the Date/Time Properties window and, in the Zip Manager Help window, click the button at the bottom marked Tell me about the dangers of updating zip files on floppy disks. The Updating Existing Zip Files topic appears. At the top of this window you'll see pair of buttons which you can click to browse through the related topics.

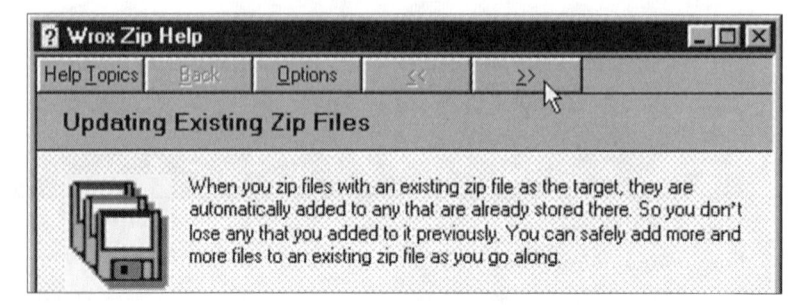

> **Updating Existing Zip Files**
>
> When you zip files with an existing zip file as the target, they are automatically added to any that are already stored there. So you don't lose any that you added to it previously. You can safely add more and more files to an existing zip file as you go along.

While you've got it open, explore the Wrox Zip Help file. Form you own opinion on how well it matches the Windows 95 interface, and whether it really does give the assistance you need to use Wrox Zip. As you work through the rest of the chapter, you might also like to consider how well we've met our own design guidelines.

An Overview of a Help Project

There are several different types of object that come together to make up a Help file. Assembling all these and linking them together in the right way requires some forward planning. Rather like building a house, it becomes a **project**, and the file that binds all the parts of the project together is called, not surprisingly, the **project file**.

Turning all the parts into a complete Help file involves **compiling** it. This converts all the different objects into a special format and then binds them together into one single file. The resulting file can be displayed by Windows Help engine, an application called `WinHelp.exe`.

> **FYI** In fact, when it's in use, a complete Help system also requires other files, though you only need to create one of these: the **Contents** file. You'll see more about **Contents** files in the next chapter.

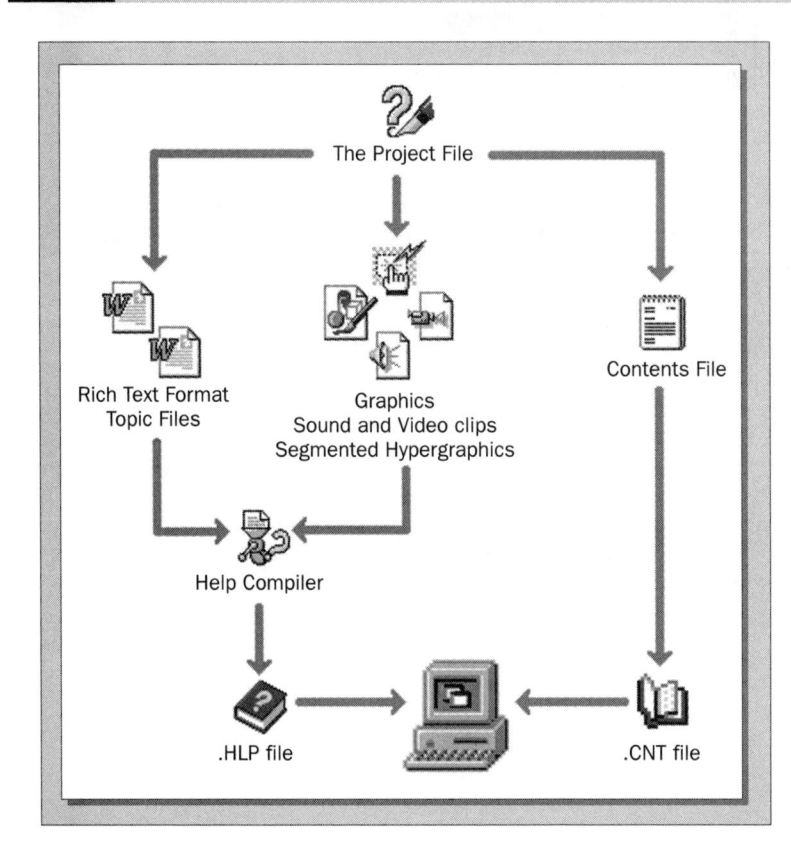

The project file contains all the information that you need to bind the different elements of the Help file together as they are compiled. This is a normal text file, whose format resembles the Windows `.ini` file we saw in Part 1. It contains sections for each different part of the Help project, such as listing the files that make up the topic and defining the types of window that display the topics.

In the next chapter, we'll take a look at how the project file is organized and how we compile a Help file. In this chapter, we're going to concentrate on just one part of the Help project: the topic file.

The Tools You Need

For every project, you need the correct tools to help you get your job done. There are three things you must have to start building Help files:

- A word processor that handles rich text format files
- A copy of Windows 95 Help Compiler or Help Workshop (Version 4)
- A little artistic skill and a lot of patience

A Word Processor

It's probably safe to assume (as you've bought this book) that you have a copy of Microsoft Word. It handles rich text format (`.rtf`) files well, having been developed along with Windows Help system. You'll also find that current versions of WordPerfect will produce `.rtf` files.

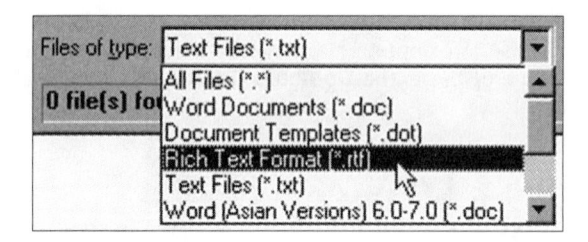

> **FYI** You have to install a separate filter that reads and writes rich text format files with Word, because it's not the default when you install Word or Microsoft Office. If you don't see the **Rich Text Format** (.rtf) option in the list of file types (in the **Open** dialog), run the Word setup program again and make sure it's selected in the **Text Conversion Filters** section.

The Help Compiler

You'll also need a copy of the latest version of Microsoft's Windows 95 Help Compiler or Help Workshop. Help Workshop is the new name for the Version 3 Help Compiler from Windows 3.x.

Help Workshop consists of two main programs. `Hcw.exe` is the graphical interface for creating your project files and managing the various elements of a Help file. It makes creating Help files much easier than in earlier versions where you had to create the project file yourself.

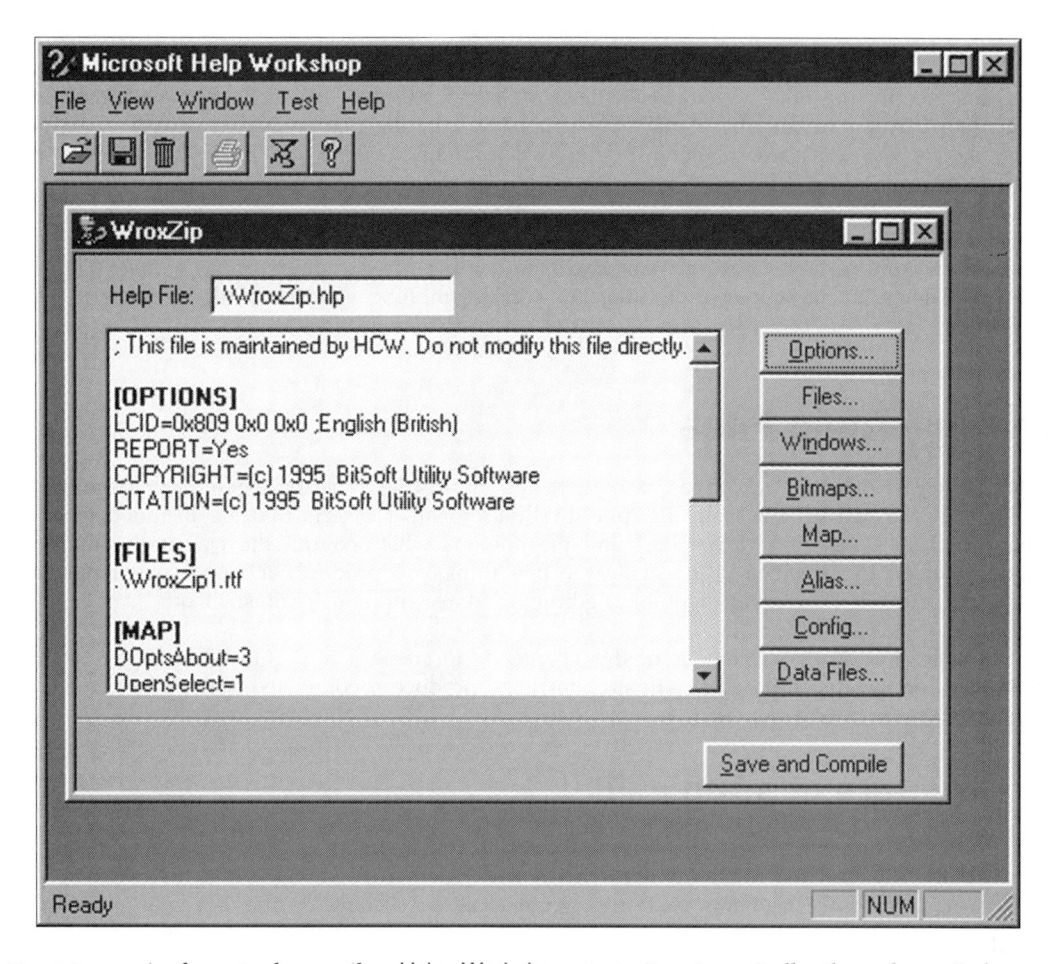

Hcrtf.exe is the actual compiler. Help Workshop starts it automatically, then closes it down once the compilation is complete. You can create your own project files and run **Hcrtf** directly.

To create graphics which have hot spots that users can click to get more information, you'll need another program: **Shed.exe**. This wonderful name belies its real use. **Shed** actually stands for **Segmented Hypergraphics Editor**.

In Windows 95, Help files can include images with as many colors as the user's display hardware can handle. You can use high resolution true-color graphics if you wish. However, these don't always look good on lower specification machines when the colors have to be dithered. To overcome this, another program, called **Mrbc.exe** (Multiple Resolution Bitmap Compiler), allows you to include the same image in different resolutions within the Help file.

Help Workshop contains all these files, plus its own Help files.

> **FYI** We haven't supplied **Help Compiler** with this book. You'll also find it's included with almost all Microsoft programming systems, such as Visual Basic, Visual C++, etc. and with many other software suppliers' products. If you haven't already got a copy you can buy the Microsft WinHelp developer's guide which contains the software.

The Final Ingredients

We can't supply the final ingredients—artistic skill and patience. You'll need some artistic ability because when you're building a Help file you have a far freer approach than with Word macros and dialogs. But don't worry, there are standard guidelines which will help you get your Help files looking just like those provided with other applications—and sometimes a lot better!

You'll need patience because, like programming, creating Help files can be infuriating at times. As well as pure text, you can include macros and other objects which bring it alive. This often means that you spend a long time adjusting and recompiling your Help file to get it looking just right.

Creating Topic Files

The main part of any Help project is creating the **topic files**. These are the `.rtf` documents that contain all the text for the Help file, plus the links to other objects that are included (such as graphics, sound files and video clips) and the pointers which control the way each different topic is joined to the others. It's usually the first thing you produce, and once you have the basic file ready it's a case of compiling, editing, and recompiling to finish it off.

So, our objective in the remainder of this chapter is to create a topic file which is ready to be compiled for the first time. Our ultimate aim is to produce a completed Help file to go with the `PrintBothSides` macro you first met in Chapter 6.

The Structure of a Topic File

The topic file contains almost all of the information that determines how your Help file will appear, and the way the different topics are linked together. Each individual topic is displayed in a window, and the user moves from topic to topic by clicking on the 'hot spot' areas of each one.

A **hot spot** can be words that are underlined and colored green, a pushbutton, or a graphic. You can even have graphics that jump to different topics depending on which area you click. Usually, the mouse pointer changes to a 'finger' when you are over a hot spot part of a topic.

You define the parts of a topic that form these links by formatting them in a special way when you create the topic file, or by including special commands in the file. As a simple example, here's a section of a topic file showing some links to other topics. Each topic is separated from the next by a hard page break, one that's inserted by the user rather than by Word and doesn't change as text is added to the topic or removed from it.

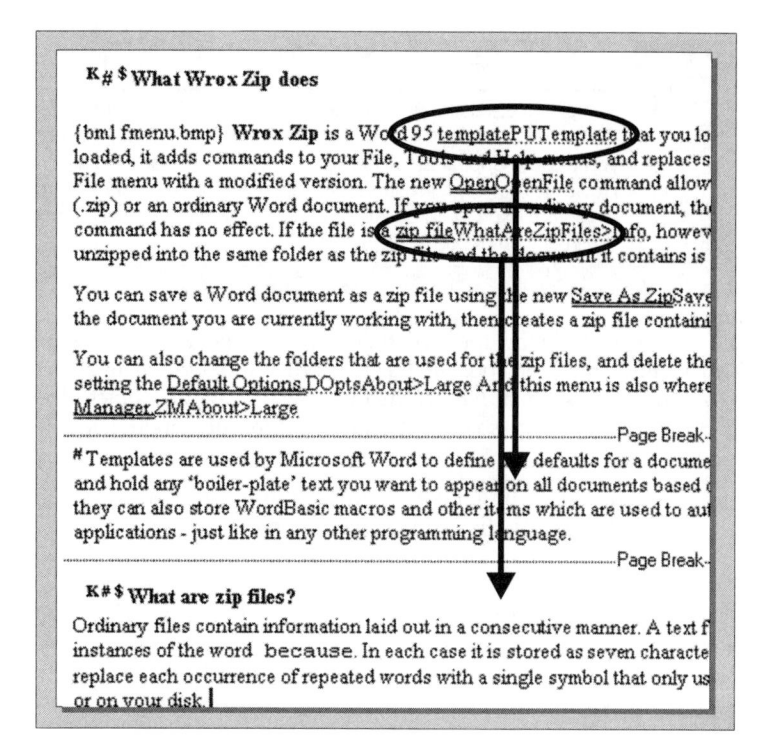

The Help file knows which topic (page) to jump to because each one has a **topic identifier** assigned to it. You assign a topic identifier by including a footnote in the topic. The text of the footnote is then used as the topic identifier. Footnotes play a major role in the way a Help file is constructed and displayed. Rather than a number, each footnote marker is a special character. A hash sign (#) is used for a topic identifier.

Other footnote characters identify the title of the topic, the keywords that appear in the index, the default window type, the macro that runs when the topic is opened, and the sequence in which the user can browse through the topics. You'll meet each of these as we continue to build our new Help file during this and the next chapter.

An Overview of Jumps and Pop-ups

Jumps and **pop-ups** are placed directly in the topic file, where they appear on screen when the Help file is in use. The difference between a jump and a pop-up is simply the way the topic they refer to is displayed. A jump changes the current topic to the one specified for that jump instruction, while a pop-up displays the new topic in a small window which appears to stand out in front of the first topic. It remains on screen until the user clicks again, anywhere in the windows.

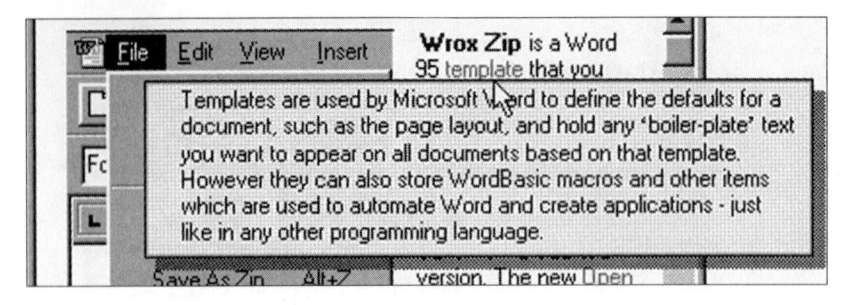

However, the differences in the way the two types are implemented are minor. Both use underlined text to identify the 'hot spot' in the Help file, and hidden text to identify the topic that they refer to. And there's no difference in the structure of the topics themselves, though each one is laid out in such a way so that it suits the type of window it's displayed in.

Simply setting the formatting of the text creates the hot spot and makes the mouse pointer change when it's over it. All you need to do is to tell the Help file which topic you want to pop up or jump to.

Planning a Help File

You'll no doubt realize by now that it takes quite a lot of planning to create a successful Help file. You can convert existing documentation if you have it, but it often still needs a lot of work. And if you're starting from scratch, the most usual first thought is 'Where do I start?'

In general, most Help files have a 'Getting Started' or 'Welcome' topic which acts as a starting point for the Help file. It can introduce new users to the application in a natural way, keeping the learning curve as shallow as possible. Alternatively, you may have a single window or dialog in the application that forms the focus, like our **PrintBothSides** macro. In this case, you can build the whole Help file around this as a starting point.

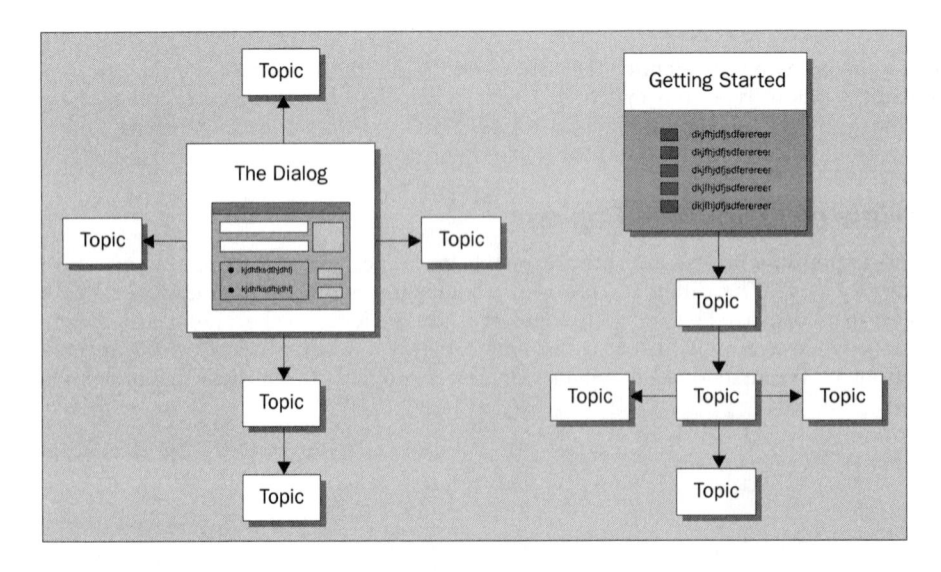

Some of the important points to bear in mind while you plan a Help file are:

- Make it easy to get back to where you came from. Avoid dead ends if possible. If you have a series of topics covering some function of the application, add a jump to the 'introduction' topic at the end.

- Make it obvious where different types of information are available. If you have a set of topics covering the syntax of commands, link them together but keep them separate from the 'Getting Started' or 'tutorial' parts.

- Keep topics short and concise. Unlike a book, users expect to find and grasp the nuggets of information they need quickly, rather than having to sit down and read it all.

- Use plain language and add pop-up windows to explain any terms that they may not be aware of. Using a pop-up window means they don't lose their place in the Help file while reading the extra information.

- Try and think how people will use the application and anticipate where they may need extra assistance. You can write a special topic for just this.

Setting the Styles

Much of modern program design is about style. To the Word developer, style might mean the specification of a paragraph's font, pitch, format and line spacing. With Help files, though, style means more than just that. We're into the 'arty' stuff again, which involves making your Help file match and complement Windows 95's look and style.

For example, here's the 'Welcome' topic that's displayed when the WroxPBS Help file is used. It uses small buttons with simple text descriptions so that you can quickly get to the area you want help on. From here, you can also go direct to the Contents or Index in the Help Topics window.

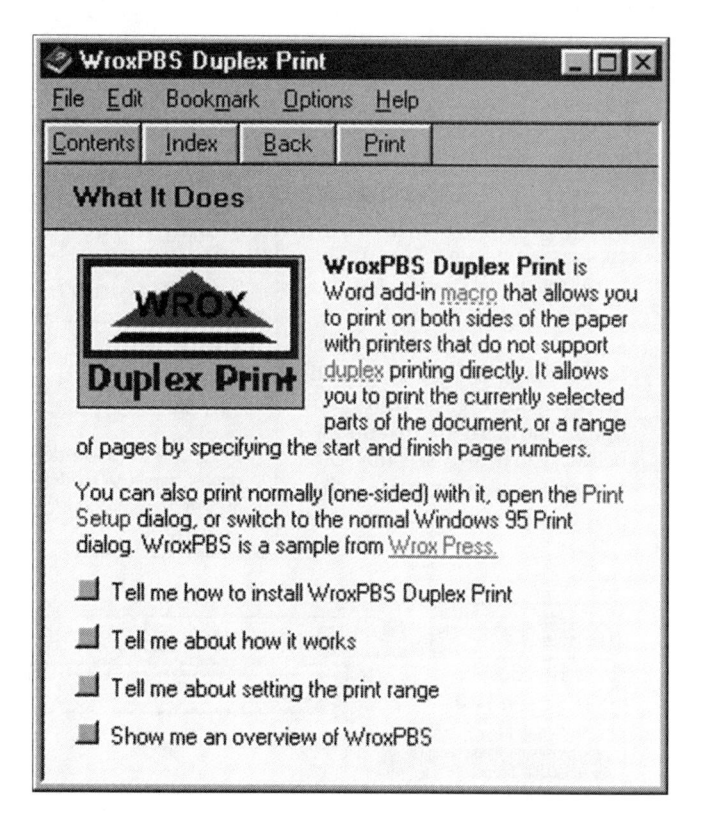

337

These small Windows 95-style buttons are also used to lead you to other related topics. Each time, the text makes it obvious what the other topic covers.

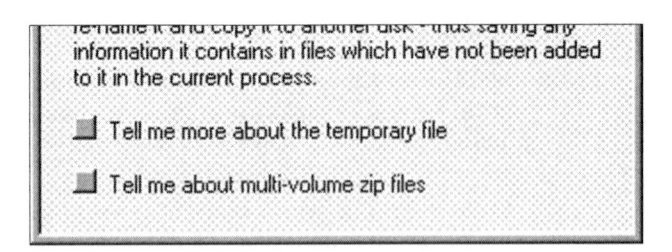

The standard text style in Windows 95 Help is 8pt MS Sans Serif, indented from the left and right margins. In some places it also uses extra line spacing. The Tip heading has 6pt before and 2pt after, and the following text is formatted as Bullets. This style is often used to give extra information about a topic.

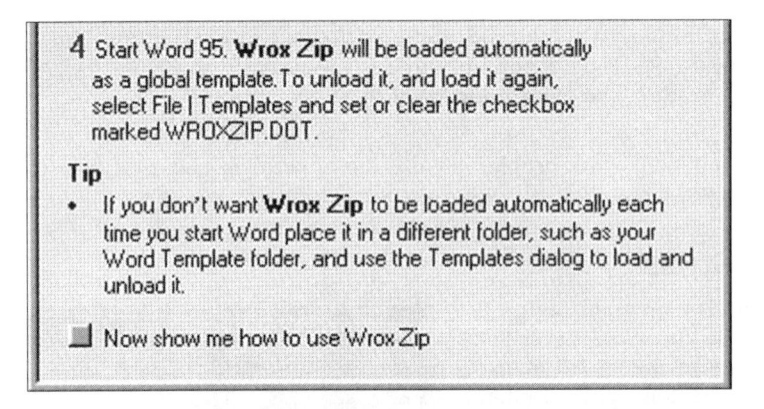

You can also include non-scrolling headings. The Windows 95 style uses 10pt bold MS Sans Serif, with a line spacing of 6pt before and after. The heading background is light gray, and the body of the window light yellow. In the example below, you'll also see the Do It graphic used to start each paragraph.

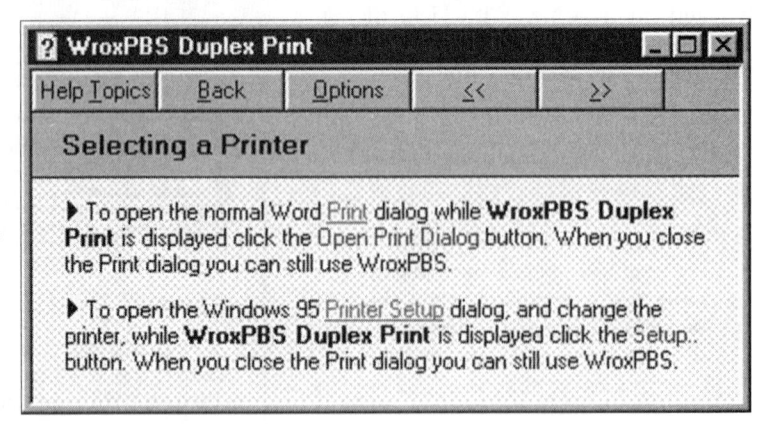

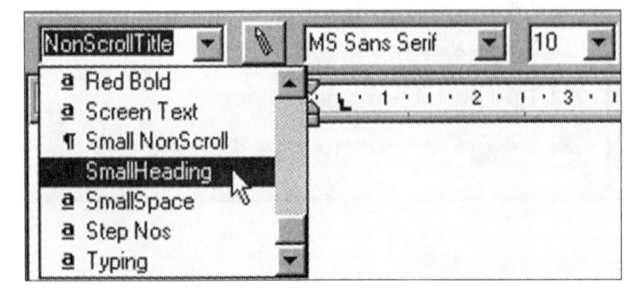

Of course, we can use Word's styles to help us get the style we want. Several of Microsoft's recommended Help file styles are included for you in the sample template that we've supplied.

Creating a Non-scrolling Title

As an example of the styles that we've included in the WroxHelp template, look at the previous screenshot from the WroxPBS Help file. The title area at the top of the window stays put when the topic is scrolled. Traditionally, the color of this is light gray, though in many Windows 95-style Help windows it's no longer used at all. However, if you have a topic which won't all fit on screen in one go, this is a useful way to keep part of it in view all the time.

> **FYI** Remember, your users may be working in a lower screen resolution mode, so a topic that fits neatly inside a window on your machine might not fit so neatly when they view it. If you don't know what the lowest resolution will be, plan to make your topics fit on a 640 x 480 VGA screen.

Creating a **non-scrolling region** like this is easy. You just format the first paragraph (normally just the title) using Word's Keep with Next style. Select Paragraph from the Format menu and click the Text Flow tab in the dialog.

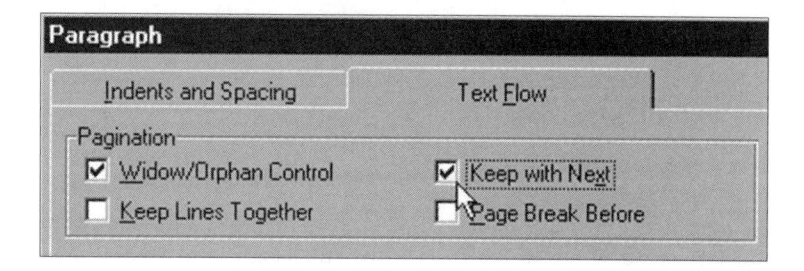

The WroxHelp template contains the style NonScrollTitle which automatically formats the text in a larger font, with extra space above and below and with the Keep with Next paragraph format.

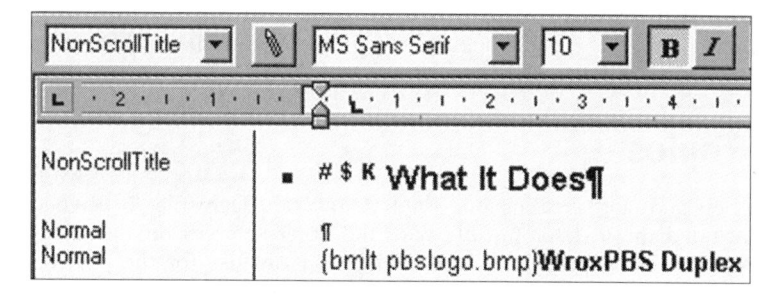

You can, of course, also place graphics or other objects in the non-scrolling region.

Using Different Window Types

One of the factors that most affects the look of a Help file is the different types of windows that the topics are displayed in. No longer is it a matter of one style of window showing all the topics. With Windows 95, we're into special window types for each type of Help topic. For example, a small window called a **procedure window**, placed high on the right-hand side of the screen, is usually used to show the steps needed to carry out a task.

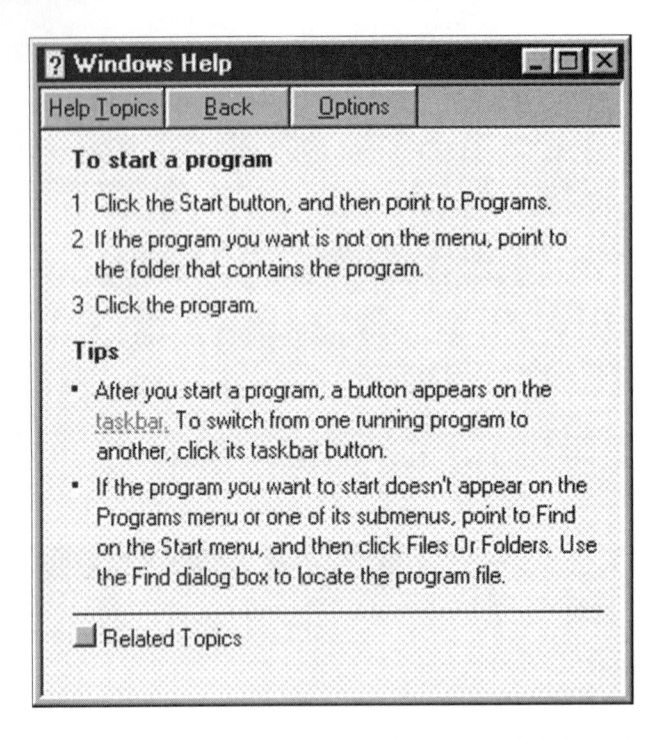

To display large topics that contain reference material or general information, you can use the Help system's default **Main** window, which fills the full height and central area of the screen. And you've already seen how some windows stay on top of all the others. You can also create windows which automatically adjust in height to suit the amount of text they have to hold. Many of the Wrox Zip Help windows do this.

You can define up to 255 different window types, though, in general, four or five should be plenty. The definition of each type is held in the project file, and you'll see more about how this is done in the next chapter.

Writing the Topics

So let's now get on and start creating our Print Both Sides Help file. To save you a lot of typing, we've included the text for the file with the other samples on the disk that accompanies this book. There are part-completed versions which you can use for the different examples in this chapter. They're stored in the **\WroxHelp** subfolder of your samples folder. Unless you changed the defaults during installation, your samples folder will be **C:\BegWord**.

A Help project can contain several topic files, but we'll only be using one. It's much easier to work with one single file, unless your project involves several hundred topics.

Topic Titles and Identifiers

Step one of a Help project involves writing the topic files, as we discussed above. Once this is done, we need to add the topic identifiers and topic titles to each topic. If you don't add a topic identifier, you won't be able to jump to that topic from another one, though you can still browse through topics that have no topic identifier. If you don't add a title to each topic, they won't appear in the full-text-search Find tab of the Help Topics window.

Topic footnote entries are placed in the topic file, at the beginning of the topic to which they refer. A **topic identifier** is a text string which uniquely identifies that topic. It's inserted as a footnote using the hash (**#**) character as the Custom Mark for the footnote entry dialog. A **topic title** is the name that appears in the Index and Find tabs of the Help Topics window, and the Topics Found dialog. It's inserted using the dollar (**$**) character as the custom mark.

Try It Out - Setting the Topic's Title and Identifier

We'll add the topic identifiers and titles to the Print Both Sides topic file. You'll need the file **WroxPBS1.rtf** which contains the text of the topic file, and the WroxHelp template which we've also supplied. You'll find this when you open **WroxPBS1.rtf**, so it should be in your **\Templates** folder.

1 Copy the file **WroxHelp.dot** from the **\WroxHelp** subfolder of your samples folder into your **\Templates** folder.

> **FYI** Unless you changed the defaults during installation, the **WroxHelp** template will be in the folder **C:\BegWord\WroxHelp**. Your **\Templates** folder will be **\Winword\Template** or **\Msoffice\Winword\Templates**, unless you changed the defaults when you installed Word 95 or Office 95.

2 Double-click on the file WroxPBS1.rtf to open it in Word. If you don't want to change the original, you can make a copy of it in another folder and load that instead. You may be prompted to confirm the conversion of the file from Rich Text Format if you have set this option in Word's Options window. If you're prompted, just click OK.

3 The first thing you'll notice is that the Word environment changes. There are several new buttons on the toolbar, new commands on the menus, and the document is displayed with paragraph markers and a style margin visible. It may also be enlarged. We'll consider all these changes in a while.

4 The insertion point will be directly before the heading of the first topic, What It Does. Select Footnote from the Insert menu and select the Custom Mark: option. Enter a hash character (#) and click OK.

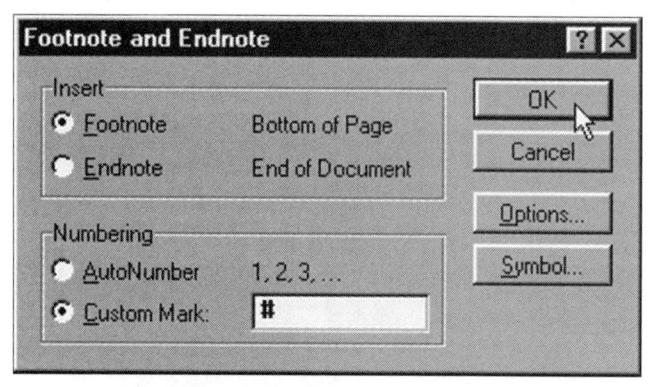

5 Word inserts the footnote marker into the document and opens the footnote window. Type the identifier for this topic, WHAT_IT_DOES.

6 Click <u>C</u>lose to go back to the document. Then repeat the process, but use a dollar character ($) for the custom mark and type the title for the topic, What It Does. Once you've closed the footnote window, you'll see the two footnote marks in the document.

7 Now let's see an easier way. Scroll down to the Installing WroxPBS topic, and place the insertion point anywhere in it. Click the new Topic ID button on the toolbar. This comes from the WroxHelp template you copied into your `\Templates` folder.

8 A dialog opens where you can enter both the title for the topic and the identifier. Fill in both the boxes, then click OK.

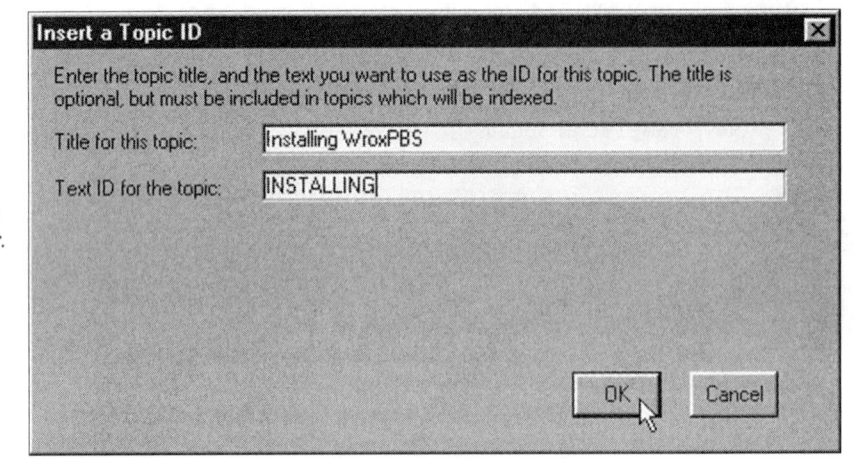

9 The macro in the WroxHelp template automatically inserts the footnotes into the document for you. If you want to see them, double-click on the footnote mark in the document to open the footnote window.

10 Finally, we can make life even easier. Scroll to the topic headed About WroxPBS, and select this heading by dragging over it with the mouse. Don't include the paragraph marker. Then click the Topic ID button on the toolbar. Now the dialog is already filled in for you, though you can edit the topic identifier if you wish.

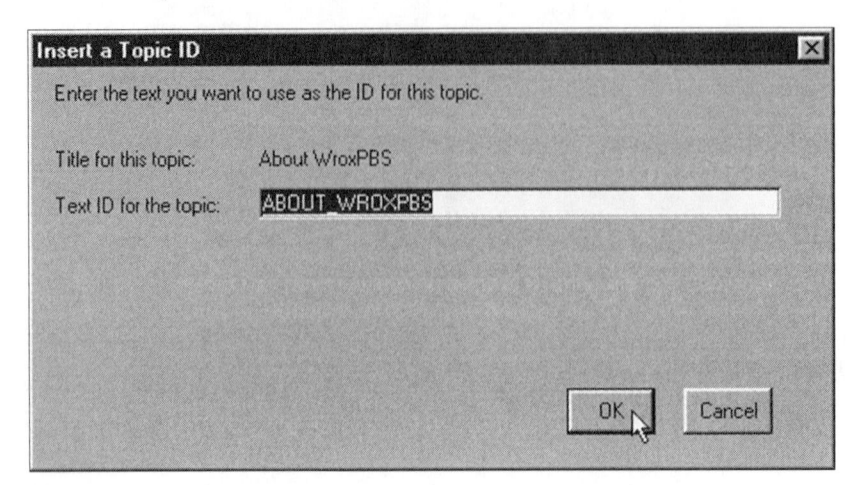

How It Works

You've seen two ways of inserting a topic identifier and title into a topic file. The first is the usual way, using Word's Footnote dialog. The second way is much more transparent and particularly aimed at creating Help files. It uses a macro stored in the WroxHelp template, which creates a custom dialog and processes the text you enter. The result is the same either way. Footnotes with the special custom footnote marks are inserted in the topic file to create the topic identifier and topic title.

The WroxHelp template also allows you to edit the topic identifier and title. If there's already one defined when you open the dialog, it's displayed and you can change it. As you've seen, if you select (highlight) some text from the topic first, then press the new **#** button on the toolbar, this text is automatically proposed as the topic title, and a topic identifier is created for you. You can carry on and insert topic titles and identifiers for the rest of the topics ready for the next example, or you can use another copy of the topic file that we've supplied as **WroxPBS2.rtf**.

What the WroxHelp Template Does

We don't intend going into much detail about the workings of the WroxHelp template because you'll see how to use its features as you work through this and the next chapter. However, you may wish to modify and add new routines, so we'll give you a brief overview.

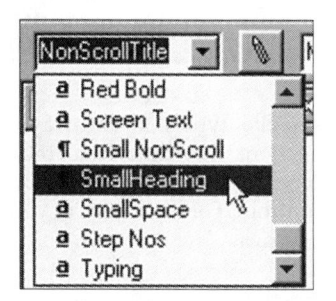

The WroxHelp template contains a set of predefined styles based on the recommendations for Windows Help files. These allow you to quickly and easily format text so that it matches other Help files and the Windows 95 interface.

The changes to the Word environment you see when you open a document based on it come from **AutoOpen** and **AutoClose** macros. The **AutoOpen** macro reads your current settings for various options and saves them in the template as AutoText entries. It then sets the options most useful for working with topic files. For example, it displays paragraph markers, tabs and hidden text, turns off the automatic spellchecker, displays the style name area and disables Automatic Word Selection and Smart Cut and Paste. It also sets the view to Normal, and the magnification to 125%. When you close the document, the **AutoClose** macro simply reads your previous settings and restores them.

Depending on the screen resolution you work in, and your own preferences, you may wish to alter the option settings in the **AutoOpen** macro to suit.

```
Sub MAIN      'AutoOpen macro
    ViewNormal
    Dim TOD As ToolsOptionsView
    GetCurValues TOD
    SetAutoText "WHStyleAreaWidth", TOD.StyleAreaWidth, 1
    SetAutoText "WHTabs", Str$(TOD.Tabs), 1
    SetAutoText "WHParas", Str$(TOD.Paras), 1
    SetAutoText "WHHidden", Str$(TOD.Hidden), 1
    ToolsOptionsView .StyleAreaWidth = "3 cm", .Tabs = 1, \
                    .Paras = 1, .Hidden = 1
```

```
        Redim TOD As ToolsOptionsEdit
        GetCurValues TOD
        SetAutoText "WHAutoWordSelection", Str$(TOD.AutoWordSelection), 1
        SetAutoText "WHSmartCutPaste", Str$(TOD.SmartCutPaste), 1
        ToolsOptionsEdit .AutoWordSelection = 0, .SmartCutPaste = 0
        Redim TOD As ToolsOptionsSpelling
        GetCurValues TOD
        SetAutoText "WHAutomaticSpellChecking", \
                    Str$(TOD.AutomaticSpellChecking), 1
        ToolsOptionsSpelling .AutomaticSpellChecking = 0
        Redim TOD As ViewZoom
        GetCurValues TOD
        SetAutoText "WHZoomPercent", TOD.ZoomPercent, 1
        ViewZoom .ZoomPercent = "125%"
    End Sub
```

The WroxHelp template also modifies the Save As menu command. You must save your topic files in Rich Text Format (.rtf). A macro, named **FileSaveAs,** runs instead of the normal **SaveAs** command the first time you save your topic file and automatically selects Rich Text Format as the file type.

There's another set of macros and corresponding toolbar buttons and menu commands which inserts the different types of custom footnote entry and allows you to edit them. Each button has the relevant footnote symbol on it.

The macros work by assembling a list of existing footnotes of a particular type into an array and displaying this in a custom dialog. You'll find the two main functions that do this in the **WHLib** macro. **FillFNArray** fills an array with the existing footnote entries, and **ShowDialog** displays the same custom dialog, but with different labels for the controls. For example, if you're inserting a **K**-type footnote, the dialog shows all the existing index entries.

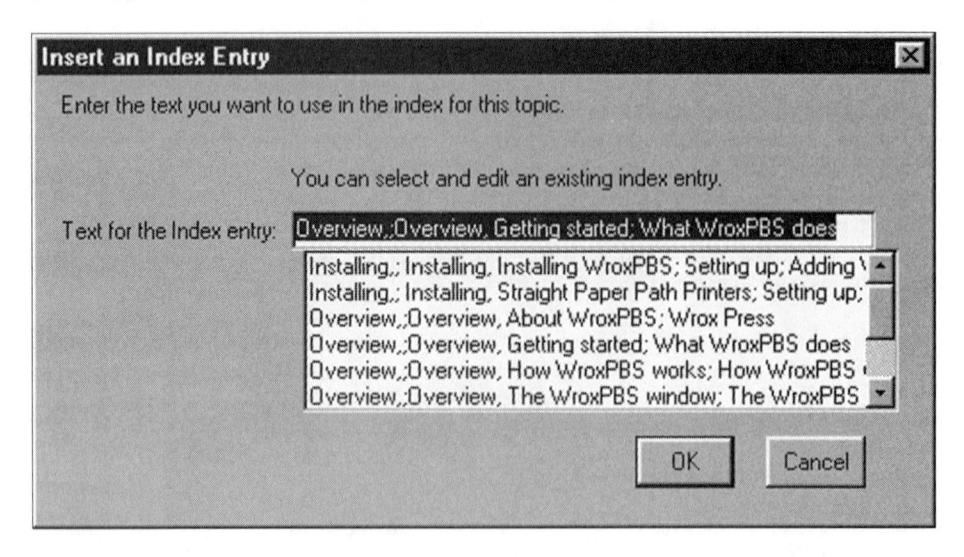

There are also toolbar buttons and menu commands devoted to inserting pop-ups, jumps, buttons and graphics. You'll see these used in the next two examples.

Linking Topics Together

A jump is defined in the topic file by formatting the hot spot text with a double underline, while a pop-up window uses single underline format. When you view the completed Help file from an application, the text that's displayed for the hot spot is colored green. (This is the default. The user can change the color of hot spots when they view the Help file.) Just to confuse you, however, jumps display a single underline, and pop-up windows display a dotted underline.

We'll add the jumps and pop-up links we need in our Print Both Sides Help file. You can use the version where you added the topic identifiers and titles in the previous example, or the file **WroxPBS2.rtf** that we've supplied with the other sample files. It has all the topic identifiers and titles already in place.

Try It Out - Linking Topics with Jumps and Pop-ups

You'll need the file **WroxPBS1.rtf** with the topic identifiers and titles inserted, or you can use the file **WroxPBS2.rtf** instead. If you use your own copy, the names of the topic identifiers will be those that you created. You'll also need to have placed the file **WroxHelp.dot** in your **\Templates** folder, as described in the previous example.

1 Open the file which contains the topic identifiers and titles (either **WroxPBS1.rtf** or **WroxPBS2.rtf**). If you don't want to change the original, make a copy of it in another folder and open that instead. First, we'll construct a pop-up link in the first topic.

2 In the first topic, select the word *duplex* by dragging over it with the mouse. Make sure that you only select the word itself, not any spaces before or after it. Then click the Pop Up button on the toolbar.

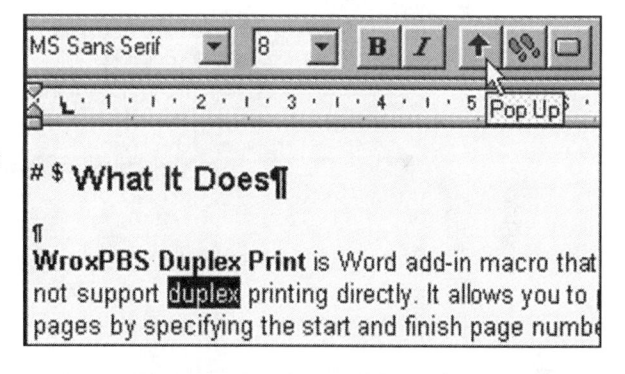

3 The Insert a Pop-up Window dialog opens, showing the text you selected and a list of the identifiers of all the existing topics within the file. Select PU_DUPLEX. This is the identifier we created for the topic that explains what *duplex* means.

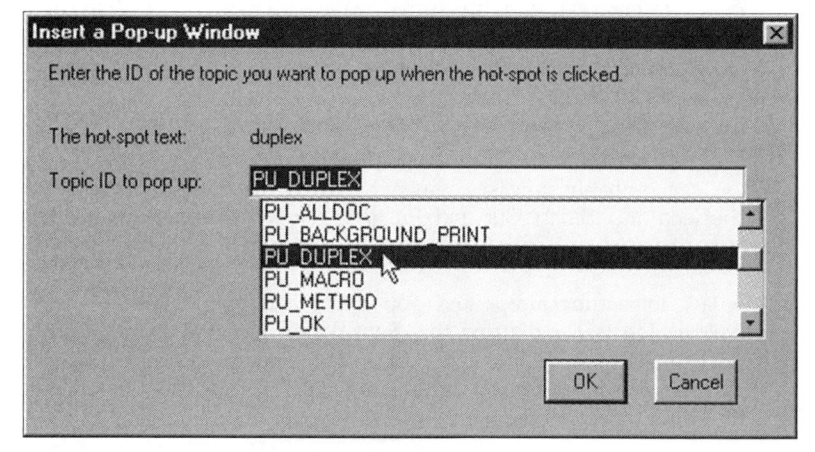

345

4 Click OK. The topic identifier is inserted into the document after the word *duplex*, and both are formatted to create the pop-up link.

5 Now we'll insert a jump. In the first topic, select the words range of pages by dragging over them with the mouse. Don't select any spaces before or after the phrase. Then click the Jump button on the toolbar.

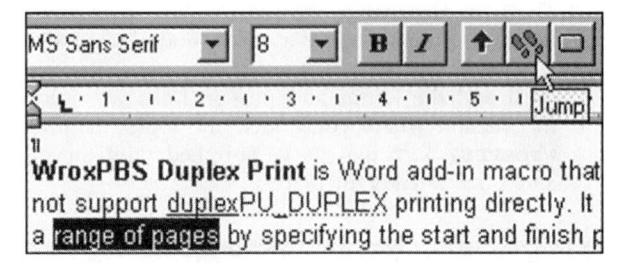

6 The Insert a Topic Jump dialog opens, again showing the text you selected and a list of the IDs of all the existing topics. Select PRINT_RANGE, the identifier we created for the topic that explains how you set the print range.

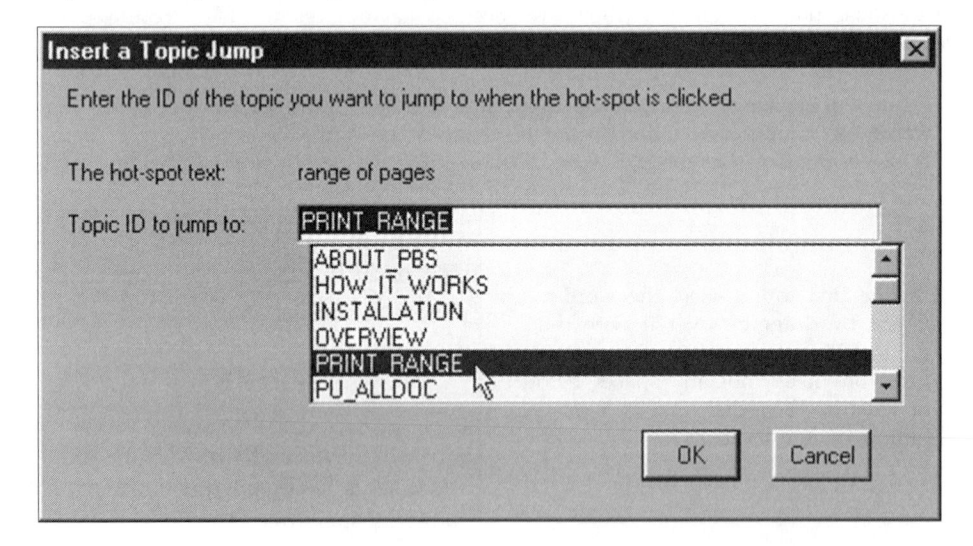

7 Click OK. The topic identifier is inserted into the document after the phrase range of pages, and the whole lot is formatted to create the jump.

What We've Done

You can probably now see why we turned off Automatic Word Selection, Automatic Spell-Checking and Smart Cut and Paste in the WroxHelp template. Having extra spaces inserted, and your underlines obscured by wavy red ones, doesn't make the job any easier.

In fact, formatting jumps and pop-ups is a fiddly business if you do it in the traditional way, by selecting the text and using the Font dialog to set it to single or double underline or hidden. So you'll probably have found the WroxHelp template's toolbar buttons very useful. They make the job quicker and easier, by automating the repetitive task of opening the Font dialog and selecting the options you want.

By formatting the existing text in the topics with single or double underlines, and adding the identifier of the other topic as hidden text immediately after it, we've created jumps which take us to another topic, and pop-ups which display another topic in a pop-up window. Of course, you'll just have to take our word for this for the time being, until we compile the Help file in the next chapter.

You can also use the Pop Up and Jump dialogs to insert the text for the hot spot, as well as the destination topic identifier. If you don't select any text before opening the dialog, you can enter it into the dialog instead. When you click OK, the macro inserts the text and the topic identifier, and formats them for you automatically.

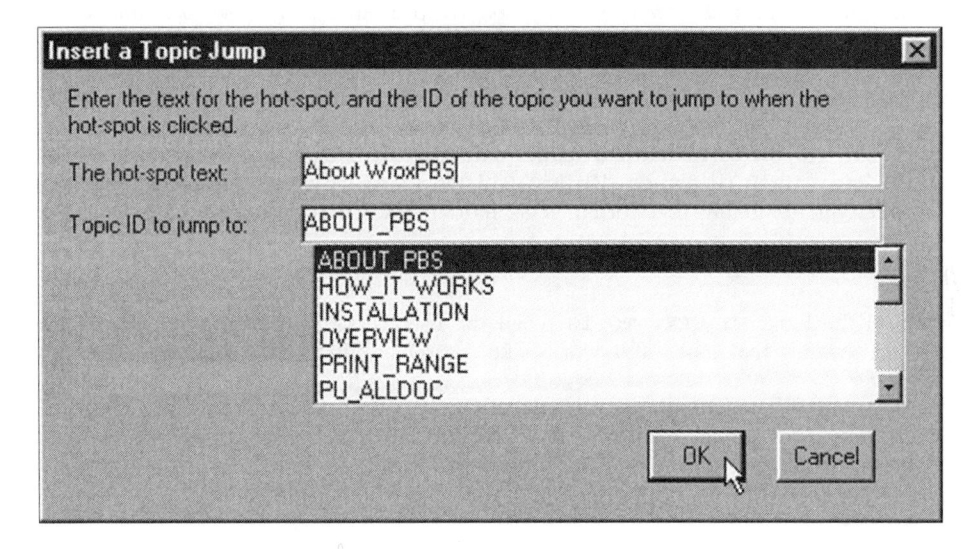

Adding Graphics and Buttons

A Help file would be very boring if it only displayed text. You can include images and graphics in a variety of ways. Probably the easiest is to simply insert them in the topic file, just like you would when using Word to produce a normal document. You can also add a **picture command** to the topic file, which specifies the image file. In this case, the Help compiler includes the file in a special part of the help file (referred to as the **baggage** section) instead of storing it in the topic.

This second method has a major advantage. If you use the same graphic twice, it will only be included once in the Help file. If you embed the same picture directly into the topic file in two different places, it will be duplicated in the Help file. If you want to use different resolution versions of the same image for different users' displays, you have to include them as a command, using the second method.

The WroxHelp toolbar contains two buttons for inserting graphics. The one on the left inserts a picture directly, by embedding it in the document, just like it does when you are placing pictures in your normal Word documents. The one on the right creates a picture command in the topic.

Adding a Graphic with a Picture Command

A command to include a graphic is simple. `{bml Mypic.bmp}` places the image **Mypic.bmp** against the left margin, where the command appears in the topic. Any text on the same line wraps to the left of the image. For example, here's part of the Wrox Zip Help file which uses this command to insert the picture of the menu:

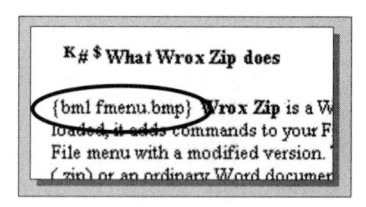

To place the graphic against the right margin, we use **bmr** instead of **bml**, and to place it in the text as though it were a character, with no text wrap around it, we use **bmc** (the **c** means *character*, not *centered*). If we want the white parts of the graphic to appear transparent, so that the background color shows through, we just add a **t**. The commands become **bmlt**, **bmrt**, **bmct**.

Formatting the graphic as underlined (either single or double) makes it into a hot spot, and we can turn it into a jump or pop-up. We just add the identifier of the topic we want to pop-up or jump to after the command and format it as hidden text. For example,

    {bml Mypic.bmp}MY_NEXT_TOPIC

will jump to the topic **MY_NEXT_TOPIC** when the user clicks on the graphic **Mypic.bmp**. So, we can create a graphic that looks and works like a toolbar button and clicking it displays the relevant topic.

This is the only way to use a button with a picture on it. If you're happy with a text caption, or no caption at all, you can use a 'real' button.

Adding a Button

The Help Compiler supports a command which creates real push buttons anywhere in a topic, not just on the button bar at the top of the window. You can also include a text caption on the button, but not a picture.

You'll have noticed in Windows 95's Help files that small blank buttons are used regularly. These are real buttons that appear to depress when you click them. They are created with a special command. For example:

    {button , JumpID(NEXT_TOPIC)}

creates a blank button 12 pixels square, and jumps to the topic **NEXT_TOPIC** when clicked.

Notice the comma after the word **button**. If you want to include a caption, you place it before the comma. In this case, you specify where to jump to by using a macro, **JumpID()**, rather than just adding the topic identifier as hidden text. The full syntax of the button command is:

{button [*caption for button*],   *macro to run* }

You don't have to jump anywhere when the button is clicked. The button command can run any macro, not just the **JumpID()** macro we used earlier. You'll see more about macros and the other things we can do when a button is clicked in the next chapter. In the meantime, let's try adding some graphics and buttons to the Print Both Sides Help file.

Try It Out - Adding Graphics and Buttons

You'll need one of the topic files we've been using in the earlier examples—the file **WroxPBS2.rtf** will do nicely. You also need the WroxHelp template to be in your **\Templates** folder, like we showed you in the previous examples.

1 Open the file **WroxPBS2.rtf**. If you don't want to change the original, make a copy of it in another folder and open that instead.

2 In the first topic, place the insertion point directly before the first words in the body of the topic, WroxPBS Duplex Print. This is where we want to insert our graphic. Then click the Bitmap button on the toolbar.

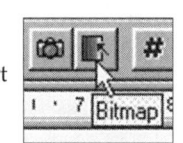

3 The normal Insert Picture dialog opens. Select the file PBSLOGO.bmp, which you'll find in the **\WroxHelp** subfolder of your samples folder.

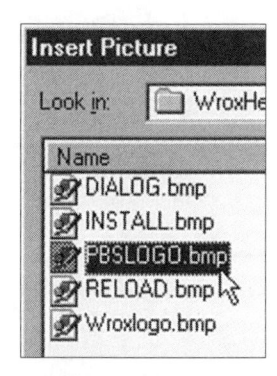

4 Click OK, and the BitMap Options dialog is displayed. Select Align Left and set the Make white areas transparent option. Note that you can only use the 'transparent' option with 16 color bitmaps.

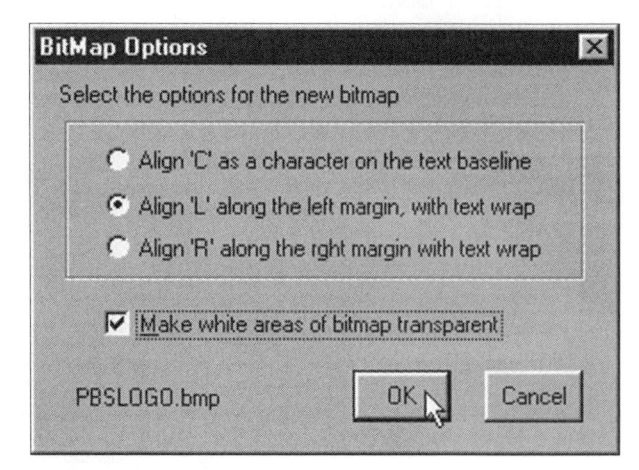

5 Click OK and the bitmap statement is placed in your topic file.

6 At the end of the first topic, add a couple of lines by pressing *Return*. Leave the insertion point on the last line. We'll place a button with a caption here.

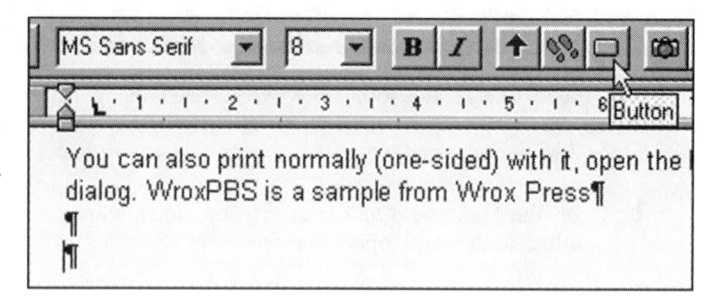

7 Click the Button button on the toolbar, and the Insert a Jump Button dialog appears. Enter the caption for the button and select the topic you want to jump to when it's clicked.

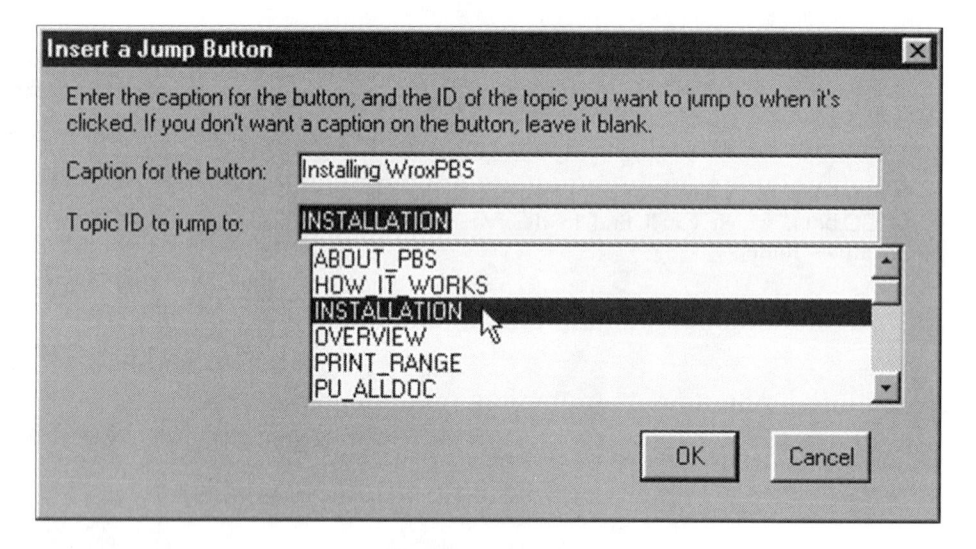

8 Click OK, and the new button is added to the topic.

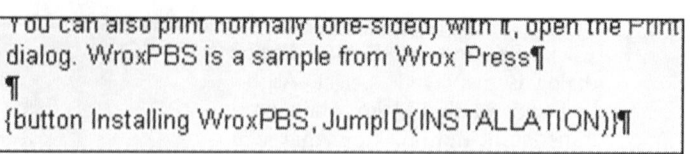

When the topic file is compiled, the new logo and button appear:

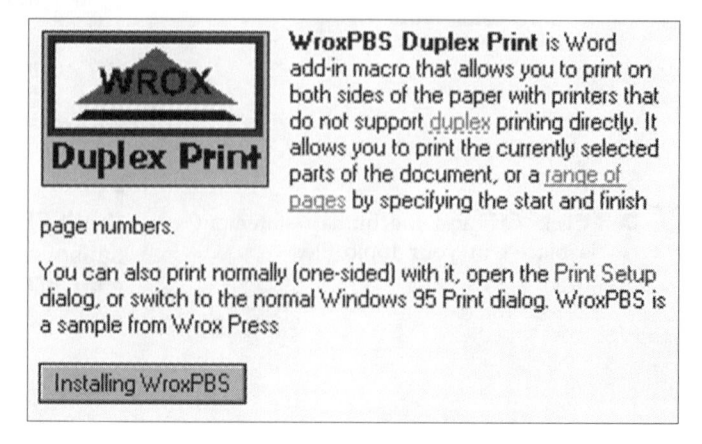

How It Works

The **WroxHelp** template has helped us to insert the graphic and button commands we need. The macros it contains make it easier to select the options we want, and, in the case of the `button` command, select the identifier of the topic we want to jump to. Of course, you can just as easily type the full commands into the topic file directly if you wish.

Before you use buttons with text captions, take a look at other Windows 95-style Help files. In general, these use only blank buttons and pictures that look like buttons. Remember, your application will be judged on its Help file as well as other factors, and you don't want it to look out of place. To create a blank button, just leave the caption empty.

One special use for graphics is where you need to include something that the normal Help file format doesn't support. For example, you can't use superscripts or subscripts in the text of a Help file, or format it as single or double underline (because it's then treated as hot spot text). Instead, you create a graphic that contains the text or formatting you want, and place this in the topic file.

Windows **Help Compiler** contains several built-in graphics for you to use. Place their name in a graphic command in your document and **Help Compiler** will use the built-in default if it doesn't find a graphic with that name in your project folder.

Other Topic Footnotes

Our **WroxPBS** topic file is now almost complete. It has the topic identifiers and titles that we need for each topic, and the jumps and pop-ups have been defined which link the topics together. We have also added the graphics that brighten it up, along with some buttons for the user to select the different topics she wants to see.

However, there are still a few things we need to do. The most obvious is to arrange for each topic to have one or more keywords attached to it, so that the user can search for a topic by using the Index tab of the Help Topics window.

Adding Index Entries to a Topic

We attach index entries, or keywords, to a topic by placing them in a footnote which uses the capital letter **K** as the Custom Mark of the Insert | Footnote dialog. These automatically appear, sorted in alphabetical order, in the Index tab of the Help Topics window. When the user selects a keyword and clicks Display, the topic containing that keyword is shown. If more than one topic contains the keyword, a list of all the matching keyword entries is shown in the Topics Found dialog, and the user can select which one they want.

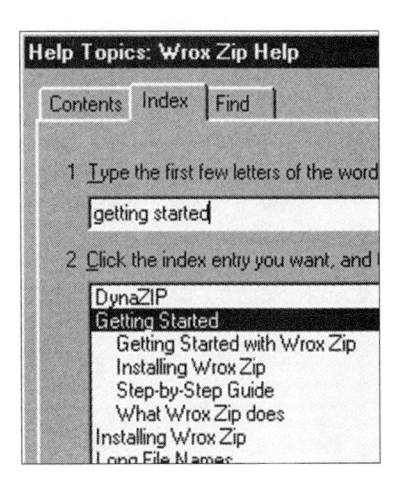

You'll notice that the keywords can be split over two levels, like the index of a book. This allows us to create headings which cover a broad range of topics. In the example here, we've used a Getting Started top-level entry to collect together the different topics that are connected with using Wrox Zip for the first time.

Try It Out - Adding Index Entries to a Topic File

We'll add an index entry to the Print Both Sides Help file. Again, you'll need one of the topic files you've been working with earlier—**WroxPBS2.rtf** will do fine. Of course, you'll need the WroxHelp template to be available in your **\Templates** folder.

1 Open the file **WroxPBS2.rtf**. If you don't want to change the original, make a copy of it in another folder and open that instead.

2 Place the insertion point anywhere in the first topic and click the Index Mark button on the toolbar.

3 In the Insert an Index Entry dialog that appears, type the words that you want to add to the Index tab of the Help Topics window, separating them with semicolons.

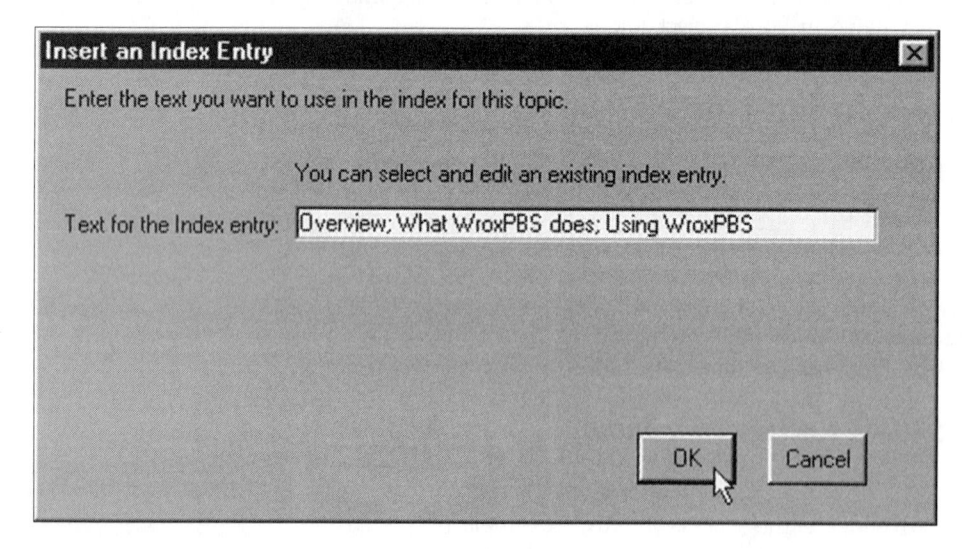

4 Click OK to insert the new index entry, then go to another topic and click the Index Mark button again. This time, the dialog shows you the all the existing index entries. You can select one and edit it.

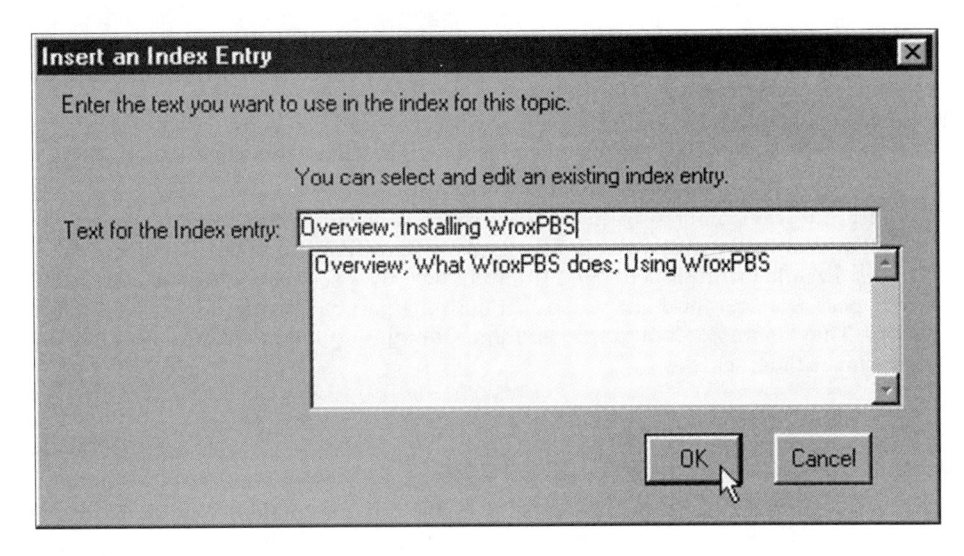

What We've Done

Adding keywords is as simple as inserting the correct footnote, and using **WroxHelp** makes it easy for you to edit the existing ones. Alternatively, you can select the footnote marker in your topic file and use the Footnotes command on the View menu to see the current entry.

The difficult part is deciding what the keywords should be. You need to add enough so that users can easily find the topic they want. They might not know the full technical name, so you should think about other words they might search for. For example, if your topic covers configuring an add-in you might want to place keywords which start with add-in, configuring, setting up and installing.

To create the two-level keywords, you have to structure the entry in a specific way. To create this series of entries in the Help Topics window,

> Configuring
> > add-ins
> > templates

you need to enter the keywords as:

> Configuring,; Configuring, add-ins; Configuring, templates

This means that you need to make sure that each topic's keywords follow the same pattern. If another topic has the keyword footnote,

> Configuration,; Configuration, default options

the Index will look like this:

> Configuring
> > add-ins
> > templates
>
> Configuration
> > default options

You should consider changing one of the topic's keywords so that they all fall under the same heading. In Windows 95, the preferred method is to use the -ing ending of a verb.

The WroxHelp template makes things easier because you can see a list of the existing keywords, select one, and edit it. This helps to ensure that they all follow the same pattern.

> **FYI** Notice the way commas are used to link the subheadings to the main heading. They don't appear in the index, but are there so that the **Help Compiler** can create the correct levels. Each keyword is separated from the next by a semicolon. If you want a keyword to appear as a first-level entry, you just omit the part before the comma, and the comma itself. The K footnote **Configuring add-ins; Configuring templates** produces two separate first-level index entries.

Specifying the Default Window for a Topic

Another type of footnote that you can use in your topic is the **default window** entry. This specifies the type of window that the topic will be displayed in when opened from the Index or Contents tab of the Help Topics window. To include a default window entry, you insert a footnote using the greater-than character (>) as the footnote mark, and enter the name of the window type you want to use.

Although we haven't discussed window types in any depth yet (that comes in the next chapter), you should be aware that you can define windows with different characteristics and create the topic so that it suits that particular window. Each window type has a name of up to eight characters. The default window type is called **Main**.

There are a couple of things to bear in mind about default window entries. If you place the footnote marker for the default window (>) before the footnote marker for the topic identifier (#) in your topic file, Help Compiler will report an error when you come to compile your Help file. If you don't give a topic a title, the default window entry usually has no effect (although this may be a temporary bug in the current version of Help Compiler).

Try It Out - Adding a Default Window Entry

We'll add a couple of default window entries to our WroxPBS topic file, even though we haven't yet defined the windows. This isn't such a bad idea, because you should have planned out what types of windows you're going to use, and which topics will be displayed in each type. Again, you'll need one of the topic files we've been using, and the WroxHelp template in your **\Templates** folder.

1 Open any of the topic files, such as **WroxPBS2.rtf**. If you don't want to change the original, make a copy of it in another folder and open that instead.

2 Place the insertion point anywhere in the first topic and click the Topic Window button on the toolbar.

3 In the Specify Default Topic Window dialog that opens, type the name of the window type that you want to be the default for that topic. Here, we've used a window called steps, that we'll be defining in the project file later.

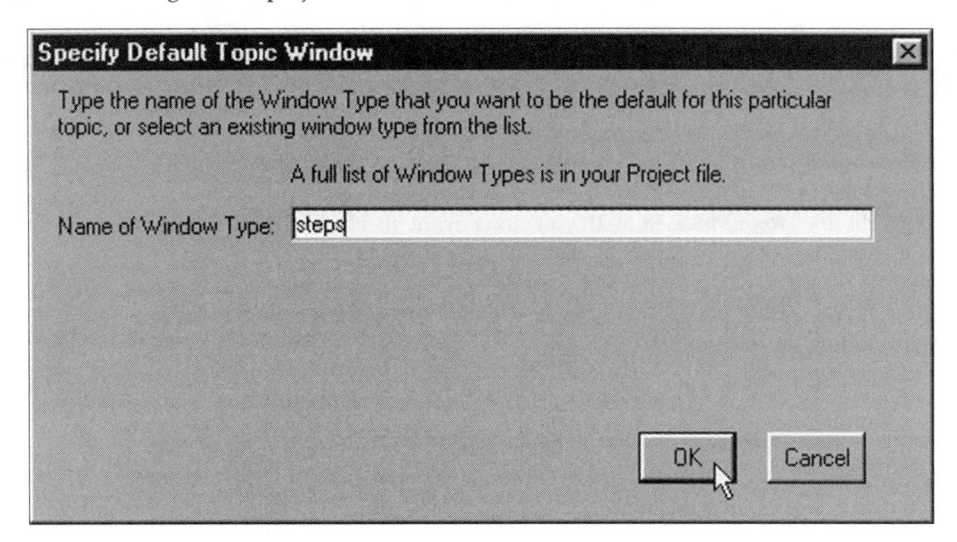

4 Click OK and the Topic Window footnote is inserted. If you look at the topic file, you can see it's been added to the other footnotes we've been creating, after the topic identifier and title footnotes markers.

5 Go to another topic and insert a Topic Window entry for it. This time, you'll see the steps window listed in the dialog, so you can select it instead of typing it in.

How It Works

The principle of adding a default window type to a topic is identical to adding any other footnote type, such as the keywords we added in the previous example. Again, the WroxHelp template has made things easier by allowing us to place the cursor anywhere in a topic, and select a window type from the list of ones we've already used. It automatically places the new footnote markers at the beginning of the topic.

> **FYI** Notice that WroxHelp doesn't query the project file for a list of window types. This would tend to slow the macro down. In WordBasic, it's difficult to store values when a macro ends. You could modify the macro to keep a list of window types in the template as AutoText entries, or in the document as document variables if you wish.

Creating a Browse Sequence

The final type of footnote that we'll be considering in this chapter is the **browse sequence** entry. To include a browse sequence entry, you insert a footnote which uses a plus sign (+) as the Custom Footnote Mark, enter the name of the sequence you want to add it to and, optionally, the position within that sequence. If you omit the position, the topics with that browse sequence name appear in the order you've entered them in the topic file, so you can change the display order by re-ordering them in the topic file.

The full syntax is *browse sequence name* [: *position number*] and the position numbers don't have to be consecutive. If you start by using 5, 10, 15, etc., you can always add others in between later.

Try It Out - Specifying a Browse Sequence

We'll create a browse sequence in our WroxPBS topic file. You'll need one of the topic files we've been using, and the WroxHelp template in your \Templates folder.

1 Open the file **WroxPBS2.rtf**. If you don't want to change the original, make a copy of it in another folder and open that instead.

2 Place the insertion point anywhere in the first topic and click the Browse Mark button on the toolbar.

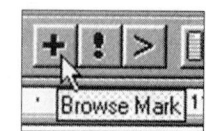

3 In the Insert a Browse Sequence Mark dialog that appears, type a number for the position of the topic in the sequence you're creating, and the name of the sequence. You can use any name you like for the sequence.

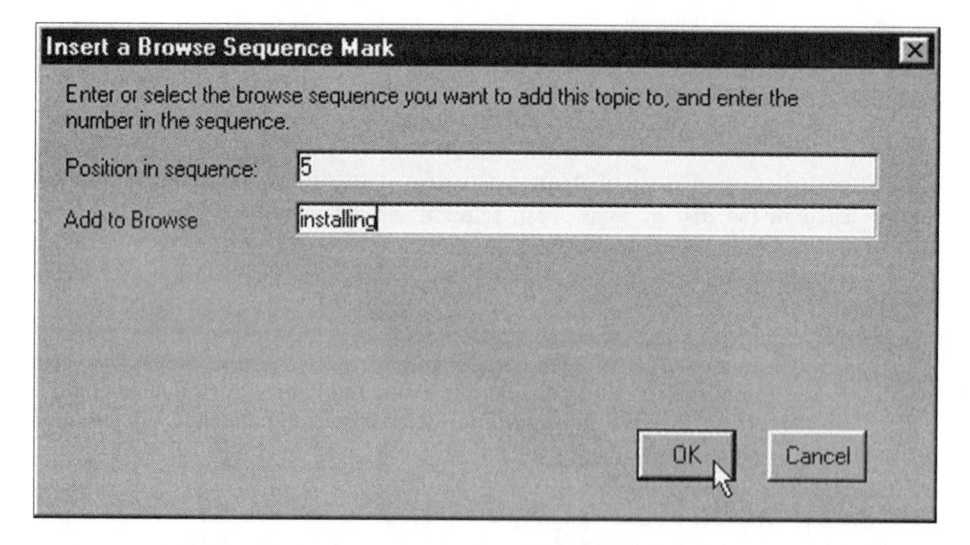

Insert a Browse Sequence Mark

Enter or select the browse sequence you want to add this topic to, and enter the number in the sequence.

Position in sequence: 5

Add to Browse: installing

4 Click OK then go to another topic that you want to add to the same sequence. Click the Browse Mark button again. Now you can see the existing entries for this (and any other) sequences.

Chapter 8 - Creating Windows 95 Help

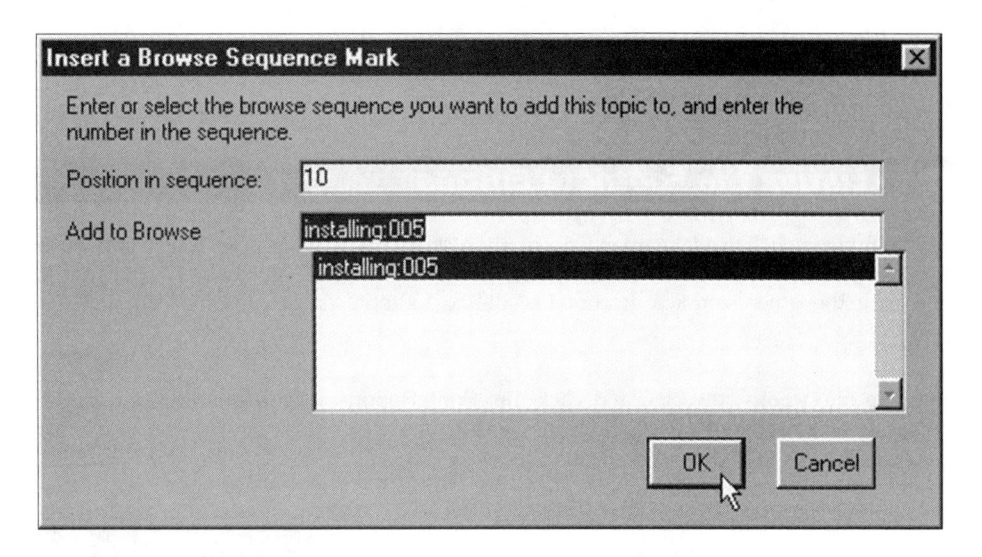

5 Type the position of this topic in the sequence, and click OK. WroxHelp automatically adds an entry using the sequence name, but with the new position. You can examine the result by double-clicking on the + footnote marker to open the footnote window.

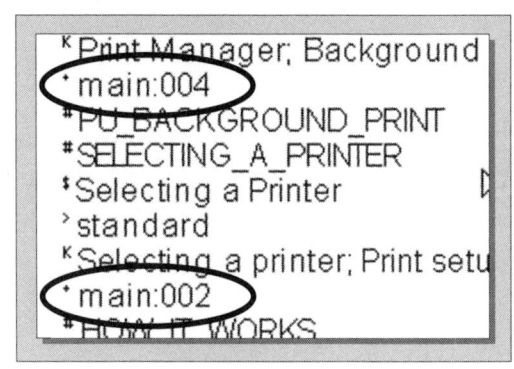

How It Works

Again, the WroxHelp template has helped us to place the new footnotes. It displays a list of the current browse sequence entries, so we can choose one and specify the position number for it. Although browse sequences seem like a good idea, remember that your users will probably be looking for particular information much of the time. Use a browse sequence for topics that are closely related and follow a theme, but don't forget to include keywords and jumps so that they can go off in another direction if they need to.

The best use of a browse sequence is for broad introduction topics which explain how complex operations work, or for tutorials which require the user to carry out a series of instructions. However, most people aren't used to using the browse buttons to any great extent, and may feel lost if there are no links to other parts of the Help file in a topic.

Printing Footnote Reports

As you'll have come to realize in this chapter, much of the way that topic files work involves footnotes. This makes working with the file that bit more difficult. Keeping the footnote window open all the time limits the space available to display your topic file. Finding the footnote you want is even harder, because the footnote markers are so small. If you try to examine all the keyword entries for a topic file containing 50 topics, you soon end up seeing double.

357

Beginning WordBasic Programming

The WroxHelp template contains a simple routine which allows you to list all the entries from a topic file in alphabetical order. The list is broken down into the different footnote types, so you can select which types you want to see.

Try It Out - Listing the Footnote Entries

For this example, you'll need to open one of the WroxPBS topic files and the WroxHelp template in your **\Templates** folder. To see it to best effect, use the file, **WroxPBS3.rtf**, that we've supplied with the other samples. It contains all the footnote entries for the complete Help file.

1 Open the file **WroxPBS3.rtf** and click the Print Reports button on the toolbar, or select Print Reports from the Tools menu.

2 The Help File Reports dialog opens. Here you select the types of footnote you want to list. We've selected all except the A-Link Entries and Topic Macros types.

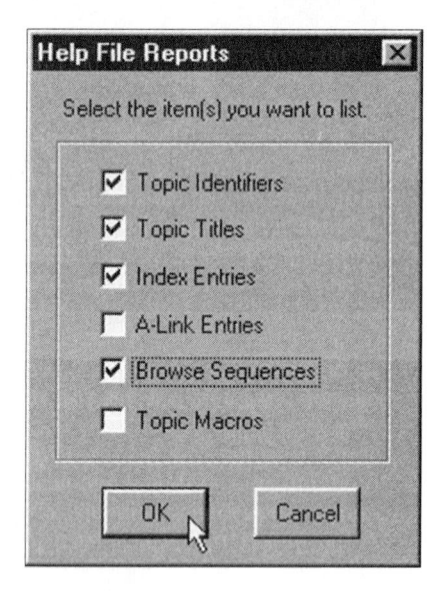

3 Click OK, and the list is created in a new document. You can save it to disk or print it as you wish. Here's part of it:

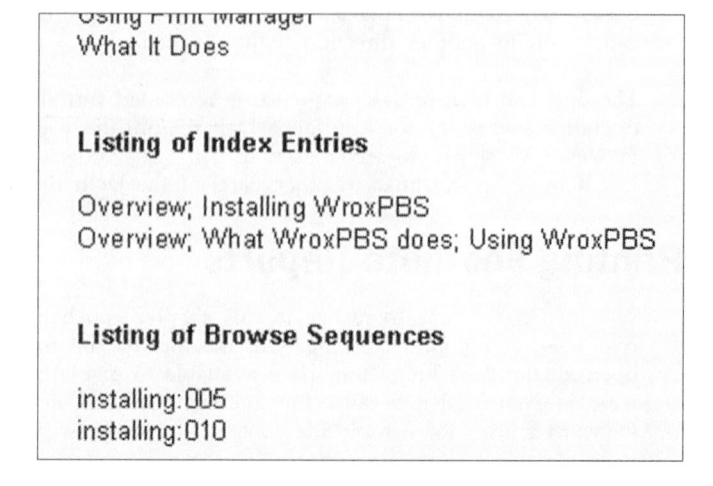

```
Using Print Manager
What It Does

Listing of Index Entries

Overview; Installing WroxPBS
Overview; What WroxPBS does; Using WroxPBS

Listing of Browse Sequences

installing:005
installing:010
```

What We've Done

In this example, you've seen another way that the WroxHelp template can make your life easier when you're creating Help files. It allows you to produce listings of the different types of footnote in a topic file, sorted alphabetically.

However, it doesn't list them by topic. If you want this information, you can open the footnote window. Here, the footnotes are listed in the order they occur in the document, so those in each topic are together. Again, you're free to modify the WroxHelp macros as you wish. What we've supplied and how you've used them in this chapter, is only our suggestion.

> **FYI** Microsoft's **Help Workshop** has a facility to list the footnotes in a compiled Help file, rather than a topic file. We'll see this in use in the next chapter.

Reference of Help File Footnote Types

If you're now confused by all the different types of footnote we've been using, don't panic. Here's a complete list of all the standard footnote types that Help Compiler supports. You'll also see one extra—the final type which uses the 'at' character (@) as the custom footnote mark. Help Compiler doesn't seem to mind a topic file containing 'unknown' footnotes, it just ignores them. We've added this type to WroxHelp to make creating another component of the Help file—the Contents list—easier. But more of that in the next chapter...

Mark	Footnote Type	What It Contains
#	Topic Identifier	The text identifier for identifying the topic in jumps, pop-ups and macros. Up to 255 characters with no spaces allowed.
$	Topic Title	The title for the topic which appears in the Find tab of the Help Topics window during a full-text search.
K	Index Keywords	Contains the keywords which appear in the Index tab of the Help Topics window. Can be up to 16000 characters long, with each keyword separated by a semi-colon.
A	A-Link Keywords	Special keywords that don't appear in any of the indexes, but are used to form links between topics and files where the precise target topic is known.
>	Default Window	Defines the window type that the topic is displayed in when opened from the Index or Contents lists in the Help Topics window.
+	Browse Sequence	Specifies where the topic is displayed as part of a sequence of topics which can be browsed in order, by using buttons on the toolbar.
!	Topic Macro	One or more macros that run whenever that topic is opened.
@	Contents List Entry	A WroxHelp-specific entry that helps to create the file which displays in the Contents tab of the Help Topics window.

We've covered some of these footnote types in this chapter, and you'll see the rest in the next one. However, before we finish, a quick word about the **A-Link** footnote.

Using A-Link Keyword Entries

Normally, you use a **K** footnote to add keywords to a topic file. These are displayed in the Index tab of the Help Topics window, and are sometimes referred to as **K-Link** entries. A special macro, called a **KLink** macro, can jump to a topic by using its **K** footnote entry, rather than by specifying the topic identifier directly.

You can also link your Help file to another one when you compile it, by setting options in the help project file (you'll see this in the next chapter). Once you've done this, you can jump to a topic in the other Help file, just as you do in your own topic file. However, unless you have the original documentation for the other Help file, you probably won't know the Topic Identifier. But the index entries in that file's **K** footnotes are shown in the Index tab of the Help Topics window when you view it. So you can use a **KLink** macro to jump to a topic in that file.

However, in both these cases, if there are several topics containing that keyword, the Topics Found dialog is displayed instead of the actual topic you want.

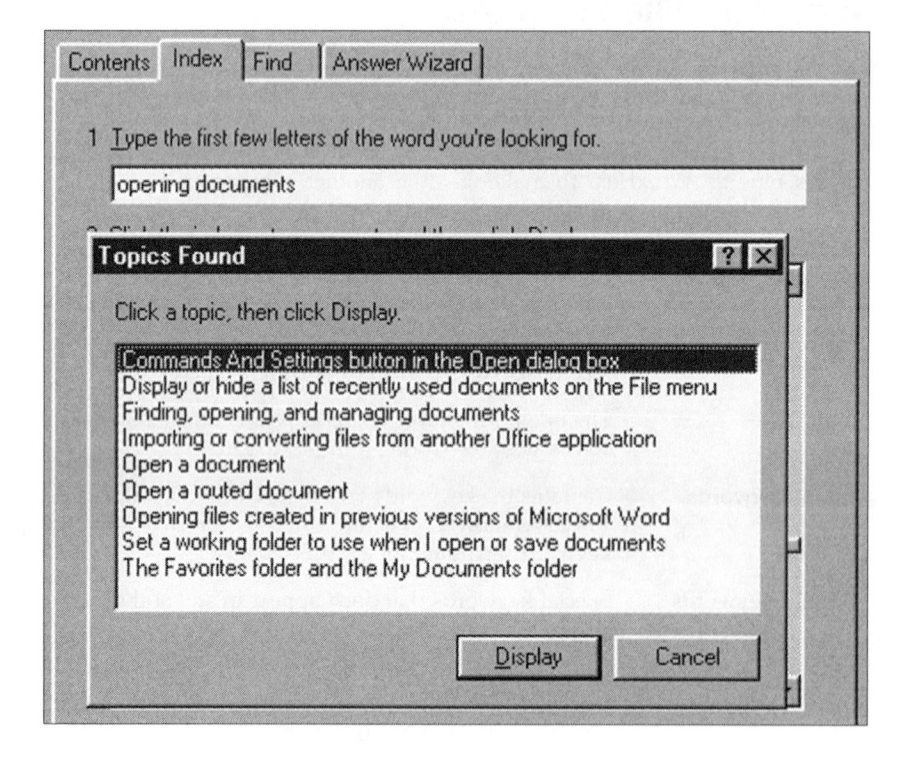

This may be what you want to happen, but if not you can get round it by using **A-Link** footnote entries. These aren't displayed in any index, and must be unique for a Help file. In this way, when you jump to a topic using the **ALink** macro and specifying one of its **A** footnote keywords, you always get that topic.

Many Help files don't contain **A** footnotes, however, and we aren't using any in the ones we'll be creating. However, we'll be looking in more depth at **K** footnotes and the way you link Help files together in the next chapter. Both have exactly the same format, but just different footnote characters.

Summary

In this chapter, we've started off the process of creating our first Help file. We began by looking at Help files and their structure in general, familiarizing ourselves with the terminology. Then we saw the components that are required, the main one being the topic file.

In fact, the bulk of this chapter has been devoted to topic files and the various footnote types that are used to form the links between the topics and the other elements in the Help project.

As we worked through the chapter, we saw:

- An overview of the Windows 95 Help system
- The different components that make up a Help file
- How the Word document forms the basis of a Help file
- The way the document is structured in a Help file

The next step is to compile our Help file for the first time and see how it looks. Before we can do that, though, we have to define the other elements of the project, by creating the project file. This is our first step in the next chapter.

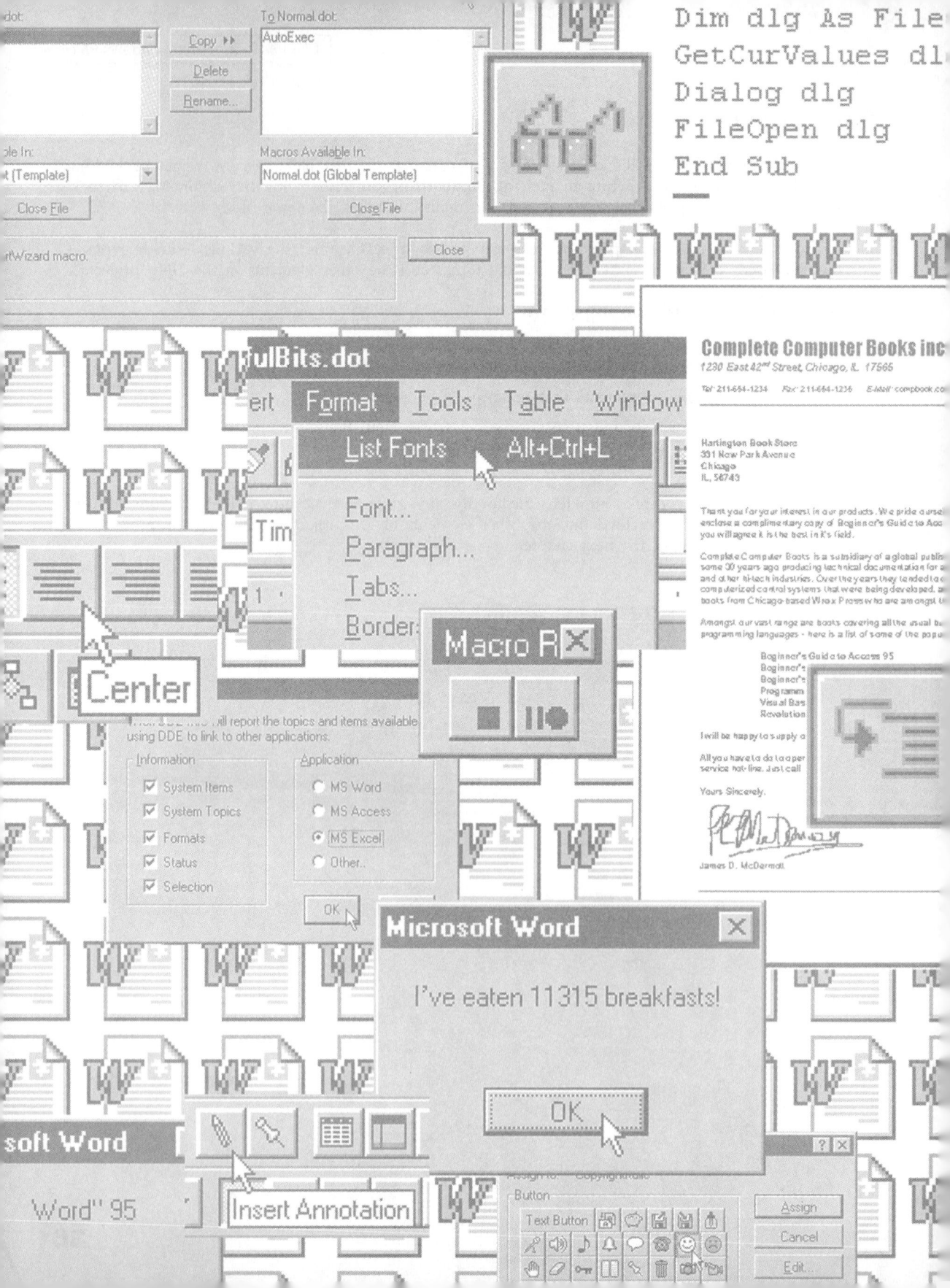

```
Dim dlg As File
GetCurValues dl
Dialog dlg
FileOpen dlg
End Sub
```

9

Compiling Windows Help Files

Introduction

In the previous chapter, we started the process of creating a Help file for our WroxPBS (Print Both Sides) add-in. At the same time, we showed you how the different components of a Help project fit together, and the basics of creating the main part of a Help project, the topic file. Now we are ready to compile it for the first time.

In this chapter, we'll move on to the other parts of a Help project. The second main component is the project file, which we'll look at in the first part of the chapter. After that we'll show how you can add other elements to a Help file, such as sound and video clips, links to other programs and graphics that respond to the user depending on which area they click. We'll also add a contents page to the Help Topics dialog.

One of the things that causes most confusion is how you can use macros to change the way a Help file works. We'll show you some simple examples that are very easy to implement, and discuss other macros that offer you the chance to add extra functionality.

Finally, we need to consider how you can link the completed Help file to your application. Although we won't be implementing full context-sensitive help, because WordBasic doesn't support it like other programming languages, we'll show you what's possible. The Wrox Zip Help file you met in the previous chapter does include a partial implementation of context-sensitive help.

So, in this chapter we'll be covering:

- How you create the project file and compile your Help file
- Ways of adding extra features, and how macros are used in a Help file
- What the contents list is, and how you create it
- How you can link your Help file to an application

First of all then, the project file…

Creating a Project File

The topic file you created in the previous chapter is only one part of a complete Help project. Although it contains the majority of the information, there are other elements which the topic file doesn't include. For example, we saw how you could use various types of window for different topics.

When you come to compile a Help file, you also have to tell Help Compiler which files are to be used and the name of the final Help file. You also need to tell it the macros that you want to run when the Help file is opened, the text for the window's title bars, the type of compression to be used and which topics are to be shown as context-sensitive help. The **project file** acts as the main reference for these and holds a whole range of other information.

Its format is similar to a normal Windows `.ini` file, with sections for each type of information. Most are optional, but you do have to supply a few items. You can create a project file using a normal text editor, or Word itself (remember to save it as a text file, though, not in Word's own document format). However, it's far easier to use Help Workshop, which is what we'll be doing in this chapter.

The Sections of a Project File

The Help Workshop main window shows you the project file as you create it and has a set of buttons which allow you to add information to each section. To start a new project, you just select <u>N</u>ew from the <u>F</u>ile menu, then select Help Project. Once you tell Help Workshop the name and folder for the new project file, it automatically creates the default entries for you.

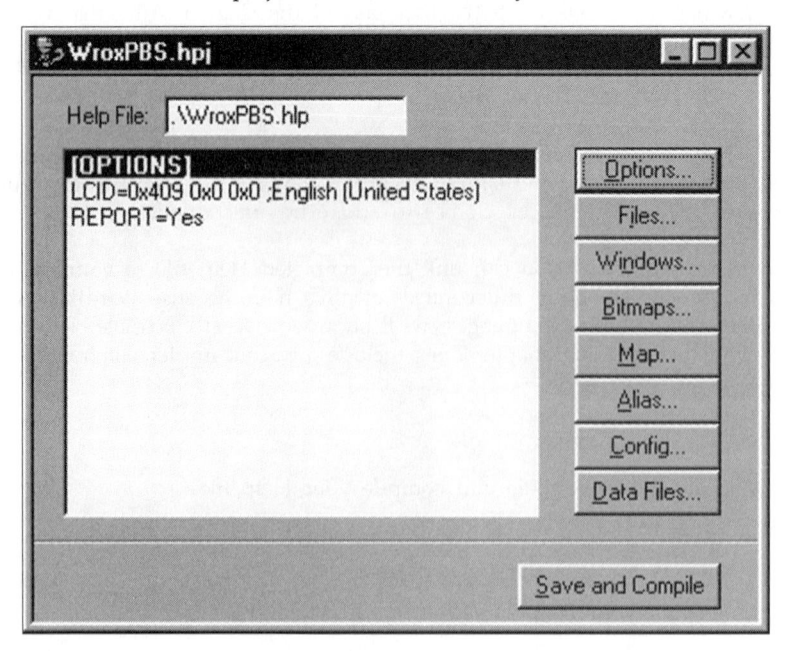

We'll take a brief look at each of the buttons in the main Help Workshop window to see what they're used for and the sections of the project file they create.

The [Options] Section

In the [OPTIONS] section of the project file, Help Workshop stores a range of information connected with how the Help file will be built, and how it will behave. These include the text for the title bar, the default topic, the sorting order for the index and other lists, the text for the About dialog, the type of compression and error reporting to be used during compilation, and whether or not to create the full text search file at the same time.

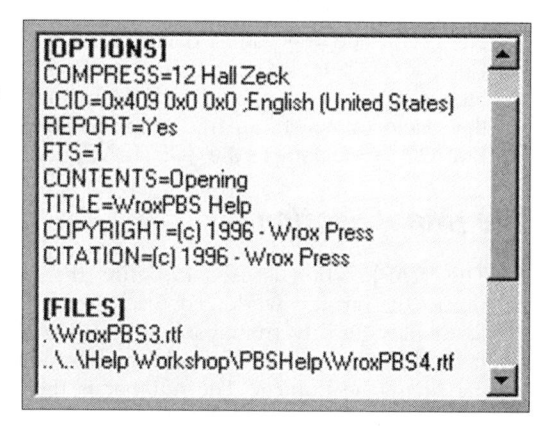

```
[OPTIONS]
COMPRESS=12 Hall Zeck
LCID=0x409 0x0 0x0 ;English (United States)
REPORT=Yes
FTS=1
CONTENTS=Opening
TITLE=WroxPBS Help
COPYRIGHT=(c) 1996 - Wrox Press
CITATION=(c) 1996 - Wrox Press

[FILES]
.\WroxPBS3.rtf
..\..\Help Workshop\PBSHelp\WroxPBS4.rtf
```

You can also specify macros that you want to run when the user selects an entry in the Index page of the Help Topics window. These are actually stored in a separate [MACROS] section of the project file. For each one, you specify the name that appears in the Index, the name that appears in the Topics Found dialog if there's more than one matching Index entry, and the macro you want to run.

> **FYI** When you distribute your Help files, you only need to supply the `.hlp` and `.cnt` files. The full-text search file for the **Find** tab of the **Help Topics** window is automatically created by the Help system the first time the user selects this tab. However, you can set **Help Workshop** to create this file, using the **FTS** tab in the **Options** dialog, and distribute it as well.

The [Files] Section

The [FILES] section simply contains a list of the topic files that you want Help Compiler to use when it's creating your Help file. You can add topic files from different folders if you wish.

The [Windows] Section

This section is used to specify the different window types for the project. For each one, you can specify the title bar text, the color and size, whether it remains on top of other windows, and the number and type of buttons, such as Help Topics, Back and Options.

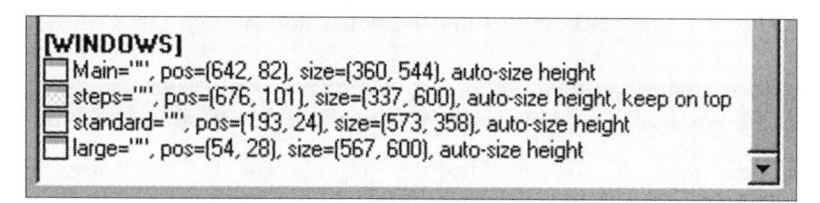

```
[WINDOWS]
Main="", pos=(642, 82), size=(360, 544), auto-size height
steps="", pos=(676, 101), size=(337, 600), auto-size height, keep on top
standard="", pos=(193, 24), size=(573, 358), auto-size height
large="", pos=(54, 28), size=(567, 600), auto-size height
```

For each window type you define, you can also add a list of Help macros that you want to run when that window is opened. These are placed in separate sections of the project file. If you add a macro to a window type called `Steps`, Help Workshop creates a section in the project file called [CONFIG - Steps].

The [Bitmaps] Section

Here, you add the names of any folders that contain bitmaps for the Help file. Normally, Help Compiler only looks for bitmaps in the same folder as the project file. If you have a set of bitmaps that you use in several Help files, you can store them elsewhere and use this option so that Help Compiler can find them. When you specify a folder, Help Workshop adds a line BMROOT= <folder> to the [OPTIONS] section of the project file.

The [Map] Section

The [MAP] section is used to define the links from your Help file to the outside world. For each topic you want to be able to display directly from your application as context-sensitive help, you add an entry which consists of the topic identifier and a unique number. The number is then used to access that particular topic.

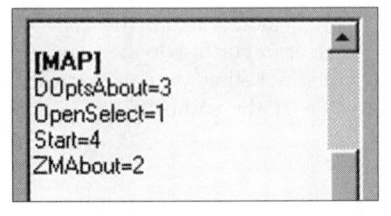

```
[MAP]
DOptsAbout=3
OpenSelect=1
Start=4
ZMAbout=2
```

The 'Alias' Section

Once you've built a topic file, it's often difficult to change a topic identifier without breaking the various links which use it. Instead, you can create an alias, or new name, for that topic identifier. Any references to the new name will be converted automatically to the original one. This is particularly useful if you have to combine two Help files.

The [Config] Section

As well as running a Help macro when a particular window is opened, you can also do so when your Help file is first opened, irrespective of which window is displayed. The [CONFIG] section is used to store the macros that run as soon as the Help file is opened.

The [Data Files] Section

The final button is used to add various types of data file to the Help file, without including them in a topic file. Each Help file has a 'baggage' section that contains items such as the sound files, video clips and bitmaps that are referred to in the topic file, but not embedded in it, say, bitmaps which have been added to a topic file using a statement like **{bml MyPic.bmp}**. The section in the project file where these data files are listed has the title [BAGGAGE].

Don't worry if you're a little lost by this quick tour of the project file. You don't need to edit it directly. In fact, Help Workshop warns you against doing this. Instead, you enter all the information using Help Workshop's dialogs. Now that you've seen what each section does, though, you should be on your way to understanding how a Help project fits together.

Try It Out - Creating the WroxPBS Project File

So, let's create the project file for our WroxPBS Help file. For this, you'll need to have installed Help Workshop and have the topic file you created in the previous chapter to hand. If you wish, you can use the completed topic file **WroxPBS3.rtf** which is in the **\WroxHelp** subfolder of your samples folder. Unless you changed the defaults during installation, this will be **C:\BegWord\WroxHelp**.

Chapter 9 – Compiling Windows Help Files

FYI — We haven't supplied **Help Compiler** with this book. You'll find that it's included with almost all Microsoft programming systems, such as Visual Basic, Visual C++, etc. and with many other software suppliers' products. If you haven't already got a copy, you can get one from the WinHelp Developer's Kit

1 In the folder where you installed Help Workshop, create a new folder called `\PBSHelp` to hold all the files we'll need for our Help project. Then copy `WroxPBS3.rtf` and all the `.bmp` bitmaps from the `\WroxHelp` subfolder of your samples folder into this new folder.

2 Start Help Workshop and select New from the File menu. In the New dialog, select Help Project.

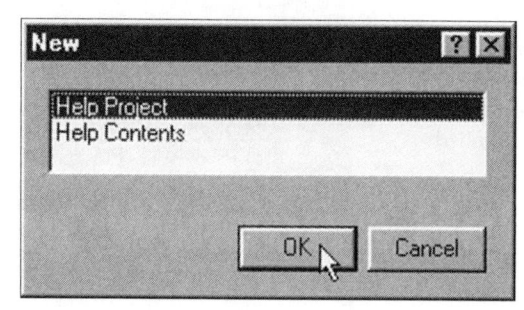

3 Click OK, then change to your `\PBSHelp` folder and enter the name WroxPBS for the name of the new project file. Click Save and Help Workshop displays the new file.

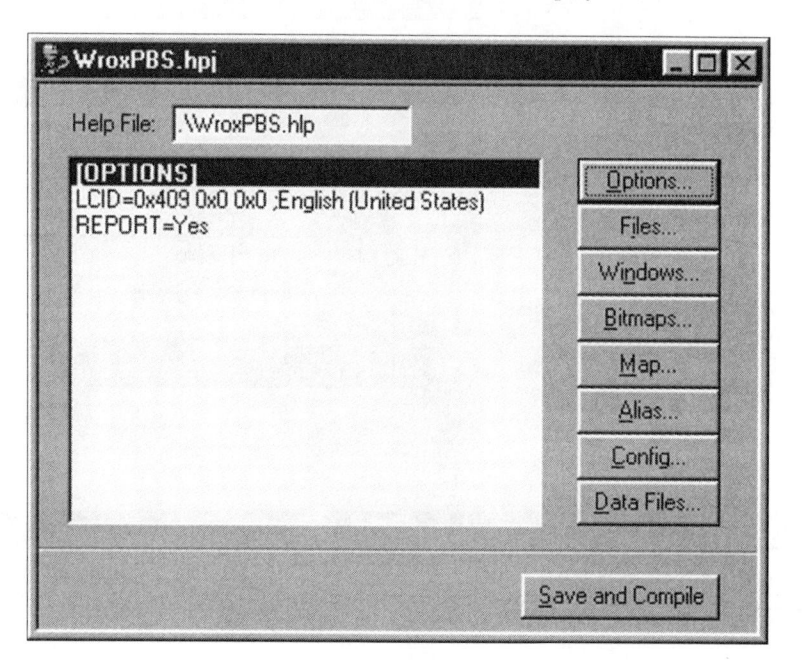

4 Click the Options button and open the General tab. Enter the title for the Help file. If you like, you can add the text for the About dialog and what you want to be added when a user copies or prints text from your Help file into another application (called the **citation**).

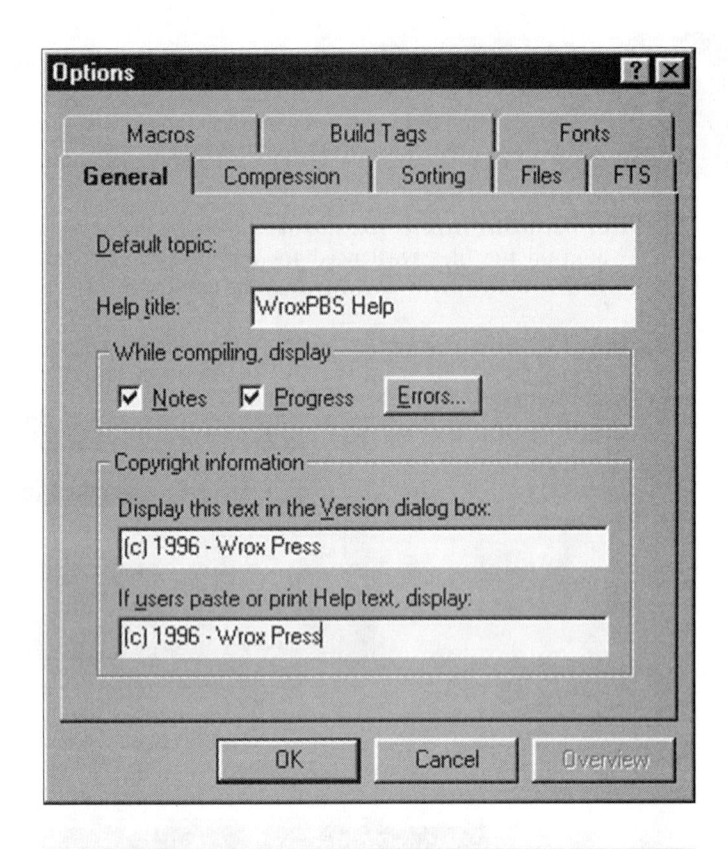

5 Open the Files tab and, in the Rich Text Format (RTF) files: section, click the Change... button:

6 The Topic Files dialog appears. Click Add, select the file WroxPBS3.rtf, then click Open. It's added to the list of Topic Files.

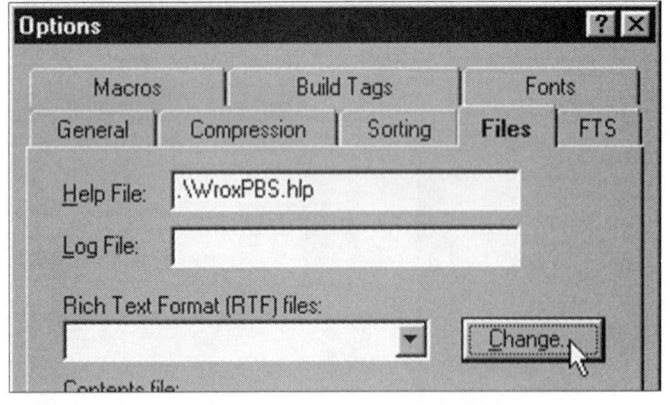

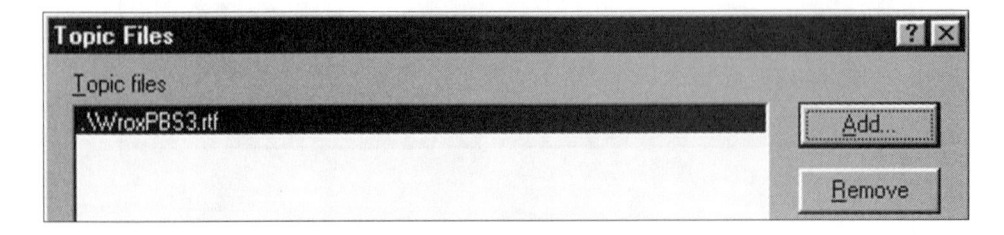

7 Close the Options dialog and look at the project file. Help Workshop has added the options we specified to the [OPTIONS] section and created a [FILES] section containing the name of our topic file:

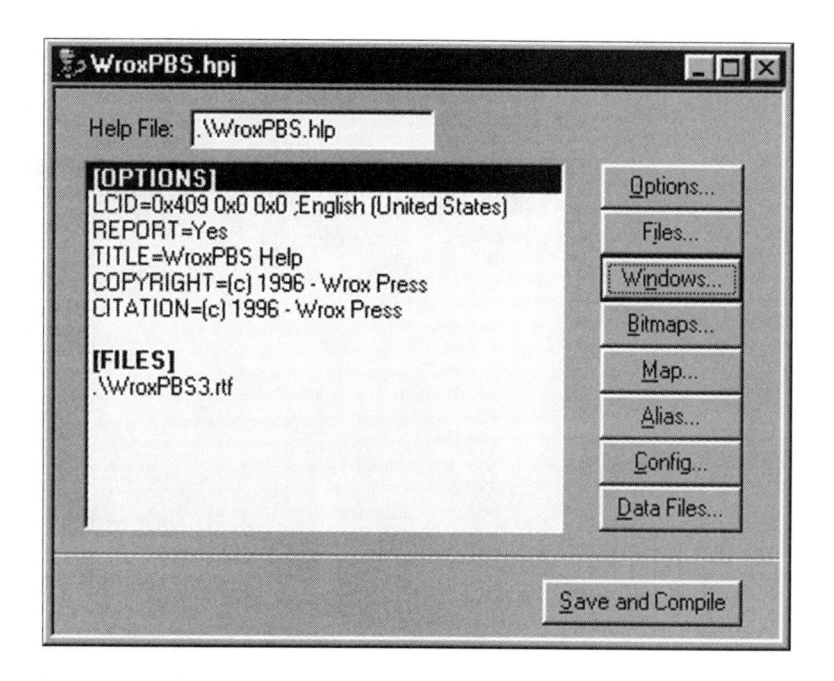

> **FYI** You can also create the [FILES] section by selecting the **Files...** button, which has the same effect as using the **Options** dialog.

8 When we produced the topic file, we added Default Window footnote entries which specified the type of window we wanted that topic to be displayed in. Now we need to define these windows. Click the Wi*n*dows... button to open the Window Properties dialog and click *A*dd... to create a new window type.

9 We'll start with the default Main window. Enter the name Main and click OK. Back in the Window Properties dialog, turn off the Keep Help window on top option, then select the Position tab and click the Auto-Sizer button.

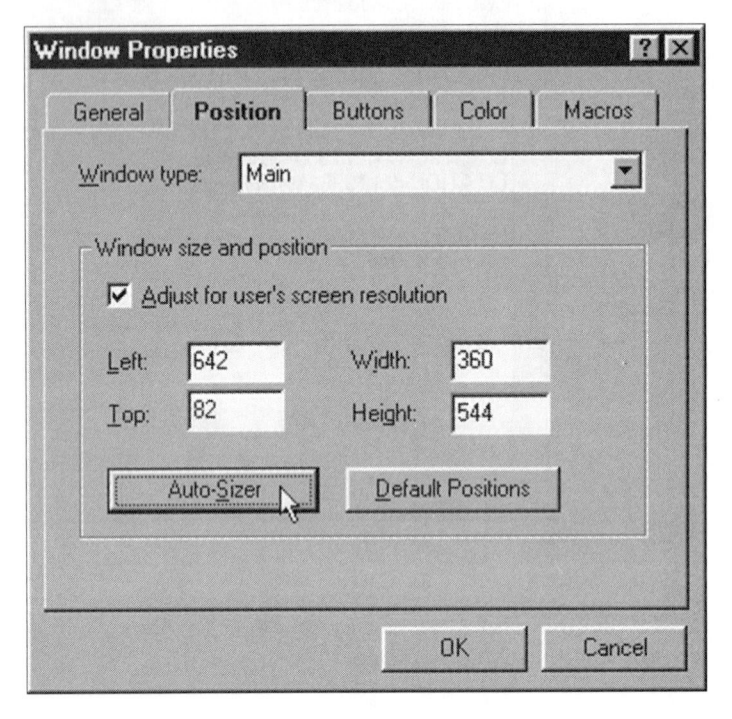

10 A 'dummy' window appears, which you can move and size to suit your topic. It's about right as it is, but this actually depends on the screen resolution you are working in. Once you're happy with the size and position, click OK and Help Workshop sets the values in the Window Properties dialog for you.

11 Click the Buttons tab and turn off the No default buttons option, then turn on the options for Help Topics, Back and Options.

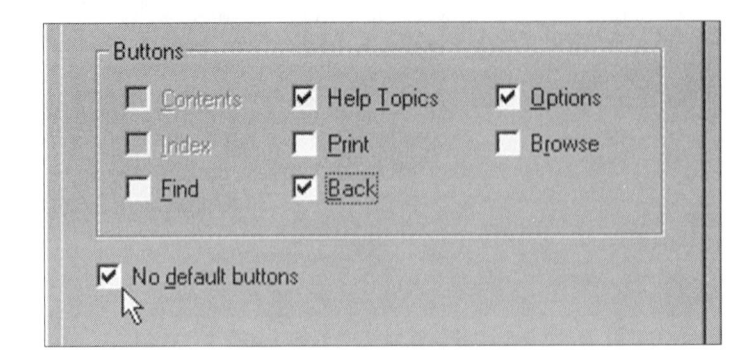

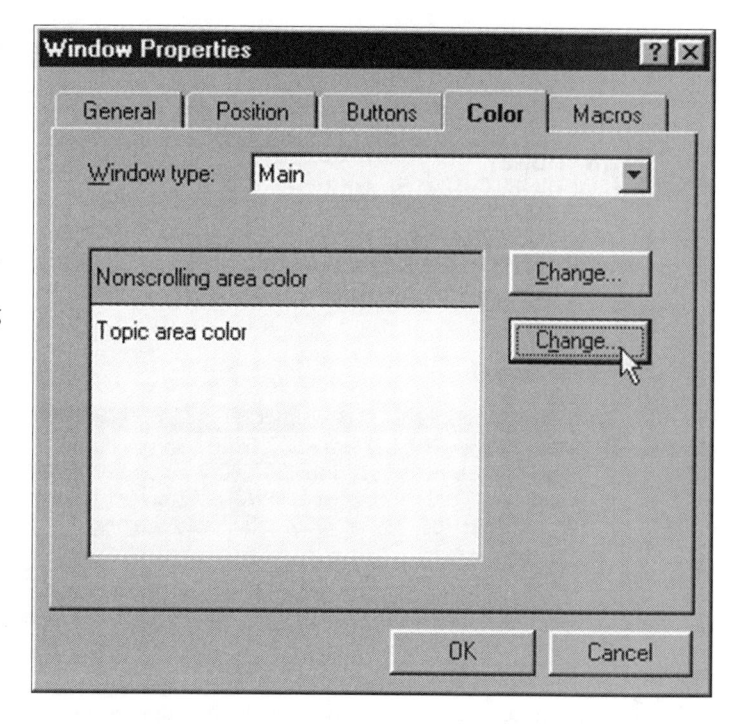

12 Now click the Color tab and change the body of the window to white by clicking the lower Change... button and selecting white in the color dialog.

> **FYI** In the previous chapter, we saw how you can create a non-scrolling title for a topic, by formatting the text in the topic file with Word's **Keep with Next** paragraph format. You can change the background color of this non-scrolling region here as well, though it only appears if there's a non-scrolling area specified in the topic file.

13 Click OK and the new window is added to the project file. Repeat the process to create three more window types. For these, you'll notice that the Auto-size height option is available. Set it for all these windows.

Window Name	Description
Standard	A medium sized window, wider than the Main window but with a yellow background, placed at the top center of the screen.
Large	A large window which fills the central area and almost full height of the screen. The background is white and Keep Help window on top is off.
Steps	A narrow yellow background window placed to the right of the screen, with Keep Help window on top turned on.

Also make sure you turn on the Browse option in the standard window's Buttons tab. Take a look over the page to see how the final project file looks.

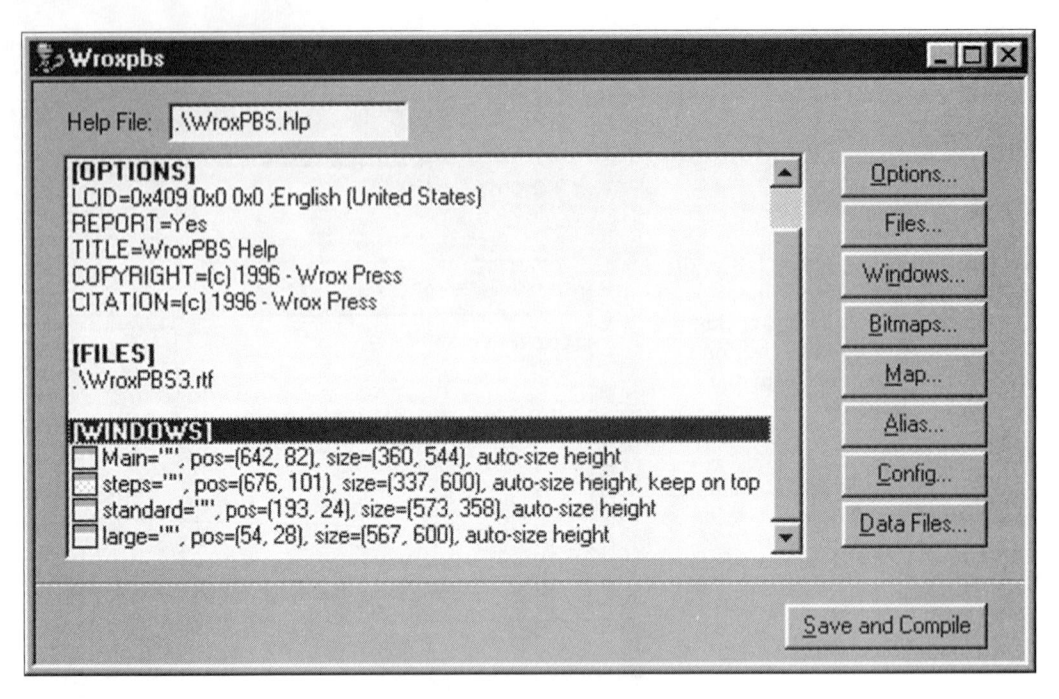

14 Finally, select <u>S</u>ave from the <u>F</u>ile menu to save our new project file. Leave Help Workshop open, though, because you'll need it for the next example.

How It Works

We've used Help Workshop to create our new project file, ready to compile the WroxPBS Help file for the first time. Help Workshop does most of the work. We only need to supply information on the topic file(s) that we want to include and define the window types that are specified in the topic file. We also specified a title for the Help file, which is displayed in the title bar of each window. Now we're ready to compile our Help project.

Compiling a Help File

Once the project file is complete, we can compile the Help file for the first time. This process collects together all the elements required, which are listed in your project and topic files, converts them into a special format, then binds them all together in one file. The completed file has the **.hlp** extension and can be opened just like any other file.

A completed Help file is actually a document, in the same sense as a spreadsheet or database file, and not a complete application. Windows starts the program **WinHelp.exe** and sends it your Help file. There can be several instances of WinHelp running at any one time, each displaying a different Help file.

Help Workshop can create a finished Help file and display it normally, or in a special mode where it's under your control. This second method has several advantages. It can show the messages that WinHelp generates as it displays your Help file and allow you to switch between topics in a different order than if you used the normal jumps built into it. This is called **Help Author** mode.

Using Help Author Mode

When Help Workshop is running in Help Author mode, it displays each topic of your Help file with the topic number (the page number in the topic file) shown in the title bar.

Instead of jumping from one topic to another, using the links you built into it or with the Index window, you can step through the topics one by one, or jump directly to one of them. Notice that the *order* of the topics is that of your topic file.

Key Combination	Effect
Ctrl+Shift+Right Arrow	Goes to the next topic in the Help file.
Ctrl + Shift +Left Arrow	Goes to the previous topic in the Help file.
Ctrl + Shift +Home	Goes to the first topic in the Help file.
Ctrl + Shift +End	Goes to the last topic in the Help file.
Ctrl + Shift +J (Jump)	Goes to a particular topic in the Help file.

The final option displays a dialog where you enter the number or topic identifier of the topic you want to jump to:

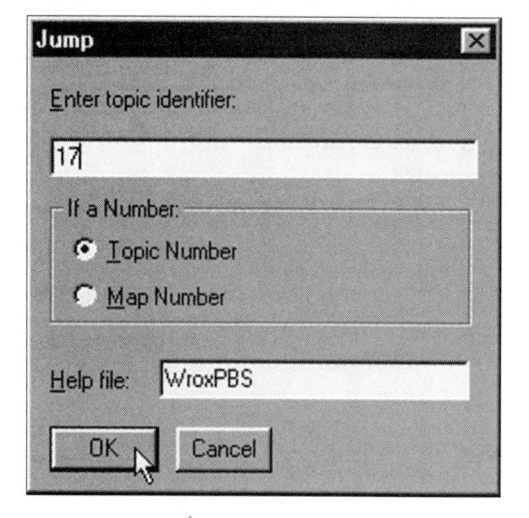

Getting Information about Topics and Hot Spots

One of the useful aspects of Help Author mode is that you can use it with other Help files, not just your own. For example, you can view the Word Help file and get information about the topics and the macros it uses.

373

Once you have a Help file displayed in Help Author mode, you just right-click on a topic and select Topic Information. Help Workshop displays a range of information about that topic. However, depending on the options selected when it was compiled, you may not be able to see the topic identifier and the name of the topic (`.rtf`) file.

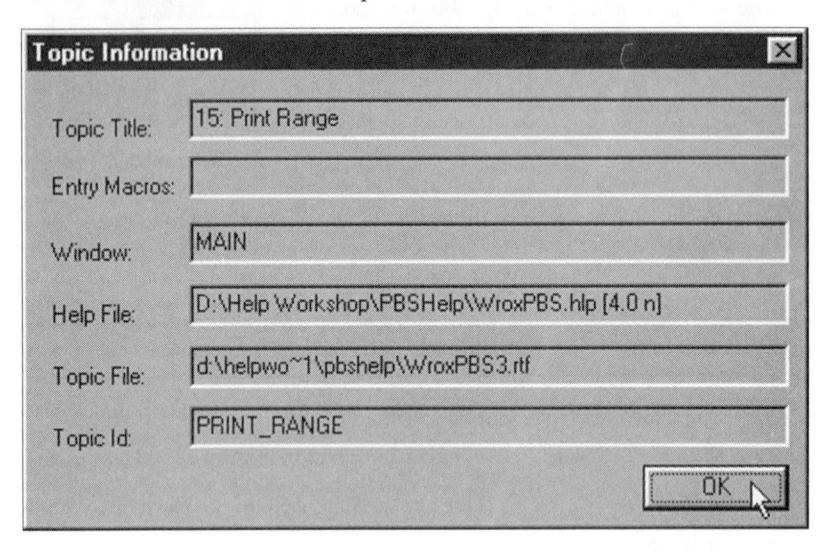

[Topic Information dialog showing:
Topic Title: 15: Print Range
Entry Macros:
Window: MAIN
Help File: D:\Help Workshop\PBSHelp\WroxPBS.hlp [4.0 n]
Topic File: d:\helpwo~1\pbshelp\WroxPBS3.rtf
Topic Id: PRINT_RANGE]

If you right-click on a hot spot in Help Author mode, the text that defines the jump or pop-up window is displayed. You can then decide if you want to make the jump or not. If the hot spot runs a macro (like the `JumpID` macro we used with a push button in our WroxPBS topic file) you can see the macro itself.

So, Help Author mode allows you not only to display your own Help files under your control, but also to get information about other people's Help files. This is an excellent way to find out how the author implemented different actions or behavior, something that you can't do with a normal application.

Viewing WinHelp Messages

While your Help file is being displayed, every action you take is carried out by `WinHelp.exe`. You can view these actions by displaying WinHelp's messages in Help Workshop. Each time you click on a hot spot, run a macro or open a topic, messages are sent between Help Workshop and WinHelp.

Select WinHelp Messages from the View menu to turn on the display of messages. This is a very useful way of pinning down problems with your Help file, as you can see the instruction being sent to WinHelp and any error messages that result. If your Help file is jumping to the wrong topic, for example, you can see which one WinHelp is trying to display.

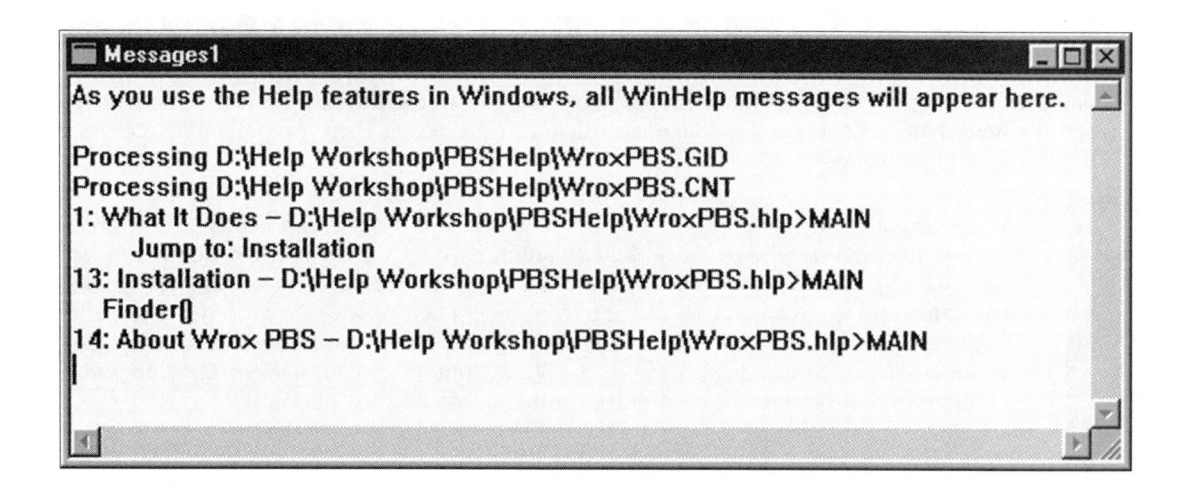

Compiling and Viewing Your Help File

Generally, you'll want to view your new Help file once it's been compiled. Click the Compile button on the toolbar and Help Workshop displays the Compile a Help File dialog. This shows the name of the project file that's currently active. Below are several options that you can set during compilation. You can speed up compilation by minimizing the Help Workshop window first, though, on a reasonably quick machine, the difference is negligible.

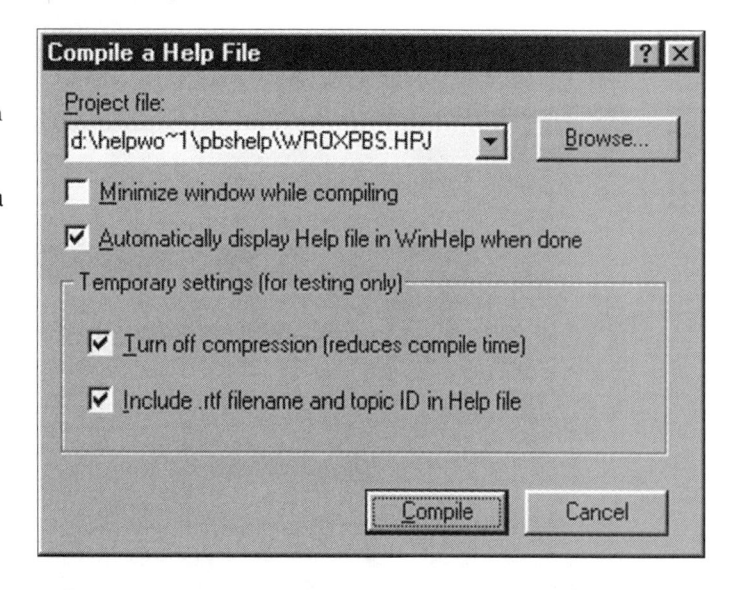

Make sure you set the second option, Automatically display Help file in WinHelp when done. This saves you having to open it afterwards to view it. The other options allow you to temporarily turn off compression of the file (if you've turned it on in the Options section), and include the topic file name and topic identifiers in the compiled Help file. You'll recall from our discussion of Help Author mode that these are generally not included in the final Help file. If you want to include them, set this option.

Finally, click the Compile button and your new Help file is created and displayed. We'll try this now with our WroxPBS Help file.

Try It Out - Compiling the WroxPBS Help File

For this Try It Out, you'll need the completed project file **WroxPBS.hpj** from the last example and the **WroxPBS3.rtf** topic file. Make sure that you are *not* in Help Author mode, i.e. it's not ticked on the File menu.

> **FYI** If you installed the Help file for **WroxPBS** when you used it in Chapter 6, you must rename the original files or move them to another folder, otherwise **Help Compiler** may not create the new file correctly. For the time being, rename the files WroxPBS.hlp and WroxPBS.cnt to OldPBS.hlp and OldPBS.cnt. Then make sure you delete the file WroxPBS.gid. All these files should be in your Windows\Help folder. The .gid file is a hidden file, so you'll need to use the View|Options... menu item in **My Computer** or **Explorer** and, in the View tab, turn on the Show all files option.

1 If you have closed Help Workshop, you'll need to open it first and load the project file **WroxPBS.hpj**. Select it from the recently used files list in the File menu, or open it with the normal Open dialog.

2 Click the Compile button on the Help Workshop toolbar and, in the Compile a Help File dialog, turn on the Automatically display Help file in WinHelp when done option.

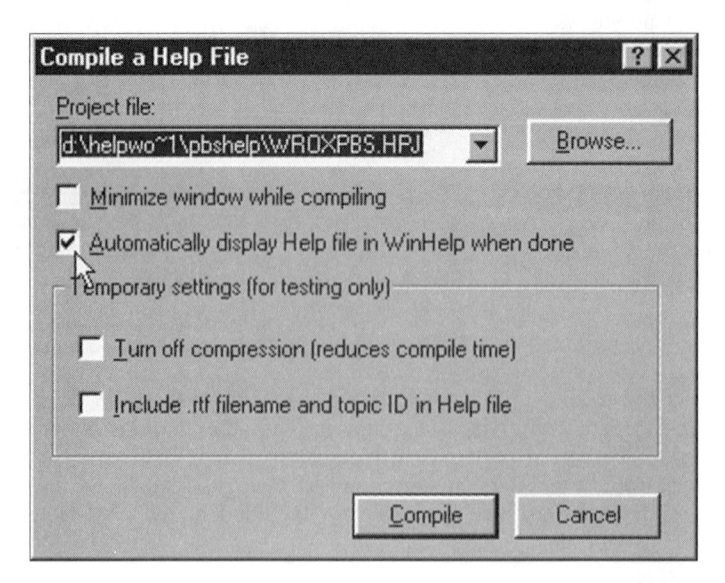

3 Click the Compile button in the dialog and Help Workshop compiles the project to create the new Help file, then displays it.

Chapter 9 - Compiling Windows Help Files

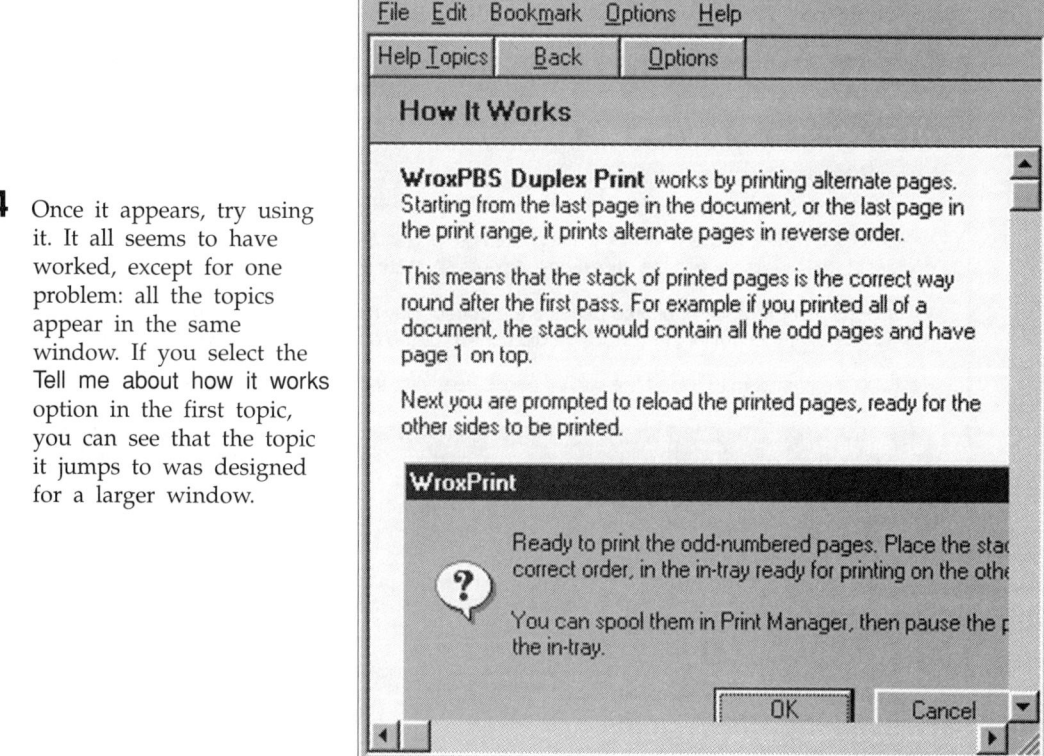

4 Once it appears, try using it. It all seems to have worked, except for one problem: all the topics appear in the same window. If you select the Tell me about how it works option in the first topic, you can see that the topic it jumps to was designed for a larger window.

5 Click the Help Topics button to open the Help Topics window. In the Index list, double-click on How WroxPBS works.

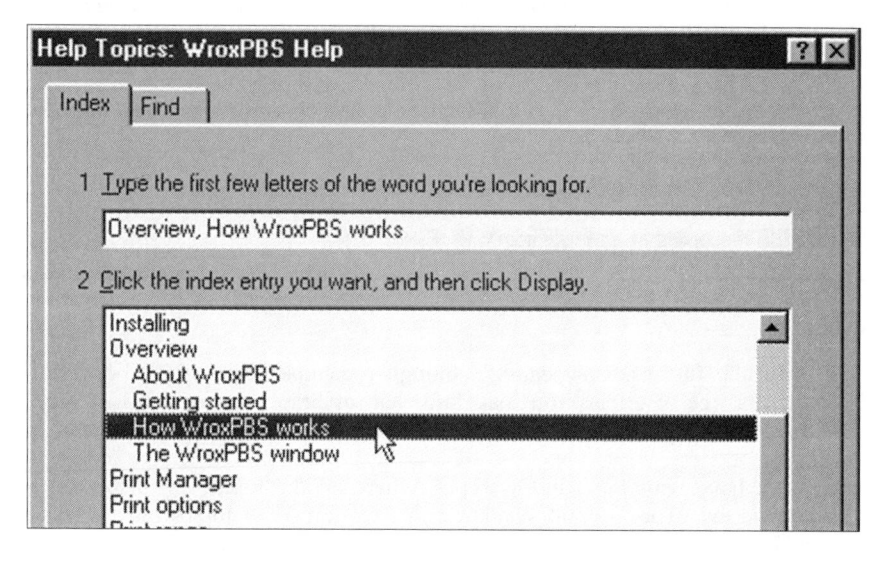

6 This time, the topic appears in the correct type of window. You can see all of the text and graphics (as long as you made the window large enough when you defined it in Help Workshop!).

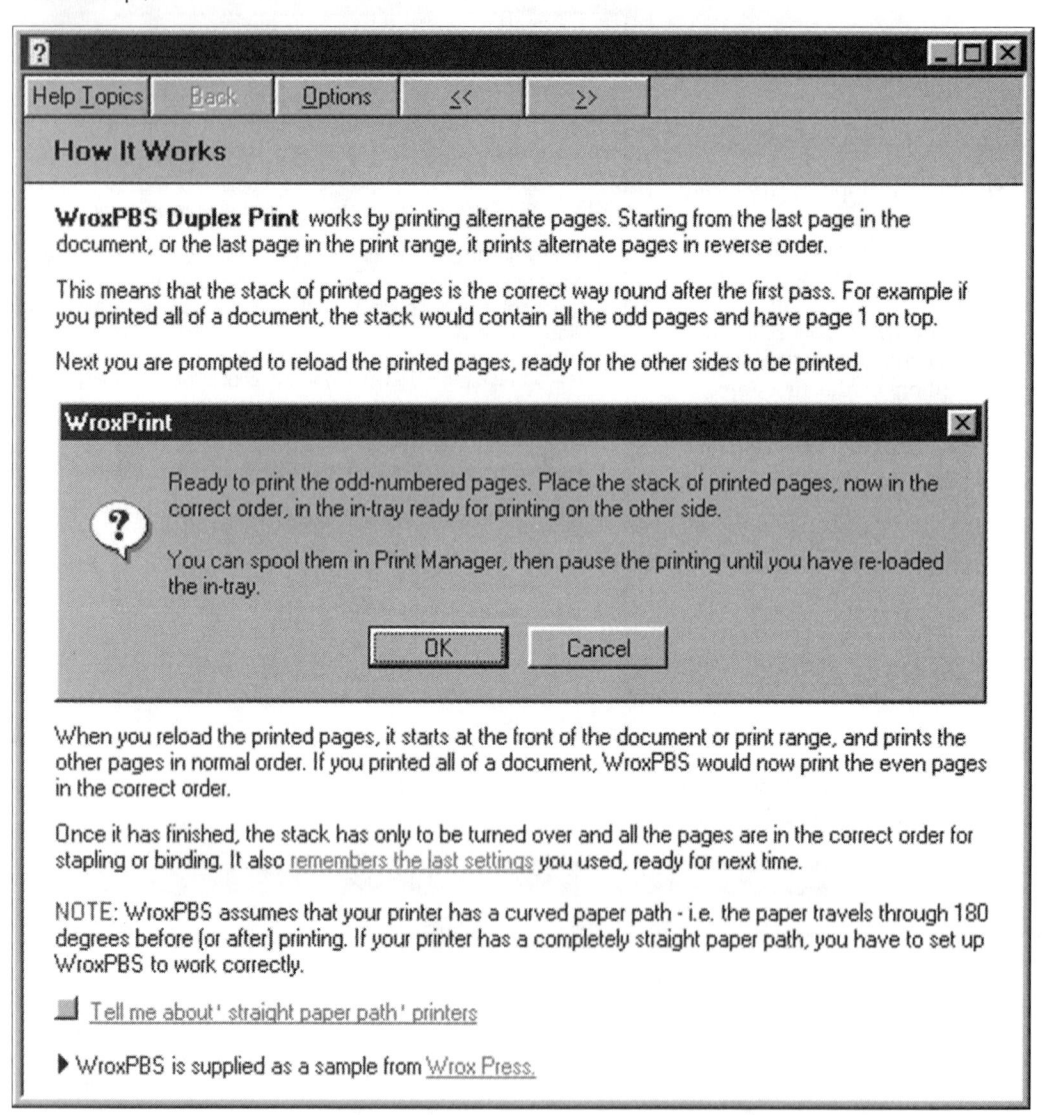

How It Works

Compiling our Help file was easy enough, though remember that you've been working with a topic file which is free of errors. You may find that, at first, you get a list of error messages when you come to compile your own files. However, that's the subject of a later section.

The problem we have with the window types, where all the topics are displayed in the same one, is to be expected. The Default Window entry we added to topics only works when that topic is opened from the Contents or Index tab of the Help Topics dialog, not when we jump to it from another topic. We'll look at how we can jump to other window types later on.

Adding Extra Features to a Help File

The new WroxPBS Help file works quite well, and is almost ready for use. However, there are a few things we still need to do to improve it. Windows 95's Help system supports several other functions that make your Help files both more attractive and easier for the user to work with. Among these are graphics that have several hot spots and sound and video clips. We'll see how to use these next.

Graphics that Respond to the User

One of the topics in the Help file for our WroxPBS utility is an overview of the dialog you see while you are using it. This has hot spots that correspond to the different controls and areas in the dialog. Clicking on one displays a pop-up window which describes what it does.

This type of graphic is called a **segmented hypergraphic** and is created with a separate part of Help Workshop, a program called **Shed.exe**. With it, you define each hot spot area and assign a pop-up window or jump to it.

Try It Out - Creating the WroxPBS Overview Graphic

We've supplied the original graphic for the WroxPBS dialog with the other samples in the **\WroxHelp** subfolder. We'll convert this into a segmented hypergraphic for use in our Help file.

1 Open Hotspot Editor. This is one of the programs included with Help Workshop. If it doesn't appear on your Start menu, run it by double-clicking on the file Shed.exe, which will be in the folder where you installed Help Workshop.

2 Select Open... from the File menu and open the file dialog.bmp which you copied into your new **\PBSHelp** folder in the previous examples. Notice that Hotspot Editor is showing its age. It still uses the Windows 2 style of File Open dialog.

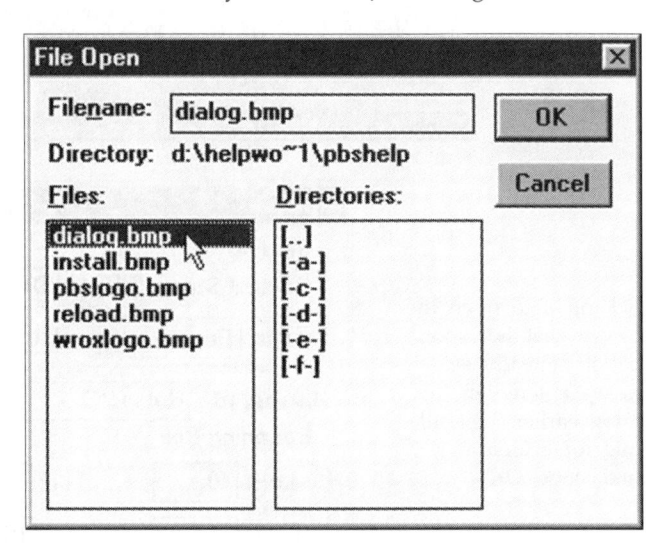

3 Hotspot Editor displays the graphic, a picture of the main WroxPBS dialog. Before we start defining the hot spot areas, we need to set the defaults. This makes the rest of the job much easier. Select P_references... from the _E_dit menu.

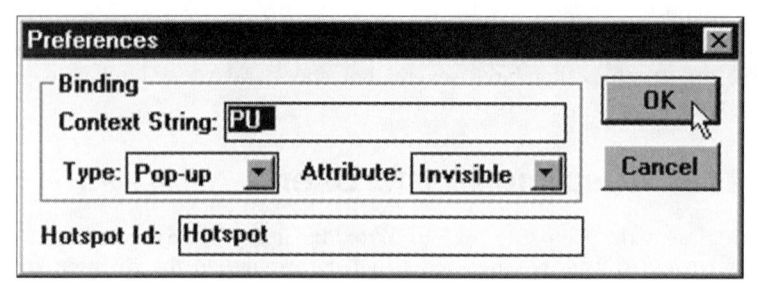

4 We're going to use a Context String (the identifier of the topic we want to jump to) which starts with PU_ We also want the type of hot spots to be Pop-ups, and we don't want their outline to be visible. Set these options in the Preferences dialog, as shown here.

5 Click OK, then, in the main window, click and drag a rectangle round the _A_ll Document option in the Print Range box. It appears as a gray rectangle with 'sizing' handles around the edges.

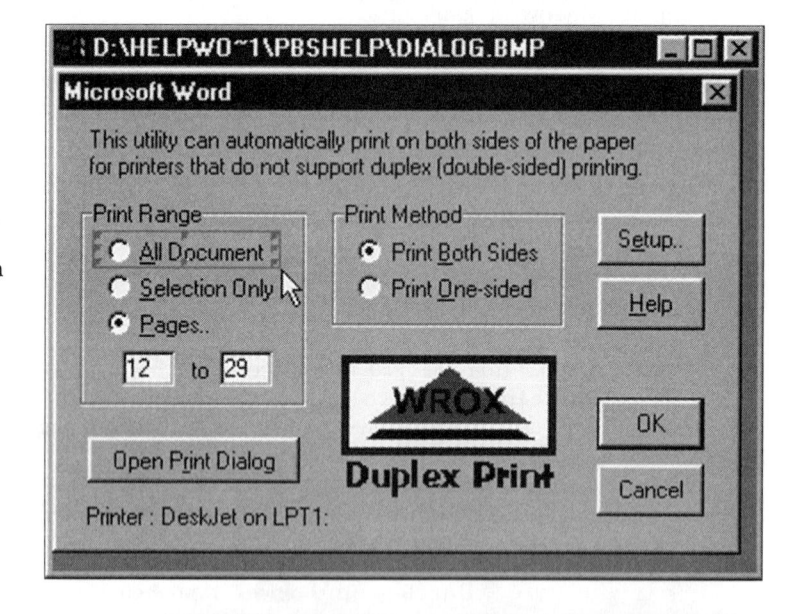

6 Now double-click on it to open the Attributes dialog for that hot spot. You can see that it's already set with the values we entered in the Preferences dialog earlier. Just fill in the rest of the topic identifier, PU_ALLDOC, and click OK.

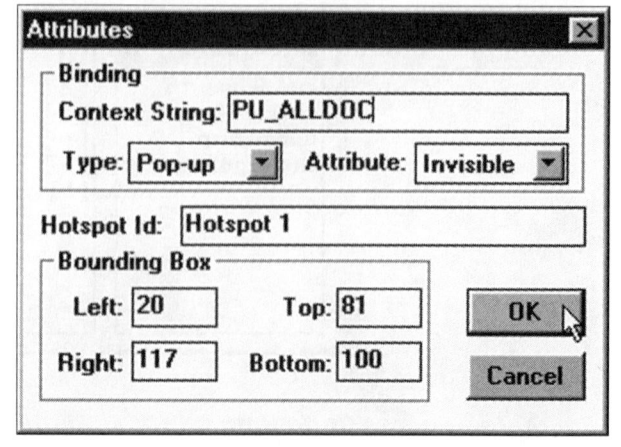

7 Now you need to repeat the process for all the other areas that you want to appear as hot spots:

Context String	Topic
PU_SELECTION	The Print Range, Selection Only option.
PU_PAGES	The Print Range, Pages.. option.
PU_METHOD	The whole Print Method option box.
PU_PRINT	The Open Print Dialog button.
PU_PRNTNAME	The label showing the printer name.
PU_SETUP	The Setup button.
PU_OK	The OK button.

8 Once you've defined all the hot spots, select Save As... from the File menu and save the new segmented hypergraphic as **Dialog.shg** in the same folder as your Help project.

9 The final task is to add it to the topic file and compile it. Open **WroxPBS3.rtf** and scroll down to topic 4, the one that starts with **{bml dialog.bmp}**. Change this bitmap command to use the new segmented hypergraphic instead, **{bml dialog.shg}**.

10 Save the topic file, start Help Workshop and load the project WroxPBS.hpj. Click the Compile button on the toolbar and set the Automatically display Help file in WinHelp when done option. Finally, click the Compile button in the Compile a Help File dialog, select the Show me an overview of WroxPBS topic and click on your new graphic.

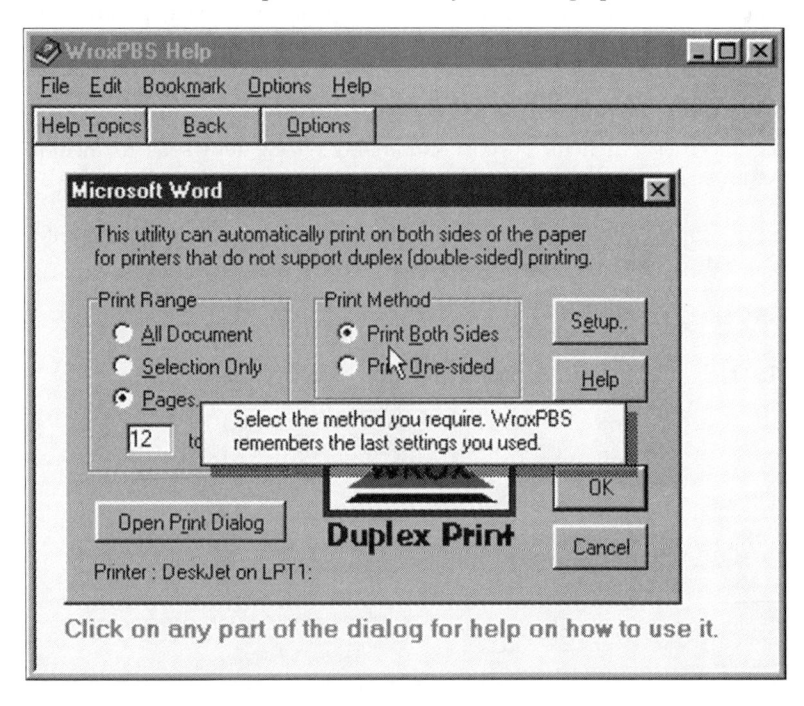

How It Works

We've created a segmented hypergraphic for our WroxPBS Help project using Help Workshop's Hotspot Editor, a program called **Shed.exe**. It's simply a matter of dragging a rectangle over the area we want to make into a hot spot, then telling Hotspot Editor the type of link, Jump or Pop-up, and the topic identifier of the topic we want to pop up or jump to.

Now, when the mouse pointer is over a hot spot, it will change to a pointing finger and clicking will display the topic defined as the context string. (In earlier versions of Help Compiler, the topic identifier was known as a **context string**.) You can also make the outlines of the 'hot' areas visible, though we chose not to.

We used the prefix PU_ simply because it makes it easier to tell which topics are destined for pop-ups rather than jumps when working with the topic file.

> **FYI** If you are creating fully context-sensitive Help, you should use the prefix **IDH_** for your topic identifiers. **Help Compiler** will then automatically check that they are all correctly mapped to a context number in the project file.

Using Sound and Video Clips

You can also liven up your Help files by including sounds and video. Having said that, this isn't a common technique in Help files. When a user is having problems with your application, they probably don't want to listen to music—they can phone a software support help line for that! But there are situations where it can be useful.

If you are trying to *teach* with a Help file, rather than just support an application, you may want to include sounds and video. Help files are particularly suited to computer-based learning situations, where you can provide an interactive tutorial. A video clip can be worth a thousand words of Help text when users are trying to get to grips with an extra tricky operation.

Adding Sounds and Video Clips to a Help File

Help Compiler includes a general-purpose command which allows us to include multimedia files in our Help topics. It's as easy as inserting the **mci** command in a topic file.

For example, we copied the **Goodtime.avi** file from the Windows 95 CD into a Help project folder and created a topic file containing just the command:

```
{mci goodtime.avi}
```

Compiling the Help file produced this, albeit over 30MB in size!

You can control the way the video clip appears. To place it aligned to the left or right margin, you use **mci_left** or **mci_right** instead. There are also arguments that define how the window looks, and the way that the file behaves:

```
{mci external, f:\win95\funstuff\highperf\goodtime.avi}
```

This will keep the size of the Help file down by not including the video clip in the compiled version. When you open the topic, it is read from the original file instead.

```
{mci noplaybar nomenu repeat play, goodtime.avi}
```

This will display the video without the playbar and start button, start it automatically when the topic is opened and repeat it once it's finished. You can use any mixture of these arguments to get the effect you want.

We haven't included sounds or video in our sample Help files, but, if you have a sound card installed, you might like to try the following example which demonstrates how it can be done.

Try It Out - Adding Sound Clips to a Topic File

You'll need a suitable sound file for this example. If you have a sound card installed on your machine, you should find the file **The Microsoft Sound.wav** in your **\Windows\Media** folder.

1. Copy the file **The Microsoft Sound.wav**, or any other sound file, into the **\PBSHelp** folder you created earlier. Then, in Word, create a new document based on your Normal template. Click the New button on the toolbar.

2. Type the command to play the sound file you're using, along with some descriptive text into the new document.

   > **Playing your tune...**
   > {mci play, The Microsoft Sound.wav}

3. Select Save As... from the File menu, change the Files of type: to Rich text Format (*.rtf), and save the document in your **\PBSHelp** folder as **soundplay**.

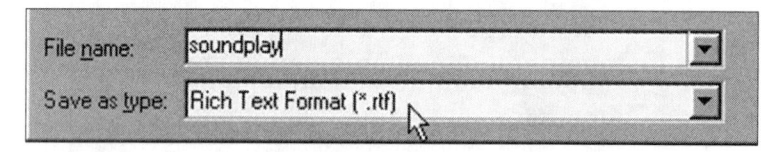

   File name: soundplay
   Save as type: Rich Text Format (*.rtf)

4. Start Help Workshop and create a new project file by selecting New from the File menu, selecting Help Project and clicking OK. Save it in your **\PBSHelp** folder as **sounds**.

5. Click the Options... button in the main project window and enter the text for the window title in the General tab of the Options dialog.

   Help title: Now Playing

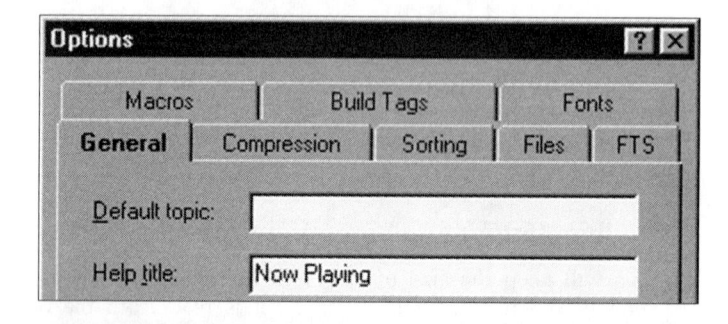

6. In the Files tab of the Options dialog, click the Change... button and add your new topic file **soundplay.rtf**.

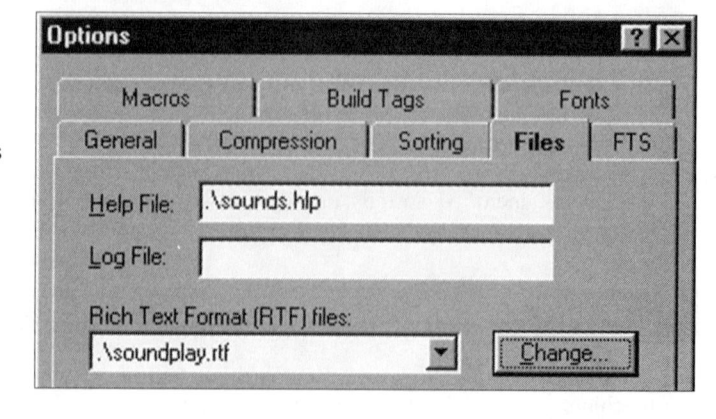

   Help File: .\sounds.hlp
   Rich Text Format (RTF) files: .\soundplay.rtf

7. Click OK to close the Options dialog, click the Compile button on the Help Workshop toolbar and set the Automatically display Help file in WinHelp when done option.

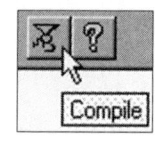

8 Click the Compile button in the Compile a Help File dialog and your new Help file appears, complete with musical introduction.

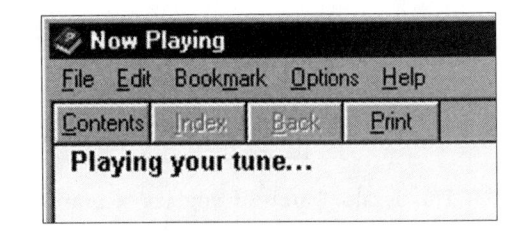

How It Works

We've used the general-purpose `mci` command in our topic file to play a sound file when the topic is opened. In fact, you can use all kinds of multimedia files. WinHelp depends on the software to do this being installed, however, so you should be careful to include them only if you know that the target machine for your Help file has the right capabilities.

If you use large sound or video files, it's worth supplying them separately from your Help file and using the `external` option in the `mci` command in your topic file. Otherwise, they're added to the compiled Help file's [BAGGAGE] section, which, very quickly, makes it grow.

If you have Office 95, you'll find a good selection of sound files in the **Valupack\Audio\Network\Music** folder. While your junior accountant might like to be greeted by **RockDude.wav**, you may prefer to use the more classical **Twilight.wav** for more serious projects!

Changing the Way Hot Spots Look and Work

As well as adding extra features to a Help file, like sounds and video, you can also change the way it looks and works by using different types of hot spots. While the segmented hypergraphic we created earlier is really best suited to use with pop-ups, you can also use various jump commands with these. However, we'll be concentrating on the normal jumps that you find in the body of your topic files.

Changing the Color of a Hot Spot

So far, we've used three different types of hot spot in a topic: the normal green underlined text, graphics which act as hot spots and real push buttons. In some cases, we've used two methods together in one link in a topic. For example, in the What It Does topic of the WroxPBS Help file, we placed a series of buttons with a text description next to each one. Clicking a button or the text next to it jumps to the same topic.

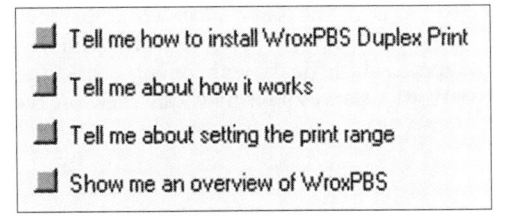

It should be obvious to the user that they can click the button, even though the mouse-pointer remains a normal arrow rather than a pointing finger. Equally, we don't really need the text to be underlined or colored green. The Windows 95 Help files use normal black text, but are still 'hot'.

385

To remove the underline and green color from the text, we just add a percent character (%) between the hot spot text and the jump instruction, and format it as hidden text.

> Tell me how to install WroxPBS Duplex Print%INSTALLATION

This is also handy if you use a graphic as a hot spot. Adding the percent character removes any underline that may be visible. If you just want to remove the green color, but leave the underline, use an asterisk (*) rather than a percent character.

Specifying the Window Type to Jump To

When we first compiled our WroxPBS Help file, we discovered a problem. When we jumped to a different topic, it appeared in the same window even though we designed it to fit a different one. To overcome this, we can specify the window type that we want the new topic to appear in as part of the jump instruction.

For a normal jump instruction, we just add a greater than (>) character, followed by the name of the window type (which must be defined in the project file) and format it as hidden text. To display the topic with the identifier **INSTALL** in a window type called **steps**, we would use:

> Tell me how to install itINSTALL>steps

In a macro jump instruction, however, we have to switch things around. For example, the **button** command uses a macro to perform the jump action. In this case, to display the **INSTALL** topic in a the **steps** window type, we use:

> { button Installing It, JumpID(>steps, INSTALL) }

Jumping to Topics in Other Help Files

When you create a jump or pop-up like those we've seen so far, WinHelp assumes that the new topic is in the same Help file and reports an error if it can't be found. Often, it's useful to be able to jump to topics in a different Help file. For example, in the Wrox Zip help file there's a topic which deals with opening documents and zip files. If the user wants help on the normal Word Open dialog, they can click on the Word Open dialog hot spot.

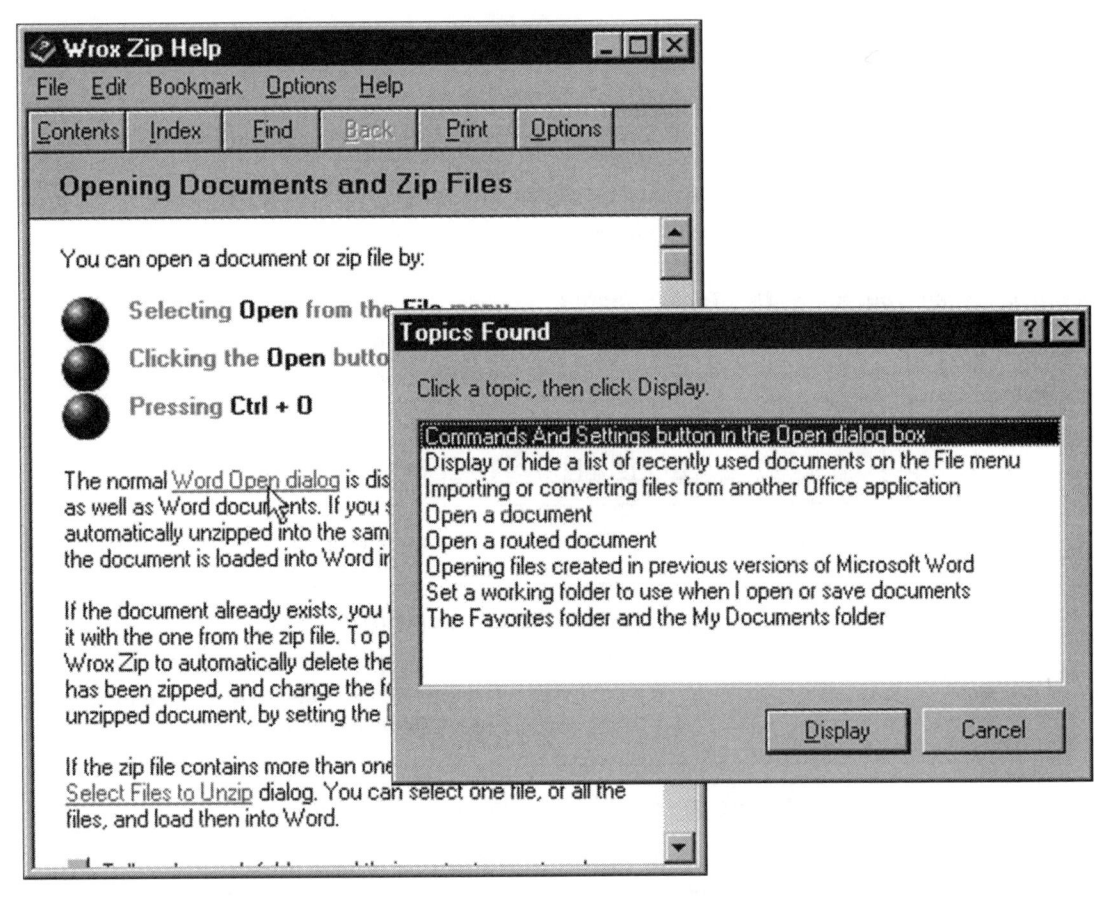

This displays the Topics Found dialog, but the topics that appear are actually in the Word Help file, not our Wrox Zip Help file. Selecting one opens that topic in our Wrox Zip Help window rather than in the normal Word Help window.

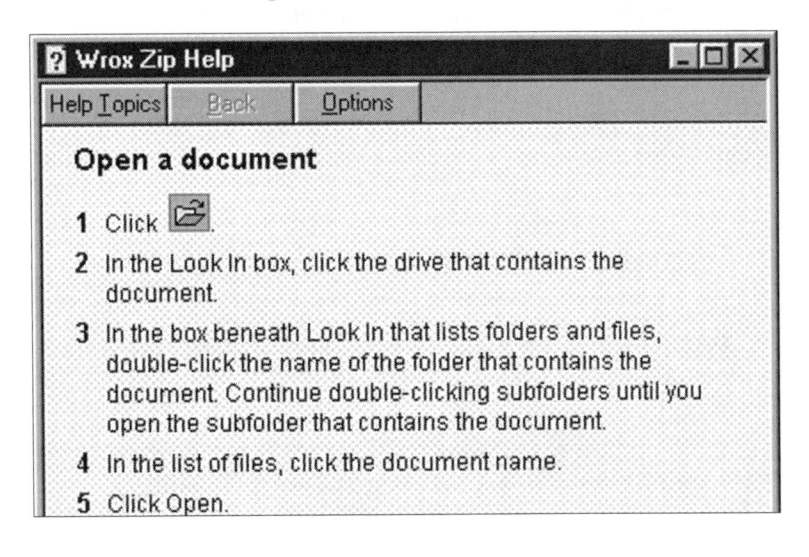

So, this gives us a way of seamlessly linking our Help file to those supplied by other software companies, not just our own. We can jump to a topic in another Help file in four ways:

- By specifying the topic identifier.
- By using a **KLink** macro and specifying the index entry.
- By using an **ALink** macro and specifying the **A**-type footnote text.
- By using the topic's hash number.

Jumping When You Know the Topic Identifier

If you know the topic identifier of the topic you want to jump to, you can add the name of the other Help file to the normal or macro jump instruction. To jump to the **INSTALL** topic in a file **MyHelp.hlp**, we use:

```
Tell me how to install itINSTALL@MyHelp.hlp
```

If we need to use a macro, such as in a **button** command, the form is:

```
{ button Installing It, JumpID( MyHelp.hlp, INSTALL) }
```

Of course, we can also specify the window type. To jump to the **INSTALL** topic, and display it in a window type called **steps**, we could use either of these methods:

```
Tell me how to install itINSTALL@MyHelp.hlp>steps
{ button Installing It, JumpID( MyHelp.hlp>steps, INSTALL) }
```

Jumping to a Topic with a KLink macro

Generally, though, we won't know the topic identifier of the topic we want to jump to. Help authors don't usually include these in the compiled Help file, as you saw earlier when we compiled our WroxPBS Help file. Instead, we can jump to a topic using the **K**-type Index footnotes they have included and which are displayed in the Index tab of the Help Topics dialog.

To jump to a topic in another Help file, which appears in the index under Installing MyApp, we could use:

```
Tell me how to install it!KLink("Installing MyApp")
```

Notice that the **KLink** macro is preceded by an exclamation mark. You have to do this whenever you use a macro in a normal hot spot. To place the **KLink** macro in a button command, we can use:

```
{ button Installing It, KLink(Installing MyApp) }
```

> **FYI** Notice that you have to use inverted commas when you use a `KLink` macro in a normal jump, but not in a button command.

Because we can always open the Index tab for a Help file, we can find the **K**-type footnote entry we want and use that in a jump instruction. This is how it works in the WroxPBS Help file. The only problem is that, if there's more than one topic with that index entry, we get the Topics Found dialog, as you saw earlier, rather than jumping directly to it.

Jumping to a Topic with an ALink macro

The other alternative allows us to jump directly to a topic by specifying its **A**-type footnote text in an `ALink` macro. The syntax of an `ALink` macro is identical to the `KLink` macro, but it displays the topic with a matching **A**-type footnote entry instead. However, many Help files, including the Word Help file, don't include **A**-type footnotes. Normally, Help authors only include these if they know other developers will need to display particular topics.

> **FYI** To use a `KLink` or `ALink` jump, we also have to add the name of the other Help file to our own Help project, so that WinHelp knows where to look. We do this in the contents list file rather than the project file. You'll see how when we look at the contents list towards the end of this chapter.

Jumping to a Topic Using its Hash Number

If you know the unique hash number of a topic, you can jump directly to it by specifying this number in a `JumpHash` macro. The hash number is defined for a topic when the Help file is being built. However, there's no reason to assume that they will stay the same in new versions, so you may find that your jumps fail with different versions of the same Help file.

Using a `KLink` jump is generally safer because, even if the Help file has changed, the Topics Found dialog will still display any that match and jump to the correct one. Of course, if the supplier updates their Help file by adding more topics to it, the Topics Found dialog will show these new topics as well.

The `JumpHash` macro is identical to the `JumpID` macro, except that you specify the hash number of the topic rather than the topic identifier:

```
{ button Installing It, JumpHash( MyHelp.hlp, 2148312939) }
```

Before you can use a `JumpHash` macro, you have to know the hash numbers for your target Help file. This and other information can be provided by Help Workshop.

Getting Information about Other Help Files

While you can get information about the **K**-footnotes in another Help file by looking at the Index tab of the Help Topics window, you can't do this to find the **A**-type footnotes, hash numbers or topic identifiers. However, Help Workshop can help you to investigate other Help files.

We used Help Author mode earlier in the chapter to examine our own Help file. You can also use it while running other people's Help files. Make sure Help Author is ticked in the File menu and select Run WinHelp.... In the View Help File dialog, select the Help file you want to run and click View Help.

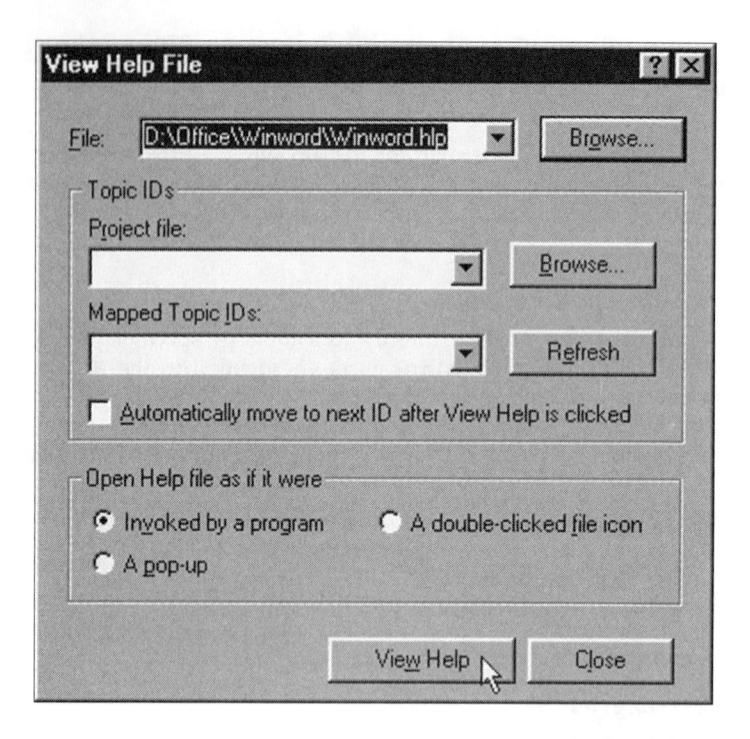

The file (here it's Word's own Help file) is displayed in Help Author mode. You can see the topic number at the top of the window, but right-clicking doesn't produce the topic identifier because when it was compiled the author chose not to include them.

Our other option is to run a report on the Help file. Select Report... from the File menu and you can select what type of information you want to know. Here, we've selected Hash numbers, but you can also get a listing of other types. We tried the A keywords option, but there are none in the Word Help file.

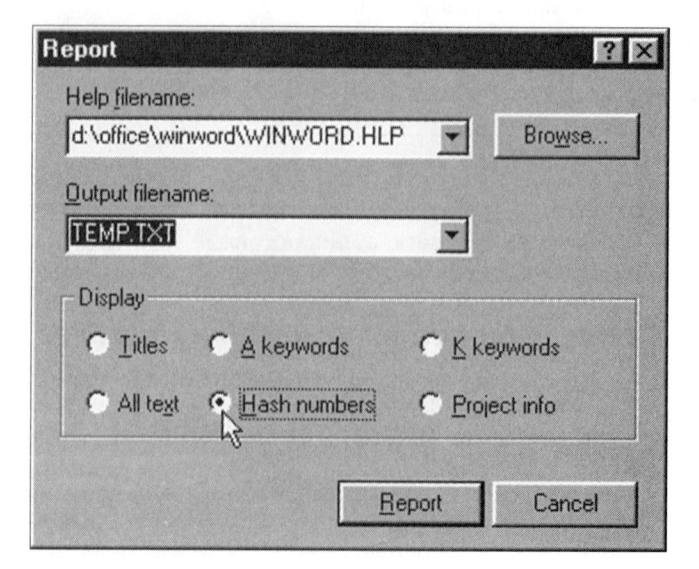

The result of the Hash numbers report is shown opened in WordPad, so you can quite easily use the **JumpHash** macro to jump to any particular topic directly if you wish.

```
Hash numbers in D:\Office\Winword\Winword.hlp

Hash #          Topic #         Topic Title
2148312939      (0x800ca76b)    1005    Entries in the File Name box
2148684251      (0x801251db)    448     Delete a data field
2149258122      (0x801b138a)    872     The Tagged Image File Format (.TIF) filter
2149503552      (0x801ed240)    6       Insert an AutoText entry
2167214671      (0x812d124f)    966     Route a document
```

Try It Out - Changing the Hot Spots in Our WroxPBS Help File

Before we go any further, we'll add some of the different types of jumps to the WroxPBS Help file, so you can see the results. You can use the routines in the WroxHelp template to help you. You'll need the **WroxPBS3.rtf** topic file and the **WroxPBS.hpj** project file that we've been using throughout this chapter.

1 Open the topic file **WroxPBS3.rtf** and, in the first topic, find the line that creates the Tell me how to install WroxPBS button and text. Delete it and leave the cursor at the start of that line.

```
¶
{button , JumpID(INSTALLATION)} Tell me how to install WroxPBS Duplex PrintINSTALLATION ¶
¶
```

2 First, we'll replace the button, but this time so that it jumps to the correct window type. Click the Button toolbar button and the Insert a Jump Button dialog appears.

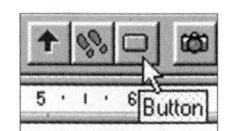

3 Select the INSTALLATION topic in the list and add the text, >steps, to it.

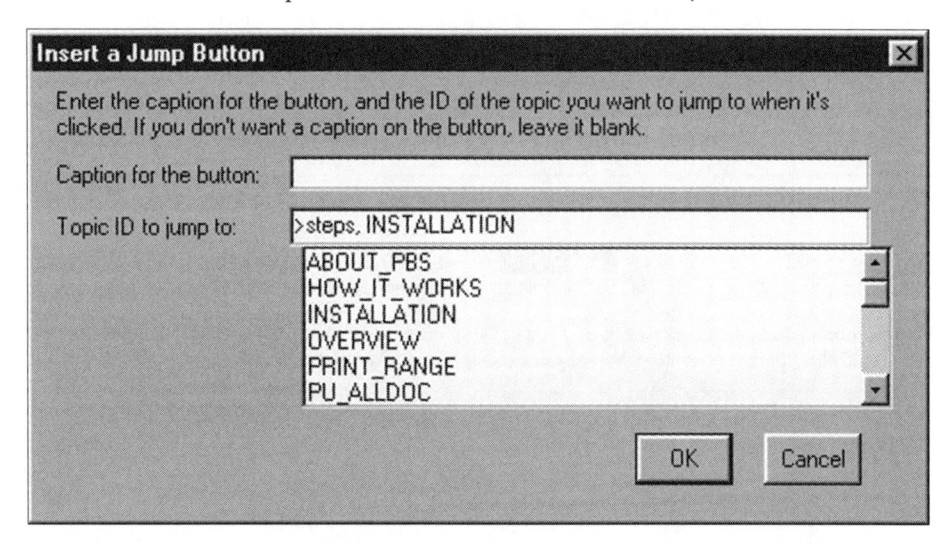

391

4 Click OK and the **button** statement is created, including the window type instruction.

```
¶
{button , JumpID(>steps, INSTALLATION)} ¶
¶
```

5 Now we'll add the text for the button and make it 'hot', but leave it looking like normal text rather than underlined and green. Click the Jump button on the toolbar to open the Insert a Topic Jump dialog.

6 Type the text for the hot spot and select the INSTALLATION topic identifier from the list. Add a % in front of it to remove the underline and green color, and add >steps after it so that we jump to the correct window type.

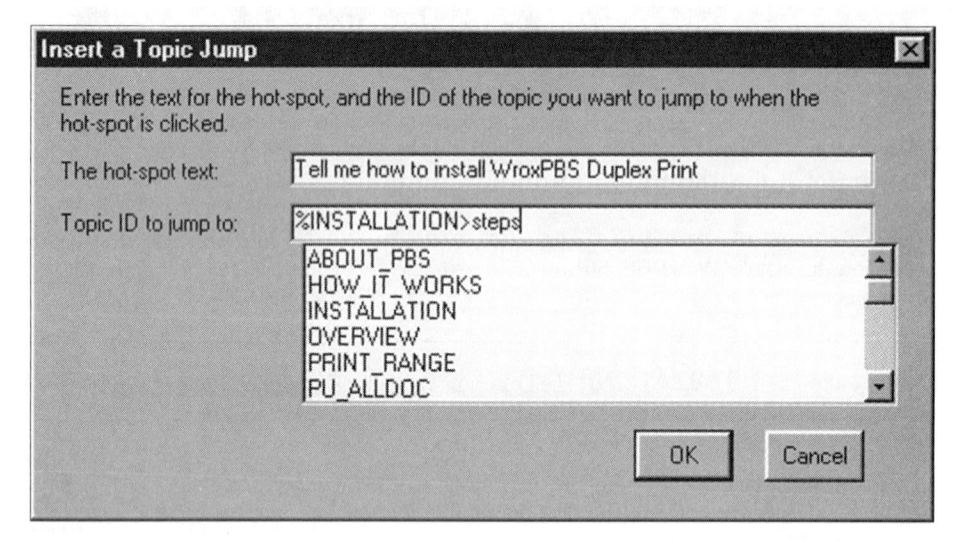

Insert a Topic Jump

Enter the text for the hot-spot, and the ID of the topic you want to jump to when the hot-spot is clicked.

The hot-spot text: `Tell me how to install WroxPBS Duplex Print`

Topic ID to jump to: `%INSTALLATION>steps`

```
ABOUT_PBS
HOW_IT_WORKS
INSTALLATION
OVERVIEW
PRINT_RANGE
PU_ALLDOC
```

[OK] [Cancel]

7 Click OK and the hot spot is created for us automatically. The final line looks like this:

```
¶
{button , JumpID(>steps, INSTALLATION)} Tell me how to install WroxPBS Duplex Print%INSTALLATION>steps ¶
¶
```

8 Scroll down to the Selecting a Printer topic. Here, we need to add **KLink** jumps to the main Word Help file. Select the words Word Print dialog.

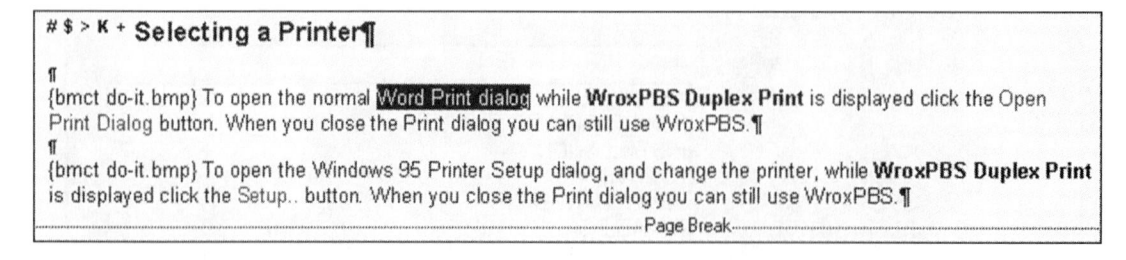

```
# $ > K +  Selecting a Printer¶
¶
{bmct do-it.bmp} To open the normal Word Print dialog while WroxPBS Duplex Print is displayed click the Open
Print Dialog button. When you close the Print dialog you can still use WroxPBS.¶
¶
{bmct do-it.bmp} To open the Windows 95 Printer Setup dialog, and change the printer, while WroxPBS Duplex Print
is displayed click the Setup.. button. When you close the Print dialog you can still use WroxPBS.¶
·····························Page Break·····························
```

9 Click the Jump button on the toolbar to open the Insert a Topic Jump dialog. Because we selected the text for the hot spot first, it's shown in the dialog. Type in the **KLink** macro we need, remembering the exclamation mark: !KLink("printing, documents")

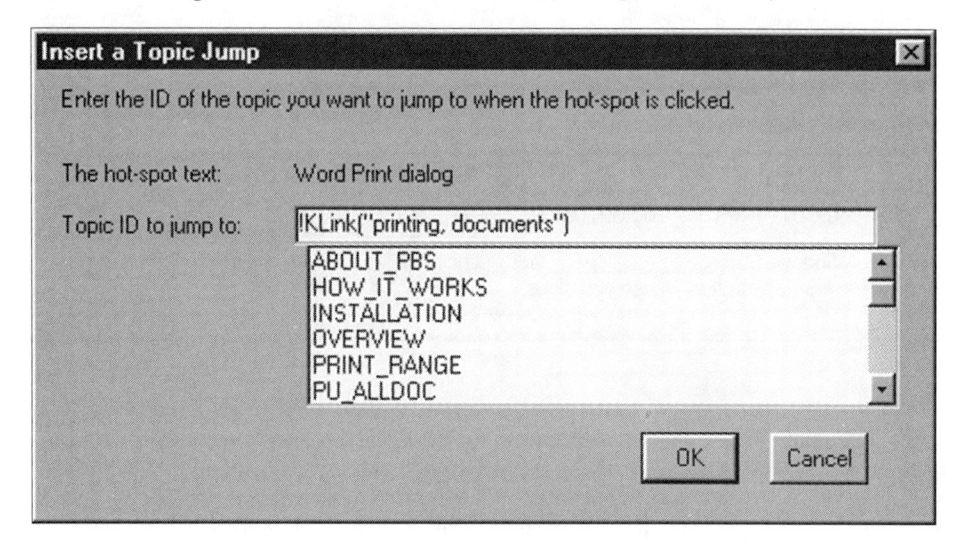

10 Click OK, then highlight the words Printer Setup dialog in the next paragraph. Click the Jump button again and, this time, enter the macro !KLink("printers, changing settings"). Then click OK. You can now see the two new jumps in the topic file.

11 Save the topic file and compile your Help file. In the opening topic, you can see the difference that the new hot spot has made. Clicking on the button or hot spot opens the new topic in the correct (steps) window.

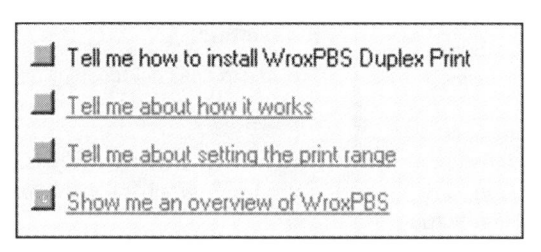

12 Open the Help Topics window and select Print setup in the Index tab to display the Selecting a Printer topic. Click on one of our new **KLink** jumps.

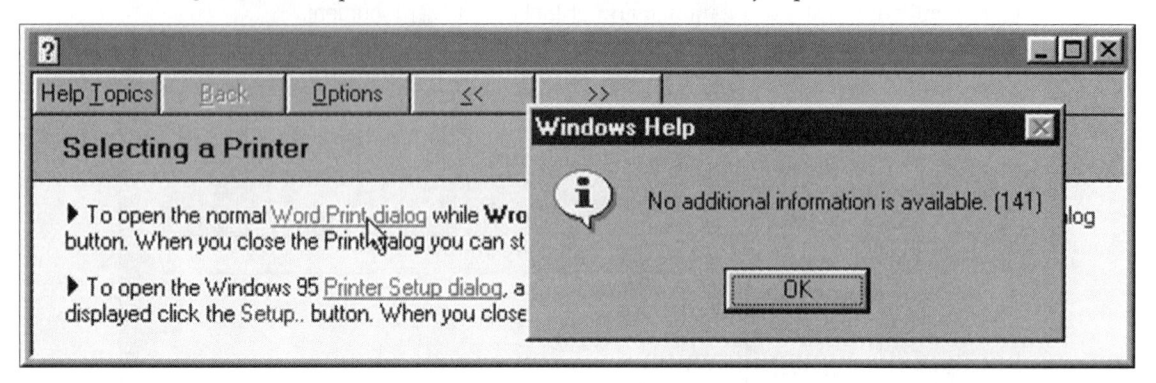

How It Works

Well, we can't really expect the **KLink** jumps to work yet because we haven't told the Help file where to look for these topics. We'll do this when we create the contents list, as you'll see later.

However, in this example, you have seen how easy it is to add more complicated types of jump to your topic files. The macros included in the WroxHelp template make it much simpler than having to type the text for each one directly into the topic file and format it afterwards.

More about Help File Macros

Throughout these two chapters, we've talked about macros and seen some of them, like **JumpHash** and **KLink**, used in topic files. Macros can add extra features or usability to a Help project. For example, we've seen how you can use them to jump to a topic in a different Help file. They can also be used to close windows that are no longer required, run other applications, and a multitude of other tasks.

We'll look at some of the most useful applications of macros in this part of the chapter. You can get a full list of Help File Macros and more information about any one of them from Help Workshop's Help file.

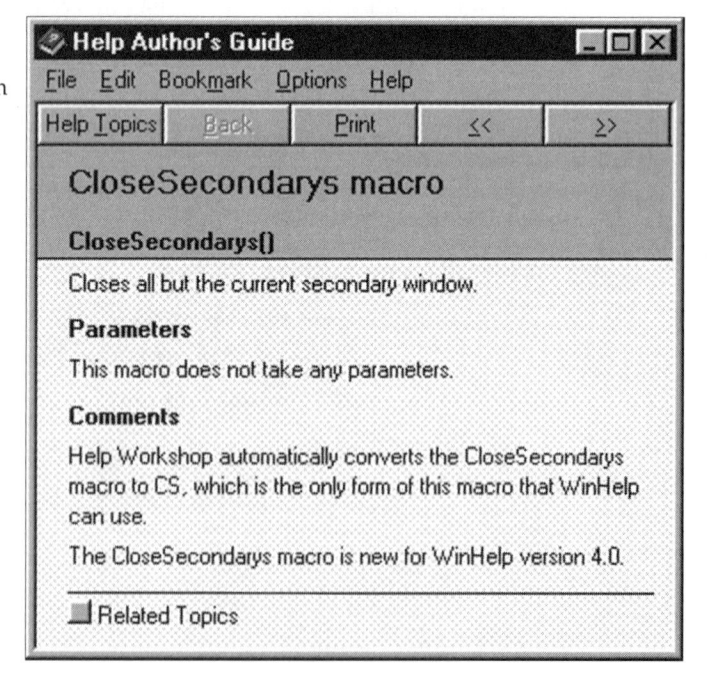

Where are Macros Used?

A macro can be used in several different places:

- In the [CONFIG] section, so that it runs when the user opens the Help file.
- In a [CONFIG - <window>] section, so that it runs when the user opens that window.
- In a hot spot in the topic file, so that it runs when the user clicks the hot spot.
- In a command that uses a macro as its argument.
- In the Macro footnote of a topic in the topic file.

To use a macro in either of the first two places, we use Help Workshop to add it to the project file. Click the Config button to add it to the [CONFIG] section, so that it runs when the user opens the Help file. To specify that it runs only when a particular window is opened, click Windows... and enter the macro in the Macros tab.

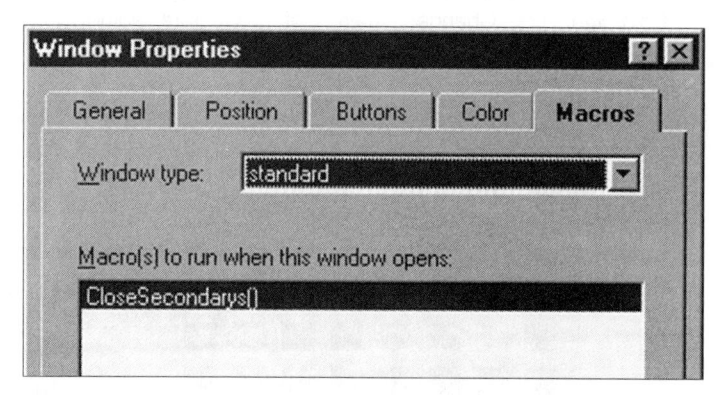

Here, we're using the **CloseSecondarys** macro. When you use several types of window in your Help file, they all remain on screen until you close them individually. You can use the **CloseSecondarys** macro to close all the other windows that may have been left open, except the for default Main window and the current window.

The third option, placing a macro in a topic file hot spot, means editing the topic file. After the underlined hot spot text, we type an exclamation mark, then the macro itself. To run several macros in turn, we just separate each one with a semicolon. For example, the topic file entry,

> Tell me about installation!CloseSecondarys();JumpID(INSTALLATION)

will close any open secondary windows, then jump to the topic with the identifier **INSTALLATION**. We've already seen how the **button** command uses a macro as its argument. In the WroxPBS topic file, we used this to display a button which jumped to the **INSTALLATION** topic when clicked:

> {button Installing WroxPBS, JumpID(INSTALLATION)}

Finally, we can include a macro in the Macro footnote of a topic, so that it runs automatically each time that topic is displayed. Let's have a look at some particular examples.

Setting the Color of Pop-ups

It's usual practice in a Help file to display pop-ups with a yellow background, yet Help Compiler sets them to white by default. You can change the color of a pop-up by using the `SetPopupColor` macro, either globally for all pop-ups or individually for each one.

The syntax is `SetPopupColor(`*red value*`,` *green value*`,` *blue value*`)`. The easiest way to determine the values for the color you want is to use the color selector in the Color tab of the Window Properties dialog.

Open Help Workshop, load the `WroxPBS.hpj` project file and click the Windows... button. In the Color tab, click Change..., then Define Custom Colors >>. Select the color you want and read off the Red, Green and Blue values from the dialog directly.

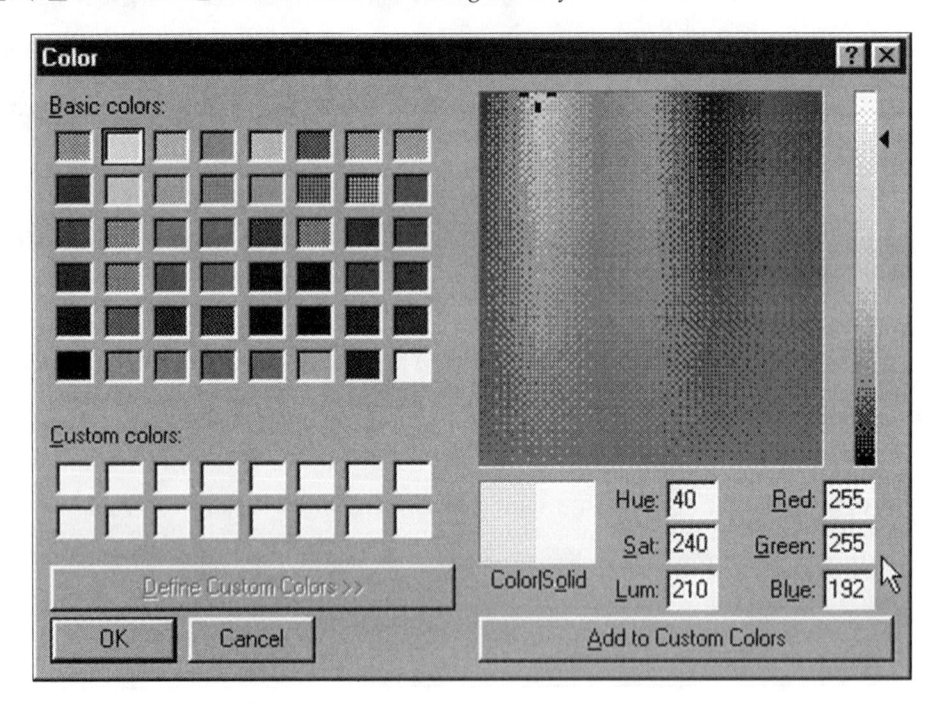

In our WroxPBS Help file, we follow tradition of using yellow for all the pop-ups. To do this, we run the `SetPopupColor` macro when the Help file first opens by placing it in the [CONFIG] section of our Help file.

Back in the main project file window, click the Config... button, then Add.... In the Add Macro dialog, enter the text SetPopupColor(255,255,192):

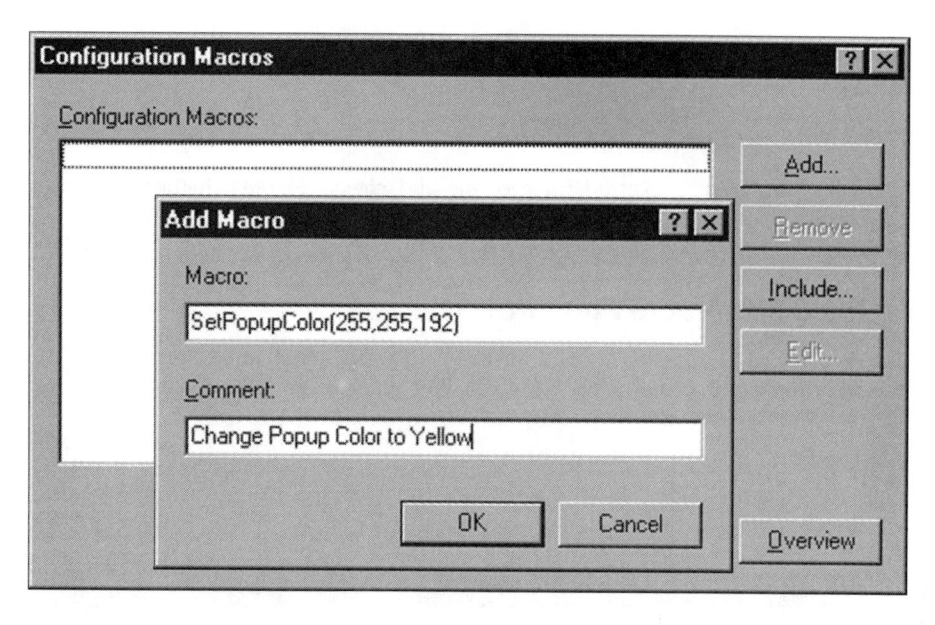

[Screenshot: Configuration Macros dialog with Add Macro sub-dialog showing Macro: `SetPopupColor(255,255,192)` and Comment: `Change Popup Color to Yellow`]

If you want to add the **SetPopupColor** macro to a particular window type, you just select the Windows button instead, open the Macro tab, select the window type you want to add it to and click Add....

However, if (for some strange reason) you want all your pop-ups to be *different* colors, you can use the **SetPopupColor** macro in your topic file, where the hot spot that opens the pop-up is. After the hot spot text, you enter an exclamation mark to indicate that it's a macro rather than the destination topic identifier, then enter the macros you need to carry out the task:

```
-in macro!SetPopupColor(0,255,128);JumpID(PU_DUPLEX) that allows y
ot support duplex!SetPopupColor(255,0,0);JumpID(PU_DUPLEX) printir
selected parts of the document, or a range of pages by specifying the star
```

Setting and Using Help File Markers

Creating a Help file is a little like writing an application in WordBasic. By including commands in the topic file, such as **bml** or **mci** (which add a bitmap, video or sound file), and by placing macros in topics, we add to the functionality of the Help file.

We can even use a form of variable to store information. Windows Help files support markers which you can create with a macro. You can then make decisions about what to do, say, when a topic is opened. For example, when users first open the Getting Started topic in the Wrox Zip Help file, the graphical Overview topic also appears to introduce them to our Help file. However, the next time they display the Getting Started topic, it doesn't appear.

We've done this by adding macros to the topic file, in macro footnotes, which run each time that topic is opened. In the Overview topic, we placed the macro,

```
SaveMark(SeenThis)
```

which creates a Help File Marker called **SeenThis** as soon as that topic is opened. In the Getting Started topic, we added the macro:

```
IfThenElse("SeenThis", , JumpID(>Large, IntroScreen))
```

This runs when the Getting Started topic opens and checks to see whether the marker **SeenThis** exists. If it doesn't, it jumps to the Overview topic, which has the topic ID **IntroScreen**. If the marker does exist, it does nothing.

Inserting Topic File Macro Footnotes

The WroxHelp template contains a routine that helps you insert topic macros. Place the insertion point in the topic to which you want to add the macro and click the Topic Macro button on the toolbar.

This opens the Insert a Topic Macro dialog. You can type the macro directly, or select and edit one that already exists in the topic file.

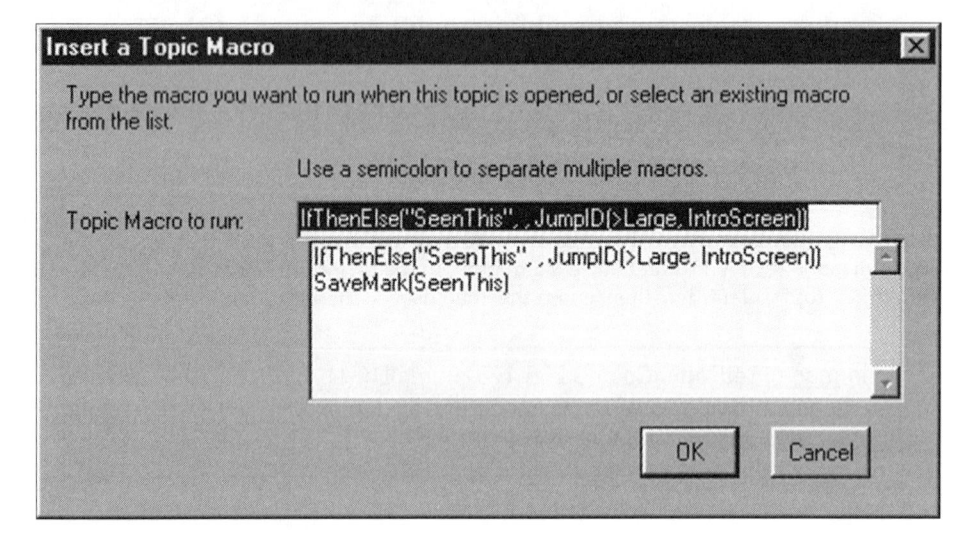

Running Other Programs

When we looked at the Wrox Zip Help file in the previous chapter, we saw how it could run other programs directly. This is a handy way to make life easier for your users. For example, we included a button in the Installing Wrox Zip topic which opens Explorer ready to copy the necessary files.

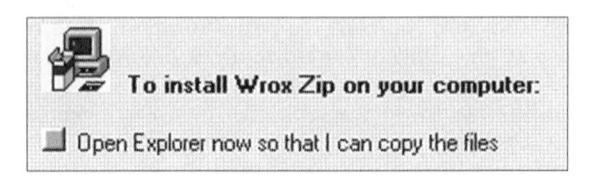

Opening an Application or Data File

To start another program or open a data file in its own application, we can use the **ExecFile** or **ShellExecute** macros. In the Wrox Zip Help file, we've used **ExecFile** in a **button** command to run the program **Explorer.exe**:

```
{button , ExecFile(Explorer.exe)}
```

If you want to 'execute' a data file by loading it into its own application, you use **ShellExecute** instead. This is a more complex but more flexible way of starting another program. You'll find full details of the arguments it requires in the Help Workshop Help file.

Opening Control Panel

Help Compiler also supports a special macro for opening the various applets in Control Panel. This can be useful if you need your user to change some settings for their computer, or just to check that everything is set up properly.

You may recall from our discussion of bitmaps in the previous chapter that Help Compiler has some built-in bitmaps that it uses automatically if it can't find one with that name in your project folder. One of these is **shortcut.bmp**, which is the standard Windows 95-style button for opening Control Panel applets. So, by inserting the text **{bmct shortcut.bmp}** in our Help file, this bitmap is automatically displayed.

To open the Date/Time Properties dialog, we used:

```
{bmct shortcut.bmp}%!ControlPanel(timedate.cpl, Date/Time)
```

This uses the **ControlPanel** macro and sends it details of the applet we want. We can also specify the tab we want to be open, though this doesn't work in some of the applets, such as the Mouse Properties dialog which varies depending on which mouse driver you have installed.

The first argument is the name of the program that *contains* the control panel applet. The second is the name of the control panel applet itself. You can also add a third argument which specifies the tab you want on top, starting with zero for the first one.

Creating a Contents List

You'll have noticed that there's no Contents tab in the Help Topics dialog of the WroxPBS Help file that we've been building. The reason is that we haven't supplied a contents list file. This is a separate file which you must supply with your compiled Help file in order for the Contents tab to be displayed. We saw what the Contents tab looks like, and how it works, when we examined the Wrox Zip Help file in the previous chapter.

What is a Contents List File?

In the previous chapter, we also looked at an overview of the components that make up a Help file. Most of these—the topics files, graphics, sound and video clips, etc.—are compiled into a single **.hlp** file. In earlier versions of Windows, this was all you had to supply for your Help system. In Windows 95, however, the contents list file, which fills the Contents tab in the Help Topics dialog, is a separate file. This normally has the same file name as the main Help file, but with the extension **.cnt**. It's a plain text file that you can create in a text editor, or directly using Help Workshop.

> **FYI** The contents file doesn't *have* to have the same name as the main Help file. That's just usual practice. However, if you create a Help system which uses several linked `.hlp` files, you may wish to use a single contents file with a different name.

Here's part of the contents list file for the Wrox Zip Help file. You can see that there's a series of lines which define how the Help and contents files fit together, followed by the lines which make up the entries in the Contents tab of the Help Topics window:

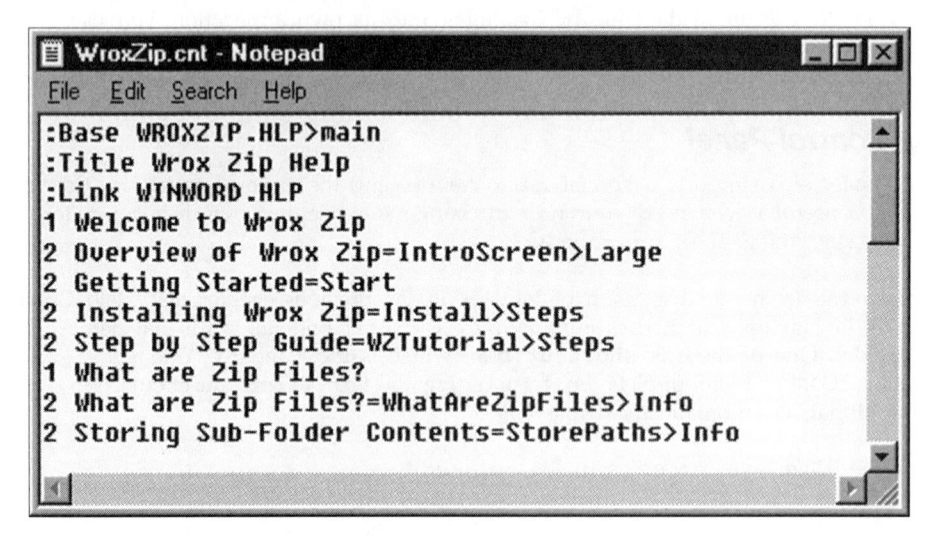

```
:Base WROXZIP.HLP>main
:Title Wrox Zip Help
:Link WINWORD.HLP
1 Welcome to Wrox Zip
2 Overview of Wrox Zip=IntroScreen>Large
2 Getting Started=Start
2 Installing Wrox Zip=Install>Steps
2 Step by Step Guide=WZTutorial>Steps
1 What are Zip Files?
2 What are Zip Files?=WhatAreZipFiles>Info
2 Storing Sub-Folder Contents=StorePaths>Info
```

Because the Contents tab can display several levels of entry, as books you can open or pages which represent topics, there's a number before each line that identifies the level. Creating the contents file isn't difficult in itself, but, because there's no link between it and the actual topic file, it can be hard to picture how the two will interact and which topics should be placed at each level.

Creating a Contents List with Help Workshop

You create a contents list using Help Workshop. Select New from the File menu and, in the New dialog, select Help Contents.

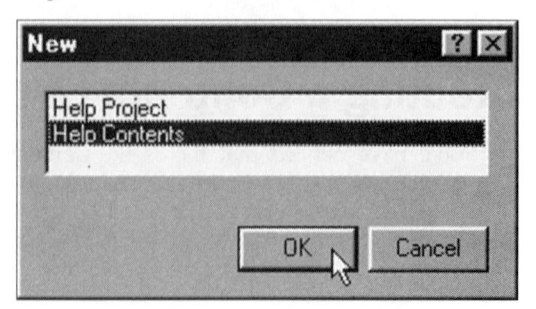

You can then enter the headings and topic entries you want for the contents list, and move them around until you get it just right. Here's the same Wrox Zip contents list loaded in Help Workshop:

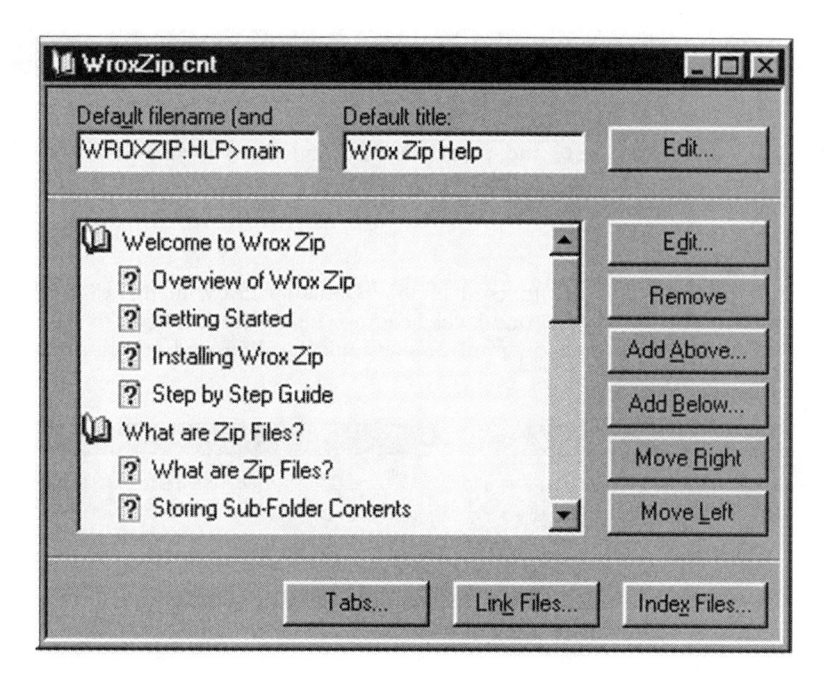

The Default Filename, shown at the top of the window, indicates which `.hlp` file the contents list links to and the window type that is the default for all the topics. The Default Title is the text shown in the title bar of our Help file windows and in the Help Topics window.

At the bottom of the window are three buttons that define the other information that the contents file can include. The only one that interests us at the moment is Link Files. This is where we have to specify any Help files we want to jump to with **KLink** or **ALink** macros. You can see how the final contents list file corresponds to these options in Help Workshop.

```
:Base WROXZIP.HLP>main
:Title Wrox Zip Help
:Link WINWORD.HLP
```

> **FYI** The **Tabs...** button allows you to create custom tabs, instead of using the books and documents graphics which are the default. The **Index Files...** button allows you to combine the index entries for other Help files with your own. Both of these are outside the scope of this book, but you can find more information from **Help Workshop**'s Help file.

Creating a Contents List with WroxHelp

To make life easier for you, we've included a set of macros in the WroxHelp template which partly automate the process of creating a contents list file. You still need to do some work on it, but it does attempt to link the topic and contents files together for you.

Try It Out - Creating the WroxPBS Contents List

1 Open the file, `WroxPBS3.rtf`, and place the insertion point in the first topic. Click the Contents Entry button on the toolbar to open the Add a Contents Tab entry dialog.

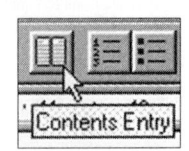

2 The first line of your topic is proposed for the Contents Entry, in this case, What It Does. We want this to appear as a second-level heading, inside the top-level book heading. Add an entry for the top-level heading in front of our topic heading and separate them with an @ character.

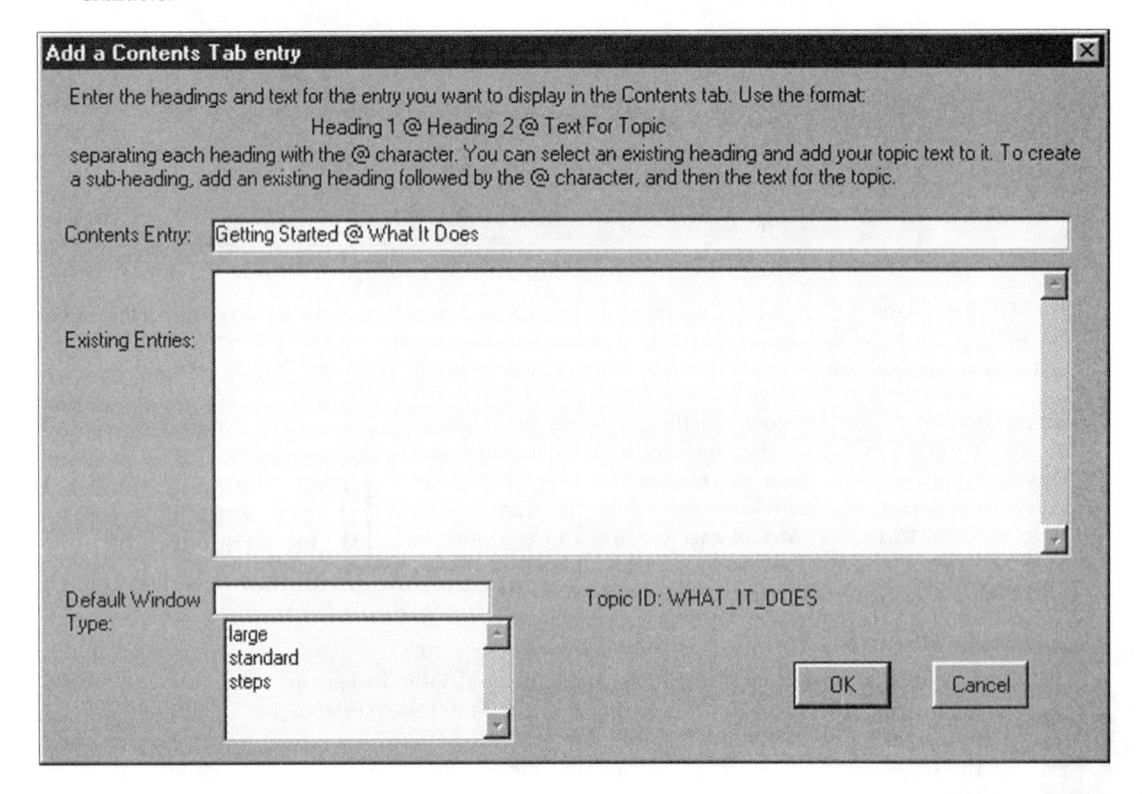

Add a Contents Tab entry

Enter the headings and text for the entry you want to display in the Contents tab. Use the format:

Heading 1 @ Heading 2 @ Text For Topic

separating each heading with the @ character. You can select an existing heading and add your topic text to it. To create a sub-heading, add an existing heading followed by the @ character, and then the text for the topic.

Contents Entry: `Getting Started @ What It Does`

Existing Entries:

Default Window Type: large / standard / steps

Topic ID: WHAT_IT_DOES

[OK] [Cancel]

3 Click OK and the new Contents Entry is added to the topic as a footnote, using a WroxHelp-specific footnote character @.

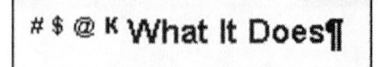

`# $ @ K What It Does¶`

4 Place the insertion point in the Installing WroxPBS topic and open the Add a Contents entry dialog again. This time, the dialog shows the first Contents Entry we added. To insert the new one under the same heading, just select it in the list. The first-level heading is added automatically.

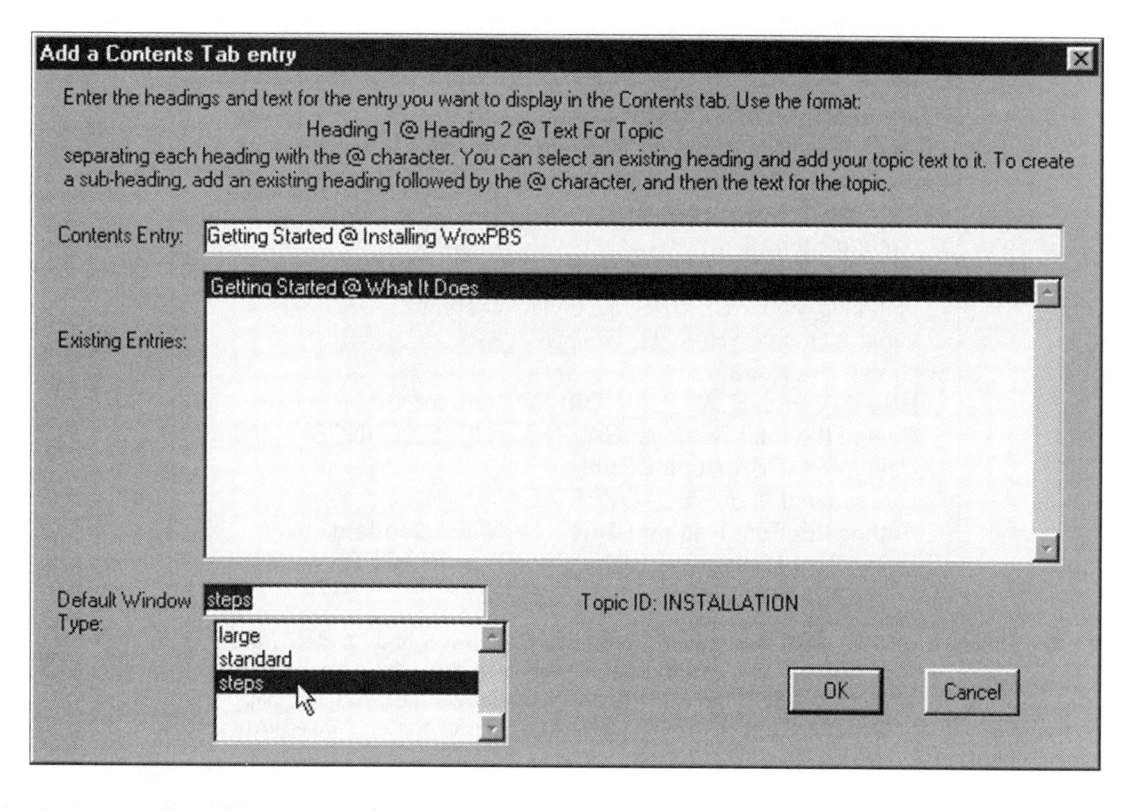

5 There's also a list of the window types we've specified in Default Window entries shown. We want our Installing WroxPBS topic to appear in a steps window, so select this. Then click OK.

6 Continue adding contents entries, using different first-level headings. Here's our final list shown in the Add a Contents entry dialog:

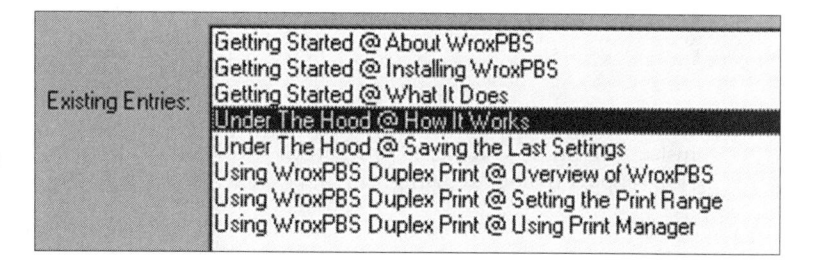

7 One you've added all the entries, select Co_ntents List from the _Tools menu. The `ContentsList` macro gathers together all the contents entries you've specified and creates the contents list text file for you in a new document. Notice that it has included the window types where we selected them.

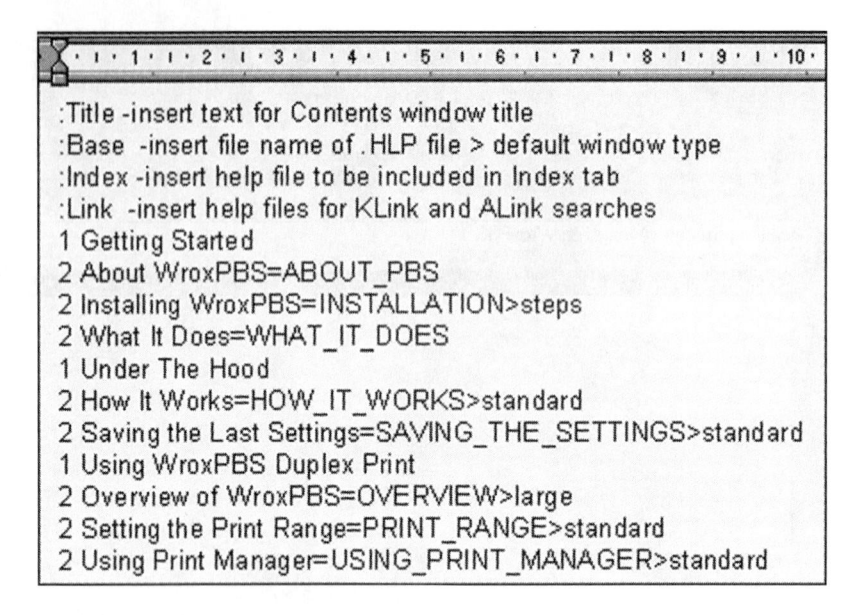

```
:Title -insert text for Contents window title
:Base  -insert file name of .HLP file > default window type
:Index -insert help file to be included in Index tab
:Link  -insert help files for KLink and ALink searches
1 Getting Started
2 About WroxPBS=ABOUT_PBS
2 Installing WroxPBS=INSTALLATION>steps
2 What It Does=WHAT_IT_DOES
1 Under The Hood
2 How It Works=HOW_IT_WORKS>standard
2 Saving the Last Settings=SAVING_THE_SETTINGS>standard
1 Using WroxPBS Duplex Print
2 Overview of WroxPBS=OVERVIEW>large
2 Setting the Print Range=PRINT_RANGE>standard
2 Using Print Manager=USING_PRINT_MANAGER>standard
```

8 To finish off, we only need to fill in the **Title**, **Base** and **Index** information. However, notice that the entries are sorted in alphabetical order within each level. You may want to swap them around. You'll have to do this manually. Once you are happy with it, save the new file as **WroxPBS.cnt** in your **\PBSHelp** project folder. Make sure you save it as a text file (not in Word's document format).

9 To see it working, just recompile your Help file. Instead of the first topic, it now opens with the Help Topics dialog, showing our new contents list.

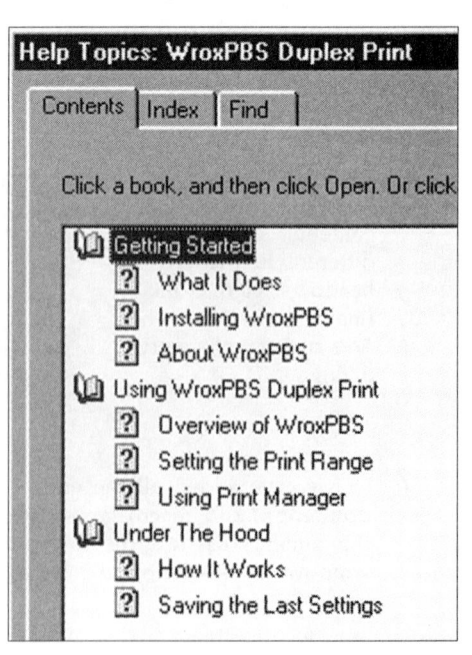

How It Works

We've shown you another way to create a contents file for your Help files, rather than using Help Workshop directly. Which method you prefer probably depends mostly on how complicated your Help files are. The final contents list file is simply a text file that contains some information about the links between the different project files and a list of the headings for the Contents tab of the Help Topics dialog.

If you open the Index tab and go to the Selecting a Printer topic, you'll find that the two **KLink** jumps we created earlier now work properly. This is because we've added the names of the two other Help files which supply the information to our contents list file.

```
:Base WroxPBS.hlp>
:Link Windows.hlp
:Link Winword.hlp
1 Getting Started
```

> **FYI** We've included the final version of the WroxPBS Help topic file with the other samples, as `WroxPBS4.rtf`. You can use it to create the Help file if you wish, or just experiment with it. It contains all the entries for creating the contents list.

Linking Help to Your Application

Before we leave Help files, we need to look at how you link the completed Help file to your application. You would normally add an entry to the default Help menu of your application to open the Help file directly, displaying either the Help Topics dialog or your own choice of starting topic.

The Wrox Zip add-in we've supplied as a sample with this book adds an entry to Word's Help menu when it's installed. This opens the Help file at the Getting Started topic and also displays a graphical 'Welcome' screen which gives an overview of what Wrox Zip does.

Alternatively, users can open the Help file by clicking a Help button in either the Zip Manager, Default Options or Select Files to Unzip dialogs. These open the relevant overview topic for that dialog, rather than the main topic, but they can still open other topics by following the jumps in the overview windows, or clicking the Help Topics button to open the Help Topics dialog.

Context-sensitive Help

This second method creates a simple form of context-sensitive help. The user gets to see a topic which is directly relevant to the dialog they are using, rather than having to find it from the Help Topics window. We can display any topic this way providing that we've already set up the links that do it in the project file.

Mapping Context-sensitive Help Topics

Click the <u>M</u>ap... button in H<u>e</u>lp Workshop's main project file dialog. The Map dialog opens.

Here, you can enter numeric values for any of your topics. In the screenshot, you can see the links in our Wrox Zip Help file:

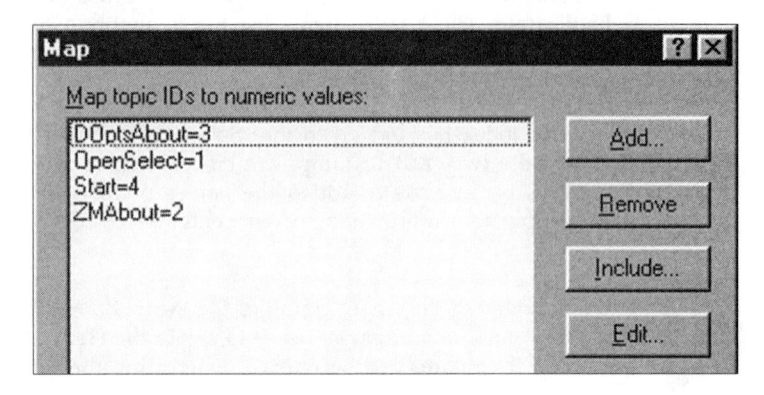

Once the Help file has been compiled, these map numbers are stored within it. We've only defined four, because these are the only entry points into the Help file that we'll be using. However, if you were implementing full context-sensitive Help, you would need to provide a numeric ID for every pop-up topic that you wanted to display when users click the What's This? button in a dialog in your application.

Opening a Help File from Your Application

To open a Help file from within an application, we use an API (Application Programming Interface) call to the WinHelp application. We tell it the name of the Help file we want to open, and we can send it one of the numbers that we mapped to a topic ID. WinHelp displays the topic that correspond to that number.

However, things aren't quite that simple. WinHelp also needs to know the handle of the window that's in use. A **window handle** is simply the number that Windows uses to identify that window in its internal workings. We can get the handle of the currently active window using another API function: `GetFocus`.

So we need to write a WordBasic subroutine in our application. First, we define the two API functions:

```
Declare Function GetFocus Lib "user32" Alias "GetFocus"() As Long
Declare Function WinHelp Lib "user32" Alias "WinHelpA"(hwnd As Long, \
    lpHelpFile As String, wCommand As Long, wData As Long) As Long
```

Now for the subroutine itself. We use a parameter `OpenHelp` which will contain a value corresponding to the context in our application. Here, we're just using two possible values, **1** to open the Help file with mapped topic number one displayed, or **0** to close the Help file when our application ends. The value for this argument is supplied by the code that runs when the user clicks a button in the application. For example, clicking the <u>H</u>elp button calls our subroutine with `ShowHelp(1)`, and the Cancel button calls it with `ShowHelp(0)`.

```
Sub ShowHelp(OpenHelp)
    If OpenHelp Then
        Command = 1            'HELP_CONTEXT
```

```
        TID = 1                 'Mapped Topic ID number
    Else
        Command = 2             'HELP_QUIT
        TID = 0                 'Zero when closing Help
    EndIf
    HelpFile$ = "WROXPBS.HLP"
    hWnd = GetFocus
    Result = WinHelp(hWnd, HelpFile$, Command, TID)
End Sub
```

You can see from the code that the two values of **wCommand** that we're sending to WinHelp are **HELP_CONTEXT (1)** and **HELP_QUIT (2)**. The **wData** argument contains the mapped topic number we want. In the first case, we send **1** and, when we're closing the Help file, we send zero.

Opening Help in Wrox Zip

The subroutine in the Wrox Zip add-in is a little more complicated because, as you saw earlier, we have four mapped topics that we can jump to:

```
Sub ShowHelp(Topic$)
    Command = 1                 'HELP_CONTEXT
    TID = 0                     'Mapped topic ID
    TWin$ = ""                  'Window type
    Select Case Topic$
       Case "About"
          TID = 4
       Case "Options"
          TID = 3 : TWin$ = ">Large"
       Case "ZipManager"
          TID = 2 : TWin$ = ">Large"
       Case "SelectFile"
          TID = 1 : TWin$ = ">Large"
       Case "CloseHelp"
          Command = 2           'HELP_QUIT
    End Select
    TWin$ = "WROXZIP.HLP" + TWin$
    hWnd = GetFocus
    Result = WinHelp(hWnd, TWin$, Command, TID)
End Sub
```

We call this subroutine with a text argument that corresponds to the context we're in. For example, clicking the Zip Manager Help entry in the Help menu executes the statement **ShowHelp("About")**, while the Help button in the Default Options dialog executes the statement **ShowHelp("Options")**. Also notice that we can specify the window type we want to display the topic in by adding it to the name of the Help file, using **WROXZIP.HLP>Large** for the Help file name argument opens the topic in a window type named **Large**.

Coping with Errors in a Help File

The final subject that we'll consider briefly is the thorny problem of errors in your Help project files. By far the most common are those that come from your topic file. It's quite likely that the first time you compile a new file, you'll be faced with more than one. What you'll see here are some tips to help you track down and correct some of the errors that you're most likely to come across.

Errors, Warnings and Notes

Help Workshop will report any problems it finds as it compiles your Help file. For example, it may give you an error message if it can't find any of the files it needs. It won't compile until you fix the problem. You may also get a warning if there's a problem that will result in your Help file not working correctly, say, a hot spot has no topic identifier attached to it. Finally, Help Compiler will show notes about things that won't stop the Help file working but will probably affect the way that it's displayed. In all cases, it tells you the topic number where it found the problem.

Error Warning	Problem and Solution
Paragraph markers formatted as hidden text.	The paragraph break won't be displayed and can spoil the layout of your topic. If you accidentally format a Page Break as hidden, two topics will be shown in one window.
Scrolling areas defined before non-scrolling areas.	This means that the non-scrolling title region won't display properly. You need to go back to the topic file and adjust the formatting.
Bitmap used in both transparent and non-transparent form.	You have used the same graphic in a **bmx** and **bmxt** command. This means that two copies will be stored in the Help file. Unless this is what you want, go back to the topic file and make sure all the bitmap commands use the same form.
Window type *x* not defined.	You are trying to jump to a window type you haven't defined in the project file. This may be a typing error in the topic file, or an ommission from the project file.

Help Files that Misbehave

Even if you don't get any messages during compilation, you can still find that your Help file doesn't look or work properly. For example:

Unexpected Behaviour	Likely Problem
Jumps go to the wrong topic or window type.	Make sure that your topic file is correct, with the jump instructions properly formatted as hidden text and no extra spaces in them. If there's punctuation after the hot spot text, include it in the hot spot itself
Text doesn't wrap in the non-scrolling window.	If you have used the Keep LinesTogether paragraph format for a non-scrolling region, the text won't wrap. Make it shorter to fit.
The command for a button or bitmap appears, rather than the button or graphic.	You have probably mistyped a **button** or **bitmap** command. If a graphic is missing, you'll see a special picture showing you a broken graphic. It looks like a hole in your topic window!
There is white space around a graphic on a colored background.	This probably means that you omitted the **t** (transparent) in the **bitmap** command that displays it.

Table Continued on Following Page

Unexpected Behaviour	Likely Problem
ALink and **KLink** jumps don't work.	You may have forgotten to specify the files that contain the topics you want to jump to in the contents list file.
Error messages appear when a macro runs.	You need to go back to the macro in question and check the syntax. Generally, the message gives you some idea of what the problem is.
The formatting of your Help file is different to that which you designed.	The layout of your topics will change, depending on the screen resolution of the system used to view it. If you design a Help file in SVGA mode and display it in VGA mode, the text is larger and less will be visible in each Help window.

Testing the Contents File

Help Workshop can test your `.cnt` file to make sure that the syntax is correct and all the jumps actually exist, though it can't tell you if they go to the wrong topic. It can also be used to test individual macros. Both of these commands are available from the Test menu.

Don't forget that you can also run your Help file in Help Author mode. This allows you to test each jump and pop-up, view the macros and execute them one by one and generally get information about individual topics. To switch to Help Author mode, select it on the File menu and run, or recompile and display your Help file.

Summary

In this chapter, we've completed the task of creating a Help file for our WroxPBS (Print Both Sides) add-in. Along the way, we've shown you what the project file is, how it's created and the different ways you can add extra features to make your Help files both more informative and more exciting.

Of course, there are many other ways for you to use the functionality of Help Workshop. Once you start creating Help files, you soon discover new techniques and tricks. Don't forget that you can use Help Workshop in Help Author mode to discover how other authors have implemented features in their Help files.

As we've worked through this chapter, you've seen:

- How you create the project file and compile your Help file
- Ways of adding extra features and how macros are used in Help file
- What the contents list is and how you create it
- How you can link your Help file to an application

This chapter marks the end of Part 2 of the book. In Part 3, we move on to look at how Microsoft Word can be used to communicate with the outside world, rather than just as a single-user tool. You'll see many of the techniques we've introduced so far being combined with other applications.

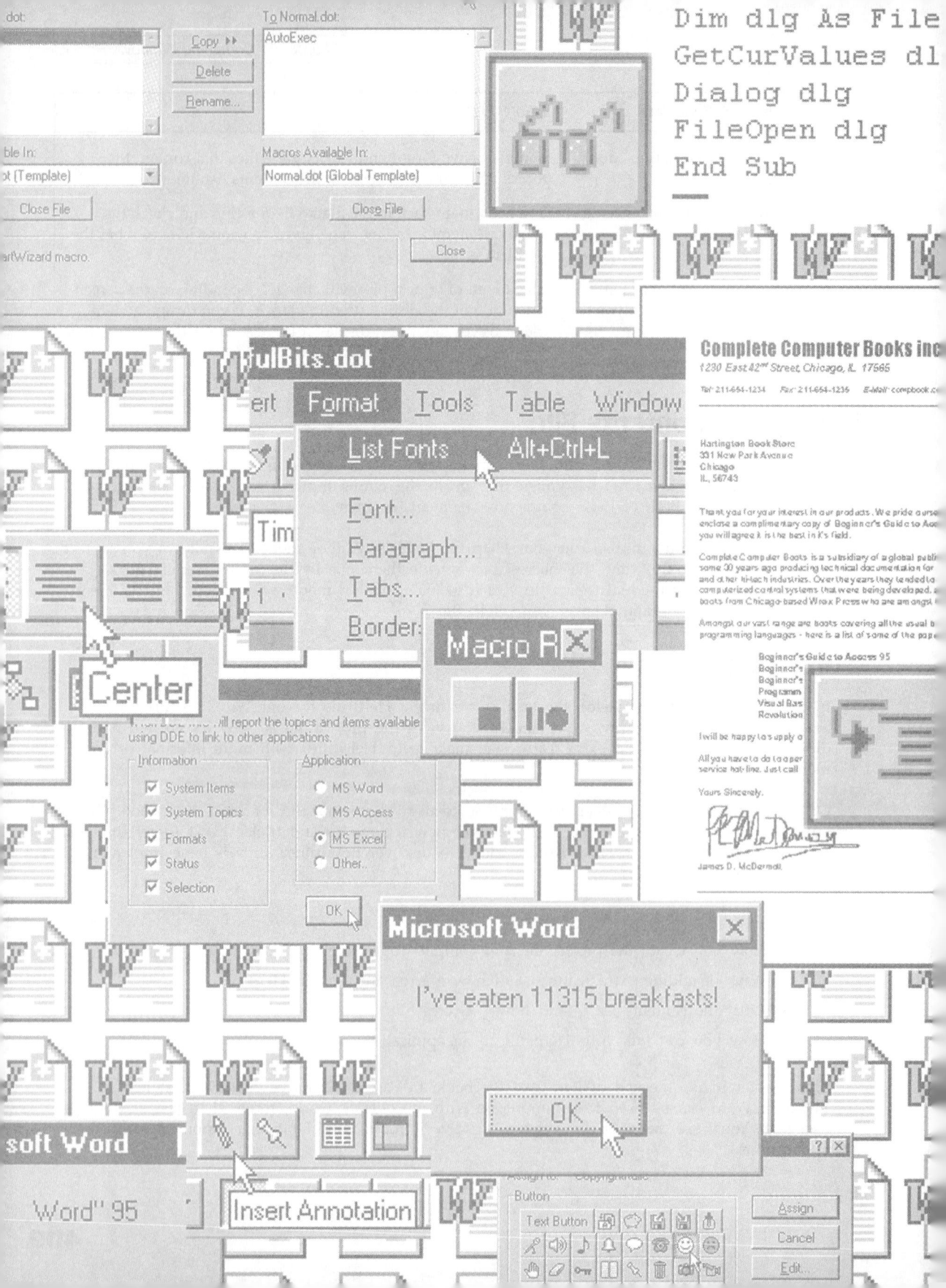

```
Dim dlg As File
GetCurValues dl
Dialog dlg
FileOpen dlg
End Sub
```

Part 3

Word and the Outside World

In the previous two sections of this book we've been working head-down with Microsoft Word as a single user, ignoring what's going on in the world around us. Our task in Part 1 was to learn the fundamentals of WordBasic and explore how it can make our life easier in a variety of ways. In Part 2, we became more adventurous. We saw how to build wizards, utilities and add-ins aimed at achieving more complex tasks and extending the power of the Word environment. Then we carried on to see how Word itself becomes just a tool, using it to create web pages and Help files.

Now in Part 3, it's time to lift our eyes from the screen and take a bit more notice of what's going on around us. You may work in an office using Word as part of a team, or you could be working alone and communicating the results of your labors to others. Whichever way, as they say in the best science fiction movies, you are not alone. These days, you are more likely to share information electronically than as printed documents, so in this part of the book we'll be looking at how Word fits into this environment.

Communicating with the 'outside world' can involve many different situations, from simply passing document files over a network or by e-mail, to integrating directly with other applications so that Word can use their methods and data. We'll see some of these possibilities in this, the final part of the book.

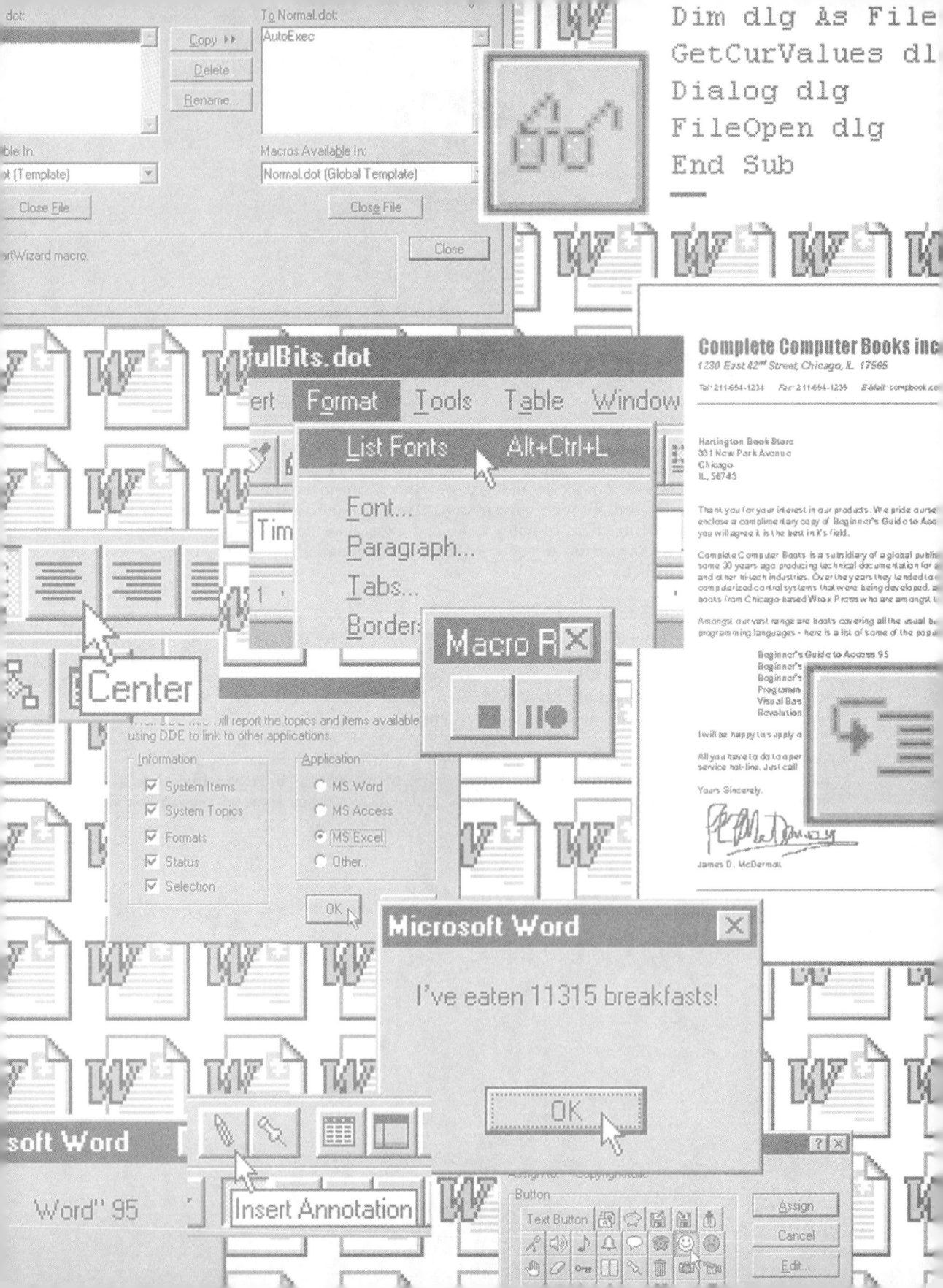

```
Dim dlg As File
GetCurValues dl
Dialog dlg
FileOpen dlg
End Sub
```

10

The Problems of Sharing Documents

Introduction

Modern working methods are all about sharing information. In a corporate environment, data is used by many different people. It could be anything from processing a customer's order to writing, editing and proofing a technical manual. The information could be stored centrally on a network server, or distributed across several computers. You may even use the 'sneaker-net' method, passing files between machines on disk or tape.

In earlier chapters, we looked at ways of passing a Word document between the various people who need to work on it. You can split a document up so that each person works on a different part, using master documents, or distribute protected copies and compile all the revisions and annotations into the original afterwards.

However, in this and subsequent chapters, we'll be looking at a different situation, where several users manipulate the original document directly or link a document to other data sources. There are several matters that you need to consider. For example, what happens when two users are editing a document simultaneously? How can you be sure that everyone follows the same 'house style' for their documents? There's also the increasing concern over the risk of viruses which can damage the data on your system.

So, in this chapter, we'll show you:

- How to organize documents and templates in a workgroup
- How to manage simultaneous editing of documents
- How to protect your data from the risk of damage by Word viruses

Along the way, you'll see more examples of how WordBasic can help to automate, control and generally manage those everyday tasks for you.

Managing Document Templates on a Network

You'll be aware that all the functionality we've been adding to Word in previous chapters uses the appropriate templates, where the macros, AutoText entries, toolbars and menu customizations are stored. If you work in an environment where users are connected to a network, it makes sense to have only one version of these templates available. This makes it much easier to maintain and update the code or styles stored in it.

Workgroup Templates

Normally, when you select New... from the File menu, Word only shows the templates available in your own **\Templates** folder and in the subdirectories below it. However, if you want to, you can set Word to include templates stored in a central location on the network or any other location. Open the Options dialog (select Options... from the Tools menu) and click the Workgroup Templates entry in the File Locations tab.

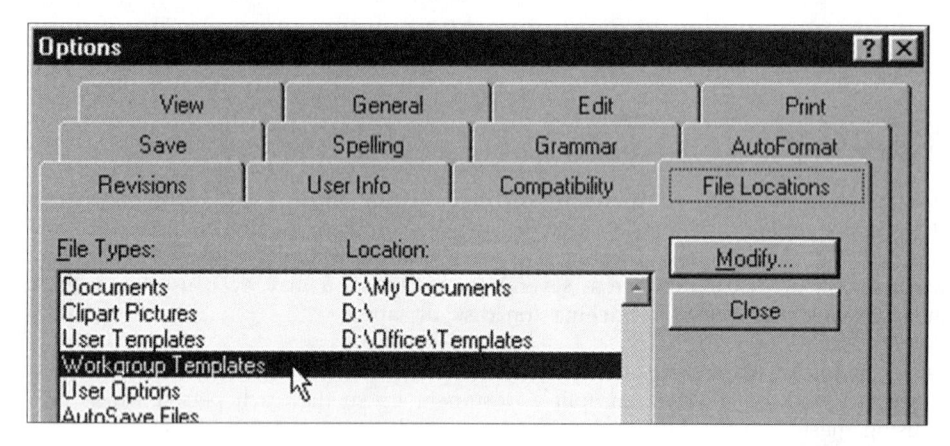

Click Modify... and use the Modify Location dialog to select the folder where the templates you want to include in the Templates dialog are stored. This can be any shared location on the network which all the users will have access to.

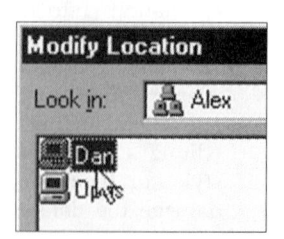

Then, delete any templates from the local machine's **\Templates** folder that are duplicated in the network template folder. That way, all users will have to open the network copy of the template.

Protecting Templates from Changes

You can protect a template from being changed by setting the Write Reservation Password (in the Save tab of the Options dialog) before you save it. Any changes made to it while it's open can only be saved if the user knows the password. You saw how this worked back in Chapter 6.

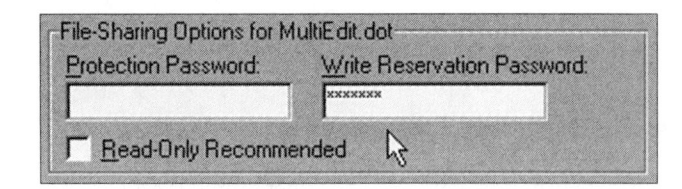

Whether the template is on a local machine or in the network's **\Workgroup Templates** folder, you can protect it this way. Users will not be able to save any changes they make to it while they have it open. If they change a 'house style' paragraph format, for example, it will not affect other users or new documents they create themselves.

However, this means that you have to be careful how you use templates to store the values required by your macros. For example, the **PrintBothSides** macro we use in the Wrox PBS Duplex Print dialog (introduced in Part 2) saves the current settings as AutoText entries in the user's Normal template. However, the macros in the WroxHelp template (that we used to create Help topic files in Part 2) save the settings here, not in the Normal template, so, if it has a Write Reservation Password, they'll be lost when the user closes it.

Instead, you can use document variables to store the values in a document, if this is appropriate, or **SetPrivateProfileString()** to store them in an **.ini** file or Window's registry.

Adding Pages to the Template Dialog

Finally, remember that you can add your own tabs to the New dialog so that it's easier to organize the templates your users need. Word (and other Microsoft Office applications) display each subfolder in the **\Templates** folder on a separate tab. By deleting the ones you don't need and adding new ones, you can set it up exactly as you wish.

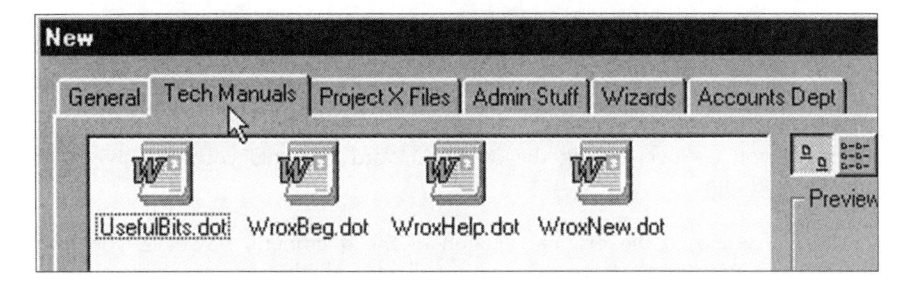

To create a new page, all you need to do is add a folder with the appropriate name to your **\Templates** folder. Keep the name fairly short to avoid it being truncated on the page tab. As long as there's at least one template in that folder, Word automatically displays the tab. To remove an existing page, you simply delete the subfolder or just delete any templates within it. It will no longer appear in the New dialog.

Sharing Documents Over a Network

When you open an existing document in Word, it isn't all loaded into memory at once. Instead, Word creates a temporary file and manipulates this. Only when you save the document is the temporary one assembled into a 'proper' Word document, replacing the original version stored on your disk. This is why, if you suffer a system failure, the original is still generally intact; you just lose the changes since the last save took place.

Simultaneous Editing of Documents

If you have more than one person editing a document simultaneously, they all have to work on their own copy. Word won't allow them to open the same document directly. If you try this, you get a message warning you that the document is in use:

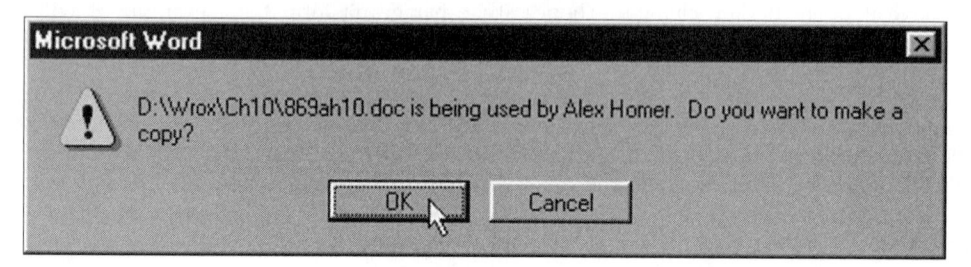

You can click OK to create a copy of the document as it currently stands and work with this copy instead of the original. However, when you come to save it, you get another warning, depending on what the other user has done while you had the document open. If they still have their copy open, you get this message:

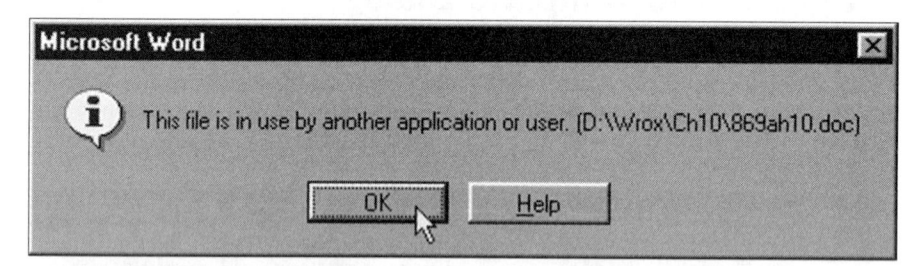

Clicking OK opens the Save As dialog, where you can specify a different name for your copy of the document. If you try overwriting the original, Word prevents you and gives you a warning that the file is read-only.

If the other user has closed the original version of the document, however, you have the option of replacing it with your copy. If you do, you will lose all the changes they made since you opened your copy, which is a sure way to decrease your popularity with your colleagues. Unless they are aware of what's happening and approve, you should choose No and create a copy with a different file name. If everyone is agreed that your version should be kept, click Yes.

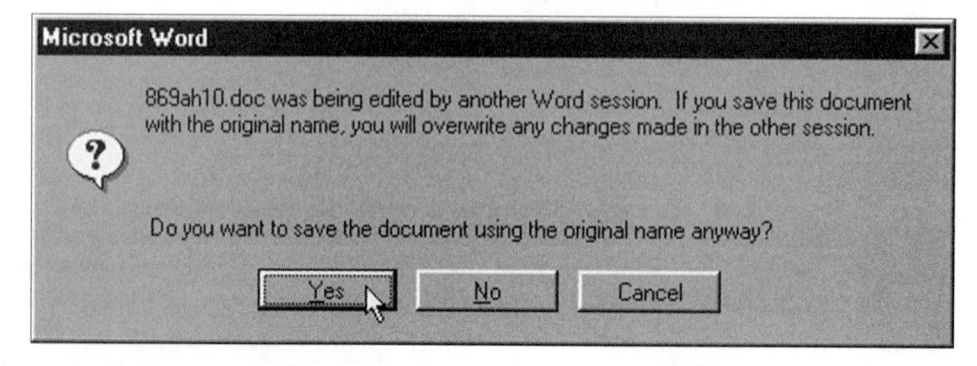

Comparing Different Versions of a Document

The result of simultaneous editing of a document is two or more copies with different names. The problem is, how do you reconcile all the different changes in the original document? The easiest way is to use Word's **compare versions** functionality. Open one of the edited document, select Revisions... from the Tools menu and click Compare Versions...

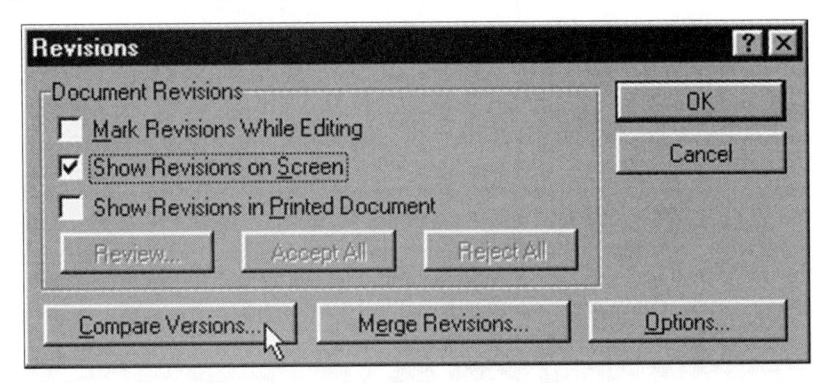

You select the original file using the normal Open dialog and Word places revision marks in the active document, showing where it differs from the other file. (We looked at revision marks in Chapter 6.) Turn on the Show Revisions on Screen option so that you can see all the places where the two documents differ. You can edit the document directly to take account of the revisions, or click the Review... button to open the Review Revisions dialog. Here, you can Find each revision and Accept or Reject them individually:

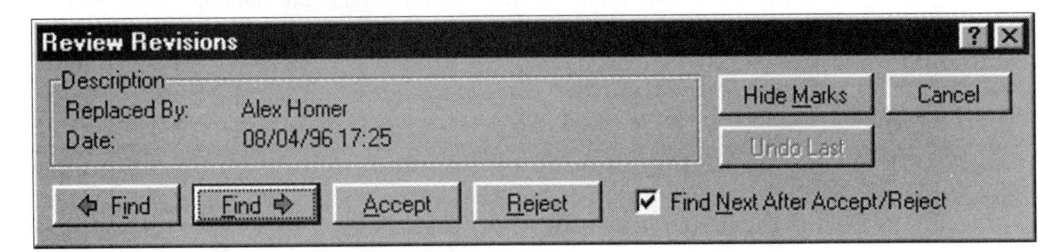

We can automate much of this process. You may find the following very useful if you regularly have a situation where several users have to edit the same document. It uses a macro to control how the documents are opened, so that the changes made by different users are regularly combined back in the original.

Automating Simultaneous Editing of a Document

We can use the WordBasic **ToolsCompareVersions** statement to compare documents in the same way as using the Revisions dialog. The problem is knowing when another version of the document has been created and what it's called. To overcome both these difficulties, we'll take over the whole process so we can control how and where each document is saved. You'll find this an interesting example of how WordBasic can completely change the behavior of Word.

The Plan for Our Wrox Multi-Edit Macro

The plan is simple enough. When a document is opened, we check to see whether it's already been opened by another user. If it has, say by user A, we create a copy in the same folder as the original, giving it a particular name so that we can identify it later. This copy is then edited by user B. If user C opens the original document, we repeat the process, using another unique and identifiable file name.

So we end up with several versions of the file. The file names will be the original name, plus a three digit number. The file **Original Name.doc** will spawn edited versions, named **Original Name 001.doc**, **Original Name 002.doc**, etc. Each time a user opens **Original Name.doc** while it's being edited by someone else, the next numbered file will be created.

Now we have to consider how to combine the changes. The best time to do this is when the original file is opened, when nobody else is editing it. We can look for any edited versions that have previously been created and compare these, one by one, to the original. We know what the files names of the edited copies will be and where they have been stored, because our macro did it in the first place. We've put together this macro for you to try.

Try It Out - Simultaneously Editing a Document with Wrox Multi-Edit

You'll need the template **MultiEdit.dot**, which is in the folder with the other sample files. Unless you changed the default when you installed the samples, this will be **C:\BegWord**.

1 Close Word if you have it running, then copy the file **MultiEdit.dot** from the samples folder into your Word **\Startup** folder. (Unless you changed the defaults when you installed Word 95 or Office 95, this will be **\Winword\Startup** or **\Msoffice\Winword\Startup**.) Now start Word so that the MultiEdit template is loaded globally. You can check it's there by looking in the Templates and Add-ins dialog.

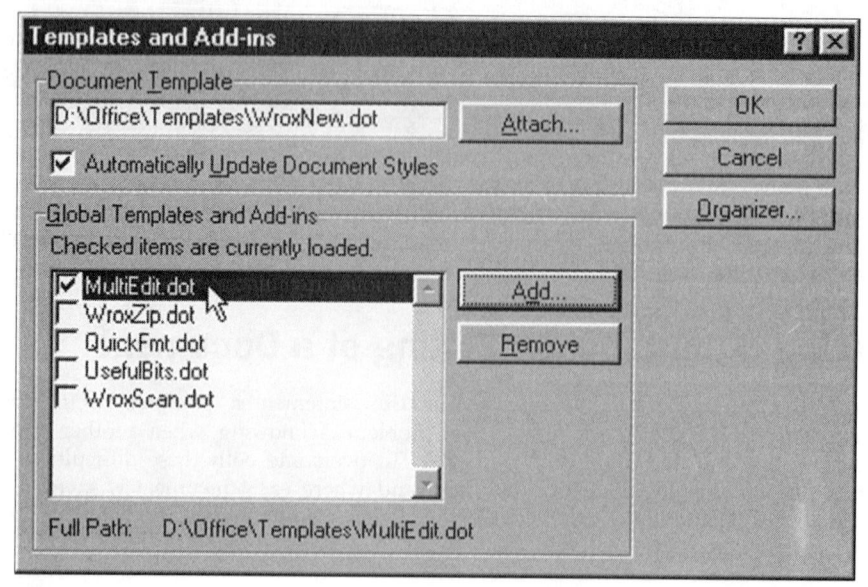

Chapter 10 - The Problems of Sharing Documents

2 Select New... from the File menu and select your Normal template, or click the New button on the toolbar, to create a new document based on the normal template.

3 Type some text into the document—a couple of lines will do. Then save it on your disk as `Test Document.doc`, in a folder where you can locate it later to 'clean up'.

> This document demonstrates the way Wrox Multi-Edit can be used to allow simultaneous editing of a document by several users. This is the original document.

4 Close the document `Test Document.doc`, then open it again in Word. This simulates the first person opening the document to edit it.

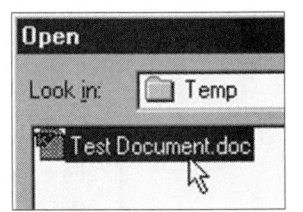

5 Now you need to start another instance of Word. This can be on another machine on the network that has access to the folder where you stored the `Test Document.doc` file. Alternatively, use the same computer by minimizing Word and starting another copy of Word from the Start menu.

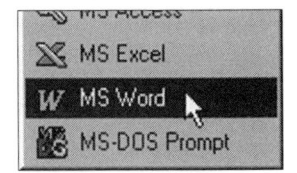

> **FYI** If you use a seperate copy of Word on another machine, make sure you place the MultiEdit template in its `\Startup` folder before you start it so that it also has access to the macro

6 In the second copy of Word, select Open... from the File menu and then open the same `Test Document.doc` file. You'll see a message warning you that it's already being edited:

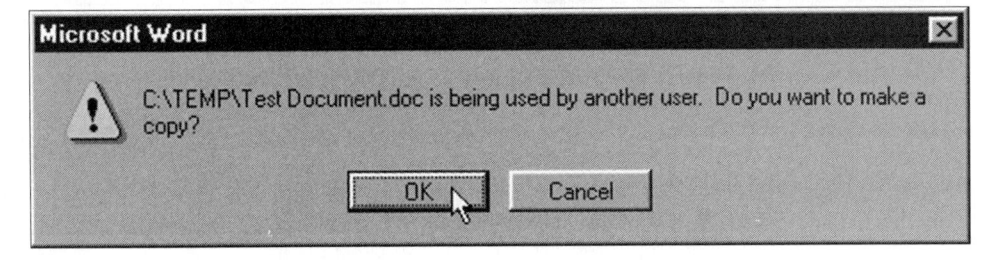

> Microsoft Word
>
> ⚠ C:\TEMP\Test Document.doc is being used by another user. Do you want to make a copy?
>
> [OK] [Cancel]

419

7 Click OK, and another message appears. Your copy of Test Document is saved as Test Document 001.doc automatically. Make one or more changes to the text and then Save and Close the document.

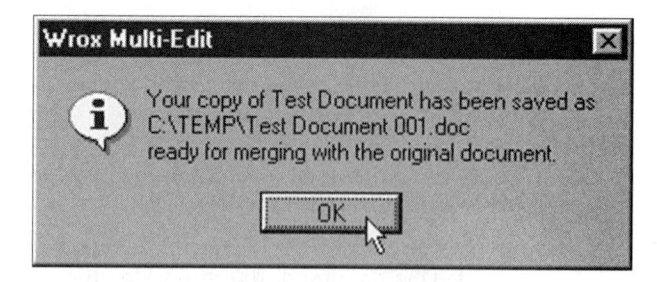

> **Wrox Multi-Edit**
> Your copy of Test Document has been saved as C:\TEMP\Test Document 001.doc ready for merging with the original document.
> [OK]

8 Now repeat the process by opening `Test Document.doc` again. Don't use the list of most recently used files in the File menu. You must use the File | Open... command or the Open button on the toolbar. This copy is automatically saved as `Test Document 002.doc`.

9 Make a different change to this text this time, then Close and Save the document, and Exit from Word.

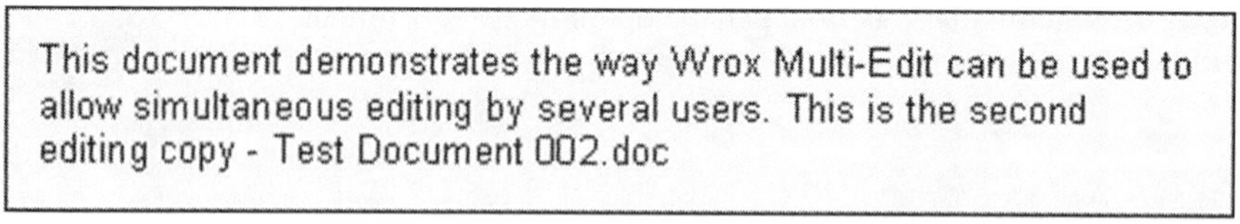

> This document demonstrates the way Wrox Multi-Edit can be used to allow simultaneous editing by several users. This is the second editing copy - Test Document 002.doc

10 Go back to the first instance of Word and close the original copy of `Test Document.doc` there.

How It Works

We now have the original document and two copies of it. Open My Computer or Explorer to see them. The two copies contain different changes to the text, so we need to compile these changes back in the original document. The macro in our MultiEdit template looks after this automatically for us, as you'll see next.

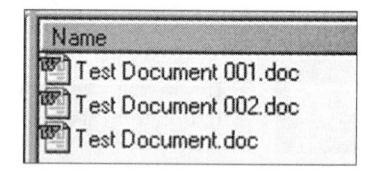

> **Name**
> Test Document 001.doc
> Test Document 002.doc
> Test Document.doc

Try It Out - Compiling the Edited Documents with Wrox Multi-Edit

You must have completed the previous Try It Out before starting this one. It shows how the original version of our `Test Document.doc` file can be updated with the changes made to the two copies.

1 Select Open... from the File menu, or click the Open button on the toolbar. Select the file `Test Document.doc` that we created in the previous example. *Don't* open in by selecting it in the most recently used files list in the File menu.

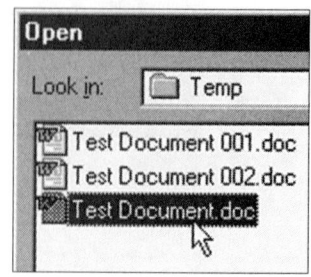

> **Open**
> Look in: [Temp]
> Test Document 001.doc
> Test Document 002.doc
> **Test Document.doc**

2 The document is opened in Word, and immediately a dialog is displayed telling you that there are other copies of the document which have been edited while the original was open:

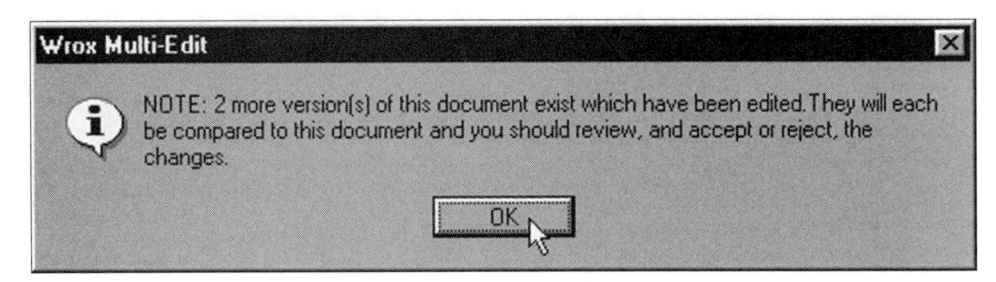

3 Click OK and the two documents are compared. When this is complete, you see revision marks showing where they differ and the Review Revisions dialog opens. The only point to watch is that we are actually comparing them the 'wrong way round', so the changes in the newer (**001**) version of the document are shown crossed out. The original version of the document is assumed to be the one you want to keep.

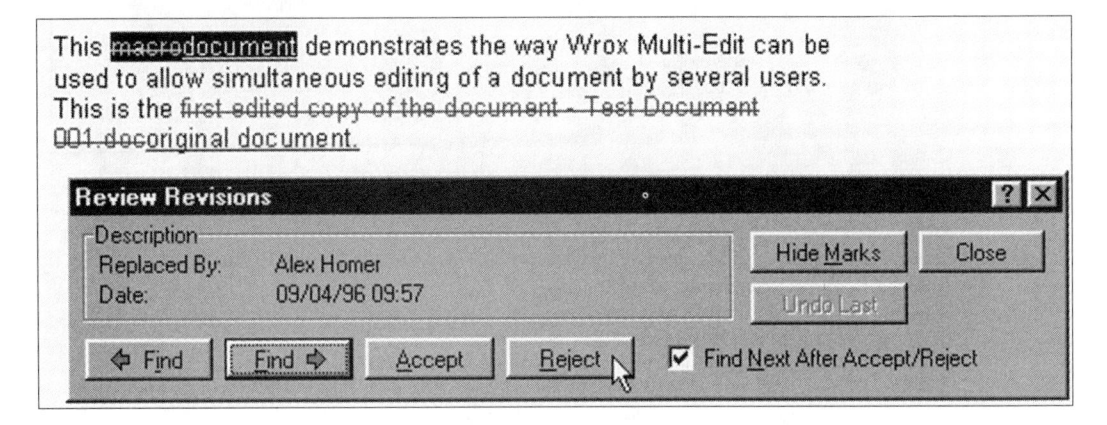

4 Click Find to move to the first revision. The word *document* was replaced by the word *macro* in the newer version, and we want to keep this change. To do so, you have to click Reject (not Accept). You'll see more about this later. Carry on clicking Reject for each revision, to update the original document.

5 When you've done them all, click Close to close the Review Revisions dialog. You are prompted to delete the other version of the document to prevent it being compared again when you next open the original document:

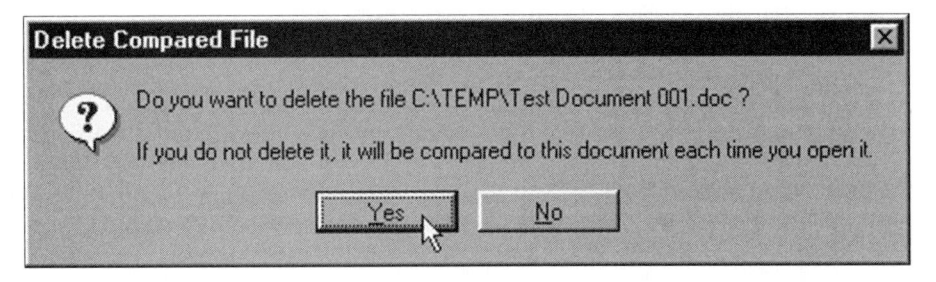

6 Click Yes to delete the document, then you get a message to say there is another edited version of the document:

> **Wrox Multi-Edit**
> NOTE: 1 more version(s) of this document exist which have been edited. They will each be compared to this document and you should review, and accept or reject, the changes.
> [OK]

7 Click OK and repeat the process of combining the documents. This time, you are combining the changes made in the second edited copy, **Test Document 002.doc**. You may get a message to say there are still revision marks in the original document. Just click Yes and continue to compare the next one.

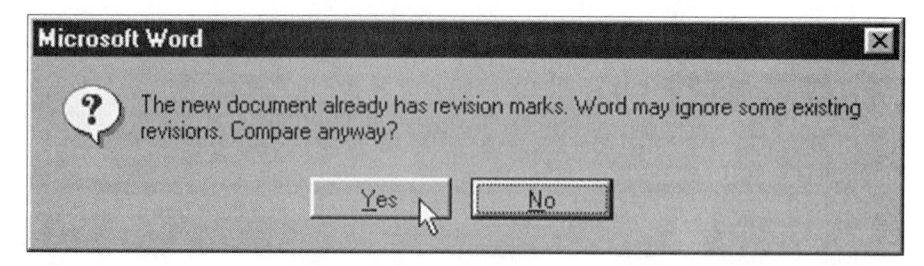

> **Microsoft Word**
> The new document already has revision marks. Word may ignore some existing revisions. Compare anyway?
> [Yes] [No]

8 Once you've reviewed the changes made to the second document, you have a fully up-to-date version of all three documents.

> This macro demonstrates the way Wrox Multi-Edit can be used to allow simultaneous editing by several users. This is the second editing copy - Test Document 002.doc

How It Works

The key to how the macro works is replacing the **FileOpen** command by our own version. That way, when a document is opened, we can check whether it's already being edited. If it is, we save the new copy using the 'next numbered' file name in the same folder. In our example, it was **Test Document 001.doc** and **Test Document 002.doc**. If the document isn't currently open elsewhere, we look for any of these files with a 'numbered' file name in the same folder as the document. If we find any, we loop through them, comparing each one to the original and displaying the Review Revisions dialog.

So, how do we know if a document is being edited elsewhere? Remember, Word creates a temporary file when it opens an existing document. All we have to do is to see if this file exists when we open our document. If it does, we know someone else is editing the document already.

An obvious way to start our macro is to use the name **AutoOpen**, so that it runs when a new document is created, but this won't work because the **AutoOpen** macro only runs once the document is opened. Even if it isn't being edited by another user, Word will create the temporary file as it opens the document, so it will always exist when the **AutoOpen** macro runs. This is why we have to take over the **FileOpen** command. We need to get the name of the file that is being opened and check for an existing temporary file before we open another copy.

We've placed all the main code in a single macro, named **OpenMultiEdit**, and created a separate **FileOpen** macro which simply runs this macro:

```
Sub MAIN   'This is the FileOpen macro
    OpenMultiEdit
End Sub
```

So now you can see why we can't use the most recently used file list (in the File menu) to open a document. It doesn't run the **FileOpen** macro.

> **FYI**
>
> You need to bear this in mind when you write macros in Word. Selecting from the most recently used file list (MRU) bypasses the normal **FileOpen** macro. So if your user has already opened the document before, your code could fail if they open it again using the MRU. You can prevent this by removing the MRU list from the **File** menu with:
>
> `ToolsOptionsGeneral .RecentFiles = 0`
>
> You can also control the number of files that appear, using
>
> `ToolsOptionsGeneral .RecentFileCount = <no.files>`

Here's the start of the **OpenMultiEdit** macro:

```
Dim Shared CFiles$(0)

Sub MAIN
    On Error Goto OME_Exit
    Dim DLG As FileOpen
    GetCurValues DLG
    If Dialog(DLG) = 0 Then Goto OME_Exit
    ThisPath$ = Files$(".")
    ThisFile$ = DLG.Name
    If Left$(ThisFile$, 1) = Chr$(34) Then
        ThisFile$ = Mid$(ThisFile$, 2, Len(ThisFile$) - 2)
    EndIf
    If Right$(ThisFile$, 4) <> ".doc" Then Goto OME_Open
```

We start by declaring a **FileOpen** dialog record and getting the current values to fill it. Then we display the dialog so that the user can select the file they want to open. If they click Cancel, we just exit from the macro, but, if they click Open, we capture the file name and current folder before we actually open the file. The Open dialog returns Windows 95-style long file names enclosed in quotation marks, so, before we go any further, we strip off any that it's added. We also check to make sure that it's a Word document being opened. If it isn't, we jump to the end of the macro and open the file normally, then exit.

Before we open a document file, we need to look for the matching temporary file. Word uses a file name which has the first two characters replaced by **~$** for this file. (If the name is less than eight characters, however, it fills it out to eight, keeping more of the original name. We'll look at this in detail in a while.) Our **GetTempFileName$()** function returns the equivalent temporary file name, and we can see whether it exists. Notice that we've used the **FileFind** statement rather than the **Files$()** function here. **Files$()** may fail to find a file if it's open in another application and, of course, the temporary file is open in the other copy of Word that is running. Once we've executed **FileFind**, we can open the document:

```
ThisFile$ = Left$(ThisFile$, Len(ThisFile$) - 4)
TempFile$ = GetTempFileName$(ThisFile$ + ".doc")
FileFind .SearchPath = ThisPath$, .Name = TempFile$
FileOpen DLG
```

Now we can see if this document is actually a copy of the original. If it is, **CountFoundFiles()** will return **1** because the **FileFind** statement found the temporary file. Word will already have displayed the dialog warning that the document is already open and opened it as a copy. So we just need to save this copy, using our special file name, and tell the user what's happening. Our macro contains the **GetFreeFileName$()** function that we introduced in Part 1. It returns the next numbered file name if the one you supply already exists:

```
    If CountFoundFiles() = 0 Then
        'not being edited - compare with other versions
        . . .
        ( we'll look at this part in a while )
        . . .
    Else
        'open by another user - save new copy
        NewFile$ = GetFreeFileName$(ThisPath$ + "\" + ThisFile$)
        FileSaveAs .Name = NewFile$
        Msg$ = "Your copy of " + ThisFile$ + " has been saved as" + NewFile$
        MsgBox Msg$, "Wrox Multi-Edit", 64
    EndIf
    GoTo OME_Exit
OME_Open:
    FileOpen DLG
OME_Exit:
End Sub
```

So, we've looked after the situation where the file is already open, but the macro also has to handle comparing the other versions if it isn't. If the **FileFind** statement didn't find a temporary file (i.e. **CountFoundFiles()** returned zero), we first need to see whether there are any other versions of the file in the same folder. Again, we use **FileFind**, supplying an argument containing the **?** wildcard characters so that it will only match files which have a number added to the name of the document:

```
        'not being edited - compare with other versions
        FindFile$ = ThisFile$ + " ???.doc"
        FileFind .SearchPath = ThisPath$, .Name = FindFile$
        FCount = CountFoundFiles()
```

Our variable **FCount** will contain the number of existing copies of the document. If it's not zero, we build a list of the names in the **Shared** array **CFiles$()**. You've seen this technique used several times before:

```
        If FCount > 0 Then                  'copies do exist -
            Redim CFiles$(FCount - 1)       'so get a list of their names
            For Loop = 0 To FCount - 1
                CFiles$(Loop) = FoundFileName$(Loop + 1)
            Next
```

Now we're ready to go. We loop for each file displaying a message, then comparing it to the active (original) document. We also switch on revision marks, so that they're visible on screen, and display the Review Revisions dialog. When the user clicks Close, we can delete the original file if we need to. Once they've compared all the copies, we hide revision marks and exit.

```
        For Loop = 0 To FCount - 1
            Msg$ = "NOTE:" + Str$(FCount - Loop) + " more version(s) of
            Msg$ = Msg$ + this document exist which have been edited."
            MsgBox Msg$, "Wrox Multi-Edit", 64
            On Error Resume Next
            ToolsCompareVersions .Name = CFiles$(Loop)
            ToolsReviewRevisions .ShowMarks
            Redim DLG As ToolsReviewRevisions
            If Dialog(DLG) <> 0 Then
                Msg$ = "Do you want to delete the file " + CFiles$(Loop)
                If MsgBox  (Msg$, "Delete Compared File", 36) Then
                    Kill CFiles$(Loop)
                EndIf
            EndIf
        Next
        ToolsReviewRevisions .HideMarks
    EndIf
```

Comparing Documents the 'Right Way Round'

We mentioned earlier on that we were comparing the original document and the copy the 'wrong way round'. Word's **ToolsCompareVerions** statement, and the Compare Versions command available in the Revisions dialog, assume that the active document (the one you currently have open) is the one that has been edited. It compares this against another document, which is assumes is the original.

In our macro, the document that is open (active) is the original, because that's the only time we can combine the changes from the other copies. The revision marks show our original document as revising the edited copy. This is why you had to click Reject to accept changes made in the copy.

How you view this depends on whether you think the original document should take precedence over the edited one. If you want to change round the way that they're compared, you would first have to open each copy listed in the **CFiles$** array in turn and compare it to the one the user had selected. Then you would have to delete them all and re-open the original. Like all the other code in this book, you are free to change it so that it works the way you need it to!

Using Logical Comparisons to Generate Values

One of the functions we've used in our **OpenMultiEdit** macro returns the name of the Word temporary file given the actual file name of the document. This is relatively easy. The rules are:

- If the file name is eight characters or more, replace the first two with `~$`.
- If the file name is seven characters, use `~$` and the last six characters of the name.
- If the file name is six characters or less, use `~$` and the whole of the name.

Here's the code that we've used:

```
Function GetTempFileName$(FName$)
   TFLen = Len(Left$(FName$, InStr(FName$, ".") - 1))
   TFPos = 1 + Abs(TFLen > 6) + Abs(TFLen > 7)
   GetTempFileName$ = "~$" + Mid$(FName$, TFPos)
End Function
```

The trick is to find the position in the name from where we want to keep the rest of it. If the name is eight characters long, we want position **3**, for seven characters, we want position **2**, and for six or less characters, we want position **1**. To get this number we've used the line:

```
TFPos = 1 + Abs(TFLen > 6) + Abs(TFLen > 7)
```

It works because when we carry out a comparison, we get the result **True** (**-1**) or **False** (**0**). The **Abs()** function returns the absolute value of its argument, converting **-1** into **1** but leaving **0** alone. So, we can add together the results. For example, if the length of the file name is seven characters, we get:

```
                    TFPos = 1 + Abs(-1) + Abs(0)
therefore:          TFPos = 1 + 1 + 0
which gives:        TFPos = 2              'the result we want
```

> **FYI** You may need to experiment with **Wrox Multi-Edit** to make it work correctly on your system. How it works depends on where the temporary files are created and how your network handles long file names. If you copy the document to a local machine and then open them there, it will also fail to find the temporary file and not perform correctly.

Protecting Yourself from Viruses

In the last few years, we've seen the rise of a new threat to all computer-based systems. As in all walks of life, there's an element of the community who seek fame and fortune through negative aspects of technology. One of these aspects is the increasing number of viruses that threaten your valuable data.

A **computer virus** is a piece of code that has two properties: it can cause damage to the system it exists on and replicate itself so that it travels to other systems. Simply running an infected application places the virus code on your system and, once there, it tags itself onto other application files. When you pass on one of these files to another person, the process is repeated on their system.

Until recently, these viruses only affected executable (program) files, but there are an increasing number of document viruses being discovered. As applications have included more powerful programming languages, such as WordBasic, virus writers have found ways of using these to create a virus which exists in a document rather than a program file. So, while you should still use an anti-virus program to scan any files you copy to your system (and many now also look for the well known document viruses), this is often not enough.

How Document Viruses Work

If you are reading this expecting to learn how to write a virus, then you'll be disappointed. We won't be providing any samples! However, you do need to appreciate how they can exist and how you protect yourself against them.

Document viruses are generally application-specific. One that affects Microsoft Access databases won't work with Lotus Approach because they use different types of application programming language. However, taking Access as an example, it's not hard to see how dangerous an unknown database can be. Access allows you to create VBA (Visual Basic for Applications) code modules within a database file. VBA contains all the functionality needed to rename or delete files, change entries in the Windows' registry, or otherwise interfere with your system as a whole. Because you can create code which runs as soon as the database file is opened, it can wreak havoc before you know what's happening.

Word, however, is different. You can only place code in macros, and macros can only be stored in a template, not directly in a document, so we should be safe enough. But no doubt you've heard about Concept, the virus that found fame by being distributed in a Word document on a Microsoft Developer's CD-ROM. Concept caused a huge uproar when it appeared, removing the comfortable 'it can't happen to me' syndrome which previously existed.

Word Document Viruses

The problem with Word isn't really to do with Word itself, it's more a problem with the Windows operating system. You saw in Part 2 how we can persuade Windows that a Word template is not really a template, but a wizard. We simply change the file extension part of the name from **.dot** to **.wiz**. Windows then quite happily shows it with a new icon and description:

Equally, replacing **.dot** with **.doc** fools Windows into thinking that it's a document, not a template. However, Word is cleverer that that. When you load the file, complete with all its macros, Word recognizes that it's a template and will calmly run any macros it contains.

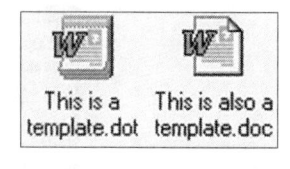

To the user, it looks just like a document. When it's open in Word, the title bar still reads This is also a template.doc. Of course, a template can contain text just like a document, so who's going to notice anyway? Even opening the Properties dialog for the document from within Word, or in My Computer or Explorer, shows that the operating system is still convinced that it's a normal document. Here's the Properties dialog for a file that we'll be looking at in this part of the chapter. It's actually a template that contains the Concept virus, and just loading it could start the process of infecting our whole system. So how can we protect ourselves?

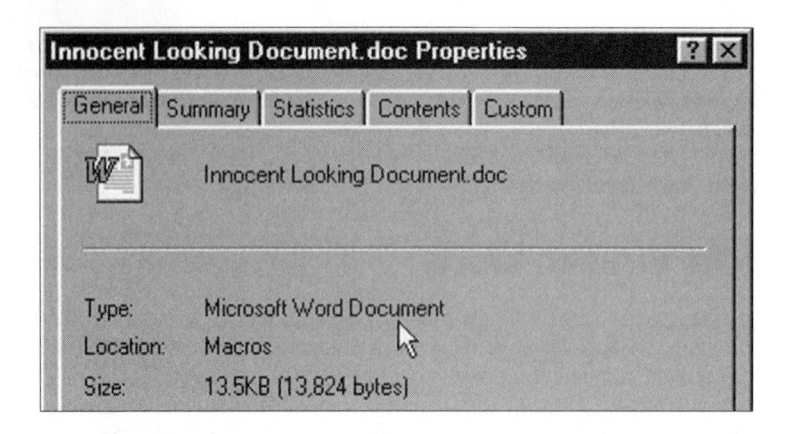

Fighting the Virus Threat

As with any illness, you don't start getting better until you treat it, and you can't start to treat it until you know you're ill. To make matters worse, the longer you wait before you start the treatment, the harder it is to recover. Computer viruses are no different. If you let one get established, it can spread right through your files, and those of your colleagues, and, then, getting rid of it becomes a huge undertaking.

There are three stages to protecting yourself from damage through viruses:

- Recognizing that you're infected.
- Removing the virus.
- Preventing other viruses getting established.

Once you know how to check for a virus, you can and should do it regularly. Even if you aren't infected at the moment, you should certainly be taking steps to prevent viruses getting a hold on your system in the future. The threat can only get worse as virus writers improve their techniques. In fact, the Concept virus appears to have been written as a warning of what is possible rather than with malicious intent. The macro that could actually do the damage contains just a **REM** statement:

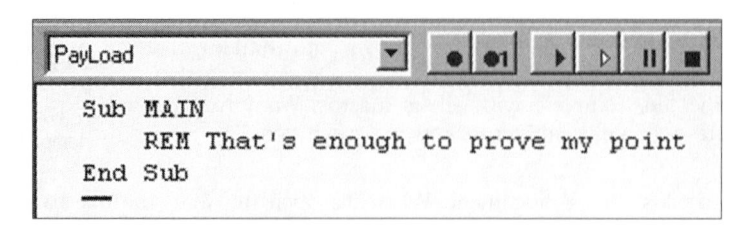

```
Sub MAIN
    REM That's enough to prove my point
End Sub
```

Recognizing that You're Infected

Once you know what to look for, the current types of Word document virus are easy enough to spot. You have three tools ready to hand in Word that can help: the Macro, Templates and Add-ins and Organizer dialogs.

Using the Macro Dialog to Check for a Virus

Select Macro... from the Tools menu and make sure that Macros Available In: is set to All Active Templates. Look at the list of macros. If there are any that you don't recognize, you should immediately be suspicious. This screenshot shows the macros that are available when the **Innocent Looking Document.dot** file we saw above is open. The AutoExec, AutoMacros, FilePrint and PrintBothSides macros are ones we've created and stored in our Normal template. But the others make up the Concept virus.

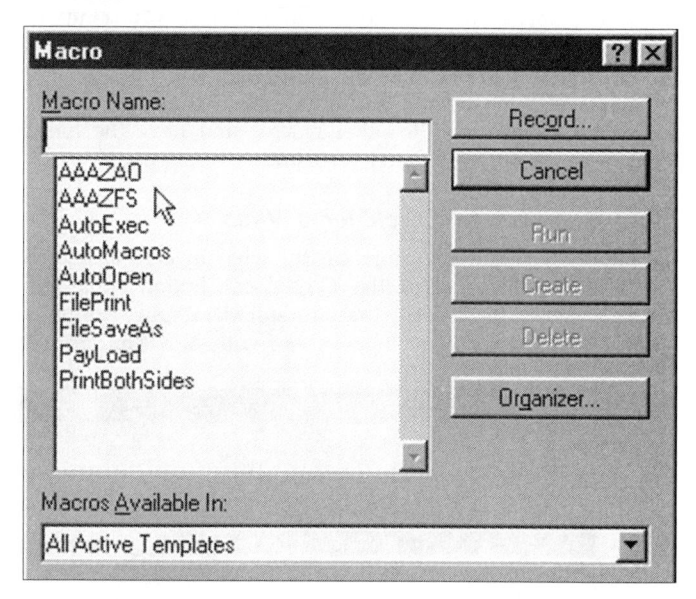

Using the Templates Dialog to Check for a Virus

One other way is to select Templates... from the File menu when you have a suspicious document open. This dialog shows the name of the template that the document is attached to. But look at the screen shot below, which again shows the Innocent Looking Document file. The Document Template entry is blank and disabled. Why? Because our innocent looking document is in fact a template. That's how it can store the macros you saw in the Macros dialog above.

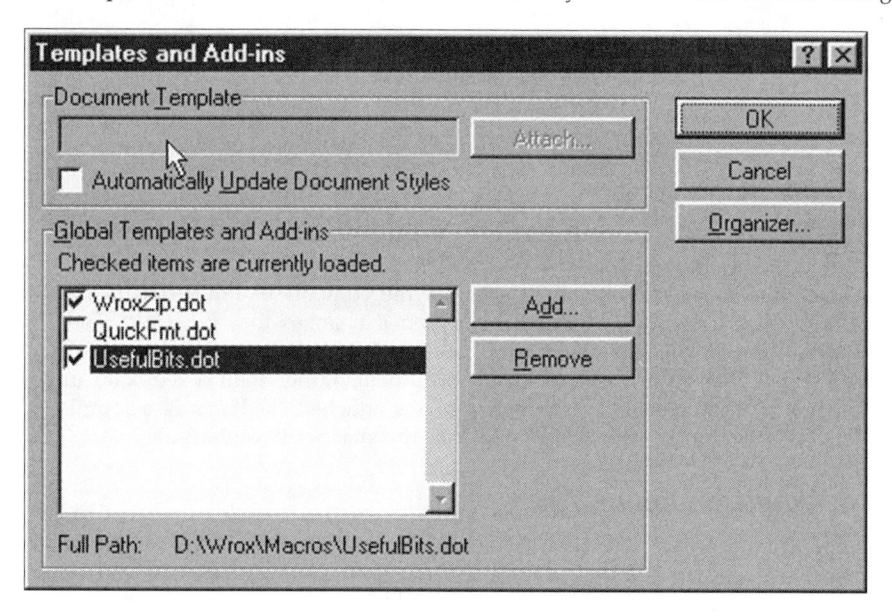

While you've got this dialog open, also take a look at the list of Global Templates and Add-ins. If a template has been copied into Word's `\Startup` folder, it will automatically be loaded and shown with a tick in the list. Make sure you know what the add-ins you've got loaded actually do. Remember that the macros in each one are available globally. You may also see **Word link libraries** listed here. These are a set of functions written in another language, such as C or C++, which are available to other macros and have the file extension `.wll` instead of `.dot`. Again, beware of any you don't recognize.

Using Organizer to Check for a Virus

Finally, you can see more clearly what macros are stored in any template by opening the Organizer dialog. Click the Organizer... button while the Templates and Add-ins dialog is open. This shows the macros that are stored in your Normal template, and the active template if this is different. Here's what it looks like with our `Innocent Looking Document.doc` file loaded:

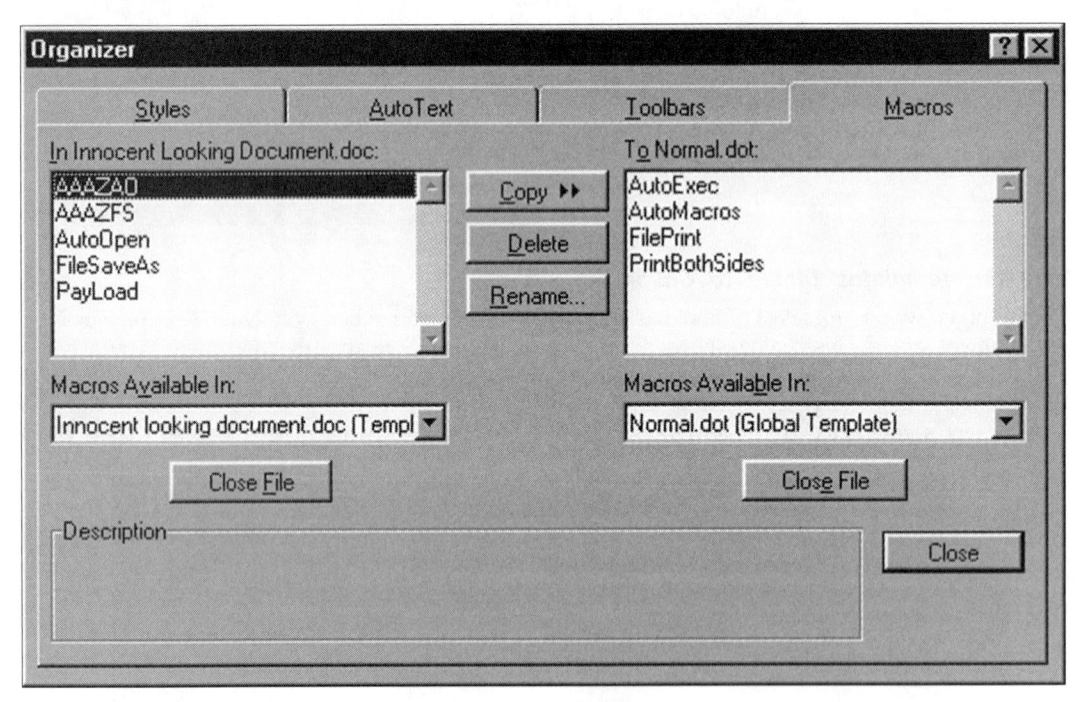

You can also use the Organizer dialog to examine the contents of other documents and templates. Click Close File, then click it again when it changes to read Open File. The Open dialog will default to looking for Word templates (`*.dot`), but you can change this to `*.doc` to open a document. If the document really is a document, rather than a template in disguise, Organizer will show the contents of the template it's attached to. If it's is a template masquerading as a document, however, you'll see the macros it contains.

Removing a Word Document Virus

To remove a document virus, you need to delete the macros that are causing it to spread. Depending on how long it is since it found its way onto your system, this can be a long and arduous task. Of course, the macros themselves could be different for different types of virus. Here are the steps that you need to go through.

Cleaning the Open Document

The first step is to deal with the document you've got open if it contains a virus. Just by saving it as it is could make the situation worse. Select the name of the open document in the Macros Available In: box and delete any 'auto' macros, such as `AutoOpen`, `AutoExec`, `AutoNew`, `AutoClose` or `AutoExit`. Also, delete any which have the same name as Word's built-in commands, such as `FileSaveAs`. Any others macros won't run by themselves, so you can either delete them or leave them alone or if you want to study the virus afterwards. Instead of deleting the macros, you can also try renaming them so that they don't run automatically, say by adding an `x` in front of the existing name, using the Organizer dialog.

Cleaning Your Normal Template

If the virus's macros have already run—and unless you check every document as you open it, they may have run without you noticing—you now have to check and remove it from all the other places it could have spread to. It only takes one infected document to start the process all over again. The key component in spreading a virus is your Normal template, which is always loaded, and any other templates you load when Word starts.

Close all open documents and open the Macro dialog again. See if the virus macros have been copied to your Normal template. (You'll know the names of the macros that caused the trouble, because you've seen them in the Macros dialog.) Then repeat the process with all the globally loaded templates listed in the templates dialog. If none are infected, you've probably caught the virus before it could spread.

Cleaning other Documents and Templates

If any of your templates are infected, you now need to check every other document and template you may have opened since it appeared. You can do this by using Window's Find dialog to find all the documents or template files on your hard disk. In the Named: box enter *.do?, which will match with all Word's **.doc** and **.dot** files. For Look In:, select the root of the drive you want to search, or your whole computer (My Computer) to search every drive.

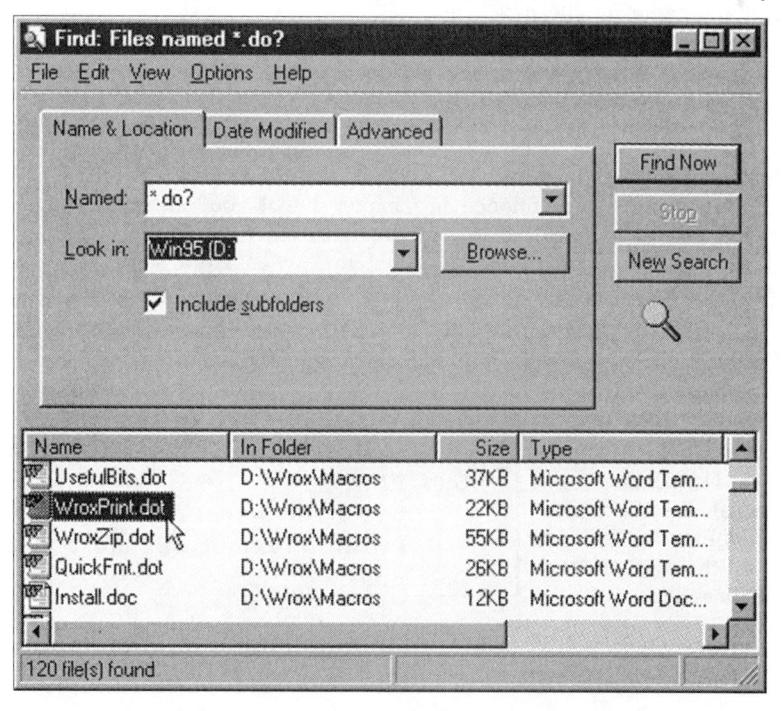

Once you've got the list of files (some of which may not be Word files), you can see when they were last modified or accessed by right-clicking on the name and selecting properties from the short-cut menu. In the General tab, you can see the date it was last changed or opened:

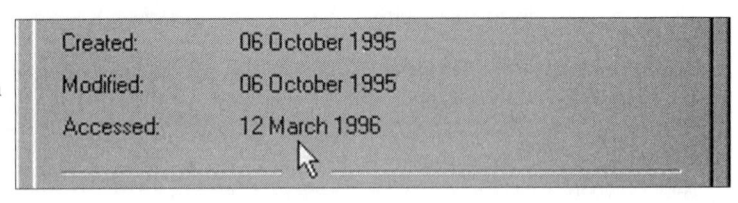

Created:	06 October 1995
Modified:	06 October 1995
Accessed:	12 March 1996

Do not open any of the files in Word. Instead, use the Organizer dialog to see what macros are in them. Once you find one that is not infected, it's very likely that any which were last modified before this one won't be infected either, so you may not have to work on all the files after all. But remember any back-ups you've made on tape or disk. Viruses can often pop up again long after you think you've removed them. Simply opening an archived document which contains the virus starts the infection off all over again.

Recovering the Original Document

Once you've disarmed the virus and cleaned up any infection, you may find you have to recover the documents that have been infected. Remember, it's likely that the virus will have saved them as templates, rather than documents. Word won't allow you to save a template back as a document, even using a macro.

The easiest way out is simply to copy the text from the original document (which is now a template) to a new document. Create a new document based on the correct template, i.e. the one it should be attached to. In the original document, select all the text with Select All on the Edit menu and copy the text. Switch to the new blank document and paste in the text. Go back to the original one and close it without saving any changes, then save the new document with the same file name as the original one. Of course, if you want to keep the old document, you can use a different file name for the new one.

Protecting Yourself from Document Viruses

There are ways that you can protect yourself from the current generation of document viruses, and probably from new ones. To establish itself on your system, a virus has to be executed when the document is loaded. It can do this using one of Word's auto macros, such as **AutoExec** or **AutoOpen**. We mentioned in Chapter 1 that you can prevent auto macros running quite easily. One way is to create an **AutoExec** macro in your Normal template which switches off auto macros. Because **Normal.dot** is loaded first when Word starts, auto macros in other templates will not run.

Turn Off AutoMacros

Creating the **AutoExec** macro is easy. Select Macro... from the Tools menu and set the Macros Available In: to Normal.dot (Global Template). For the macro name enter AutoExec, and click Create. Between the **Sub MAIN** and **End Sub** lines enter:

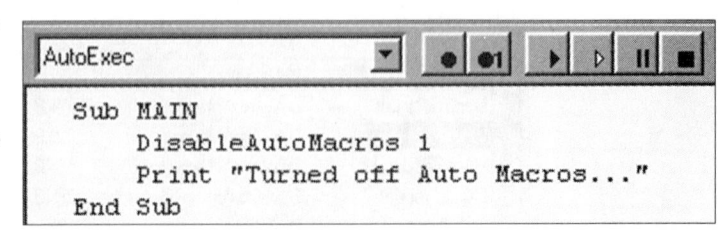

```
Sub MAIN
    DisableAutoMacros 1
    Print "Turned off Auto Macros..."
End Sub
```

Save this macro and then run it by double-clicking on it in the Macro dialog. Word switches auto macros on by default when it starts, so our new macro will switch them off after Word has loaded each time. Now a virus can't establish itself automatically when the document is loaded. (Later in the chapter we'll look at another way of controlling auto macros.)

Check the Contents of the Document

If you are the least suspicious about a document, check what's in it before you open it. Select Macro... from the Tools menu and click the Organizer... button in the Macro dialog. Click Close File, then click it again when it changes to read Open File. The Open dialog will default to looking for Word templates (*.dot) but you can change this to *.doc to open a document. If it's is actually a template in disguise, you'll see the macros it contains.

Check the File Type when You Save it

Remember from earlier chapters how you can replace any Word command with your own code, so doing almost anything with a loaded document could run a macro which will damage your system instead of executing the original command. It's likely that a virus will try to save your document as a template rather than as a document, so the first thing you should do after loading any suspect document is to select Save As... from the File menu, rather than just saving it with the toolbar button or Save command. That way, you can immediately see whether it's a template. The Save as type: box is set to Document Template (*.dot) and grayed out. Click Cancel instead of saving it.

This is often your first warning, so make a point of always checking this when you open a document for the first time.

We've supplied you with some WordBasic macros that you can use to help protect yourself from viruses. Most new anti-virus programs now check for the common Word viruses, but new viruses are likely to appear regularly in the future. We'll show you how to install Wrox Virus Scan, and how to use it.

Try It Out - Installing Wrox Virus Scan as an Add-in

You'll need the file **WroxScan.dot** for this and the next two examples. You will find it in the samples folder with the other files you installed from the disk that accompanies this book. Unless you changed the defaults during installation, your samples folder will be **C:\BegWord**.

1   Close any open documents, then close Word altogether if it is running.

2   Using My Computer or Explorer, copy the template **WroxScan.dot** into your Word **\Startup** folder. Unless you changed the defaults when you installed Word 95 or Office 95, this will be **\Winword\Startup** or **\Msoffice\Winword\Startup**.

3   Start Word again. The WroxScan template is loaded automatically, and will be loaded each time you start Word in future.

How It Works

By placing the template in Word's `\Startup` folder, we force it to be loaded as a global template each time Word starts. To remove it for the current session, select Templates... from the File menu and uncheck the box next to it. When you start Word again, though, it will be reloaded automatically.

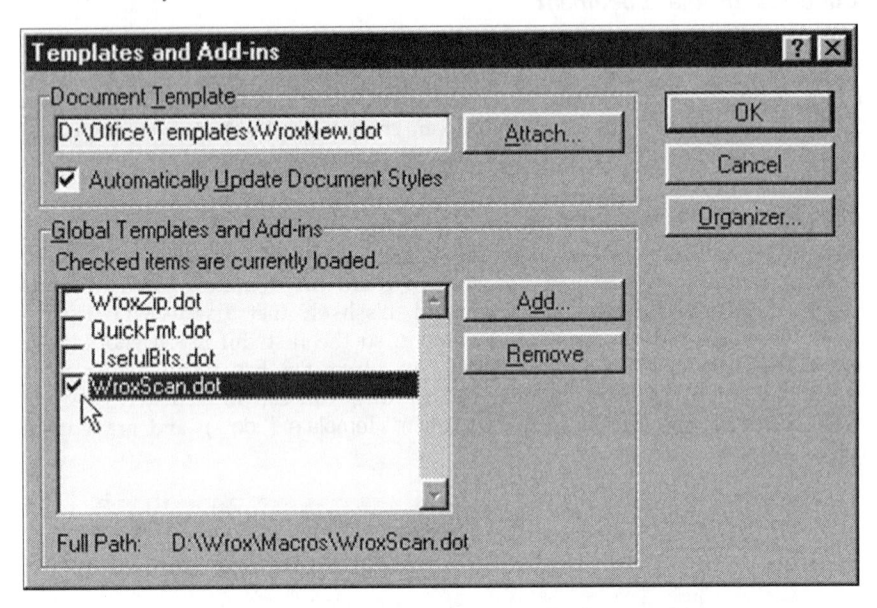

If you prefer to only load it when you want to use it, you can place it in a different folder, say your default `\Templates` folder, then you can load and unload it by checking or unchecking it in the Templates and Add-ins dialog. However, the `AutoMacros` macro, which allows you to control whether macros in other templates can run automatically, will only be available when WroxScan is loaded.

Copying the WroxScan Macros to Your Normal Template

To get the maximum benefit, you should load WroxScan every time Word starts. If you are short of memory but want the `AutoMacros` and `VirusScan` features to be permanently available, you can copy them into your Normal template instead. This saves the separate WroxScan template being loaded globally each time Word starts.

Try It Out - Installing Wrox Virus Scan in Your Normal Template

1 Open the WroxScan template by selecting Open... from the File menu. Then open the Organizer dialog by selecting Templates... from the File menu and clicking the Organizer... button.

2 Click the Macros tab, and in the list of macros select VirusScan, AutoMacros and AutoExec. Click the Copy button to copy them into your Normal template.

> **FYI** If you already have an `AutoExec` macro in your **Normal** template (you'll see it in the list in the **Organizer** dialog) don't copy the `AutoExec` macro from **WroxScan**. Instead, you need to add a line to your existing `AutoExec` macro. We'll show you how in step 6.

3 Click the Toolbar tab in Organizer and copy the toolbar WDAM into your Normal template. Then click Close to return to Word and close the WroxScan template.

4 You'll see the new toolbar WDAM which is now stored in your Normal template. Click the Close button on this toolbar to hide it.

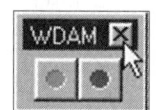

5 Select Customize... from the Tools menu and open the Menus tab in the Customize dialog. Select Macros in the Categories: list, then VirusScan in the Macros: list, and Add Below the &Templates command on the &File menu. Then repeat the process with the File(No document) menu.

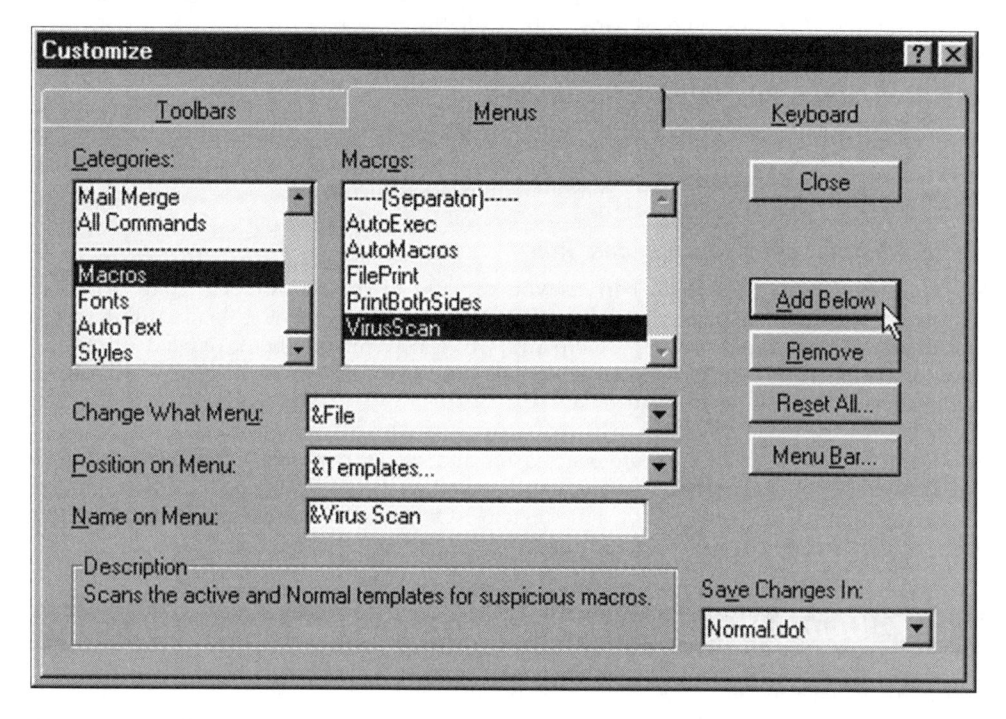

6 If you *already* have an `AutoExec` macro in your Normal template, you shouldn't have copied the new one from `WroxScan.dot`. Instead of replacing the whole macro with the new version, you need to add the following line to it:

```
AutoMacros.SetToolbarButton(0) 'No toggle
```

You must also remove any other lines in your `AutoExec` macro which contain the `DisableAutoMacro` statement, as these may prevent the new macro working properly.

> **FYI** Don't forget to remove the copy of **WroxScan** from your Word **\Startup** folder once you've copied the macros into your **Normal** template.

Uninstalling Wrox Virus Scan

If you have installed WroxScan by copying it into your Word **\Startup** folder, you can uninstall it simply by deleting this copy or moving it to another folder. By placing it in your **\Templates**, folder you can still load and unload it globally using the Templates and Add-ins dialog. Once you've moved or deleted the template, right-click on the Standard toolbar, click Customize..., and drag the Auto Macros button off it.

If you have installed WroxScan in your Normal template, you need to delete the macros again to uninstall it. Open Organizer and, in the Macros tab, delete the macros **VirusScan**, **AutoMacros** and **AutoExec** from **Normal.dot**. If you added the line **AutoMacros.SetToolbarButton(0)** to your existing **AutoExec** macro, just delete this line instead. Then open the Toolbars page and delete the toolbar WDAM. Close Organizer and right-click the Standard toolbar. Select Customize... and drag the Auto Macros button off the toolbar.

Using the WroxScan Template Macros

The two macros that you'll find most useful are **AutoMacros**, which switches auto macros on and off using a toolbar button, and **VirusScan**, which scans for any suspicious macros in a document's template, or a template masquerading as a document.

Controlling whether Auto Macros can Run

As you've seen, one of the main barriers you can use to protect yourself from viruses is to make sure you prevent any auto macros from running when a document is loaded. But this has an unfortunate side-effect. Many of the templates we've used in this book depend on an **AutoOpen** or **AutoNew** macro to work properly. If you permanently disable all auto macros, you lose the functionality and convenience they offer.

The ideal situation is to switch auto macros on and off as required. Off when you are loading an unknown document so that you can check whether it's safe, and on for the templates you use regularly and which depend on auto macros. Once you've installed the WroxScan template, you have this feature available all the time.

Try It Out - Using the Wrox Auto Macros Button

You'll need to have installed the WroxScan template for this example, either globally so that it's shown in the Templates and Add-ins dialog, or by copying the macros into your Normal template.

1 Take a look at your Standard toolbar. It should contain a button with a green dot on it. Moving the mouse-pointer over it shows the tool-tip Auto Macros:

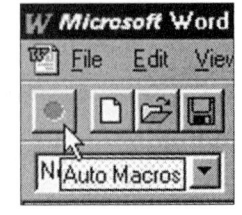

FYI If you can't see the button, select **Macro...** from the **Tools** menu and select the macro **AutoMacros** in the list. Then click the **Run** button.

2 Click the button and it changes to a red dot. At the same time, a message is displayed in the status bar at the bottom of the Word window. To prove it works, open the Book Order application we used in Chapter 5 from your samples folder. The Wizard dialog doesn't appear because the `AutoNew` macro which displays it doesn't run.

3 Close the Book Order application and click the Auto Macros button again. Auto macros are turned back on. Now try opening the Book Order application again and you'll see that it starts up automatically.

4 Click the Auto Macros button once more to turn auto macros off, then close Word altogether. When you start Word again, the button is red and auto macros are turned off. If you repeat the process when the button is green, Word starts with it in the same state and with auto macros turned on.

How It Works

The theory behind the macro is simple. We just use the WordBasic `DisableAutoMacros` statement to switch auto macros on or off. There is, however, a problem. Word doesn't have a `DisableAutoMacros()` function to tell us the existing setting, so we need to store the setting each time we change it. We could use a document variable, but it would mean each document could contain a different value. Another method is to use an AutoText entry in the Normal template. The code you can see below, however, uses an **.ini** file to store the setting.

We created the `Wroxword.ini` file in Chapter 5, with our `WroxPic` macros, so we'll add a section to it for our `AutoMacros` value. You can open the **.ini** file in NotePad to see what it looks like when the `AutoMacros` macro has run.

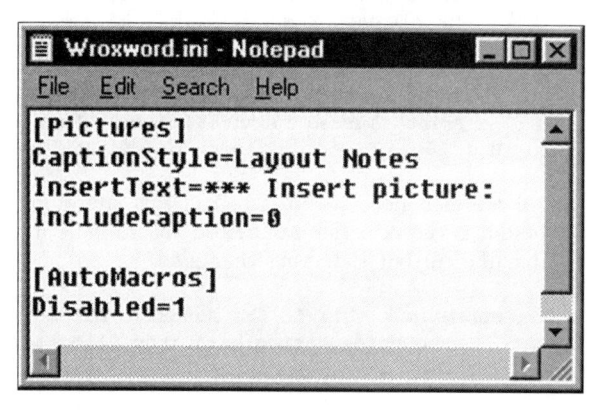

```
[Pictures]
CaptionStyle=Layout Notes
InsertText=*** Insert picture:
IncludeCaption=0

[AutoMacros]
Disabled=1
```

The main routine for `AutoMacros` is called `SetToolbarButton` and takes an argument, `Toggle`. If this is `True`, it reverses the state of the button and executes a `DisableAutoMacros` statement with an appropriate argument, **1** to turn auto macros off and **0** to turn them back on again. If `Toggle` is `False` (**0**), it simply updates the button face without changing the setting of auto macros. It also writes the new setting back into the **.ini** file afterwards.

Because other macros can turn auto macros on and off, the Auto Macros button will not reflect the true setting when this happens, because it can't detect the current state of auto macros. However, it will read the **.ini** file and set the button correctly each time Word starts. If you click the Auto Macros button twice, it will 'catch up' again.

Here's the main `SetToolbarButton` procedure. As well as reading the .**ini** file, setting auto macros with the `DisableAutoMacros` statement and then updating the .**ini** file afterwards, it prints a message in the status bar. Of course, it has to change the picture on the toolbar button, even create a new button if this is the first time it has run or if the user has accidentally removed it.

> **FYI** If we don't check that the button exists first, we end up changing the picture of the button that is currently at the left of the toolbar, probably the **New** document button.

```
Sub SetToolbarButton(Toggle)
    Active = 1
    If LCase$(Right$(MacroFileName$(), 10)) = "normal.dot" Then Active = 0
    If ToolbarButtonMacro$("Standard", 1, Active) <> "AutoMacros" Then
        AddButton "Standard", 1, 2, "AutoMacros", 0, Active
        AddButton "Standard", 2,, "", 0, Active
    EndIf
    'get current setting from INI file
    INIFileName$ = DefaultDir$(9) + "\WROXWORD.INI"
    Auto$ = GetPrivateProfileString$("AutoMacros", "Disabled", \
                                                    INIFileName$)
    If Len(Auto$) Then
        AutoSetting = Val(Auto$)
        If Toggle Then AutoSetting = Abs(Not(- Abs(AutoSetting)))
    Else
        AutoSetting = 1       'running for the first time
    EndIf
    CopyButtonImage "WDAM", AutoSetting + 1, Active
    PasteButtonImage "Standard", 1, Active
    DisableAutoMacros(AutoSetting)
    'now update the INI file
    SetPrivateProfileString("AutoMacros", "Disabled", \
            LTrim$(Str$(AutoSetting)), INIFileName$)
    If AutoSetting Then Auto$ = "OFF" Else Auto$ = "ON"
    Print "Turned "; Auto$; " Auto Macros."
End Sub
```

All we than need to do is to call this subroutine when Word starts, and when the Auto Macros button is clicked. The `AutoExec` macro calls it with an argument of **0** each time Word starts, so that the current state isn't changed:

```
Sub MAIN    'This is the AutoExec macro
    AutoMacros.SetToolbarButton(0)'No toggle
End Sub
```

The `AutoMacros` macro uses an argument of **1** to toggle auto macros on and off when the toolbar button is clicked:

```
Sub MAIN    'This is the AutoMacros macro
    SetToolbarButton(- 1)    'Toggle state
End Sub
```

Creating Toolbar Buttons in WordBasic

WordBasic contains statements and functions that we can use to manipulate toolbars in Word. In the example above, we added a new button to the Standard toolbar with:

```
If ToolbarButtonMacro$("Standard", 1, Active) <> "AutoMacros" Then
    AddButton "Standard", 1, 2, "AutoMacros", 0, Active
    AddButton "Standard", 2,, "", 0, Active
EndIf
```

This uses the **ToolbarButtonMacro$()** function to retrieve the name of the macro currently attached to a toolbar button. The syntax is:

```
ToolbarButtonMacro$(ToolbarName$, Position, Context)
```

The toolbar we want is called Standard, and the position is **1**, the first from the left. In our macro, we've used the **MacroFileName$()** function to return the full path and name of the template containing the macro which is currently running. If the last ten characters are **Normal.dot** we know that our macro has been copied into the user's Normal template, so we set the variable **Active** to **0**. Otherwise, the macro is running from a global template, so we set it to **1**. We can then use this variable for the *Context* argument in our procedure.

> **FYI** The **MacroFileName$()** function is useful for discovering the path and filename of a document's template. Just bear in mind that templates can be loaded globally as well as attached to a document. So, the result depends on which template the macro is actually stored in.

If we need to add the button, we use the **AddButton** statement. This takes a range of arguments depending on what type of button you want to add. The Word help file contains full details of them all. In our case, we add a button to the Standard toolbar at position **1**. The third argument is the *Category* and setting this to **2** means that we want the button to run a macro. The third argument is the name of the macro and the fourth is the button picture (chosen from the standard set of built-in button faces). We don't want a picture at this stage, so we set this argument to zero. Finally, the fifth argument is the *Context*, as you saw earlier.

We also add a space on the toolbar at position **2**. In this case, we only need to supply arguments for the toolbar name, position, picture and context. Setting the macro name argument to an empty string produces a space instead of a button. The **AddButton** argument can also be used to create text buttons if we need them.

Changing the Picture on a Toolbar Button

We also need to set the picture on the toolbar button, both when it's created and when the macro changes the setting for auto macros. This is done by copying the face from another button and pasting onto our button. Now you see where the hidden toolbar WDAM comes in. It simply holds the two button faces we want to use:

```
CopyButtonImage "WDAM", AutoSetting + 1, Active
PasteButtonImage "Standard", 1, Active
```

We copy the button face to the clipboard, using the **CopyButtonImage** statement with the name of the source toolbar, the position of the button and the *Context*. Then we paste it to the Standard toolbar with **PasteButtonImage**, supplying the position of the target button and the *Context* again.

> **FYI** For a full list of all the statements and functions you can use to manipulate toolbars and menus, search the Word Help file for **toolbars, WordBasic statements and functions**. Alternatively, click on the statement in the macro window and press *F1* for help on a particular one.

Scanning a Suspicious Document for Viruses

Rather than just look for the common types of Word document virus, by checking the names of the macros Wrox Virus Scan actually checks each macro and reports any instructions that might be used to damage your data. It also warns you if a macro can't be opened. It could, for example, be encrypted like those in the WroxZip template we introduced in Chapter 5.

Try It Out - Using Wrox Virus Scan

We'll use Wrox Virus Scan to check out a template that contains a macro we know contains some suspicious lines. Don't worry, it can't damage your data because there's a **GoTo** statement at the beginning which jumps straight to the end, so the code in the macro can't run. The macro is in the WroxScan template with the other macros that we've been using.

1 Open the file **WroxScan.dot** from your samples folder. Select <u>V</u>irus Scan from the <u>F</u>ile menu. The introduction message tells you what Wrox Virus Scan will do:

2 Click OK. You'll see the names of the macros in your Normal template appear briefly in the Word title bar (if you have Word maximized) as they are opened and scanned for suspicious entries. Afterwards, a message tells you the results of the scan:

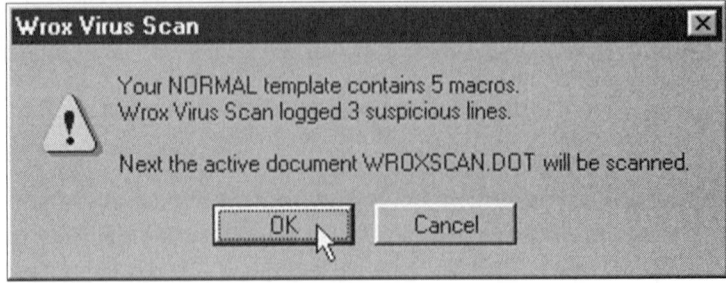

3 Click OK again and the process is repeated for the macros in the active document or template. If it was a normal document, you would get a message saying there are no macros to scan. In our case, it's a template and you can see that it contains a lot of suspicious entries:

Chapter 10 - The Problems of Sharing Documents

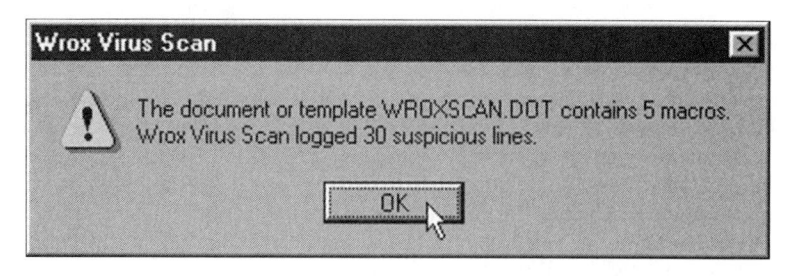

> **Wrox Virus Scan**
>
> ⚠ The document or template WROXSCAN.DOT contains 5 macros.
> Wrox Virus Scan logged 30 suspicious lines.
>
> [OK]

4 Click OK and a report is generated, showing you the entries that WroxScan marked as suspicious. This includes any that could change data outside Word or otherwise damage your system.

Wrox Virus Scan Results
Documents/templates: WROXSCAN.DOT and Normal.dot
Printed on 07/04/96

The macro NORMAL:PrintBothSides contains the 'ToolsMacro' instruction:
> ToolsMacro .Name = "FilePrintSetup", .Run
WARNING: This statement can copy, delete or run other macros.

The macro NORMAL:PrintBothSides contains the 'Declare' instruction:
> Declare Function GetFocus Lib "user32" Alias "GetFocus"() As Long
WARNING: This can execute Windows' low-level API functions directly.

The macro NORMAL:AutoMacros contains the 'SetPrivateProfileString' instruction:
> SetPrivateProfileString("AutoMacros", "Disabled", \
WARNING: This can change settings in Window's Registry or an INI file.

The macro WROXSCAN.DOT:SuspiciousMacro contains the 'Kill' instruction:
> Kill "ThatFile"
WARNING: The 'Kill' statement can delete files from your disk.

The macro WROXSCAN.DOT:SuspiciousMacro contains the 'Name' instruction:
> Name ThisName$, ThatName$
WARNING: The 'Name' statement can re-name existing files on your disk.

The macro WROXSCAN.DOT:SuspiciousMacro contains the 'Open' instruction:
> Open "ThisFile"
WARNING: This could open an existing file and change it, or create a new one.

---

5 If you want a hard copy of the report, click the Print button on the toolbar. Otherwise you can save it as a Word document for future reference.

How It Works

Instead of looking for known viruses by checking for macros with particular names, Wrox Virus Scan flags up any lines in a macro which can damage your data. It doesn't flag up lines which can change the contents of a Word document while it is open. If it did, almost every line would be suspicious, because most macros are designed to change the document they operate on! There are around twenty WordBasic statements and functions which are included in the scan. The sample macro **SuspiciousMacro** in the WroxScan template obligingly contains one of each. It's these, plus a couple out of the **PrintBothSides** and **AutoMacros** macros in our Normal template, which are flagged by Wrox Virus Scan.

You can change the list of words that are treated as suspicious and exclude particular macros from the scan by editing the **WroxScan** macro yourself. In fact, you may want to develop it further, so we've included another version for you to try. But more of that later.

There's a lot of code in **WroxScan**, so rather than printing it all we'll show you how the parts fit together. You can open it in the usual way from the Macros dialog to study it. It uses five **Shared** variables. The array, **SearchWords$**, holds the suspicious words we're looking for, and **SWCount** the number of these words we've set up. The array, **Reports$**, will hold the suspicious lines we find, and the warning messages that go with them. You can change the size of this array here if you get error messages when **WroxScan** runs, but there should be enough room for even the most complex macro's suspicious entries as it is. The other two variables hold the number of **Reports$** entries created so far, and the name of the active document or template when the macro starts:

```
Dim Shared SearchWords$(0)
Dim Shared SWCount
Dim Shared Report$(250)
Dim Shared Recount
Dim Shared ActiveTemplate$
```

The start of the scan process in **Sub MAIN** simply displays the various messages and calls the **CheckMacros()** function twice, once with the argument **"Normal"**, then again with the argument **"Active"**. If **Recount** is still zero after this, it means that we've found no suspicious lines:

```
Sub MAIN
'. . .
   SetSearchWords
   Recount = 0
   ActiveTemplate$ = UCase$(WindowName$())
   Msg$ = "Your NORMAL template contains" + Str$(CheckMacros("Normal"))
   Msg$ = Msg$ + " macros." + Chr$(13)
   LogCount = Recount
   If LogCount > 0 Then
      Msg$ = Msg$ + "Wrox Virus Scan logged" + Str$(Recount) + " lines."
      IconType = 48
   Else
      Msg$ = Msg$ + "Wrox Virus Scan found no suspicious instructions."
      IconType = 64
   EndIf
   MsgBox Msg$, "Wrox Virus Scan", IconType
. . .
   'repeat for active document or template
. . .
```

```
        If Recount = 0 Then
            Msg$ = "No suspicious entries found."
            MsgBox Msg$, "Wrox Virus Scan", 64
        Else
            PrintResults 'create new document & print contents of Report$()
        EndIf
    End Sub
```

The **SetSearchWords** subroutine reads the various entries into the **SearchWords$** array. The word to search for is in column **0**, and the warning text in column **1**. You can edit these, add new ones or remove existing ones as you wish. Remember to alter the value of **SWCount** to match:

```
Sub SetSearchWords
    SWCount = 21
    Redim SearchWords$(SWCount - 1, 1)
    SearchWords$(0, 0) = "Kill"
    SearchWords$(0, 1) = "This statement can delete files on your disk."
    SearchWords$(1, 0) = "Name"
    SearchWords$(1, 1) = "This statement can re-name your existing files."
    'etc...
End Sub
```

The process of checking a document or template starts with the **CheckMacros()** function. This loops through the macros sending each one to our **OpenMacro()** function, including the name of the template (**TName$**).

```
Function CheckMacros(MType$)
    If MType$ = "Normal" Then
        MCount = CountMacros(0, 0, 0)
        TName$ = "NORMAL:"
        For Macro = 1 To MCount
            OpenMacro(TName$, MacroName$(Macro, 0, 0, 0), 1)
        Next
    EndIf
    . . .

    'repeated for the active document or template
    . . .
    CheckMacros = MCount
End Function
```

The **OpenMacro** subroutine tries opening each macro. If it's encrypted, we can't scan it, so we store a warning in the **Report$** array instead. (The WordBasic **IsExecuteOnly()** function tells us whether a macro is encrypted.) Otherwise, we try and open it using the **ToolsMacro** statement. If we succeed, we pass the name of the macro to our **ScanMacro()** function. If we can't open it, we again add an entry to the **Report$** array. Notice that we can bypass the scan for certain macros. This is helpful for macros in your Normal template which you know will be flagged up as including suspicious entries, but really are safe. The value of **MType** is **1** for macros in the Normal template, so we test the name of the macro as well as the value of **Mtype**:

```
Sub OpenMacro(TName$, MName$, MType)
    On Error Goto OM_Err
    If MName$ = "VirusScan" And MType = 1 Then Goto OM_Exit
```

```
            If MName$ = "VirusScanAll" And MType = 1 Then Goto OM_Exit
            If IsExecuteOnly(TName$ + MName$) Then
                Msg$ = "The macro " + TName$ + MName$ + " is encrypted."
                Report$(Recount) = Msg$
                Recount = Recount + 1
            Else
                ToolsMacro .Show = MType, .Name = MName$, .Edit
                ScanMacro(TName$ + MName$)
                DocClose
            EndIf
            Goto OM_Exit
        OM_Err:
            Msg$ = "The macro " + TName$ + MName$ + " cannot be opened."
            Report$(Recount) = Msg$
            Recount = Recount + 1
        OM_Exit:
        End Sub
```

Here's the bit that does the real work. We use **EditFind** once for each word in the **SearchWords$** array. The basic method is shown below, but if you check out the macro itself, you'll see that it's a lot more complex. For example, if the word is in inverted commas, or part of a **REM** statement, we can disregard it. If it's preceded by a full stop, it's an argument for another statement (such as **.Name**). If it's followed by an equals sign, it's not a statement, so again can be ignored.

```
        Sub ScanMacro(MName$)
        For SWNumber = 0 To SWCount - 1
            SWord$ = SearchWords$(SWNumber, 0)
            StartOfDocument
            EditFind .Find = SWord$, .WholeWord = 1, .Replace = "", .Direction = 0
            While EditFindFound()
                SelType 1
                StartOfLine
                EndOfLine 1                                    'select the whole line
                TextLine$ = CleanString$(Selection$())    'and get it in TextLine$
                . . .
                'Check if it really is a suspicious line
                'If so, create the warning message in Msg$
                . . .
                Report$(Recount) = Msg$       'and out in it the Report$() array
                Recount = Recount + 1
                LineDown
                StartOfLine
                EditFind .Find = SWord$
                RetVal = 0
            Wend
        Next
        End Sub
```

Scanning Every Document on Your System

If a virus has got a firm hold, it can affect all the files on your system over a period of time. We've put together another version of the **VirusScan** macro which scans all the documents and templates on your system while you make yourself a cup of coffee.

You've already seen in Parts 1 and 2 of this book several routines that can be used as components for this new macro. For example, the DrivInfo template we used in Chapter 5 contains macros that will create a list of the drives installed on your system. Earlier in that chapter, we saw how the WordBasic **FileFind** statement could be used to collect a list of file names matching a pattern.

The sample **VirusScanAll** macro builds a list of both fixed and removable drives on your system, using a version of the **MakeDriveList()** function we saw in **DrivInfo.dot.** It then runs the **FileFind** statement twice on each disk, once to find Word documents and again to find template files. The resulting list is built up in an array.

Then all we have to do is open them in Word one by one and run the normal **VirusScan** macros against them, storing all the results in another array. Once we've scanned them all, we can create a new document and print the results.

Running Wrox VirusScanAll

To start the **VirusScanAll** macro simply select it from the File menu while you have the WroxScan template loaded globally. After an introduction message, it starts to build a list of files. You can see the progress in the Word status bar at the bottom of the window. Depending on the size and number of drives you have installed, this can be quite a long job because it looks first for **.doc** (document) files and then for **.dot** (template) files.

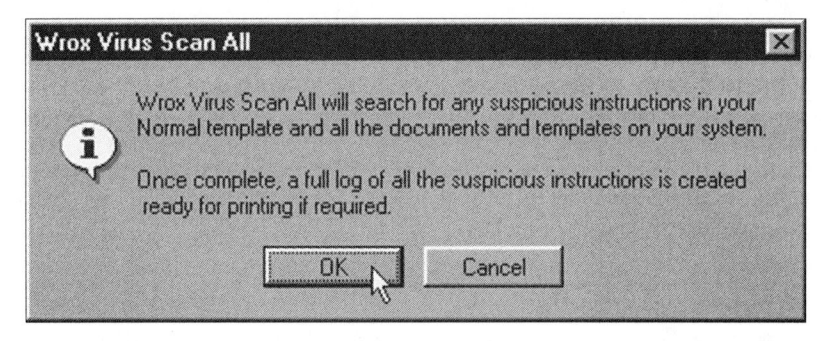

Once the list is complete, it disables auto macros, then loads and scans each document. If you have Word maximized, you can see the names appearing in the Word window title bar. If the file is a normal Word document, WroxScan scans the macros in the template that is attached to it. These are the ones that will be visible in the Macro window and available while that document is active, so if you have several documents attached to the same template, this template is scanned once for each document. Remember that we have to scan all the documents because they could actually be templates disguised as documents, containing their own macros.

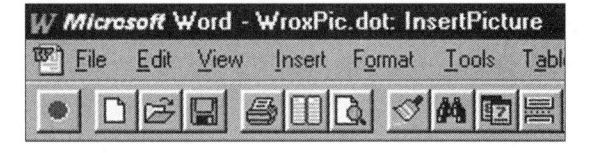

Finally, a new document appears containing the list of suspicious lines, just like with the single document scan we used earlier. The maximum number of files the macro can handle as it stands is 1000. It can store and print up to 2000 warning reports. If you find you're getting an error message, -"Cannot create drive list", you can change the values for **MaxList** and **MaxReport** in the first few lines of the macro.

You can include a floppy disk or CD-ROM in the scan simply by placing it in a drive before you start the scan. Network or remote drives, however, are not included in the scan. You could easily adapt the macro to scan just a particular drive, or you could even add code to display the list of the available drives in a custom dialog and allow the user to choose which one to scan.

Of course, you can also copy the **VirusScanAll** macro into your Normal template if you wish. You'll need to create the menu entries for it afterwards. Remember to add it to the File (No document) menu, as well as to the normal File menu. The **VirusScanAll** macro works best if you run it with no document loaded.

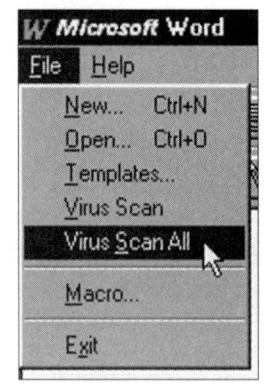

Summary

In this chapter, we've started to think about using Word as part of a team, rather than as a single user. Problems such as the simultaneous editing of documents, maintaining a house style and protecting from viruses are all tasks you must start to consider in this type of environment.

In the first part of the chapter, we saw how and where we should store the templates that these users will need, then we went on to look at how Word behaves when it has to handle files being updated by several users.

Finally, we devoted a lot of space to looking at how the new types of document virus can affect your system. You can imagine on a network which contains thousands of files how big a task it would be to check and disinfect each one. Even if you have existing systems in place to protect you from the normal executable file viruses, you should be planning how to defend yourself against document viruses now. They are easier for an amateur to produce, can be harder to find because you probably won't be expecting an attack from this quarter and, most importantly, they can be just as damaging as other viruses. You have been warned!

So, we've covered:

- How to organize documents and templates in a workgroup
- How to manage simultaneous editing of documents
- How to protect your data from the risk of damage by viruses

Chapter 10 - The Problems of Sharing Documents

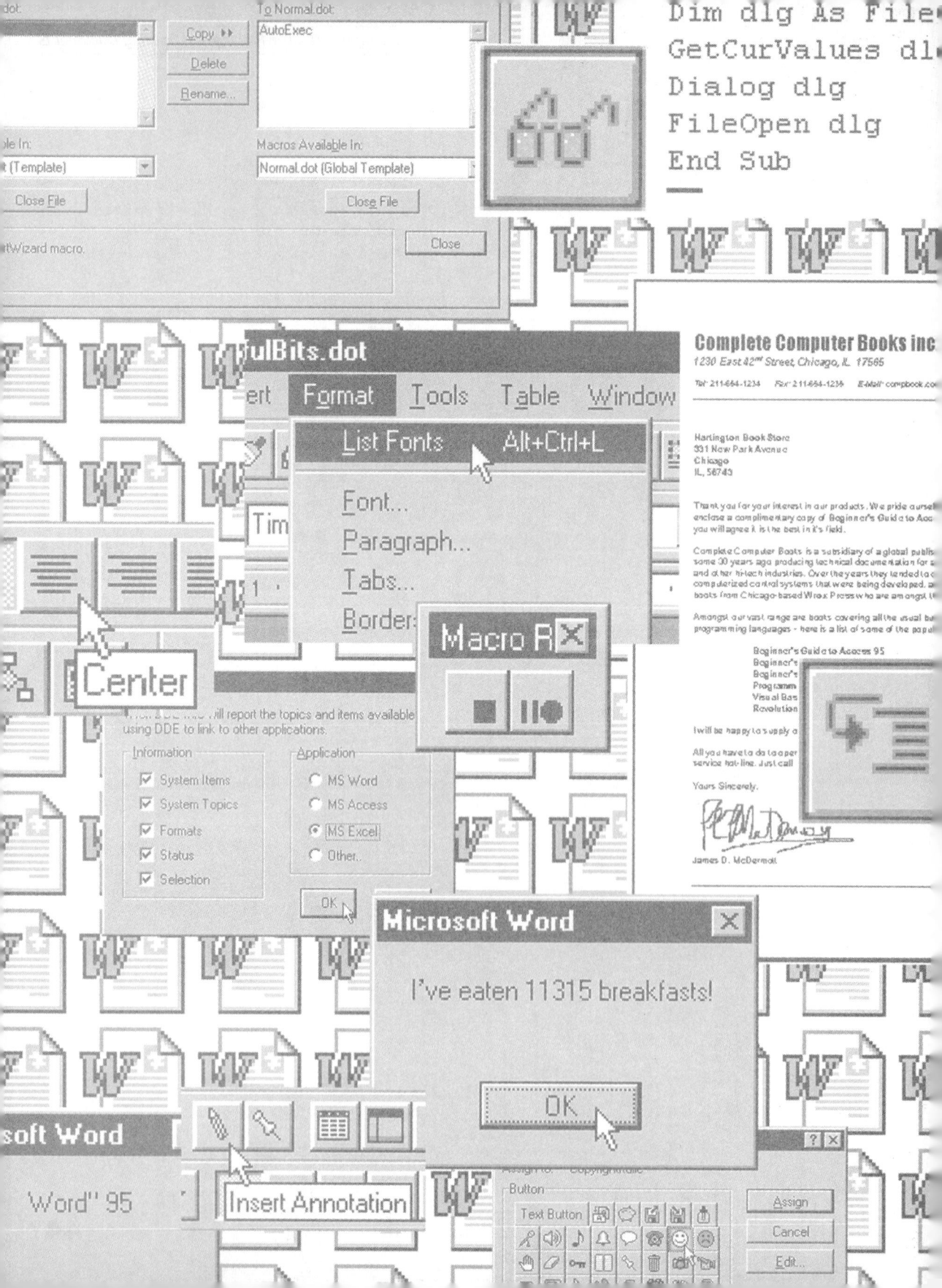

```
Dim dlg As File
GetCurValues dl
Dialog dlg
FileOpen dlg
End Sub
```

Complete Computer Books inc
1230 East 42nd Street, Chicago, IL. 17585
Tel: 211-664-1234   Fax: 211-664-1235   E-Mail: compbook.co

Hartington Book Store
331 New Park Avenue
Chicago
IL, 56743

Thank you for your interest in our products. We pride ourselt
enclose a complimentary copy of Beginner's Guide to Acc
you will agree it is the best in it's field.

Complete Computer Books is a subsidiary of a global publis
some 30 years ago producing technical documentation for a
and other hi-tech industries. Over the years they tended to c
computerised control systems that were being developed, a
books from Chicago-based Wrox Press who are amongst th

Amongst our vast range are books covering all the usual bu
programming languages - here is a list of some of the popul

Beginner's Guide to Access 95
Beginner's
Beginner's
Programm
Visual Bas
Revolution

I will be happy to supply a

All you have to do to open
service hot-line. Just call

Yours Sincerely,

James D. McDermott

---

ulBits.dot

ert F̲ormat T̲ools T̲able W̲indow

List Fonts   Alt+Ctrl+L

Font...
Paragraph...
Tabs...
Borders

Macro R ✕
■ ▮▮

Information
☑ System Items
☑ System Topics
☑ Formats
☑ Status
☑ Selection

Application
○ MS Word
○ MS Access
● MS Excel
○ Other..

OK

Microsoft Word ✕

I've eaten 11315 breakfasts!

OK

Insert Annotation

Button
Text Button

Assign
Cancel
Edit...

Using Fields and Forms in Word

Introduction

One thing that you would least expect Word to do is to display, gather and organize data. Traditionally, this has been the domain of database applications like Microsoft Access® and Lotus Approach®. However, Word contains features that can make it ideally suited to this type of task. You've no doubt already used Word fields in your documents, even if only to insert the date or page numbers. But there's a lot more you can do with them. You can even create multimedia documents that play video clips and sounds.

You can use Word to create forms, just like the paper-based equivalent. Users can enter and edit information, and it can then be stored as a file on disk or passed to another application. DDE (Dynamic Data Exchange) and ODBC (Open Database Connectivity) make it easy to retrieve and store information like this.

In later chapters, we'll see how DDE and ODBC are used in Word, but, first, we need to investigate how we set up and use forms. In this chapter, we'll show you how to create and merge them.

So we'll be looking at:

- What Word fields are and how they can be used
- How we can create electronic forms and use different types of fields
- How to protect and automate electronic forms
- How to save the data from a form as a file on disk

We'll start with a look at some of the common types of Word fields that you'll already have used in your documents.

What are Word Fields?

As well as normal text, you can insert many different items into a Word document, features like pictures or equations and OLE objects like an Excel spreadsheet. These are usually visible when you're editing the document, appearing just the same as they will when you print it. Some of the things you use in your documents every day aren't actually stored in the document, though. For example, the page number you place in the footer section of a document is a field, containing only an instruction, not the actual page number. It just looks like a page number because you're viewing the result of the field, not the field itself.

Viewing the Field or the Result

To see the actual field, or as it's usually called, the **field code**, you have to switch on Field Codes in the View tab of the Options dialog. Select Options... from the Tools menu and turn on the Field Codes option. Now look at your page number, where you'll see the instruction that creates it. Here's the footer section of one of our manuscripts in Word, in Normal view showing the results of the fields:

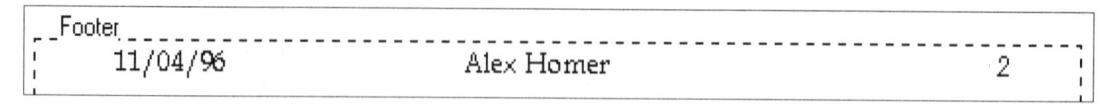

```
Footer
    11/04/96              Alex Homer                           2
```

Here's the same thing, but with Field Codes turned on in the Options dialog:

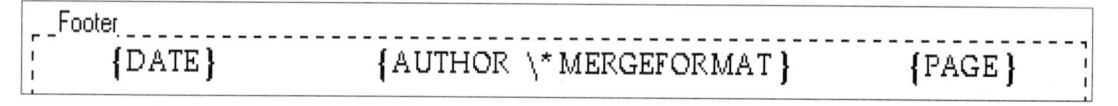

```
Footer
    {DATE}         {AUTHOR \* MERGEFORMAT}          {PAGE}
```

Placing the insertion point in a field causes the whole field to be shaded light gray, unless you've changed the settings in the Field Shading: section of the Options dialog. The default for this option is When Selected, which means that the field is shaded when you place the insertion point in it. If you like, you can also opt to have the fields Always or Never shaded.

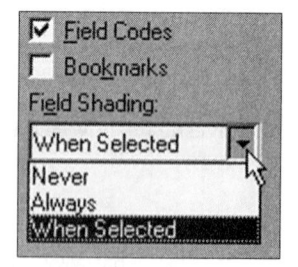

The Field Codes option in the Options dialog turns the view of *all* the field codes in your document on and off. You can do the same through the keyboard, or use it to turn *individual* fields on or off. You'll find, though, that using the Options dialog can save you a lot of time when you're working with fields in a document.

According to the Word Help file, to toggle the view of field codes for the *selected* field only, you press Shift + F9, and to toggle the view of *all* field codes, you press Alt + F9. What it fails to mention is that this only works in Normal view. In Page Layout view, Word toggles *all* the fields for both Shift + F9 and Alt + F9. You can also use the short-cut menu. Right-click on a field and select Toggle field Codes. In WordBasic, you use the **ToggleFieldDisplay** statement in a macro to display the field codes or the result, which is the same as pressing Shift + F9.

Types of Word Field

There are around eighty different types of field available, but many of these are ones you're not likely to meet when you're using Word for general tasks. Some are included to maintain backward compatibility with earlier versions of Word which didn't have the built-in functionality that the latest version offers.

In earlier chapters, you've already seen us use several types of field. For example, we used the {INCLUDETEXT} and {RD} fields in Chapter 6 to show how large documents can be manipulated. In the section of the same chapter which looked at indexing a document, we used the {XE} and {INDEX} fields to insert the index entries and the index itself.

Word fields can be divided into three broad categories:

- Simple types of field that can display information
- Button fields that can carry out an action or run a macro
- Form fields that are used to gather information

We'll look at the first two types briefly, showing you some of the ways they can be created and used from WordBasic. The remainder of this chapter, however, will focus on the third type.

Using Simple Field Types to Display Information

The field that displays your page numbers is a simple field. These are mainly used to display information which is not part of the text you enter, but is created by or stored in Word itself. The common examples are shown in the table below:

Field Type	What It Does
{ DATE }	Displays the current date set in the operating system.
{ TIME }	Displays the current time set in the operating system.
{ INFO }	Displays any of several different types of information about the document. See the list below.
{ PAGE }	Displays the current page number.
{ PAGEREF }	Displays the page number of a bookmark located elsewhere in the document.
{ BOOKMARK }	Displays the text marked by a bookmark elsewhere in the document.
{IF}	Displays one of two values, depending on the result of a comparison.
{COMPARE}	Displays 1 or 0, depending on the result of a comparison.
{FORMULA}	Displays a calculated numeric result.

Using { DATE } and { TIME } Fields

Although they have different field codes, these two are basically the same. As we saw in Part 1, the operating systems stores the date and time as a serial number. By default, the {DATE} field displays this so that it only shows the date, and the {TIME} field so that you can only see the time. This is because they use the Regional Settings section of Windows Control Panel to determine the correct format. You can, though, change the way the date or time is displayed.

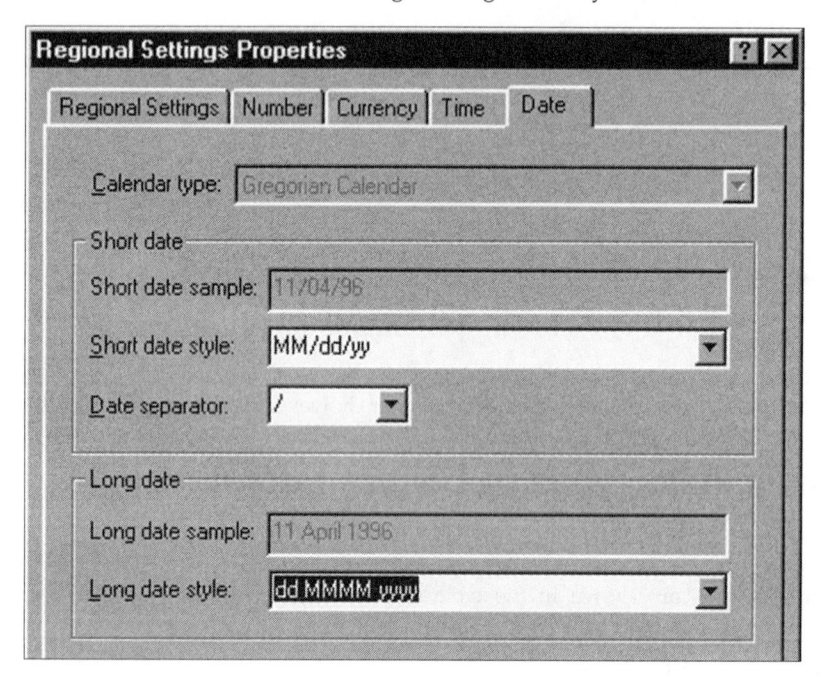

Changing the Format of {DATE} and {TIME} Fields

When you place a field in a Word document, you can include other instructions that control what or how information is displayed. The general form of the field codes in simple field types is:

```
{ FIELDTYPE [ \ format ] }
```

where **FIELDTYPE** identifies the type of field you want, and *format* controls how the information is displayed.

The *format* uses characters to represent the way parts of the date or time are displayed. Together, they make up a format string which, for a date or time field, is preceded by the @ character:

Format String	What It Does	Example
\@ "h"	Displays hours as one or two digits in 12-hour clock format.	1, 2, 3 ... 10, 11, 12
\@ "hh"	Displays hours as two digits in 12-hour clock format.	01, 02, 03 ... 10, 11, 12
\@ "H"	Displays hours as one or two digits in 24-hour clock format.	0, 1, 2 ... 21, 22, 23
\@ "HH"	Disaplays hours as two digits in 24-hour clock format.	00, 01, 02 ... 21, 22, 23
\@ "m"	Displays minutes as one or two digits.	1, 2, 3 ... 57, 58, 59
\@ "mm"	Displays minutes as two digits.	01, 02, 03 ... 57, 58, 59
\@ "AM/PM"	Displays uppercase AM or PM.	AM or PM
\@ "am/pm"	Displays lowercase am or pm.	am or pm
\@ "d"	Displays the day as one or two digits.	1, 2, 3 ... 29, 30, 31
\@ "dd"	Displays the day as two digits.	01, 02, 03 ... 29, 30, 31
\@ "ddd"	Displays the day as a 3-letter abbreviation.	Mon, Tue, Wed ... Sat, Sun
\@ "dddd"	Displays the full name of the day.	Monday ... Sunday
\@ "M"	Displays the month as one or two digits.	1, 2, 3 ... 10, 11, 12
\@ "MM"	Displays the month as two digits.	01, 02, 03 ... 10, 11, 12
\@ "MMM"	Displays the month as a 3-letter abbreviation.	Jan, Feb, Mar ... Oct, Nov, Dec
\@ "MMMM"	Displays the full name of month.	January ... December
\@ "yy"	Displays the year as two digits.	95, 96 ... 03, 04, 05
\@ "yyyy"	Year as four digits.	1995, 1996 ... 2004, 2005

Here are some examples of {DATE} and {TIME} fields, and their result:

```
{ DATE \@ "dddd d MMMM yyyy, h:mm am/pm" }   -> Monday 12 June 1996, 9:32 am
{ DATE \@ "'Today is 'dddd" }                -> Today is Monday
{ DATE \@ "mm/dd/yy hh:mm" }                 -> 06/12/96 09:32
{ TIME \@ "mm/dd/yy hh:mm" }                 -> 06/12/96 09:32
```

Notice that you have to enclose the format string in quotation marks. If you want to include text as well, like the second example, you enclose this in single inverted commas within the format string. Bear in mind that the case of the letter M is important, it can mean Months or minutes. For the other format characters, however, case doesn't matter. Notice how both the {DATE} and {TIME} fields give the same result if you provide the same format string.

Using {INFO} Fields

You've seen how each Word document has a set of properties. To view them, select Properties from the File menu. The {INFO} field is used to display these properties in a document and can also be used to update some of them. One of the strange things is that the field type {INFO} is optional with this field. The syntax is:

    { [INFO] InfoType ["NewValue"] }

InfoType is the name of the property and **NewValue** is the new setting for it if you want to change the existing value.

The properties you can use for **InfoType** are the same as those in the Properties dialog and those that you can manipulate with **DocumentProperty** statements in WordBasic:

Property	What It Displays
TITLE	The title of the document.
SUBJECT	The subject of the document.
AUTHOR	The author of the document.
MANAGER	The name of the manager.
COMPANY	The name of the company.
CATEGORY	The category of the document.
KEYWORDS	The keywords used to identify the document.
COMMENTS	The comments about the document.
TEMPLATE	The document template.
CREATETIME	The creation date.
LASTSAVEDTIME	The date the document was last saved.
LASTPRINTED	The date the document was last printed.
LASTSAVEDBY	The name of the last person to save the document.
REVISIONNUMBER	The number of times the document has been saved.
TOTALEDITINGTIME	The number of minutes the document has been open.
PAGES	The number of pages in the document.
PARAGRAPHS	The number of paragraphs in the document.
LINES	The number of lines in the document.
WORDS	The number of words in the document.
CHARACTERS	The number of characters in the document.

Table Continued on Following Page

Property	What It Displays
BYTES	The size of the document in bytes.
NAMEOFAPPLICATION	The name of the associated application; for example, "Microsoft Word for Windows 95".
SECURITY	The level of document protection.

If you supply a value for the **NewValue** argument, this updates the information stored in that property for the active document or template. You can only use the **NewValue** argument with the **TITLE**, **SUBJECT**, **AUTHOR**, **COMMENTS** and **KEYWORDS** Properties. For example:

```
{ AUTHOR }                    -> Alex Homer
{ AUTHOR "Tom Smith" }        -> Tom Smith (and changes the Author property)
```

Changing the Format of Text Fields

You can control how the text contents of fields are displayed. For example, you can change the capitalization using special format strings preceded by an asterisk character.

Format String	What It Does
* caps	Makes the first letter of each word a capital.
* firstcap	Makes the first letter of the first word only a capital.
* lower	Makes all the letters lowercase.
* upper	Makes all the letters uppercase.

```
{ AUTHOR \* caps }            -> Alex Homer
{ AUTHOR \* firstcap }        -> Alex homer
{ AUTHOR \* lower }           -> alex homer
{ AUTHOR \* upper }           -> ALEX HOMER
```

You can also set the formatting of the text. Adding the *** charformat** instruction displays the contents of the field using the same formatting as the first letter of the field code. You can also omit the *** charformat** instruction altogether and get the same result by just formatting the first character.

{*A*uthor} ⟶ *Alex Homer*

If the results of a field change, you can force Word to apply the formatting of the previous result to the new result by using the ***mergeformat** instruction. For example, if you format the name displayed by { AUTHOR * mergeformat } by setting it to italic, Word retains the italics even if the author name changes.

Changing the Format of Numeric Fields

Of course, some fields produce a numeric, rather than textual, result. As you'll have guessed by now, you can also control the way that numbers are displayed by using a format string. There are a range of standard formats which are useful for converting a number into a text-type format. Note that they all convert the number to the nearest integer value, except for *** dollartext**.

Format String	What It Does	Example
* alphabetic	Displays the lowercase alphabetic character equivalent.	1 displays as a, 2 as b, etc.
* Alphabetic	Displays the uppercase alphabetic character equivalent.	1 displays as A, 2 as B, etc.
* arabic	Displays cardinal numerals.	1, 2, 3 ... 15 ... etc.
* cardtext	Displays the cardinal text equivalent.	one, two ... fifteen ... etc.
* dollartext	Displays cardinal text with fractional part as hundredths.	thirty six and 25/100
* Hex	Displays hexadecimal numbers.	F82B, 2AC, 10A, etc.
* OrdText	Displays ordinal text.	seventeenth, thirty-first, etc.
* Ordinal	Displays ordinal arabic text.	17th, 30th, 1st, etc.
* roman	Displays lowercase Roman numerals.	mcmlxiv
* Roman	Displays uppercase Roman numerals.	MCMLXIV

```
{ Page \* cardtext }    ->    twelve
{ Page \* Roman }       ->    XII
{ Page \* ordinal }     ->    12th
```

You can also control the way the result is displayed as a number. To do this, you create a format string which defines how many of the individual parts of the number should be displayed and in what form. These format strings are preceded by a hash character.

String	What It Does	Example
\# "0"	Displays a number or a zero.	{ 3.4 \# "$00.00" } -> $03.40
\# "#"	Displays a number or a space.	{ 3.4 \# "$##.##" } -> $ 3.4
\# "x"	Displays a number or nothing.	{ 3.4 \# "$xx.xx" } -> $3.4
\# "-"	Displays a minus sign, or a space if positive.	{ -5 \# "-0" } -> -5
		{ 5 \# "-0" } -> 5
\# "+"	Displays a minus sign or a plus sign.	{ -5 \# "+0" } -> -5
		{ 5 \# "+0" } -> +5

If you specify fewer characters than there are decimal places in the number, it's rounded to that many decimal places first. However, if you specify fewer characters than there are significant figures in the number (figures before the decimal place), Word automatically displays all the significant figures.

You insert decimal places and thousands characters as literal text within the format string, along with currency characters. If you want to include ordinary text, you enclose it in single inverted commas, as we did in the {DATE} field example. By mixing the characters, you can get exactly the display format you want:

```
{ 12345.6 \# "$-#,##0.00" }          -> $ 12,345.60
{ 14.758 \# "$xx0.##" }              -> $14.76
{ 26 \# "'Part number: '0000.##" }   -> Part number: 0026
```

If you want numbers to line up correctly in columns, you should be using the - and # characters so that positive numbers with less characters are padded with spaces. If you're placing the numbers is normal text, use the x character and omit the - character so that blank spaces are removed from the resulting number.

You can specify different formats for a number if it turns out to be positive, negative or zero. Word evaluates the result and uses the relevant numeric format string. To specify the three different formats, you separate each one from the others with a semicolon as \# **"PositiveFormat; NegativeFormat; ZeroFormat"**. You can use just the first two, omitting the zero format if you wish:

```
{ 4.6 \# "0.00;(0.00);'zero'" }      -> 4.60
{ -4.6 \# "0.00;(0.00);'zero'" }     -> (4.60)
{ 0 \# "0.00;(0.00);'zero'" }        -> zero
```

Using {PAGE} and {PAGEREF} Fields

The {PAGE} field inserts the current page number into the document. The {PAGEREF} field inserts the number of the page where a particular bookmark is, as a reference to that page. For example, imagine that page 17 of a document contains a word that is marked by the bookmark **TheWord**. On page 24, we place a {PAGE} and a {PAGEREF} field, and get the following results:

```
{ PAGE }                 -> 24
{ PAGEREF TheWord }      -> 17
```

There are similar fields which allow you to reference footnotes and endnotes in a document. Of course, you can change the way the numeric result of all these fields is displayed by using the various number type format-string options that you saw in the previous section.

Using {BOOKMARK} Fields

The {BOOKMARK} field simply displays the contents of a bookmark which is located elsewhere in the document. It allows you to duplicate text in another part of a document. For example, if the word *Duplication* is marked by the bookmark **TheWord**, we can place the same text elsewhere using:

```
This shows { TheWord } of text .    ->   This shows Duplication of text.
```

You don't include the field type, **BOOKMARK**, in this field, just the name of the bookmark. Again, you can change the formatting of the result using the various format strings you've already seen, depending on whether the result is a number or text. In the following examples, the bookmark **TheWord** marks the number 17 in our document.

```
{ TheWord \# "0000.00" }             -> 0017.00
{ TheWord \*ordtext \*caps }         -> Seventeenth
```

457

Notice how we've used two instructions in the second example to get the initial letter capitalized.

Using {IF} and {COMPARE} Comparison Fields

All the fields we've looked at so far take an existing value from within Word and display it in the document. However, you can use types of field which calculate their own value. This can be as a result of a comparison, like in these two field types. Both evaluate an expression or condition and display a different result depending on the outcome. The {IF} field displays one of two values:

```
{ IF TheWord = "Yes" "The word is Yes" "The word is not Yes" }
```

The field code instruction is in three parts, separated by spaces. The first is the expression, which will evaluate to either **True** or **False**. If it's **True**, the second part is displayed; if it's **False**, the third part. In the expression above, if the bookmark **TheWord** marked the word Yes, the field would display The word is Yes. It also works if the text marked by the bookmark is actually a number. If **TheWord** marks the characters 17 in a document, this next field will display It's less that 20.

```
{ IF TheWord < 20 "It's less than 20" "It's at least 20" }
```

In both these cases, we've used a bookmark in the comparison. You can also use another field or a mathematical expression involving text, numbers, fields and bookmarks. If you refer to a bookmark that doesn't exist, however, the field displays the warning message: Error! Bookmark not defined. And you can't use the **NOT** operator to reverse the truth of the comparison, as you can in WordBasic. Instead, you have to switch round the order of the other two parts of the statement:

```
{ IF NOT TheWord >= 20 "Less than 20" "At least 20" }    <- DOESN'T WORK
{ IF TheWord >= 20 "At least 20" "Less than 20" }        <- OK
```

The {COMPARE} field works in a similar way to {IF}. It contains only the comparison expression, however, and returns **1** if the comparison evaluates to **True**, or **0** if evaluates to **False**. If **TheWord** is a bookmark, we can use the following:

```
{ COMPARE TheWord = "Yes" }   ->   1 if the word is Yes, or 0 if not
```

Both the {COMPARE} and {IF} fields will accept wildcards in text strings. You can use the normal ***** and **?** wildcard characters to represent any other characters, as you do in a file name. The ***** wildcard represents any number of characters (or none at all) and **?** represents a single character.

```
{ IF TheWord = "Word*" "It starts with Word" "Doesn't start with Word" }
```

Any word starting with *Word*, no matter how many letters it has, will give the result, It starts with Word.

```
{ COMPARE TheWord = "Word?" }   ->   1 for Words Wordy etc, or 0 for Wordly
```

Only five character words starting with *Word* will give the result 1; everything else will give zero.

Using {FORMULA} Calculated Fields

As well as comparing values and displaying the result in the document, you can use a type of field that calculates its own new value: the {FORMULA} field. The syntax for this type of field is:

    { = formula [\# formatstring] }

The **formula** is a mathematical expression which can include text, numbers, fields and bookmarks. If you want to control the way the result is displayed, you use the optional **formatstring** section. The result will be numeric, so the format string will start with **\#**.

For an example, imagine we have a document which contains two bookmarks, **Sales** and **Costs**. These mark the numbers in the document which are our sales and costs for the year. We can display the result of calculations on the contents of these bookmarks using {FORMULA} fields:

    { = Sales - Costs \# "'Annual Profit: '$ #,##0.00" }
    { = Costs / 12 \# "'Average monthly costs: '$ #,##0.00" }

Here's the result of the example above. The fields themselves could, of course, be placed within the body of the text in a document. They would blend in as though they had been typed directly, except that if you change the sales or costs figures to update the report, the profit and monthly costs are automatically updated as well.

> Sales: $ 43,467.74
> Costs: $ 29,559.40
> Annual Profit: $ 13,908.34
> Average monthly costs: $ 2,463.28

Instead of placing the fields in the text, we can create a table and place them there. Now Word almost becomes a spreadsheet. You type values into the cells of the table as you would in a spreadsheet, then place {FORMULA} fields where you would normally enter a formula in a spreadsheet, and Word will calculate the values for these cells. This is one of the most useful places to use {FORMULA} fields. We'll be looking at an example of this later on in the book.

When are the Contents of Fields Updated?

If you've been trying out the various examples above, you may have come up against a couple of problems. If you edit the field codes or change the contents of a bookmark they refer to, the result displayed in the field isn't updated automatically, but some fields, such as the page numbers in the footer of your documents, are updated automatically.

To update a field you can click on it and press *F9*, or right-click and select Update Field. Word can also update all the fields in a document before it's printed. This feature is turned off by default, which speeds things up, but you can turn it on in the Print tab of the Options dialog—select Options... from the Tools menu.

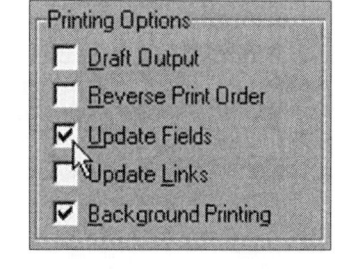

To update the contents of a field using WordBasic, you place the **UpdateFields** statement in your macro. If the selection contains more than one field, they're all updated.

Inserting Fields Manually into a Document.

In Part 2 we saw how to insert fields using the Field dialog—select Fi*e*ld... from the *I*nsert menu. This allows you to find the type of field you want and add the formatting string or other instructions to it. The check box in the bottom left will add the *mergeformat instruction (which preserves field formatting when a new value is entered in a field) if it's checked when the field is inserted into the document.

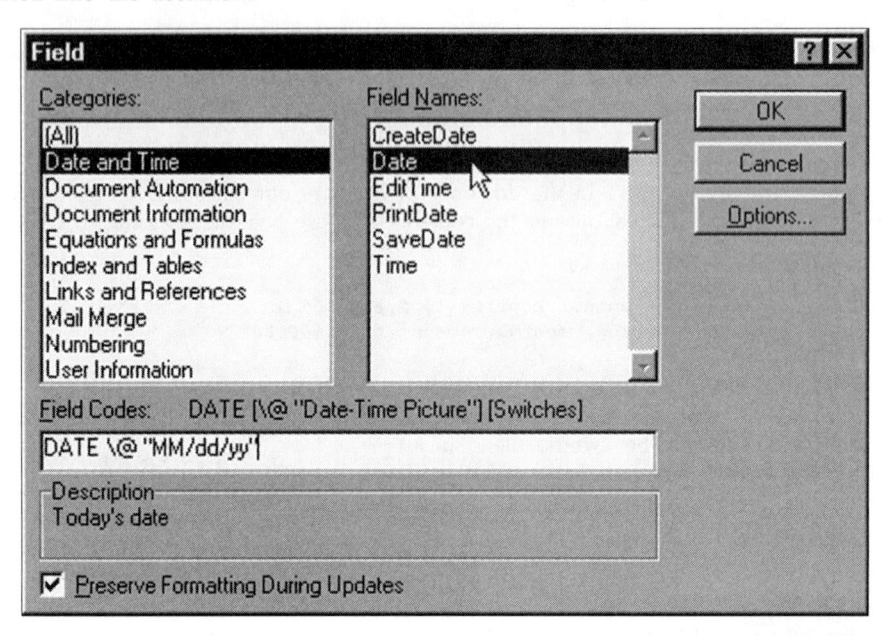

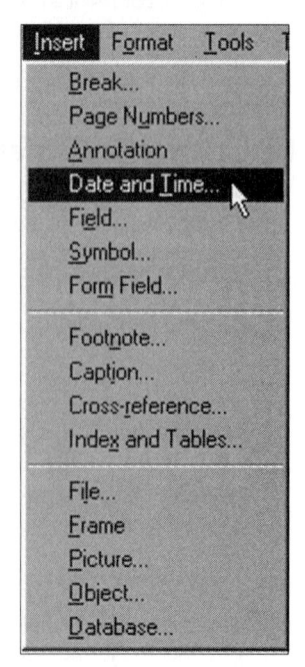

You can also insert fields manually by typing them directly into a document. However, typing the opening and closing braces (the curly brackets) doesn't work. Instead you have to press *Ctrl + F9* to place an empty field with the pair of braces at the insertion point. Word automatically switches to Field Codes view, where you can type the field codes in directly. Once you've done so, press *F9* to update the field contents, then *Shift + F9* to view the result.

Of course, there are other ways to insert fields. The *I*nsert menu has a range of commands for inserting all kinds of fields directly, from Date and *T*ime... and Cross-*r*eference..., to Fi*l*es and Database.... However, each of these creates the normal field codes appropriate for that type of field and just makes it easier to supply the extra instructions needed. You can insert any of these fields using the Fields dialog:

Inserting Fields with WordBasic

The WordBasic statements which insert fields in your document broadly mirror those on Word's Insert menu. The standard one is `InsertField` and is easy to use:

```
InsertField .Field = "DATE"    ->    { DATE }
```

When we're creating a formatting string we have to be a bit more careful. We must enclose the string itself in quotation marks and any literal text in inverted commas. So to create a field that displays The date is: 04/07/96, we need the field codes: **{ DATE \@ "'The date is:'MM/dd/yy" }**. We can build this string in a variable first. This macro inserts the date at the current insertion point:

```
Sub MAIN
    FmtStr$ = "DATE \@ " + Chr$(34) + "'The date is: 'MM/dd/yy" + Chr$(34)
    InsertField .Field = FmtStr$
End Sub
```

Rather than use `InsertField`, we can just use `InsertDateField` or `InsertTimeField`. These statement take no arguments, and the formatting of the field they produce matches that set in your Regional Settings in Control Panel. Similarly, WordBasic has the `InsertPageNumbers` statement. This takes three arguments and allows you to create a {PAGE} field automatically in the header or footer section of your document. The Word Help file contains details of all the `Insert` statements which can be used to create fields—search on fields in WordBasic, inserting.

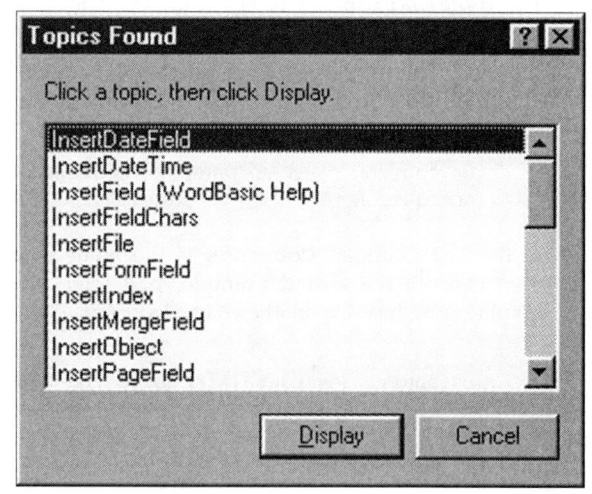

As with Word's various menu commands, the WordBasic `InsertField` statement can be used to insert most types of field. There is also the `InsertFieldChars` statement which inserts an empty field with the pair of braces leaving the insertion point between them and switches to Field Codes view. With both of these statements it just means you have to understand the optional instructions that are needed for that type of field. But as we're supposed to be 'developers', rather than just plain 'users', then this should be one of our aims anyway...

Using Button Fields to Carry Out an Action

So, we can display information using fields and, in some cases, update the properties of our document with an {INFO} field. But we can also use other types of field which carry out some action rather than just displaying text.

Field Type	What It Does
{GOTOBUTTON}	Jumps to another place in the document when double-clicked.
{MACROBUTTON}	Runs a macro when double-clicked.

We'll take a look at both of these as they offer an easy way to create interactive documents that can 'come alive', like the multimedia files that we're seeing so much of.

Using {GOTOBUTTON} Fields

The {GOTOBUTTON} is useful if you want the reader to be able to jump to different parts of the document. It gives you another way to create hypertext documents, like we saw with web pages and Help files in Part 2. The syntax is:

```
{ GOTOBUTTON destination displaytext }
```

The *destination* can be a bookmark, page number, or item such as a footnote or annotation - the same as you can use with the **EditGoTo** statement. The *displaytext* is the text or graphic that you want to appear in the document. Everything after the *destination* and the following space are treated as *displaytext*, irrespective of any spaces it contains. Double-clicking the text or graphic in the document moves the insertion point to the specified location in the document.

```
{ GOTOBUTTON Contents Jump to Contents Page }
{ GOTOBUTTON p10 Jump to page 10 }
```

In the first example, **Contents** is the name of a bookmark placed in the contents page of the document. In the second example, **p10** refers to the tenth page in the document. To use a graphic, you insert it in the *displaytext* part of the field.

```
{ GOTOBUTTON Contents [graphic] Go to the Contents page }
```

This displays the button plus the text after it. You can omit the text, of course. However make sure that any text (and/or graphic) will all fit on one line, because otherwise the field will display an error message and will not work correctly.

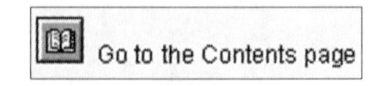

> **FYI** We've supplied the graphic you can see above, and others, in the **Fields** subfolder of your samples folder so that you can experiment with creating these buttons.

Using {MACROBUTTON} Fields

Once you understand how {GOTOBUTTON} fields work, {MACROBUTTON} fields are easy. They're identical in syntax but instead of supplying a bookmark, page number, or other item, you use the name of the macro you want to run when the text or graphic is double-clicked.

```
{ MACROBUTTON macroname displaytext }
```

The macro **macroname** runs when you double-click the field. It must be available, i.e. stored in the active document's template, a global template, or your Normal template. The **displaytext** is the text or graphic that appears in the document. It works in the same way as the {GOTOBUTTON}, and the same limits and conditions apply.

Running a macro when a button is clicked gives you a lot more opportunities than just jumping to another place in the document. Anything you can do with WordBasic is available with a double-click in the document. For example here's how part of a multimedia document might look:

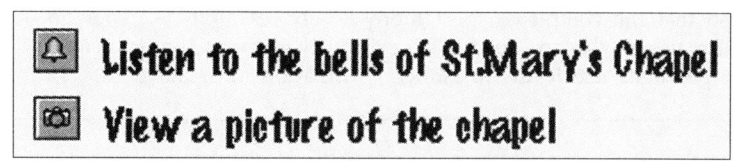

> 🔔 **Listen to the bells of St.Mary's Chapel**
> 📷 **View a picture of the chapel**

Double-clicking the first button runs a macro which uses WordBasic's **Shell** statement to start Media Player and play the sound:

```
Sub MAIN
    Shell "SndRec32.exe /play /close TheBells.wav"
End Sub
```

Double-clicking the second button runs a macro that displays the picture. This could be a video clip that you display using the **Shell** statement again:

```
Shell "mplayer.exe /play /close Chapel.avi"
```

Or it could be a graphic file displayed in Windows Paint Brush application. You could even use the macro to create a custom dialog containing a **Picture** control, and show the picture and a caption.

Using Single-clicks to Activate a Button Field

One problem with the {GOTOBUTTON} and {MACROBUTTON} fields is that you have to double-click them to carry out the action. When you click them once, they just become shaded. People are used to web pages and Help files where they only have to click once on the 'hot' text or graphics. You can change the Options settings for Word to allow a single click to operate the {GOTOBUTTON} and {MACROBUTTON}. You can only do this with a macro because there's no setting in the Options dialog to change it. Here's the macro, which you can name **AutoOpen** so that it runs when the user opens the document:

```
Sub MAIN    'Run this macro to set it to single-clicks
    ToolsOptionsGeneral .ButtonFieldClicks = 1
End Sub
```

To set it back to the default, you run a similar macro when they close the document. Call this macro **AutoClose**:

```
Sub MAIN    'Run this macro to set it back to double-clicks
    ToolsOptionsGeneral .ButtonFieldClicks = 2
End Sub
```

What are Electronic Forms?

We've looked at some of the popular types of field that you can use in normal Word documents. Now we'll move on to the specific types of field that have one main purpose: creating electronic forms. An **electronic form** is basically a Word document that contains form fields, as well as any other text and graphics that make up the document.

Electronic forms can be used to produce order forms, invoices, survey sheets, or for any activity that uses paper-based forms. Often, the Word document will contain tables which are formatted with borders so that the completed form more closely resembles a paper document. Forms are an ideal way for users who are not highly computer-literate to interact with your applications. Most database packages use forms to gather information from the user.

When you create a form like this in Word, the user can only type or change the values in the specific areas where you've placed form fields. They can't edit the rest of the document or change the layout. This is because you protect the document using features similar to those we examined in Chapter 6. Select **Protect Document...** from the **Tools** menu and turn on the **Forms** option. You can also enter a **Password** for the document so that other users can't turn off the protection without this password.

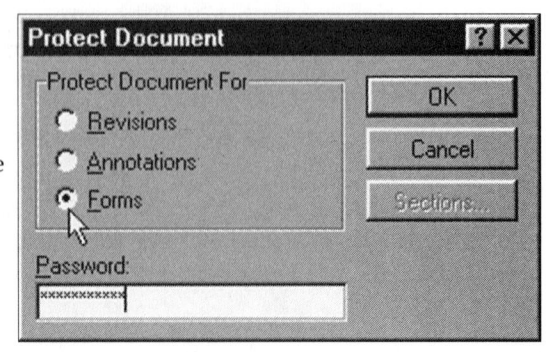

We would normally create a form like the Complete Computer Book Inc. invoice as a template rather than as a document. The template holds all the text, tables and graphics so that when the user creates a document based on it, all this is already in the new document. Protecting the template for Forms will mean that the document is also protected, allowing the user to just move from one control to the next with the Tab key filling in values as they go, just like a paper-based form.

The other reason for using a template is that you'll probably want to use macros to automate the form. These can change the values in the form fields and generally interact with the user while they're filling in the form. For example, if they're filling in a survey form and one of the questions asks if they own a car, you could enable or disable other fields which ask about car insurance because whether they're applicable depends on the value the user enters in the first field.

What are Form Fields?

Form fields are used to display a control on a form, in a similar way to the controls we used in custom dialogs in Part 1. The user can manipulate these controls, just as they do in a dialog. There are three types of field especially designed for use on forms:

Field Type	What It Does
{ FORMCHECKBOX }	Displays a check box control on a form.
{ FORMDROPDOWN }	Displays a drop-down list box control on a form.
{ FORMTEXT }	Displays a text box control on a form.

Inserting Form Fields using Word Menus and Commands

To insert a form field, select Form Field... from the Insert menu. Word displays the Form Field dialog where you specify the type of field and set the options for it. This dialog also has a Show Toolbar button that displays the Forms toolbar. You'll need this displayed as you work with the fields on a form.

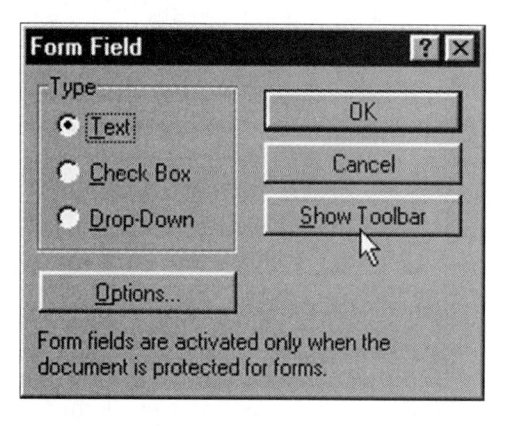

The Forms toolbar has buttons for inserting the three different types of field and setting the options for them. It also provides buttons for inserting tables and frames, formatting them and protecting the document. You can, of course, display this toolbar by selecting Toolbars... from the View menu and checking the Forms toolbar entry in the list.

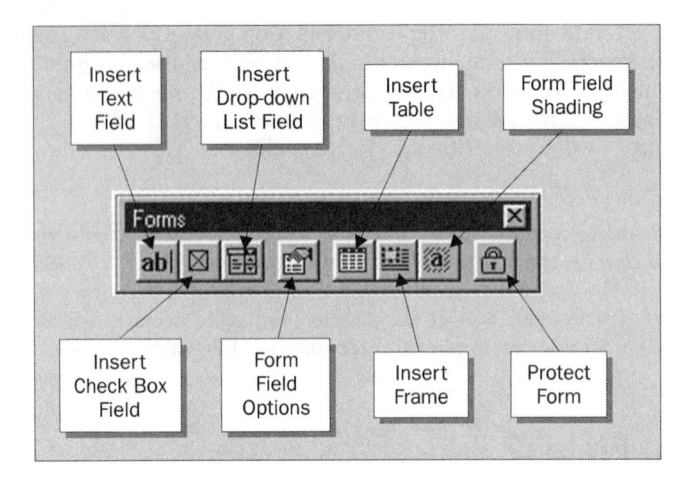

[Diagram of Forms toolbar with labeled buttons: Insert Text Field, Insert Drop-down List Field, Insert Table, Form Field Shading, Insert Check Box Field, Form Field Options, Insert Frame, Protect Form]

Each field has a set of options or properties which control how the field appears and behaves. The options available are different for the three types of field. You can also add Help features to them so that the user can get assistance as they use your form. You can display text in the status bar at the bottom of the Word window, or in a dialog that appears when they press *F1*. As an example, here's the options dialog for a **Text** field:

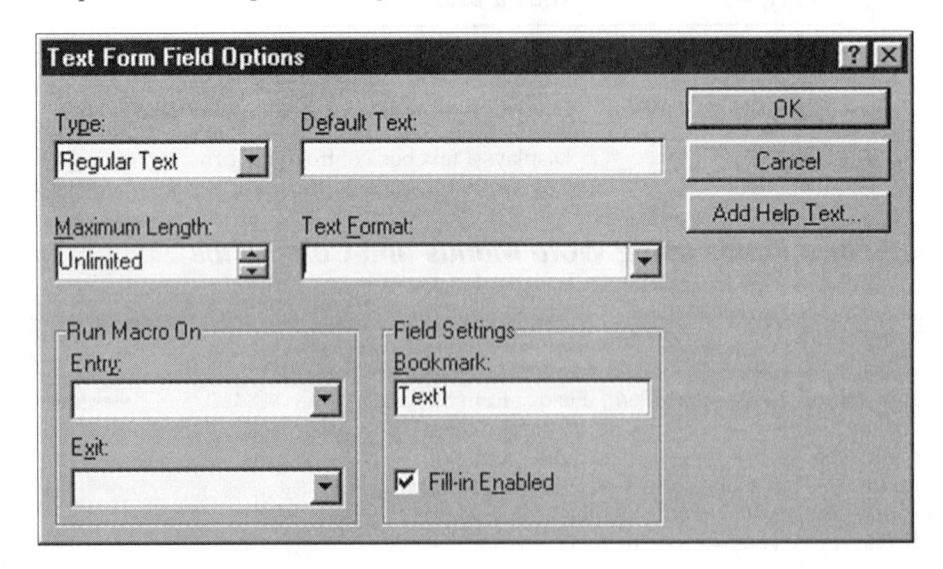

[Screenshot of Text Form Field Options dialog with fields: Type (Regular Text), Default Text, Maximum Length (Unlimited), Text Format, Run Macro On (Entry, Exit), Field Settings (Bookmark: Text1, Fill-in Enabled checked), and OK, Cancel, Add Help Text buttons]

You'll see how the different options are used later in this chapter. For the time being, though, notice the settings in the bottom left of the dialog. A form field can run any macro you specify when the insertion point is placed in it (On Entry) and/or when it loses the focus (On Exit). This is how we automate our form to make it react to the user, and make working with it easier for them.

Inserting Form Fields with WordBasic

You can insert form fields and set their options using WordBasic statements. Once the fields are in place and the document is protected, you can also use WordBasic to set and retrieve the values in each of the form fields and move the insertion between them. You can see that, in some ways, using form fields is just like using custom dialogs, the only difference being the statements and functions. Here's a summary of the WordBasic statements that are used with form fields:

Statement	What It Does
`CheckBoxFormField`	Inserts a check box form field at the current insertion point with the default settings for its options.
`TextFormField`	Inserts a text box form field at the current insertion point with the default settings for its options.
`DropDownFormField`	Inserts a drop-down list form field at the insertion point with the default settings for its options.
`FormFieldOptions`	Sets the options for the currently selected field.
`InsertFormField`	Inserts a form field of any type at the current insertion point and sets its options, all in one go.
`EnableFormField`	Sets a form field to be enabled (so that it can be used) or disabled.
`AddDropDownItem`	Adds an item to a drop-down list field.
`RemoveDropDownItem`	Removes an item from a drop-down list field.
`RemoveAllDropDownItems`	Removes all the items from a drop-down list field.
`GetFormResult()`	Returns the value (1 or 0) from a check box field, or the index of the selected item in a drop-down list.
`GetFormResult$()`	Returns the contents of a text box field, or the text of the selected item in a drop-down list.
`SetFormResult`	Changes or updates the value displayed in a form field and optionally sets the field's default value.
`ClearFormField`	Deletes the text in a text form field.

So, we can create a drop-down list form field at the current insertion point and build the list of items it displays, using this macro:

```
Sub MAIN
MyHelp$ = "Select your operating system"
DropDownFormField       'insert a drop-down list field
CharLeft 1, 1           'and select it
FormFieldOptions .Entry = "Macro1", .Exit = "Macro2", \    'set the options
            .Name = "OpSystem", .Enable = 1, \             'for the field
            .OwnHelp = 1, .HelpText = MyHelp$, \
            .OwnStat = 1, .StatText = MyHelp$
AddDropDownItem "OpSystem", "Windows 95"                   'add the items to
AddDropDownItem "OpSystem", "Windows NT"                   'build the list
AddDropDownItem "OpSystem", "OS/2"
AddDropDownItem "OpSystem", "Unix"
End Sub
```

Notice how we have to select the field before we use the **FormFieldOptions** statement. When it's been inserted with **DropDownFormField**, the insertion point is left immediately after the field. In this example we're specifying the **OnEntry** and **OnExit** macros and enabling the control by setting its **.Enable** argument to **1**. Word identifies each form field in a document by marking it with a bookmark. We specify the name for that bookmark in the **.Name** property. Here we've set it to **OpSystem**. If you don't specify a name, Word creates one of its own, such as **DropList1** or **Check2**.

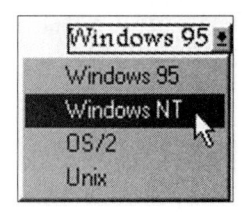

Remember that we can specify the Help text that is shown in the status bar, or when the user presses *F1*. In our example we've specified the same text for both in the variable **MyHelp$** at the beginning of the macro. In the **FormFieldOptions** statement we tell Word that we want to use our own Help entries by setting the **.OwnHelp** and **.OwnStat** arguments to **1**. Then we just have to supply the text we want displayed for the **.HelpText** and **.StatText** arguments.

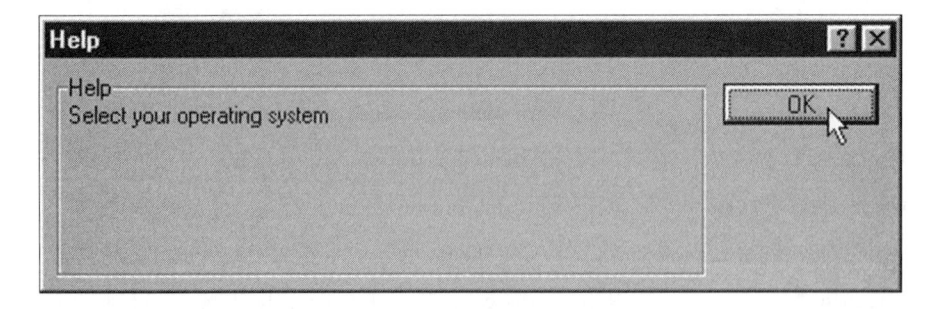

Finally, we create the list by using multiple **AddDropDownItem** statements, supplying the name of the bookmark that marks the field and the text we want to add.

> **FYI** If the macro names you specify for the **.OnEntry** and **.OnExit** arguments don't exist or aren't available in the current context, you'll get a **Bad Parameter** error message when you try to run the macro.

Alternatively, we could use the **InsertFormField** statement and supply all the options required in one go. This single statement inserts a text-type form field and sets its options. This time, we haven't specified any Help entries:

```
InsertFormField .Entry = "Macro1", .Exit = "Macro1", \
                .Name = "UserName", .Enable = 1, .TextType = 0, \
                .TextDefault = "unspecified", .TextWidth = 15, \
                .TextFormat = "Uppercase", .Type = 0
```

You can see how similar the arguments are to the **FormFieldOptions** statement. In this case, though, we have specified a value for the **Type** argument. Setting it to **1** creates a check-box-type field, **2** creates a drop-down list field, and **0** (or omitting it altogether) creates a text-type field. So we could have omitted it here. Because this is a text field, we can use other optional arguments to set the **TextType**, **TextDefault**, **TextWidth** and **TextFormat**.

TextType Value	Style
0	Normal text
1	Number
2	Date
3	Current Date
4	Current Time
5	Calculation

`TextDefault` is the text that's shown in the field as the default. `TextWidth` controls the maximum number of characters that can be entered in the field. Set it to the number required or to `0` for any number (unlimited). `TextFormat` can be used when `TextType = 1` to specify how the text will be displayed. The same options are available as with a normal Word text field: "`Uppercase`", "`Lowercase`", "`First Capital`" and "`Title Case`".

A full list of all the arguments for the `InsertFormField` statement is in the Word Help file. There are arguments that are used to specify the options when you create check box and drop-down list fields, as well text-box types like we've done here. Once you've inserted a form field, you can change the values of any of the options later using the `FormFieldOptions` statement in your macro.

Remember that the document will not behave like a form until you protect it. In Chapter 6 we saw how you can use WordBasic to do this. The statements `ToolsProtectDocument` and `ToolsUnprotectDocument` change the protection of the active document. For example,

```
ToolsProtectDocument .DocumentPassword = "Secret", .Type = 2
```

protects the document, turning it into a form, and,

```
ToolsUnprotectDocument .DocumentPassword = "Secret"
```

removes the protection. If your document has more than one section and you want to protect individual sections, you use the `ToolsProtectSection` statement after you've protected the document to remove protection from the relevant section. For example, to protect all except section **2**, you could use:

```
ToolsProtectDocument .DocumentPassword = "Secret", .Type = 2
ToolsProtectSection .Protect = 0, .Section = 2
```

The Wrox Reader Survey Form

To show you how you can use Word forms, we'll build a sample form in this chapter and automate it using macros. In the next chapter we'll show you how we can use the data we collect, both in Word and in other applications. You can use Word forms for almost any purpose, either as a way of replacing paper-based systems or as a totally new application. The individual controls can be can enabled and disabled depending on the values the user enters in the form. Form fields can be used to enter numbers or text, so you can create order forms and invoices that automatically total their values.

Having said that, we've chosen an example that doesn't involve numbers, because you'll often use either a database or spreadsheet application for focused tasks like these. Word forms are more suited to those areas where there's no specially designed application, allowing you to build one that exactly matches your needs.

We use our application to collect information from all those who read our books, because, after all, monitoring customer satisfaction with your company's products is a primary requirement in today's competitive business climate. Here's our completed survey form **Survey.dot**, as seen in Word. You'll find it in the **\Fields** subfolder of your samples folder.

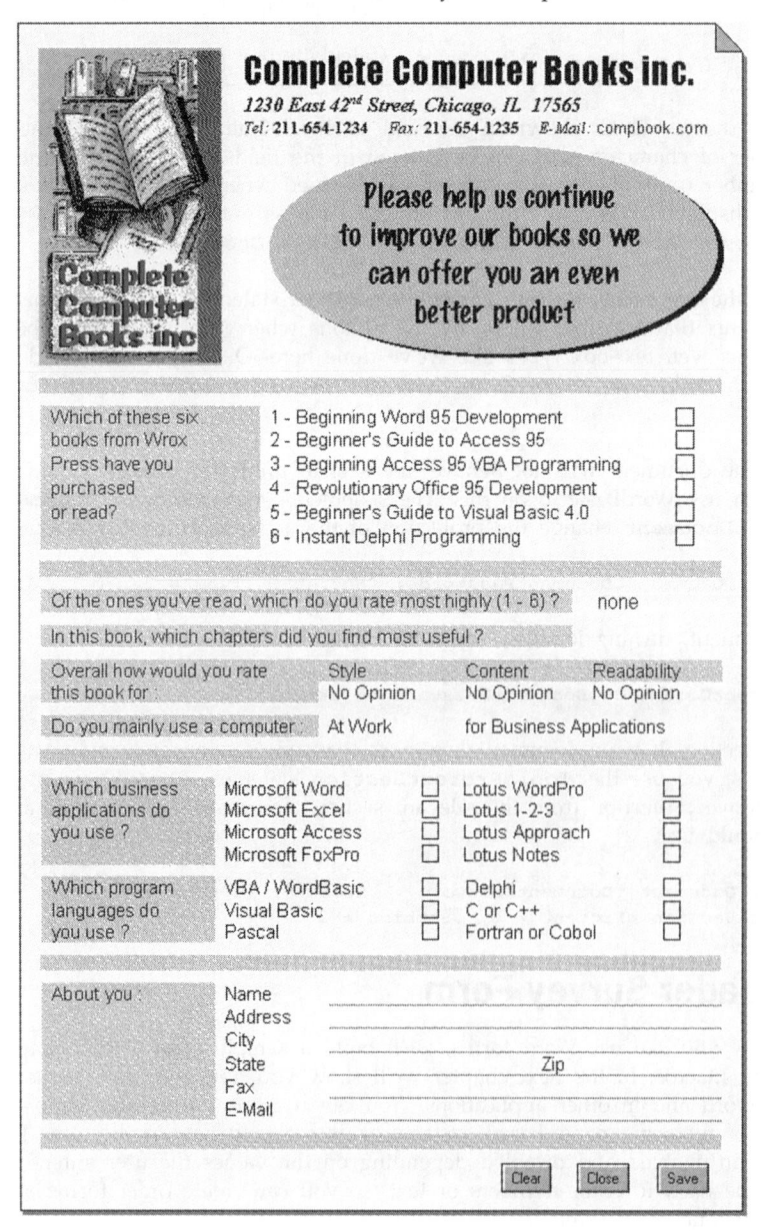

Creating the Survey Form

Although you can write macros that insert fields into a form, as you saw in an earlier section, this is really only useful if you're creating lots of forms. In this case, you could use WordBasic to build a tool that creates custom forms for you. In general, however, you'll create the form itself using Word's menu and toolbar commands, then automate it with WordBasic afterwards. This is what we did with our Survey form.

Try It Out - Creating the Wrox Survey Form

In this example, we'll show you how we created the Survey form. We've supplied the graphics that we used in the **\Fields** subfolder of your samples folder. In case you want to see it without creating it yourself, we've also included the complete template, **Survey.dot**.

1 Select New... on the File menu, select Template in the Create New section of the dialog and click OK to create a new template. Save it as **Survey.dot** on your disk. Then select Toolbars... on the View menu, place a check against Forms and click OK to show the Forms toolbar.

2 Create a two-column one-row table at the top of the new template using the Insert Table button on the Forms or Standard toolbar. Insert the graphic **Books.bmp** in the first column and type the company name and address in the second.

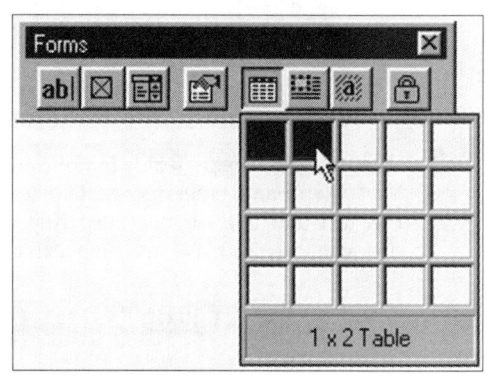

3 Insert three blank lines under the table. With the insertion point on the second of these, click the Borders button on the Formatting toolbar and set the Shading for the line to 20%. Now insert another table to hold the book names— make it three columns by six rows and size it as shown below. Type the question for this part of the form in the first column and enter six book titles in the second. Then select the first column and set the Shading for it to 20%.

4 Now we can insert the check box fields. Place the insertion point in the last column of the first row and click the Check Box Form Field button on the Forms toolbar. Then double-click on the new field to open the Check Box Form Field Options dialog. Enter the name Field1 for the Bookmark.

5 Click the Add Help Text... button, and the Form Field Help Text dialog opens. Select Type Your Own:, and enter some Help text. There are two pages in this dialog: one for the Status Bar text and one for the Help Key (F1) text. Enter some Help text in both of these. Notice that you can also use an AutoText Entry instead of typing it directly.

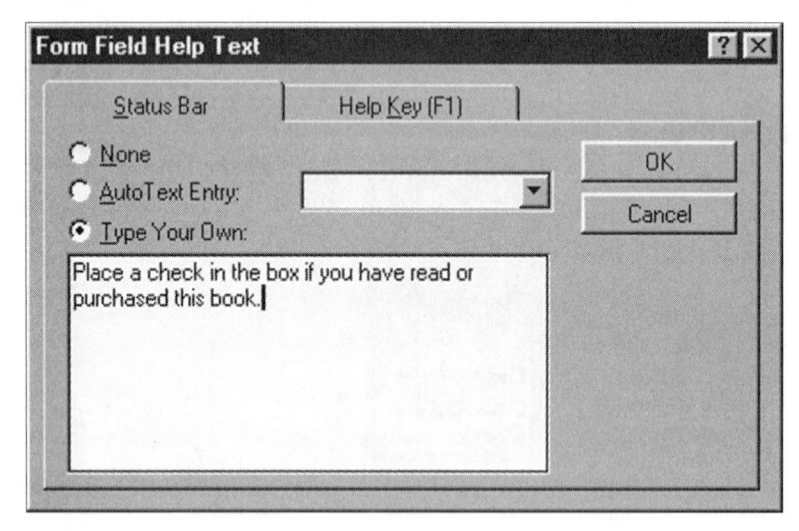

6 Close the Help Text and Options dialogs. We need the same type of control for the other five rows of this table, so click on the new control to select it and then copy it to the clipboard. Then click in the next row of the table and paste a copy of the control into the cell. Repeat this for the other rows, then double-click on each in turn and enter the name for their Bookmarks—use Field2 to Field6 for these.

Which of these six books from Wrox Press have you purchased or read?	1 - Beginning Word 95 Development	☐
	2 - Beginner's Guide to Access 95	☐
	3 - Beginning Access 95 VBA Programming	☐
	4 - Revolutionary Office 95 Development	☐
	5 - Beginner's Guide to Visual Basic 4.0	☐
	6 - Instant Delphi Programming	☐

> **FYI** You may be concerned that we aren't using more descriptive names for the fields. Be patient and you'll see why later on. Just make sure you name each field using the word **Field**, followed by a consecutive number — **Field1**, **Field2**, **Field3** etc.

7 Insert another three blank lines, formatting the second one with 20% shading again. Then insert two two-column one-row tables, separated by a single blank line. Enter the questions and size and format the tables.

| Of the ones you've read, which do you rate most highly (1 - 6) ? | |
| In this book, which chapters did you find most useful ? | |

8 Now we can add the two controls for these questions. Click in the last column of first table and click the **Drop-Down Form Field** button on the **Forms** toolbar. Then double-click the new field and set the options for it. We need the list to include the word none and the numbers 1 to 6, as shown below. Also, don't forget to set the **B**ookmark and enter the help text you want for the field.

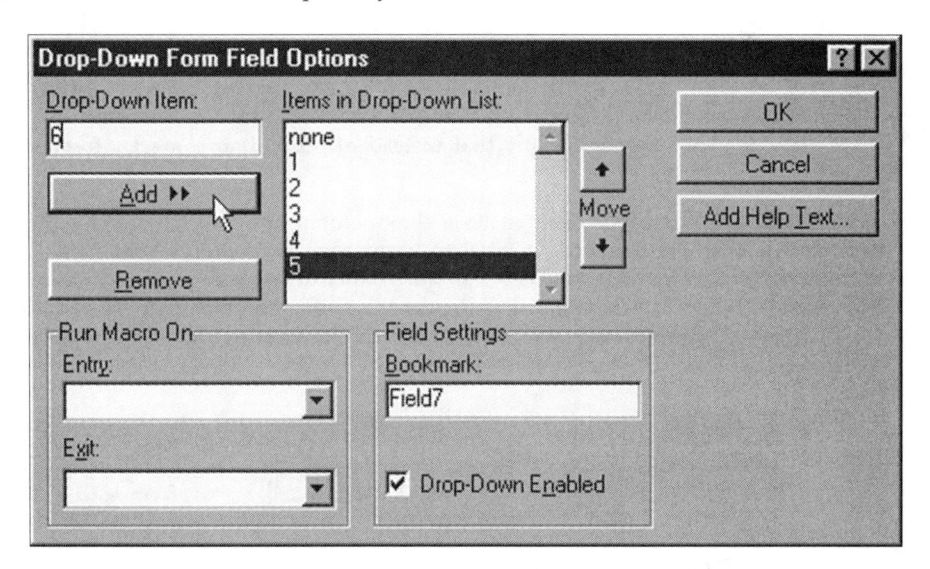

9 Close the dialogs, then click in the last column of the second table and click the Text Form Field button on the Forms toolbar. Then double-click the new field and set the Type to Regular Text and Maximum Length to 15. Change the Bookmark to Field8, and make sure you *clear* the Fill-in Enabled check box for this field. Leave the other options blank.

10 Carry on inserting the tables and blank lines to separate them, and the fields for the form's controls. Format each section however you want, but try and keep it simple. You should define one or more styles for the text, and use these rather than formatting individual pieces of text separately.

> **FYI** Word sometimes has problems handling a lot of different character formatting within tables. If you get a message that the template is too complex, make sure you have defined a style for your text and apply that instead of individual character formatting.

11 At the bottom of the document, create a three-column one-row table. Place the insertion point in the first cell and press *Ctrl-F9* to insert a normal empty Word field. Type **MACROBUTTON ClearForm** between the braces, then insert the graphic **Clearbtn.bmp** immediately before the closing brace. Repeat this with the other two, using **CloseForm** with the graphic **Closebtn.bmp** and **SaveData** with **Savebtn.bmp**. The graphics are in the **\Fields** subfolder of your samples folder.

12 Switch Field Codes view off with *Alt-F9* and save the template. Then click the Protect Form on the Forms toolbar and your new form comes to life. You can use *Tab* and *Shift-Tab* to move around and set the values of the various controls. To get rid of the gridlines on screen, select Gridlines on the Table menu so that it's not ticked. When you've finished experimenting, click the Protect Form button again.

How It Works

We've created the outline of our Survey form, using mainly the buttons on the Forms toolbar. While we haven't taken you through every step of creating every control, you should have produced a form that is workable, if not exactly the same as ours. You've seen how easy it is to insert and set the options for fields, and you're ready to go on designing your own.

We used the following values for the other drop-down list fields in our Survey template. We also cleared the Fill-in Enabled option for the Style, Content and Readability drop-down list fields when we created them.

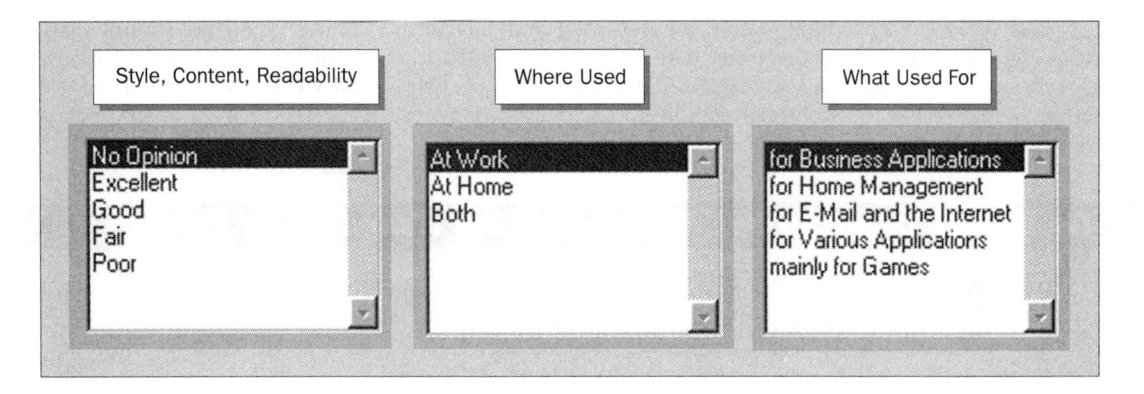

Style, Content, Readability	Where Used	What Used For
No Opinion Excellent Good Fair Poor	At Work At Home Both	for Business Applications for Home Management for E-Mail and the Internet for Various Applications mainly for Games

We also added a decorative slogan to the top of the form, under our company name and address. This is just an oval created with Word's drawing tools, with a light-gray fill and shadow effect, but no border. To use the drawing tools, select the Drawing toolbar in the <u>V</u>iew | <u>T</u>oolbars... dialog.

You'll notice that you can't use the field for entering the chapter numbers while the form is protected. This is because we cleared the Fill-in E<u>n</u>abled checkbox when we created it. You'll see why in the next section.

The three {MACROBUTTON} fields we placed at the bottom of the document form the command buttons. While a document is protected for forms, these fields can still be used. We still need to create the macros for these because, if you try the buttons, you'll find that they don't work at the moment.

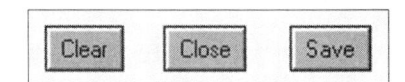

Once the form template is complete, you can place an icon on the desktop that creates a new copy of the form (as a new document) automatically when double-clicked. In My Computer or Explorer, right-click on your new template and drag it onto the desktop. Click twice (slowly) on the name under the icon and change it to whatever you need. It's as easy as that.

Automating the Survey Form

We can now use our new form to collect information. The user creates a new document based on our **Survey.dot** template and its form level protection is applied automatically. They can press *Tab* and *Shift+Tab* to move between the field controls, and enter values or set and clear the check boxes. However, consider the situation where they enter a value for the chapters they found most useful, but haven't selected which of the books they are referring to. This makes the data meaningless.

Of the ones you've read, which do you rate most highly (1 - 6) ?	none
In this book, which chapters did you find most useful ?	11, 12

We can automate our form using **OnEntry** and **OnExit** macros that run when the user moves from one control in the form to another. These can set values in other controls, or enable and disable them as appropriate. This way, we can ensure that the results make sense and that they're are actually useful.

Each field has an option setting for the Entry and Exit macro names. When the control that the field displays receives the focus (i.e. when the user tabs to it or clicks on it using the mouse), the macro whose name appears in the Entry option of Form Field Options dialog will be executed. When the control loses the focus, the macro whose name is specified in the Exit option will be run.

Try It Out - Using an OnExit Macro in the Wrox Survey Form

We'll use exit macro for the field control where the user selects which book they found most useful to make sure that the value in the 'chapters' control makes sense. At present the control for entering the most useful chapters is disabled and can't be used at all. We'll see how it should work We'll use the completed Survey template that we've supplied to see how it should work.

1 Copy the file **Survey.dot** from the **\Fields** subfolder of your samples folder into your default **\Templates** folder with your other Word templates. Then create a new survey form by selecting New... from the File menu and double-clicking Survey.dot.

2 Don't select any books in the first section. Instead, try clicking on the control after the question '.. which chapters did you find most useful ?'. You can't place the insertion point there because it' disabled at the moment. The three drop-down lists for Style, Content and Readability are also disabled.

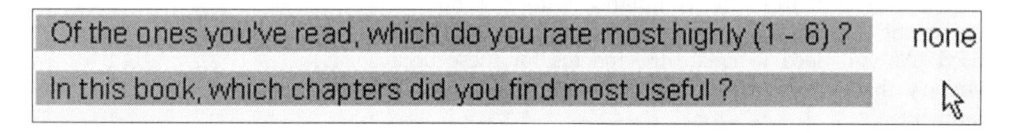

3 Click on the word 'none' in previous question and a drop-down list appears. Select book 2.

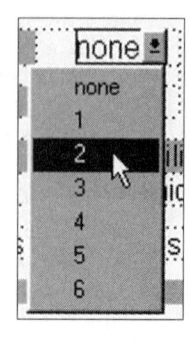

4 Press the *Tab* key to move to the next control. The 'chapters' control is now enabled, and the insertion point moves there so that you can type in the numbers. You'll also notice that the book you've chosen is checked in the list of titles above. The drop-down Style, Content and Readability lists are now available.

Which of these six books from Wrox Press have you purchased or read?	1 - Beginning Word 95 Development 2 - Beginner's Guide to Access 95 3 - Beginning Access 95 VBA Programming 4 - Revolutionary Office 95 Development 5 - Beginner's Guide to Visual Basic 4.0 6 - Instant Delphi Programming	☐ ☒ ☐ ☐ ☐ ☐

Of the ones you've read, which do you rate most highly (1 - 6) ?	2		
In this book, which chapters did you find most useful ?			
Overall how would you rate this book for :	Style No Opinion	Content No Opinion	Readability No Opinion

5 Enter some text, like 12, 13, and select some values for Style, Content and Readability. Then open the drop-down list in the previous question again and select 'none'. Press the *Tab* key, and the 'chapters' response you entered is removed and the text box becomes disabled. At the same time the Style, Content and Readability lists are set to No Opinion and also disabled, and the focus moves to the question after them.

How It Works

So that we can ensure the validity of the data in the form, we control which fields the user can enter data for, depending on the answers they provide to other questions. We're using the response they provide to the question about which book they thought most useful to control whether the questions about which were the most useful chapters and the overall ratings of the book are available.

It's all done with a macro named `ChapterSelect`. The first step is to create the macro, then we open the Form Field Options dialog for the 'best book' control and enter this macro for the E*x*it option. It will run when the user presses *Tab* to leave this control, or when they click on a different control after changing the value.

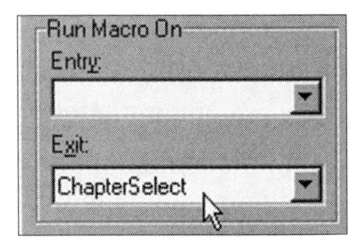

The macro itself just has to set the enabled state of the controls and clear the values if the user has selected 'none'. So first we get the setting of the 'best book' control, using `GetFormResult$`:

```
Sub MAIN                                    'the SelectChapter macro.
BestBook$ = GetFormResult$("Field7")        'get the value of the field.
```

Then we can decide which part of the **If-Then-Else** loop we need to execute. If the value is 'none' we need to clear the 'chapters' control and disable it. We also have to deal with the three list controls for Style, Content and Readability. Because we used consecutive numbers in the field names, we can manipulate them using a **For-Next** loop. The expression **"Field" + LTrim$(Str$(Loop))** creates the name of the field, such as **Field9**.

However, we can't use the **SetFormResult** statement in this loop for all the controls, because we have to supply a different argument for text and drop-down list fields. So we deal with **Field8** (the 'chapters' control) separately first:

```
    If BestBook$ = "none" Then                          'no book selected, so:
        EditGoTo "Field12"                              'move to Field12.
        SetFormResult "Field8", ""                      'clear Field8 'chapters'..
        EnableFormField "Field8", 0                     'and disable the control.
        For Loop = 9 To 11
            TheField$ = "Field" + LTrim$(Str$(Loop))    'set the values in the
            SetFormResult TheField$, 0                  'list fields to No Opinion
            EnableFormField TheField$, 0                'and disable them.
        Next
```

Notice that we have to move the focus away from the control before we disable it. This is easily done using the **EditGoTo** statement that you've seen before, which supplies the name of the bookmark to move to. This is, of course, the name of the field, because this is a bookmark which marks the field itself.

If the user selects a book number in the list, we need to enable the controls again. We'll take the opportunity to set the 'purchased or read' check box for that book as well. If they thought it was the best one, we can safely assume that they read it! To enable the controls, we can loop through all of them, as we did to disable them. Because the **EnableFormField** is the same for all types of control, we can do them all in the same loop this time.

Then we go to the 'chapters' field, ready for them to enter a value. At the same time, we convert the number of the book they chose into a bookmark name and set the appropriate check box with a **SetFormResult** statement:

```
    Else
        For Loop = 8 To 11
            TheField$ = "Field" + LTrim$(Str$(Loop))    'enable the 'chapters' and
            EnableFormField TheField$, 1                'the list controls.
        Next
        EditGoTo "Field8"                               'go to 'chapters' control.
        BookNum = Val(BestBook$)                        'get the book number
        If BookNum Then
            BMName$ = "Field" + LTrim$(Str$(BookNum))   'build the field name..
            SetFormResult BMName$, 1                    'and set it for the book
        EndIf
    EndIf
End Sub
```

We also need to create macros that runs when the form is created and closed. These turn off the display of gridlines, improving the appearance of the document on screen, and set the number of clicks required to activate a button field to **1**. Remember, you normally have to double-click a Word button field to run the macro it contains. We want the user to be able to single-click the Clear, Close and Save buttons on our form.

```
Sub MAIN        'the AutoNew macro
    ToolsOptionsGeneral .ButtonFieldClicks = 1
    TableGridlines 0
    SetDocumentDirty 0
End Sub

Sub MAIN        'the AutoClose macro
    ToolsOptionsGeneral .ButtonFieldClicks = 2
End Sub
```

We don't need to turn **TableGridlines** back on, because Word does that automatically when we open another document. The other statement in the **AutoNew** macro tells Word that the document doesn't have to be saved once it's been loaded. You'll see more of this later on.

Saving the Data from a Form

OK, so we've got the form working and the user can enter the information we want to collect. Now we have to consider what we're going to do with his information. When a document is protected for forms, the Save commands on the File menu work in a different way from a normal document.

If the user saves the form normally, we end up with a file on disk which is in Word document format, albeit containing form fields and being protected. We can print this, but the idea is to get away from a paper-based system. Instead, we can set the Save Data Only for Forms option that tells Word to save only the values in the form fields, not the whole document. It creates a file on disk which has the extension **.txt**, and contains just the values from each of the controls as a comma-delimited text file.

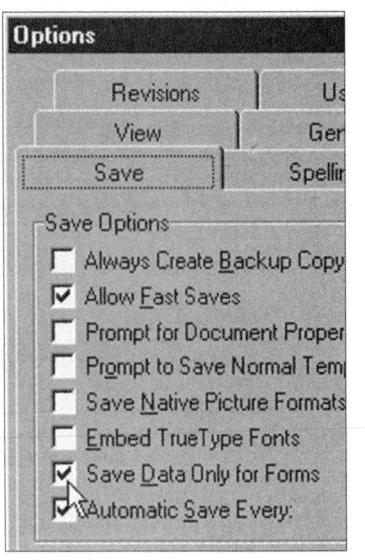

> **FYI**
>
> A comma-delimited text file contains a series of values laid out as a line of text. Values which are text (strings) are enclosed in quotation marks, and each value is separated from its neighbors with a comma. This kind of file often has the extension **.csv** (comma separated values) and can be opened in other applications as a pure data file.

This is idea if we only want to save the data from one form. We can use the WordBasic **ToolsOptionSave** statement, with the **.FormsData** argument set to **1**, to turn on saving of forms data only:

```
ToolsOptionsSave .FormsData = 1
```

Alternatively, we can take over the Save As... command on the File menu by replacing it with our own macro. In the macro we use the **FileSaveAs** statement with the **.FormsData** argument set to **1**:

```
FileSaveAs .Name = "Survey.doc", .FormsData = 1
```

Storing Data from Several Forms

This method is fine for saving the data from one form, but if you save the data from a form, then change the values in the controls and save the data again, you find that the File menu now has only Save and Save Copy As.... If you Save the data, you overwrite the original file. If you Save Copy As..., Word adds a number to the end of the file name and you create a separate file with the new data.

We want to build up a file containing lots of survey results so that we can analyze them and make sure our books are meeting our customers' expectations. So we have to find a way to save the data ourselves.

Manipulating Text Files with WordBasic

Word contains a set of statements that can read and write directly to a file on disk. We can use these to build our survey results file. Here's a summary of the commands you can use to work with disk files. You'll find a full description of each in Word's Help file.

Statement	What It Does
Open	Creates a new file or opens an existing one ready for use.
Read	Reads data from a file removing quotation marks from text values.
Input	Reads data from a file leaving quotation marks around text values.
Input$()	Reads a specified number of characters from a file into a string.
LineInput	Reads a complete line of text up to the carriage return from a file.
Write	Writes data to a file, enclosing string values in quotation marks and separating values with commas.
Print	Writes data to a file., but doesn't enclose string values in quotation marks, and separates values with *Tab* characters.
Close	Closes one or all open files.
Eof()	Returns **True** (**-1**) if the end of a file has been reached.
Lof()	Returns the length of an open file in bytes.
Seek()	Returns the current position in the file.
Seek	Moves the current position in a file to a new specified position.

FYI
> Notice that the WordBasic `Print` statement writes to a file separating the values with *Tab* characters. This is a popular format that can be read by almost all other applications. However, there's no WordBasic statement that reads files of this type directly. The only method is to use `LineInput` to read the complete line, then parse the string and break it up into individual values using your own code.

We're going to use the `Print` statement to create a tab-delimited text file for maximum compatibility with other applications. Our macro that adds the values from the form to the file on disk runs when the user clicks the Save button on the form. However, we also need to protect them from losing the data if they accidentally close the form before the data has been saved.

Checking whether a Document has been Saved

As soon as you make any changes to a newly opened document, Word sets an internal flag which marks it as dirty. This isn't a reflection on your writing style, but an indicator that the user should be prompted to save the changes before closing it. Each time it's saved, the dirty flag is reset. If you save a document, then close it immediately, the prompt doesn't appear.

We can use this flag ourselves to see whether the document needs to be saved. The WordBasic built-in function `IsDocumentDirty()` returns `True` (`-1`) if the document contains changes that haven't been saved. We can save the document ourselves, or prompt the user to save it.

```
If IsDocumentDirty() Then MsgBox "You need to save the document"
```

If they chose not to save it, we can then use the `SetDocumentDirty` statement to clear the flag so that Word doesn't prompt to save it when they close it:

```
SetDocumentDirty 0    'clears the dirty flag and prevents the Save prompt.
SetDocumentDirty 1    'sets the flag, marking the document as dirty.
```

There are equivalent `IsTemplateDirty()` function and `SetTemplateDirty` statement that work the same way with the template that the document is based on.

How Our Macros Work

So let's have a look at the way the macros in the Wrox Survey Form work. When the user clicks the Close button, we check to see whether the form is dirty. If it is, we prompt them to save the data in the form, and if they select Yes, we run the `SaveData` macro that adds the values in the fields to our data file. It also clears the dirty flag, so they won't be prompted to save the data again, and closes the form.

```
Sub MAIN   'CloseForm
    If IsDocumentDirty() Then
        Msg$ = "Do you want to save the current entries ?"
        If MsgBox(Msg$, "Wrox Survey", 36) = - 1 Then SaveData
    EndIf
    SetDocumentDirty 0          'clear the dirty flag
    On Error Goto FC_Exit
    FileClose                   'and close the document
FC_Exit:
End Sub
```

The Clear button on our survey form runs the **ClearForm** macro. This also checks to see whether the current values have been saved, and prompts the user to save them if not. To reset all the controls to their default values, we just need to unprotect the form and protect it again, turning off screen updating to make it look smoother. Unless you supply **1** for the **.NoReset** argument, the **ToolsProtectDocument** statement automatically resets them all to their default values. If you have protected the form's template with a password when you created it, you also have to supply the password here. When a document is protected, users can't open the Macro dialog to see the macros, so they won't be able to see the password you've used. This way, you don't compromise your document security. Once we've reset the values, we clear the dirty flag so that they won't be prompted to save it until they've entered new values.

```
Sub MAIN    'ClearForm
If IsDocumentDirty() Then
    Msg$ = "Do you want to save the current entries ?"
    If MsgBox(Msg$, "Wrox Survey", 36) = - 1 Then SaveData
EndIf
Screenupdating 0                        'turn off screen updating
ToolsUnprotectDocument                  'remove protection
ToolsProtectDocument .Type = 2          'protect it resetting all fields
SetDocumentDirty 0                      'clear the dirty flag
Screenupdating 1                        'turn screen updating back on
End Sub
```

The Save button runs the **SaveData** macro, and here we save the values in the field controls and again clear the dirty flag. First, we check to see whether a value has been entered in the {Name} field on the form. If not, we display a message, move the focus to that control and exit from the macro. When the user saves the data, we'll clear the existing values in the fields afterwards, so this prevents them saving blank forms:

```
Sub MAIN     'SaveData
    On Error Goto Write_Err
    If GetFormResult("Field29") = "" Then
        Msg$ = "You haven't entered a name for this form."
        MsgBox Msg$, "Wrox Survey", 48
        Goto Write_Exit
    EndIf
```

Next we set the name of our data file in the variable **TheFile$** and display a message in the status bar. Now we're ready to save the values from the fields. We've got 34 fields to save, and we can loop through them because we named them all in the same way, **Field1** to **Field34**. (Now you can see why we did this!) The expression **"Field" + LTrim$(Str$(Loop))** creates the field names for us, and we get the value stored in each one with the **GetFormResult$()** function.

First, we have to open the disk file. The **Open** statement takes the name of the file (stored in the variable **TheFile$**) and a file number that we use to refer to the open file in our macro. We've used **#1**, but WordBasic allows up to four files (**#1** to **#4**) to be open at once. We can also specify the way we want the file opened. We've used **Append** so that the data will be added to the end of the file. (If it doesn't already exist, a new file is created automatically.) Other options are **Input**, which allows us to read data from the file, and **Output**, which deletes any existing file with the same name and creates a new one each time.

```
TheFile$ = "Survey.txt"
Print "Saving the current entries to the file "; TheFile$
NumFields = 34
```

```
      Open TheFile$ For Append As #1            'open the file
      For Loop = 1 To NumFields
         TheField$ = "Field" + LTrim$(Str$(Loop))  'build the field name
         If Loop = NumFields Then               'last field so ..
            Print #1, GetFormResult$(TheField$)    'print value and RETURN
         Else                                   'otherwise ..
            Print #1, GetFormResult$(TheField$),   'print value and TAB
         EndIf
      Next
      Close
```

The **Print** statement outputs the value as a string (because we retrieved it from the control as a string using the **GetFormResult$()** function) and for the first 33 values, we follow this with a comma, which tells the **Print** statement to add a *Tab* character after the value in the file. To make sure we don't add an extra *Tab* character to the end of the line, we use **Print** without a comma for the last value, which adds a carriage return to the file.

Once we've written all the values, we close the file using the **Close** statement, then clear the current values. Because it only needs a few lines to do this, it's not worth calling the **ClearForm** macro. We might as well do it directly, which also makes the macro run faster. Then we clear the dirty flag and exit. The rest of the code is just an error trap to handle any errors that may occur:

```
      Screenupdating 0
      ToolsUnprotectDocument
      ToolsProtectDocument .Type = 2
      SetDocumentDirty 0
      Screenupdating 1
      Goto Write_Exit
Write_Err:
      Close
      Msg$ = "Cannot write to file " + TheFile$
      MsgBox Msg$, "Wrox Survey", 48
Write_Exit:
End Sub
```

The **Close** statement will accept the number of a file and only close that file. Omitting it, as we've done here, just closes all the open files. You should try out the Wrox Survey Form, and create a data file so that you can see it all working. Once you've saved a few forms, open the file **Survey.txt** into NotePad to see what it looks like.

> **FYI**
>
> As it stands, the macro saves the file **Survey.txt** in the current folder. You can set the current folder by opening another document from the folder where you want the survey results file to be built. In fact, you should consider changing the **SaveData** macro so that it always works with the same file, otherwise you won't be able to guarantee that all the entries end up in the same place.
>
> Change the line **TheFile$ = "Survey.txt"** to one appropriate for your system, such as **TheFile$ = "C:\Temp\Survey.txt"** or similar.

If you look in the Macros dialog, you'll find that we've also taken over several of Word's normal commands with our own macros. The reasoning is simple. If the user selects Save from the File menu instead of using the Save button on the form, we end up saving a copy of the form as a Word document. If they close the form by using the Word menu command, it will prompt them to save the form, again as a Word document.

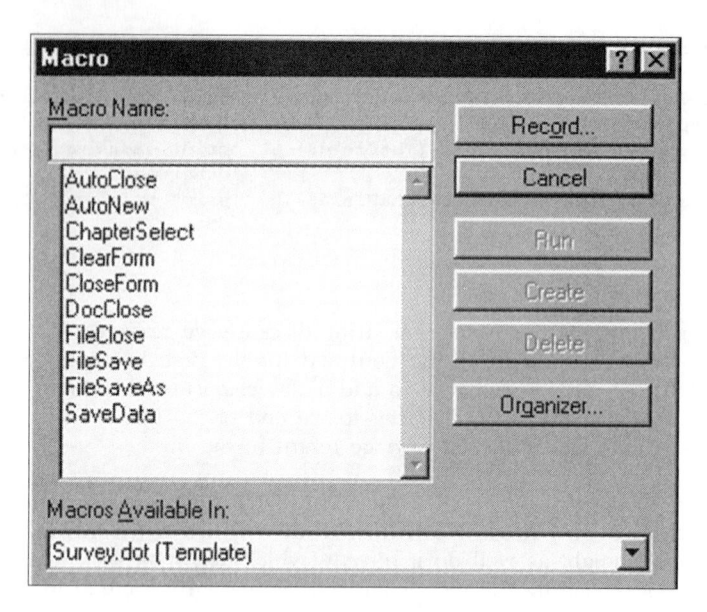

We've added macros to the **Survey.dot** template for **DocClose** (which runs when you click the close button at the top right of the document window), **FileClose**, **FileSave** and **FileSaveAs**. The first two run the **CloseForm** macro, and the other two run the **SaveData** macro.

This way, we take over full control of the interface. However, there's a minor problem. If you take over all the Save commands, you won't be able to save any changes that you make to the design of the template! We've purposely left the **FileSaveAll** command (Save All on the File menu) alone, so we can use this to save any changes we make as we develop the application.

> **FYI** Before you can open the Macros dialog you have to unprotect the form. We haven't password-protected it, so you can use the button on the Forms toolbar to unprotect it and protect it again afterwards.

Summary

In this chapter, we've introduced a lot of new concepts and, in many places, have referred you to the Word Help file. As you start to use the underlying power of Word, you find out just how many options you have available. We could never get them all into a book this size. Instead we've concentrated on a real-world solution which shows you just what you can achieve with very little effort and surprisingly small amounts of WordBasic code.

In this chapter we've seen:

- What Word fields are and how they can be used
- How we can create electronic forms and use different types of fields
- How to protect and automate electronic forms
- How to save data from a form as a file on disk

We ended the chapter rather abruptly, having built a form-based application which creates a data file on disk. This is intentional because, in the next couple of chapters, we'll show you how Word and other applications can take advantage of this data to help you and your company maintain the competitive advantage you need in today's business environment.

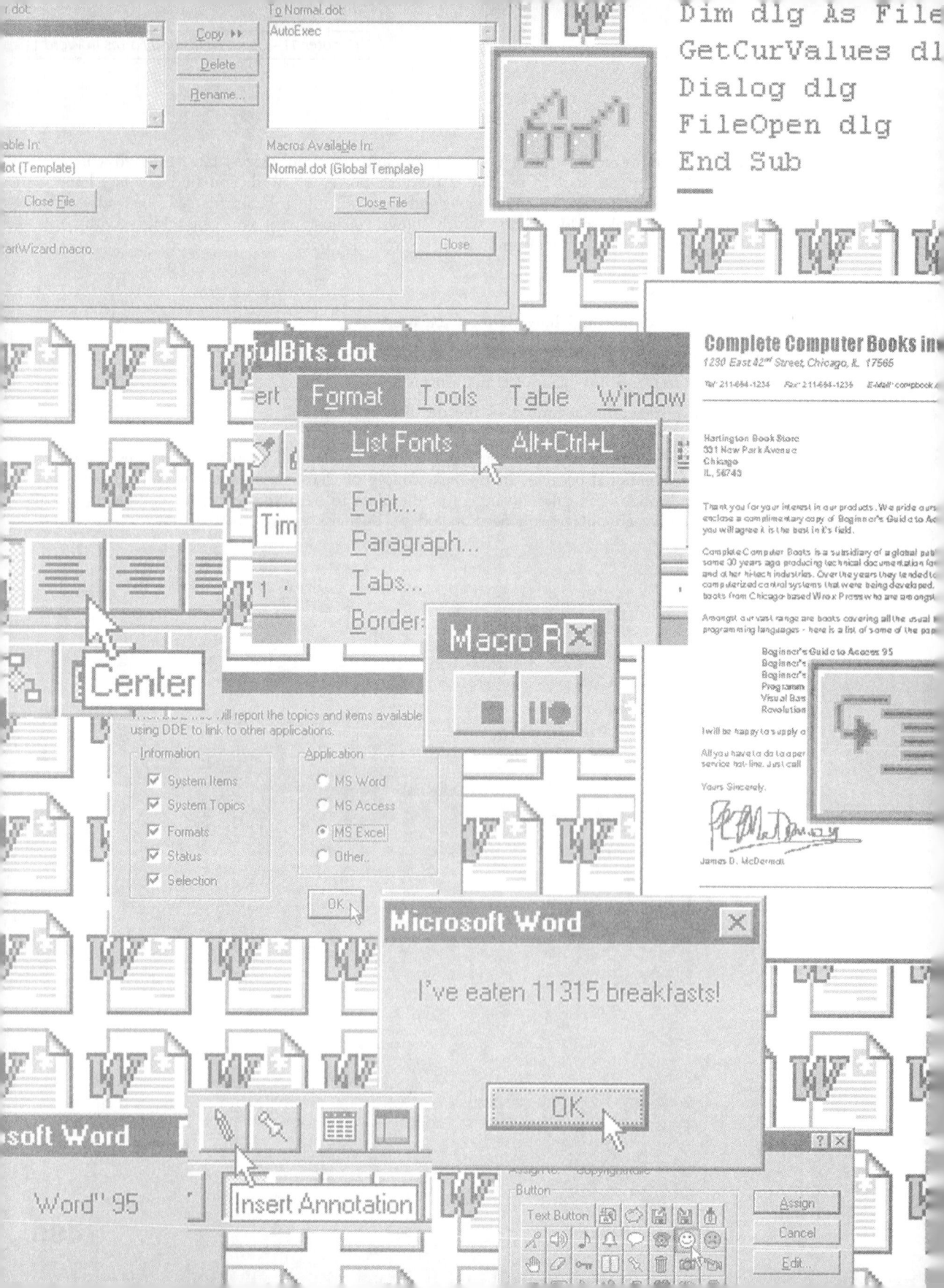

```
Dim dlg As File
GetCurValues dl
Dialog dlg
FileOpen dlg
End Sub
```

12

Sharing and Analyzing Data

Introduction

In the last chapter, we built a system which can collect opinions from our customers (the people who read our books), and store them in a file on disk. This makes use of the electronic forms features of Word, something different from the mode you probably use every day. But it's no good gathering data like this unless you intend to make some use of it. If it just sits on your disk, eating up valuable space, you're wasting your time collecting it.

In this and the next chapter, we'll look at the different ways you can use the data you collect. Our examples are based on the results produced by our Survey form, but they are equally applicable to any other types of data you accumulate. Of course, the data doesn't have to have come from a Word form. You can use Word to analyze data collected by any other method, as long as the file is in a format which Word can read. We looked at the different Word file-handling methods briefly in the previous chapter, and you'll see some more examples in this one.

We'll be using two of the other Microsoft applications that are part of Office 95. In some cases, as with Dynamic Data Exchange, the methods we describe will only work directly with these specific applications, but you may be able to adapt them to work with other programs. Most applications from other manufacturers will at least allow you to import the data from a disk file and analyze it there.

So, in this chapter we'll look at:

- How we can use our survey results to produce reports in Word
- How to import the survey data into other Office 95 applications
- The background to DDE and OLE, and how we can use them in Word
- Using DDE with WordBasic in detail, including several examples

We'll be saving OLE for the next chapter, where we continue looking at how our Survey data can be shared between different types of application and used for different purposes.

Using the Wrox Survey Results

Collecting data is a waste of time. It usually requires some effort from the user and can reduce the efficiency of your system if it takes up valuable processing time. In a non computer-based system, all you end up with is filing cabinets full of paper. If you collect it electronically, you just get files that eat up disk space.

The only thing that makes collecting data worthwhile is when you turn it into information. You use information to steer your business properly, make decisions about future policy and maximize your company's potential. This is the only reason that corporations are willing to spend the millions of dollars they do on information systems, data warehouses and all the other buzzword applications of the day.

Even so, if you're running the local golf club, or need to keep your home accounts in order, having the right information available is still a great benefit. Collecting your club members' opinions on how the 10th green should be improved will ensure you take the right decisions, and having all the members' names and addresses handy will mean you can automatically write to everyone, asking for their contribution towards the cost of the improvement!

Turning Data into Information

The real difference between data and information is how relevant it is to what you want to know. In theory, you can extract information from your data which isn't useful, but it's still information. For example, our survey results could suggest that, statistically, more people use C++ for programming in New York than in Arkansas. As a book publisher, this isn't going to change the way we produce our books, but it's vital information for a chain of books stores if they are going to stock the books that people want to buy.

Before we look at particular examples of how we can get information from our data, we'll consider an overview of what you can do using simple methods. Most of the Office 95 applications will import each other's data files directly. For example, you can import an Excel spreadsheet directly into Access or Word. Most major manufacturer's products will read the data files produced by their, and other company's, programs.

Once you get the data into the other application, you can analyze it and extract information from it. In Access, you can create queries and reports and include charts created by Microsoft Graph. In Excel, you can manipulate it, consolidate it, create scenarios and produce really complex charts. In Word itself, you can use it for reports and mail merge it to provide standard letters. These are only some of the possibilities. You can use Microsoft Query if you have it installed, or send the data to a mainframe-based system or network database, such as FoxPro or Oracle™.

Chapter 12 - Sharing and Analyzing Data

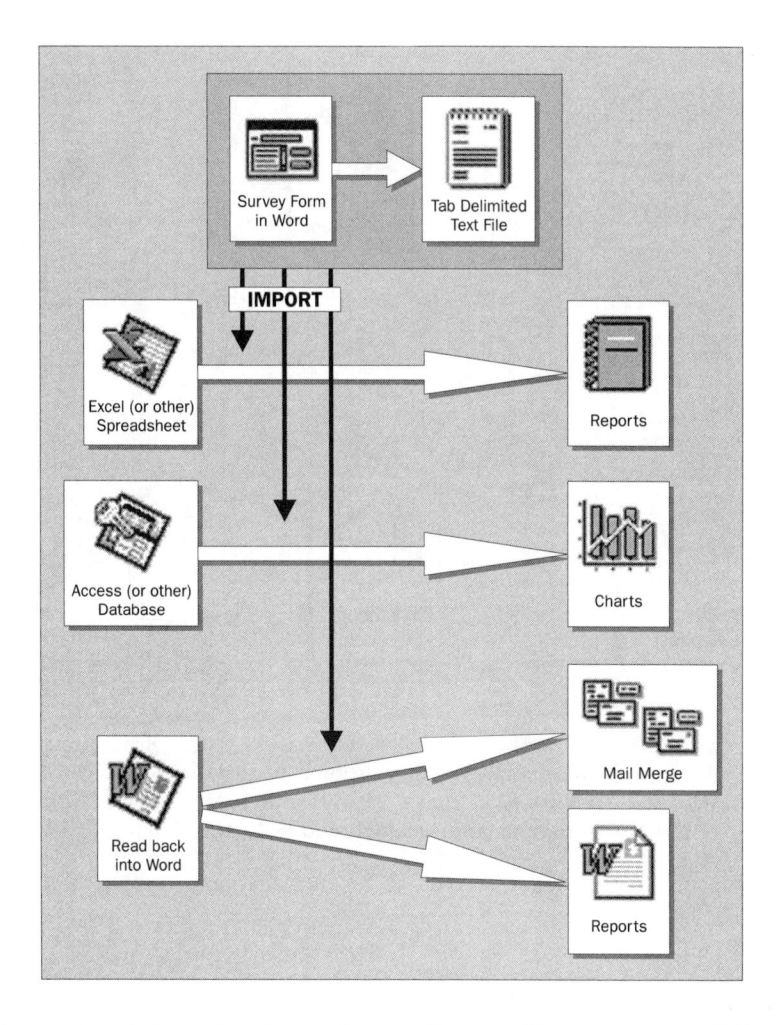

[Figure: Diagram showing Survey Form in Word → Tab Delimited Text File, with IMPORT arrows flowing to Excel (or other) Spreadsheet, Access (or other) Database, and Read back into Word. Outputs include Reports, Charts, Mail Merge, and Reports.]

Word can also retrieve information from other applications. There are many different ways of doing this, from the simple to the exotic. Word supports **OLE** (Object Linking and Embedding), though, at the moment, not as fully as the other Office 95 applications. It also allows you to use **DDE** (Dynamic Data Exchange) directly and **ODBC** (Open Database Connectivity) through a Word link library add-in.

Word also has built-in functionality which allows it to communicate with Microsoft Exchange to handle e-mail. Through another add-in it can also use **MAPI** (Messaging Application Programming Interface) methods to access other mail systems. The following graphic shows how some of these methods fit together, and the most likely uses you'll make of them. We won't be covering all these in detail, but we'll try and give you some starters for exploring further.

489

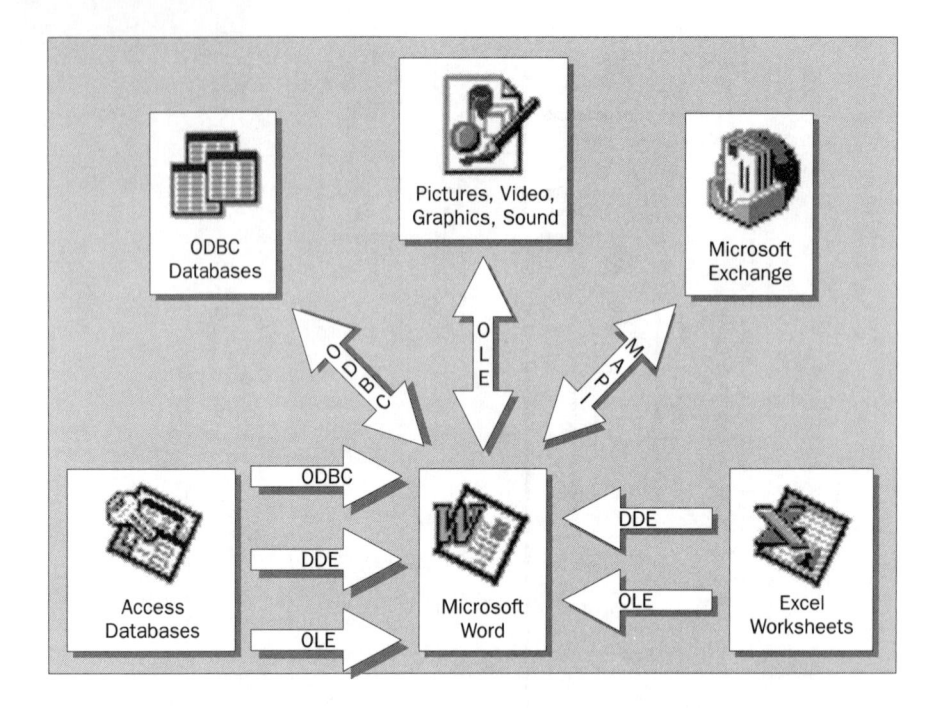

> **FYI** To use ODBC and MAPI with Word, you need to install special Word link libraries, `Wbodbc.wll` and `Wbmapi.wll`. These are available to developers through Microsoft's Developer Network program and are included with the *Microsoft Word Developer's Kit*.

Analyzing Data in Word

As a first step, we'll look at how our survey results can be used in Word. While it's by no means a substitute for a 'proper' database or spreadsheet application, Word can produce attractive and useful reports by analyzing the data using WordBasic, presenting it as a document. We've included an example for you to try, and we'll show you how it's put together. Before we look at the report, however, we should consider how we're going to read the data that we unceremoniously dumped into the **Survey.txt** file in the last chapter.

Disk Files and WordBasic

You'll recall from the last chapter that WordBasic supports two main methods of writing data into a text file on disk. We could use the **Write** statement which automatically surrounds text values with quotation marks and separates each of the values with commas. These individual values, which can be text or numbers, together make up a record. Each record in the file is terminated with carriage return and linefeed characters, **Chr$(13)** and **Chr$(10)**. This type of file is called a **comma-delimited file**, and may have a **.txt** or **.csv** (comma separated values) file extension.

```
Open "C:\Test.txt" For Output As #1
TheName$ = "Word"
TheNumber = 95
Write #1, TheName$, TheNumber
Close #1
```

test.txt - Notepad
`"Word", 95`

WordBasic also offers the **Print** statement. This places the values in the file, but doesn't enclose text in quotation marks. It also separates the values with *Tab* characters, rather than commas. This type of file is referred to as a **tab-delimited file**, and usually has the **.txt** file extension.

```
Open "C:\Test.txt" For Output As #1
TheName$ = "Word"
TheNumber = 95
Print #1, TheName$, TheNumber
Close #1
```

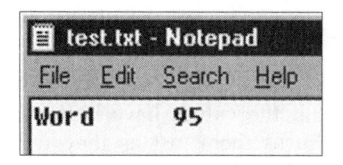

test.txt - Notepad
`Word    95`

We chose a tab-delimited file for our survey data because it's easier to produce the format we want with a loop in WordBasic. Using the **Write** statement produces a file which has each value in a separate record, on a separate line. The comma at the end makes no difference to the way the file is written, and neither does a semicolon.

```
Open "C:\Test.txt" For Output As #1
For Loop = 1 To 5
    Write #1, Str$(Loop),
Next
Close #1
```

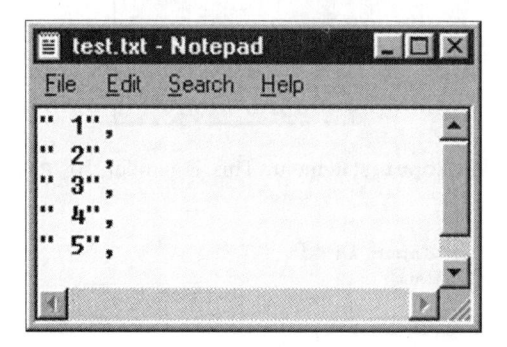

test.txt - Notepad
```
" 1",
" 2",
" 3",
" 4",
" 5",
```

The **Print** statement, however, will add values to the same line until you explicitly send a carriage return to the file. This is what we wanted from our Survey form because we looped through each of the fields writing them to the file one by one. Thus, each line of fields stored one record of information:

```
Open "C:\Test.txt" For Output As #1
For Loop = 1 To 5
    Print #1, Str$(Loop),
Next
Print #1, ""
Close #1
```

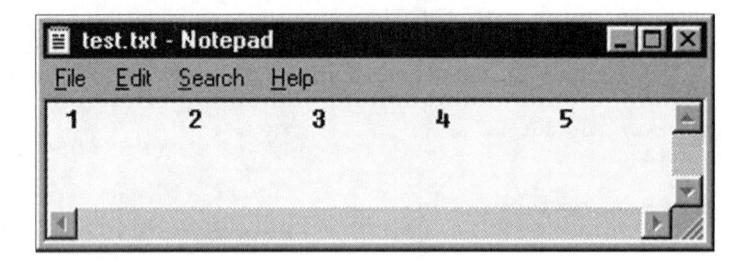

Reading Disk Files in WordBasic

When we come to read the data in a text file from WordBasic, we can use one of four different built-in statements and functions. If the values have been written to the file with the **Write** statement, the **Read** statement returns them just as they were written. It removes quotation marks from text values automatically, which makes it easy to retrieve data from a text file.

```
Open "C:\Test.txt" For Input As #1
Read #1, TheName$, TheNumber
Close #1
MsgBox TheName$ + Str$(TheNumber)
```

Somewhat less useful is the **Input** statement. This is similar to **Read**, but it doesn't remove the quotation marks:

```
Open "C:\Test.txt" For Input As #1
Input #1, TheName$, TheNumber
Close #1
MsgBox TheName$ + Str$(TheNumber)
```

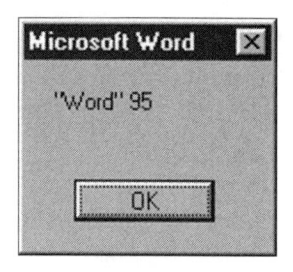

[Dialog: Microsoft Word — "Word" 95 — OK]

The **Input$()** function works completely differently, despite the similar name. It reads only the specified number of characters from the file, including the comma or *Tab* delimiter characters, and you have to supply this argument when you call the function:

```
Open "C:\Test.txt" For Input As #1
TheResult$ = Input$(5, #1)
Close #1
MsgBox TheResult$
```

[Dialog: Microsoft Word — "Word — OK]

If you have to deal with files created by traditional mainframe-type databases, you'll find the **Input$()** function useful. Often, these files are of **fixed width format**, which means that each record has the same number of characters and there are no separators between the individual values or the records themselves. The values are padded with spaces to fill the allocated space. You retrieve individual values and whole records by specifying the exact number of characters you need, then removing these extra spaces. You would then have to use a WordBasic string-handling function to retrieve the individual fields from within the records.

Finally, we can use the **Line Input** statement (yes, there *is* a space in the statement name). This returns everything up to, but excluding, the next carriage return:

```
Open "C:\Test.txt" For Input As #1
Line Input #1, TheResult$
Close #1
MsgBox TheResult$
```

[Dialog: Microsoft Word — "Word", 95 — OK]

Retrieving Data from Our Survey File

In Chapter 11, we mentioned that there is no WordBasic statement which can read tab-delimited files directly, and we've seen this again in the previous section. So how do we get our survey data back? The answer is to read the whole record in one go and parse out the individual values ourselves with WordBasic. This isn't as complicated as it sounds.

Each value in the file is separated from its neighbors by a *Tab* character, which we can find using the **InStr()** function. This returns the position of the first occurrence of a substring within a string, and we've used it this way regularly in previous chapters. It starts the search for the substring from position **1**, the first character, in the source string. However, we can supply a value for the optional **Index** argument, which defines a different starting point for the search.

Here's how we've used it in our Results template to get individual values from the records in our **Survey.txt** file. We created a function, **GetLineValue$()**, which takes two arguments: the 'field' number and the string to find it in. It returns the value as a string. If we want it to be numeric, we can convert it later using WordBasic's **Val()** function, a nice compact function that's relatively quick and would make an excellent candidate for your own UsefulBits library template:

```
Function GetLineValue$(ValNo, TheLine$)
    Start = 1                                   'position in the string
    For Loop = 1 To (ValNo - 1)                 'move to required value
        Start = InStr(Start, TheLine$, Chr$(9)) + 1
    Next
    If ValNo = NumVals Then                     'if its the last value
        Finish = Len(TheLine$) + 1              'use the rest of the string
    Else                                        'else find next Tab character
        Finish = InStr(Start, TheLine$, Chr$(9))
    EndIf
    GetLineValue$ = Mid$(TheLine$, Start,(Finish - Start))
End Function
```

The idea is to retrieve the data for a single field within the record. The entire record is stored in **TheLine$**, so we need to find the start and end points of the value we want within the string. By using **InStr()** with the extra **Index** argument, we can loop through the *Tab* characters until we've passed **(ValNo - 1)**, one less than the number of the value we want. If **ValNo** is zero when the routine is called, the loop doesn't execute at all. The function isn't protected from calls where **ValNo** is greater than the number of actual values in **TheLine$**. You could add code to check for this first, or make sure you only use it with valid arguments.

Once we've pinpointed the start of the value, we find the end by looking for the next *Tab* character, or, if it's the last value, using the length of the string. The variable **NumVals** is a global **Shared** variable that's declared at the beginning of the macro. Then, when we've got the start and end points, we pull the value out of the string using the **Mid$()** function.

We can use this function to get any value from a record by reading the whole record into a string and sending it, together with the field (value) number we want, to the function. So, we need to read the whole string from the file. The **Line Input** statement does just this:

```
Line Input #1, ValLine$                         'read the whole line, and
TheResult$ = GetLineValue$(4, ValLine$)         'get the fourth value from it
```

Knowing when to Stop

One other problem is knowing when we have processed all of the records and have reached the end of the file. If we execute a **Line Input** statement (or any other statement that reads from a file) after we've reached the end of the file, we'll get an error. We could trap this error, but a neater way is to use the **Eof()** (End Of File) function. This returns **False (0)** if there are more records in the file, or **True (-1)** if we've already read the last one:

```
Open "C:\Test.txt" For Input As #1          'open the file
While Not Eof(#1)                           'while not at end of file
   Line Input #1, TheResult$                'read the whole record
Wend                                        'and do it again
Close #1                                    'close the file
```

Remember to close the file afterwards. If you don't, you won't be able to open it in the same macro, though Word will usually close it for you when the macro ends. This could, however, damage the file, so you should *never* rely on it If you are writing to it, rather than reading from it, leaving it open is an easy way to create 'lost clusters' on your disk and lose the data altogether.

When you are manipulating files, you should also provide an error trap, because you can't rely on the file always being in the same place, or even the disk being available. In the error trap, you might want to use the **Close** statement without specifying the file number so that it closes all open files, not just the one you specify. If you have a typo in your macro, you may end up leaving a different file open!

Try It Out - The Wrox Survey Results Report

So let's get on and see some file-handling at work. You'll need the Results template for this example, which you'll find in the **\Fields** subfolder of your samples folder. You'll also need to have a file of survey data created by the Survey application we used in the previous chapter. If you haven't created one of your own, you can use the completely fictitious sample file we've supplied. It's called **Survey.txtM** and is in the same folder as the Results template.

1 Copy **Results.dot** from the **\Fields** subfolder of your samples folder into your default **\Templates** folder. Unless you changed the defaults when you installed Word 95 or Office 95, this will be **\Winword\Template** or **\Msoffice\Templates**.

2 Select <u>N</u>ew... from the <u>F</u>ile... menu and double-click on the Results template. (Don't use the New button on the toolbar.) The Results application starts automatically. At the bottom of the window, in the status bar, you'll see the file being processed.

> Analyzing line 11 of file C:\Begword\Fields\Survey.txt

FYI If you have turned off auto macros, the Results application won't start running automatically. In this case, select <u>M</u>acro... on the <u>T</u>ools menu and double-click on **UpdateResults**. You may also need to change the following line (the first line after Sub MAIN in the UpdateResults macro) if you have installed the sample files in a different folder, or want to use your own Survey data file: MyFile$ ="C:\Begword\Fields\Survey.txt"

3 Once the whole file has been processed (it's quick because there are only 27 records in the file), you see the finished report. It analyzes readers' opinions of our books, according to the data in the Survey file.

Complete Computer Books inc.
1230 East 42nd Street, Chicago, IL 17565
Tel:211-654-1234   Fax:211-654-1235   E-Mail:compbook.com

Reader Survey Report 1995 - 1996

I am pleased to report the results of the recent reader survey of our six latest titles. The total number of responses to the survey up to Saturday 20 April was 27.

Our customers had purchased or read a total of 64 of our books and overall they scored us at 6 for style, 7 for content and 5 for readability, giving an overall average score for the three categories of 56%.

A table containing the full breakdown by title is included below and I look forward to your comments on what has been an excellent result yet again.

Total Number of Responses : 27

Book:	1	2	3	4	5	6	Overall
No. purchased or read:	9	11	12	9	13	10	64
Of these, chosen as best:	44%	36%	41%	33%	46%	30%	
Avg. score for Style:	6	5	6	5	5	7	6
Avg. score for content:	7	7	5	6	6	6	7
Avg. score for Readability:	4	4	6	5	5	7	5
Avg. score Overall:	57%	53%	57%	53%	53%	67%	56%

List of Titles:

1 - Beginning Word 95 Development
2 - Beginner's guide to Access 95

Remember that information like this can only ever reflect the data you've collected and may not represent 'real life'. Only a proportion of your customers will return the survey slips you provide, so you can never be sure you have a representative sample. One of the hardest tasks in doing any type of survey is getting that representative sample of responses.

It's generally accepted that people who are quite pleased with your products, and even those who rate them very highly, won't tell you. The ones who will always tell you are those who are not happy, for all sorts of reasons. So, if you can score above half marks for anything, it's a sign that you're doing well.

How It Works

There can't be many management reports you have to produce which are as easy as that! The **UpdateResults** macro, which runs automatically when the Report template is opened, reads the data in the file, analyzes it to get the results and inserts these into a new document. This is a fairly simple example of what can be done, but it provides that kind of vital information which can help to keep your business on track.

Designing the Results Template

The Results template contains the boilerplate text and graphics for the report, and the fields which are used to place the data from the survey. We created the template like any other document and inserted the fields manually using the Word menus. At the bottom is the table where the results are actually placed by the macro

Book:	1		Overall
or read:	9		{=sum(left)}
as best:	44%		
for style:	6		{=sum(left)/6\##0}
content:	7		{=sum(left)/6\##0}
readability:	4		{=sum(left)/6\##0}
Overall:	{=sum(B4:B6)*10/3\##0%}		{=sum(B4:G6)*10/18\##0%}

The values in columns 1 to 6, with the exception of the last row, are produced by the macro and placed in the table using WordBasic. The cells in the column for book 1 contain fields which are marked by bookmarks named **ROW1** to **ROW5**, and the macro uses these to figure out where to place the results. The other values in the table are produced by **calculated fields**, as you can see from the diagram which shows parts of the table in Field Codes view.

To calculate the first few values for the Overall column, we've used the **sum** function within the calculated field. The argument `left` tells the function to add together all the values in cells to the left of it. In the middle rows of this column, we've divided the total by six, because there are six books, and formatted it to show the result to the nearest whole number.

```
{ =sum(left) }            'total for the row to the left
{ =sum(left/6 \# #0) }    'same but divide by 6 and show as nearest integer
```

You see now how we can use Word tables like a spreadsheet. In the last row, we want to show the average for each book for the three categories (Style, Content and Readability) as a percentage. We've done it using the **sum** function again, and divided by three. As each score is out of ten, we only need to multiply the result by ten (instead of 100) to get the percentage, and we use a format string to show the percent sign in the cell as well.

Notice how we refer to the cells that we want to add together, just like in a spreadsheet. **B4:B6** is the cells in the fourth, fifth and sixth rows of the second column. In the Overall column, we've used **B4:G6** to include the cells in the fourth, fifth and sixth rows of all the columns from the second to the seventh (**B** to **G**).

The upper part of the template contains the text preamble. Here, we've used bookmark-type fields, which refer to the values in the table. For example, the total number of books that were purchased or read in the first row of the Overall column is marked by the bookmark **COUNT**. Over the page you'll see the text in Field Codes view, so that you can see the fields we've used.

> I am pleased to report the results of the recent reader survey of our six latest titles. The total number of responses to the survey up to { DATE \@ "dddd d MMMM" } was { TOTAL }.
>
> Our customers had purchased or read a total of { COUNT } of our books, and overall they scored us at{ STYLE } for style,{ CONTENT } for content, and{ READ } for readability, giving an overall average score for the three categories of { OVERALL }.
>
> A table containing the full breakdown by title is included below, and I look forward to your comments on what has been an { IF OVERALL > "50%" excellent acceptable } result yet again.

To get today's date, we've included a **DATE** field. Also look at the last field here. It's an **IF** type, which checks the value in the overall opinions cell of the table. If it's above 50% the report displays **excellent**, otherwise it shows **acceptable**. How's that for automated document production?

Creating the Macro

The Results template contains four macros, three of which interest us at the moment. We've used an **AutoNew** macro that runs when a new document is created from the template, and an **AutoOpen** macro that runs when the document is opened. That way, the user can save a copy, and it's still updated each time they open it. Both of these simply run the **UpdateResults** macro that does all the work. We'll look at this macro in stages.

The first step is to see how we actually analyze the data in the file. We've written a subroutine, called **FillResultArray**, which collects the results, analyzes them and stores them in an array ready for inserting into the report. This way it's easier to separate the tasks of reading the data file and actually inserting the values into the document.

The macro declares two **Shared** variables when it runs. **Result** is our array, which will hold five values for each book. To make life easier (and because it's only a small array) we've declared it as five rows and six columns, so that we don't have to keep subtracting one from the indexes to cope with row and column zero. We use one location, **Result(0, 0)**, to hold the total number of responses as we process them. This saves having to return it as a separate variable.

	Column 0	*Columns 1 to 6 - one for each book*
Row 0	Total No. of Responses	
Row 1		Quantity Purchased or Read.
Row 2		Number of times chosen as the best
Row 3		Total marks for Style
Row 4		Total marks for Content
Row 5		Total marks for Readability

```
Dim Shared Result(5, 6)      'array to hold the results of the analysis
Dim Shared NumVals           'total number of fields on form and in file
```

The other **Shared** variable, **NumVals**, is the number of fields (values) in our file records and the number of fields on the original Survey form. This is used in our **GetLineValue$()** function, and we set it to **34** when the macro starts running. Then we can set up the error trap, turn on the hourglass cursor and open the file:

```
    Sub FillResultArray(TheFile$)
       NumVals = 34                           'set the number of values per record
       On Error Goto FRA_Err
       WaitCursor 1                           'show an hourglass cursor
       Open TheFile$ For Input As #1          'and open the file
```

Now we use the **Eof()** function to check whether there are any records in it. This forms the start of the loop that will read every record in the file. If we've got some records to work with, we read the first into **ValLine$**, update the number of responses in **Result(0, 0)** and stuff a message in the status bar so that the user knows that something is happening.

```
    While Not Eof(#1)                              'while we've got records
       Line Input #1, ValLine$                     'read the whole record
       Result(0, 0) = Result(0, 0) + 1             'update the total number
       Print "Analyzing line"; Result(0, 0); " of file "; TheFile$
```

The next step is to pull out and examine the first six values, which correspond to the 'purchased or read' question for each book. If we get **1**, it means the check box was set, so we increment the score for that book in row **1** of the array. To get the individual values from the line, we use our **GetLineValue$()** function, that we described earlier.

```
            For Loop = 1 To 6    'for each book
               If GetLineValue$(Loop, ValLine$) = "1" Then
                  Result(1, Loop) = Result(1, Loop) + 1       'purchased or read
               EndIf
            Next
```

Question 2 asks the reader to 'choose the best of these'. We get the value they select from field **7** of the file. Applying the **Val()** function to it gives the book number, or zero if the response was 'none'. If we get a number above zero, we can increment the value in row **2** of the array for that particular book:

```
            Best = Val(GetLineValue$(7, ValLine$))            'chosen as best
            If Best > 0 Then
               Result(2, Best) = Result(2, Best) + 1
```

Now we collect the scores for Style, Content and Readability. These are in fields **9**, **10** and **11** of the record, so we'll use a loop to examine each one in turn. Depending on the opinion, we allocate a score and add it to the existing score in the appropriate row of the **Result** array. Then we can go back to the beginning of the loop and read the next record:

```
              For Loop = 9 To 11       'style, content and readability
                 Opinion$ = GetLineValue$(Loop, ValLine$)
                 Select Case Opinion$
                    Case "Excellent"
                       Score = 10
                    Case "Good"
                       Score = 6
                    Case "Fair"
                       Score = 4
                    Case "Poor"
                       Score = 1
                    Case Else
                       Score = 0
                 End Select
```

```
                    Result(Loop - 6, Best) = Result(Loop - 6, Best) + Score
            Next
        EndIf
    Wend
```

The last job is to close the file, restore the normal cursor, then jump to the end of the macro. The rest is just the error handling code:

```
    Close #1                            'close the file
    WaitCursor 0                        'restore the cursor
    Goto FRA_Exit                       'and jump to the end
FRA_Err:
    Close                               'close all open files
    Msg$ = "Cannot read file " + TheFile$
    MsgBox Msg$, "Wrox Survey", 48
FRA_Exit:
End Sub
```

So, we've got a routine that fills our array with values All we need to do is to put them in the right places in the document. Here's the **Sub MAIN** part of the macro. It first sets the name of the file, which you may need to change to match the file you are using. Of course, you could replace it with an **InputBox$()** call, use the **FileOpen** dialog, or even create a custom dialog to get the name from the user each time. Next, we call the **FillResultArray** routine and check whether we've got any results by examining **Result(0, 0)**. If we don't, we jump to the end of the macro, display a message and exit:

```
Sub MAIN
    MyFile$ = "C:\Begword\Fields\Survey.txt"   'set the filename
    ScreenUpdating 0                           'turn off screen updating
    FillResultArray(MyFile$)                   'analyze the file
    If Result(0, 0) = 0 Then Goto No_Data      'jump to the end
```

The **EditGoTo** statement, used with the name of a bookmark in the document, places the insertion point at that location. We can then use an **Insert** statement to place the value in the document. We actually placed Word fields in the document and marked these by bookmarks. This prevents the bookmark disappearing when the text is inserted, which is useful when we want to refer to it again from elsewhere in the document. To insert the values in the table, we go to the second cell in each row (which is marked by a **ROWx** bookmark) and use the **NextCell** statement to step along the row:

```
        EditGoTo "TOTAL"                            'total number of responses
        Insert LTrim$(Str$(Result(0, 0)))
        For TRow = 1 To 5                           'fill in table
            EditGoTo "ROW" + LTrim$(Str$(TRow))     'the row in the table
            For Book = 1 To 6
                TheValue = 0                        'set default value
                Select Case TRow
                Case 1                              'purchased or read
                    TheValue = Result(1, Book)
                    Insert LTrim$(Str$(TheValue))
                Case 2                              'chosen as best
                    If Result(1, Book) > 0 Then     'prevent divide by zero error
                        TheValue = Result(2, Book) * 100 / Result(1, Book)
                    EndIf
                    Insert LTrim$(Str$(Int(TheValue)) + "%")
```

```
            Case 3, 4, 5                       'style, content or readability
                If Result(2, Book) > 0 Then    'prevent divide by zero error
                    TheValue = Result(TRow, Book) / Result(2, Book)
                EndIf
                Insert LTrim$(Str$(Int(TheValue)))
            End Select
            NextCell                           'goto next table cell
        Next
    Next
```

Notice how we have calculated and formatted the values differently, depending on where they are going in the table. Row **2** is calculated as a percentage of the total 'purchased or read' for that title, while rows **3**, **4** and **5** are calculated as an average of the 'chosen as best' total.

Finally, we need to update the fields in the document so that they reflect the new values. We select the whole document, then execute the **UpdateFields** statement. However, our document contains an **IF** field that depends on fields occurring after it, so we have to update it after we've updated the others. Rather than selecting just the one we want to update, the easiest way is to issue two **UpdateField** statements:

```
        EditSelectAll                   'select all the document
        UpdateFields                    'update all the fields, then
        UpdateFields                    'update again for {IF} field
        SelType 1                       'remove selection
        ScreenUpdating 1                'turn screen updating back on
        Print "Finished..."
        Goto Done                       'and exit
No_Data:
        Msg$ = "No survey results found"
        MsgBox Msg$, "Wrox Survey", 48
Done:
End Sub
```

We've spent a lot of time on this example because it contains a lot of new material. You've seen how we can work with text files in WordBasic, a method for analyzing data and storing it in an array, and the ways you can insert data into a document, including using a table like a spreadsheet. Next, we'll see how we can use a 'real' spreadsheet application and a 'proper' database.

Using the Survey Results in Excel and Access

Turning data into information can either be very simple, or extremely complicated. We can't guess what your business needs to know, but, in this section, we'll show you how you can share the data you collect between applications. We'll be using the Survey data we collected in the last chapter, but you can, of course, use the general techniques with your own data. You don't have to start from a file created in. We'll be looking at how you get information from other applications back into Word later on.

If you use Word, you'll probably also have access to other components of Microsoft Office 95. We'll be using Excel and Access here, but, if you use applications from other manufacturers, you'll probably find that the methods we describe will still work. You'll have to consult the individual application's documentation for exact details.

Importing the Data into Excel

Getting tab-delimited data, like the type in our Survey file, into Excel couldn't be easier. In fact, it's one of the reasons we chose this format. Just start Excel, open My Computer or Explorer, find the file **Survey.txt** in the **\Fields** subfolder of your samples folder and drag it onto the Excel window. It's imported automatically.

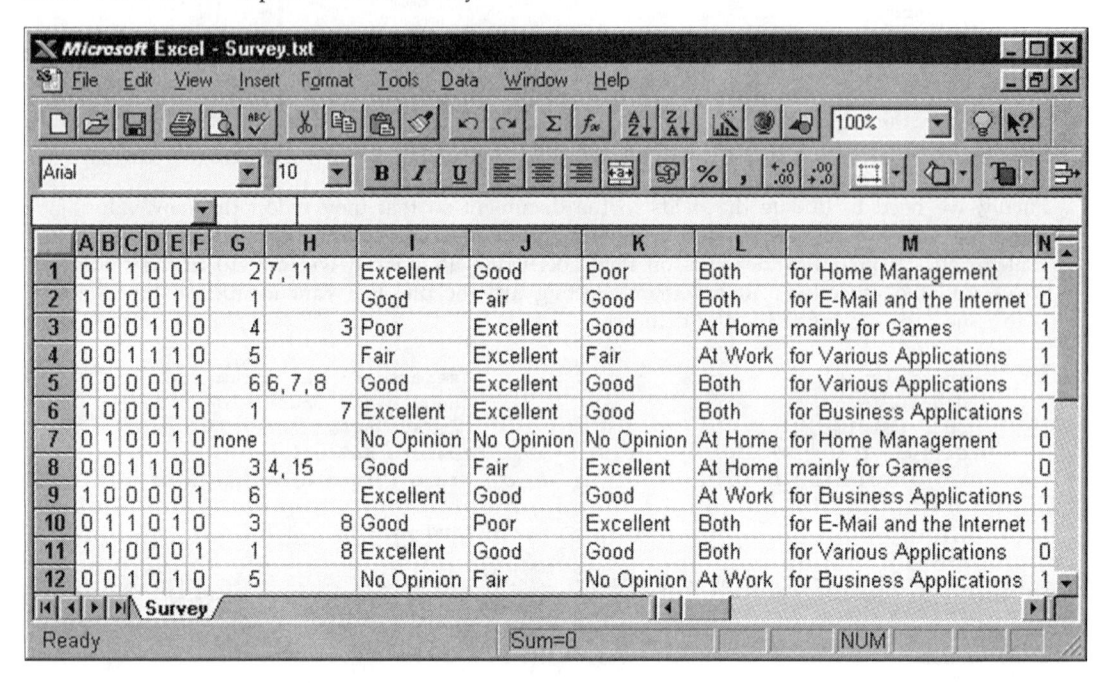

	A	B	C	D	E	F	G	H	I	J	K	L	M	N
1	0	1	1	0	0	1	2	7, 11	Excellent	Good	Poor	Both	for Home Management	1
2	1	0	0	0	1	0	1			Good	Fair	Good	Both	for E-Mail and the Internet	0
3	0	0	0	1	0	0	4	3	Poor	Excellent	Good	At Home	mainly for Games	1
4	0	0	1	1	1	0	5		Fair	Excellent	Fair	At Work	for Various Applications	1
5	0	0	0	0	0	1	6	6, 7, 8	Good	Excellent	Good	Both	for Various Applications	1
6	1	0	0	0	1	0	1	7	Excellent	Excellent	Good	Both	for Business Applications	1
7	0	1	0	0	1	0	none		No Opinion	No Opinion	No Opinion	At Home	for Home Management	0
8	0	0	1	1	0	0	3	4, 15	Good	Fair	Excellent	At Home	mainly for Games	0
9	1	0	0	0	0	1	6		Excellent	Good	Good	At Work	for Business Applications	1
10	0	1	1	0	1	0	3	8	Good	Poor	Excellent	Both	for E-Mail and the Internet	1
11	1	1	0	0	0	1	1	8	Excellent	Good	Good	Both	for Various Applications	0
12	0	0	1	0	1	0	5		No Opinion	Fair	No Opinion	At Work	for Business Applications	1

Select Save As... from the File menu, change the Files of type: to Microsoft Excel Workbook (*.xls), and you've got an Excel spreadsheet containing the data from the Survey file. Other spreadsheet applications may not support drag-and-drop like this, which means that you'll have to open the file in the normal way, using Open.... on the File menu. If you're lucky, your application will recognize the format automatically, though you may have to give it a little guidance.

Using File | Open... in Excel starts the appropriate Import Wizard. (There may be an equivalent in other applications you use.) Here, it's recognized the tab-delimited format of our Survey file without any help from us. If your data file is in comma-delimited (or other) format, Excel will also have a go at deciphering it for you.

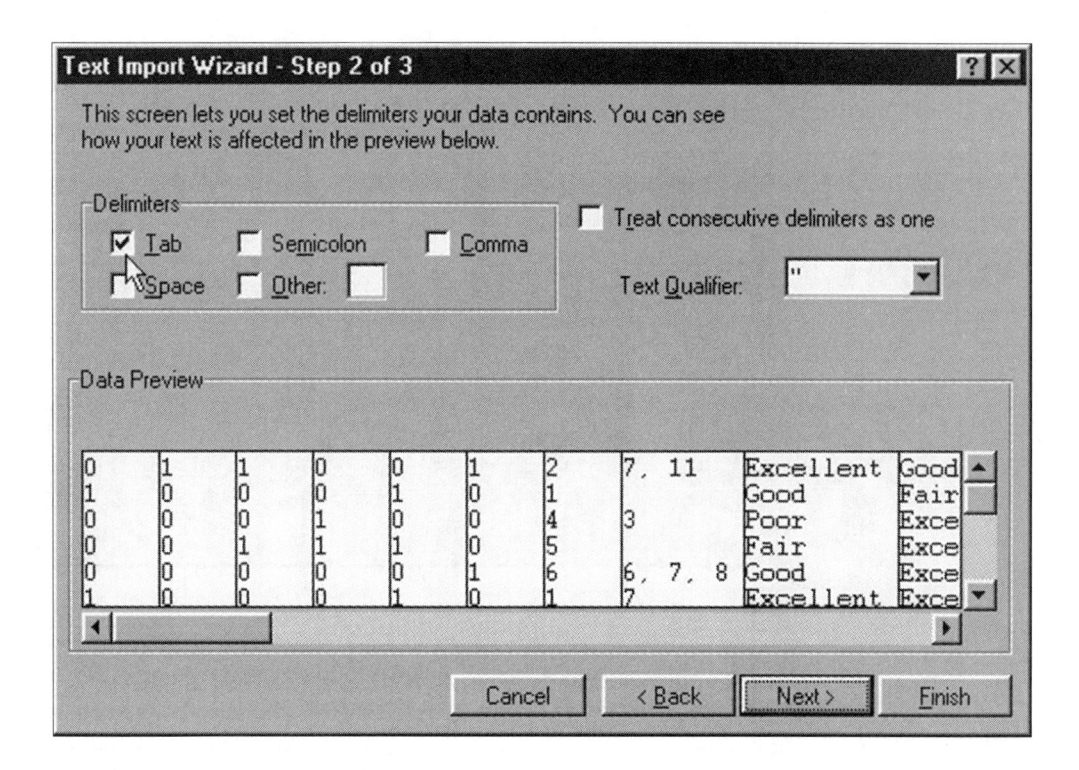

Analyzing the Data in Excel

Once the data is safely inside Excel, you can analyze it. Our survey data contains details of which applications our readers use regularly. They had the opportunity to check several boxes for the common business and programming applications:

Which business applications do you use ?	Microsoft Word	☐	Lotus WordPro	☐
	Microsoft Excel	☐	Lotus 1-2-3	☐
	Microsoft Access	☐	Lotus Approach	☐
	Microsoft FoxPro	☐	Lotus Notes	☐
Which program languages do you use ?	VBA / WordBasic	☐	Delphi	☐
	Visual Basic	☐	C or C++	☐
	Pascal	☐	Fortran or Cobol	☐

We'll see whether there's any correlation between the books they've purchased and the applications they use. We've added a page to the Excel spreadsheet where we've created a simple analysis of the data. It calculates the percentage of the total number of responses, of readers for each book and users of the relevant application. We've also taken the opportunity to calculate what value of our total sales this represents, based on the price of each book.

The values in the Analysis page of the workbook are gathered from the Survey page. The Total No of Responses cell uses the formula =COUNT(Survey!A:A) to count the number of values, while the cells in the Total Number Purchased and Total No Using This App rows use formulas like `=SUM(Survey!P:P)` to total the whole columns on the other sheet. If you want to see the Excel spreadsheet for yourself, it's in the **\Fields** subfolder of the samples folder.

Wrox Reader Survey Results 1995 - 1996

Total No of Responses: 27 Total Sales Value: $ 2,295.80

	Word 95 Development	Guide to Access 95	Access 95 VBA	Office 95 Development	Guide to Visual Basic 4.0	Delphi Programming
Total Number Purchased	9	11	12	9	13	10
No. Books Purchased	33%	41%	44%	33%	48%	37%
Price Each	$ 34.95	$ 34.95	$ 36.95	$ 49.95	$ 34.95	$ 24.95
Total Value	$ 314.55	$ 384.45	$ 443.40	$ 449.55	$ 454.35	$ 249.50
Total No Using This App	14	12	12	11	13	3
No. Using This App	52%	44%	44%	42%	48%	11%

Creating a Chart

Having analyzed the data, we can produce the inevitable charts. Here's one that clearly shows the relationship between application users and book purchasers:

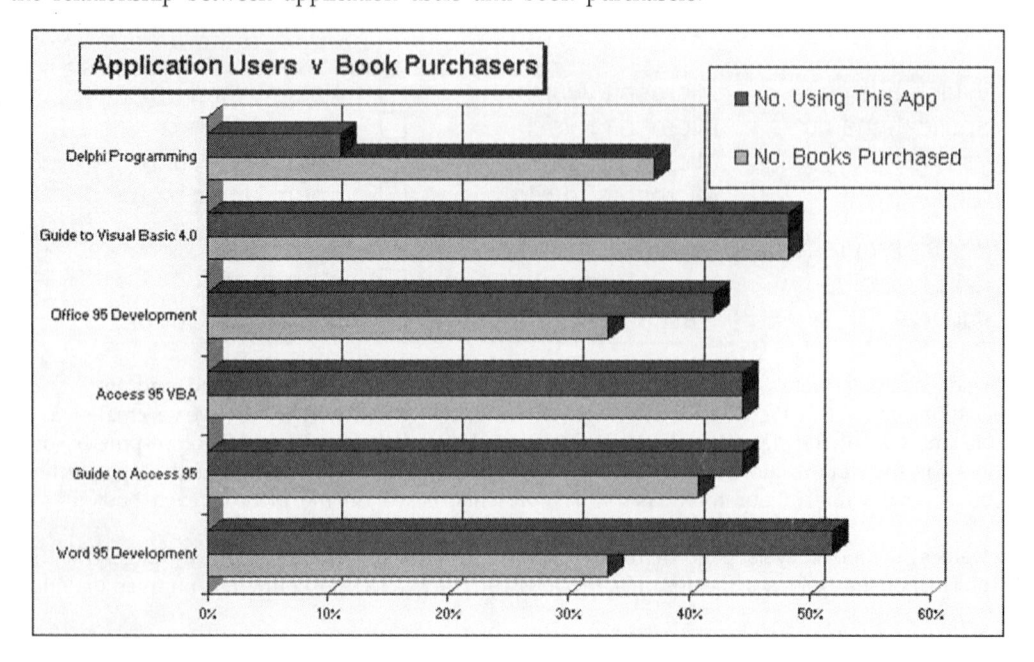

Here's another example of how information can only ever reflect the data you collect and may not represent 'real life'. The chart shows that only 11% of our readers program in Delphi, yet 37% bought our book about it. Perhaps they liked the picture on the cover!

Importing the Data into Access

Getting our survey data into Access isn't quite as easy as it was with Excel. For a start, we have to create a database for it. There's no concept of 'Untitled' in Access as there is in other applications; you have to provide a database file on disk to work with. So, the first step is to start Access and select Blank Database from the introduction dialog. Change to the folder where you want the new database stored and enter a name. Our example database file, which is in the **\Fields** subfolder of your samples folder, is called **Survey.mdb**.

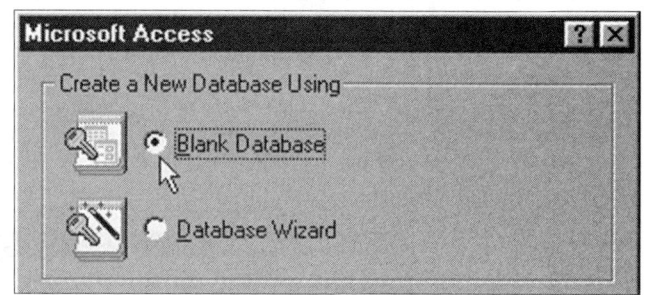

Once you've created the new file, you have just an empty database window. Here's the next hitch: it doesn't support drag-and-drop from My Computer or Explorer. Instead, you have to select Get External Data from the File menu, then click Import.... Change the Files of type: to Text files and click the Import button to start Text Import Wizard.

Even with the wizard, things aren't plain sailing. Obviously Access isn't expecting tab-delimited data because it treats our file as though it's comma-delimited. In the second screen of the wizard, the Delimiter character is set to Comma, so we need to select Tab instead.

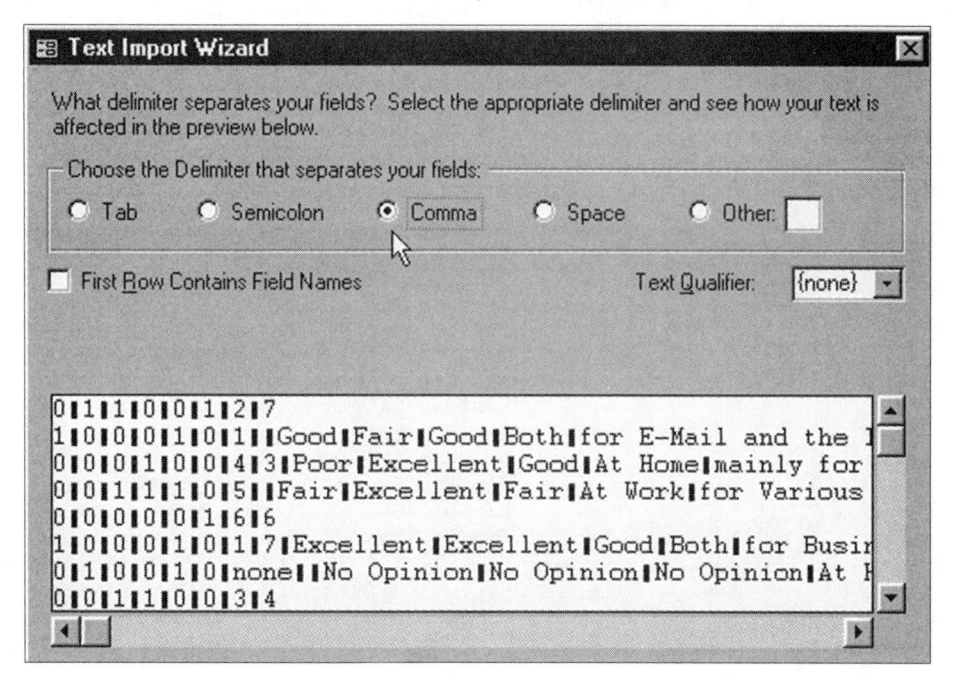

If the first row of our file contained the names of the fields, we could get Access to use these name for the columns (fields) in the new table, but it doesn't, so we leave this option unchecked. We can also specify the Text Qualifier. Remember that the WordBasic **Write** statement surrounds text values in quotation marks. Here, we tell Access what the file uses. In our case, the Text Qualifier is {none} because we created the file with the **Print** statement instead.

Once we select the Tab option for the delimiter, Access recognizes the data file properly, but we still have lots to do. The wizard asks which table you want to put the data in (even though the database is empty), and lets you select the data types for each column.

Access needs to know what data type each field should be, and will assume **Long Integer** (numeric) for any that have numbers in the first record. Then, when we import data which has text in this field in other records, it will produce an import error. So, in our case, we need to change the data types for the 'chosen as best' in Field7, and the Zip Codes in Field32, to Text. Notice how, because we used the name **Fieldxx** in our Word form, it matches the field name Access automatically allocates. This should make renaming the fields later much easier.

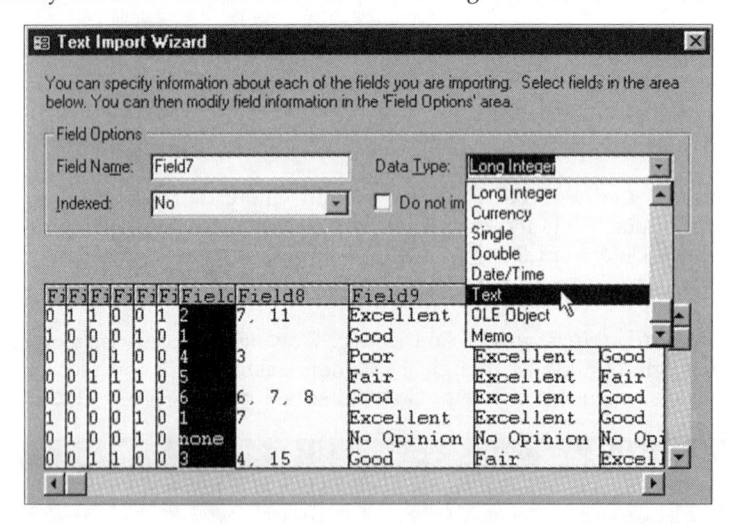

The final hurdle appears when Access prompts you to specify a primary key. This is the value used to uniquely identify each record, and, in most cases, you can let Access create it automatically. Finally, the wizard imports the data into the new table:

Using the Data We've Collected in Access

While we expect most people to be at least a little familiar with Excel, Access is a different matter. We don't intend this to be a guide to using Access, so we'll be showing you what is possible rather than how to achieve it. Check out the other Wrox Press books about Access if you want to learn more. *The Beginner's Guide to Access 95* and *Beginning Access 95 VBA Programming* both take you through the steps of learning Access from the start.

A database is often used simply for storing information, which makes it a good place to keep a list of existing and potential customers. We've already got that data from our survey, so all it needs is a little summarizing and tidying up. We've renamed the fields and created a query, named MakeAddressList, which summarizes the number of Microsoft and Lotus applications each person uses, and the number of different languages. We dropped the opinions on each book, but kept a note of which ones they had read. If we need the data on their opinions later, it's still in the original table. The next screenshot shows part of the table of results from the MakeAddressList query.

Creating a Customer List Report

Now we've got a more manageable set of data, we can use this to create a report in Access. We used Report Wizard to create the Customer List report, a section of which you can see below. It lists our customers by State and includes a count of the different types of application they use, where they use a computer and which of our books they've read.

We also took the opportunity to sum the number of application types in the report footer because the results could be useful. For example, from our fictitious data we find that our respondents use 42 Microsoft applications, 30 Lotus applications and 39 programming languages. So, if we only produce books about Microsoft applications, we could be missing a huge market opportunity, and the large number of people who use a programming language of some type means that we also need to keep up to date here.

Getting the Information Back into Word

Now that you've seen some brief examples of how we can use the data from our Word Survey form in other applications, we need to step back and consider some of the problems that can arise. When you export the data into other applications, you run the risk of losing contact with it. For example, what happens as we collect more survey data? If you decide to maintain a customer list in Access, how do you know that the data in Excel is current?

You need to decide up front how you're going to store and manipulate information. Otherwise, it can become disseminated across different applications and, on a network, across different computers. Maintaining a single up-to-date version of the data is the most important part of your task.

To be able to use data from a single source, we can take advantage of the new technologies which have been creeping into applications over the last few years. Although one of these methods, Dynamic Data Exchange, is becoming rather long in the tooth, it's still a mainstay in inter-application data exchange. We'll take a look at some background, then see how we can use the different methods in Word.

An Overview of DDE and OLE

Dynamic Data Exchange (DDE) was the method that Windows applications first used to communicate with each other. An application becomes the **client** by **initiating**, or starting, a DDE conversation with another application, which then becomes the **server**. To start the conversation, it opens a **channel** and, once this is established, it can send instructions and data to, or retrieve information from, the other application. Each channel defines a single **topic** and there can be several channels open at the same time, between the same or different applications. The application and topic for a channel can't change during a conversation, and each channel must be closed when the conversation is complete.

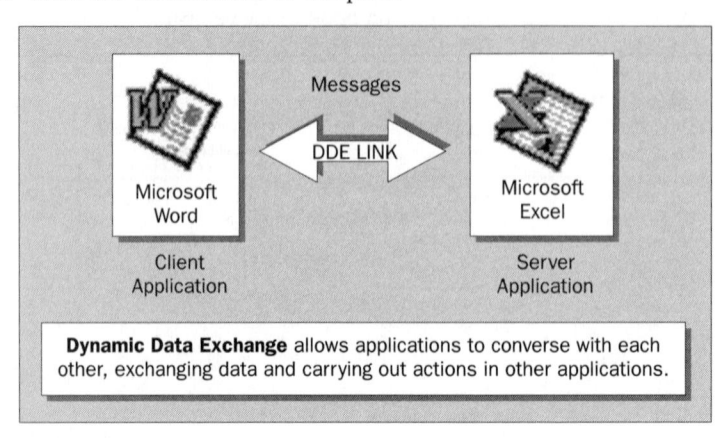

Dynamic Data Exchange allows applications to converse with each other, exchanging data and carrying out actions in other applications.

Object Linking and Embedding (OLE), on the other hand, is a much more recent innovation. It's based on the continuing development of Microsoft's **Component Object Model** (COM) which embraces all the aspects of creating and maintaining **compound documents**. You'll no doubt be aware that a document in a Windows application can contain data created in different applications. In Word, you can include WordArt objects, equations, sounds and pictures in your documents, as well as objects created by many other applications. To be able to store these in its data file, Word uses a specially structured format which is closely defined by COM. The standards also cover the way that applications use the clipboard to copy data, how they implement drag-and-drop, and how OLE Automation passes information.

OLE falls into two distinct categories. The traditional method, usually referred to as **OLE Documents**, covers the embedding or linking of data in a document which is created and maintained by a different application to the one that created the original document. For example, if you insert an Excel spreadsheet into a Word document, you can edit it by double-clicking on it to activate it, but it's Excel that actually does all the work. If you don't have Excel installed and properly set up in the Windows registry, you can't edit the data.

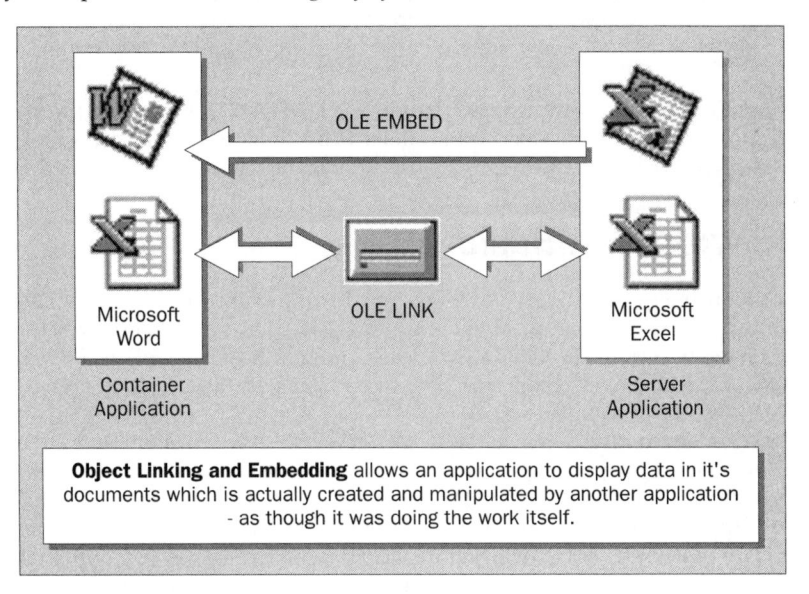

OLE EMBED

Microsoft Word — OLE LINK — Microsoft Excel

Container Application

Server Application

Object Linking and Embedding allows an application to display data in it's documents which is actually created and manipulated by another application - as though it was doing the work itself.

The most recent implementation of OLE, called **OLE2**, allows an application to use **in-place activation**. In this case, instead of seeing a copy of Excel open, as you would under traditional OLE, Word appears to seamlessly 'become' Excel. The menus, toolbars and other screen furniture change to look like Excel while you're working with the object. Applications that don't support OLE2 still open in a separate window, and the object in the original document is grayed out while you're editing it.

The second category of OLE embraces many of the other COM properties. Amongst them is **OLE Automation**, a new method designed to eventually replace DDE. Like DDE, you send instructions to the other application to control it, but by creating an instance of the other application as an **object** first. Then you can use all the methods and functionality of the other application to manipulate the data, and pass it back to the calling application when complete.

At present WordBasic doesn't support OLE Automation for working with other applications, but you can use VBA in other applications to manipulate Word this way. We won't be spending time on OLE Automation in this book, but it's well covered in the other publications from the Wrox Press range.

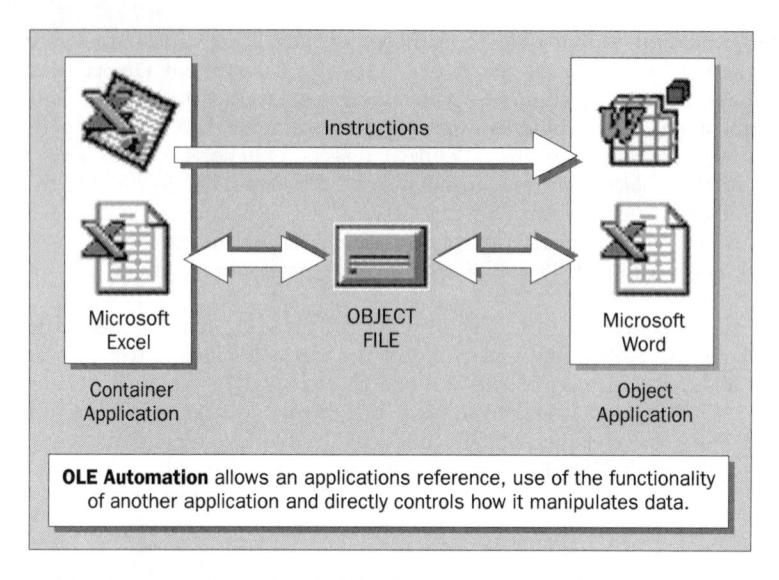

OLE Automation allows an applications reference, use of the functionality of another application and directly controls how it manipulates data.

We'll finish up this chapter with a detailed look as how DDE can be used in WordBasic, because until Word gains its Visual Basic for Applications (VBA), this is what you've got to work with. In the next chapter, we'll see how you can use OLE as it's presently supported by Word.

Using DDE with WordBasic

There is no menu interface in Word to allow you to use DDE directly; everything has to be done with macros. You can see an obvious example of DDE in operation when you install applications on your system. In Windows 3, each program's icon lived in a group inside Program Manager, which you could add or remove using DDE.

Program Manager has survived the move to Windows 95. If you select Run on the Start menu and enter Progman.exe, it pops up, just like stepping back in time. The DDE methods it used are still supported in Windows 95. To show you how you can use these to install your own documents or applications, we've included an example for you to try. Documents based on the Results template you used earlier will automatically add themselves to your Start menu. This is useful because, unlike the Documents menu, they don't 'disappear off the end' as other documents are opened.

Try It Out - A Self-installing Document Using DDE

1 Open My Computer or Explorer, and go to the **\Fields** subfolder of you samples folder. Unless you changed the defaults during installation, this will be **C:\BegWord\Fields**. Double-click on the file **Results.dot** to create a new survey results document.

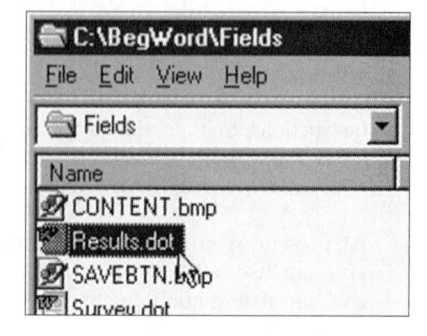

2 Select Save As... from the File menu, change to the folder where you want to store the file and enter a name for it.

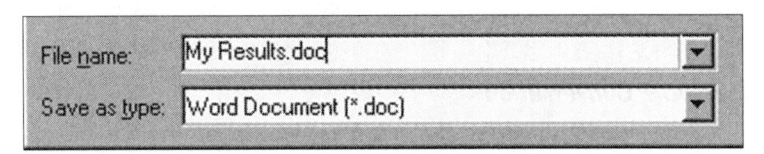

3 Click Save and close the document. You'll see the Start Menu window open, with a named short-cut for your new document:

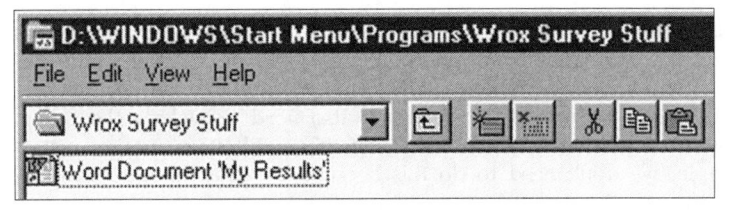

4 Close the Start Menu window, then close Word. Click the Start button on Windows Taskbar, select Programs and click the new Wrox Survey Stuff group. You'll see an entry for the document:

5 Click this entry, and Word starts with the document loaded.

How It Works

The Results template has a **FileSaveAs** macro which replaces the original Word command. First, it carries out the usual actions of getting the current values for the dialog and displaying it. If the user clicks Save, it saves the document as normal, but, then, it executes some extra code. Here's an outline of the macro:

```
Sub MAIN
On Error Goto FSA_Exit
Dim dlg As FileSaveAs                        'declare a FileSaveAs record
GetCurValues dlg                             'get the current values
Result = Dialog(dlg)                         'display the dialog
If Result Then                               'user clicked Save ..
    FileSaveAs dlg                           '..so save the document
    If GetDocumentVar$("Installed") <> "Yes" Then
        '
        ' Install on Windows Start menu
        '
        SetDocumentVar "Installed", "Yes"
        FileSave    'save changes caused by updating the document variable
    EndIf
EndIf
FSA_Exit:
End Sub
```

511

Once the file is saved, the macro checks the value of a document variable called **Installed**. If this is **Yes**, the file has already been saved once and the macro has run previously, so the next part of the code is skipped. If it hasn't been saved before, we need to install it on the Start menu.

The Stages of a DDE Conversation

To use DDE, we go through a series of steps. First we check whether the application is running. If it isn't, we have to start it. If we were communicating with Excel, for example, we would use:

```
If Not AppIsRunning("Microsoft Excel") Then Shell "Excel.exe"
```

Word's **AppIsRunning()** function returns **True (-1)** if the application whose window title you specify is already running, and **False (0)** if not. It doesn't matter if the window title includes the name of an open document. The **Shell** statement starts the application that you specify, and, if it isn't listed in the registry, you may also need to include the full path to it. If the application is already running, the **Shell** statement will start another instance of it. (In our Results example, we don't need to do this because the Start menu manipulation is done by Windows itself, and it's obviously already running.)

When we know that the application is running, we can open a channel to it using the **DDEInitiate()** function. This returns the channel identifier that we'll need to use later on, so we store it in a variable. Note that many applications, including Excel and Access, have a setting in their Options dialog which can prevent them from accepting a DDE link. You must make sure this is cleared before you attempt to start the conversation.

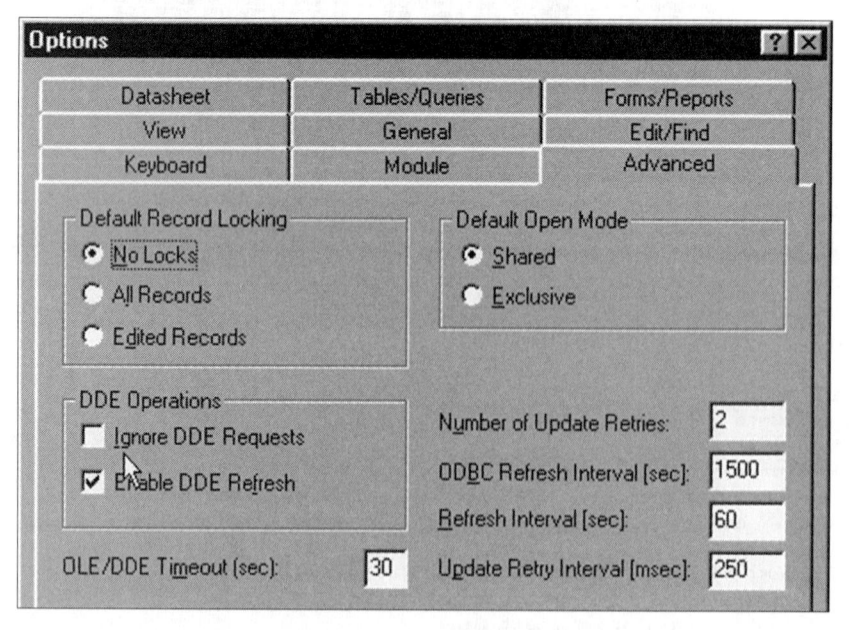

The **DDEInitiate()** function requires the name of the application we want to talk to and the topic we want to talk about. In most cases, the application name is the same as the file name but without the file extension. The topic, though, varies widely, but most applications support a **system topic**, which we'll look at later. In our Results template, the application we start the conversation with is **progman**. The topic has the same name.

```
Channel = DDEInitiate("progman", "progman")    'open the DDE channel
```

If **Channel** is greater than zero, we know that the operation succeeded, so we can start to communicate with the other application. To create a program group and short-cut, we have to send commands to the **progman** application using the **DDEExecute** statement. We supply the channel number and a string containing the command:

```
Command$ = "[CreateGroup(Wrox Survey Stuff)]"   'create the command string
DDEExecute Channel, Command$                    'and execute the command
```

You can see that the command, **CreateGroup**, takes the name of the new group as its argument, and the whole thing is enclosed in square brackets. If the group already exists, it is just activated. To create the short-cut, we use the **AddItem** command. We can also remove existing short-cuts with the **RemoveItem** command. **AddItem** requires two arguments: the full path and file name of the target file and a description for the menu. (You can also select a different icon, but we've left it as the default by omitting this extra argument.) To remove an item, you only specify the description.

Actually getting the arguments is the fiddly part because you have to enclose long file-name strings in quotation marks, so there's some string handling to do first. We get the name and path of the file from the **DocumentStatistics** dialog record:

```
Redim dlg As DocumentStatistics             're-declare the dialog record
GetCurValues dlg                            'get the current values
TheName$ = dlg.FileName                     'get the name of the file
Desc$ = Left$(TheName$, Len(TheName$) - 4)  'remove the .doc extension
Desc$ = Chr$(34) + "Word Document '" + Desc$ + "'" + Chr$(34)
  'now build the path, adding '\' if required then the file name
ThePath$ = dlg.Directory
If Right$(ThePath$, 1) <> "\" Then ThePath$ = ThePath$ + "\"
ThePath$ = ThePath$ + TheName$
  'enclose it in quotation marks if required
If (InStr(ThePath$, " ")) And (Left$(ThePath$, 1) <> Chr$(34)) Then \
                    ThePath$ = Chr$(34) + ThePath$ + Chr$(34)
  'finally build the command string and execute it
Command$ = "[AddItem(" + ThePath$ + "," + Desc$ + ")]"
DDEExecute Channel, Command$
```

Finally, we must close the channel. Otherwise, it remains active until Word is closed, wasting memory and resources. If you leave too many channels open, you'll find that DDE operations stop working. To close a specific channel, we use the **DDETerminate** statement, supplying the channel number.

```
DDETerminate Channel
```

If you want to ensure all channels are closed, especially if you fear that an error trap in a macro could prevent a channel being closed properly, you use the **DDETerminateAll** statement. This closes all channels that you have opened in WordBasic since you last started Word.

Using DDE with Our Survey Spreadsheet

We can quite easily communicate with Excel via DDE, retrieving information from spreadsheets for use in our documents. We can also send information to Excel from Word, executing commands or changing the data in a spreadsheet.

For example, our **Survey.xls** file calculates the total revenue from the data we collected, by multiplying each book purchased by the price. Suppose we needed to update the prices by 10% to account for an increase in computer book tax. We'll do this with DDE, then retrieve the new total.

Try It Out - Updating the Survey Spreadsheet Using DDE

You'll need the DDEOLE template for this example, from the **\Fields** subfolder of your samples folder. Unless you changed the defaults when you installed the sample, this will be **C:\BegWord\Fields**.

1 Open the DDEOLE template in Word, select Macro... from the Tools menu and select the macro ExcelUpdate. Click the Run button to start it.

2 After a few seconds you'll see a button appear on the Taskbar for Microsoft Excel. Then the Microsoft Word button will start flashing, to indicate that it's displaying a message box.

3 Switch to Word, and the message box tells you the new total for the books after a 10% increase in the price.

4 Switch to Excel and look at the Analysis page. You can see the new prices have been inserted in the spreadsheet cells. Close it without saving the changes.

	Word 95 Development	Guide to Access 95	Access 95 VBA	Office 95 Development	Guide to Visual Basic 4.0	Delphi Programming
	0	11	12	9	13	10
	0%	41%	44%	33%	48%	37%
$	38.45	$ 38.45	$ 40.65	$ 54.95	$ 38.45	$ 27.45

Total Sales Value: $ 2,179.38

One of the problems with DDE is that applications may time-out and fail to make contact if the system is busy. Your WordBasic macro doesn't wait for Excel to finish loading, so you get errors if Excel isn't ready for it. We've used the loop **For Wait = 1 To 10000 : Next** to delay the macro, but you may need to increase the value of the loop if you find errors are occurring. Alternatively, start Excel yourself and load the workbook first. If you've installed the samples in a different folder, you'll also have to edit the second line in the macro:

```
ThePath$ = "C:\BegWord\Fields\"
```

How It Works

After we've set the file name and the path to it, we check whether Excel is already running. If it isn't, we start it. Notice that we've used the optional **WindowStyle** argument to make it start up minimized, as just a button on the Taskbar. This argument only works with some applications. We have to wait while Excel gets itself going, and you may have to adjust the value in the loop if you keep getting errors. It depends on how much memory you have free and on the general speed of your disk and hardware.

```
Sub MAIN      'the UpdateExcel macro
TheFile$ = "Survey.xls"
ThePath$ = "C:\BegWord\Fields\"     'change this if installed elsewhere
If Not AppIsRunning("Microsoft Excel") Then
    Shell "Excel.exe", 2                    'start Excel
    For Wait = 1 To 10000 : Next            'and wait while it loads
EndIf
```

The next step is to load the Survey file. Of course, Excel could already be running, so we need to see if the file we want is already loaded. We open a channel to the System topic and get a list of all the available topics. This uses the **DDERequest$()** function, which returns the data as a string. If there are several items in the string, they are separated by *Tab* characters. The **Topics** topic will contain a list of all the open workbooks and their pages. By using the **InStr()** function to look for the name of our file, we can whether it's already loaded.

```
Channel = DDEInitiate("Excel", "System")      'open the channel
Loaded$ = DDERequest$(Channel, "Topics")      'get a list of the topics
If InStr(Loaded$, TheFile$) = 0 Then
    Command$ = "[OPEN(" + Chr$(34) + ThePath$ + TheFile$ + Chr$(34) + ")]"
    DDEExecute Channel, Command$
EndIf
DDETerminate Channel                          'close this channel
```

If it's not loaded, we tell Excel to load it by sending an **[OPEN]** command. The string we have to send is **[OPEN("C:\BegWord\Fields\Survey.xls")]**, surrounding the file name in quotation marks, so we build this in **Command$** first, then send it to Excel with **DDEExecute**. Then we can close the channel, because we need to use a different topic for the next part of the macro. DDE doesn't let you change the topic of an open channel.

The new topic we need is the Analysis page of our Survey workbook. We open a channel to it using **DDEInitiate("Excel", "[Survey.xls]Analysis")**. Notice that the topic doesn't include the path, only the file name:

```
Channel = DDEInitiate("Excel", "[" + TheFile$ + "]Analysis")
```

With our new channel, we can read the data in Excel. To access a cell we have to use the "**RC**" (Row/Column) form rather than the more usual "**A1**" form. We want the cells **G2** to **G7**, so the equivalent is **R7C2** to **R7C7**. However, rather than get them all in one go, as a tab-delimited string, and then try to manipulate them, we'll read them one at a time and put the new values back. This makes the macro much simpler. We've used a loop to create the cell references 'on the fly':

```
For Loop = 2 To 7                                   'for each price cell
    CellRef$ = "R7C" + LTrim$(Str$(Loop))           'create the cell ref.
    ThePrice$ = DDERequest$(Channel, CellRef$)      'get the value from it
    NewPrice = Val(Mid$(ThePrice$, 3)) * 1.1        'add 10%
    DDEPoke Channel, CellRef$, Str$(NewPrice)       'and put it back
Next
```

Remember that values are returned as strings, and, because they are currency format, we need to strip off the leading **"$ "** first. We have to put them back in as strings, using the **DDEPoke** statement. This time, Excel will look after formatting them as currency for us.

> **FYI** If you retrieve the values from a block of cells using DDE, each value is separated from its neighbors by a *Tab* character. Each row is terminated by a carriage return, just like the tab-delimited text file we created with our **Survey** application.

Finally, we get the new total from the spreadsheet and close the channel. We can then display the result in a message box and exit. Of course, you could just as easily use the returned value in a document. We'll see this in the next section.

```
TheTotal$ = DDERequest$(Channel, "R3C7")            'get the new total
DDETerminate Channel                                'and close the channel
Msg$ = "The new total value of purchases is "
MsgBox Msg$ + TheTotal$, "Wrox Survey", 64          'display the result
End Sub
```

Using DDE with Our Survey Database

While you could freely request and poke values into an open Excel spreadsheet, you can't use the same techniques in Access. Instead, you send it a command which opens a data set, or creates a new one, and then retrieve this data set. For example, you can retrieve the contents of an Access table or query just by initiating a DDE link directly with it. To retrieve the contents of the Survey table from the **Survey.mdb** database we created earlier, we could use:

```
Channel = DDEInitiate("MSAccess", "SURVEY; TABLE Survey")
TheData$ = DDERequest$(Channel, "All")
```

The data set is returned in tab-delimited form, with each row terminated by a carriage return. This example assumes, of course, that you've already started Access and opened the database. As well as opening a table, you can retrieve the data that results from running an existing **QUERY**, or create your own query as an **SQL** statement and execute this directly.

Here's an example that creates an **SQL** query and executes it against the Survey database. The results are inserted into a formatted table in a new document. Much of the code should now be familiar, so we'll only spend time on the new parts. First, try running the macro. It's in the **DDEOLE.dot** template in the **\Fields** subfolder of your samples folder. The query is called AccessCustomer, and, when you run it, it creates this table:

Name	E-Mail	Fax
Ade Sill	asill@sales.indycorp.com	404-894-5123
Amanda Perkins	mandy@Lis.pitt.edu	412-983-9165
Andrea Turner		619-968-3385
Andrew Jordan	ajordan@novell.com	801-958-3875
Bruce Spring	bspring@aol.com	718-374-1163
Chuck Smith	crsmith3@aol.com	216-956-3812
David Brown	drbrown@mindspring.com	404-868-9656
Dino Zacci	it.coopers.co.ca	705-793-56294
Dom McRobb	dmcrobb@msn.com	714-992-8114
Eddie Fisher		360-468-2967
Franklin John	fjohns?...	415-999-20...

The principle behind the macro is similar to using Excel. First, we have to check whether Access is already running, and, if not, start it. Access usually displays an introduction screen, where you select the database you want to work with, so we have included the **SendKeys** statement to clear this by simulating the user pressing the *Escape* key:

```
Sub MAIN      'the AccessCustomer macro
On Error Goto AC_Err
If AppIsRunning("Microsoft Access") = 0 Then    'if Access is not running
    Shell "MSAccess", 2                          'start it minimized
    For Loop = 1 To 10000 : Next                 'and wait while it loads
    SendKeys "{esc}", 0                          'clear the intro screen
EndIf
```

Once we've got Access going, we open a channel to the **System** topic, and use this to open the database we want. Again, if you installed the samples in a different folder, you'll have to change the line that creates the command string. If we can't open the channel, we jump to the error handler section at the end of the macro:

```
SysChannel = DDEInitiate("MSAccess", "System") 'open the system channel
If SysChannel = 0 Then Goto AC_Err
 'open the database using the System channel
Command$ = "[OpenDatabase C:\BegWord\Fields\Survey.mdb]"
DDEExecute SysChannel, Command$
```

Now the clever part. We create an SQL query string which selects the full name, e-mail address and fax number from the Survey table and sorts them by name. Then we run it by opening a new channel with it as the topic. Access runs the query and creates the data set, then we retrieve it using **DDERequest** with the special value **"Data"** as the item:

```
Command$ = "SURVEY; SQL SELECT DISTINCTROW FullName, EMail,"
Command$ = Command$ + " Fax FROM Survey ORDER BY FullName;"
DataChannel = DDEInitiate("MSAccess", Command$)
Result$ = DDERequest$(DataChannel, "Data")
```

If the query fails, or if there's no data, we get an empty string as the result, so we can display an error message. If we do get a result, we create a new document and put the information into it. You can see how we insert the titles for the table separated by *Tab* characters, so that when the text in the document is converted to a table they will be placed in the correct cells. To get the formatting, we've taken advantage of Word's Table AutoFormat capabilities, as you'll see in the code over the page.

```
    If Result$ <> "" Then
        FileNewDefault
        Bold 1                                          'insert headings for table
        Insert "Name" + Chr$(9) + "E-Mail" + Chr$(9) + "Fax"
        InsertPara
        Bold 0
        Insert Result$                                  'insert results from Access
        EditSelectAll                                   'select all the document
        TableInsertTable .ConvertFrom = 1               'and convert it to a table
        TableAutoFormat .Format = 3                     'then format it
        SelType 1                                       'and remove the selection
    Else
        Msg$ = "No Data Retrieved"
        MsgBox Msg$, "Access Customer", 64
    EndIf
```

Finally, we can close all the channels we've opened and close down Access (assuming that we managed to start it). The rest is the error handling code:

```
Goto AC_Exit
AC_Err:
Msg$ = "Cannot communicate with Microsoft Access"
MsgBox Msg$, "Access Customer", 48
AC_Exit:
DDETerminateAll     'close all the channels, and then close Access
If AppIsRunning("Microsoft Access") Then AppClose "Microsoft Access"
End Sub
```

> **FYI** If you haven't met SQL before, you should think about learning it. It's rapidly becoming the standard way to manipulate database files and is fully supported in Microsoft Access. In fact, in certain circumstances, you can even execute an SQL query against an Excel spreadsheet. If you are new to Access and want to know more about SQL, *The Beginner's Guide to Access 95* from Wrox Press contains an SQL primer and shows you how to use it.

Hints and Tips for DDE with Word

Despite its age, Dynamic Data Exchange (DDE) is a powerful technique. Even as Word changes in new releases to encapsulate Visual Basic for Applications (VBA), you'll still find that DDE provides a useful way of communicating with other applications, especially non Microsoft and custom built applications. DDE is excellent for establishing links to custom-built site-specific software. In this section, we'll give you some more background information that will help you explore DDE's capabilities, and look at some of the pitfalls. First, though, we'll give you a summary of the DDE statements and functions available in Word:

Function or Statement	What It Does
`DDEInitiate(`*Application$*`, `*Topic$*`)`	Opens a channel to an application about *Topic$*. Returns the channel number, or zero if it can't be opened.
`DDERequest$(`*ChanNum, Item$*`)`	Requests information from another application. Returns data as a string, or an empty string if it's unsuccessful.
`DDEPoke` *ChanNum, Item$, Data$*	Sends *Data$* to another application. *Item$* defines where the data should be placed. in Excel, this is the cell reference in row/column form.
`DDEExecute` *ChanNum, Command$*	Sends a command to the other application. The command must be one that it recognizes.
`DDETerminate` *ChanNum*	Closes a DDE channel.
`DDETerminateAll`	Closes all DDE channels opened by Word in this session.

Finding the Topic You Need

Every application that supports DDE has a `System` topic to which you can always connect. You can use this topic to get a list of the other topics that are supported, though not always all of them. Generally the names of all open documents are available as topics, together with the different items in that document. For example in Excel each workbook page is a separate topic, and in Access the tables and queries are available as topics. Word can also act as a DDE server as well as a client in the way we've been using it, and all open documents are available as topics.

There are standard topics available which are supported in many applications:

`SysItems`	Returns a list of the items available in the `System` topic.
`Topics`	Returns a list of all the currently available topics.
`Status`	Returns Ready or Busy (not supported by all applications).
`Formats`	Returns a list of all the supported clipboard formats.
`Selection`	Returns the currently selected range of cells (Excel).

Finding the Command You Need

When you want to execute a function or carry out a command in the other application, you have to know which commands it supports. These vary widely between all applications; even the Microsoft Office applications differ from each other. For example, to open the file **MyDocument** from drive `C:`, each one uses a different syntax:

In Access:	`[OpenDatabase C:\MyDocument]`
In Excel:	`[OPEN("C:\MyDocument")]`
In Word:	`[FileOpen "C:\MyDocument"]`

The documentation for the target application should show the DDE commands that it accepts, but this is often not the case. You have to either experiment by trying the normal commands that the application's macro language uses, or seek help from technical support sources. At least Access provides some of the answers in its Help file, as you can see overleaf.

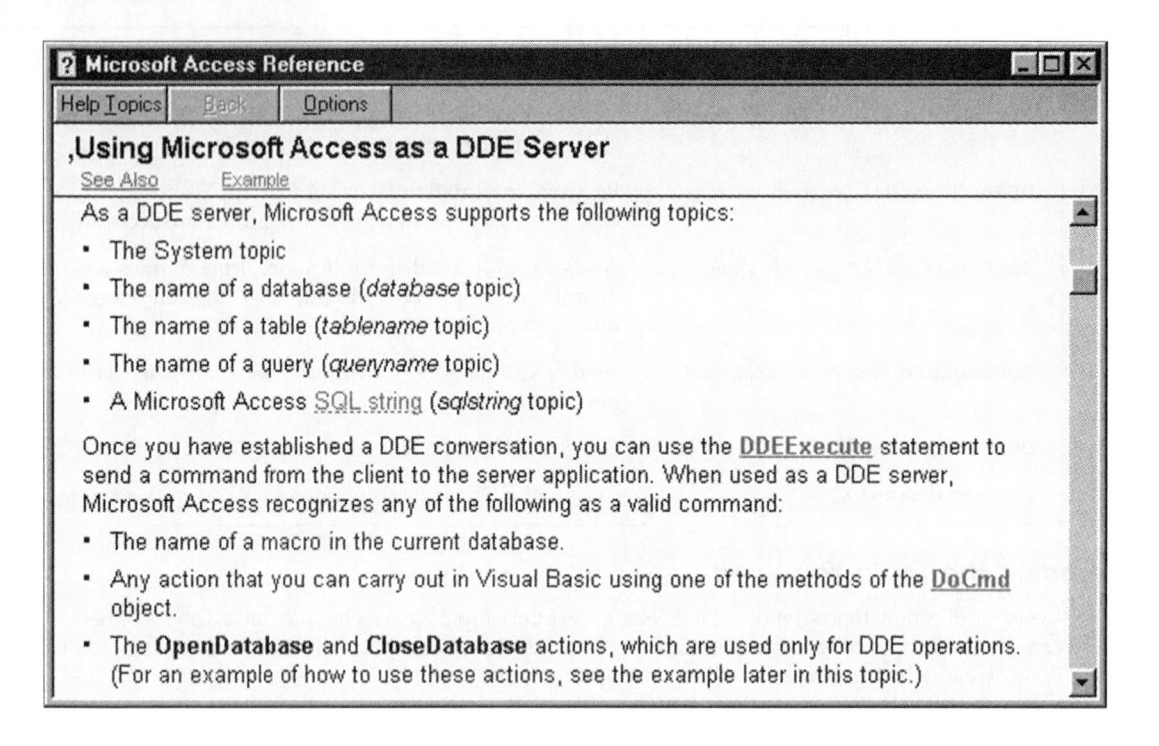

Poking About in Other Applications

Excel is quite unusual in that it lets you manipulate the contents of a spreadsheet directly, as you've seen in a previous example. Access, on the other hand, won't let you use **DDEPoke** at all. Word is quite happy accepting poked data, but will only insert it in an empty bookmark, but you can retrieve a list of bookmarks from Word using the **DDERequest()** function. Again, you'll have to consult the documentation from your applications to find out exactly if, and where, you can insert data directly.

Handling Errors in DDE Operations

DDE operations are prone to errors. Because a separate copy of the application has to be loaded, the conversation can fail because the other application has not finished loading, or is busy elsewhere. Remember that, in Access, we had to clear the introduction screen after loading before it would open the database. To effectively use DDE, you should take pains to gain a thorough understanding of the application with which you wish to communicate.

How long it takes an application to load and start responding depends on the available memory and resources of the computer that it's running on. You may not be able to run any of the samples we've supplied if your system is pushed for memory space. With the size of modern applications, 16 MB is becoming the minimum for DDE to work reliably.

There are also other possibilities. The user could close down the application you've opened before your macro has finished, and an error will occur. If they don't have the application installed, or it's not set up correctly in Windows registry, the operation will obviously fail.

So you need to implement error handling in your macros. Use an **On Error** statement at the start, and check the channel number returned by each **DDEInitiate()** function call to make sure it succeeded. If a **DDERequest$()** function call fails, you'll get an empty string. This could be an indication that the process didn't work, but could be a valid result, depending on what you were hoping to retrieve. In Excel, an empty cell will return an empty string, so you need to be careful how you handle this.

The Wrox DDE-Info Application

To end, here's a sample application that you'll find useful if you work with DDE regularly. It allows you to investigate the topics and methods that an application supports. You can try it against any application. If it doesn't support DDE you'll just get an error message.

Try It Out - Using the Wrox DDE-Info Application

You'll need the DDEOLE template from the **\Fields** subfolder of your samples folder for this example. Unless you changed the defaults when you installed the samples, the template will be in **C:\BegWord\Fields**.

1 Open the **DDEOLE.dot** template from the **\Fields** subfolder of your samples folder, and select Macro... from the Tools menu. In the Macro dialog select the macro DDEInfo and click Run.

2 The main Wrox DDE-Info dialog appears, where you can select the Application you want to examine and the Information you want to know. Make sure that all the check boxes are ticked and select the MS Excel application.

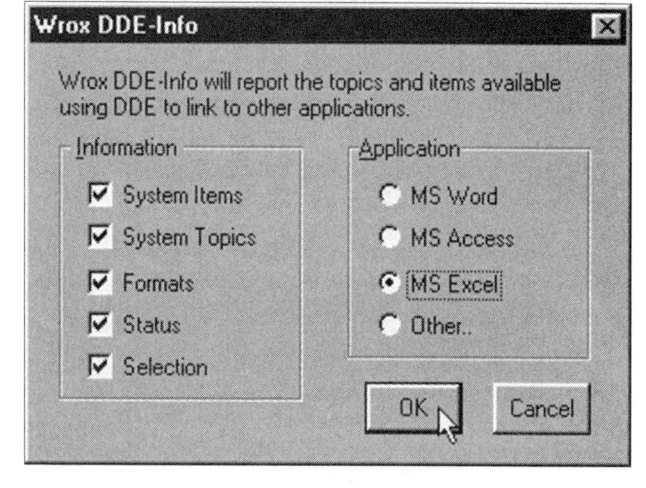

3 Click OK, and the macro asks if you want to load a document or file in the application first. Click Yes.

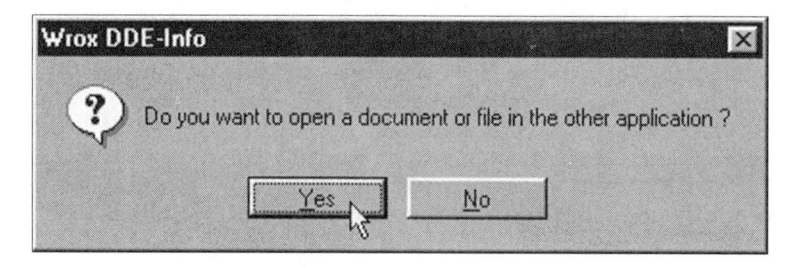

4 In the Open dialog, change to the `\Fields` subfolder of your samples folder if it's not already the current folder. Double-click the file `Survey.xls`, which is the only one displayed because the macro has set the File name entry to *.xl? so that it matches Excel spreadsheet files.

5 Excel starts, with the Survey spreadsheet loaded. Once the macro has finished (when the hard disk is idle), you can close Excel. In Word, there's a new document containing the DDE information retrieved from Excel:

Listing of System Items for Microsoft Excel
SysItems
Topics
Status
Formats
Selection
Protocols
EditEnvItems

Listing of currently available Topics for Microsoft Excel
[Survey.xls]Analysis
[Survey.xls]Chart
[Survey.xls]Survey
System

Listing of available Clipboard Formats for Microsoft Excel
XLTable
Microsoft Excel 5.0 Format
Wk1
CSV
Text
Rich Text Format

The current Status of Microsoft Excel is:
Ready

The current Selection for Microsoft Excel is:
[Survey.xls]Survey!R1C1

If you want to load a different type of file, such as `.wks`, into Excel, you can change the File name entry in the Open dialog. Alternatively, start Excel (or one of the other Microsoft applications) and load the data file first. The macro will use the currently running copy of the application for the DDE operations.

You may not be able to so this with Access, however, if the database you load changes the window title from Microsoft Access to a customized name. In this case, the macro will try to start another instance of Access, because the `IsAppRunning()` function won't detect the currently running instance.

When you select Other.. for the Application, the macro doesn't know the window title of the application you choose, so it will always try and start a new instance. If you choose to open a document, the macro will only work if that document type is correctly registered in Windows.

We don't intend explaining how the `WroxDDE-Info` macro works, because it's all techniques that you've already seen. If you want to examine it, you can open it in Edit view from the Macro dialog.

Summary

You may have been surprised to see in this chapter how easily we can share data between applications. In the early days of office-type business applications, such as spreadsheets and word processors, you often ended up buying separate specialist programs which just converted data from one format to another. Putting a chart in a text document could be a nightmare, involving starting and closing different applications each time to get it looking just right. If you still have to interface with a mini- or main-frame system, you may well find similar problems.

One of the reasons that the 'office' bundles have become so popular (besides the aggressive pricing policy) is the ease with which the individual applications interact, and share data and information. In the next chapter, we'll be showing you how it goes a lot deeper than you've seen so far. The whole future of application design philosophy is changing in line with the background of Compound Object Model (COM) technology. In the next few years, we'll start to see smaller independent applications, which combine to offer the power of the bloated disk-hungry monsters of today.

In the chapter we've looked at:

- How we can use our survey results to produce reports in Word
- Ways of importing the survey data into other Office applications
- The background to DDE and OLE, and how we can use them in Word
- Using DDE with WordBasic in detail, including several examples

Next, we need to consider the other major method of sharing data between applications: Object Linking and Embedding (OLE). This will form the main thrust of the next chapter, so grab a mug of coffee, put your feet up, and we'll continue the story...

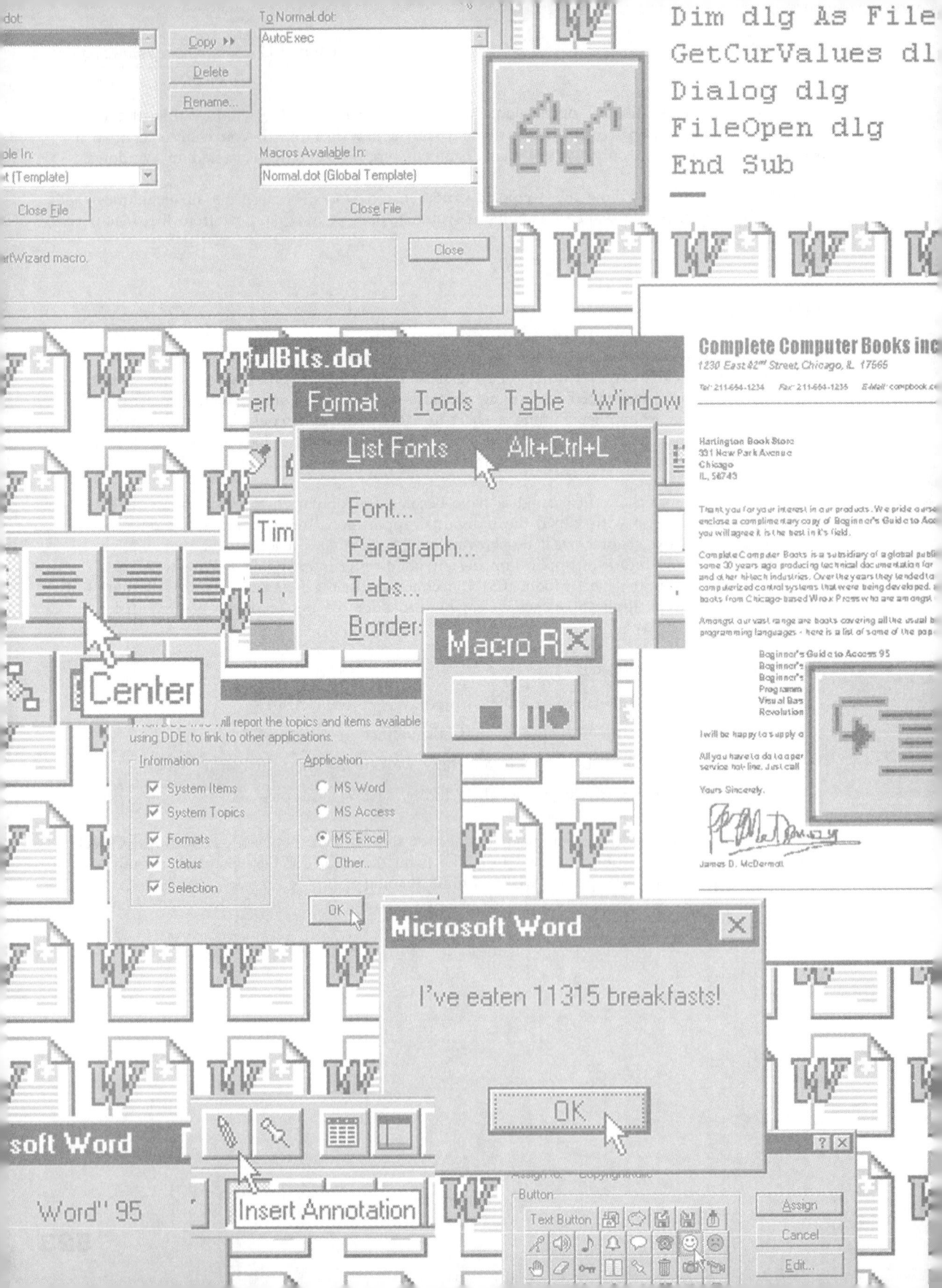

```
Dim dlg As File
GetCurValues dl
Dialog dlg
FileOpen dlg
End Sub
```

I've eaten 11315 breakfasts!

13

Using Objects in Your Documents

Introduction

In the previous chapter, we started to consider how we handle data in a multi-application environment, and turn it into information which will benefit our business. We talked about the ways we can share data between different applications, and looked at how Dynamic Data Exchange (DDE) works. Although it does suffer from some disadvantages, DDE will probably form the keystone for using data manipulated by Excel or Access, or a similar application, with Word. In fact, many of the built-in Word processes use DDE to pass data between applications.

In this chapter, we'll move on to look at **Object Linking and Embedding** (OLE) as it's presently supported by Word. This technology provides a far more flexible and transparent way to create compound documents which display data produced by several applications. We'll also take a brief look at how OLE Automation works, though you can't take advantage of this in WordBasic. You'll have to wait until Word gets its own implementation of VBA (Visual Basic for Applications) before you can exploit this exciting new technique.

While we're looking at OLE, we'll also catch up with an 'odd-ball' Word command which is part of the compound document philosophy: **InsertDatabase**. This is a kind of half-way house method for inserting and linking data from another source.

So, in this chapter, we'll cover:

- How OLE works, and how we can use it in Word
- Other Word commands for inserting and linking data
- The ways we can use OLE from WordBasic

The Future of Object Technology

One of the ideals that we discussed in the previous chapter was to have only one working copy of our data in a multi-application environment. If the sales department keeps a customer list in Access, and the accounts department uses Excel to store their copy, you are almost bound to have problems with integrity of the data if you allow both departments to update it simultaneously. Each will make different changes to their files, rapidly getting out of step, with neither version reflecting the true current situation.

To overcome this, modern applications allow far more flexibility in the way data can be moved between them and presented in a variety of ways. You've seen some examples already in this book. The key to it all is to keep just that one single up-to-date version of the data and pass copies to other applications that need to use it. Only the original version is updated, so each application always gets the current information. When we were using DDE in the last chapter, this was the stage we reached when we updated our reports using data stored in either Excel or Access.

What is an Object?

Unless you've been living in a cave for the last few years, you can't fail to have heard about the latest ideas in programming technology. **Object-oriented programming** (OOP) is supposed to be the future for all languages. It's already making it's mark in large commercial systems where it can increase the speed of application development and reduce the number of errors in the final application. The principle is simple enough. Instead of creating each function you need from scratch, you use a library of prebuilt objects which have been thoroughly tested and debugged. You simply slot them into your code and use them directly.

Without going into too much technical detail, we can define an **object** as something which contains its own data, along with the methods required to manipulate that data. For example, a spell checker object would have all the data needed to tell whether the text you sent it contained any errors, and would know how to correct it. All you need to do is to tell the object what text you want it to work on. In the future, you won't buy huge applications like Word, you'll just buy a pack of objects and slot them together to build a word-processor that does exactly what you want.

In a compound document, the objects we work with tend to be things like spreadsheets, database records, pictures, sounds and more esoteric items like equations. They are classed as objects because the container application (in our case, Word) doesn't have the functions required to manipulate these objects directly. It depends on the application that originally created the data to do all the work.

What is Object Linking and Embedding?

When we place an object in a Word document, we have to be able to load it back into the application that handles that object (the server) when we want to edit it. Windows uses the registry to keep details about each type of object that your system supports. The kinds that are available depend on what other applications you have installed and, to some extent, how you have set them up.

Notice that handling an object such as a spreadsheet using OLE is different to importing it into Word. When you copy or import cells from a spreadsheet into a document, Word uses its own file converter to read the spreadsheet file and stores the information in a table in the document.

When you use OLE, Word stores information about where the object came from so that it can activate that application and load the data back into it when you want to edit it.

We looked at the broad differences between DDE and OLE in the previous chapter, so let's now take a closer look at where the data itself gets stored when you use each method.

Reviewing the Steps of a DDE Operation

As far as data handling is concerned, you normally use DDE only to retrieve data from a file that already exists. The process in outline is simple enough. Using WordBasic, you start the server application (in this example, Excel) and tell it to load the data file you want to work with. You then retrieve the information you want from the file while it's open. All that gets stored in your document is the data you've retrieved. If other users change the original data, you have to run the process again to get the latest version.

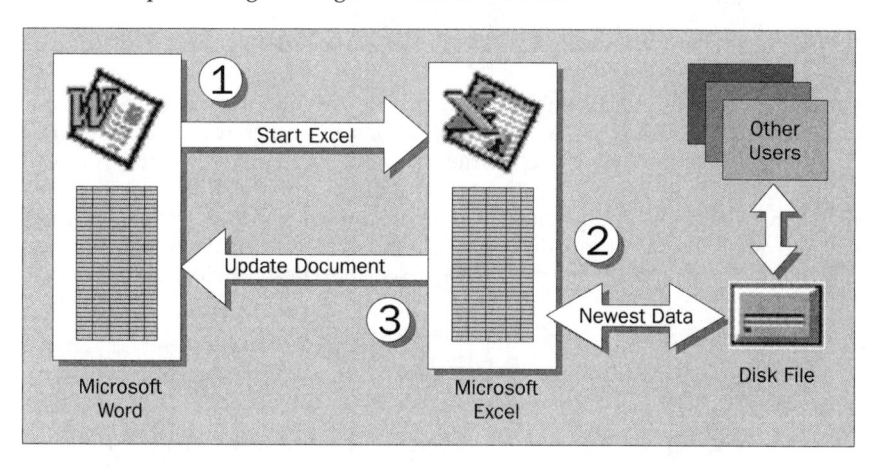

Linking and Embedding with OLE

OLE is a more complex process, but gives far more flexibility in the way you can store the information. There are two distinct methods of inserting an object into your documents. You can embed it so that a copy of the data is stored in the document, or link it so that the data remains stored on disk in its original form. In the following descriptions, we've used Excel, but any application that can act as an OLE server gives the same result. However, some may not support OLE2, so you don't get the benefit of in-place activation as you do with Excel. In this case, they open up as though you had run them normally from the Start menu, i.e. in a new window rather than as part of Word.

You would generally make use of embedding when you want to create a new object. Word starts the relevant server application (in our example below it's Excel), then the Word menus and screen furniture change to those of Excel and you create the new object just as you would an ordinary worksheet. However, when you click outside the worksheet object, the data is stored in your Word document, not as a file on disk. Double-clicking the worksheet in Word lets Excel takes over again and you can edit it. When you're finished editing, the updated data in placed back in the document.

However, if you decide to copy the data into a new worksheet and save it as an Excel file, it becomes totally disconnected from Word. Other users won't see any changes you make in your Word document, and you won't see any they make when you view the embedded worksheet in Word.

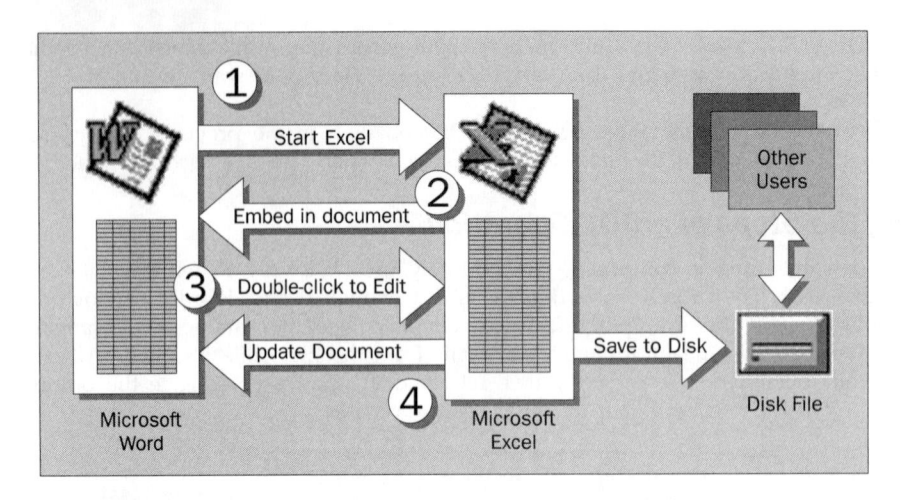

The other method of using OLE, linking the data file to your document, works quite differently. Notice that the diagram below shows the applications the other way round, because you have to create the file first. You can't create it 'on the fly' from within Word. Once you've created and saved the file, rather than embedding the actual data, you insert a link to it into your Word document. Then, when you double-click in your document, Word starts the original server application and loads the file from disk into it. Once you've edited the file, it's saved back to disk again, so both you and other users always see the latest version.

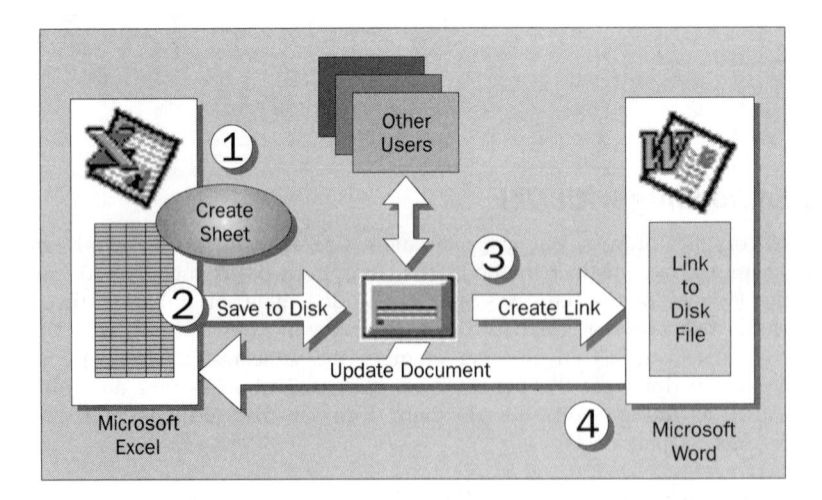

From this brief look at how OLE stores information, it's obvious that we can benefit by using linking in a multi-user or multi-application environment to make sure that we only have one copy of the data. By linking our documents to external data files, we also reduce the size of the actual document file because the object's data doesn't need to be stored in it. If we embed picture objects or large data files, the size of the document grows alarmingly quickly.

The only problem with linking is that we have to have all the other files available. If they've been deleted or moved, or if we pass the document to someone else, the link is broken and we can't view or update them in the document. Because of the way the link works, we don't get in-place activation when we link files to a document, even if the server supports OLE2.

Embedding does have its uses, though. For example, Word doesn't have any built-in features for manipulating equations directly. It depends on the Microsoft Equation Editor application, **Eqnedt32.exe**, which is stored with the other OLE server applications in your **\Program Files\Common Files\Microsoft Shared** folder. If you start Equation Editor from My Computer or Explorer, you'll find that the only way to save the data from it is to copy it into your document. Like many purpose-designed OLE server applications, it's designed to be used only for creating embedded objects in your documents.

Of course, embedding your documents makes them a lot more portable. Other people can view the data you've embedded in them because it travels in the document file. Providing that they have the appropriate server applications installed on their system, they can also edit them.

Using Word's Menus to Work with Objects

We'll take a brief look at how you insert various types of object into a Word document using the menu commands and other methods. This isn't a tutorial on using Word in the traditional way, but will allow you to see how we achieve the same types of tasks when we come to use WordBasic to automate the operations.

Most of Word's OLE commands are on the Insert and Edit menus. The Insert menu allows us to create a new object or insert an existing one, and the Edit menu gives us the commands we need to manipulate it once we've got it in the document. The Object item on the Edit menu is only available when you have an object selected in your document, and the Links... command will only then be available if there are any linked objects in the document. Depending on the type of object, the text of the last menu command changes. In our case, the object type is a Linked Bitmap Image Object.

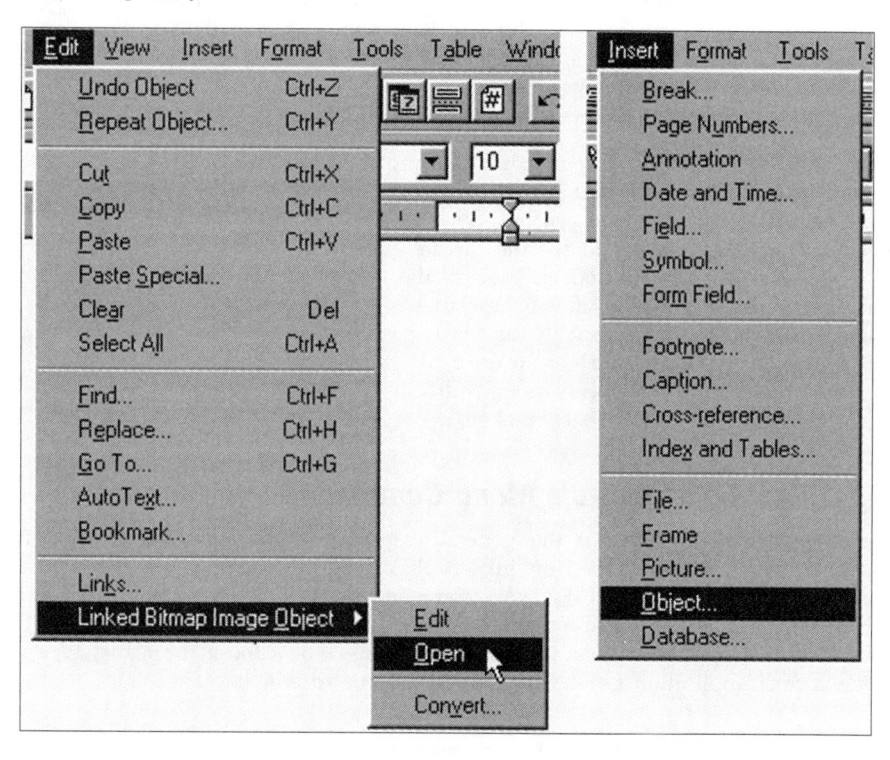

Inserting Objects into Your Documents

Word's menu commands offer a minefield of possibilities when you're inserting objects. Some of them can only insert embedded objects, while some can insert an object that is either embedded or linked. However, to make matters more confusing, you can insert a linked object, but at the same time include the current data it contains. Let's have a look at the Insert menu's OLE commands.

Insert | File... is designed to include other text files, including Word documents, in your document. Insert | Frame is not really an OLE command as such, but is used to insert a bounding frame in which you place pictures or other objects. It allows you to resize and reposition them freely within your document.

Inserting a Picture

Insert | Picture... is a short-cut way of using OLE to insert a picture file into your document, though many people probably use it without realizing that OLE is at work behind the scenes. Once you've inserted the picture that is embedded in your document, double-clicking on it loads the Microsoft Draw application to let you edit it. The problem here is that you could well have created the picture in a different application (such as Microsoft Paint), so loading Draw is not terribly useful.

However, you can insert a linked picture file using Insert | Picture.... On the right of the Insert Picture dialog are two check boxes. Setting the Link To File check box means that a link to the picture file on disk will be inserted into the document, so that, if the original file is updated, so will the picture in your document. By default, Word also includes a copy of the picture embedded in the document; you can think of it as being embedded and linked. When the original changes, though, Word will automatically replace the embedded copy with the new version.

If you don't want to include the embedded copy of the picture in the document, once you've set the Link To File option, you can uncheck the Save with Document option. You still get to see the picture as it will look when it's printed, and, as long as the original picture file is available, it will be shown each time you open the document. If the file is moved or deleted, however, you get an error message and the picture disappears from your document because the link has been broken.

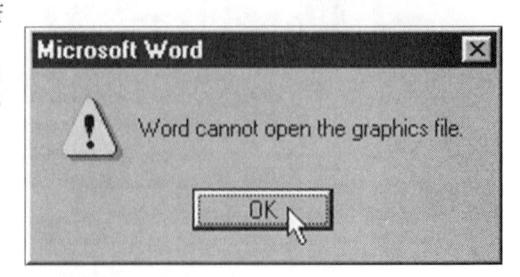

Inserting Objects with Word's Menu Commands

The Insert | Object... command is the 'general' way of inserting any type of object into your document. It allows you to embed or link an object and control how it's displayed and stored in the document. Using the Insert | Picture... command doesn't give you as much control as this general method. You can achieve a similar effect to Insert | Picture... by inserting a Picture object with the Insert | Object... command. This time, because you choose the actual type of object you want, the correct application is loaded when you come to edit it.

Embedding Objects

When you first open the Object dialog, you see the Create New page, showing a list of the types of object available on your system. Many of these will be the default Microsoft object types that are installed with Windows 95, Word 95 and Office 95. Your list should include types such as Equations, WordArt, Graphs, Wave Sounds, Bitmaps, Video Clips, MIDI Sequences, and, of course, the various types of Excel and Word documents.

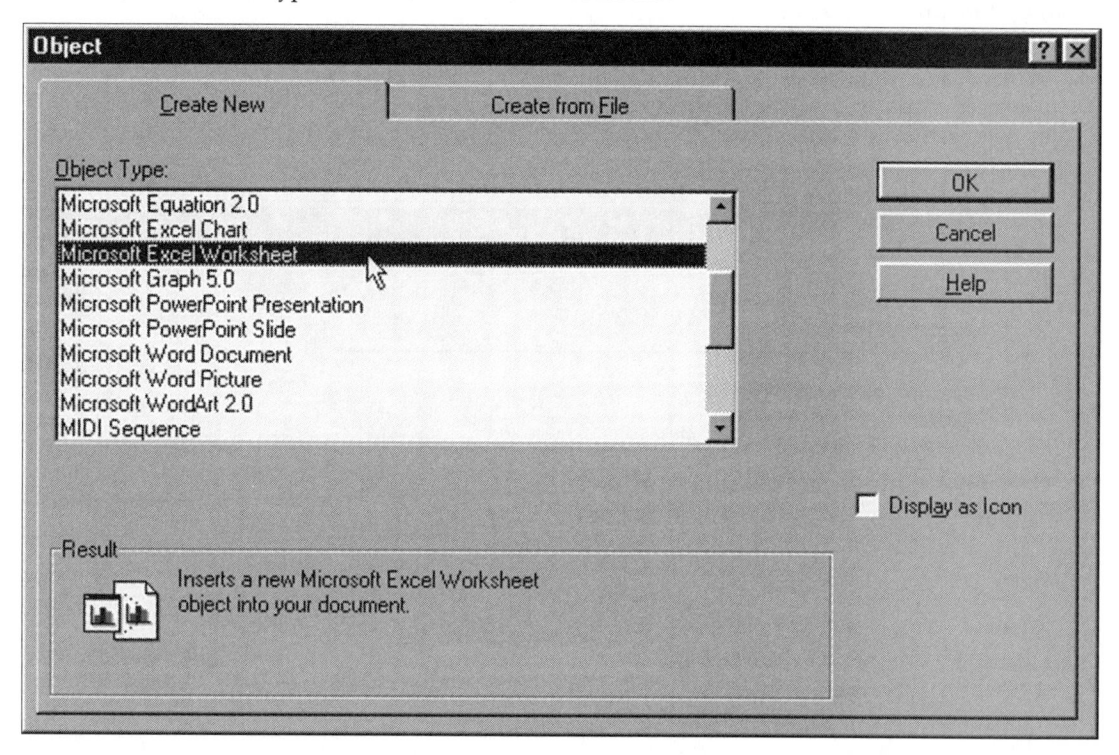

Selecting one and clicking OK starts the relevant server application, and you create the new object. When you close the server, the object is embedded in your document. Normally, your new object is embedded so that you see it as it appears in the server application. For example, if the server is Excel, you get a miniature Excel worksheet in your Word document. However, you can set the Display as Icon check box so that, instead, Word only displays an icon. Double-clicking the icon still opens the object in the correct server for editing.

Of course, some objects are always inserted as icons. If you think about it, it's difficult to display a Wave Sound object any other way. If you set the check box, you can select which icon you want to be used in the document. With certain types of object it actually changes the way they are displayed. For example, with a Wave Sound, you only get the icon itself in your document unless you set the Display as Icon check box, where you can also specify the caption that you want displayed with the icon.

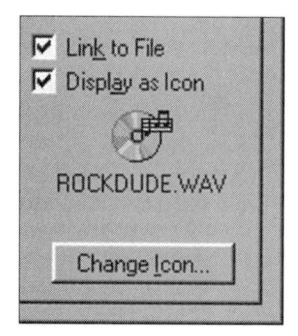

You'll also find that setting the Display as Icon check box can change the way the server application appears. Even if it supports OLE2, it can't show the object within the Word document because this will only contain an icon of the new object. So, instead of in-place activation, you find that the server starts up in its own window, as it would if you ran it from the Start menu.

Linking Objects from Files

The second page of the Object dialog, Create from File, is where you insert an existing object. Rather than creating the file, you're actually creating an object based on it in the document. All you need to do is select the file using the Browse... button, decide whether you want to link it by setting the Link to File check box, and click OK. If you don't set Link to File, the object is embedded in the document and becomes a separate copy from the file on disk.

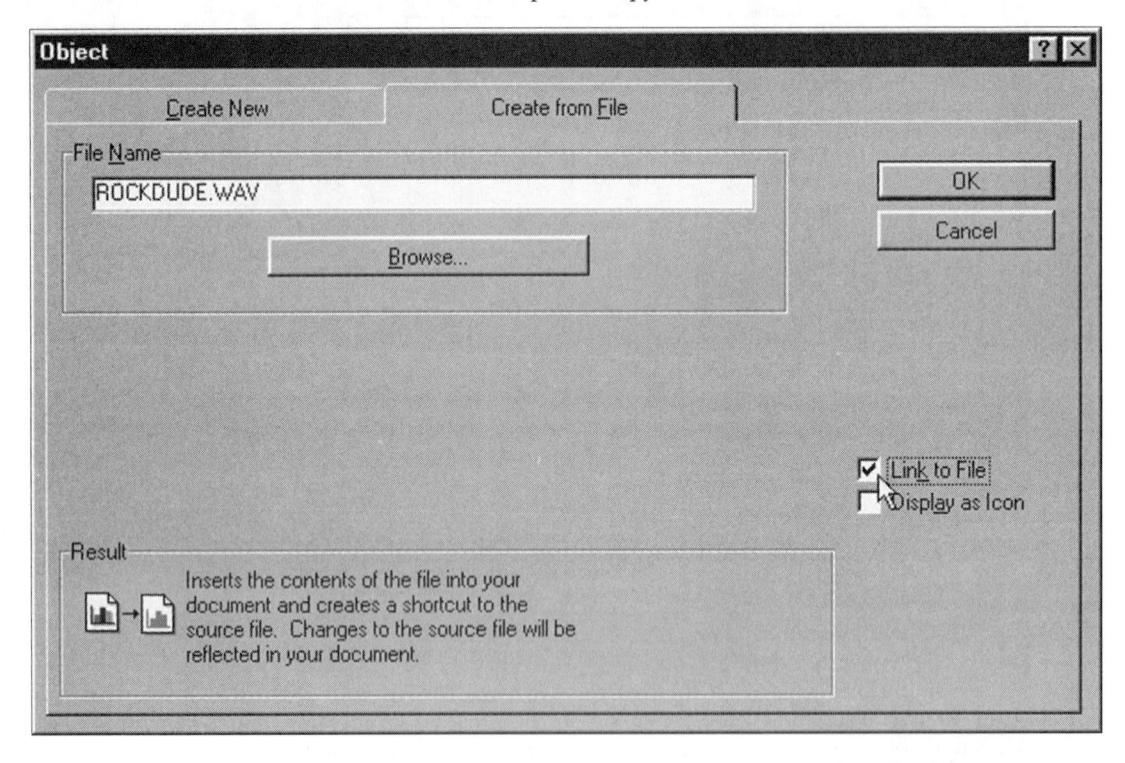

Again, you can specify that the object is displayed as an icon and change the icon itself to one from the data file or any other icon that takes your fancy. Here, we're linking the file **RockDude.wav** (from the **\Valupack\Audio\Network\Music** folder of the Office 95 CD) to our document so that it wakes up our editor when he reads it!

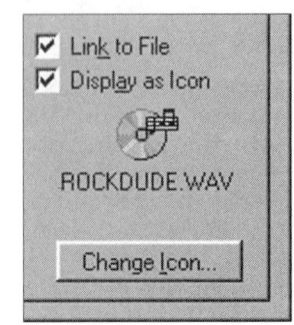

Using Drag-and-drop to Embed Objects

OLE also supports the drag-and-drop actions that are becoming ever more a part of using Windows. This is also probably the easiest way to embed an existing object into your document, but you can't link to an object file on disk, as you can when you use the other methods. Drag-and-drop always embeds objects.

Simply open My Computer or Explorer, select the file you want, drag it onto the Word window and drop it in the document. Word automatically embeds it, though you may not see it appear until you switch to and activate the Word window.

Using the Paste Special Command to Insert Objects

The final method of inserting an object is to copy it to the clipboard in the source application and paste it into Word. When the clipboard contains data that Word recognizes, the Paste and Paste Special... commands on the Edit menu are available. Selecting Paste simply copies the data into Word. If you copy part of an Excel worksheet, for example, it's inserted into the document as values in a table. However, if you select Paste Special..., Word opens the Paste Special dialog, where you can select how you want the object or data to be inserted. Depending on the type of data, you get a range of choices:

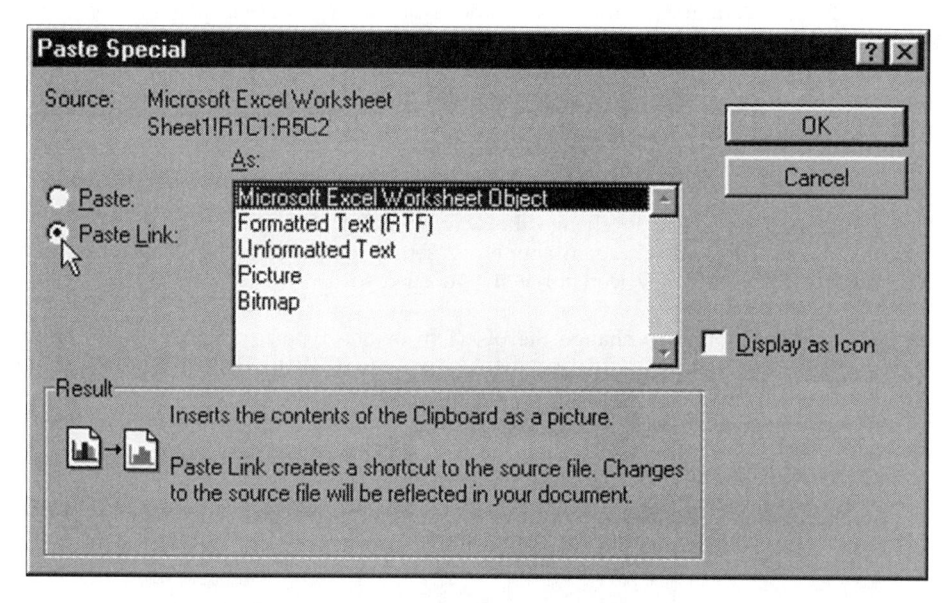

Here, you can see the choices for an Excel worksheet. We can insert it into the document as an Excel Worksheet Object so that, when you double-click it, Excel is activated to allow the values to be edited. Other alternatives are Formatted Text, Unformatted Text, and as a Picture or Bitmap. However, bear in mind that you get a different selection of object types to choose from depending on what type of data you've copied to the clipboard.

Formatted Text inserts the values in a table, just like when you use the normal Paste command. Unformatted Text inserts the values separated by *Tab* characters and carriage returns, just like tab-delimited text. Using the Bitmap option inserts a graphic of the values which looks like a table, and using Picture inserts a graphic which looks like tab-delimited. In these last two cases, double-clicking starts the Draw application, not Excel.

Rather than embedding it, you can, of course, link the new object by selecting Paste Link in the dialog. If you set the Display as Icon check box, an appropriate icon in displayed in the document instead of the actual values.

> **FYI** The Paste option in the Paste Special dialog is not the same as the Paste command on the Edit menu. In the Paste Special dialog, selecting Paste embeds the object into your document. The Paste command on the Edit menu just copies the data into the document.

Working with Objects in Your Document

Having got the object safely into your document, you'll find there are different ways to edit and manipulate it, depending on the object type. Most objects respond to a double-click by opening the server application with the data loaded. If they are OLE2-compliant (and the object is not displayed as an icon) the server starts with in-place activation, otherwise it opens in a new window.

However, when you double-click them, the various Sound-type objects play, and you may find others on your system which respond in the same way. To edit this type of object, you have to use the final command on the Edit menu (which will show the type of object such as Wave Sound) or right-click on it and select Edit from the short-cut menu. This menu also contains an Open (or Play) option which is equivalent to double-clicking the object.

Converting Objects to a Different Type

The Convert dialog allows you to change the way an object is displayed in the document. You can change it to an icon or back again simply by setting or clearing the Display as Icon check box. You can also choose a new icon for it if you need to.

You may also get the option to change the object from one type to another. For example, here we're converting an embedded Word Document object into a Word Picture type object. Take care, though, because many of these conversions are one-way only. In this case, once you've converted it, you can't get the original back if the only copy is embedded in your document. The list of object types to which you can convert may be different for linked and embedded objects.

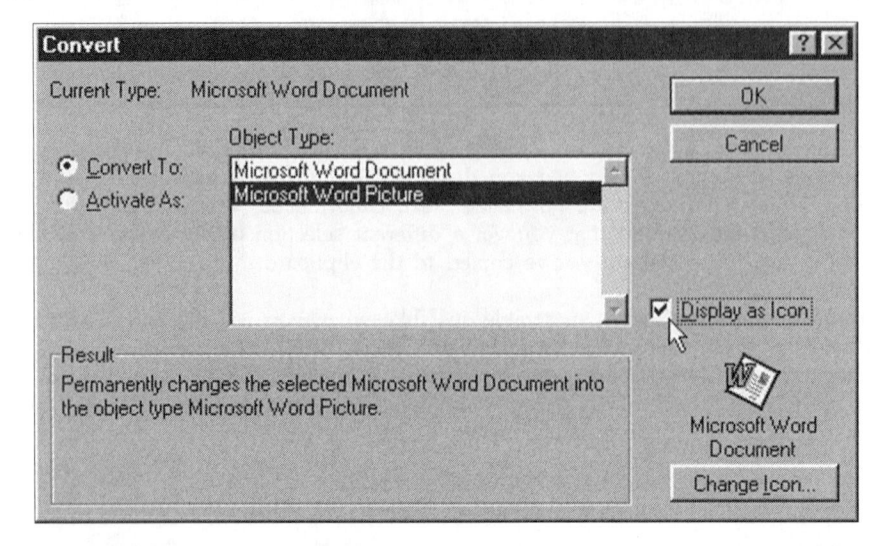

Managing the Links to Objects

One other operation you can perform is to maintain the connections for objects which you've inserted in your document and that are linked to files on disk. If you move the original files or pass the document to someone on another computer, the links will be broken, which means that the files will not be where Word expects to find them. To correct this, you use the Lin<u>k</u>s... option on the <u>E</u>dit menu.

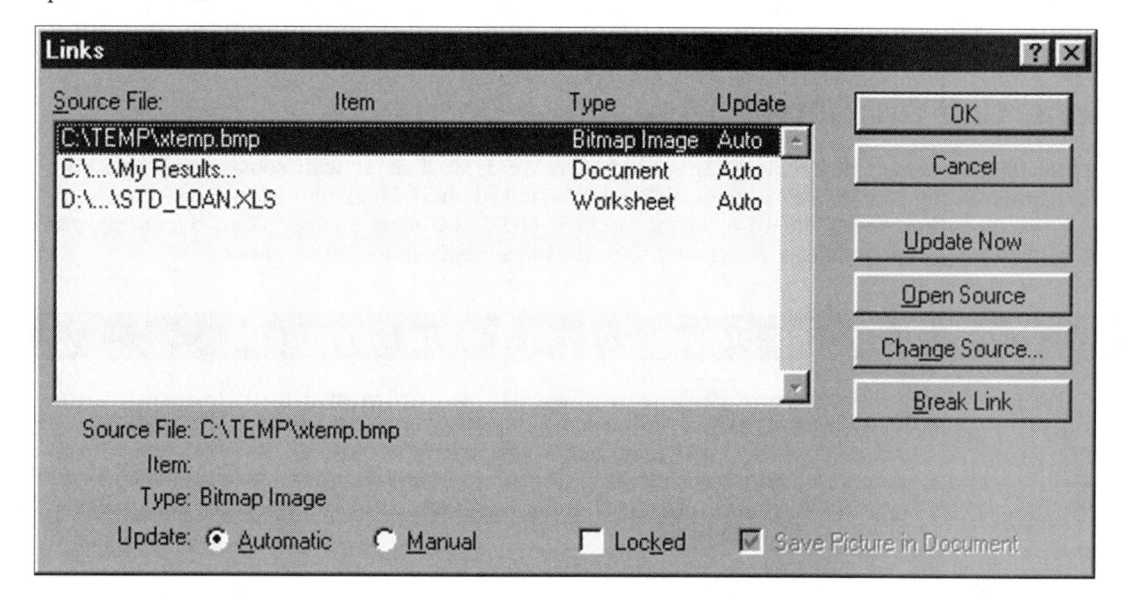

The rather intimidating Links dialog shows all the linked objects in your document and lets you change the way they behave and set their properties. You can use the push buttons to update the selected object, open it for editing in its server (source) application, change the link itself to point to another file (useful if you've moved the object file or document), and break the link to the file on disk.

At the bottom of the dialog are radio buttons which let you set the Update mode. <u>A</u>utomatic causes the object to be updated when the source file changes and <u>M</u>anual prevents updates to the object until you select Update on the Edit or short-cut menus (or click the Update Now button in this dialog). By setting the check box here, you can also set the Loc<u>k</u>ed property of the object so that it can't be edited. By clearing the Save Picture in Document option (for a linked graphic), you instruct Word not to save the graphic data in the document, making the document file smaller. This is equivalent to clearing the Save with Document check box in the Insert Picture dialog you saw at the beginning of this section.

Non-conformist Server Applications

As you use OLE in Windows 95, you soon start to see the different ways that objects created by different server applications behave, and the different ways the servers themselves behave. For example, some server applications allow you to save the object you are editing as a file on disk. Sometimes, doing so breaks the link between the object and your Word document. Considering that the specifications for OLE are bound up in Microsoft's Component Object Model (COM) definition, you would expect them to all behave in the same way.

535

It would be comforting to think that it's only server applications that don't support OLE2, or those that are 'leftovers' from Windows 3.x and not designed for Windows 95, that suffer from these inconsistencies. However, if you try Microsoft's own Paint application, which is part of Windows 95, you'll find that it has some strange habits. As an example, try inserting an existing bitmap into a document and setting the Link to File check box. If you edit the object, then close Paint and select No when prompted to save the changes, the document is still updated to show the new version, yet the file on disk doesn't change. This probably isn't what you expect to happen!

Inserting Our Survey Data into a Document

Having seen in outline how OLE is used with Word, we'll try it with some of the data we gathered from our reader survey. We'll insert a linked Excel chart into a document and some data from our Access database. In this section, you'll also meet another Word command, Insert | Database..., that makes working with data in other applications much easier.

Try It Out - Using the Survey Data in a Word Document

You'll need the files, **Survey.xls** and **Survey.mdb**, that we created in the previous chapter for this example. They're stored in the **\Fields** subfolder of your samples folder. Unless you changed the defaults, this will be **C:\BegWord\Fields**.

1 Create a new Word document by clicking the New button on the Standard toolbar. If you want to add some introductory text for the report, you can type it in now. Leave the insertion point at the end of the document.

2 The easiest way to insert just part of an Excel workbook is to use Paste Special.... Start Excel from your Start menu and load the **Survey.xls** file. Switch to the Chart page, click on the chart to select it, then copy it to the clipboard.

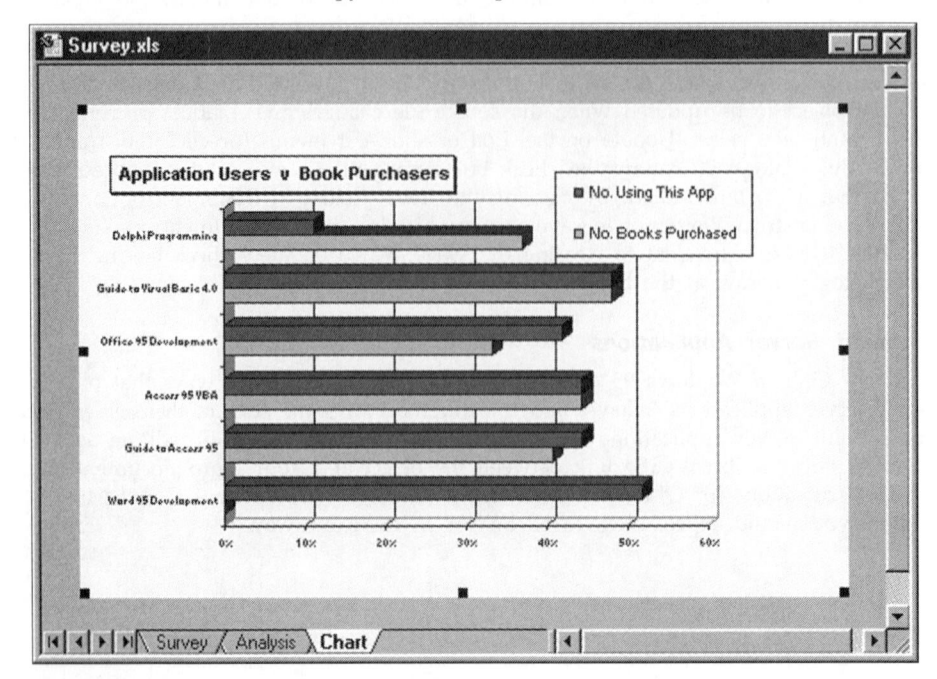

3 Back in your Word document, select Paste Special... from the Edit menu to open the Paste Special dialog. Select Microsoft Excel Chart Object and set the Paste Link option so it will be updated when the original copy (in Excel) changes.

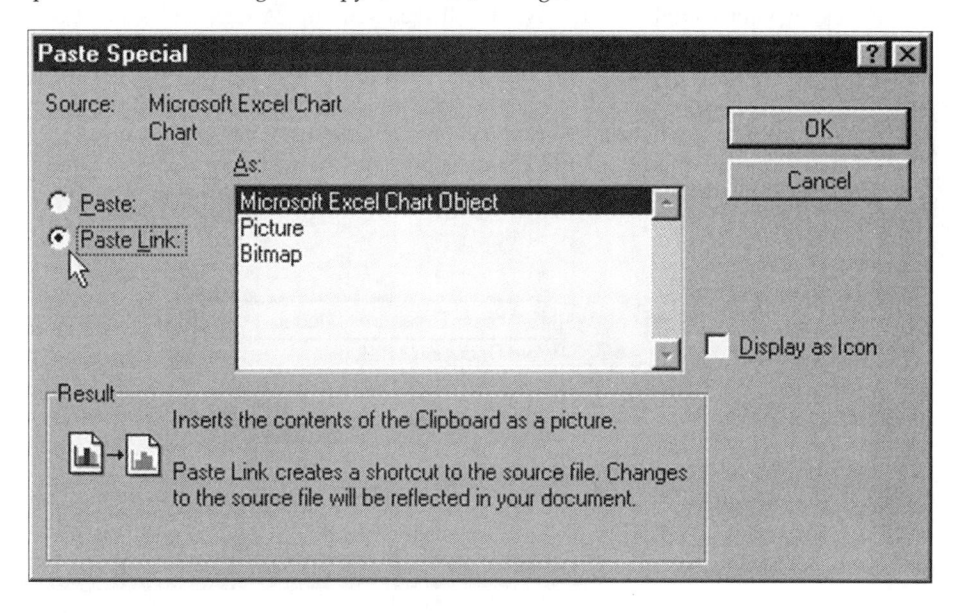

4 Click OK to insert the chart into the document.

> **FYI** Below the new chart, we need to add a table with some of our customers' names and details. We'll do this using the Insert | Database... command. This very useful command places a table in your document containing data from another source, which could be a Word document, Access database, Excel worksheet, or almost any other application to which Word can connect.

5 Press *Return* a couple of times and add some more explanatory text to your document if you wish. Leave the insertion point at the end again and select Database... from the Insert menu.

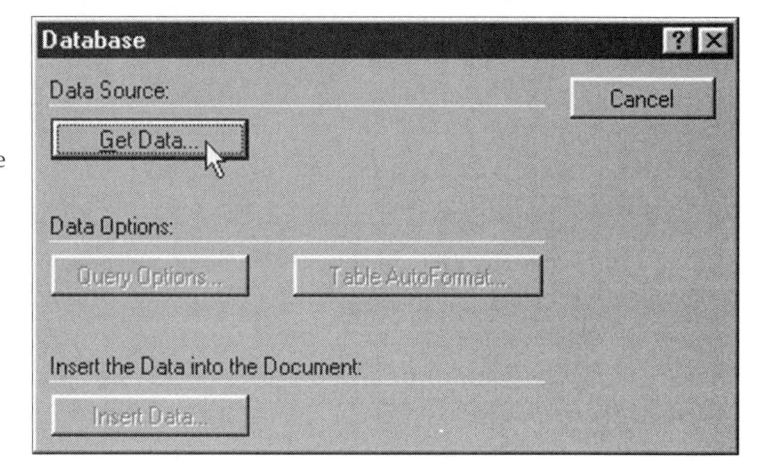

6 The Database dialog is the control center for the whole operation. First, click the Get Data button to select the data source. In the Open dialog that appears, set the Files of type: to MS Access Databases (*.mdb) and Open the **Survey.mdb** database from the **\Fields** subfolder of your samples folder. Word will then start up Access and send it a series of DDE commands. You can watch the status bar to see how it's progressing.

> **FYI** If you don't have Microsoft Access database engine installed on your system, you'll find that this option is not available. If this is the case, the rest of this example may not work for you, but follow along anyway, because you'll still be able to glean some useful information from it.

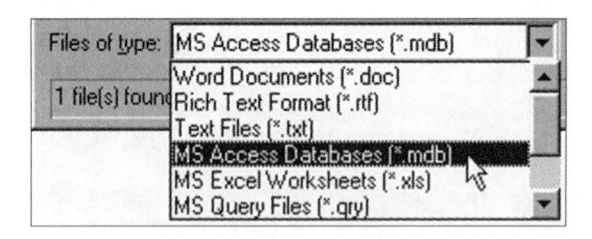

7 The next dialog shows the tables and queries in the database. Select the table Survey.

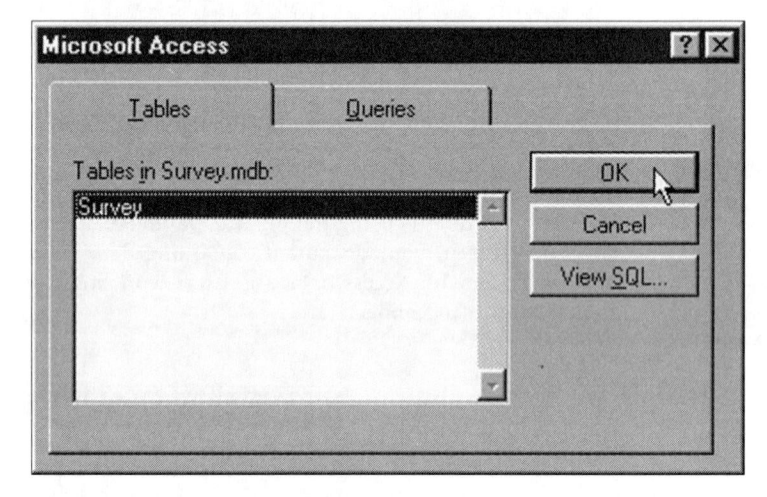

8 Click OK, then, back in the Database dialog, click the Query Options... button. Click the Select Fields tab so that you can select the fields you want. Click the Clear All button to clear all the selected fields, then use the Select >> button to add the FullName, Fax and E-mail fields. The Include Field Names option will provide a nice heading for the table that we're producing. (The captions on the buttons change, depending on which list you're selecting from.)

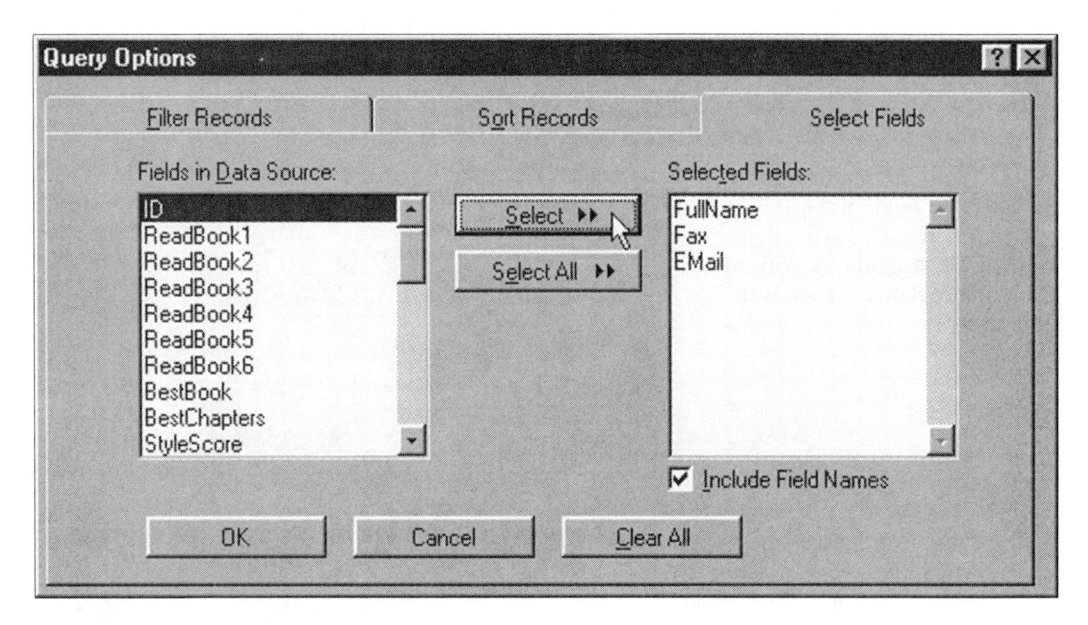

9 Click OK, then, back in the Database dialog, click the TableAutoFormat... button. Select the format you want. In our case, we used Simple 3.

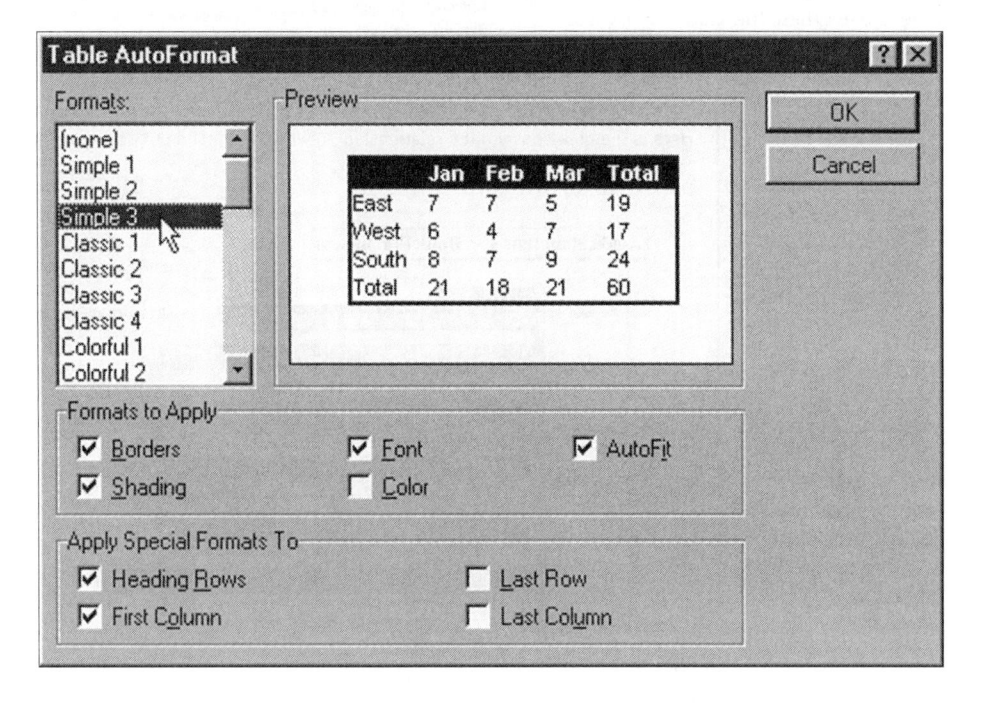

10 Click OK to close the Table AutoFormat dialog, and we're back in the Database dialog with all the options set ready to go.

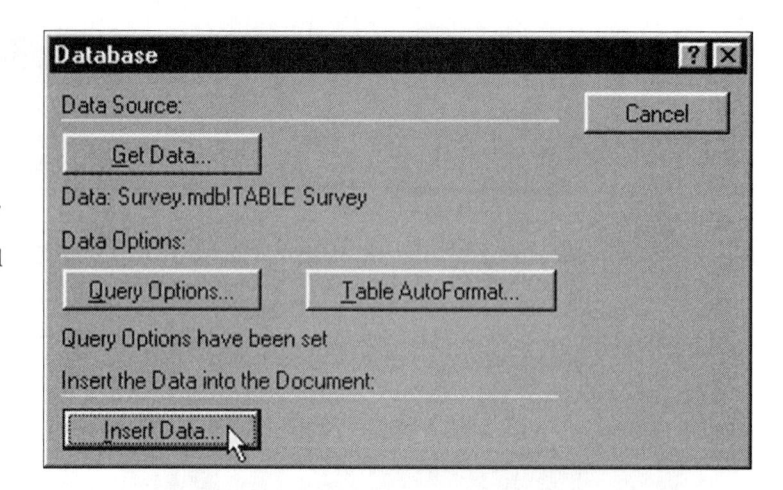

11 Click Insert Data and the final dialog allows us to select the records we want. Enter 5 to 8, and make sure you set the Insert Data as Field option, which will allow you to update the values in the table when the data in Access changes.

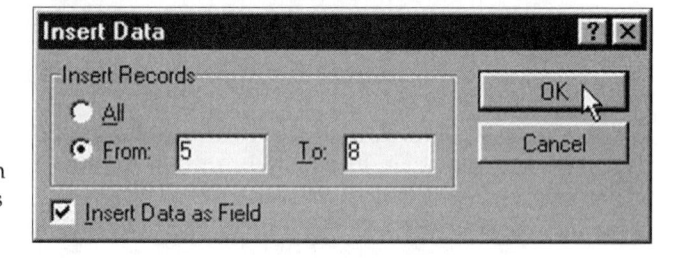

12 Click OK, and the table is created. If you watch the status bar, you'll see the commands being sent to Access to collect the data:

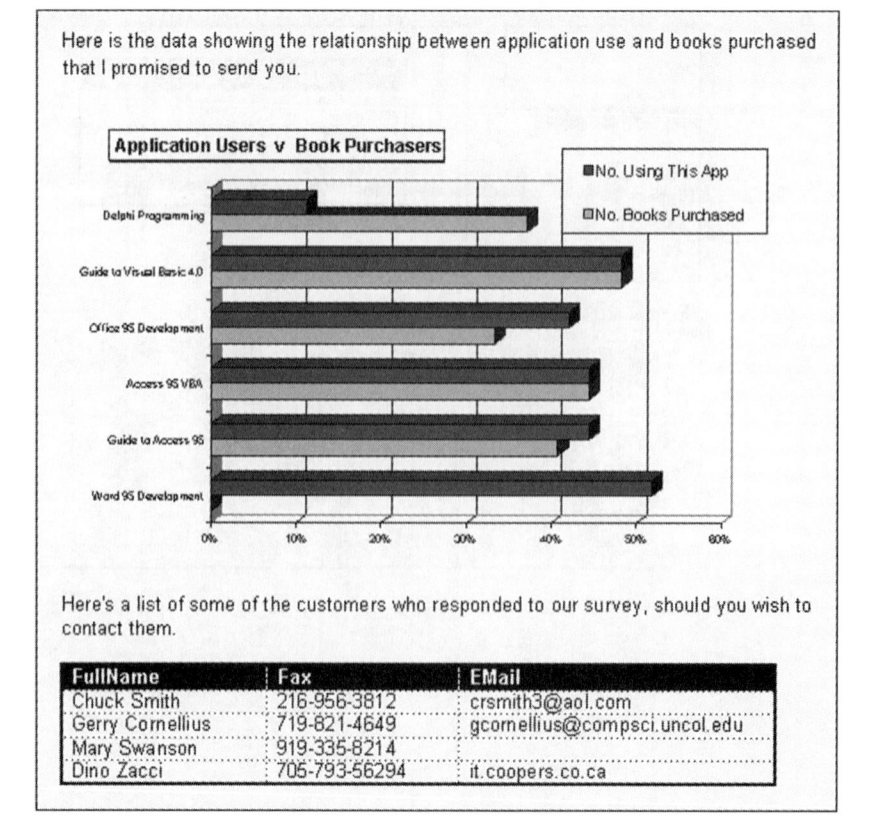

How It Works

In this example, we've inserted an Excel chart in our document as an OLE object, using the Paste Special... command and selecting the Paste Link option. If you try changing the formatting of the chart in Excel, you'll see the chart in your document change as well.

To get the data from Access, we used the Insert | Database... command. In fact, this doesn't use OLE at all. In our case, it communicated with Access using DDE. You can see this happening in Word's the status bar while you're setting the options or if you click in the table and press *F9* to update it. You'll see Access start up and a DDE link being established. Word is doing much the same as we did with our **AccessCustomer** macro in the previous chapter, but this is certainly easier to set up. See, there are still some things that are just plain easier to do with DDE!

> **FYI** Because it uses DDE, you have to explicitly update the table with *F9* when the data changes, though Word will update it before printing if you've set the Update Fields option in the Print tab of Word's Options dialog.

The Insert | Database... command also allows you to connect to and retrieve data from other sources. This could be an Excel worksheet, a table in a Word document, or any database which supports ODBC (Open Database Connectivity) methods. Notice also that we set the Insert Data as Field option in the Insert Data dialog because we want the data to be updated when the source information (in the database) changes. If you don't set this, the data is just inserted as a normal Word table, as though you had copied and pasted it from Access.

How Word Stores Objects

Before we go on to look at using OLE with WordBasic, we ought to consider how Word actually stores the objects we've been inserting. If you open the document we created in the previous example and press *Alt-F9* to show the field codes, you can see that Word stores the objects as fields. The first is a **{LINK}** field which displays the Chart page of our **Survey.xls** workbook. The second is a **{DATABASE}** field which collects the data from our **Survey.mdb** database.

```
{ LINK Excel.Chart.5 "C:\\BegWord\\Fields\\Survey.xls" "Chart" \a \p }

{ DATABASE \d "C:\\BegWord\\Fields\\Survey.mdb" \c "TABLE Survey" \s "SELECT
[FullName], [Fax], [EMail] FROM [Survey]" \f "5" \t "8" \l "3" \b "183" \h }
```

The two main types of field used with OLE in Word are the **{EMBED}** and **{LINK}** fields, though there are other types which can be used to insert data into your documents and update it when the source changes. The **{DATABASE}** field in the example we saw uses DDE to update the information, though, in some cases, it might use ODBC or other methods. We'll have a look at these fields in more detail, then consider the WordBasic statements we can use to create them and work with them.

The {EMBED} Field

This field inserts an OLE object so that it's embedded in the document, as when you use either the Insert | Object... command or Edit | Paste Special.... The syntax is:

    { EMBED ClassName [Switches] }

where **ClassName** is the special name used in the registry to identify the server application's object, such as **Excel.Sheet.5**, and **[Switches]** affect how the object appears when you update it after you've changed the size or cropping of it in the document:

Switch	What It Does
\s	Changes the embedded object back to its original size when the field is updated.
* MERGEFORMAT	Applies the sizing and cropping of the previous result to the new result when you update the field.

For example, the field **{ EMBED Excel.Sheet.5 * MERGEFORMAT }** displays an Excel worksheet object embedded in a document. When you insert an equation into your document, Word places the field **{ EMBED Equation.2 }** in it. To see a list of the available classes, run Registry Editor and look in the HKEY_CLASSES_ROOT key.

> **FYI** To start Registry Editor, select Run from your Start menu, enter regedit then click OK. Click on the plus sign next to HKEY_CLASSES_ROOT and scroll down through the list. Don't change any values, though, or you could stop OLE working properly for that object.

The {LINK} Field

This field inserts an OLE object so that it is linked to the document. It can also optionally store a picture of the data (as it stands at that point in time) in the document. It's equivalent to using the Insert | Object... command or Edit | Paste Special with the Link to File option set. The syntax of the field is:

    { LINK ClassName "Filename" [Range] [Switches] }

where **ClassName** is the special name used in the registry to identify the server application's object, such as **Excel.Sheet.5**, and **"Filename"** is the path and name of the file to link to. You have to use double slashes in the name to prevent Word treating them as switches. **[Range]** identifies which part of the source file is to be linked. In an Excel workbook, it can be a cell reference or a named range, and in a Word document it's a bookmark. **[Switches]** is used to control the way the data is stored and displayed in the document:

Switch	What It Does
\a	Updates the field automatically when the source file changes.
\b	Inserts the linked object as a bitmap.
\d	Prevents graphic data being stored with the document.
\p	Inserts the linked object as a picture.
\r	Inserts the linked object in rich text format (RTF).
\t	Inserts the linked object in text-only format.

In our example, we used the following field to insert a chart from an Excel workbook. The **\a** switch means that the information will be updated in Word whenever the chart in Excel changes.

```
{ LINK Excel.Chart.5 "C:\\BegWord\\Fields\\Survey.xls" "Chart" \a \p }
```

Other Types of Fields

There are other types of field that are used to insert data into a document, so that it's updated as the source changes.

The {DATABASE} Field

To insert the data from our Survey database, we used a **{DATABASE}** field. The syntax for this is simple:

```
{ DATABASE [Switches] }
```

It's the complexity of the switches and the number of options available that makes it hard to work with. It actually uses SQL (Structured Query Language) to manipulate the data in the source application, using an SQL statement stored in the field.

Switch		What It Does
\d	"*Location*"	This holds the path and file name of the database, except when using a query against an SQL database via ODBC.
\c	"*Connection*"	This is the connection string used to access an ODBC data source.
\s	"*SQL*"	This is the Structured Query Language statement used to manipulate the data source. Each quotation mark in the string must be preceded by a backslash (\), for example **"select * from \"My Table\""**.
\f	"*StartNumber*"	This specifies the number of the first record to insert into the document i.e. **\f "27"**.
\t	"*EndNumber*"	This specifies the number of the last record to insert into the document i.e. **\t "62"**.

Table Continued on Following Page

Switch	What It Does
\h	This switch adds column headings to the data in the new table. The headings are the field names of the data retrieved.
\b *"Attributes"* and \l *"Format#"*	This is used to control the column width and formatting of the table in the document. You can select a predefined format or build you own by adding values together which each represent one particular format attribute. See the Word help file for a full list.

In our previous example we used the following field to insert some of the records from our Access Survey database.

```
{ DATABASE \d "C:\\BegWord\\Fields\\Survey.mdb \c "TABLE Survey" \s "SELECT
[FullName], [Fax], [E-mail] FROM [Survey]" \f "5" \t "8" \l "3" \b "183" \h }
```

The {INCLUDEPICTURE} Field

One other field that you'll come across is **{INCLUDEPICTURE}**, which provides a way of inserting graphics into a document. You create an **{INCLUDEPICTURE}** field using the Insert | Picture... command and setting the Link to File check box. The syntax of the field is:

```
{ INCLUDEPICTURE "Filename" [Switches] }
```

where **"Filename"** is the full path and file name of the picture file on disk, and **[Switches]** controls how the graphic is stored and displayed.

Switch	Explanation
\c *Converter*	The name of the graphics filter you want to use (excluding the **.flt** filename extension). If you don't include it, Word selects a suitable filter automatically if there is one.
\d	Prevents Word storing the graphics data in the document.

Note that the **{INCLUDEPICTURE}** field appears to work like an ordinary OLE object, but when you double-click on a graphic, the Draw application opens. In many cases, the graphic may have been created in another application. You should open and edit the original graphic file in this application, then reload the new version by updating the field in Word with F9.

To link a picture file to a document and prevent Word storing the data in the Word file (which reduces the size of the file), we could use:

```
{ INCLUDEPICTURE "C:\\BegWord\\Pictures\\Defaults.bmp" \d }
```

Manipulating Objects with WordBasic

WordBasic contains statements which broadly mirror the commands on Word's menus, and which you can use to insert and manipulate all kinds of objects directly. However, unless you intend building an application that creates compound documents of some kind (say a wizard), you'll generally find that it's easier to use the menu commands rather than create a macro each time you want to insert an object or edit it.

WordBasic Statements for Manipulating Objects

To make things easier to follow, we've divided the various WordBasic statements that you use to manipulate OLE objects and insert data into three groups.

- General statements for inserting objects
- Statements for inserting specific objects
- Statements for manipulating objects

General Statements for Inserting Objects

These are the statements that you'll use most of the time to insert objects or data from another application or file. Each mirrors its respective dialog (or several dialogs), allowing you to carry out the complete action in one go. For each statement there are arguments for the options available in the dialogs. You can find a full list of these arguments by searching Word's Help file for the statement name.

Statement	What It Does
`InsertObject`	This is equivalent to the options available in the Object dialog. You can use it to start a server for creating a new object, or to insert an existing object from a file. It allows you to link or embed the object.
`EditPasteSpecial`	This is equivalent to the options in the Paste Special dialog when there is data available on the clipboard. It allows you to link or embed the object.
`InsertDatabase`	This is equivalent to the options in the Database dialog where you specify all the settings required to connect to another database and retrieve data from it. It uses DDE or other methods (rather than OLE) to update the data displayed by the {DATABASE} field it produces.
`InsertPicture`	This inserts a Picture object in the document. This can be embedded or linked with an {INCLUDEPICTURE} field.

Examples

The following statement inserts our Survey worksheet as a linked object into the active document at the current insertion point. The class name you use must match one of the object server classes available on your system. If you have different applications installed, or even different versions, you'll have to change the class name.

```
InsertObject .FileName = "C:\BegWord\Fields\Survey.xls", .Link = 1, \
             .Class = "Excel.Sheet.5"
```

As a simpler example, the following statement opens Microsoft Paint and creates a new embedded object:

```
InsertObject .Class = "Paint.Picture"
```

The class name, `Paint.Picture`, refers to Microsoft Paint, though the older class name `PBrush` seems to do the same thing. The next example, using `EditPasteSpecial`, uses a picture stored on the clipboard to create an OLE object of type `PBrush`, even though we've specified `Paint.Picture` as the class.

```
EditPasteSpecial .Class = "Paint.Picture", .DataType = "Object"
```

The **InsertDatabase** statement is notoriously difficult to code in WordBasic. The easiest way is to click the Record Next Command button on the Macro toolbar and perform the action using the Insert | Database... command. Here's the statement which creates the **{DATABASE}** field you saw in example document we created earlier, as recorded in a macro:

```
InsertDatabase .Format = 3, .Style = 183, .LinkToSource = 1, \
        .Connection = "TABLE Survey", \
        .SQLStatement = "SELECT FullName, Fax, EMail FROM [Survey]", \
        .SQLStatement1 = "", .PasswordDoc = "", .PasswordDot = "", \
        .DataSource = "C:\BegWord\Fields\Survey.mdb", .From = "5", \
        .To = "8", .IncludeFields = 1
```

You'll see that there are two **SQLStatement** arguments. String arguments are limited to 255 characters, but SQL statements are often longer than this. All you do in this case is split the SQL statement into two (so that both are less than 255 characters) and assign the second half to **SQLStatement1**.

Finally, to insert a picture in a document and link it to the file on disk so that it's updated if the file changes, we can use:

```
InsertPicture .Name = "C:\BegWord\Pictures\Defaults.bmp", .LinkToFile = 1
```

If we want to use the dialog form of any of these statements, we do it in the usual way. This example allows the user to select a picture to be inserted, but forces it to be inserted as a linked file irrespective of the setting they choose for the Link to File option. This is because we set the value of the **LinkToFile** option in the macro after displaying the dialog but before inserting the picture.

```
Sub MAIN
    Dim IPDRec As InsertPicture     'declare the dialog record
    GetCurValues IPDRec             'get the current settings
    If Dialog(IPDRec) Then          'display the dialog
        IPDRec.LinkToFile = 1       'set the LinkToFile option
        InsertPicture IPDRec        'and insert the picture
    EndIf
End Sub
```

Statements for Inserting Specific Objects

While the previous statements can be used to display a dialog or carry out the action directly, there are also specific statements which just create new objects in a particular server application. When the user closes the server, the object is embedded in the document; there's no option to link it. The statements take no arguments, so are easy to use.

Statement	What It Does
`InsertChart`	Starts Microsoft Graph and embeds the new chart.
`InsertDrawing`	Starts Microsoft Draw and embeds the new drawing.
`InsertEquation`	Starts Equation Editor and embeds the new equation.

Table Continued on Following Page

Statement	What It Does
`InsertExcelTable`	Starts Microsoft Excel and embeds the new worksheet.
`InsertSound`	Starts Sound Recorder and embeds the new sound.
`InsertWordArt`	Starts Microsoft WordArt and embeds the new WordArt.

Statements for Manipulating Objects

Once the object is in the document, you can manipulate it by selecting it and executing one of the following statements. Because the objects are stored in fields, you can find an object by using `EditGoTo` with a `Destination` argument of `"d"` (*field*), as well as by using `"o"` (*object*) or `"g"` (*graphic*).

```
EditGoTo "o 'PBrush'"    'go to the next PBrush object
EditGoTo "d 'LINK'"      'go to the next LINK field
EditGoTo "g"             'go to the next graphic
```

The statements that manipulate objects are pretty well self-explanatory:

Statement	What It Does
`ActivateObject`	Opens or plays the selected object in its server application, as though it had been double-clicked.
`EditObject`	Opens the object in its associated server for editing. Unlike `ActivateObject`, it doesn't play a sound or similar object.
`EditPicture`	Opens a graphic object in Microsoft Draw.
`FileClosePicture`	Closes Draw and embeds the picture in the document.
`ConvertObject`	This is equivalent to the options in the Convert dialog. Allows you to convert the selected object to another type, or change the way it's displayed.
`EditLinks`	This is equivalent to the options in the Links dialog. Allows you to update or open the object, change or break the link, set the Update mode and Loc<u>k</u>ed property, and control whether the graphic data is saved in the document.

Examples

`ActivateObject`, `EditObject` and `EditPicture` are all single statements that take no arguments. They operate on the currently selected object in the active document. `FileClosePicture` is used only when the active window is a Word picture editing window and, again, takes no arguments.

To convert an object from one type (`Class`) to another, you select it in the document and use `ConvertObject`. This example converts the currently selected Word Document object to a Word Picture object:

```
ConvertObject .ActivateAs = 0, .Class = "Word.Picture.6"
```

You can also use it to change the way an object is displayed, as an icon or a picture. The following statement changes the icon for the selected object to the 'desktop' one in Explorer and sets a new caption for it in the document.

```
ConvertObject .IconNumber = 3, .IconFilename = "EXPLORER.EXE", \
             .Caption = "My Desktop", .DisplayIcon = 1
```

The **EditLinks** statement is a lot more versatile. You'll see it in use in the final example of this chapter, but, in the mean time, here are a couple of examples. There are three arguments that are equivalent to the 'action' buttons in the Links dialog: **UpdateNow**, **OpenSource** and **KillLink**. To change the source file for the link, you use the **FileName** argument. To change the Update Mode, you set the **UpdateMode** argument to **0** (Automatic) or **1** (Manual). Finally, you can set the **Locked** property to **0** or **1** with the **Locked** argument and the Save Picture in Document option with the **SavePictureInDoc** argument.

This example changes the update mode of a linked object, based on part of the Analysis page of our **Survey.xls** workbook, to manual. It leaves the object unlocked and saves a picture of it in the document. Notice that the **Link** argument is set to **"\Sel"** to refer to the currently selected object in the document:

```
EditLinks .UpdateMode = 1, .Locked = 0, .SavePictureInDoc = 1, \
          .UpdateNow, .Link = "\SEL", .Application = "Excel.Sheet.5", \
          .Item = "Analysis!R1C1:R11C8", .FileName = "Survey.xls"
```

Like all dialog statements, we only have to supply arguments where we want to change the current or default values. For example, the next statement opens the same linked object in its source application, using the **.OpenSource** argument. Because we didn't select the object in the document first, we've set the **.Link** argument to **"1"** to refer to the first item in the Links dialog list.

```
EditLinks .OpenSource, .Link = "1", .Application = "Excel.Sheet.5", \
          .Item = "Analysis!R1C1:R11C8", .FileName = "Survey.xls"
```

To show you how WordBasic can provide a benefit when using OLE, we've supplied some sample macros which use WordBasic's OLE and other commands to enhance the built-in Word menu commands. You can save time and effort by creating simple macros if you regularly have to manipulate compound documents. You can use these to make it easier for others to create a particular kind of object, or control what types of object they can use and how they are inserted.

Keeping Your Document Logo Up-to-date

As a starter, here's a method that inserts our logo into a document. We always place it right at the beginning, after a horizontal line. Because we regularly update the logo, we want to be sure that each document displays the latest version. If we inserted the logo in a template, only new documents based on that template would have the latest version. Instead, we use WordBasic to insert a link to it in the document. That way, when the logo changes, all our existing and new documents will automatically have the latest version.

Chapter 13 - Using Objects in Your Documents

Try It Out - Linking a Logo to Your Documents

You'll need some of the files from the **\Fields** subfolder of your samples folder for this example. Unless you changed the defaults, this will be **C:\BegWord\Fields**. If you installed the samples on a different disk, or in a different folder, you'll get the error message 'Cannot find logo file' when you run the macro. If you do, you'll have to change the first line of the **InsertLogo** macro in the template to show the correct path before you start.

1 In My Computer or Explorer, go to the Fields subfolder of your samples folder and double-click on the file DDEOLE.dot to create a new document based on this template.

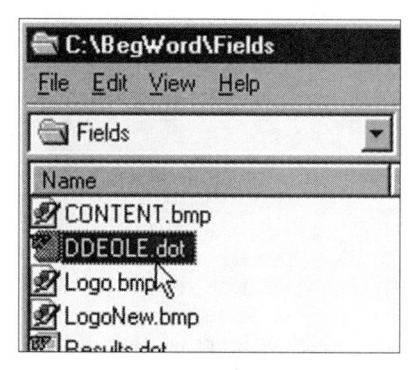

2 You'll see a new toolbar, called OLE-DDE. If it's not visible, right-click on any other toolbar, select Toolbars... and place a tick next to DDE-OLE in the list of available toolbars.

3 Type some text into the new document, then click the Insert Logo button on the new toolbar. The logo is inserted into your document automatically.

4 Now we'll change the source logo file. Select Save As... from the File menu, enter a name for the new document and click Save. Then close it with the Close button at the top right of the document window.

549

5 Back in My Computer or Explorer, click twice (slowly) on the file Logo.bmp. This is the file that our document logo object is linked to. Rename it to LogoOld.bmp. Then rename the file LogoNew.bmp to Logo.bmp. This will be our new logo file.

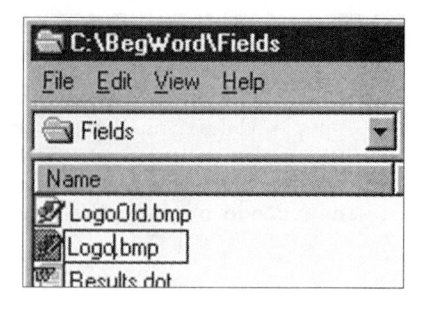

6 Open the document you've just created again. Now it shows the new version of our logo.

How It Works

This example shows how you can completely automate the task of inserting a particular type of object, using the `InsertObject` statement. First, we set the path and name of the object file in the variable `LogoFile$`, then go to the start of the document. As good house-keeping, we save the current value of line style set in the Borders dialog and change it to our new setting:

```
Sub MAIN
    LogoFile$ = "C:\BegWord\Fields\Logo.bmp"
    If Files$(LogoFile$) = "" Then Goto Insert_Err
    StartOfDocument
    SavedStyle = BorderLineStyle()      'save the current line width
    BorderLineStyle 4                   'set it to 3pt. Width
```

Now we can set the top border of the current line, reset the line style back to it's original setting and change the paragraph to right-aligned:

```
    BorderTop                           'draw the border
    BorderLineStyle SavedStyle          'reset the line width
    RightPara                           'set right alignment
```

To insert the logo, we use `InsertObject`, specifying the file name and setting the `Link` option to `1`. We also have to specify the `Tab` (page) in the Object dialog, and the `Class` of the object we want to insert:

```
        InsertObject .FileName = LogoFile$, .Link = 1, .Tab = 1, \
                .Class = "PBrush"
```

Finally, we insert a carriage return, set the paragraph style back to left-aligned and insert a blank line. The error trap is used to catch the situation where the logo cannot be found by the **Files$()** function at the start of the macro:

```
    InsertPara                      'set left alignment and
    LeftPara                        'move the insertion point
    InsertPara                      'down past new logo
  Goto Insert_Exit
  Insert_Err:
    Msg$ = "Cannot find logo file" + Chr$(13) + LogoFile$
    MsgBox Msg$, "Insert Logo", 48
  Insert_Exit:
  End Sub
```

Because we force the object to be linked to the source file, changes to the file are reflected in any existing documents that used the macro, as well as in new ones.

Maintaining an Audit Log of Data Use

Using the same centrally stored data in each document, rather than having multiple copies which can get out of step with each other, is most important. However, as a system administrator, you ought to know where the data is being used. By taking over the Word commands that insert an object into a document, we can provide a log file showing who used it, where, and when.

Try It Out - Keeping Track of Corporate Data Use

You'll need the template **DDEOLE.dot** for this example, and the files **Survey.xls** and **Survey.mdb** that we created in the previous chapter. They will be stored in the **\Fields** subfolder of your samples folder. Unless you changed the defaults when you installed them, this will be **C:\BegWord\Fields**. This example will require you to have a copy of Microsoft Access installed on your system.

1 In My Computer or Explorer go to the Fields subfolder of your samples folder and double-click on the file DDEOLE.dot to create a new document based on this template.

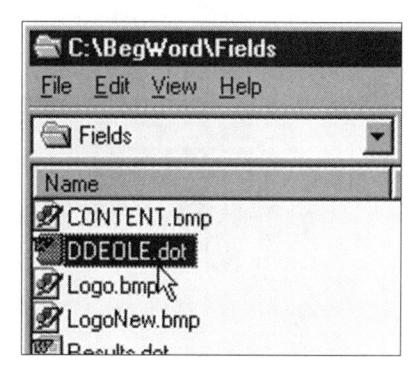

2 You'll see a new toolbar, called OLE-DDE appear. If you can't see it, right-click on any other toolbar, select Toolbars... and place a tick next to DDE-OLE in the list of available toolbars.

3 Type some text into the new document, then click the Insert Corporate Data button on the new toolbar. Because this is a new document, you'll be prompted to save it first. Enter a name for the document, say Furtive Data.doc, and click Save.

4 Now the Database dialog opens to start the process of inserting any kind of data into the document. We'll use the sample Survey data. Click Get Data, change the Files of Type: to MS Access Databases (*.mdb), select the file Survey.mdb from the Fields subfolder of your samples folder, then select the Survey table in the following dialog.

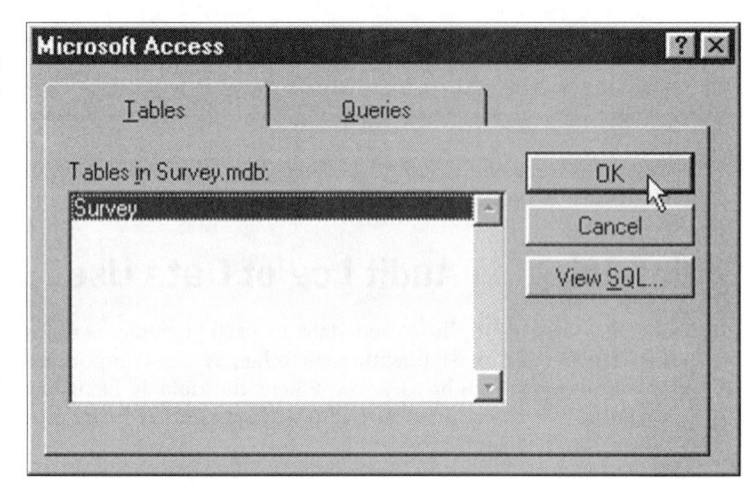

5 Back in the Database dialog click Query Options... and, in the Select Fields page, choose the name and address fields to be included in the result.

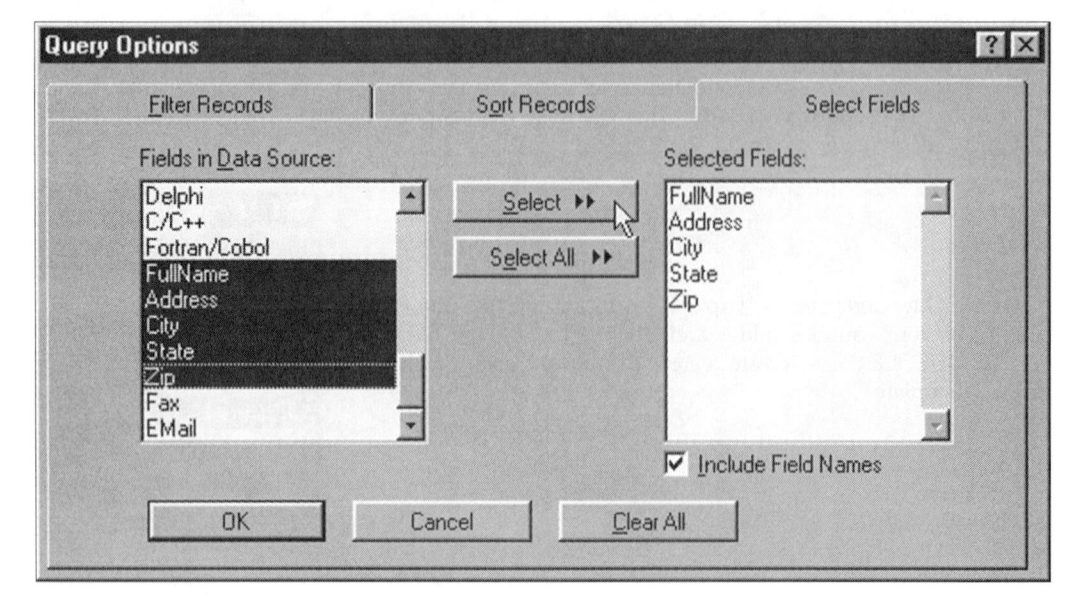

6 Then open the Sort Records tab. Select the Zip field in the Sort By list and set the sort order to Ascending.

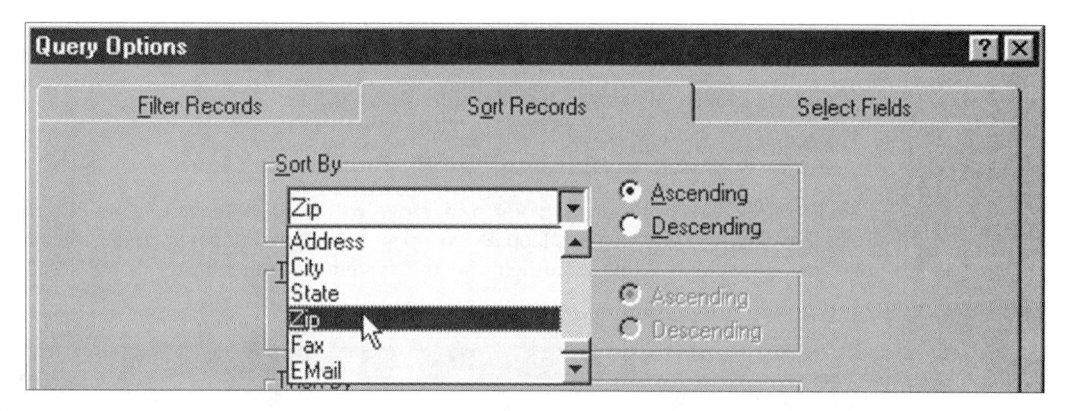

7 Open the Filter Records tab and in the first row select State for the Field, Equal To for the Comparison, and enter CA for the Compare To value. We'll only be using records for California. Then Click OK to go back to the Database dialog.

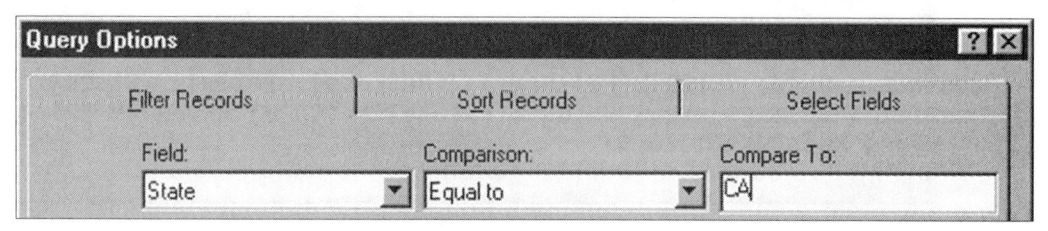

8 If you want to set a format for the table, do this now by clicking the Table Auto Format button in the Database dialog. We chose Simple 3 format for our example. Then click Insert Data and enter 1 and 5 in the From and To boxes of the Insert Data dialog. Don't set the Insert Data as Field option.

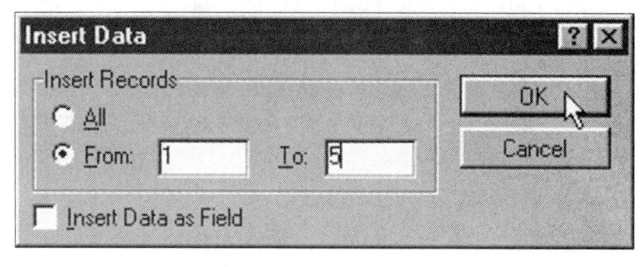

9 Click OK and, after some rummaging about on the hard disk, Word inserts the new table into our document:

This is some data I've lifted from our corporate database without telling the system administrator. Please keep it to yourself!

FullName	Address	City	State	Zip
Richard Beckinsdale	100 N Sepulveda Blvd	El Segundo	CA	90245
Jools Holland	1302 Fairmount Ave	La Crescento	CA	91214
Trevor McDonald	1948 Redhill Ave	Costa Mesa	CA	92626
Don McRobb	527 N Adlena Drive	Fullerton	CA	92633
Franklin Johns	560 Marsh Road	Menlo Park	CA	94025

10 Click on the table in the document and press *F9*. You'll see Access start up again and update the data in the table, even though we didn't specify that the data be inserted as a field.

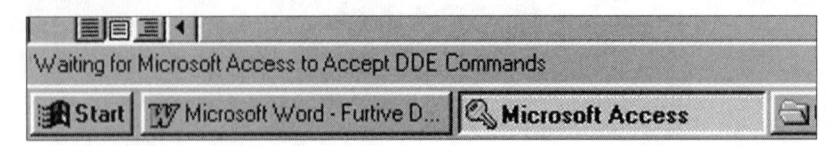

11 Now go back to My Computer or Explorer and move to the root folder of your C: drive. Find and double-click on the file AuditLog.txt to open it in NotePad. It contains details of the data you've just inserted in your document, so the system administrator can tell it's been used!

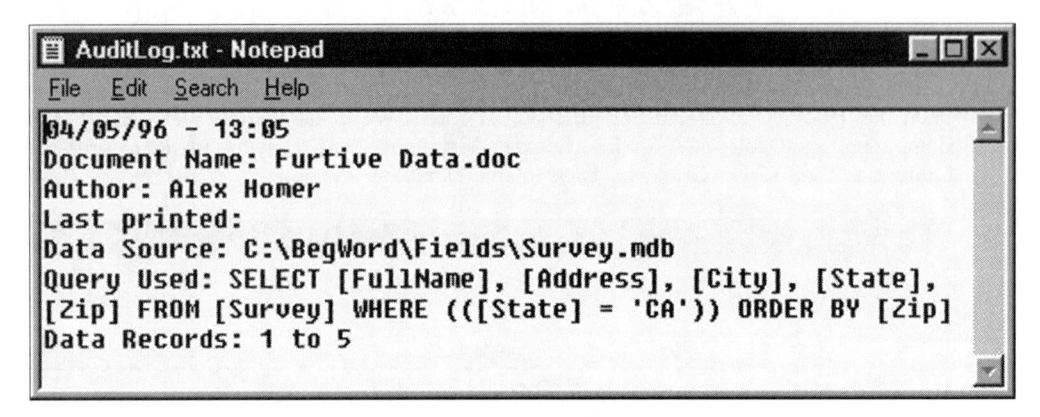

```
04/05/96 - 13:05
Document Name: Furtive Data.doc
Author: Alex Homer
Last printed:
Data Source: C:\BegWord\Fields\Survey.mdb
Query Used: SELECT [FullName], [Address], [City], [State],
[Zip] FROM [Survey] WHERE (([State] = 'CA')) ORDER BY [Zip]
Data Records: 1 to 5
```

12 Close the AuditLog.txt file in NotePad. Then carry on and insert some more data by clicking the Insert Corporate Data button on the DDE-OLE toolbar, but this time use different files. Try using data from the file **Survey.xls** and others - you get a different set of pages in the Query Options dialog for each type of file. Afterwards, look in **AuditLog.txt** file. Each time you insert data the details are appended to the end of the file.

How It Works

Although this is a more complex macro, much of it is concerned with creating the text for the log file. At the beginning of the macro, we set the path and name of the log file. You can change this to suit your system. Then we set an error trap in case the user selects Cancel as they're saving the document, or if the macro can't access the log file. If either of these happens, data isn't inserted into the document.

```
Sub MAIN
AuditLog$ = "C:\AuditLog.txt"
On Error Goto IDB_Err
```

Now we can get the name of the document from its window title. If it hasn't been saved yet, we force the user to save it so that the name is updated, together with the document properties that we'll be using to identify it in the log file. New documents don't have the **.doc** file extension, so we can use this as the test. Once we've saved it, we get the new file name from the window title.

```
    TheDoc$ = WindowName$()                 'get name of document
    If Right$(TheDoc$, 4) <> ".doc" Then
        Dim FSARec As FileSaveAs            'save if its a new document
        GetCurValues FSARec                 'to update the properties
        Dialog FSARec
        FileSaveAs FSARec
        TheDoc$ = WindowName$()             'then get document name
    EndIf
```

Now we declare a dialog record, get the current settings for it and display the **Database** dialog. If the user clicks Cancel, we skip the rest of the macro, but if they click OK in the final InsertData dialog, we can start the process of building the log file entry. Notice that if they haven't printed the document yet, the **LastPrinted** document property contains a random value, but it always starts with **01/01**. We can test for this to prevent the log file storing a random result.

```
    Dim IDBRec As InsertDatabase            'declare dialog record
    GetCurValues IDBRec                     'get current settings
    If Dialog(IDBRec) Then
        'create the entry for the log file
        Log$ = Date$(Now()) + " - " + Time$(Now()) + Chr$(13)
        Log$ = Log$ + "Document Name: " + TheDoc$ + Chr$(13)
        Log$ = Log$ + "Author: " + GetDocumentProperty$("Author") + Chr$(13)
        LastPrint$ = GetDocumentProperty$("LastPrinted")
        ' returns rubbish starting with 01/01 if it's not been printed
        If InStr(LastPrint$, "01/01") = 1 Then LastPrint$ = ""
        Log$ = Log$ + "Last printed: " + LastPrint$ + Chr$(13)
```

The **Log$** variable now contains the information about the user and the document. We get the details about what they are inserting from the dialog record. This includes the path and name of the data source, the SQL statement and the record numbers:

```
        Log$ = Log$ + "Data Source: " + IDBRec.DataSource + Chr$(13)
        Log$ = Log$ + "Query Used: " + IDBRec.SQLStatement
        Log$ = Log$ + IDBRec.SQLStatement1 + Chr$(13)
        If IDBRec.From > "" Then
            DataRecs$ = IDBRec.From + " to " + IDBRec.To
        Else
            DataRecs$ = "All"
        EndIf
        Log$ = Log$ + "Data Records: " + DataRecs$ + Chr$(13) + Chr$(13)
```

Now that we've got the log file entry, we add it to the **AuditLog** file. We **Open** it in **Append** mode, **Print** the entry and **Close** it again:

```
        Open AuditLog$ For Append As #1     'open the log file
            Print #1, Log$                  'write the entry
        Close #1
```

Before we actually insert the data, we make sure that it will be inserted as a field, even if the user doesn't set this option in the Insert Data dialog. All we have to do is set the **LinkToSource** field in the dialog record directly. Then we simply execute the **InsertDatabase** statement using our dialog record.

```
        IDBRec.LinkToSource = 1                'set the Link option
        InsertDatabase IDBRec                  'and do it...
    EndIf
    Goto IDB_Exit
    IDB_Err:
      Close
      Msg$ = "Cannot use corporate data at the current time"
      MsgBox Msg$, "Insert Corporate Data", 48
    IDB_Exit:
    End Sub
```

If any part of the process fails and raises an error, the data is not inserted in the document. Instead, the user gets a message telling them that the task cannot be completed. Of course, in our sample DDEOLE template, there's nothing to stop the user inserting data using a different command. However, you could easily take over the Insert | Database command completely by just naming the macro **InsertDatabase** and removing all the other OLE commands from the menus.

Sharing Your Compound Documents

One of the problems that we've already found occurs when you need to send a copy of a compound document to someone else. If you've inserted part of a worksheet or some database records stored centrally on your network server, you can freely pass copies of the document around your workgroup and the links will still be correct. However, if you want to e-mail it to a colleague on the other side of the globe, you need to make sure that he or she has the latest copy of the data to which you've included links in your document.

One of the easiest ways to do this is by replacing the links in the document with the latest version of the data, and therefore actually embedding it in the file. That way, you can just send the complete document without having to worry about sending any linked files. If they won't need to edit it, you can insert the data as pictures instead.

Try It Out - Converting Linked Data in Documents to Result Graphics

You'll need the template **OLEDDE.dot** from the **\Fields** subfolder of your samples folder for this example. Unless you changed the defaults when installing them, your samples folder will be **C:\BegWord\Fields**.

1 In My Computer or Explorer go to the Fields subfolder of your samples folder and double-click on the file DDEOLE.dot to create a new document based on this template.

2 You'll see a new toolbar, called OLE-DDE, appear. If you can't see it, right-click on any other toolbar, select Toolbars... and place a tick next to DDE-OLE in the list of available toolbars.

3 Type some text and insert some linked objects into the new document. To insert a linked object, select Object... from the Insert menu and open the Create from File tab in the Object dialog.

4 Click Browse... and select a file from your disk. Here, we're using the picture **CAMERA.bmp** from the **\Fields** subfolder of the samples folder.

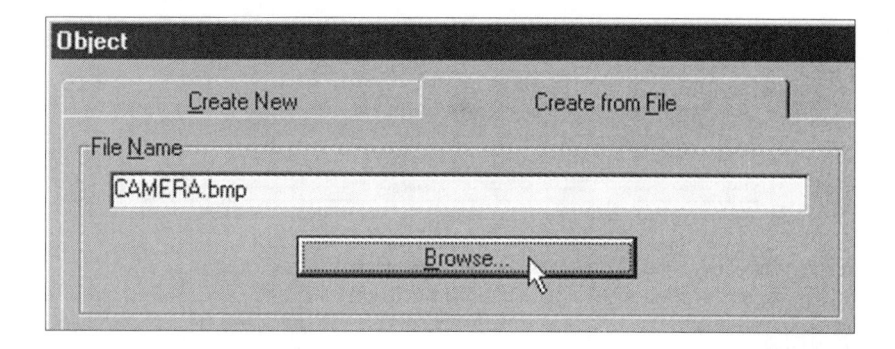

5 Make sure that you set the Link to File check box in the Object dialog, then click OK to insert the object.

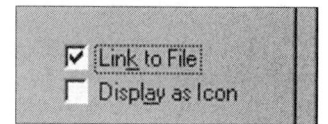

6 Carry on and insert some other objects. Try the **Survey.xls** Excel worksheet. Remember, you can insert part of an application's data file by opening that file in the original application, copying it to the clipboard and selecting Paste Special... from Word's Edit menu to link it to your document.

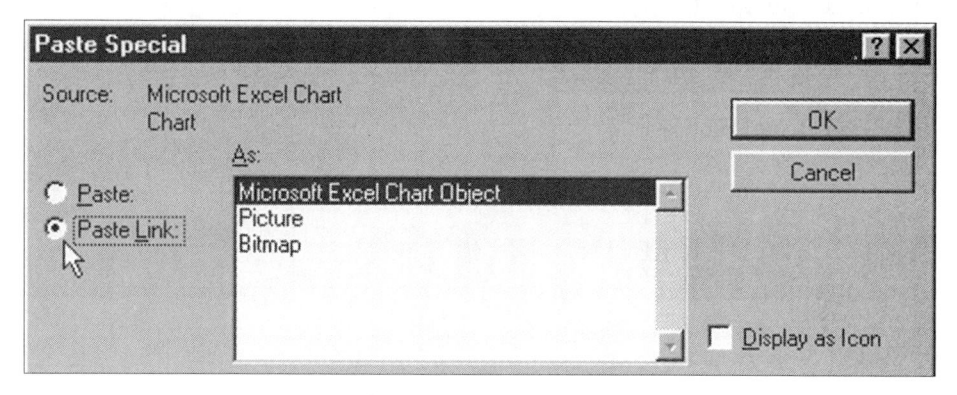

7 Once you've got some objects in your document, press *Alt-F9* to view the Field Codes they've produced. You'll see that they are all **{LINK}** fields of various types.

This is an example of how you can change linked objects into embedded objects.

{ LINK Paint.Picture "C:\\BegWord\\Fields\\CAMERA.bmp" "" \a \p }

This is very useful for sending someone a copy which they don't need to be able to edit.

{ LINK Excel.Sheet.5 "C:\\BegWord\\Fields\\Survey.xls" "" \a \p }

You can even include parts of a data file.

{ LINK Excel.Chart.5 "C:\\BegWord\\Fields\\Survey.xls" "Chart" \a \p }

8 Press *Alt-F9* again to return to normal view, then click the Update For Mailing button on the new toolbar:

9 It takes a while because Word has to activate each object's server application in turn. After some time, the status bar displays a message indicating that the job is done:

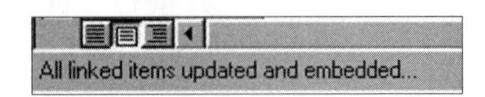

10 Press *Alt-F9* to view the field codes again. Now they are all **{EMBED}** fields of type **Word.Picture.6**. The data is included in the document so that you don't have to distribute the source files. They can't be edited in their original application because they're stored as pictures of the object, not as the original data file.

This is an example of how you can change linked objects into embedded objects.

{ EMBED Word.Picture.6 }

This is very useful for sending someone a copy which they don't need to be able to edit.

{ EMBED Word.Picture.6 }

You can even include parts of a data file.

{ EMBED Word.Picture.6 }

How It Works

This macro is quite simple. All we do is use the **EditLinks** statement to carry out the tasks you would normally do with the Update Now and Break Link buttons in the Links dialog. We can do this two ways. We can use the position of the entries in the Links dialog list (where 1 is the first, 2 is the second, etc.), or we can select each object in turn in the document by searching for **{LINK}** fields.

We've used the second method so that you can see how easy it is to find any kind of field in a document. If your document includes pictures inserted with the Insert | Picture dialog, which produces **{INCLUDEPICTURE}** fields, you'll need to search for and select these as well as the **{LINK}** fields.

First we go to the start of the document and plant a bookmark called **Temp**. Then we use **EditGoTo** to find the first **{LINK}** field. To see if we found one, we check whether the current insertion point is the same as the Temp bookmark. If it's not, the function **CmpBookmarks ("Temp", "\Sel")** returns **False**:

```
Sub MAIN
StartOfDocument
EditBookmark .Name = "Temp", .Add         'mark current position
EditGoTo "d 'LINK'"                        'got to next LINK field
While CmpBookmarks("Temp", "\Sel")         'if we moved, we found one
```

Before we do anything else, we replace the **Temp** bookmark with a new one here, then select the {LINK} field we've found. To update a {LINK} field, we use the **EditLinks** statement with the **UpdateNow** argument. To replace it with a picture, we use the **KillLink** argument. In both cases we tell **EditLinks** that the bookmark **"\Sel"** (the current selection in the document) contains the object that we want it to work on:

```
    EditBookmark .Name = "Temp", .Add       'so mark the new position
    CharRight 1, 1                           'select the field
    EditLinks .Link = "\Sel", .UpdateNow    'update it
    EditLinks .Link = "\Sel", .KillLink     'and replace with a picture
```

Finally, we use **EditGoTo** again go to the next {LINK} field. The **While-Wend** loop continues to execute as long as **EditGoTo** keeps moving the insertion point, i.e. while there are more {LINK} fields in the document:

```
    EditGoTo "d 'LINK'"                     'then go to the next one
Wend
Print "All linked items updated and embedded..."
End Sub
```

Once we've done them all, we can print a message in the status bar and exit.

Using Word as an OLE Server

So far, in the last two chapters, we've been considering how Word is used as the container application for DDE and OLE operations. In DDE, a Word macro uses statements and functions to start the server application, insert and retrieve information, then close it again. In OLE, a Word document has various objects inserted into it which are created and maintained by their own server application.

Word can also act as an OLE server for other applications. You can insert a Word Document or Word Picture object into any other application that supports OLE. If it's OLE2-compliant, Word will also give in-place activation. So, in Access, for example, you can offer your users a far more functional text-editing capability than the normal Access text box controls can manage.

Inserting a Word object into another application's document is normally done in much the same way as you inserted objects into your Word documents in this chapter. In Excel and Access, for example, you can use the Insert | Object... or Edit | Paste Special... commands, or just drag-and-drop a Word **.doc** file into the container application's document.

A Brief Look at OLE Automation

As we've discovered in this and the previous chapter, the basis of object technology is to produce objects which contain not only their own data, but also the methods for manipulating that data. With our OLE examples we've seen plenty of data, but the methods we've used consisted of loading the server application in its entirety, and leaving the user to manipulate it and update the data in the container application when they've finished.

While the server application is open, our only way of controlling it is to use the WordBasic **SendKeys** statement to send individual keystrokes to it. Because we're not in complete control, we can't rely on what the user will do in the server application while it's open.

The answer is an extension to OLE, called **OLE Automation**. Applications which support this expose the methods that they contain, as well as the data in their documents, and these methods can be accessed by other applications. By using the exposed methods of the server, the client application can directly control the whole process.

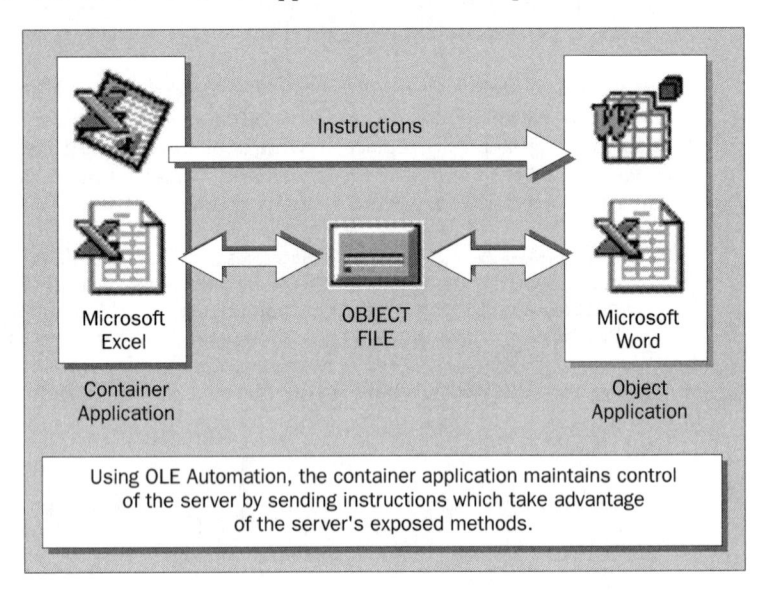

Using OLE Automation, the container application maintains control of the server by sending instructions which take advantage of the server's exposed methods.

WordBasic doesn't support OLE Automation with Word as the client, but many other application programming languages, such as Visual Basic and VBA, do. However, Word exposes its own data and methods, so you can use it as an OLE Automation server. We'll take a brief look at how you can use Word as a server with the Visual Basic and very similar VBA (Visual Basic for Applications) programming languages.

OLE Automation and Visual Basic

To start an instance of Word and get access to its data and methods, we declare an object variable in Visual Basic or VBA and assign the **Word.Basic** OLE object to it :

```
Dim WordObject as Object
Set WordObject = CreateObject("Word.Basic")
```

Once we've created the new object in VB, we can use it to manipulate Word directly through the methods of WordBasic's macro language. We can execute almost any WordBasic statement or function and run our own macros.

A couple of points to keep in mind are that the server will normally be started hidden and with no document open (unless you are creating a reference to a copy that's already running). OLE Automation operations are normally carried out against a hidden server, but if you want to show Word, you can execute the WordBasic **AppShow** statement with the name of the window you want to show as the argument:

```
WordObject.AppShow "Microsoft Word"
```

In general, the syntax for accessing the methods of the server is to use the object variable that refers to it, followed by a full stop, then the method and its arguments. So, to open a new document in Word where we've created the instance referred to by **WordObject**, we can use:

```
    WordObject.FileNewDefault
    WordObject.Insert "Some Text for a new document"
```

From there on in, it's just like you were working in Word. The object variable in VB refers to the instance of Word that you've started. You just have to remember to precede each statement or function with the object variable's name. To make this easier, you can use the **With** construct. For example:

```
    With WordObject
       .Style "Heading 1"
       .Insert "This is a Heading"
       .InsertPara
       .Style "Normal"
       .Insert "This is some body text."
    End With
```

When the object variable goes out of scope in the container application, which, unless it's been declared as a global (or public) variable will generally be when the procedure ends, the server application closes. You can also close it by setting the object variable to the special value **Nothing**:

```
    Set WordObject = Nothing
```

So you can see just how powerful a technique this is, with all kinds of uses. As an example, you can use functions such as Word's grammar and spell checkers directly on data from another application, controlling the whole process from VB. Of course, you can create your own macros in WordBasic, then run them from the client application.

Remember also that the Word document you are working with can be stored in an OLE control in the container application. In this case, you don't have to start a separate instance of Word directly; you just activate the OLE object from the container application.

OLE 'Gotchas' with Word and WordBasic

There are a few things you have to be aware of when you use Word as an OLE Automation server.

Running Your Own Macros

You can't send arguments to a macro that you've created yourself. You have to store the values somewhere first, for example in Document Variables, then call the macro and have it retrieve them. To start a macro, you use the WordBasic **ToolsMacro** command, specifying the name of the macro and the value **True** to run it:

```
    WordObject.ToolsMacro "MyMacro", True
```

Using Word Dialogs

You can quite happily use the normal Word statements which display dialogs with OLE Automation, but bear in mind that, if you're working with a hidden object and you display a dialog, the whole process stops until the user responds. If Word is not the active application, the dialog may not be visible and the OLE process will fail. Generally, you would only use this sort of automation when the user was actively editing the document. This would ensure that they could react to the dialogs.

However, you can't use the statements and functions which create and manipulate custom dialogs in the container application's code (in this case VB). But, if you want to, you can run a WordBasic macro which creates a dialog.

Statement and Function Names

WordBasic functions that return a string value end with a dollar sign (**$**). When you execute that function from VB, you have to either omit the dollar sign, or enclose the function name in square brackets:

```
TheDocumentName = WordObject.[WindowName$](0)
TheDocumentName = WordObject.WindowName(0)
```

If the WordBasic statement or function has the same name as a VB statement or function, you also have to enclose it in square brackets to prevent VB reporting a syntax error or executing its own version.

Statement and Function Arguments

Versions of Visual Basic prior to version 4.0 do not support named arguments (yet WordBasic has done so for many years!). So you cannot use something like this:

```
WordObject.FileSaveAs .Name = "My New Document"
```

Instead, you have to supply the arguments in the order that the statement expects them. Although you don't have to supply all the optional arguments, you do have to include them (or use a comma to indicate the ones you aren't supplying) up to the last one you need. To make more sense of this, imagine that you're using the **FormatDropCap** statement you saw in Part 1 of the book. This takes four arguments, so in Visual Basic and above you can use:

```
WordObject.FormatDropCap .Position = 1,. Font = "Deco", .DropHeight = 2, \
                         .DistFromText = 5
```

However, in Visual Basic or earlier, you have to use:

```
WordObject.FormatDropCap 1, "Deco", 2, 5
```

If you don't want to specify the **Position**, **Font** or **DropHeight**, but do want to specify the **DistFromText** you have to use:

```
WordObject.FormatDropCap , , , 5
```

However, if you only want to specify the **Position** and **Font** and not the **DropHeight** or **DistFromText**, you can omit these arguments altogether:

```
WordObject.FormatDropCap 1, "Deco"
```

To make matters worse, the order of the arguments given in the Word documentation and Help file are not always correct! If you intend to use OLE Automation seriously and are currently running older versions of VB, you should consider upgrading to VB4 or above.

Summary

The techniques and methods of OLE, together with DDE, that we covered in depth in the previous chapter, allow you to create compound documents that combine information from many different applications. More than this, they allow you to maintain the integrity of your information sources by using only one master data file as the source for all your documents, rather than keeping similar copies of it in different applications.

Using OLE and DDE methods with Word means that you can produce attractive documents and reports, which are always up to date. We've also shown how you can use WordBasic to automate and control the use of objects and data by creating simple macros. We looked at:

- How OLE works and how we can use it in Word
- Other Word commands for inserting and linking data
- The ways we can use OLE from WordBasic

Our examples were mainly based on the data we collected with our Survey form and, in the final chapter of this book, we'll show you some more ways that you can use Word to take advantage of the information that you've gathered. We'll look at how you use mail merge and some simple techniques for communicating information by e-mail via Microsoft Exchange.

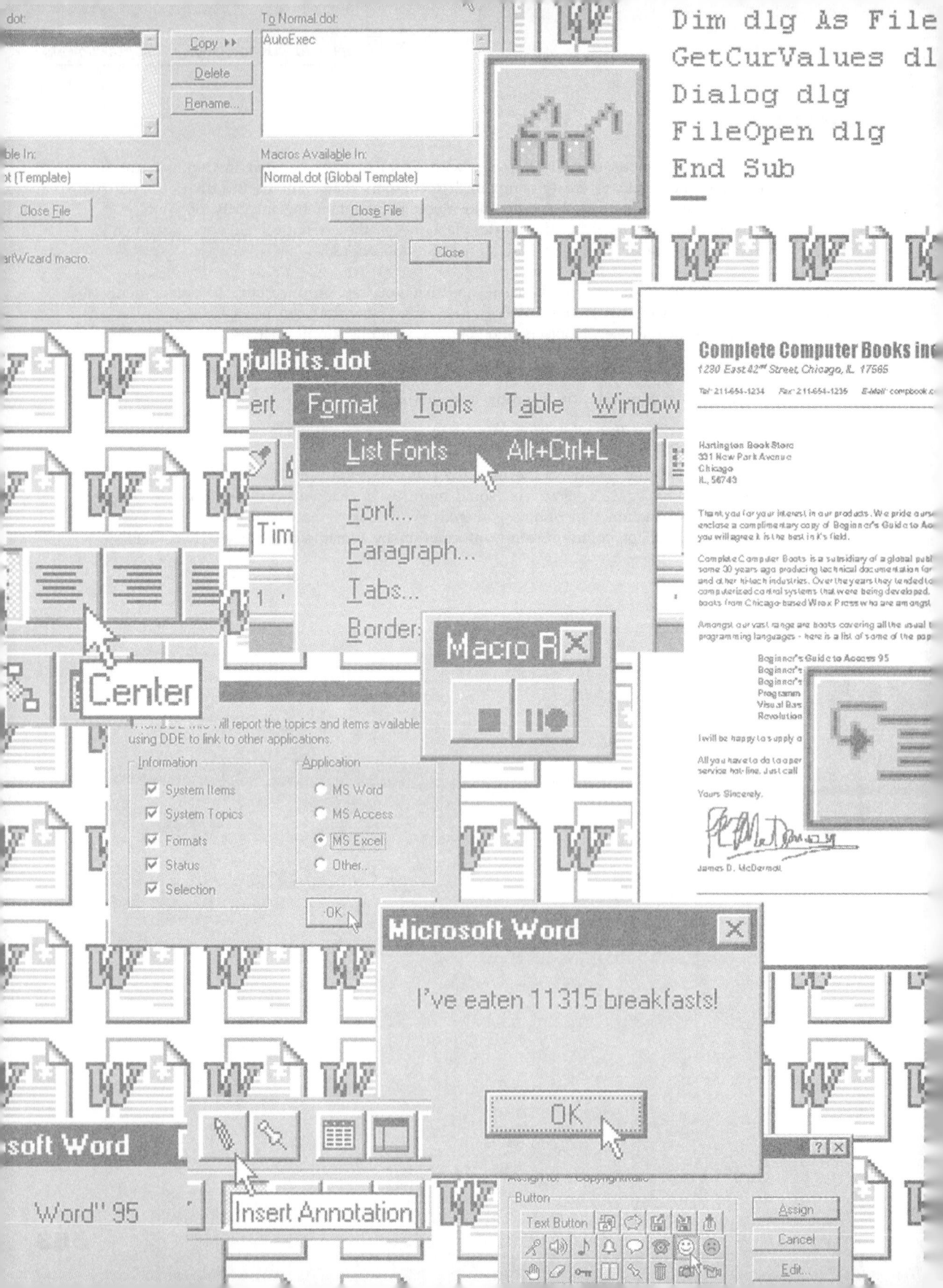

```
Dim dlg As File
GetCurValues dl
Dialog dlg
FileOpen dlg
End Sub
```

14

E-mail, Address Books and Mail Merge

Introduction

So far, in this section of the book we've been looking at how you use Word in a multi-user and multi-application environment. We've seen ways of passing documents around a local area network, and of using information in a variety of applications and their documents. For example, we used the data from our reader survey in Excel and Access, as well as in Word itself.

One of the most exciting things about Windows 95 is the way it's bringing all the different methods of communication together within the operating system itself rather than by using add-in packages. No longer do you need different applications to handle faxes, e-mail, or the transfer of files between users on a network. In this chapter, we'll see how you can use Word in this environment to make your everyday tasks easier.

Windows 95 also allows you to manage information about your personal or business contacts in one central address book. This makes life a great deal easier, because you no longer have to worry about how you get the information from one application to another. There's no more need for copying 'phone numbers from your personal organizer application into your fax application. They can all be stored in one place, ready for use with any application.

We'll also be finishing up the book with a look at mail merge. If you've ever wondered how so many companies find the time to write you those nice personalized letters offering their latest earth-shattering products, you'll discover the secret here. By the end of this chapter you'll be flooding the world with 'junk mail' along with the best of them.

So in this chapter you'll see:

- How Windows 95 can link Word to the electronic world outside
- How to manage your contacts and send e-mail and faxes directly from Word
- How mail merge can help you to target your documents for maximum effect

Chapter Fourteen

Using an Address Book

One of the main aims of Windows 95 was to concentrate application-wide functions into the operating system. One of these functions is the handling of contact information. Windows 95 contains a new system-level application called **Microsoft Exchange**, which can integrate all the communication functions of your machine into one system and store all your contact details in its **Personal Address Book**. Of course, you can still use separate stand-alone applications to manage your contact information, electronic mail and faxes in Windows 95, but once you start using Exchange you'll find it generally offers a more complete all-round solution.

For example, we use two electronic mail systems and a built-in fax modem, as well as being linked to a local area network (LAN). All our contact information is stored in a Personal Address Book, so sending a message is simply a matter of selecting the correct recipient. Exchange automatically looks after addressing the message and routing it via the correct service.

Of course, your own system will differ from our set-up, but in this section and the next we'll aim to show you what you can do when you're using Exchange, and introduce you to some of the ways it can help you work more efficiently.

The Microsoft Exchange Personal Address Book

Before we start looking at how you can use Word with Exchange, we'll take a brief look at the way Exchange can make using electronic communication methods easier by storing the details of your contacts. This isn't a guide to using Exchange, but will help you to understand what we have to do to communicate with it.

The Default Address Book

Word communicates with your default address book, and uses it to store and retrieve information. When you install Windows 95 you have the option of installing Microsoft Exchange, which contains an address book that can serve as your default address book. This is classed as a **service** in Exchange, and is called **Personal Address Book**. It's the option we have chosen for our set-up.

> **FYI** Even if you haven't installed Exchange, you may still be able to use the Word macro examples we've supplied. Microsoft Office 95 contains a personal information manager called Schedule+. You can use its address book as your default address book instead of Exchange.

Using Personal Address Book

The Exchange Personal Address Book can hold a variety of information about your contacts. There are four pages for every contact. The first lists everything from their name and address to their company, department and the name of their assistant. The second page contains almost every kind of 'phone or fax number you can think of, and the third allows you to enter a page-full of notes as free text.

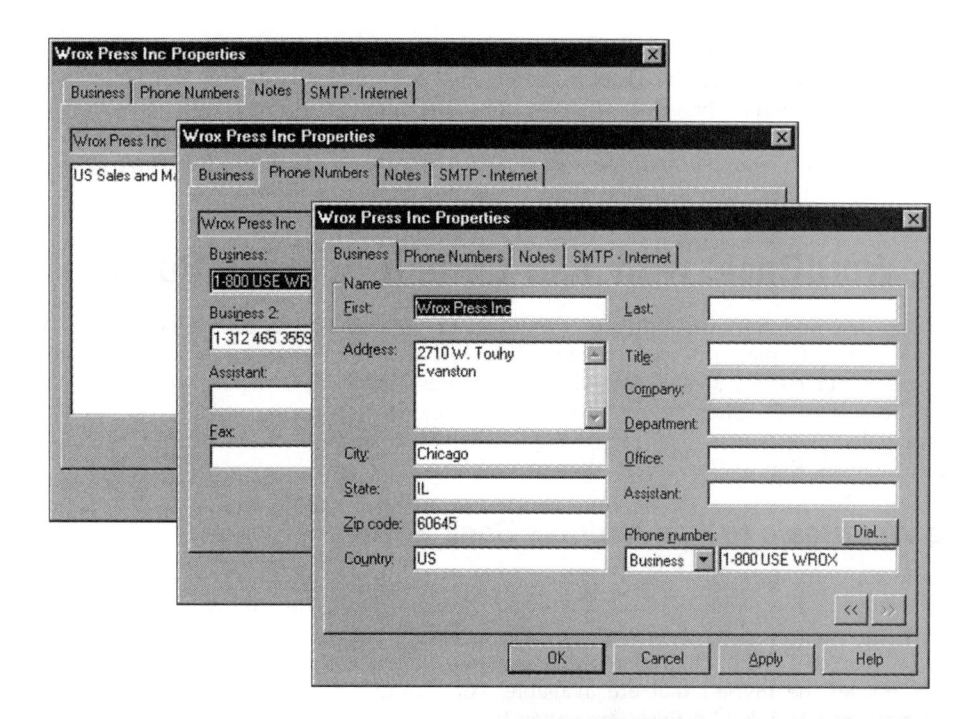

The fourth page will be different depending on the type of address you are storing. When you add a new contact to your Personal Address Book, you have to specify the address type by selecting it from a list of the available services.

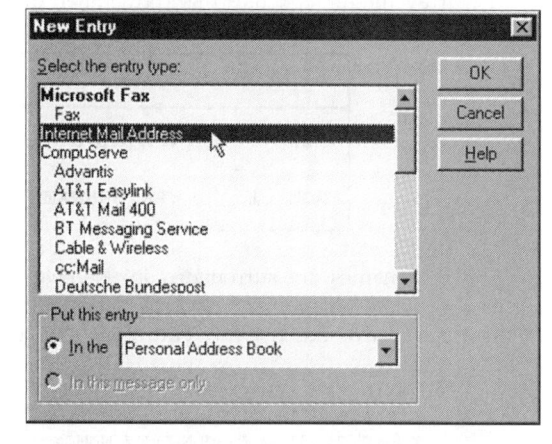

If you use e-mail via the Internet and select the **Internet Mail Address** option, this fourth page will be headed **SMTP - Address**. If you select a closed 'bulletin board' system, such as CompuServe or AOL, you'll find the service name used as the heading. If you're storing the details of another user on your network, or creating an entry just for sending faxes, you'll see a different page again:

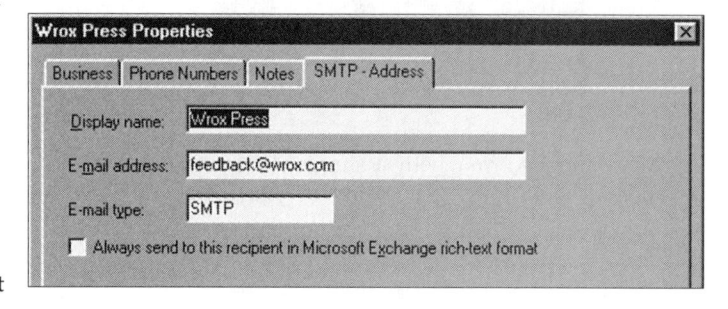

You don't have to supply information for every field in the address book, though you must include what's known as the Display name, the name that's shown in the list of addresses, identifying that entry. This Display name must be unique for every different service entry in your address book. Of course, you also have to specify the primary e-mail address (or fax number) for each entry. When you create and send a new message, Exchange uses the address type of the recipient you select to send it via the correct service.

Using WordBasic with Your Default Address Book

You can add and retrieve addresses to and from your default address book using WordBasic macros. For example, you could write a macro that takes the currently selected text in a document and creates a new entry in your address book. This means, however, that your macro must be able to decipher which part is the name, street address, city, etc., so it's likely to be useful only when you're handling documents that are in a standard format. We'll take a look at the techniques that are involved, though.

Using WordBasic to Add Address Book Entries

To add an entry to your default address book, you use the **AddAddress** statement. This takes one argument: the name of a two-dimensional string array containing the information you want to add. In the first column of the array you place the names of the fields, and in the second, the data for that field. This means that you only have to supply the information for fields you want, not all the myriad that are available. For example, to set the First: and Last: name entries, the array might look like this (remember that all array dimensions start at zero):

	Column 0	Column 1
Row 0	<PR_GIVEN_NAME>	ALEX
ROW 1	<PR_SURNAME>	HOMER

The field names are surrounded in <> characters, and you can include as many or as few rows as you wish, but you do have to declare the array with the number of fields you are using—you can't leave the last few empty. So we could code the example above like this:

```
Sub MAIN
   Dim Addr$(1, 1)
   Addr$(0, 0) = "<PR_GIVEN_NAME>"
   Addr$(0, 1) = "Alex"
   Addr$(1, 0) = "<PR_SURNAME>"
   Addr$(1, 1) = "Homer"
   AddAddress Addr$
End Sub
```

We've supplied you with a simple demonstration that adds our own contact details to your address book, making it easier for you to tell us what you think of our books.

Chapter 14 - E-mail, Address Books and Mail Merge

Try It Out - Adding Our Contact Details to Your Address Book

For this example, you'll need the template **E-Mail.dot**, which we've supplied in the **\Fields** subfolder of your samples folder. Unless you changed the defaults during installation, this will be **C:\BegWord\Fields**. You'll also need to have Microsoft Exchange installed, with Internet Mail or CompuServe set up as a service.

1 If it's not already running, start Exchange by double-clicking the icon on your desktop. Log on if prompted. This prevents you having to log on and choose a profile when you run the macro.

2 Open the file **E-Mail.dot** from the **\Fields** subfolder of your samples folder. The Wrox Address toolbar will appear. If you can't see it, select Toolbars... from the View menu and place a tick next to it in the list of available toolbars.

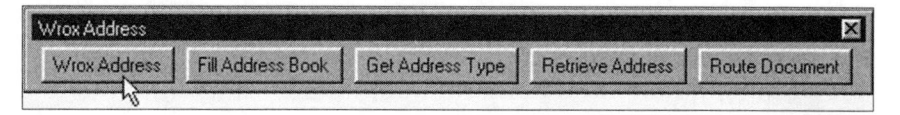

3 Click the Wrox Address button. If you have Schedule+ installed, you may be prompted to log on to it, in which case, just click OK. Then switch to Exchange and click the Address Book button to open your address book.

4 You'll see the new entry for Wrox Press in your address book, together with our telephone numbers. Double-click on it and you can see that the macro has added our e-mail address, phone and fax numbers, and postal address information.

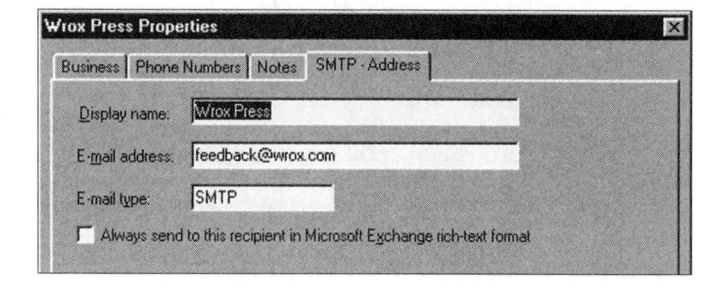

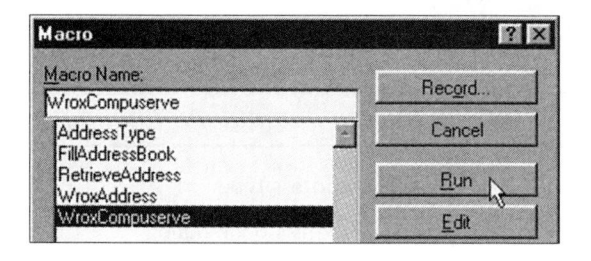

If you get an error message, it may be because you already have an entry for Wrox Press, or that you don't have Internet Mail set up as an available service. If you use CompuServe instead, you can run the **WroxCompuserve** macro by opening the Macro dialog, selecting this macro and clicking the Run button. This creates an entry for Wrox Press using our CompuServe e-mail address rather than the Internet one.

569

> **FYI** If you have access to both services and run both the macros, you'll see that they create two entries with the same display name. This is only possible because they use different services. Display names must all be unique *within* each service.

How It Works

This is a very simple demonstration of how you can add information to Personal Address Book from WordBasic. It uses the technique we described earlier of creating a two-dimensional array and placing the field names and their values in it. We execute the **AddAddress** statement using the name of the array.

```
Sub MAIN
    Dim Addr$(9, 1)
    Addr$(0, 0) = "PR_DISPLAY_NAME"
    Addr$(0, 1) = "Wrox Press"
    Addr$(1, 0) = "PR_ADDRTYPE"
    Addr$(1, 1) = "SMTP"
    Addr$(2, 0) = "PR_GIVEN_NAME"
    Addr$(2, 1) = "Wrox Press"
    Addr$(3, 0) = "PR_STREET_ADDRESS"
    Addr$(3, 1) = "2710 West Touhy Avenue"
    Addr$(4, 0) = "PR_LOCALITY"
    Addr$(4, 1) = "Chicago"
    Addr$(5, 0) = "PR_STATE_OR_PROVINCE"
    Addr$(5, 1) = "IL"
    Addr$(6, 0) = "PR_POSTAL_CODE"
    Addr$(6, 1) = "60645-9911"
    Addr$(7, 0) = "PR_PRIMARY_TELEPHONE_NUMBER"
    Addr$(7, 1) = "800 814 4527"
    Addr$(8, 0) = "PR_PRIMARY_FAX_NUMBER"
    Addr$(8, 1) = "312 465 4063"
    Addr$(9, 0) = "PR_EMAIL_ADDRESS"
    Addr$(9, 1) = "feedback@wrox.com"
    AddAddress Addr$()
End Sub
```

Personal Address Book Field Names

Here's a list of the field names (or **properties**, as they're called in the Help file) that you can use. Each one corresponds to one of the text boxes you see in the different pages of Personal Address Book.

Field Name in Address Book	What It Contains
PR_ADDRTYPE	Electronic mail address type
PR_DISPLAY_NAME	Text shown in Address Book dialog
PR_GIVEN_NAME	Given name, or first name
PR_SURNAME	Surname, or last name
PR_INITIALS	The addressee's initials

Table Continued on Following Page

Field Name in Address Book	What It Contains
PR_LOCATION	Room, building or flat number
PR_STREET_ADDRESS	House number and street address
PR_STATE_OR_PROVINCE	State, county or province
PR_LOCALITY	City, town or locality
PR_POSTAL_CODE	Zip code or postal code
PR_COUNTRY	Country name
PR_EMAIL_ADDRESS	Electronic mail address
PR_TITLE	Job title
PR_COMPANY_NAME	Company name
PR_DEPARTMENT_NAME	Department name within company
PR_OFFICE_LOCATION	Office location
PR_PRIMARY_TELEPHONE_NUMBER	Main telephone number
PR_HOME_TELEPHONE_NUMBER	Home telephone number
PR_OFFICE_TELEPHONE_NUMBER	Office telephone number
PR_OFFICE2_TELEPHONE_NUMBER	Alternative office telephone number
PR_CAR_TELEPHONE_NUMBER	Car telephone number
PR_CELLULAR_TELEPHONE_NUMBER	Mobile telephone number
PR_BEEPER_TELEPHONE_NUMBER	Beeper telephone number
PR_RADIO_TELEPHONE_NUMBER	Radio telephone number
PR_OTHER_TELEPHONE_NUMBER	Any other telephone number
PR_PRIMARY_FAX_NUMBER	Main fax number
PR_BUSINESS_FAX_NUMBER	Business fax number
PR_HOME_FAX_NUMBER	Home fax number
PR_COMMENT	Text for the Notes tab for this entry

Creating Address Book Entries from Existing Data

Because it's simple to create new entries in Personal Address Book and get the relevant information into the correct fields, you can easily import existing data with a WordBasic macro. This could be useful if you currently store your data in another application, such as Lotus Organizer™. All you need do is to export it as a text file, read this file with WordBasic and assign the appropriate parts to each field in your address book. As an example, we've supplied a macro that reads the data from our reader survey file, **Survey.txt**, and inserts a new entry in Exchange's Personal Address Book for each reader.

Try It Out - Adding Our Reader Survey Data to Exchange

For this example, you'll need the template `E-Mail.dot`, which we've supplied in the `\Fields` subfolder of your samples folder. Unless you changed the defaults during installation, this will be `C:\BegWord\Fields`. You'll also need to have Microsoft Exchange installed, with Internet Mail set up as a service.

1 If it's not already running, start Exchange by double-clicking on the icon on your desktop. Log on if prompted. This prevents you having to log on and choose a profile when you run the macro.

2 Open the file `E-Mail.dot` from the `\Fields` subfolder of your samples folder. The Wrox Address toolbar will appear. If you can't see it, select Toolbars... from the View menu and place a tick next to it in the list of available toolbars.

3 Click the Fill Address Book button. If you have Schedule+ installed, you may be prompted to log on to it. If this happens, just click the OK button. In the status bar, you'll see the names being added one by one. Once it's finished, switch to Exchange and click the Address Book button to open your address book.

> **FYI** If you *have* installed the samples in a different folder, you'll need to change the first line after `Sub MAIN` in the `FillAddressBook` macro to reflect the new location of the file `Survey.txt` before you run the macro:
>
> `TheFile$ = "C:\BegWord\Fields\Survey.txt"`

4 You'll find that it now contains entries for all the people who responded to our survey, together with your existing entries.

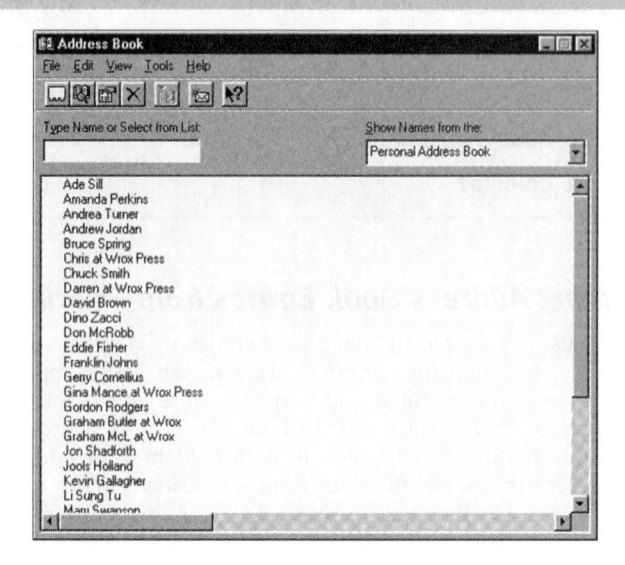

5 Double-click on one of the new entries to open its **Properties** window, and check out the pages of the dialog. You'll see that it's added their name and address, and their fax number and e-mail address.

How It Works

This macro again uses the **AddAddress** statement to create new entries in your default address book. The basic plan is to examine every line in the **Survey.txt** file and pull out the address details. We can then build the array of values for **AddAddress** from these. You saw in the previous chapter how we read a text file like this and extract the values, so we won't describe these techniques in detail again here.

Here's the **MAIN** routine in the macro. It loops through the **Survey.txt** file, reading each line and sending it to our **FillAddrArray** subroutine. Once it has filled the array **Addr$** with the values for each field of that entry, it uses our own **AddThisAddress()** function to put the entry into Exchange. If this function returns **False** (0), we display a message.

```
Dim Shared Addr$(9, 1)           'array to hold the new address values
Dim Shared PABEmailType$         'the Address Type for each new address
Dim Shared NumVals               'number of values in each line of file

Sub MAIN
   TheFile$ = "C:\BegWord\Fields\Survey.txt"  'set the file name
   PABEmailType$ = "SMTP"                     'and the Address Type
   NumVals = 34                               'and the no. of values
   On Error Goto FAD_Err
   Open TheFile$ For Input As #1              'open the Survey file
   While Not Eof(#1)                          'more lines to read
      Line Input #1, TheLine$                 'read the whole line
      FillAddrArray(TheLine$)                 'fill the array
      If Not AddThisAddress Then              'and create the entry
         Msg$ = "Cannot add entry for " + Addr$(0, 1) + Chr$(13)
         Msg$ = Msg$ + "It may already exist in the address book."
         MsgBox Msg$, "Wrox Address", 64
      EndIf
   Wend                                       'go back for next line
   Close #1                                   'close the file
   Print "Finished."
   Goto FAD_Exit
FAD_Err:
   Close                                      'close all files
   Msg$ = "Cannot update the Address Book :" + Str$(Err)
   MsgBox Msg$, "Wrox Address", 48
FAD_Exit:
End Sub
```

To fill the array, we call the **FillAddrArray** subroutine. This uses the **GetLineValue$()** function that we wrote and used in the previous chapter to extract a particular value from a line of tab-delimited text. We send it the number of the field and the complete line as arguments. The first call is with field (value) **28** which is the name of the reader who returned the survey form. Because they entered their whole name in one field, we have to split it at the first space character to separate off their first name, as you'll see over the page.

```
Sub FillAddrArray(TheText$)
    FullName$ = LTrim$(RTrim$(GetLineValue$(28, TheText$)))
    SpacePos = InStr(FullName$, " ")
    If SpacePos > 0 Then
        Forename$ = Left$(FullName$, SpacePos - 1)
        Surname$ = Mid$(FullName$, SpacePos + 1)
    Else
        Forename$ = ""
        Surname$ = FullName$
    EndIf
```

We can then carry on and get the rest of the details by calling **GetLineValue$()** for each field we want. We haven't repeated the code of this function here, so refer back to the previous chapter if you want to see how it works:

```
    Addr$(0, 0) = "PR_DISPLAY_NAME"
    Addr$(0, 1) = FullName$
    Addr$(1, 0) = "PR_ADDRTYPE"
    Addr$(1, 1) = PABEmailType$
    Addr$(2, 0) = "PR_GIVEN_NAME"
    Addr$(2, 1) = Forename$
    Addr$(3, 0) = "PR_SURNAME"
    Addr$(3, 1) = Surname$
    Addr$(4, 0) = "PR_STREET_ADDRESS"
    Addr$(4, 1) = GetLineValue$(29, TheText$)
    Addr$(5, 0) = "PR_LOCALITY"
    Addr$(5, 1) = GetLineValue$(30, TheText$)
    Addr$(6, 0) = "PR_STATE_OR_PROVINCE"
    Addr$(6, 1) = GetLineValue$(31, TheText$)
    Addr$(7, 0) = "PR_POSTAL_CODE"
    Addr$(7, 1) = GetLineValue$(32, TheText$)
    Addr$(8, 0) = "PR_PRIMARY_FAX_NUMBER"
    Addr$(8, 1) = GetLineValue$(33, TheText$)
    Addr$(9, 0) = "PR_EMAIL_ADDRESS"
    Addr$(9, 1) = GetLineValue$(34, TheText$)
End Sub
```

We also use the **AddThisAddress()** function. Remember that you can't add two entries with the same display name and address type, so our macro will fail if any of the readers' details already exist in the address book. However, it's difficult to check in code whether they already exist. If we try and retrieve an entry that doesn't exist, Exchange displays a dialog which prompts for more information. That's not what we want to happen, so we just try adding the new entry, and let the error trap in this separate function catch any that fail. We're assuming that they fail because a similar entry already exists:

```
Function AddThisAddress
    On Error Goto ATA_Err
    Print "Adding entry for "; Addr$(0, 1)
    AddThisAddress = 0
    AddAddress Addr$()
    AddThisAddress = - 1
ATA_Err:
End Function
```

Finding the Correct Address Type

One of the problems that you'll meet when you come to add new entries to the address book is knowing what the address type to use with `PR_ADDRTYPE` actually is. For Internet Mail it's `SMTP`, and for CompuServe it's `COMPUSERVE` — quite obvious really. However, some aren't that simple. We've included a macro with the samples that returns the address type for any existing entry, so you can use it to create more of this type. If you haven't already got an entry of the type you want, you can create a new one using Exchange's menus and the New Entry dialog.

Try It Out - Finding Address Types in Personal Address Book

For this example, you'll need the template `E-Mail.dot`, which we've supplied in the `\Fields` subfolder of your samples folder. Unless you changed the defaults during installation, this will be `C:\BegWord\Fields`. You'll also need to have Microsoft Exchange installed.

1 If it's not already running, start Exchange by double-clicking it's icon on your desktop. Log on if prompted. This prevents you having to log on and choose a profile when you run the macro.

2 Open the file `E-Mail.dot` from the `\Fields` subfolder of your samples folder. The Wrox Address toolbar will appear. If you can't see it, select Toolbars... from the View menu and place a tick next to it in the list of available toolbars.

3 Click the Get Address Type button. If you have Schedule+ installed, you may be prompted to log on to it, in which case, just click the OK button. The Select Name dialog appears:

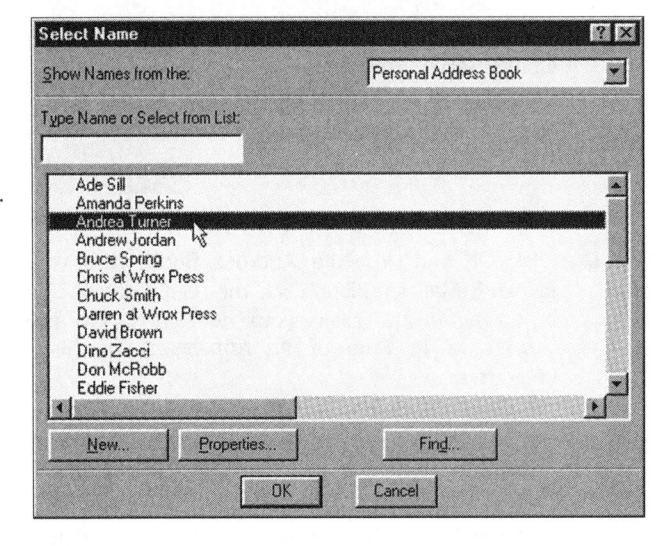

4 Select a name from the list by double-clicking on it. The Select Name dialog closes and a message box shows you the correct value for the `PR_ADDRTYPE` field for that user. In our case, it's an Internet Mail address.

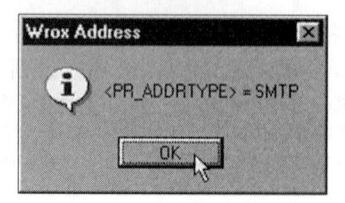

If you have a different service installed, such as CompuServe, you can repeat this to get its address type. If you don't have an existing entry of that type, you just create a new one first ....

5 Switch to Exchange and open the Address Book. In the Address Book dialog click the New Entry toolbar button.

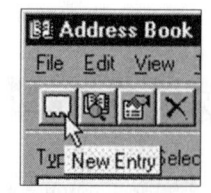

6 In the New Entry dialog select the service you want to find out about. Here, we've chosen CompuServe's own network.

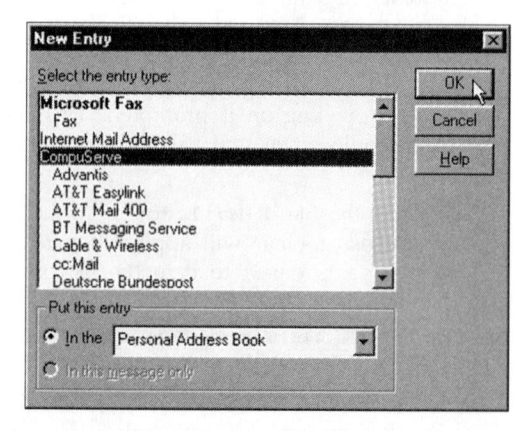

7 Click OK and in the New CompuServe Properties dialog, enter a Display Name and a dummy E-mail Address.

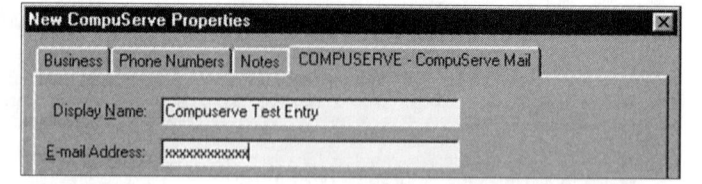

8 Click OK and close the Address Book window. Back in the E-Mail template, click the Get Address Type button again and select your new entry. The message box shows the value of **PR_ADDRTYPE** for this type of address:

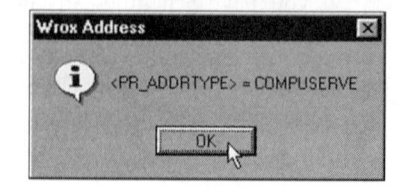

How It Works

This macro is very simple, but uses a WordBasic function we haven't met so far: **GetAddress$()**. This returns an address made up of different fields, or properties. All we have to do is tell it which fields we want. Because we haven't provided a value for the first argument—the display name we're looking for—it automatically displays the Select Name dialog. Once we've chosen a name, it returns the value of the **PR_ADDRTYPE** field, which we can display in a message box.

```
Sub MAIN
    Result$ = GetAddress$("", "<PR_ADDRTYPE>")
    If Result$ <> "" Then
        Msg$ = "<PR_ADDRTYPE> = " + Result$
    Else
        Msg$ = "Entry not found."
    EndIf
    MsgBox Msg$, "Wrox Address", 64
End Sub
```

Retrieving Information from Personal Address Book

So, as well as create new entries, we can also retrieve values from the default address book. In fact, there are two ways we can do this in WordBasic. The simplest one mirrors the actions of the Insert Address button on the Standard toolbar.

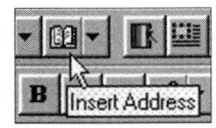

Clicking the main body of the button opens the Select Name dialog, just like the **GetAddressType** macro we used earlier. As before, if you have Schedule+ loaded, you may need to log on first. Once you select an entry, Word inserts the name and address into the active document at the current insertion point. Alternatively, you can click the down-arrow part of the button to open a list of the most recently used names and select one there. In WordBasic, the **InsertAddress** statement carries out the same action as clicking the main part of the button, and takes no arguments.

The GetAddress$() Function

A more complicated but more powerful and flexible way to retrieve information from your default address book is to use the **GetAddress$()** function that you saw in the previous Try It Out. This takes several arguments that control how it finds the address and which dialogs it displays:

> **GetAddress$(**Name$, AddressProperties$, UseAutoText, DisplaySelectDialog, SelectDialog, CheckNamesDialog, MRUChoice, UpdateMRU**)**

Argument	What It Does
Name$	The name to search for.
AddressProperties$	You use this property to specify a list of the fields you want to return. Include **Chr$(13)** to force a new line where required, and enclose text in quotation marks. For example: "<PR_GIVEN_NAME> <PR_SURNAME>" + Chr$(13) + "<PR_STREET_ADDRESS>" + ", " + "<PR_LOCALITY>" Alternatively, you can create the string as an AutoText entry, set the **UseAutoText** argument to **1**, and specify the name of the AutoText entry in **AddressProperties$**. If this argument is omitted altogether, Word looks for the default AutoText entry called **AddressLayout**. If it doesn't find it, it uses a standard layout for the address.

Table Continued on Following Page

Argument	What It Does
UseAutoText	This is used in conjunction with **AddressProperties$**. **0** indicates that **AddressProperties$** specifies the layout of the address book properties. **1** indicates that ithe property contains the name of an AutoText entry that defines the layout.
DisplaySelectDialog	This is used to control whether the Select Name dialog box is displayed. **0** means that it isn't displayed. **1** or omitted means that it is displayed. **2** returns the previously selected address.
SelectDialog	This controls how the Select Name dialog is displayed. **0** or omitted displays the dialog on Browse mode. **1** displays it in Compose mode with just the To: box. **2** displays it in Compose mode with both the To: and CC: boxes.
CheckNamesDialog	This controls whether the Check Names dialog is displayed when the value of **Name$** is not specific enough to completely distinguish an address book entry. **0** means that it will not be displayed at all. **1** or omitted means that it's displayed if required.
MRUChoice	This is used to determine which list of most recently used addresses to use as the address list. **0** or omitted uses the list of delivery addresses. **1** uses the list of return addresses.
UpdateMRU	This controls whether the new address is added to the list of most recently used addresses: **0** or omitted means that they're not added **1** means that they are added.

The **GetAddress$()** function can be difficult to use, and you may have to experiment to get the effect you want. With the current version of Exchange you sometimes find it impossible to suppress the dialog boxes completely. If you use a particular address format regularly, you should consider creating an AutoText entry for it and using its name for the **AddressProperties$** argument. You can generally omit most of the arguments, as we did in the **GetAddressType** macro earlier.

Using Addresses in Your Documents

Having seen the theory behind the **GetAddress$()** function, let's see it in action. This simple example allows you to select which fields you want to include in an address when you insert it into your document, rather than having to accept the defaults set by the Insert Address button on the Standard toolbar.

Chapter 14 - E-mail, Address Books and Mail Merge

Try It Out - Using an Address from Exchange

For this example, you'll need the template **E-Mail.dot**, which we've supplied in the **\Fields** subfolder of your samples folder. Unless you changed the defaults during installation, this will be **C:\BegWord\Fields**. You'll also need to have Microsoft Exchange installed with some addresses available in it.

1 Start Exchange by double-clicking it's icon on your desktop. Log on if prompted. This prevents you having to log on and choose a profile when you run the macro.

2 Open the file **E-Mail.dot** from the **\Fields** subfolder of your samples folder. The Wrox Address toolbar will appear. If you can't see it, select Toolbars... from the View menu and place a tick next to it in the list of available toolbars.

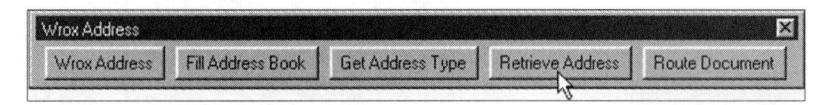

3 Click the Retrieve Address button. If you have Schedule+ installed, you may be prompted to log on to it. If you are, just click the OK button. The macro displays our custom Wrox Address dialog, where you can select a name and specify which fields you want to include in your document.

4 Click OK without entering a name to search for, and the Select Name dialog opens. Select an entry from the list by double-clicking on it.

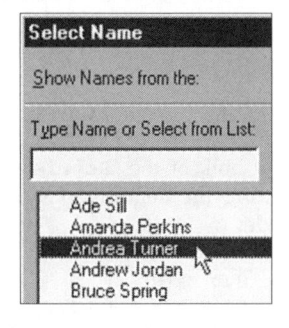

5 The address is inserted into your document at the current insertion point, containing the fields that you ticked in the Wrox Address dialog.

Andrea Turner
475 Lasso Circle
San Ramon
CA
94583

579

6 Now click the Retrieve Address button again, but this time type in part of a name. If you've added the Survey data to your default address book, try dav. Also make sure you tick the E-mail option.

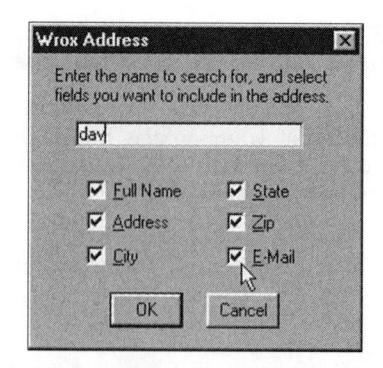

7 Click OK. This time, you'll see the Check Names dialog, because there's more that one name that matches.

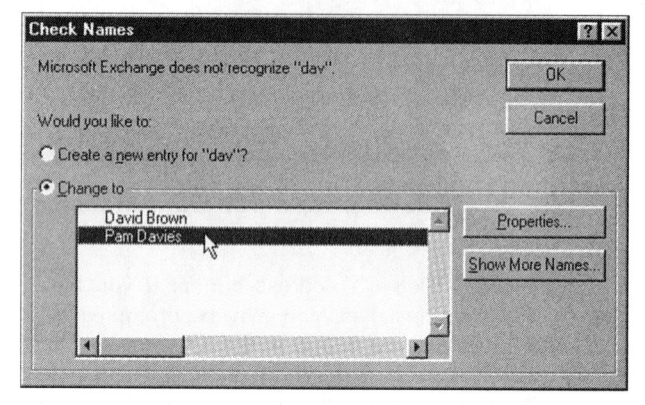

8 Select one of the entries in the Check Names dialog and click OK. Their address, including the E-mail address, is inserted in the document. If there was only one match, Word would have inserted the name without displaying the Check Names dialog.

```
Pam Davies
9 Town & County Village
San Jose
CA
95128
pdavies@fuel.exxon.com
```

How It Works

The bulk of the `RetrieveAddress` macro is concerned with creating the custom dialog and setting the default options for it. These should require no extra explanation by now, so here's the code:

```
Sub MAIN
On Error Goto MAD_Err
Info$ = "Enter the name to search for, and select fields you want to include in
the address."
Begin Dialog UserDialog  100, 50, 300, 180, "Wrox Address"
    Text 20, 6, 270, 42, Info$, .txtInfo              'define the
    TextBox 40, 40, 210, 17, .txtSearch               'custom dialog
    CheckBox 50, 75, 90, 16, "&Full Name", .chkName
    CheckBox 50, 95, 90, 16, "&Address", .chkAddr
    CheckBox 50, 115, 80, 16, "&City", .chkCity
    CheckBox 180, 75, 90, 16, "&State", .chkState
    CheckBox 180, 95, 90, 16, "&Zip", .chkZip
```

```
        CheckBox 180, 115, 90, 16, "&E-Mail", .chkEmail
        OKButton 70, 145, 70, 24
        CancelButton 160, 145, 70, 24
    End Dialog
    Dim dlg As UserDialog                       'declare a dialog record
    dlg.txtSearch = "> Click OK to select a name"  'and set the default
    dlg.chkName = 1                             'values for the controls
    dlg.chkAddr = 1
    dlg.chkCity = 1
    dlg.chkState = 1
    dlg.chkZip = 1
```

Now we display the dialog. If the user clicks OK, we build up the string that defines the address layout we want in the variable **Addr$**. To force each onto a new line, we add a **Chr$(13)** character to the end of the field names:

```
    If Dialog(dlg) Then                         'display the dialog
        Addr$ = ""
        If dlg.chkName Then Addr$ = "<PR_GIVEN_NAME> <PR_SURNAME>" + Chr$(13)
        If dlg.chkAddr Then Addr$ = Addr$ + "<PR_STREET_ADDRESS>" + Chr$(13)
        If dlg.chkCity Then Addr$ = Addr$ + "<PR_LOCALITY>" + Chr$(13)
        If dlg.chkState Then Addr$ = Addr$ + "<PR_STATE_OR_PROVINCE>" + Chr$(13)
        If dlg.chkZip Then Addr$ = Addr$ + "<PR_POSTAL_CODE>" + Chr$(13)
        If dlg.chkEmail Then Addr$ = Addr$ + "<PR_EMAIL_ADDRESS>" + Chr$(13)
```

Now we look at the value in the text box. If it still starts with **>**, we know they want to open the Select Name dialog to search for a name, so we set the value of a variable **DoSearch** to **1**. If they have entered some text, we set **DoSearch** to **0**. This variable is then used as the **DisplaySelectDialog** argument for the **GetAddress$()** function and we insert the result into our document. Because we've omitted the rest of the arguments, **GetAddress$()** will automatically display the Select Name dialog on Browse mode when **DoSearch** is **1**, and show the Check Names dialog if the text is not specific enough to define only one entry. The rest of the macro is just the error-handling code:

```
        If Left$(dlg.txtSearch, 1) = ">" Then
            DoSearch = 1                        'display Select Name dialog
        Else
            DoSearch = 0                        'don't display the dialog
        EndIf
        Insert GetAddress$(dlg.txtSearch, Addr$, 0, DoSearch)
    EndIf
    Goto MAD_Exit
MAD_Err:
    Msg$ = "Cannot retrieve the address :" + Str$(err)
    MsgBox Msg$, "Wrox Address", 48
MAD_Exit:
End Sub
```

Using Word as Your Electronic Mail Editor

So now, if you don't like the look of the standard Exchange interface, you can use WordBasic to create you own routines for managing the entries in your default address book. You can also install Word as the default editor for your e-mail messages. Whether you want to do so depends on the machine that you're using. If you've got less than 16-MB of memory on board, you can find this is a painful process, but it does let you send e-mail which contains all kinds of formatting. But if you just want spell checker functionality, remember that it's already built into the standard Exchange editor.

For more details, search the Word Help file for mail, electronic mail editor and select Using Word as an electronic mail editor. Word also contains a series of statements that will manipulate the messages in your Inbox in this situation. For more details of these statements, search the Word Help file for MailMessage and select the one you want.

Sending Documents with Exchange

Once you've got your contacts' details into Exchange, you can send e-mail and faxes to them very easily. Although WordBasic contains statements which can automate this, more often than not you'll use the normal Word menu commands. There are two commands on Word's File menu that you can use to send documents by e-mail direct from Word: Send... and Add Route Slip... items

Sending E-mail Direct from Word

The File | Send... command is the simplest way to send a document via e-mail. It inserts a copy of your document into a new mail message and you just have to select the recipient by clicking the To: button, and fill in the Subject: and any other text you want. If your document only contains simple text, this is inserted in the body of the message, but if it contains formatting or pictures, it's automatically inserted as an **attachment**, like this:

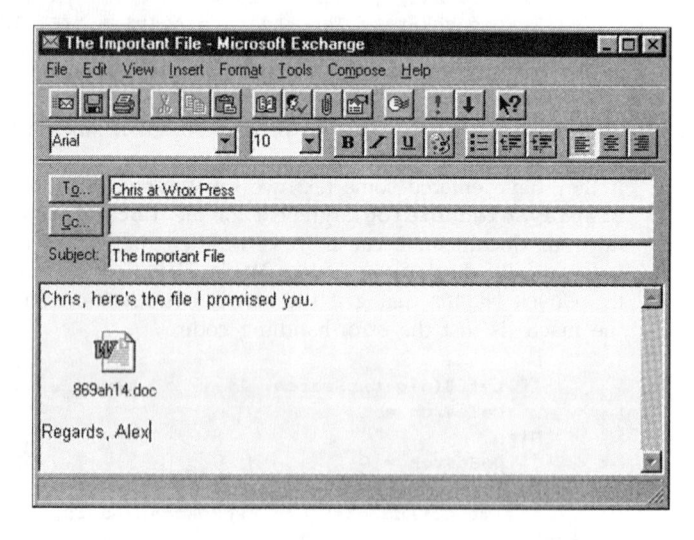

In Word's Options dialog you'll find the Mail as Attachment option. When this is set, your documents are always sent to Exchange as a file that is attached to the message, rather than as normal text. Of course, if you're sending them in rich text format over a service that only supports normal ASCII, like Internet Mail, they will always be sent as an attachment which needs to be encoded appropriately. There's a variety of ways to do this, such as **UUEncodeing**, the details of which would require a book in itself. Exchange will make some attempt to choose an appropriate format, but, quite often, sending files with e-mail is a hit and miss affair.

> Chapter 14 – E-mail, Address Books and Mail Merge

FYI UUEncoding is a method of sending files over a network which only supports text, such as ASCII codes in e-mail. The whole file is translated into a different format which can be safely transmitted as ASCII code, and must be undecoded at the other end. Exchange automatically unencodes files which are received in UUEncoded form.

There is a single WordBasic statement, **FileSendMail**, which mirrors the File | Send... command. It takes no arguments.

Routing a Document from Word

The second option is to **route** a document. This allows you to control who sees the document, in what order, and how they can modify it. You would normally use it when you have several people, such as editors and reviewers, working on a document. To route a document, you choose Add Routing Slip from the File menu.

You can route a document in different ways. Here's an example of a routing slip for a document that has three recipients. We've selected the One After Another option, so each recipient is numbered in the order that they'll see it. Alternatively, we can select All at Once so that they can all work on it at the same time. We've also set the Return When Done and Track Status options so that the document will come back to us when the last person has finished with it, and we'll be automatically informed by e-mail as each person mails it to the next.

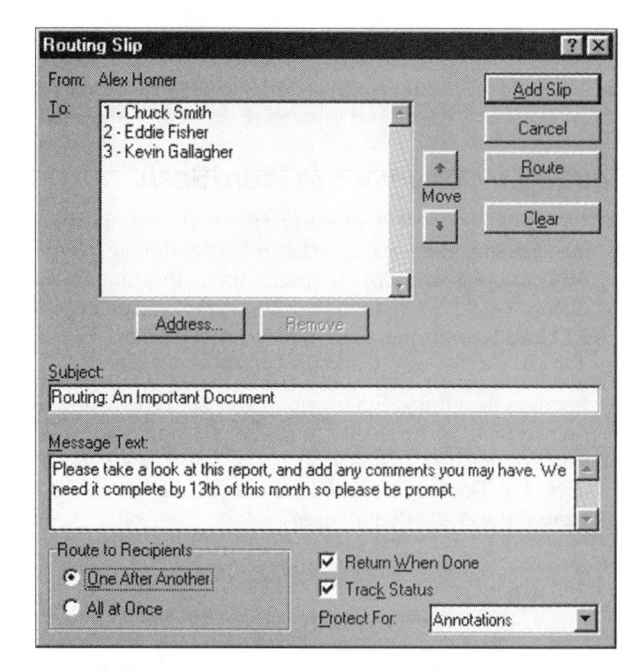

In the lower right-hand corner of the dialog, you can see that we've protected the document for annotations. You can select Revisions, Annotations, Forms or (none) here to specify how the document should be protected. Word automatically applies the protection when the document is sent. We looked at what effect each type of protection has in earlier chapters.

Clicking the Route button sends the document on its way. If you had selected All at Once for the routing method, a copy would be sent to all the recipients. In our case, only one copy is sent—to Chuck Smith, who is the first on the list. Switching to Exchange and opening the new e-mail message reveals that it contains the document itself as an attached file, together with instructions on how the recipient should pass on the document to the next recipient.

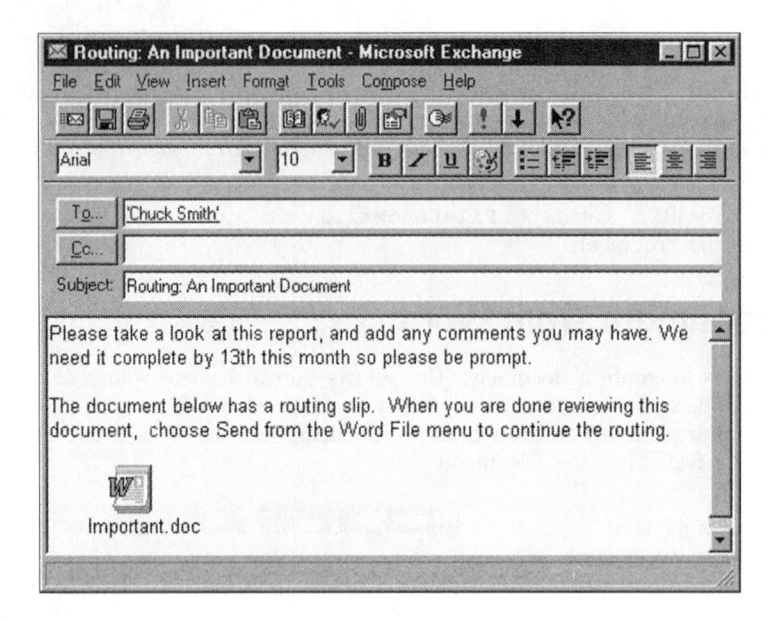

Routing a Document in WordBasic

We can use the `FileRoutingSlip` dialog statement in WordBasic to achieve the same effects as the Routing Slip dialog. The E-Mail template contains a macro for you to try, called `RouteDocument`, which routes the active document in exactly the same way as the Routing Slip dialog. You'll need to have the correct recipients set up in Exchange. You can do this with the `FillAddressBook` example we saw earlier.

Because the Track Status option is set, you'll also have to have your own e-mail address set up in your default address book, so that it can be attached to the document before it's sent. To run the macro, click the Route Document button on the Wrox Address toolbar. Here's the code that it uses:

```
Sub MAIN
    TheSubject$ = "Routing: An Important Document"
    TheMsg$ = "Please take a look at this report . . . be prompt."
    FileRoutingSlip .Subject = TheSubject$, .Message = TheMsg$, \
                    .AllAtOnce = 0, .ReturnWhenDone = 1, \
                    .TrackStatus = 1, .Protect = 2, .AddSlip
    FileRoutingSlip .Address = "Chuck Smith", .AddRecipient
    FileRoutingSlip .Address = "Eddie Fisher", .AddRecipient
    FileRoutingSlip .Address = "Kevin Gallagher", .AddRecipient
    FileRoutingSlip .RouteDocument
End Sub
```

We first use the `FileRoutingSlip` statement to add a new routing slip to the active document. Here, we specify the subject, message text and settings for the various options in the Routing Slip dialog. The statement finishes up with the `AddSlip` argument.

Next, once for each recipient, we use `FileRoutingSlip` with the `AddRecipient` argument and supply their display name for the `Address` argument. Exchange will verify that the address we supply corresponds to an entry in the default address book, or display the Check Names dialog for any it can't find. Remember, you have to have your own address available when the Track Status option is set

Finally, we send the document using `FileRoutingSlip` with the single `RouteDocument` argument. The macro protects the active document for annotations, because we've used `2` for the `Protect` argument. This means that you have to select Unprotect Document from the Tools menu after it's run before you can edit the document again. Of course, you could add the `ToolsUnprotectDocument` statement to the end of the macro to do this automatically if you wish.

The `FileRoutingSlip` statement also accepts arguments for manipulating existing routing slips and removing part or all of the recipient list. For a full list of these arguments, search the Word Help file for the `FileRoutingSlip` statement.

Sending Faxes from Word

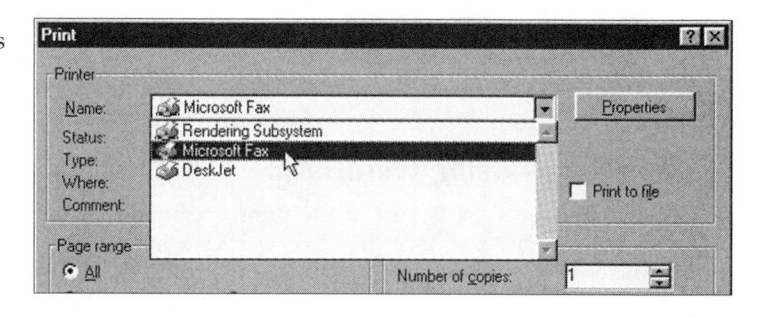

One other way of communicating electronically is by **facsimile** (or **fax** as we all know it). Not everyone has recognized the benefits of e-mail yet, so you may be forced down this 'old-technology' route occasionally! Windows 95 contains the software for managing your faxes, and you can store details of the recipients in your default address book. Microsoft Fax installs itself as a special kind of printer driver, so sending a fax is as easy as selecting Microsoft Fax in the Print dialog.

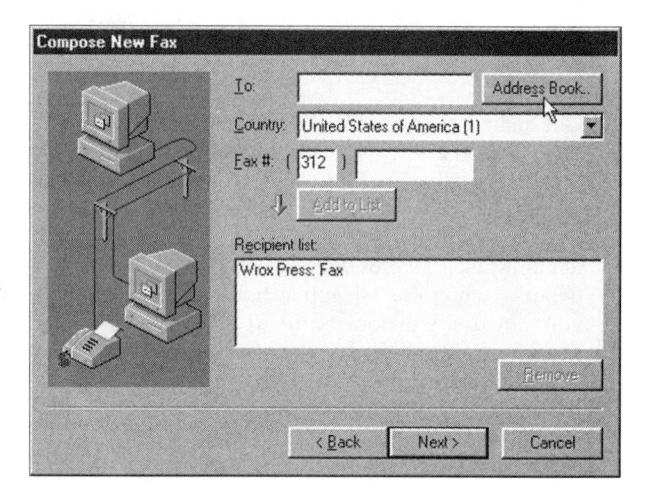

Clicking the OK button then either starts Fax Wizard or opens the Compose New Fax dialog, depending on how you've set up Microsoft Fax. Both contain an Address Book button, where you can select a recipient from your address book, providing that you've already set up the recipient with an address type of FAX. If you select an entry which has a different address type, such as SMTP, Exchange will route the document via that service instead.

585

You can type the recipient's details directly into the Compose New Fax dialog, though, and select more that one recipient if you wish. The faxes are placed in your Outbox in Exchange, and sent automatically. You'll see the Fax Status window showing the progress of each one:

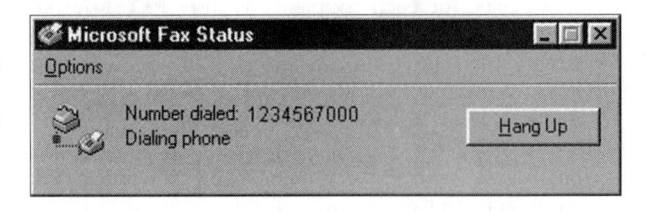

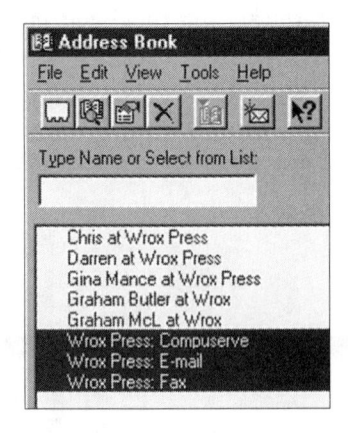

When you add multiple entries for a contact to your default address book, for different address types such as their e-mail address and fax number, you should consider using a display name which reflects the address type. This makes selecting the correct entry much easier.

Sending Faxes Using WordBasic

Because sending a fax is part of the print operation in Word, you can use the normal WordBasic printing methods to achieve the same task in a macro. The only difference is that you have to set Microsoft Fax as the current printer first, using the **FilePrintSetup** statement. Then you can print the document in the normal way. If you want to control which pages are sent, or set other options, you can use the normal **FilePrint** statement instead of **FilePrintDefault**:

```
Sub MAIN
    FaxName$ = "Microsoft Fax on FAX:"
    FilePrintSetup .Printer = FaxName$, .DoNotSetAsSysDefault = 1
    FilePrintDefault
End Sub
```

Our macro changes the current printer for the active Word session to Microsoft Fax, then prints the document using the default settings in the Print dialog. Microsoft Fax becomes the current printer for all your Word documents until you close and restart Word, when it returns to the printer set as your system default.

Omitting the **.DoNotSetAsSysDefault** argument causes Microsoft Fax to be set as the system default printer for all applications, so, if you only want to change the active printer for one fax, you can use a dialog record to get the name of the current printer and then restore it afterwards. You'll find this macro, named **SaveAsFax**, in the **E-Mail.dot** template we've supplied with the sample files:

```
Sub MAIN
    FaxName$ = "Microsoft Fax on FAX:"
    Dim FPS As FilePrintSetup
    GetCurValues FPS
    DefaultPrinter$ = FPS.Printer
    FilePrintSetup .Printer = FaxName$
    FilePrintDefault
    FilePrintSetup .Printer = DefaultPrinter$
End Sub
```

If your set-up differs from the standard one, you can also use this method to get the name of the Microsoft Fax printer system. Simply set Microsoft Fax as your default printer, add a **MsgBox** statement to the macro that displays the value of **DefaultPrinter$**, and run it.

Using Mail Merge with Word

Our final subject in this book is **mail merge**, which, in many ways, brings together the different techniques that we've worked with throughout the book. Mail merge is a very powerful way of maximizing your company's business potential in a competitive world, while minimizing the cost. The trick is to focus your selling efforts towards the people most likely to spend their hard-earned cash on your products.

When you advertise in a general circulation paper or magazine, you can expect only a small proportion of the readers to be interested in what you have to say. By choosing special-interest publications, however, you can target the audience you want more accurately. However, this doesn't even come close to the effect of actually writing personally to those potential customers who you know are most likely to buy. This is why the majority of your morning post consists of 'junk mail', so as you carelessly toss it unread into the bin, just remember that you've been specially chosen to receive that letter!

What is Mail Merge?

The theory behind mail merge is very simple, and it's been around in various forms for a long time. However, modern applications like Word can produce mail-merged letters which are far more attractive and personalized than some of the older systems. Using mail merge, you take a **data source**, which can be anything from a spreadsheet or database file to a normal Word document or a text file, and produce a separate letter or other document for each **record** in it. So, if your address list in Access has 200 entries, you can produce a **form letter** to everyone in one go, rather than having to type or copy 200 different addresses.

However, mail merge can do a lot more than that. Instead of just letters, you can print envelopes, labels, or lists of any kind, or send the text as a fax or an e-mail message. In fact, the possibilities are almost boundless. The figure on the following page shows you just some of them.

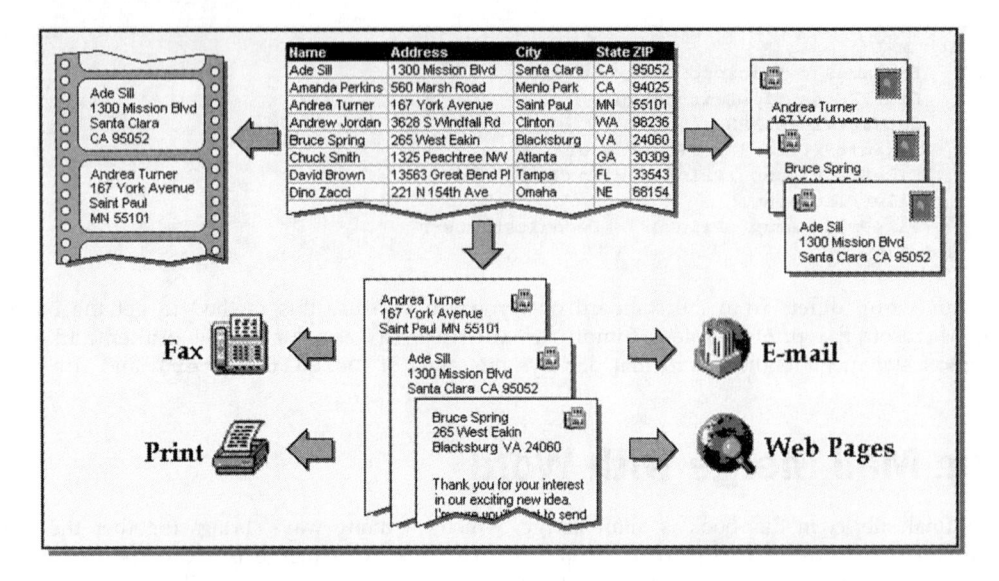

Mail merge works by inserting fields into a main document. These are a special type of field called a {MERGEFIELD}, and refer to a particular field (or column) in the file which forms the data source. For example, if the data source contains a field named **FullName**, we could insert a field in our document like this,

    { MERGEFIELD FullName * charformat }

to display the value of **FullName** for each record. (Notice the distinction here between *field* as the thing between two 'curly brackets' in a Word document, and *field* as the 'column' of data in the data source.)

In the way that the values they display actually appear, the fields you use in the Word document behave like all other fields. You can also use the normal formatting arguments with them. In our example above, we've added the *** charformat** argument to make sure that the values are displayed in the same font and style as the rest of the text in the document.

Using Mail Merge with Our Survey Data

We've supplied you with an example of how mail merge can be used. You can try this out, then experiment by adding different fields to the main document or by using different data sources. We have based the data for the mail merge on the query we created in an earlier chapter in Access. However, using Access as the data source directly can be slow, especially if you have less than 16-MB of memory on your system, and unless you purchased Office 95 Professional, you may not even have Access available.

So, instead we've exported the results of the Access **MakeAddressList** query to a text file called **Merge.txt**, using the Microsoft Word merge format. This is basically a tab-separated file, but with text values enclosed in quotation marks. The format is recognized by Word and makes the mail merge operation a lot quicker. If you want to use Access instead, you can choose this as the data source instead of our text file. Using Word to do a mail merge is very flexible because of the many forms with which it can accept data into the document.

Try It Out - Setting Up a Mail Merge from the Survey Data

For this example, you'll need the template **MailMerge.dot**, which we've supplied in the **\Fields** subfolder of your samples folder. Unless you changed the defaults during installation, this will be **C:\BegWord\Fields**. On some systems this example may fail and give you a warning that the data file we'll be using is in an unexpected format. The most likely explanation for this will be the presence of the Microsoft Desktop Database driver for text files and the absence of Word's own text file converter. In case you do have these problems we have supplied a second text file that uses a comma-separated format called **MergeCom.txt**.

1 Open the file **MailMerge.dot** from the **\Fields** subfolder of your sample folder. Then select Mail Merge... from the Tools menu to open the Mail Merge Helper dialog. This is the nerve-center for setting up a mail merge operation.

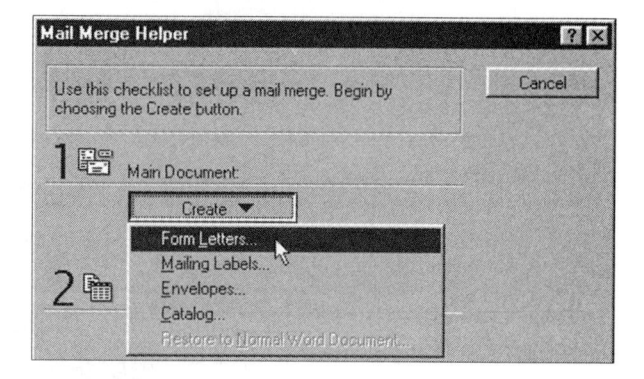

2 Click the Create button in the Main Document section, and select Form Letters. Word asks if you want to use the current document, or create a new one. Select Active Window to use the current document.

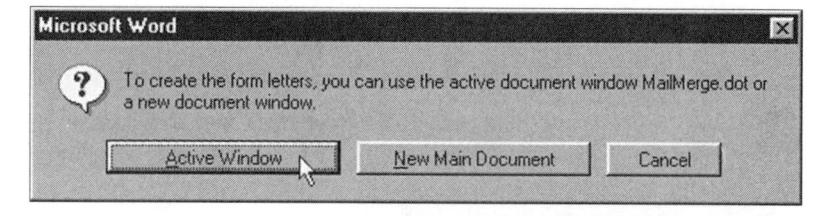

3 Back in the Mail Merge Helper dialog, we now need to select the data source. Click the Get Data button and select Open Data Source....

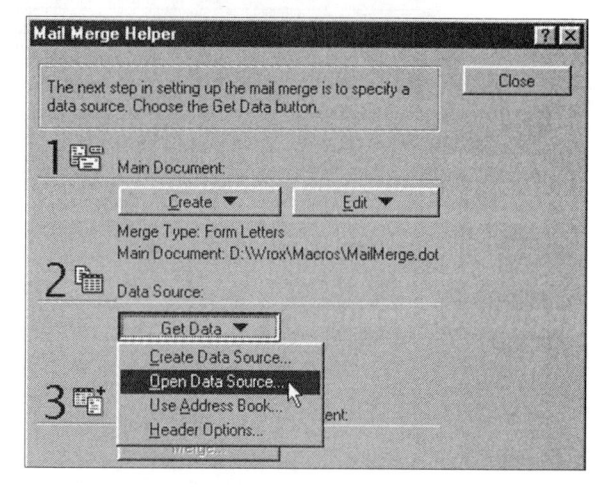

4 In the Open Data Source dialog, change the Files of type: to Text Files (*.txt) and select the file **Merge.txt** from the **\Fields** subfolder of your samples folder.

5 Back in Mail Merge Helper again, we can now select which records from the data source we want to include in the mail merge. Click the Query Options button and set the options as below so that we only include records for people who use Lotus applications and have read our book about word-processing.

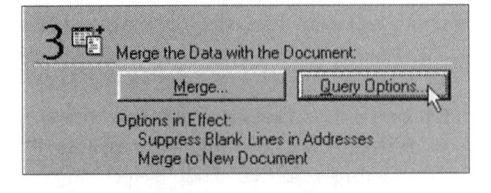

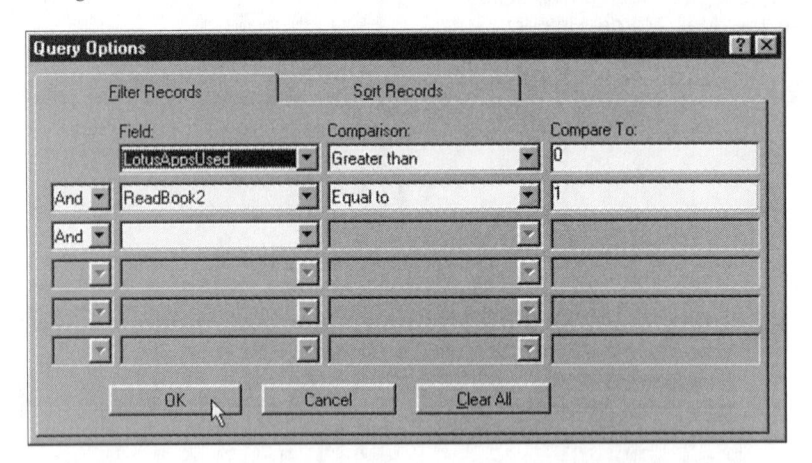

6 Now we're ready to start the mail merge, but first close the Mail Merge Helper dialog and look at the document. It contains fields such as «FullName» and «Address» at the top, plus a few in the body of the letter. Word has also displayed the Mail Merge toolbar.

7 Click the View Merged Data button, and now the fields in the document are replaced by the data from the first record in our data file.

Complete Computer Books inc.
1230 East 42nd Street, Chicago, IL 17565
Tel: 211-654-1234   Fax: 211-654-1235   E-Mail: compbook.com

Your one-stop shop for the best in computer books

Zuned Kasu
84 Golfwood
Bellwin
MO 63021

May 11, 1996

Dear Reader,

Thank you for your help with our recent reader survey. The results will assist us in making our books even better, and you can be sure we will be letting you know about all the new developments. In fact Martin in our sales department is waiting by the phone to hear from you.

As a regular user of a computer both at home and work for e-mail and the internet I am sure you appreciate just how important it is to keep up to date with new applications. And although we have not provided much support for Lotus applications in the past, you will be pleased to know that we have a new title on the way - especially designed for Lotus application users like you. And we'll make sure that it's available from a book shop in Bellwin so that you can

8 Click the arrow buttons on the toolbar to scroll through the records. You'll see the name and address change, and if you keep your eye on the second paragraph you'll also see the first and last lines of this change, reflecting where that reader uses their computer, what they use it for and the town where the book shop is located.

9 First, we'll print the letters. Click the Merge To Printer button on the Mail Merge toolbar. Word opens the standard Print dialog where you can select the printer you want to send them to.

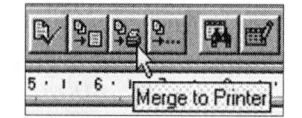

FYI You can select Microsoft Fax or your own fax driver here, but if you do, you'll have to enter the fax number for each person as they are merged. We'll see a better way to do this later on.

10 Click OK in the print dialog, and a dialog prompts you for the name of the person who will be manning the sales desk for this title. Enter a name and click OK. Don't press *Return*. You have to click the OK button with the mouse. The result: nine letters ready to be mailed!

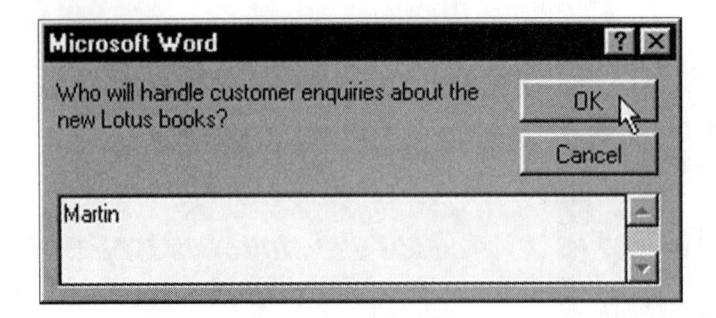

What We've Done

The result of our mail merge is nine letters that appear similar, except for the name and address, but have other subtle differences. As we perform the mail merge, the fields in the main document display the values from the records in the data source file. By placing Word {MERGEFIELD} fields at strategic points in the document, we can make it seem like we are writing a personalized letter.

When you collect data for future mail merging, bear this in mind to make sure you get the maximum benefit. For example, we only used one field in our Survey file for the reader's name, rather than storing their forename and surname separately. If we had done so, we could have used a {MERGEFIELD} at the beginning of the letter to include their name, rather than just Dear Reader.

Here's how the main document looks before you view the merged data. Most of the fields are visible, though there are some that are displaying their result. The name of the salesperson is shown, but, as you saw in the example, it's only set when you start the actual mail merge. The first line of the second paragraph shows where the reader uses their computer, rather than the field itself:

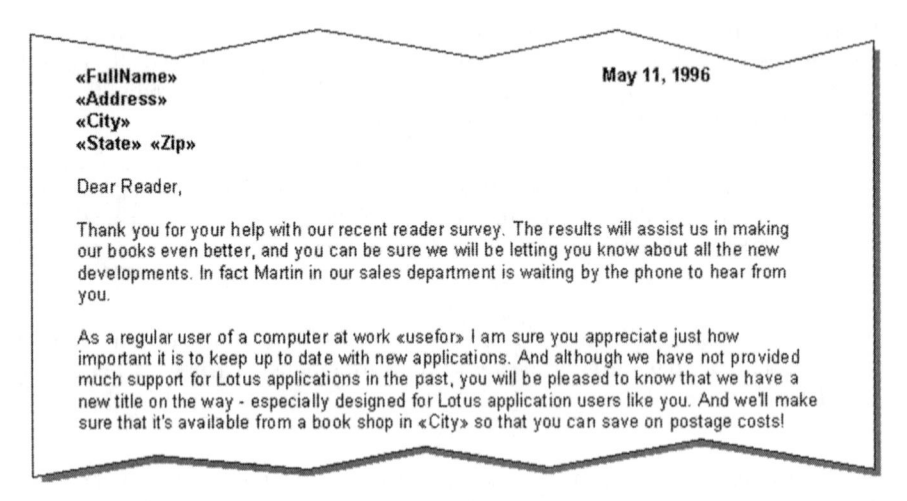

«FullName»   May 11, 1996
«Address»
«City»
«State» «Zip»

Dear Reader,

Thank you for your help with our recent reader survey. The results will assist us in making our books even better, and you can be sure we will be letting you know about all the new developments. In fact Martin in our sales department is waiting by the phone to hear from you.

As a regular user of a computer at work «usefor» I am sure you appreciate just how important it is to keep up to date with new applications. And although we have not provided much support for Lotus applications in the past, you will be pleased to know that we have a new title on the way - especially designed for Lotus application users like you. And we'll make sure that it's available from a book shop in «City» so that you can save on postage costs!

This is because these two fields are not simple {MERGEFIELD} types. To get the result we want, we've used normal Word fields, but included the {MERGEFIELD} within them. The next figure shows how the document appears when you press *Alt-F9* to display all the field codes:

```
{ MERGEFIELD FullName \* charformat}          { TIME \@ "d MMMM, yyyy" }
{ MERGEFIELD Address \* charformat }
{ MERGEFIELD City \* charformat }
{ MERGEFIELD State \* charformat } { MERGEFIELD Zip \* charformat }

Dear Reader,

Thank you for your help with our recent reader survey. The results will assist us in making
our books even better, and you can be sure we will be letting you know about all the new
developments. In fact { FILLIN "Who will handle customer enquiries about the new Lotus
books?" \o \d "the staff" } in our sales department is waiting by the phone to hear from you.

As a regular user of a computer { IF { MERGEFIELD UseWhere } = "Both" "both at home
and work" { MERGEFIELD UseWhere \* Lower \* charformat }} { MERGEFIELD UseFor \*
Lower \* charformat } I am sure you appreciate just how important it is to keep up to date with
new applications. And although we have not provided much support for Lotus applications in
the past, you will be pleased to know that we have a new title on the way - especially
designed for Lotus application users like you. And we'll make sure that it's available from a
book shop in { MERGEFIELD City \* charformat } so that you can save on postage costs!
```

The date field is one you've seen before, and the reader's name and address at the head of the letter is simply made up of the appropriate fields from the data source. The `\* charformat` argument prevents Word changing the font or style from those we used to format the main document. This can often happen when you merge from a text file, so you should always include it unless you actually want the style of the source to be used instead. In the body of the letter, we've also repeated the «City» field, and used the field:

{ MERGEFIELD UseFor * Lower * charformat }

to display the place where the reader uses their computer. Notice here we've added the * Lower argument because the text in the file starts with a capital letter and we want all lower-case. The other two fields are more complicated than this. To display the place the computer is used we've used the {IF} field, which you first saw in Chapter 11. Why? Well, the text file contains just the word Both when the computer is used at home and at work. This won't fit in with our letter, so we need to change it. The field we've used is:

{ IF { MERGEFIELD UseWhere } = "Both" "both at home and work " { MERGEFIELD UseWhere * Lower * charformat }}

This checks the value of the UseWhere field in the data source for that record, and if it's Both, it displays the text we want, both at home and work. If it isn't Both, it just displays the value from the UseWhere field, again in lowercase.

Remember from Chapter 11 that the values displayed in a field aren't changed until you update the field, either by opening or printing the document, or by pressing F9. During a mail merge operation Word reads the values from the current record and updates all the fields in the document automatically, so they reflect the values for the current record. Each time a new record is read, the values in the field change. This is why mail merge can produce different letters from one document.

However, the real power is in the use of 'intelligent' fields, like the {IF} field in our document. The other intelligent field we've used is one you haven't seen in this book so far: the {FILLIN} field. And it has a similar stable-mate, the {ASK} field. Both of these are designed for mail merge, though you can also use them in **forms**.

Prompting for a Value when a Field is Updated

The {ASK} and {FILLIN} fields are very similar. When they are updated, they can display a prompt where you either accept the default text, or type in a new value. This value can then be used in the document, and because all the fields are updated at the beginning of a mail merge, the prompt is displayed then.

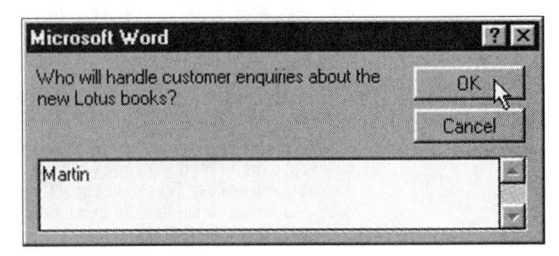

The difference between the fields is what they do with their result. The {FILLIN} field places it directly in the document, where the field itself is located. The {ASK} field stores it in a bookmark, the name of which you provide in the field. In a mail merge operation, both of them can be set to prompt once only, at the start of the merge, or once for every record.

```
{ FILLIN "Prompt" Switches }
{ ASK BookmarkName "Prompt" Switches }
```

Prompt is the text you want to display as the prompt in the in the dialog box, and *BookmarkName* is the name of the bookmark where you want to store the result of an {ASK} field. *Switches* can be any of the appropriate formatting switches, plus two special ones:

Switch	What It Does
\d "Default"	Specifies the default result if nothing is entered in the dialog.
\o	Only displays the prompts once at the start of the mail merge operation, instead of once for every record.

If you want to display the value you get from the user in more than one place in the same document, you should use an {ASK} field and reference the bookmark in all the places where you want the result. If you try to do this by placing more than one {FILLIN} field in a document, you'll be prompted once for every occurrence of the field. In our example we want to prompt for the name of the salesperson who is handling the new book. We used the field:

```
{ FILLIN "Who will handle customer inquiries about the new book?" \o \d "the staff" }
```

This prompts for the salesperson's name, using a default value of "**the staff**". We included the **\o** switch so it's only displayed once. However, as you'll see in the next example, this switch may not have any effect during a merge to Exchange.

Inserting Fields into a Main Document

You can insert any of the mail-merge specific fields, and others, using Word's menu commands. There are also buttons on the Mail Merge toolbar which insert the various mail merge fields into your document. To insert fields from the data source, you simply click Insert Merge Field and select them from the list. To insert other types of field, you can still use the normal Insert | Field... command, but the Insert Word Field button on the Mail Merge toolbar also handles the most popular mail merge fields.

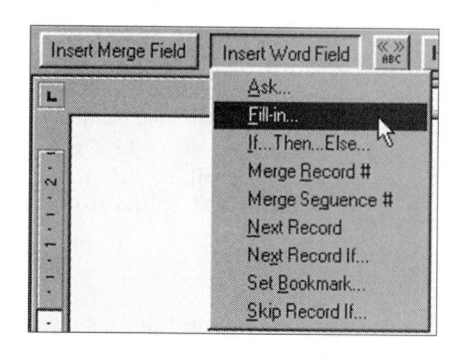

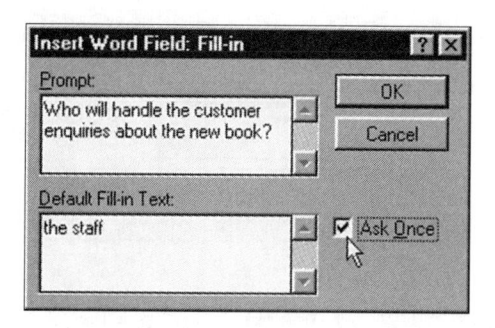

For example, you can use this button to insert the {ASK} and {FILLIN} fields rather than typing them in directly. A dialog lets you fill in all the details and specify whether to prompt once only or once for each merged document.

The other types of field you can see on this list are used to display specific information in the document about the merge, such as the record number, and control which records are included. For example, you can skip a record if the value in a particular field meets some condition. If you only want to send your document to readers in California, you can use the Skip Record If dialog to insert a field which does just that.

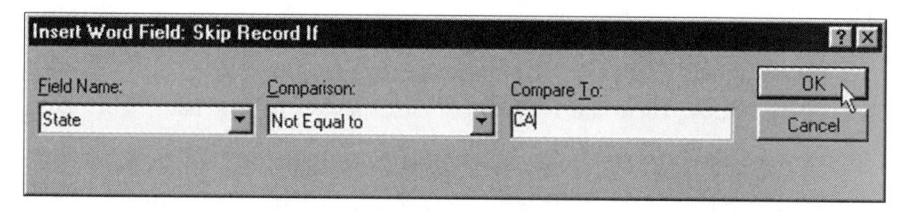

Having seen how mail merge works, it's time to consider how we can send the document as directed e-mail or faxes instead of paying for postage.

Try It Out - Sending Mail-merged Documents by E-mail

You'll need the MailMerge template that you created in the previous example, with the data source and query options set up. To send the results as e-mail, you'll also need to have Microsoft Exchange installed with the addresses from our Survey file available in it. The `FillAddressBook` macro will have done this for you in an earlier example.

1 If you've closed the MailMerge template from the previous example, open it again. Then open the Merge dialog with the button on the Mail Merge toolbar.

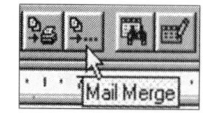

2   Here we can select how we want the merged letters to be sent. We could merge them to a new document or to the printer like the last example. However, we want to send them as e-mail, so select the Electronic Mail option from the list.

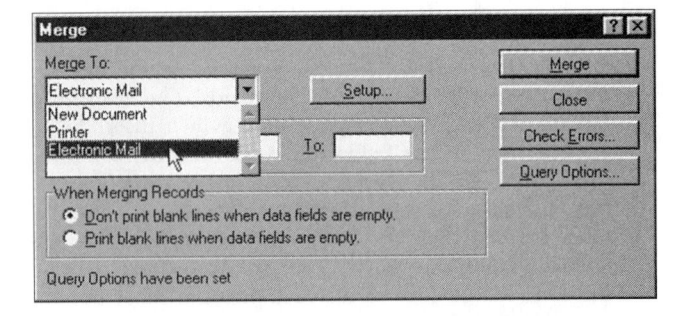

3   Click the Setup button to open the Merge To Setup dialog. We have to tell Word which field in the data source contains the display name we want it to use when the documents are sent to Exchange. Select the FullName field and enter the text for the Subject line of the message. Make sure you uncheck the Send Document as an Attachment option, then click OK.

4   Back in the Merge dialog, we're ready to go. Click the Merge button and Word displays the prompt for the salesperson. Enter a name and click OK.

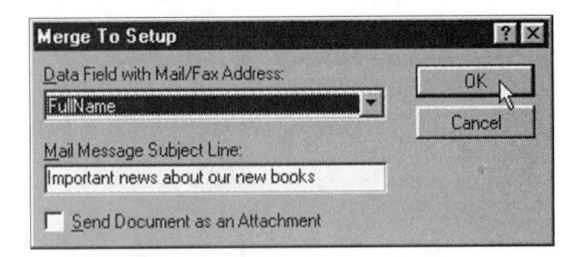

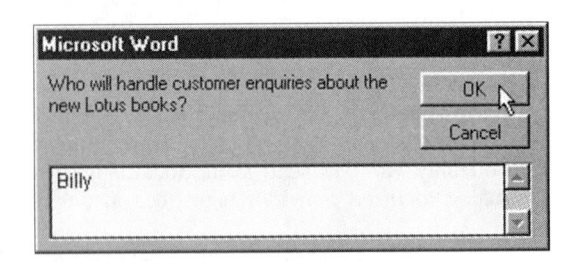

5   Merging the data this time takes a little longer, but when it's complete, open Exchange and look in your Outbox. There are nine e-mail messages ready to send.

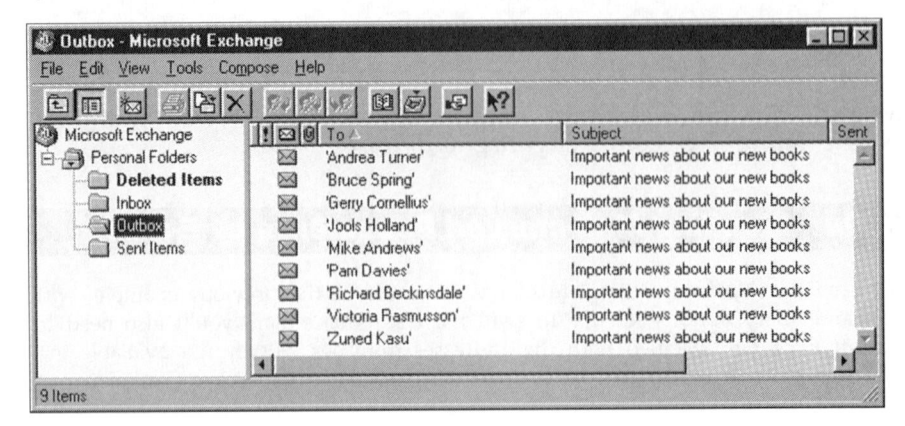

> **FYI** Depending on how you have Exchange set up, you may be prompted to log on to Exchange and select your profile. You may also be asked for the name of the salesperson for each message, instead of just once. This appears to be a problem related to the Word/Exchange interface in the present versions.

6 Open one of the messages by double-clicking on it. You'll see that Word has removed all the graphics and formatting and just included the text. It's not very tidy, but the layout was designed for printing rather than using e-mail. If you know that you're only going to e-mail them, you can design the main document to suit.

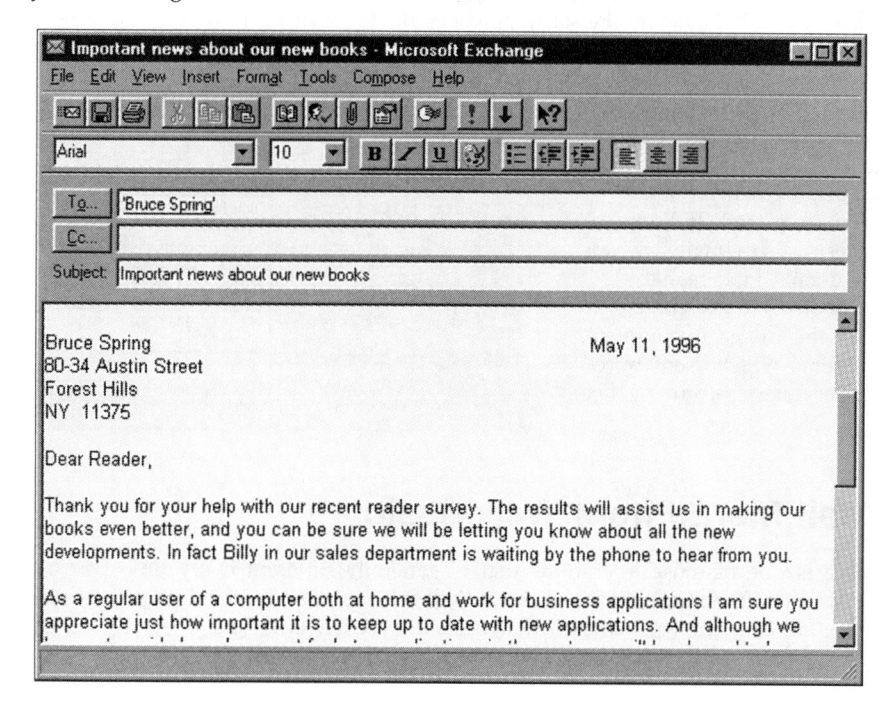

How It Works

The only difference between this example and the previous one is where we send the merged documents. The Merge dialog allows us to select Electronic Mail instead of a Printer or New Document. In order for Word to be able to create the mail messages, we have to tell it who to send them to. We do this by setting up their names and e-mail addresses in Exchange first, then in the Merge To Setup dialog, we select the field in the data source which contains the display name we've used in Exchange.

For example, we used Bruce Spring as the display name in Exchange when we created his entry in our Personal Address Book. (The `FillAddressBook` macro we described earlier in this chapter did this automatically.) In our data source, the record for this reader contains Bruce Spring in the `FullName` field. This is why we selected the `FullName` field in the Merge To Setup dialog. If we had selected the `Email` field, Exchange would have created a generic e-mail entry with that address, but not known which service to send it by. This is only likely to succeed on a Local Area Network (LAN), and is not specific enough for use where you have several services available.

In this example, we sent our documents as text-only e-mail messages. If you want to send them as formatted text, as an attachment to the message, you can use the Merge To Setup dialog to specify this. All you need to do is set the Send Document as Attachment option while you have this dialog open.

Sending Merged Documents by Fax

You've probably realized by now how we send our documents by fax instead of e-mail. Remember from our discussion of Personal Address Book and Exchange that you have to specify the **address type** when you create an entry. All our readers' entries are set up as Internet Mail, but we could just as easily have specified them as Microsoft Fax. In fact the `FillAddress` macro that inserted them into Personal Address Book could be changed to create them as fax entries instead of SMTP.

Then, when you perform the mail merge and place the resulting documents in Exchange, they will automatically be sent as faxes rather than as e-mail. If Eddie Fisher doesn't use e-mail, we can enter his details in Personal Address Book as a fax entry. Then after the merge is complete, the documents will be sent by e-mail to everyone else, but by fax to Eddie.

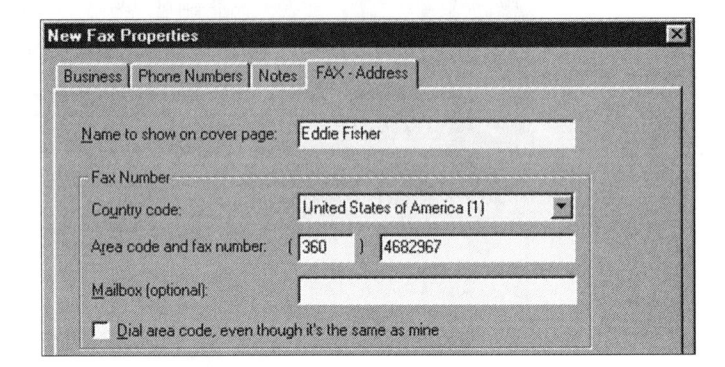

Using Mail Merge from WordBasic

Mail merge is one of those operations that is generally different every time you use it. You will probably use a different main document and data source, and different query options. These settings are stored with your document template, so each time you open it you can just start the merge. If the data source can't be found when you open the document, Word will prompt you to locate it.

However, you can write macros that convert a normal document into a mail merge-ready one, rather than using the Mail Merge Helper dialog. WordBasic contains almost 40 statements and functions which mirror the various dialogs, menu commands and buttons.

You can insert the special mail merge fields into a document using the `InsertMergeField` statement, which just takes the name of the field in the data source as an argument:

```
InsertMergeField .MergeField = "FullName"
```

The easiest way to create a macro that sets up a mail merge and then carries it out is to use the macro recorder to record the actions you take in Mail Merge Helper and modify the result. Here's the equivalent to the actions we took in setting up our Survey mail merge in the previous example. We recorded it, then removed some of the arguments that we don't need to specify (because we're accepting their default values):

```
Sub MAIN

    'Make the active window a Form Letters mail merge main document
    MailMergeMainDocumentType 0

    'Open the data source and attach it to the main document
    MailMergeOpenDataSource .Name = "C:\BegWord\Fields\Merge.txt", \
                    .LinkToSource = 1

    'Set the Query Options with an SQL statement
    SQL$ = "SELECT * FROM C:\BegWord\Fields\Merge.txt WHERE "
    SQL$ = SQL$ + "((LotusAppsUsed > 0) AND (ReadBook2 = 1))"
    MailMergeQueryOptions .SQLStatement = SQL$, .SQLStatement = ""

    'Start the merge to Electronic Mail
    MailMerge .CheckErrors = 1, .Destination = 2, .MergeRecords = 0, \
            .From = "", .To = "", .Suppression = 0, .MailMerge, \
            .MailSubject = "Exciting news about our new book", \
            .MailAsAttachment = 0, .MailAddress = "FullName"

End Sub
```

You can see that the statements reflect the options and settings for each section of the Mail Merge Helper dialog:

MailMergeMainDocumentType 0 is equivalent to clicking the Create button in the Main Document section and selecting Form Letters.

MailMergeOpenDataSource .Name = "C:\BegWord\Fields\Merge.txt", .LinkToSource = 1 is equivalent to clicking the Get Data button, selecting Open Data Source and selecting the Merge.txt file

MailMergeQueryOptions .SQLStatement = SQL$, .SQLStatement = ""** is equivalent to clicking the Query Options button and setting the conditions for including the records in the merge. In our example, we've set the equivalent SQL statement in a variable **SQL$, and specified it as the **SQLStatement** argument. (Like most WordBasic statements that accept SQL strings, if the statement is longer than 255 characters, you have to split it in two and use **SQLStatement1** for the remainder.)

Finally, we can start the merge. The **MailMerge** statement is equivalent to the Merge button in Mail Merge Helper, and takes a variety of arguments equivalent to the options in the Merge and Merge To Setup dialogs. In our example, we've specified **CheckErrors = 1** so that any errors are reported during the merge, **.Destination = 2** to specify Electronic Mail, **MergeRecords = 0** to include all the records which match our query, **From = ""** and **To = ""** because we don't want to specify a start and end record, **Suppression = 0** to prevent blank lines being printed where the fields are empty, and **MailMerge** as the command to carry out the merge operation. If we omit this, the statement will set the options but not start the merge.

The other three arguments to the **MailMerge** statement are only used when the destination is Electronic Mail. **MailSubject = "Exciting news about our new book"** specifies the subject line for the messages, **MailAsAttachment = 0** sends them as text-only, and **MailAddress = "FullName"** specifies the field in the data source which contains the Display Name we've set up in Exchange.

For a full list of all the WordBasic statements and functions, search the Word Help file on mail merge, WordBasic statements and functions and select Mail Merge Statements and Functions.

Summary

In this final chapter, we've continued to work with the information that we have to give our business a competitive advantage. Modern communication methods are slowly making letter writing a thing of the past, and Word can help you switch to the electronic future by sending documents as e-mail messages and faxes. As you are typing your latest novel, or writing that sales report, you only have to hit the New button on the toolbar, type a memo, and select Send from the File menu. Word creates the electronic message, prompts for the address, and with a single click it's on the way, either by e-mail or fax.

Centralizing your contact information in Exchange also allows you to use mail merge with e-mail and fax. You can specifically target potential customers, rapidly distribute urgent information to selected people, or send all the members of your tennis club an invitation to the annual dinner. The possibilities are endless.

In this chapter, we've looked at:

- How Windows 95 can link Word to the electronic world outside
- How to manage your contacts and send e-mail and faxes directly from Word
- How mail merge can help you to target your documents for maximum effect

By now, you should be a lot more comfortable with Word as a development environment, not just as a word processor. In fact, we've really only just scratched the surface in this book. You can now go on to develop business solutions that would, perhaps, have previously seemed impossible.

Chapter 14 – E-mail, Address Books and Mail Merge

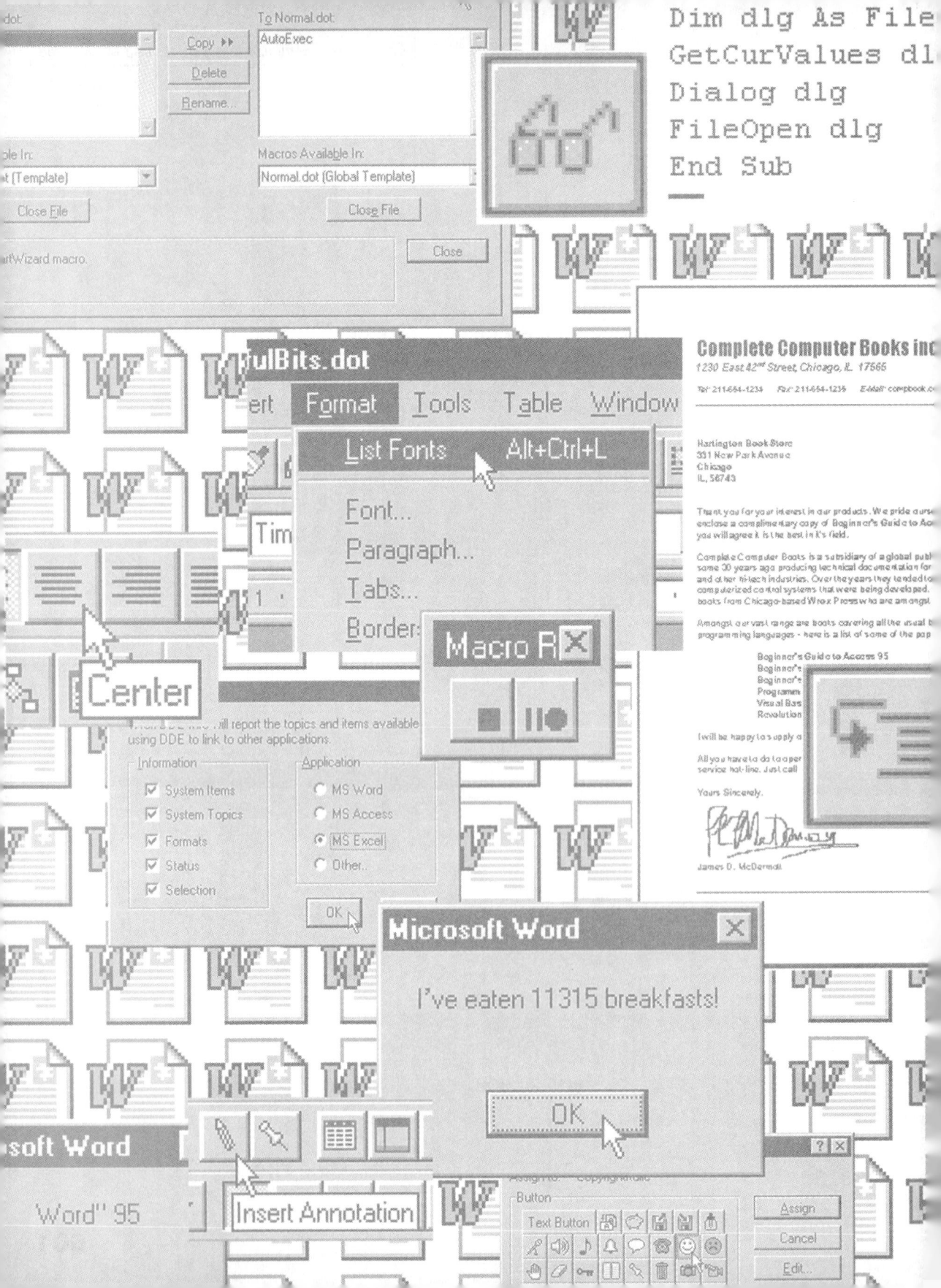

```
Dim dlg As File
GetCurValues dl
Dialog dlg
FileOpen dlg
End Sub
```

Beginning WordBasic Programming

Index

Symbols

#, topic identifier footnote 340
$, functions returning a string value 56
$, topic title footnote 341
%, hotspots, changing appearance of 386
*, hot spots, changing appearance of 386
*, numeric operator 44
* MERGEFORMAT, EMBED switches 542
+, numeric operator 44
+, string concatenation operator 44
-, numeric operator 44
.csv, comma-delimited files 490
.doc, normal document files 14
.dot, template files 14
.gid, help file 376
.htm 281
.html 281
.ini 167
.rtf, rich text files 332
.txt, comma-delimited files 490
.txt, tab-delimited files 491
.wiz, wizard files 210
.wks, Excel files 522
.wll, add-ins 19
.zip, zip files 213
/, numeric operator 44
:, index entry levels 251

;, keyword separator 354
<, comparison operator 44
<=, comparison operator 44
<>, comparison operator 44
=, comparison operator 44
>, comparison operator 44
>, footnote for default window 354
>, hot spots, specifying window to jump to 386
>=, comparison operator 44

A

A footnote 360
\a, LINK switches 543
A-Link macro 360
    jumping to a topic in another Help file 389
Access
    Wrox survey results 501
        inserting into a document 536
Action 124
ActivateObject 547
active template 14
add-ins 211
    .wll 19
    AddAddIn() 61
    AddInState() 61
    ClearAddIns() 61
    CountAddIns() 61
AddAddIn() 61

AddAddress 568, 570
AddButton 439
AddInState() 61
address book
    default 566, 568
    Electronic Mail editor 581
    entries
        creating from existing data 571
        finding correct address type 575
        using in a document 578
    field names 570
    retrieving information 577
    using 566
AddThisAddress() 573, 574
Alias 366
AllTheControls 113, 117
AND 45
annotations 241, 245
API 218
    calls
        GetDriveType() 220, 222
        GetVolumeInformation() 223, 224
        MakeDriveList() 226
    Gdi32.dll 219
    Help files
        opening from an application 406
    Kernel32.dll 219
    procedures 225
    Shell32.dll 219
    User32.dll 219
    Win32 API 219
    Winmm.dll 219

AppActivate 299
AppIsRunning() 512
Application 191, 195, 203
Application Programming
            Interface. see API
applications 187
    distributing 32
        macros, encrypting 32
    help contents, browsing and
                            running 326
    Help files
        linking to 405
        opening from application 406
    what is a Word application? 7
    Wrox DDE Info 521
AppShow 560
arguments 57
    named 59
    optional 59
    passing by value 58
    passing by reference 58
    using with functions and
                    subroutines 51
arrays 40
    declaration 42
    multi-dimensional 41
        declaration 42
    resizing
        ReDim 42
    turning into tables 74
ASK field 594
AtEndOfDocument() 141
AtStartOfDocument() 105, 141
attachment 582
AuditLog.txt 553
Auto Indexing 251
AutoClose 179, 247
AutoCorrect 22
AutoExec 179
    protection from viruses 432
AutoExit 179
AutoMacros 434, 436
AutoMarkIndexEntries 251, 257
AutoNew
179, 235, 247, 290, 295, 498

AutoOpen
179, 210, 247, 422, 498
    protection from viruses 432
AutoText 165, 216
    Zip Manager 218
AutoTextName$() 165

B

\b, DATABASE switches 543
\b, LINK switches 543
BBFunction() 129
Begin Dialog UserDialog 112
BetterBox$() 120
BetterInputBox 120
BlankWiz.dot 190
block quotes 284
    web page lists
        definition 288
        ordered 285
        unordered 285
bml commands 366
body 280
Bold() 63
Book Order.dot 211
BOOKMARK field 457
bookmarks 153
    adding, deleting and going to 154
    comparing 157
    copying and editing 156
    definition 153
    going to a point in a document 158
    ROWx 500
    stepping through a document 159
    Word's predefined, list of 156
BorderBottom 81
break points, setting 71
browser 297
buffer 223
BuildDocumentIndex 257
built-in dialogs 11, 98
    displaying 102
        Dialog 102
built-in functions 11, 14, 47

AppIsRunning() 512
arguments 51
AtEndOfDocument() 141
AtStartOfDocument() 105, 141
AutoTextName$() 165
Bold() 63
CharColor() 145
CharLeft() 137
Chr$() 91
CmpBookmarks 158, 558
common, list of 52
CountAutoTextEntries() 165
CountDocumentVar$() 166
CountFonts() 79
dates and nesting functions 54
DDEInitiate() 512
DDERequest$() 515
Default$() 262
Dialog() 106, 119, 123
difference between a function
            and a statement 51
DisableAutoMacros() 437
DlgText$() 130, 133
DlgText() 146
EditFind() 160
EditFindFound() 151, 160, 256
Eof() 495, 499
executing directly 11
File$() 84, 424
FilePrint() 264
FilePrintDefault() 264
Font$() 79, 145
FontSize() 145
GetAddress$() 576, 581
    arguments 577
GetAutoText$() 165
GetDocumentVar$() 166
GetDocumentVarName$() 166
GetPrivateProfileString$() 167
GetPrivateProfileString() 262
HighlightColor() 145
InputBox$() 93
Instr() 515
Int() 77

IsAppRunning() 522
IsExecuteOnly() 443
Italic() 51
Left$() 51, 98
Len() 62, 98
LTrim$() 208
MacroName$() 439
Mid$() 59, 494
MsgBox() 91
Now() 23, 57, 61
ParaDown() 159
RepeatFind() 160
return values 39
Rnd() 77
Selection$() 148, 256
SelInfo() 76, 148
SelType() 148
SentRight() 137, 139, 159
SetDocumentVar() 166
SetPrivateProfileString() 167
Str$() 23
String$() 224
StyleName$() 145
terminology 50
Time$() 55
user-defined procedures 54
using 50
Val() 494, 499
Word as OLE server 562
WordRight() 159
Year() 23
built-in statements
47, 112, 138, 142, 293, 296
   ActivateObject 547
   AddAddress 568, 570
   AddButton 439
   AppActivate 299
   AppShow 560
   Auto 165
   AutoMarkIndexEntries 251, 257
   Begin Dialog UserDialog 112
   BorderBottom 81
   CharLeft 136
   Close 495

common, list of 49
ConvertObject 547
CopyButtonImage 439
DDEExecute 515
DDEExecute() 513
DDEInitiate 515
DDERequest 517
DDERequest$() 515
DDETerminate 513
Default$() 262
Dialog 102
difference between a statement
            and a function 51
Dim 41
DlgEnable 130
DlgListBoxArray 237
DlgText 133, 146
DlgValue 237
DlgVisible 200
DocClose 296
DocumentProtection() 243
EditAutoText 165
EditBookmark 153, 155
EditClear 142
EditCut 142
EditFind 149, 256, 263, 298, 444
EditFindClearFormatting 150
EditFindFont 150
EditFindHighlight 256
EditFindLang 150
EditFindPara 150
EditFindStyle 150
EditGoto 158, 160, 161, 257, 263, 547, 558
EditLinks 547, 558, 559
EditObject 547
EditPasteSpecial 545
EditPicture 547
EditReplace 152
EditReplaceClearFormatting 152
EditReplaceFont 152
EditReplaceLang 152
EditReplacePara 152
EditReplaceStyle 152

FileClose 296
FileClosePicture 547
FileFind 445
FileOpen 176, 214, 422
FileRoutingSlip 584
FileSave 248
Find 150
finding the right one to use 48
Font 80
GetAddress$() 577
GetCurValues 101
Highlight 258
Input 89
Insert 47, 500
InsertAutoText 165
InsertChart 546
InsertDatabase 525, 545
InsertDrawing 546
InsertEquation 546
InsertExcelTable 546
InsertIndex 257
InsertMergeField 598
InsertObject 545, 550
InsertPicture 545
InsertSound 546
InsertTableOfContents 250
InsertWordArt 546
Instr() 494
Italic 47, 59
LineInput 89, 493, 494
manipulating objects 545
   general statements 545
   statements for inserting specific
      objects 546
   statements for manipulating
      objects 547
MarkIndexEntry 250
MsgBox 90, 587
NextCell 500
On Error Goto 72, 106
On Error Goto 0 72
On Error Resume Next 73
PasteButtonImage 439
Picture 114

Print 88, 492
ReDim 42
RepeatFind 151
Replace 150
ResetChar 147
SelectCurSentence 142
SelectCurWord 142
SelInfo() 294
SendKeys 517, 560
SetAutoText 165
SetDocumentProperty 248
SetDocumentVar 166
SetEndOfBookmark 157
SetPrivateProfileString 167
SetStartOfBookmark 157
Shell 299, 512
Spike 142
StartOfDocument 140
ToolsMacro 265, 443, 561
ToolsOptionsView 257
ToolsProtectDocument 243
ToolsUnprotectDocument 243
UpdateFields 501
Word as OLE server 562
Write 490
button command 348
button fields 461

C

', commenting code 60
\c, DATABASE switches 543
\c, INCLUDEPICTURE
    switches 544
calculated fields 497
    FORMULA 459
    sum 497
CancelButton 115
carriage returns
    StripReturns$(), removing
      from a string 97
case-sensitivity 241
    comparison operators 44

HTML tags 284
CCTIndex.doc 256
channel 508
character data types. *see* strings
CharColor() 145
CharLeft 29, 136
CharLeft() 137
chart 504
CheckBox 115
CheckMacros() 442
Chr$() 77, 91
    CleanString$(), removing
      from string 97
citation 368
Classname 542
CleanStrings$() 97
ClearAddIns() 61
ClearForm 482
client 508
client side image maps 313
Close 495
CloseSecondarys 395
CmpBookmarks 158, 558
code
    commenting 60
    controlling execution 61
      WordBasic control structures 62
    line breaks 50
CollectIndexTerms 256
ComboBox 115
comma-delimited files 490
    .txt, .csv 490
commenting 60
    REM 60
COMPARE field 458
compare versions 417
comparison operator
    < 44
    <= 44
    <> 44
    = 44
    > 44
    >= 44

comparison operators 44
    case-sensitivity 44
Component Object Model (COM)
    see also OLE
compound data types
    records
      dialog records 99
compound documents 509
    sharing 556
concordance files 251
condition 62
construct. *see* control structures
Contents List file 399
    Help Workshop 400
    WroxHelp 401
context 14
    active template 14
    built-in functions 14
    dialog record 126
    global 14
    Normal template 14
context string. *see* topic identifier
context-sensitive help 323, 405
    mapping topics 406
control structures
    controlling execution of code 62
    For–Next 64
    Goto 67
    If–Then–Else 62
    labels 67
    nesting 67
    Select–Case 63
    While–Wend 66
      Do–Loop, Repeat–While and
      Repeat–Until 66
ControlID$ 123
controls
    custom dialogs 114
    FilePreview 226
    moving and resizing 110
    web page 310
      List Box 311
      option groups 311
      Text Box 311

wizards
    adding and removing controls 194
    naming convention 197
    numeric identifiers 195, 199
    panels of controls 192, 199
    Picture control 198
    Text control 195
ConvertObject 547
CopyButtonImage 439
Copyright macro example 20
CountAddIns() 61
CountAutoTextEntries() 165
CountDocumentVar$() 166
CountDrives 221
CountFonts() 79
CountPictures 160
CountSentences 138, 140, 154
CreateIndexEntries 257
CreateMasterDocument 235
cursor
    position
        determining at start of macro 139
        determining in table 148
custom dialogs 12, 107
    ComboBox
        filling with values 117
    creating your own 108
    definition 107
    dialog definition
        editing 116
        Name argument, case-sensitivity in 116
    Dialog Editor
        installation 108
    Dialog(), controling which button is default 119
    displaying 118
    ListBox
        filling with values 117
    OptionButton
        Option group 117
    using 113
    checking which button was pressed 118
    Default button, setting 117
    limits on types of controls 113
    Tab Order button, setting 117
    values, using 119
customer list report 507

D

\d, DATABASE switches 543
\d, INCLUDEPICTURE switches 544
\d, LINK switches 543
\d, mailmerge switches 594
data
    Access
        customer list report 507
        importing data into Access 505
        using in Access 507
    analyzing
        disk files and Wordbasic 490
    Excel
        analyzing in Excel 503
        creating a chart 504
        importing into Excel 502
    getting it back into Word from other applications 508
    DDE 508
    information, turning data into 488
    OLE
        inserting data into a document 536, 541
    retrieving
        from other applications 489
        from survey file 494
    Wrox survey results 488
        Excel and Access, using results in 501
data blocks. see complex data types
data source 587
data types 39, 506

compound
    arrays 40
    records 99
dialog records 41, 99
elementary 39
    number data types 39
    strings (character data types) 40
DATABASE field 541, 543
    Switches
        \b 543
        \c 543
        \d 543
        \f 543
        \h 543
        \l 543
        \s 543
        \t 543
DATE field 452
    changing format 452
Date() 247
dates 54
    nesting functions 54
DDE 449, 489
    conversation, stages of 512
        system topic 512
    overview 508
    reviewing the steps of a DDE operation 527
    self-installing document 510
    with WordBasic 510
    Word, hints and tips
        finding the command you need 519
        finding the topic you need 519
        functions and statements 518
        handling errors in DDE operations 520
        poking about in other applications 520
    Wrox survey results database
        Survey.mdb 516
    Wrox survey results spreadsheet 513
        Survey.xls 513

607

DDEExecute 515
DDEInitiate 515
DDEInitiate() 512
DDEOLE.dot
514, 516, 521, 549, 551
DDERequest 517
DDERequest$() 515
DDETerminate 513
declaration
   arrays 42
      multi-dimensional 42
   variables 41
      shared variables 43
Default$() 262
Dialog 102
dialog definition 111
   case-sensitivity in Name
             argument 116
   dynamic dialogs 122
   editing 116
Dialog Editor
   installation 108
dialog records 41, 99
   context 126
   finding the name of a dialog 101
   getting the current value into 101
      GetCurValues 101
Dialog() 106, 123
   custom dialogs
      controling which button
             is default 119
   dynamic dialogs
      understanding Dialog()
             arguments 123
Dialog.bmp 379
Dialog.shg 381
dialogs 107
   see also message boxes
   built-in 11, 98
      displaying a built-in dialog 102
      checking how a dialog is closed 106
   custom 12
      creating your own 108
      definition 107

      using 113
   dialog definition
      numeric identifiers and controls 128
   dialog records 99
      finding the name of a dialog 101
   Dialog() 106
   dynamic 122
      dialog definition 122
      Escape key, managing 123
      password dialog 131
   FilePreview 194
   focus 117
   Macro 16
   wizards
      displaying dialog 198
   Word as OLE server 561
   WordBasic procedures 126
Dim 41
DisableAutoMacros() 437
disk files 490
DlgEnable 130
DlgListBoxArray 237
DlgText 133, 146
DlgText$() 130, 133
DlgText() 146
DlgValue 237
DlgVisible 200
DLLs 219
   DLL function, using in Word 219
   drives, identifying type 222
   hard drives, getting information about 220
   returning string values from 223
DocClose 296
document 414
   better printing 264
      Print Dialog, creating your own 265
      WroxPBS 265
   built-in properties 247
      LastSavedBy 248
      LastSavedTime 248

   checking whether a document has been saved 481
   compound 509
      sharing 556
   controlling changes to 244
      adding Edit History 245
      annotations 245
      revisions 244
   current word or sentence, selecting 142
   custom properties
      WroxUsrLastEdit 248
   determining where the end is 141
   document properties 168
      functions, creating custom properties 168
   document variables 163
   document viruses
      fighting the threat 428
      Word document viruses 430
   fields
      inserting fields manually 460
      inserting fields with WordBasic 461
   indexes 250
   managing large documents 230
      master documents and subdocuments 230
   managing pictures 258
      InsertPicture 263
      WroxPic 258
   networks
      comparing different versions of a document 417
      simultaneous editing 416
         automated 417
      viruses, protecting yourself from 426
   objects
      selecting and moving 137
   OLE 509
      inserting data into a document 541

original text, preventing
			changes to 243
protecting 241
	annotations 241
	passwords 241
	revisions 241
saving information globally 162
self-installing 510
storing information in 166
table of contents, creating 249
	InsertTableOfContents 250
text
	bookmarks 153
	deleting 142
	formatting 143
	inserting 142
	moving and selecting 136
	searching and replacing 149
	sentences, counting the
			number of 138
using objects in 525
document files
	.doc 14
document properties 168
	functions, creating custom
			properties 168
document templates
	managing on a network 414
	protecting from changes 414
	template dialog, adding
			pages to 415
document variables 38, 163
document viruses 32, 427
	fighting the threat 428
	how they work 427
	scanning a suspicious
			document 440
	Wrox VirusScan 440
	Wrox VirusScan All 445
	Word document viruses 427
drag-and-drop
	embedding objects 533
DriveInfo.dot 225

drives
	identifying type 222
DriveType 220
DrivInfo.dot 445
DropCaps 102
DropListBox 115
dynamic data exchange. *see* DDE
dynamic dialogs 122
	dialog definition 122
	Dialog()
		keeping dynamic dialog
			displayed 123
		understanding the
			arguments 123
	Escape key, managing 123
	password dialog 131
dynamic lists 237
Dynamic Password 131
dynamic-link libraries 219
DynaZIP 212

E

e-mail
	Exchange
		sending documents direct
			from Word 582
		sending mail merge
			documents 595
	UUEncodeing 582
E-Mail.dot 569, 572, 579
Edit History 245
Edit History.dot 246
EditAutoText 165
	arguments 165
EditBookmark 153, 155
	arguments 153
EditClear 142
EditCut 142
EditFind 149, 256, 263, 298, 444
	arguments 149
EditFind() 160
EditFindClearFormatting 150
EditFindFont 150

EditFindFound() 151, 160, 256
EditFindHighlight 256
EditFindLang 150
EditFindPara 150
EditFindStyle 150
EditGoTo 158, 160, 161,
	257, 263, 293, 547, 558
EditLinks 547, 558, 559
EditObject 547
EditPasteSpecial 545
EditPicture 547
EditReplace 152
EditReplaceClearFormatting 152
EditReplaceFont 152
EditReplaceLang 152
EditReplacePara 152
EditReplaceStyle 152
electronic form 464
Electronic Mail editor 581
elementary data types 39
Else keyword 62
ElseIf keyword 63
EMBED field
	Classname 542
	* MERGEFORMAT 542
	\s 542
embedding 527, 531, 533
	drag-and-drop 533
	Paste 533
	Paste Special 533
encryption
	document viruses 32
	macros 32
End Dialog 112
End Sub 43
Eof() 495, 499
Eqnedt32.exe 529
error handling 68
	break points, setting 71
	finding errors in code
		single-stepping 70
	Help files 407
	On Error Resume Next 73

run-time errors 72
    On Error Goto 72, 106
    On Error Goto 0 72
    variables, viewing their values 71
Escape key
    dynamic dialogs 123
Excel
    creating a chart 504
    Wrox survey results 501
        inserting into a document 536
Excel.Sheet.5 542
ExcelUpdate 514
Exchange
    Personal Address Book 566
    sending documents 582
        e-mail direct from Word 582
        faxes from Word 585
        routing 583
    service 566
ExecFile 399
Explorer.exe 399
expressions
    numeric operators
        precedence 46
external, mci option 385

F

\f, DATABASE switches 543
faxes 585, 586
    mail merge documents 598
field code 450
fields
    ASK 594
    BOOKMARK 457
    button
        carrying out an action with 461
        using single-clicks to
            activate 463
    calculated 459, 497
    COMPARE 458
    DATABASE 541, 543
    DATE 452
        changing format 452

EMBED 541
field code 450
field or the result, viewing 450
FILLIN 594
form 464, 465
    electronic form 464
    inserting using Word menus
        and commands 465
    inserting with WordBasic 466
    Wrox Reader survey form 469
FORMULA
    calculated fields 459
GOTOBUTTON 462
how Word stores objects 541, 544
    DATABASE 543
    EMBED 541
    INCLUDEPICTURE 544
    LINK 542
IF 458
INCLUDEPICTURE 544, 558
INCLUDETEXT 238
    InsertFile 240
INFO 545
inserting into a document
        manually 460
inserting into a document
        with WordBasic 461
LINK 541, 558
MACROBUTTON 462
MERGEFIELD 588
numeric
    changing format 455
PAGE 457
PAGEREF 457
RD 240
    InsertField 241
simple
    displaying information 451
text
    changing format 455
TIME 452
    changing format 452
types of 451
updating contents 459

what are? 450
XE 251
File$() 84, 424
FileClosePicture 547
FileFind 445
FileList.dot 190, 195, 203
filename, creating a unique 81
FileNew 76
FileOpen 176, 214, 216, 422
FilePreview 115, 194, 226
FilePrint 264
FilePrint() 264
FilePrintDefault 264
FilePrintDefault() 264
FileRoutingSlip 584
files
    .doc 14
    .dot 14
    .gid 376
    .htm 281
    .rtf 332
    .wiz 210
    .wks 522
    .wll 19
    AuditLog.txt 553
    CCTIndex.doc 256
    comma-delimited 490
        .txt, .csv 490
    concordance 251
    Contents List 399
    Dialog.bmp 379
    Dialog.shg 381
    Eqnedt32 529
    Explorer.exe 399
    fixed width format 493
    Goodtime.avi 382
    Hcw.exe 332, 333
    Help
        creating your own 321
        overview of a Help project 331
        topic files 334
        Windows 95 322
    HTML text 279, 295
    imgmap.gif 314

IndexMe.doc 251
ini
   storing information in 167
Load.bmp 261
Merge.txt 588
MergeCom.txt 589
myfile.zip 307
MyPage.htm 280
PBSLOGO.bmp 349
PicDemo.doc 259
Progman.exe 510
project
   creating your own 364
RockDude.wav 532
sequential 89
Shed.exe 333, 379
shortcut.bmp 399
soundplay.rtf 384
Survey.htm 312
Survey.mdb 505, 516, 551
   inserting into a document 536
Survey.txt 495, 502, 571
Survey.xls 513, 551
   inserting into a document 536
tab-delimited
   .txt 491
TagList.doc 293
Wbmapi.wll 490
Wbodbc.wll 490
WroxHome.htm 276
WroxPBS.cnt 265, 376
WroxPBS.gid 376
WroxPBS.hlp 265, 376
WroxPBS.hpj 376, 381, 391
WroxPBS1.rtf 341, 345
WroxPBS2.rtf 352, 354
WroxPBS3.rtf 358, 366, 376, 391, 402
WroxPBS4.rtf 405
zip 211, 212
   .zip 213
   DynaZIP 212
   opening and saving 213

Wrox Zip 211
   Zip Manager 216
FileSave 248
FileSaveAs 511
FillAddressBook 572, 595
FILLIN field 594
FillTagArray 293
Find 150
fixed width format 493
focus 117
Font 80
Font$() 79, 145
fonts, creating a list of available 78
FontSize() 145
footnotes
   Help file construction 335, 351
   # 340, 389
   $ 341
   A 360
   K 351
   Macro 395
   list of 359
   printing footnote reports 357
For–Next 64
form fields 464, 465
   Wrox Reader survey form 469
   automating 475
   checking whether a document has been saved 481
   creating 471
   macros, checking how they work 481
   OnExit macro 476
   saving data 479
   storing data 480
form letter 587
FormatFont 47, 59
formatting text 143
forms 594
   web page 310
FORMULA calculated fields 459
ftp 303

ftp.compbook.com 307
functions 51
   $ 56
   AddAddIn() 61
   AddInState() 61
   AddThisAddress() 573, 574
   arguments 51, 57
      named 59
      optional 59
      passing by reference 58
      passing by value 58
   BBFunction() 129
   BetterBox$() 120
   Bold() 63
   built-in 11, 14, 50
      common functions 52
      Now() 23
      return values 39
      Str$() 23
      subroutines, creating your own 54
      terminology 50
      user-defined procedures 54
      using 50
      Year() 23
   CheckMacros() 442
   Chr$() 77
   CleanString$() 97
   ClearAddIns() 61
   CountAddIns() 61
   CountDrives 221
   creating your own 56
   Date() 247
   DLL
      using DLL functions in Word 219
   FillTagArray 293
   GetDocList 236
   GetDocumentProperty$() 236
   GetDriveLabel$() 223, 224
   GetFile$() 218
   GetFreeFileName$() 82

GetLineValue$() 494, 498, 573
GetNameOnly$() 225
GetPathOnly$() 225
GetTempFileName$() 424
GetTheTime() 57
GetTheTime$() 61
InStr() 97
IsFixedDrive() 221
IsMacro() 76
Left$() 51
Len() 62
MakeDriveList() 221, 445
Mid$() 59
MyDialog() 122
NextPanel() 200
Now() 57, 61
OpenMacro() 443
PrevPanel() 200
ScanMacro() 443
Str$() 54
StripReturns$() 97
sum 497
Time$() 55
Time() 247
ToolbarButtonMacro$() 439
user-defined
    parentheses 56

G

GetAddress$() 576, 581
    arguments 577
GetAddressType 577
GetAutoText$() 165
GetCurValues 101
GetDocList 236
GetDocumentProperty$() 236
GetDocumentVar$() 166
GetDocumentVarName$() 166
GetDriveLabel$() 223, 224
GetDriveType() 220, 222
GetFile$() 218
GetFreeFileName$() 82

GetHTMLTag 292
GetLineValue$() 494, 498, 573
GetNameOnly$() 225
GetPathOnly$() 225
GetPrivateProfileString$() 167
GetPrivateProfileString() 262
GetTemplFileName$() 424
GetTheTime$() 61
GetTheTime() 57
GetVolumeInformation() 223, 224
gid 376
global context 14
Goodtime.avi 382
Goto 67
GOTOBUTTON field 462
GrabAnnotation 245
graphics
    inserting into a document 530
    segmented hypergraphics 379
    web pages 301
        alligning text with images 301
        alternative text for images 303
        clickable image maps 312
        formats 302
        hot images 305
        quick-loading images 303
GroupBox 115

H

\h, DATABASE switches 543
hard drives
    DLLs
        getting information about
            hard drives 220
Hcrtf.exe 333
Hcw.exe 332
head 280
Help Author 372
    topics and hot spots, getting
        information about 373
Help compiler 332
Help contents, browsing and

running applications 326, 356
Help files
    citation 368
    compiling 372, 375
        Help Author 373
        WinHelp.exe 372
    creating your own 321
        adding graphics and buttons
            347
        Browse sequence 355
        contents list 399
        default window for topic 354
        different window types 339
        graphics that respond
            to the user 379
        hot spots, changing how they
            look and work 385
        index entries 351
        jumps and pop-ups 345
        linking topics 345
        non-scrolling title 339
        project file 364
        setting the styles 337
        sound and video clips 382
        writing the topics 340
    error handling 407
    linking Help to your
            application 405
    macros 394
        where they are used 395
    markers, setting with Macro
        footnotes 397
    opening from application
            window handle 406
    opening in Wrox Zip 407
    other Help files, getting information
        about 389
    overview of a help project 331
        tools you'll need for the project
            332
    running other programs with 398
        applications and data files 399
        Control Panel 399

testing the contents 409
viewing 375
Windows 95 322
different types of help 322
Help Topics window 324
Help Workshop 364
Contents List, creating 400
default project file entries 364
Help Project
[BAGGAGE] *see also* [Data Files]
[Bitmap] 366
[Config] 366
[Data Files] 366
[Files] 365
[Map] 366
[OPTIONS] 365
[Windows] 365
Help files, compiling 375
Hotspot Editor 379
investigating other Help files 389
Highlight 258
HighlightColor() 145
highlights 251
hot spots 334
changing their appearance 385
% 386
* 386
jumping to topics in other Help files 386
specifying window to jump to 386
> 386
steps window type 386
WroxPBS 391
Hotspot Editor 379
htm 281
HTML
HTML text files, web pages as 279
hypermedia documents 273
hypertext documents 273
hypertext links 303
web addresses, understanding 303

saving document as text file 295
tables
reading contents with WordBasic 293
using 307
what is? 275
page description language 275
html 281
http 303
hypergraphics 379
hypermedia documents 273
hypertext documents 273, 322
hypertext links 303, 304, 306
Hypertext Markup Language. *see* HTML

I

IF field 458
If–Then–Else 62
NOT 62
image maps 312
web page
client side image maps 313
server-based interface applications 313
imgmap.gif 314
in-place activation 509
INCLUDEPICTURE field 544, 558
\c 544
\d 544
INCLUDETEXT 238
InsertFile 240
index entries, Help files 351
indexes 250
concordance file 251
editing 255
XE fields 251
IndexMe.doc 251
INFO field 454
ini
storing information in 167

Input 89
input/output statements
see also MsgBox, Print and InputBox
InputBox 90
InputBox$()
message box, entering information 93
Inquiry Handling System example 7
Insert 20, 47, 142, 500
InsertAddress 577
InsertAutoText 165
InsertChart 546
InsertDatabase 545
InsertDrawing 546
InsertEquation 546
InsertExcelTable 546
InsertField 241
InsertFile 240
InsertIndex 257
InsertLogo 549
InsertMergeField 598
InsertObject 545, 550
InsertPicture 263, 545
InsertSound 546
InsertTableOfContents 250
InsertWordArt 546
InStr() 97, 494, 515
Int() 77
Internet 273
browsers 297
Internet Explorer 275
Netscape 275
why you need to know about 274
World Wide Web 274
web page 275, 279
WroxWeb HTML Assistant 290
Internet Explorer 275
Internet Mail 582
Intranet 273
Is keyword 64
IsAppRunning() 522
IsExecuteOnly() 443

IsFixedDrive() 221
IsMacro() 76
Italic 29, 47, 59
Italic() 51

J

JumpHash 389
jumps 335, 345

K

K footnote 351
K-Link macro 360
    jumping to a topic in another Help file 388
keywords
    Else 62
    ElseIf 63
    ReDim 237
    REM 60
    Shared 43
    Then 62
keywords. *see* index entries, Help files

L

, line breaks in code 50
\l, DATABASE switches 543
labels 67
    On Error Goto 72
large window type 371
LastSavedTime 248
Left$() 51, 98
Len() 62, 98
line breaks in code, 50
LineInput 89, 493, 494
LINK field 541, 542, 558
    \a 543
    \b 543
    \d 543
    \p 543
    \r 543
    \t 543

linking 527
    from files 532
    objects in documents 535
    Paste Link 534
ListBox 115
    web page 311
ListFont 79, 88
ListFonts 169, 171
Load.bmp 261
logical operators 45
    AND 45
    NOT 45
    OR 45
LTrim$() 208

M

macro
    FileSaveAs 511
Macro dialog
    checking for viruses 429
    Word document viruses template cleaning 431
Macro footnote 395
    Help File markers, setting and using 397
    pop-ups, setting the color of 396
    topic file Macro footnote, inserting 398
MACROBUTTON field 462
macros
    [Config] 366
    A-Link 360
    AllTheControls 113, 117
    and WordBasic, overview 11
    built-in functions 11
    Application 191, 195, 203
    AutoClose 179, 247
    AutoExec 179, 432
    AutoExit 179
    AutoMacros 434, 436
    AutoNew 179, 235, 247, 290, 295, 498

AutoOpen 179, 247, 422, 432, 498
BetterInputBox 120
BuildDocumentIndex 257
ClearForm 482
CloseSecondarys 395
CollectIndexEntries 256
control structures
    useful macro building techniques 73
Copyright macro example 20
CountPictures 160
CountSentences 138, 140, 154
CreateIndexEntries 257
CreateMasterDocument 235
customizing button 28
DriveType 220
DropCaps 102
Dynamic Password 131
encrypting 32
ExcelUpdate 514
Execfile 399
FileOpen 214, 216
FilePrint 264
FilePrintDefault 264
FillAddressBook 572, 595
GetAddressType 577
GetHTMLTag 292
GrabAnnotation 245
Help files and footnotes 394
Insert 20
InsertField 241
InsertFile 240
InsertLogo 549
InsertPicture 263
JumpHash 389
K-Link 360
labels, referring to code 67
ListFont 79, 88
ListFonts 169, 171
Macro dialog 16
macro editing window
    font and style 32
making available to users 169
    adding to menus 173

adding to toolbars 171
key combination, setting 169
macros that run
    automatically 179
replacing Word commands 176
NewInputBox 111, 119
OnEntry 468, 476
OnExit 468, 476
OpenMultiEdit 423
PrintBothSides 264, 268
QuickFormat 143, 164
RandomTable 76
recording automatically 26
    recording the next command 26
RemoveIndexEntries 257
Results.dot
    creating the macros 498
RetrieveAddress 580
RouteDocument 584
running as Word starts 179
SaveAs Zip 214
SavedAsFax 586
screen updating 141
SetPopupColor 396
SetWroxDefaults 262
ShellExecute 399
stopping while running 34
storing 13
    context 14
    the different macro types 17
    using correct template 17
SuspiciousMacro 442
TimeFunction 61
UpdateResults 498
VirusScan 434, 436
VirusScanAll 445
Word as OLE server 561
    ToolsMacro 561
WordLength 64
writing your first 19
Wrox DDE-Info 523
Wrox multi-edit 418
Wrox Reader survey form 481
WroxCompuserve 569

mail merge 587
    ASK 594
    data source 587
    FILLIN 594
    form letter 587
    inserting fields into a main document 595
    MERGEFIELD 588
    prompting for a value when a field is updated 594
        \d, \o switches 594
    record 587
    sending documents as faxes 598
    sending documents by e-mail 595
    using 588
    what is? 587
MailMerge.dot 589
MailTo 303
Main window 340, 354
MakeDriveList() 221, 226, 445
MAPI 489
MarkIndexEntry 250
master document 230
    commands 232
    creating automatically 233
    dynamic lists, using in a dialog 237
    other ways of building 238
        INCLUDETEXT fields 238
        RD 240
MasterDoc.dot 233
mci commands
    external 385
menus
    adding macros to 173
    working with objects 529
        Paste, Paste Special and Paste Link 533
Merge.txt 588
MergeCom.txt 589
MERGEFIELD 588
MERGEFORMAT (*) 542
Message Application Programming Interface 489
message boxes

icons 90
InputBox 90
InputBox$() 93
    entering information 93
MsgBox 90
MsgBox()
    actions, offering a choice of 91
messages
    WinHelp 374
Mid$() 59, 494
MOD, numeric operator 44
MsgBox 90, 138, 587
    icons 90
    status bar, outputting information to 91
MsgBox()
    offering a choice of message box actions 91
multi-dimensional arrays 41
    declaration 42
Multi-Edit.dot 418
MyDialog() 122
myfile.zip 307
MyPage.htm 280

N

named arguments 59
naming convention
    wizard controls 197
navigation buttons
    wizards 201
nesting control structures 67
nesting functions 54
Netscape 275
networks
    document templates
        managing 414
    documents
        viruses, protecting yourself from 426
    Intranet 273
    sharing documents 415

comparing different versions of
a document 417, 425
simultaneous editing 416
simultaneous editing,
automated 417
NewInputBox 111, 119
NextCell 500
NextPanel() 200
non-scrolling title 339
Normal template 14
macros, storing 17
NOT 45
If–Then–Else 62
Now() 23, 57, 61
number data types 39
numeric fields
changing format 455
numeric identifiers
dialog definition and controls 128
wizard controls 195, 199
numeric operator
/ 44
numeric operators 44
* 44
+ 44
- 44
MOD 44
precedence 46
parentheses 46

O

object linking and embedding.
see OLE
object-oriented programming.
see OOP
objects
and non-conformist server
applications 535
compound documents, sharing 556
document
inserting data into 536
working with 534
embedding 527, 531
drag-and-drop 533

Paste 533
Paste Special 533
future of object technology 526
linking 527
from files 532
managing links
in documents 535
Paste Link 534
moving and selecting
list of functions 137
OLE 526
storing in Word 541
DATABASE 543
document logo example 548
INCLUDEPICTURE 544
LINK 541
maintaining an audit log
of data use 551
what are? 526
WordBasic
manipulating objects 544
working with using Word's
menus 529
inserting objects into
documents 530
ODBC 449, 489
OKButton 115
OldPBS.cnt 376
OldPBS.hlp 376
OLE 489, 509, 525
see also objects
Automation 509
Visual Basic 560
Word as server 559
DDE
reviewing the steps of a
DDE operation 527
documents 509
embedding 527, 531
drag-and-drop 533
Paste 533
Paste Special 533
future of object technology 526
linking 527
from files 532

objects in documents 535
Paste Link 534
objects 526
compound documents 556
maintaining an audit log
of data use 551
non-conformist server
applications 535
storing in Word 541
using Word's menus with 529
WordBasic, manipulating
objects with 544
working with in your
document 534, 536
OLE2 509
in-place activation 509
servers
using Word as an OLE
server 559
what is? 526
On Error Goto 72, 106
On Error Goto 0 72
On Error Resume Next 73
OnEntry 468, 476
OnExit 468, 476
OOP
see also objects
Open Database Connectivity. see
ODBC
OpenMacro() 443
operators 43
comparison 44
logical 45
numeric 44
precedence 46
string concatenation 44
option button 311
option groups
web page 311
optional arguments 59
OptionButton 115
OR 45
Organizer 15
checking for viruses 430

P

\p, LINK switches 543
page description language 275
PAGE field 457
PAGEREF field 457
ParaDown() 159
parentheses
  and functions 51
  and precedence 46
  user-defined functions 56
passing by reference 58
passing by value 58
password dialog 131
passwords 241
  case-sensitivity 241
Paste 533
Paste Special 533
PasteButtonImage 439
PBSLOGO.bmp 349
Personal Address Book 566
  default address book 566
    WordBasic 568
  Electronic Mail editor 581
  entries
    creating from existing data 571
    finding correct address type 575
    using in a document 578
  field names 570
  retrieving information 577
  using 566
PicDemo.doc 259
Picture 114
picture command 347
Picture control 115, 198, 206
pictures 258
  managing in a document 258
    InsertPicture 263
    WroxPic 258
pop-up windows 323, 335, 345
pop-ups
  Macro footnote
    setting the colour of
      pop-ups 396

precedence 46
  parentheses 46
PrevPanel() 200
Print 57, 492
  status bar, putting information in 88
PrintBothSides 264, 268
printing 264
  Print Dialog, creating your own 265
  Word's printing commands 264
  Wrox PBS 265
Procedure window 339
procedures 50
  running procedures in other macros 60
  Sub MAIN and End Sub 43
  user-defined 54
Progman.exe 510
project files
  Help
    [Bitmaps] 366
    [Config] 366
    [Data Files] 366
    [Files] 365
    [Map] 366
    [OPTIONS] 365
    [Windows] 365
    Alias 366
    creating your own 364
  Help Workshop 364
  window types 371
  WroxPBS 366
properties
  see also field names
  document 168
protocol types 303
pseudo-random numbers 77
publishing
  Word in a publishing environment
    better printing 264
    controlling changes to your document 244

    indexes and tables of contents 249
    managing large documents 230
    pictures, managing in a document 258
    protecting your documents 241
PushButton 115

Q

QBE (Query By Example). *see* Graphical Query Generator
QuickFmt.dot 143, 164
QuickFormat 143, 164

R

\r, LINK switches 543
radio buttons. *see* OptionButton
random numbers, creating 77
RandomTable 76
RD field 240
  InsertField 241
record 587
records 99, 587
  see also complex data types
ReDim 42
ReDim keyword 237
reference document field. *see* RD field
REGEDIT.EXE 168
registry 38
  REGEDIT.EXE 168
  storing information in 167
Registry Editor 542
REM keyword 60
RemoveIndexEntries 257
RepeatFind 151
RepeatFind() 160
Replace 150
reports
  customer list 507
ResetChar 147

resolution 339
Results.dot 495, 510
 macros 498
RetrieveAddress 580
revisions 241, 244
Rnd() 77
RockDude.wav 532
RouteDocument 584
routing 583
ROWx 500
rtf 332
run-time errors 72
 On Error Goto 72, 106
 On Error Goto 0 72
 On Error Resume Next 73

S

\s, DATABASE switches 543
\s, EMBED switches 542
Samples, folder 64
SaveAsZip 214
SavedAsFax 586
ScanMacro() 443
scope 43
screen unit 112
screen updating 141
searching and replacing 149
 finding all instances in a document 151
 format, specifying 150
segmented hypergraphics 379
Select–Case 63
 Is 64
 To 64
SelectCurSentence 142
SelectCurWord 142
Selection$() 148
SelInfo() 76, 148, 294
SelType() 148
SendKeys 517
Sendkeys 560
SentRight() 137, 139, 159

sequential files 89
server-based interface applications 313
servers
 OLE
  using Word as 559
service 566
SetAutoText 165
SetDocumentDirty 296
SetDocumentProperty 248
SetDocumentVar 166
SetDocumentVar() 166
SetEndOfBookmark 157
SetPopupColor 396
SetPrivateProfileString 167, 262
SetPrivateProfileString() 167
SetStartOfBookmark 157
SetWroxDefaults 262
Shared keyword 43
shared variables
 declaration 43
Shed.exe 333
 Hotspot Editor 379
 segmented hypergraphics 379
Shell 299, 512
Shell32.dll 219
ShellExecute 399
shortcut.bmp 399
simple fields 451
single-stepping through code 70
SortArray 80
soundplay.rtf 384
sounds
 Help files 382
Spike 142
SQL 546, 599
standard window type 371
StartOfDocument 140
Startup directory
 templates, loading globally 19
statements 51
 BorderBottom 81
 built-in 47

common statements 49
 Dim 41
 finding the right one to use 48
 Font 80
 ReDim 42
 FormatFont 47, 59
 Italic 59
 SortArray 80
 Stop 71
status bar 88
 inputting information from 89
 MsgBox, outputting information to status bar 91
 putting information in 88
steps window type 371, 386
Stop 71
Str$() 23, 54
string concatenation operator
 + 44
String$() 224
strings 40
 CleanString$(), removing Chr$() 97
 DLLs
  returning string values from 223
 StripReturns$(), removing carriage returns 97
strings
 see also variables
StripReturns$() 97
StyleName$() 145
Sub MAIN 43
subdocument 230
 controlling updates 231
 creating automatically 233
subroutines 50
 creating your own 54
sum 497
SuppValue 124
Survey.htm 312
Survey.mdb 505, 516, 551
 inserting into a document 536
Survey.txt 495, 502, 571
Survey.xls 513, 551
 inserting into a document 536

SuspiciousMacro 442
system topic 512

T

\t, DATABASE switches 543
\t, LINK switches 543
tab-delimited file 491
table of contents 249
   InsertTableOfContents 250
Table Wizard 188
tables
   cursor, determining position in table
      list of common procedures 148
   HTML 293
      using in web page 307
   list of common procedures 147
   turning arrays into 74
TagList.doc 293
tags 280
   combining different 289
   formatting
      block formatting tags 284
      logical and physical tags 283
   how WroxWeb uses the tag list entries 295
   miscellaneous
      comments 317
      fonts, colors, sound and video 315
Template Dialog
   checking for viruses 429
templates 74
   .dot 14
   active 14
   BlankWiz.dot 190
   Book Order.dot 211
   cleaning to remove viruses 431
      recovering original document 432
   context 14
   DDEOLE.dot 514, 516, 521, 549, 551

document
   managing on a network 414
   template dialog, adding pages to 415
DriveInfo.dot 220, 225, 445
E-Mail.dot 569, 572, 579
EditHistory.dot 246
loading globally 18
   Startup directory 19
macros, storing 17
MailMerge.dot 589
MasterDoc.dot 233
MultiEdit.dot 418
Normal 14
   cleaning to remove viruses 431
QuickFmt.dot 143, 164
Results.dot 495, 497, 510
   macros 498
storing 31
storing information in 164
template Organizer 15
Wrox Zip.dot 327
WroxHelp.dot 341
WroxIndex 251
WroxPic.dot 258, 259
WroxScan.dot 433, 440
text
   bookmarks 153
      addng, deleting and going to 154
      comparing 157
      copying and editing 156
      definition 153
      going to a point in a document 158
      Word's predefined, list of 156
   current word or sentence, selecting 142
   deleting 142
   formatting 143
      web page 281
   inserting 142
   moving in a document 136

   saving information globally and in documents 162, 166
      document variables 163
   searching and replacing 149
      finding all instances in a document 151
      format, specifying 150
   selecting in a document
      list of functions 136
   sentences, counting the number of 138
Text control 115, 195
   web page 311
text fields
   changing format 455
Text Import Wizard 505
TextBox 115
The Microsoft Sound.wav 383
Then keyword 62
TIME field 452
   changing format 452
Time$() 55
Time() 247
TimeFunction 61
To keyword 64
ToolbarButtonMacro$() 439
toolbars
   adding macros to 171
   buttons
      changing their positions 173
      creating in WordBasic 439
ToolsMacro 265, 443, 561
ToolsOptionsView 257
ToolTip
   automatic addition 29
topic 508
topic files 334
   button command 348
   default window 354
   index entries 351
   jumping to topics in another Help file 386
   when you know the topic

identifier 388
Macro footnotes, inserting 398
picture command 347
sound clips 383
structure 334
   hot spots 334
   jumps 335
   pop-ups 335
   topic identifier 335
topic identifier 340
   # 341
   alias 366
   jumping to topics in another Help file 388
topic title
   $ 341
training card help 326
Try It Outs 418, 556
   A Self-Installing Document using DDE 510
   Activating Your Browser with WroxWeb HTML Assistant 297
   Adding a Default Window Entry 354
   Adding Graphics and Buttons 349
   Adding Our Contact Details to Your Address Book 569
   Adding Our Reader Survey Data to Exchange 572
   Adding Sound Clips to a Topic File 383
   Adding the ListFonts Macro to the FormatMenu 174
   An Inquiry Handling System 7
   Auto Indexing with WroxIndex 251
   Automating the Copyright Text 20
   Changing the Hot Spots in Our WroxPBS Help File 391
   Changing the Style of the Macro Editing Window 33
   Compiling the Edited Document with Wrox Multi-Edit 420
   Compiling the WroxPBS Help File 376
   Controlling the Drop Cap Dialog 102

Counting Sentences in a Document 138, 140, 154
Counting the Number of Pictures in a Document 160
Creating a Master Document with Wrox MasterDoc 233
Creating a Table of Random Numbers 74
Creating a Toobar Button for the ListFonts Macro 171
Creating the File List Dialog Function 203
Creating the Wrox Survey Form 471
Creating the WroxPBS Contents List 401
Creating the WroxPBS Overview Graphic 379
Creating the WroxPBS Project File 366
Creating Unique File Names 82
Defining Our File List Wizard Dialog 195
Designing a 'Better Input Box' Dialog 108
Finding Address Types in Personal Address Book 575
Finishing Off Our File List Wizard 206
Finishing Our 'Better Input Box' Dialog 120
Getting Drive Information Using the API 220
Improving Our Copyright Macro 23
Inserting, Listing and Removing Pictures 259
Installing Wrox Virus Scan as an Add-in 433
Installing Wrox Virus Scan in your Normal Template 434
Installing Wrox Zip 211
Keeping Track of Corporate Data Use 551
Linking a Logo to Your Documents 549
Linking Topics with Jumps and

Pop-ups 345
Listing Available Fonts 79
Making Our 'Better Input Box' Dynamic 128
Printing on Both Sides with a Single-side Printer 266
Recording a Macro 27
Replacing Word's FileOpen Command 176
Saving and Opening a Zip File 213
Sending Mail-merged Documents by E-mail 595
Setting the Topic's Title and Identifier 341
Setting Up a Mail Merge from the Survey Data 589
Setting Up the ListFonts Key Combination 169
Setting Wrox Zip's Defaults 215
Specifying a Browse Sequence 356
The Sample 'QuickFormat' Utility 143
The Wrox Survey Results Report 495
Updating the Survey Spreadsheet Using DDE 514
Using an Address from Exchange 579
Using an OnExit Macro in the Wrox Survey Form 476
Using InputBox$ and MsgBox 95
Using the Sample Blank Wizard Template 190
Using the Survey Data in a Word Document 536
Using the Template Organizer 15
Using the Wrox AutoMacros Button 436
Using the Wrox DDE Info Application 521
Using the Wrox Zip Help File 326
Using Wrox Virus Scan 440
Viewing the Sample Web Pages 276

txt 490, 491

U

Uniform Resource Locator. *see* URLs
UpdateFields 501
UpdateResults 498
URLs 304
UUEncodeing 582

V

Val() 494, 499
variables 38
 arrays 40
  declaration 42
 declaration 41
  Dim 41
 document 38
 error handling
  viewing variable values 71
 naming 38
 number data types 39
 scope 43
 shared
  declaration 43
 strings 40
variables
 see also data types
video clips
 Help files 382
viruses 426
 document 32
 how they work 427
 protecting yourself from 432
 recovering original document after cleaning 432
 scanning for viruses 440
 Word document viruses 427, 430
 Wrox VirusScanAll 445
 fighting the threat 428
  Macro Dialog 429
  Organizer 430
  Template Dialog 429
  Wrox Virus Scan 433
VirusScan 434, 436
VirusScanAll 445
Visual Basic
 OLE Automation 560

W

Wbmapi.wll 490
Wbodbc.wll 490
web page 275
 adding extra features 307
 as HTML text files 279
 browser 275, 297
 creating, making it easier 290
 fonts, colors, sound and video 315
 graphics 301
  alligning text with images 301
  alternative text for images 303
  clickable image maps 312
  formats 302
  hot images 305
  quick-loading 303
 links to another part of the same page 306
 links to different pages 304
 lists
  definition 288
  ordered 285
  unordered 285
 structure 299
  defining areas of the page 280
  formatting text 281
  tags 280
 using forms and controls 310
  List Box 311
  option groups 311
  Text control 311
 using tables 307
 web addresses 303
  ftp 303
  http 303
  local formats 304
  MailTo 303
  www 304
While–Wend 66
Win32 API 219
window handle 406
windows
 project file types 371
Windows 95
 different types of help 322
  context-sensitive 323
  Help contents, browsing and running application 326
  Help Topics window 324
  hypertext document 322
  pop-up windows 323
  training card help 326
 Help files 322
WinHelp.exe 372
 Help Author 372
  topics and hot spots, getting information about 373
 WinHelp messages, viewing 374
wizards
 .wiz 210
 controls
  adding and removing 194
  naming convention 197
  numeric identifiers 195, 199
  panels of 192, 199
  Picture 198, 206
  Text 195
 creating 190
 definition 188
 dialog, displaying 198
 FileList.dot 190, 195, 203
 hints, displaying 209
 making them available 210
 navigation buttons
  enabling 201
 structure 189
 Table 188
 Text Import 505

user's options, controlling 199
user's selections, checking 202
wks 522
Word Developer's Kit 48
Word document viruses
   removing 430
      open document cleaning 431
      template cleaning 431
word processor 332
WordBasic
   analyzing data 490
   and macros, overview 11
      built-in functions 11
   built-in functions 50
   data types 39
   DDE 510
   dialog procedures 126
      context, dialog record 126
   disk files, reading 492
   expressions 45
   extending the power of 218
   fields
      form fields, inserting into a document 466
      inserting into a document 461
   HTML
      reading the contents of a table 293
   language fundamentals 38
      built-in statements 47
      operators 43
   mail merge 598
   objects
      manipulating 544
   routing a document 584
   sending faxes 586
   toolbars
      creating toolbar buttons 439
   use of
      built-in dialogs 11
      built-in functions, executing directly 11
      custom dialogs 12
   using to add address book 568

variables 38
wizards
   definition 188
WordLength 64
WordRight() 159
workgroup templates 414
World Wide Web 274, 297
   ftp 303
   http 303
   local address formats 304
   MailTo 303
   web page 275
   www 304
Write 490
Wrox DDE Info application 521
Wrox DDE-Info 523
Wrox multi-edit macro 418
Wrox Reader survey form 469
   automating 475
   checking whether a document has been saved 481
   creating 471
   macros, checking how they work 481
   OnExit macro, using 476
   saving data 479
   storing data
      WordBasic, manipulating text files with 480
Wrox survey 488
Wrox Virus Scan 433, 440
   installing 434
   uninstalling 436
Wrox Zip 211, 326, 400
   default options, setting 214
   opening Help 407
   saving and using values in a template 216
Wrox Zip.dot 327
WroxCompuserve 569
WroxHelp
   Contents List, creating 401
WroxHelp.dot 341
WroxHome.htm 276

WroxIndex.dot 251
WroxPBS 265, 391
   graphic 379
   project file 366
      window types 371
WroxPBS.cnt 265, 376
WroxPBS.gid 376
WroxPBS.hlp 265, 376
WroxPBS.hpj 376, 381, 391
WroxPBS1.rtf 341, 345
WroxPBS2.rtf 352, 354
WroxPBS3.rtf 358, 366, 376, 391, 402
WroxPBS4.rtf 405
WroxPic.dot 258, 259
WroxScan.dot 440
Wroxscan.dot 433
WroxUsrLastEdit 248
WroxWeb HTML Assistant 290
www 304

X

XE fields 251

Y

Year() 23

Z

zip file 211, 212
   DynaZIP 212
   opening and saving 213
   Wrox Zip 211
      default options, setting 214
      saving and using values in a template 216
   Zip Manager 216
      getting filenames and paths in WordBasic 217
      saving paths as Auto Text entries 218

HTML

```
<TITLE> </TITLE>
<Hn>    </Hn>                    headers  ALIGN = center/right/left
<P>     </P>                     paras
<HR>    <BR>                     horiz rule / line break
<!--    -->                      comments
<EM>    </EM>                    italic
<STRONG> </STRONG> <B></B>       bold
<TT> or <CODE> or <KBD> or <SAMP>   monospaced font
<STRIKE>  <U>                    strike out / underline
<SUB> <SUP>                      sub / superscript
<BLOCKQUOTE>                     set off quotes
<PRE>                            maintain preformatted text
<BASEFONT SIZE = "n">            default n=3
<FONT SIZE = "n">                for selected text
<BIG>  <SMALL>                   relative font-size
<FONT FACE = "choice1"> </FONT>  revert choices
<BODY BGCOLOR="#000000" TEXT="#rrggbb">    hex code
<FONT SIZE = onye FACE = "font" COLOR = "hexcode" or a package
After BODY use LINK to change colors of unvisited links
     VLINK                       visited
     ALINK                       in use click
<BLINK> </BLINK>                 makes text blink
<IMG SRC = "image.location">
<ALT = "text in place of image">
<A HREF = "image.location"> midbrackets between of full size image </A>
LOWSRC = "image low res"         locate low resolution image
```

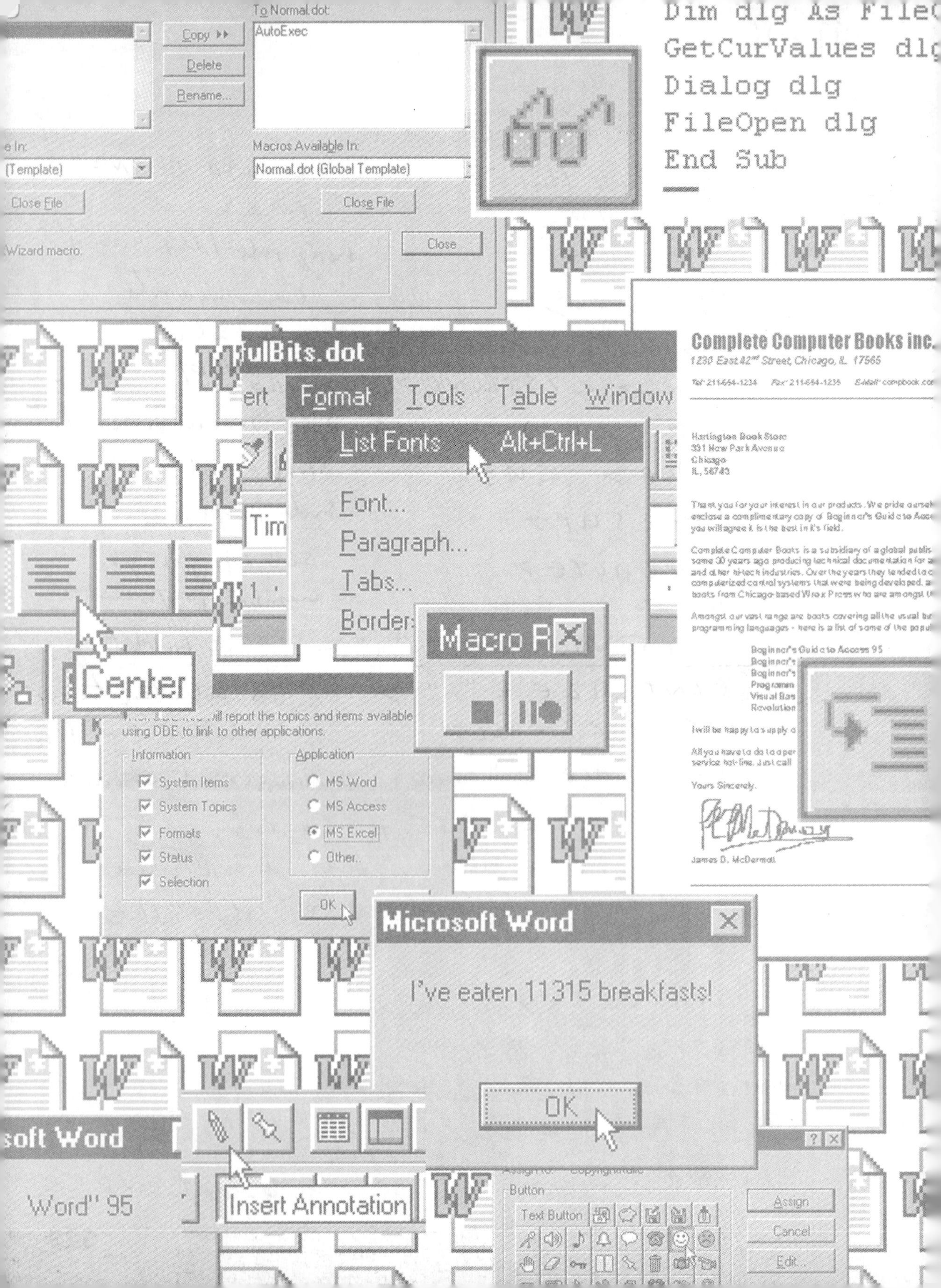
To Normal.dot:
Copy
Delete
Rename...
AutoExec
Macros Available In:
Normal.dot (Global Template)
Close File
Close
Dim dlg As File
GetCurValues dlg
Dialog dlg
FileOpen dlg
End Sub
ulBits.dot
Format
Tools
Table
Window
List Fonts
Alt+Ctrl+L
Font...
Paragraph...
Tabs...
Borders
Macro R
Center
Complete Computer Books inc.
1230 East 42nd Street, Chicago, IL 17565
Harlington Book Store
331 New Park Avenue
Chicago
IL, 56743
Yours Sincerely,
James D. McDermott
using DDE to link to other applications.
Information
System Items
System Topics
Formats
Status
Selection
Application
MS Word
MS Access
MS Excel
Other..
OK
Microsoft Word
I've eaten 11315 breakfasts!
OK
soft Word
Word" 95
Insert Annotation
Button
Text Button
Assign
Cancel
Edit...

WROX

Register Beginning WordBasic Programming and sign up for a free subscription to The Developer's Journal.

A bi-monthly magazine for software developers, The Wrox Press Developer's Journal features in-depth articles, news and help for everyone in the software development industry. Each issue includes extracts from our latest titles and is crammed full of practical insights into coding techniques, tricks and research.

Fill in and return the card below to recieve a free subscription to the Wrox Press Developer's Journal.

Beginning WordBasic Programming Registration Card

- Name
- Address
- City / State/Region
- Country / Postcode/Zip
- E-mail
- Occupation
- How did you hear about this book?
  - [ ] Book review (name)
  - [ ] Advertisement (name)
  - [ ] Recommendation
  - [ ] Catalogue
  - [ ] Other
- Where did you buy this book?
  - [ ] Bookstore (name) / City
  - [ ] Computer Store (name)
  - [ ] Mail Order
  - [ ] Other

- What influenced you in the purchase of this book?
  - [ ] Cover Design
  - [ ] Contents
  - [ ] Other (please specify)
- How did you rate the overall contents of this book?
  - [ ] Excellent
  - [ ] Good
  - [ ] Average
  - [ ] Poor
- What did you find most useful about this book?
- What did you find least useful about this book?
- Please add any additional comments.
- What other subjects will you buy a computer book on soon?
- What is the best computer book you have used this year?

Note: This information will only be used to keep you updated about new Wrox Press titles and will not be used for any other purpose or passed to any other third party.

869 Tick here if you don't want a subscription to The Developer's Journal or to recieve further support for this book. [ ] 869

WROX

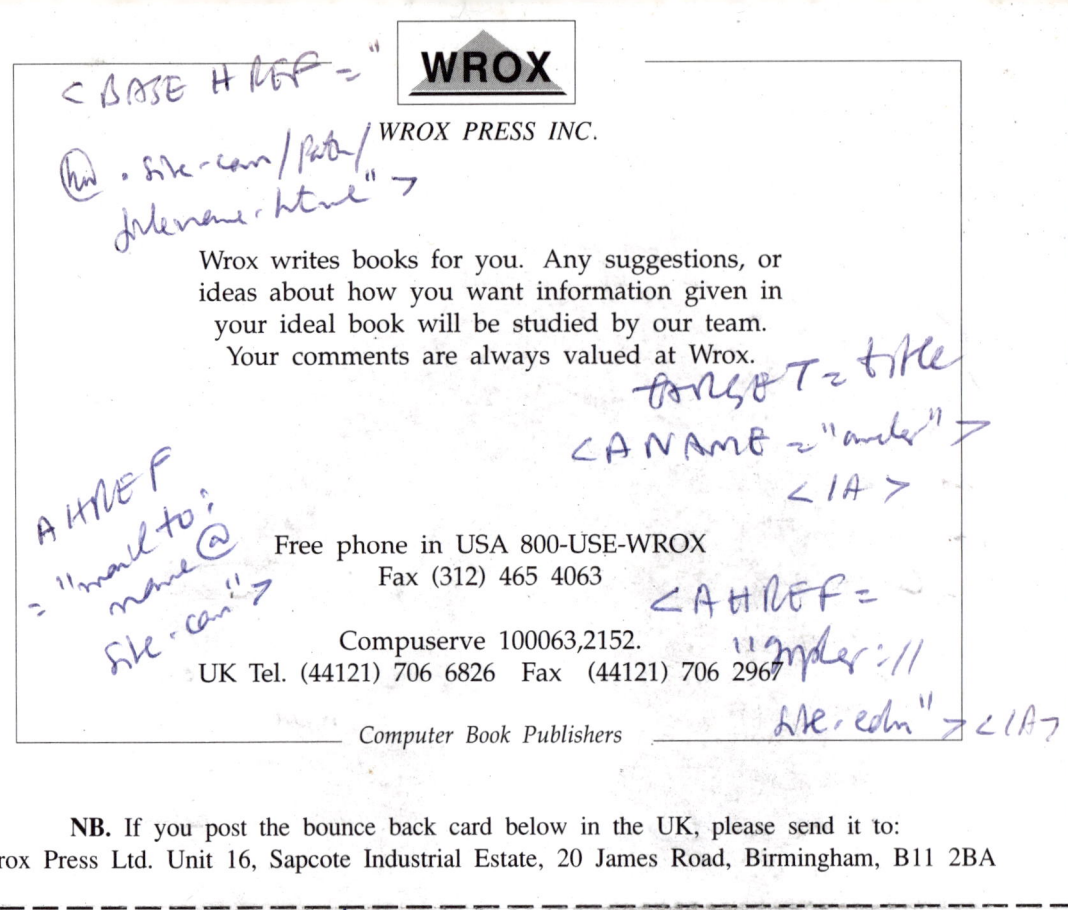

WROX PRESS INC.

`<BASE HREF="`
`(http://.site.com/path/filename.html">`

Wrox writes books for you. Any suggestions, or ideas about how you want information given in your ideal book will be studied by our team. Your comments are always valued at Wrox.

FORGOT = title
`<A NAME="anchor">`
`</A>`

A HREF
= "mailto:
name @
site.com">

Free phone in USA 800-USE-WROX
Fax (312) 465 4063

`<A HREF=`
`"#anchor"`

Compuserve 100063,2152.
UK Tel. (44121) 706 6826   Fax (44121) 706 2967

`site.edu"></A>`

Computer Book Publishers

NB. If you post the bounce back card below in the UK, please send it to:
Wrox Press Ltd. Unit 16, Sapcote Industrial Estate, 20 James Road, Birmingham, B11 2BA

HTML Tags
Address
Anchor
Block Quote
Credit
Defining
Instance

Division
Example
Footnote
Heading Block
Note

Paragraph
Pre-Formatted text

DD definition
Term
DL defn list

BUSINESS REPLY MAIL
FIRST CLASS MAIL   PERMIT #64   LA VERGNE, TN

POSTAGE WILL BE PAID BY ADDRESSEE

WROX PRESS
2710 WEST TOUHY AVE
CHICAGO IL 60645-9911

NO POSTAGE
NECESSARY
IF MAILED
IN THE
UNITED STATES

`<A HREF="news:
newsgroup">`

`<A HREF="url.address">`

`<OL TYPE=`
`UL`